THE DRAMATIC WORKS IN
THE BEAUMONT AND
FLETCHER CANON

Already published

VOLUME I

The Knight of the Burning Pestle
The Masque of the Inner Temple and Gray's Inn
The Women Hater   The Coxcomb
Philaster   The Captain

THE
DRAMATIC WORKS IN
THE BEAUMONT AND
FLETCHER CANON

GENERAL EDITOR
FREDSON BOWERS

Linden Kent Professor of English Literature, University of Virginia

VOLUME II

THE MAID'S TRAGEDY   A KING AND NO KING

CUPID'S REVENGE   THE SCORNFUL LADY

LOVE'S PILGRIMAGE

CAMBRIDGE
AT THE UNIVERSITY PRESS
1970

Published by the Syndics of the Cambridge University Press
Bentley House, 200 Euston Road, London N.W.1
American Branch: 32 East 57th Street, New York, N.Y.10022

Library of Congress Catalogue Card Number: 66–10243

Standard Book Number:
521 07253 0

Printed in Great Britain
at the University Printing House, Cambridge
(Brooke Crutchley, University Printer)

CONTENTS

Foreword   *page* vii

THE MAID'S TRAGEDY   I
  Edited by ROBERT K. TURNER, *Professor of English,*
  University of Wisconsin–Milwaukee

A KING AND NO KING   167
  Edited by GEORGE WALTON WILLIAMS, *Professor*
  of English, Duke University

CUPID'S REVENGE   315
  Edited by FREDSON BOWERS, *Linden Kent Professor*
  of English Literature, University of Virginia

THE SCORNFUL LADY   449
  Edited by CYRUS HOY, *Professor of English, University*
  of Rochester

LOVE'S PILGRIMAGE   567
  Edited by L. A. BEAURLINE, *Professor of English,*
  University of Virginia

FOREWORD

These volumes contain the text and apparatus for the plays conventionally assigned to the Beaumont and Fletcher canon, although in fact Fletcher collaborated with dramatists other than Beaumont in numerous plays of the canon and some of the preserved texts also represent revision at a later date by various hands. The plays have been grouped chiefly by authors; this arrangement makes for an order that conveniently approximates the probable date of composition for most of the works.

The texts of the several plays have been edited by a group of scholars according to editorial procedures set by the general editor, who closely supervised in matters of substance as well as of detail the initially contrived form of the texts. Thereafter the individual editors have been left free to develop their concepts of the plays according to their own views. We hope that the intimate connexion of one individual, in this manner, with all the different editorial processes will lend to the results some uniformity not ordinarily found when diverse editors approach texts of such complexity. At the same time, the peculiar abilities of the several editors have had sufficient free play to ensure individuality of point of view in its proper role; and thus, we hope, the deadness of compromise that may fasten on collaborative effort has been avoided, even at the risk of occasional internal disagreement.

The principles on which each text has been edited have been set forth in detail in 'The Text of this Edition' prefixed to volume I, pp. ix–xxv, followed by an account on pp. xxvii–xxxv of the Folio of 1647. Necessary acknowledgements will be found in the present volume in each Textual Introduction.

F. B.

Charlottesville, Virginia
1970

vii

THE MAID'S TRAGEDY

edited by

ROBERT K. TURNER, Jnr.

TEXTUAL INTRODUCTION

The exact date of the composition of *The Maid's Tragedy* (Greg, *Bibliography*, no. 357) is uncertain, but the play was probably in existence by 31 October 1611 when Sir George Buc, Master of the Revels, wrote on another dramatic manuscript: 'This Second Maiden's Tragedy (for it hath no name inscribed) may, with the reformations, be publickly acted.' Buc's terminology suggests that he had recently licensed *The Maid's Tragedy* itself.[1] The first specific mention of the play, however, occurs in a record of the payment made to John Heminge on 20 May 1613 for the presentation at court of 'fowerteene severall playes', among them *The Maid's Tragedy*.[2] On these two pieces of evidence it is usually held that the play was written about 1610. Fletcher seems to have contributed only four of the eleven scenes: II.ii, IV.i, and V.i and ii.[3]

The copy was entered, under the hands of Buc and the wardens of the Stationers' Company, to Richard Higgenbotham and Francis Constable on 28 April 1619; and Q1, with separate press-variant imprints for Higgenbotham and Constable, was printed in the same year by Nicholas Okes and another unidentified printer.[4] A second edition, for Constable alone, was printed by Purslowe in 1622.[5] On 27 October 1629 the copy was transferred to Richard Hawkins, who brought out Q3, printed by Augustine Mathewes, in 1630. Although there is no record of the transfer of the copy to him, Henry Shepherd, possibly acting on behalf of Hawkins's widow, published Q4 in 1638; the printer of this edition appears from his initials in the

[1] E. K. Chambers, *The Elizabethan Stage* (1923), III, 224.

[2] *Ibid.* IV, 180.

[3] Cyrus Hoy, 'The Shares of Fletcher and His Collaborators in the Beaumont and Fletcher Canon', *Studies in Bibliography*, XI (1958), 94.

[4] No printer's name appears on the title-page. That the first section of the book (sheets B–G) was printed by Okes is shown by the appearance on B1 of an ornament known to have been in his stock and the continuity of running-titles from sheet B through sheet G (see W. W. Greg, *A Bibliography of the English Printed Drama to the Restoration*, II [1951], 499–500).

[5] Greg, II, 500. The identification of the printer again depends on an ornament.

I-2

imprint to have been Edward Griffin, Jnr.[1] Ursula, the widow of Richard Hawkins, assigned the copy to Robert Mead and Christopher Meredith on 29 May 1638, and they, in turn, assigned it to William Leake on 25 January 1639. Leake published Q5, printed by Elizabeth Purslowe, in 1641 and Q6, printer unknown, probably in 1660.[2] Q7 appeared with the suspiciously plain imprint '*LON-DON*, || Printed in the Year 1661'; it is perhaps one of Kirkman's fraudulent reprints. The play was included in the Beaumont and Fletcher Second Folio of 1679, and Q8, the last edition before 1700, was printed in an unknown shop for Richard Bentley and S. Magnes in 1686. The early editions are lineally related to each other except for F2 and Q8, both of which descend independently from Q6.

Questions of textual authority are confined to the first three editions, the rest being completely derivative. Q3, a line-for-line reprint of Q2, is also largely derivative, but it introduces about seventy substantive variations into the text, two of which must have been editorial and about twenty of which may have been editorial. Among the twenty possible editorial variants are additions and cancellations of one or more words which do not affect meaning greatly but which tend to regularize metre, other synonymous or near-synonymous substitutions of little importance, and a half-dozen reversions to the readings of Q1. Occasionally, as in I.i.135 and IV.ii.190, quite obvious sophistications of the Q2 text are found. In the first of these instances, Q1 and Q2 read

> *Amintor*. She had my promise...

but Q3 reads

> *Evadne*. She had my promise...

As Evadne is not present in this scene and as her name appears earlier only twice in the text and not at all as a speech-prefix, it is highly improbable that the Q3 error could have arisen through the compositor's memorial failure. Instead, it seems likely that an

---

[1] *Ibid.* II, 501.
[2] There were two issues of this edition: one bears on I4ᵛ an advertisement of books which were known to have been first printed in 1659 and 1660. Greg therefore argues that the edition was printed in 1660, although the title-page of both issues is dated 1650 (*ibid.* II, 502).

editorial alteration of the 'She' of Amintor's speech to 'Evadne' (incorrectly, as Aspatia is being referred to) was indicated, which the compositor, misconstruing, set as a speech-prefix. The second instance had its origin in Q1, where the speech-prefix *Mel.* was set for IV.ii.190, the last line on I2, and again, incorrectly, for IV.ii. 191, the first line on I2ᵛ. The superfluous second prefix was retained by Q2, which printed on H4ᵛ:

> *Mel.* Marke his disordered words, and at the Maske
> *Mel.* *Diagoras* knowes he rag'd...

Attempting to correct this mistake, Q3 wrongly altered the first of these prefixes to *Kin.*, the King being one of the speakers in the scene.

The hand of a reviser is even more clearly seen at III.ii.144–5 and V.iii.269. In the first of these passages, the Q1–Q2 reading 'goe as high | As troubled waters' is altered to 'swell... | As the wilde surges'. In the second the Q1–Q2 reading 'My last is said' becomes in Q3 'My senses fade'. Any case for the authority of the Q3 alterations would have to rest heavily on these two changes in the text, but one is reluctant to think that if the exemplum of Q2 which was to serve as Q3 copy had been compared with an authoritative manuscript there would not have been more completely new readings introduced. It seems most likely that these and many of the other changes in Q3 were made by an editor after consultation of Q1 but chiefly after his own taste, and the fact that the Stationer's Censure prefixed to Q3 is in the form of a poem suggests that the composer, apparently Hawkins, might have felt qualified occasionally to improve on Beaumont and Fletcher's lines:

The Stationers Censure.

Good Wine requires no Bush, they say,
And I, No Prologue such a Play:
The Makers therefore did forbeare
To have that Grace prefixed here.
But cease here (Censure) least the Buyer
Hold thee in this a vaine Supplyer.
My Office is to set it forth
Where Fame applauds it's reall worth.

Except as a very occasional source of necessary and reasonable emendations when both Q1 and Q2 are corrupt, Q3—like the later editions—can be ignored.[1]

Because Q1 and Q2 are the basic documents for the establishment of the text, they warrant careful attention. Q1 collates A^2 B–L^4. Of it Greg noted, 'The text was printed in two sections, B–G and H–L, in slightly different types: in the first the speakers' names [the speech-prefixes] are set in small-caps, in the second in italic, but they are not indented in either. This might suggest that the copy was divided between two compositors, and that there had been an earlier edition. It is, however, more likely that composition was interrupted, and that on resumption the original type was not available, or possibly that the work was completed at another press.'[2] Several of these points may be clarified. First, there is no evidence of an earlier edition aside from the division of the copy for Q1, and it has been shown many times since Greg wrote that copy could be readily divided between two or more compositors setting from manuscript. Secondly, there can be no doubt that, as Greg said, the book was printed in two parts. In addition to the differences he observed in type and typography, there is variation in the speech-prefix abbreviations, the tag for Calianax being CAL. in the first section and predominantly *Call.* in the last and that for Aspatia being invariably ASP. in the first and *Aspat.* in the last; and there is a clear difference in the running-titles between the two sections, two skeletons being employed in each. Third, gathering A (A1–1^v blank, A2 title page, A2^v the list of speakers) is linked to the last section of the book rather than the first by the spelling 'Callianax' on A2^v, the form usually adopted in sheets H–L but never adopted in sheets B–G. Sheets B–G can be ascribed to Okes by means of an ornament on B1, but sheets H–L and A seem to have been printed in another shop.[3]

---

[1] The 1618 edition of *The Shoemaker's Holiday* provides an analagous case of heavy printing-house editing. See Fredson Bowers (ed.), *The Dramatic Works of Thomas Dekker*, I (1953), 11.

[2] *Op. cit.* II, 499–500.

[3] I previously believed that these sheets too were printed by Okes for reasons given in my 'Printing of Beaumont and Fletcher's *The Maid's Tragedy* Q1 (1619)', *Studies in Bibliography*, XIII (1960), 216–17. Of the items of evidence presented there,

Okes's part of Q1 was composed by formes in the order

B(o)–B(i)–C(i)–C(o)–D(o)–D(i)–
E(i)–E(o)–F(o)–F(i)–G(o)–G(i).

Typographical and spelling evidence indicates that Compositor A set sheets B–F (I.i.1–III.ii.170) and page G3 (III.ii.304–IV.i.1) from one case; in G some variation of spelling and the fact that the outer rather than the inner forme was first composed suggests that Compositor B may have set G1–2^v and G3^v–4^v (III.ii.171–III.ii.303 and IV.i.2–IV.i.107).[1] There seem to have been some difficulties over the printing. One of these, a purely mechanical matter, arose from Okes's selection of the particular italic fount which supplied the running-titles, a fount which appears to have had enough lower-case letters to set eight running-titles (*The Maydes Tragedy.* on both recto and verso) but only five M's and ten T's. The compositor was therefore obliged to shift capitals from the running-titles of each forme returned by the press to the running-titles already imposed in the skeleton of the next subsequent forme. This procedure would have caused a press delay, although perhaps only a brief one, between the machining of each forme.[2] More important are indications that the compositor purposely delayed the distribution of wrought-off type. Ideally, when B(o) was returned from the press, B(i) should have been ready to print, after the necessary capitals were set into the running-titles and the type-pages locked into the chase. Thus while the press was at work on B(i), the compositor should have been able to distribute type from B(o) in order to set C(i), the

only one seemed conclusive—that the roman letter of sheets H–L of *The Maid's Tragedy* Q1 is identical with that used in Okes's edition of Daniel's *Whole Works* (*STC* 6238). I am now convinced that the founts from which the two books were composed are not identical, nor have I encountered the H–L type in Okes's other books with which I am familiar. It is an ordinary roman the capitals of which have been augmented with letters from a fount of a somewhat larger size and heavier appearance. Type answering this description and of approximately the same size was used by George Purslowe for *The Maid's Tragedy* Q2, but I have been unable to make positive identification of any broken letters appearing both in Q2 and in sheets H–L of Q1. A sampling of books printed about 1619 by E. Griffin, J. Legate, and B. Alsop, with whom both Higgenbotham and Constable did other business between 1617 and 1621, has failed to locate the unidentified fount.

[1] See 'The Printing of... *The Maid's Tragedy* Q1 (1619)', pp. 203–14.
[2] See 'Reappearing Types as Bibliographical Evidence', *Studies in Bibliography*, XIX (1966), 206–8.

next forme, from a full case, and one should be able to find recognizable types from B(o) throughout C(i). As the following chart shows, B(o) was distributed just when it should have been, but every one of the subsequent formes later than it might have been, except F(i), which was distributed on time only because F(o) was not distributed at all:[1]

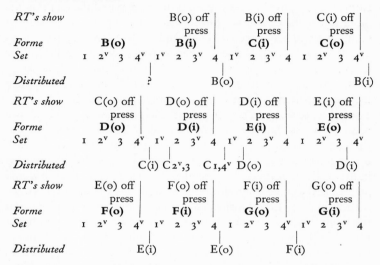

RT's show		B(o) off press	B(i) off press	C(i) off press
Forme	**B(o)**	**B(i)**	**C(i)**	**C(o)**
Set	1 2ᵛ 3 4ᵛ	1ᵛ 2 3ᵛ 4	1ᵛ 2 3ᵛ 4	1 2ᵛ 3 4ᵛ
Distributed	?	B(o)		B(i)

RT's show	C(o) off press	D(o) off press	D(i) off press	E(i) off press
Forme	**D(o)**	**D(i)**	**E(i)**	**E(o)**
Set	1 2ᵛ 3 4ᵛ	1ᵛ 2 3ᵛ 4	1ᵛ 2 3ᵛ 4	1 2ᵛ 3 4ᵛ
Distributed	C(i) C2ᵛ,3 C1,4ᵛ D(o)			D(i)

RT's show	E(o) off press	F(o) off press	F(i) off press	G(o) off press
Forme	**F(o)**	**F(i)**	**G(o)**	**G(i)**
Set	1 2ᵛ 3 4ᵛ	1ᵛ 2 3ᵛ 4	1 2ᵛ 3 4ᵛ	1ᵛ 2 3ᵛ 4
Distributed	E(i)	E(o)	F(i)	

Furthermore, the unusual alternation in composing the first formes of succeeding sheets (that is, outer and inner, then inner and outer, and so on) suggests that the workman, within the limitations of composition by formes, set adjoining pages consecutively whenever he could. He would thus have created, presumably in order to compensate for errors in casting off, slightly more favourable conditions for adjusting text to space than if he had regularly set either the inner or the outer forme first.

In sheets H–L there are a few indications—for example, a suspicious amount of white space on K2ᵛ—that two compositors were at work, but the evidence generally points to one compositor

[1] These conclusions are based upon a study of type reappearances which goes beyond that reported in 'The Printing...of *The Maid's Tragedy* Q1 (1619)', pp. 203–14.

8

setting from one case. Skeleton III imposed H(o), I(i), K(o), and L(o); Skeleton IV, H(i), I(o), K(i), and L(i). As H(o) type reappears throughout sheet I, it is likely that sheet H was set by formes outer first, and this creates the supposition that sheet I too was set by formes (also outer first, because I[o] type reappears before I[i] type), although there is no proof of the method by which I was composed. If I(o) were set first, it is rather odd that it was not imposed in Skeleton III, which would have been freed upon the distribution of H(o); but its imposition in Skeleton IV may mean only that composition was lagging behind presswork to such an extent that when I 4^v was completed both skeletons were available. If H were probably and I possibly set by formes, it nevertheless seems clear that K was set *seriatim*: in K I(o) type reappears only in pages 3–4^v, indicating that these were set after the others of that sheet. In L K(i) type reappears only in L4; there is thus no way to tell how that sheet was set. An order of composition which accounts for this evidence is shown in the following chart, but too many alternate possibilities exist to permit inference about the compositor's response to his copy. H(o), not shown, is assumed to have been set first; there is no evidence pertaining to A:

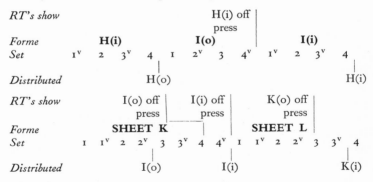

The causes of the printers' problems (or Okes's, at least) are not far to seek: an examination of the Q1 text shows that underlying it there must have been a manuscript partly mislined and illegibly written. Q1 is not only corrupt in many single words and phrases but also it lacks some eighty apparently authoritative lines found in

Q 2. Many of these omissions are scattered throughout the text, but some are concentrated, notably the following:

I.ii.140–49. Ten lines of Cinthia's speech promising the masque audience 'a contented houre' and asserting her rivalry with Phoebus. Night's speech follows without a serious logical hiatus.

I.ii.234.1–248. A measure, a song, and two short speeches of Neptune and one of Cinthia introducing the song. The omitted Third Song is not substantially different in theme or manner from the Second Song, which Q 1 includes. The action of Q 1 follows without difficulty.

II.i.67–89. Two songs by Aspatia and Dula, with several closely related short speeches. The Q 1 action proceeds logically in spite of the omission.

II.ii.7–10. Three and a half lines spoken by Aspatia about fidelity in love. This omission is probably related to the longer one a few lines below. Line 7 is metrically incomplete in Q 1, but the progression of thought is adequate.

II.ii.15–27. The last three words in l. 15, the subsequent eleven lines, and the first four words of l. 27, in which Aspatia warns her gentlewomen against man's inconstancy. In Q 1 the fragments of ll. 15 and 27 are run together to make a single hypermetrical line, but the thought follows satisfactorily.

III.i.203–6. One speech each by the King, Evadne, and Amintor. No damage is done to metre or to sense.

IV.i.81–6. Six lines of Melantius' attack on Evadne's unchastity. The entire speech is printed incorrectly as prose in both Q 1 and Q 2. The sense is not greatly affected by the Q 1 omission.

There are, in addition, two variations affecting the assignment of speeches that deserve mention here. At I.i.139.1 Q 1 omits the entrance of the Messenger and gives his speech (l. 140) to Amintor. In II.i the First Lady has a slightly greater part in Q 1 than in Q 2: in Q 1 she speaks the part of l. 14 which Q 2 assigns to Dula and the part of l. 125 which Q 2 assigns to *Omnes*. In both texts, however, she has three other speeches, l. 111 and parts of ll. 109 and 110.

Some of these differences between Q 1 and Q 2 may result from errors of transmission, but on the whole they look as though they lie beyond such a cause. Certain of the passages omitted from Q 1 seem to have been part of the original composition: the damage to metre done by the omissions at II.ii.7 and II.ii.15 suggests that the excluded matter was once part of the text, and (the songs in I.ii and

II.i perhaps excepted) the differences seem too insignificant to be accounted for as augmentations of an early version. On the other hand, they are neither offensive enough to have been removed by censorship nor sufficiently thorough or far-reaching to be the sum of material cut for a theatrical abridgement of the full text. Yet it is striking that none of the passages removed leaves a serious break in the logic of the action, and the inference from this fact must be that the text was deliberately and thoughtfully cut, one can only suppose with performance in view. Thus it would seem that the Q1 text is based on one that had been partially abridged and otherwise altered; if so, it is likely that at one point in its history some of the material now included was marked for omission. Of particular interest in this respect is I.ii.180–1, where Q1 reads, awkwardly, 'Bid them draw neere to have thy watrie race | Led on in couples ...' and Q2, 'These are our musicke: next thy watrie race | Bring on...', the reference in both texts evidently being to the 'vernall blasts and gentle winds' of l. 177. Possibly the Q1 reading was cobbled up to replace the Q2, but a change in the text represented by Q2 would have been necessary only if the songs that follow had been excised. In Q1, however, two of the three songs appear. It may be, too, that the word 'safer' at IV.i.72 appears anomalously in Q1 as 'Safer' because it was added in the Italian hand to a passage basically in secretary script.

Cutting suggests theatrical provenience; however, there are few features of Q1 that connect it with the theatre and some features that point away from such a connection. Among the former one may count the specification of a noise (*Knock within*, I.ii.21), the occasional making explicit of business (*e.g.* [*Exeunt*]. . .*other dore*, I.ii.33; *Enter* Eolus *out of a Rock*, I.ii.185.1; *Ties his armes to the bed*, V.i.35); and the precise designation of instruments to produce musical sounds (*Hoboyes*, I.ii.98; *Recorders*, I.ii.109; *Hoboies*, IV.ii.0.1). Yet Q1 is not very thorough in the indication of *withins* and *asides*, and it omits about twenty other stage-directions that are necessary to the action. It contains three indefinite directions (*Enter* Aspatia *passing with attendance*, I.i.58; *Musique*, I.ii.206; . . . *Guard*, V.ii.11.1), and one that is mistaken (*a Lady* for *Ladyes*, IV.1.0.1). Although the naming of specific musical instruments may hint at a bookkeeper's notation, there is little else in Q1 to encourage one to think it descended from a theatrical manuscript.[1] The most prominent feature of Q1 is the corruption of its language. Some of its readings are blatantly wrong; others, which considered by themselves are acceptable, are seen to be wrong, or at least inferior, when Q2 provides a better reading. Of the incorrect Q1 readings, a small number doubtless arose from ordinary faults of transmission (e.g. *villanie* for *villaine* [V.i.103], a transposition or misreading; and *should'st* for *can'st* [III.i.209], induced by *should'st* in the preceding line). But the greatest single cause of corruption in Q1 seems to have been misreading of the handwriting of the manuscript. The following are examples of what may be termed simple misreading:

Confusion of final -s and -e
welcome *for* welcoms (I. i.18 and I.ii.179), arme *for* arms (IV.ii.222)

Confusion of final -l and -s
fils *for* fill (I.i.99), vessels *for* vessell (I.ii.183), call *for* cals (III.i.62)

A letter for a final flourish
Weighes *for* Weigh (I.i.56), hands *or* hand (I.ii.87), friends *for* friend (III.ii.97), commendations *for* commendation (IV.i.8 and 16), chopt *for* chop (IV.ii.48), faults *for* fault (IV.ii.103)

Minim misinterpretations
sect *for* set (I.ii.274), sun flaring *for* same flashing (I.ii.275), sun *for* sin (II.i.179), Instant *for* Instruct (II.i.245), e'ne *for* 'em (II.i.345), rustie *for* restie (II.ii.87), wilde *for* vilde (III.i.221), plead *for* plaid (III.ii.102), stick *for* strike (III.ii.136)

Confusion of final -d and -e
judge *for* judgd (I.ii.13), wind(e) *for* wine (I.ii.159), faind *for* fine (II.ii.29)

Miscellaneous
force *for* fetcht (I.ii.168), cannot *for* can but (II.i.228), left *for* lost (II.i.346), Good, good *for* Good gods (II.ii.2), furie *for* fully (II.ii.32), black *for* back (II.ii.44), lies *for* lied (III.i.226), fault *for* fate (III.i.259), knowne *for* borne (III.ii.153), farewell *for* scandall (III.ii.159), theile lie *for* they lied (IV.i.45), world *for* worth (IV.ii.124), that *for* thou (IV.ii.138), Too *for* Tis (IV.ii.216), meet *for* melt (IV.ii.235), selfe *for* flesh (V.iii.182), grow *for* grope (V.iii.221).

[1] R. C. Bald, *Bibliographical Studies in the Beaumont and Fletcher Folio of 1647* (1938), notes that '...a general direction like *Music* is probably from the author, but...a specific direction for the kind of music required and the instruments to play it comes much more naturally from the prompter' (p. 107).

Beyond these, however, lie two more serious kinds of error—omissions and substitutions—which may have arisen in part from a more complex kind of misreading. A few omissions in Q I apparently came about, as has been seen, through deliberate cutting of the text; others undoubtedly arose from eyeskip or memorial failure on the part of the compositor. But there remains a small number which perhaps arose because the compositor, unable to decipher words in his copy, left them out, particularly when the passage made reasonably good sense without them. The following may be examples:

Omissions
Their King (I.i.8), to Rhodes (I.i.13), too (I.i.17), with armes (I.i.43), Pray stay (I.ii.10), so, so (I.ii.21—Q *1 leaves a blank*), with you (I.ii.26), wiser... than his own (I.ii.40), to my love and freedom to you (III.ii.302), Oh heare me gently, it was (IV.i.125), No more, (IV.i.126), this sword... peace (IV.ii.165–6), and...shed (V.iii.147–9).

Yet there would have been occasions upon which the compositor could not omit words without leaving ugly breaks in the sense of the passage. Sometimes, therefore, when he could not understand a reading, he may have introduced words of his own that were more-or-less sensible in context or at least similar in form to what he saw in his copy. The following may be examples, although, as will be suggested later, some of these variants may have been the result of revision:

Substitutions
blowes abroad bringst *for* blood abroad buyest (I.i.14)

        ...this Lady sir,
Sits discontented with her watrie eyes bent on the earth,
In unfrequented woods are her delight,
Where when she sees a bancke stucke full of flowers,
Then she will sit, and sigh, and tell
          for
        Yes, but this Lady
Walkes discontented with her watrie eyes
Bent on the earth; the unfrequented woods
Are her delight, and when she sees a bancke
Stucke full of flowers, she with a sigh will tell (I.i.86–90)

13

swound *for* sigh (I.i.97)
sports *for* peace (I.i.145)
there is no roome *for* and theres roome (I.ii.30)
that have *for* and how (I.ii.120)
those *for* these mortals (I.ii.132)
losses *for* blushes (I.ii.226)
kisses *for* coynesse (II.i.212)
the place she was in *for* that desart, and (II.ii.68)
tongue *for* cunning (III.ii.69).

In addition to corrupt readings, Q1 contains a very considerable amount of mislineation. In this connection the beginning of the play seems particularly revealing. The dialogue between Lysippus and the gentlemen (sig. B1: I.i.1–11) commences with two short lines, but it soon settles down to reasonably regular verse, if one takes into account the readings supplied to these passages by Q2. Q1, however, lines Lysippus' speech at I.i.5–6 (which is correctly rendered) as verse but the rest as prose, except the words 'Noble *Melantius*' (l. 12), which occupy a line to themselves. Melantius' reply to Lysippus (I.i.20–5), which begins at the foot of B1, is verse to which Q2 contributes no change; Q1 lines it as prose through 'e-' (the first letter of the word 'ever', l. 23), at which point the page ends. Yet when Melantius' speech resumes at the head of B1ᵛ with 'ver was to you . . .', it is lined as verse, as is the rest of the text of I.i. Apparently whoever cast sheet B off simply did not know what to make of this material. There must have been some clear verse lines in it (witness ll. 5–6) but the rest evidently seemed to be prose or verse so irregularly lined that it was best treated as prose. In Melantius' speech some verse lines could be discerned, but the caster-off seems, for appearance's sake, to have designated the material falling on B1 as prose and the remaining lines, those falling on B1ᵛ, as verse. Such mislineation is scattered throughout the rest of the quarto. It is not concentrated in the work of a particular compositor; it occurs quite as often in the first formes as it does in the second; it is found here and there in sheets K and L, which may have been set *seriatim*; and in many instances the mislined passages occupy the same number of lines of type as they would have done correctly lined.

The characteristics of Q1 discussed so far may suggest that it preserves the text of a memorial reconstruction—perhaps, because misreading seems to have been a corrupting factor, the foul papers of such a text. The Q1 version suffers, as has been shown, from omissions and substitutions, which in many instances may have arisen as well from the faulty memory of a reporter as from the manipulations or guesswork of a compositor. It is, moreover, shorter than the Q2 version; it shows vague signs of theatrical cutting; and it is in part mislined. All these may be evidence of a report.

The question of how bad a text must be before it is technically 'bad' is a vexing one, but an estimate of Q1's possible 'badness' may be made by means of a brief comparison of it and the central part of *Philaster* Q1, which, it was argued in the first volume of this series (pp. 386–96), does seem to have been a fairly good memorial reconstruction. The relevant part of *Philaster* is roughly five hundred lines shorter than *The Maid's Tragedy* Q1. Between the corresponding parts of *Philaster* Q1 and Q2 there are approximately 775 substantive variants, including sixty-five speeches differently assigned. Major characters in *Philaster* Q1 are generically designated (*e.g.* 'Princesse' for Arethusa, 'Boy' for Bellario). The stage-directions of the report tend to be descriptive, and its version of the action of the play occasionally differs from the corresponding Q2 version. Between *The Maid's Tragedy* Q1 and Q2, however, there are about 425 substantive variants, of which only a few arise from differences in the assignment of speeches. Except for the most minor, all characters are named. There is some, but no great, variation in stage-directions, as will be indicated more fully below. As reflected in the variant stage-directions and speech assignments, there are some differences in action between Q1 and Q2, but they amount to little. Q1 lacks (as indeed does *Philaster* Q1 to any pronounced degree) what are regarded as the classical stigmata of reports, including severe abbreviation of the text, anticipation and recollection, gag, and echoes of other plays. The whole matter would be clearer if one knew how strong a compulsion was felt by the man who prepared the copy for Q2 to bring Q1 readings into agreement with those of the new authority with which he was comparing the first edition, but as it stands Q1 seems too good to be bad.

Unlike mislineation, which is found in various parts of Q1, corrupt readings are more prevalent in the beginning than in the end of the text, a condition that could imply either that Okes's Compositor *A* coped less successfully with his part of the copy than did the compositor of sheets H–L or that the manuscript was in worse shape at the beginning than at the end. Perhaps both these implications are to be accepted, yet because Q1 corruptions are often not detectable without recourse to the superior readings of Q2 and because there is no assurance that readings of the new witness were introduced into the Q2 copy with equal care, it may be that there are more incorrect readings in sheets H–L than one can recognize. The safest hypothesis would seem to be that the manuscript from which Q1 was printed was reasonably uniform but contained patches—for example, the beginning of the first act and the masque—which were especially difficult. This supposition is supported by the fact that throughout the text—through the scenes of the two authors and through the stints of the several compositors—there runs much the same system of light, and some-times rather insensitive, punctuation, in which the comma is used in many instances where heavier stops would normally have been employed. Since the accidentals of any print were largely the com-positor's responsibility, one can ascribe pointing that reveals a misunderstanding of the language to compositorial lapses, but it appears that all the compositors were sufficiently influenced by the punctuation of the manuscript for Q1 generally to preserve it. One must then imagine an essentially authoritative manuscript, lightly punctuated, sometimes hard to read, sometimes incorrectly lined, sometimes heavily worked over, and containing some passages marked for excision that nevertheless made their way into the quarto. These are the characteristics of rough foul papers.

If such papers did underlie Q1, one can explain some readings which are nonsense or near-nonsense and which seem to have come into being because the compositor, failing to see or to make out another version of a cancelled word or phrase, conflated an authorial first shot with a second. At I.ii.120 Beaumont may have planned a clause to modify 'persons', written 'that have' and perhaps more, cancelled the words he had down, and substituted 'and how many longing eies'. The compositor rendered this as 'that have many longing eies'. At I.ii.122 'can I not' looks like a false start that should have been replaced by 'I could not'. At I.ii.272 the first version may have been 'Once more heave' or something similar; these words, changed to 'Heave up', were set as 'Once heave'. The Q1 readings at I.ii.180, I.ii.197, III.i.151–3, III.ii.69, and V.iii.221 may be further examples of such conflation.

Fletcher's linguistic preferences, ordinarily pronounced, are, however, significantly absent from Q1; moreover, as has been pointed out, such other features of the text as the punctuation suggest that the Q1 copy was homogeneous. Prominent traces of Fletcher's hand may have been suppressed in a transcript of both authors' working drafts, but it is hard to conceive of a transcript of the entire play made for any purpose that, first, would be seriously illegible and, secondly, would contain authorial changes. Perhaps at some stage of composition the authors had a copy made of their working papers, but it seems both more direct and more consistent with the features of Q1 discussed here to suppose that Beaumont rewrote Fletcher's scenes, perhaps to integrate them more firmly into the context of his own composition and that in doing so he suppressed the linguistic characteristics that usually mark Fletcher's work. It is thus most likely that Q1 was printed from Beaumont's autograph, which represented the play in a late, but not the final, stage of composition.[1]

The Q1 text, then, apparently was based on a difficult document, and a better version of the play might exist today if Q2 had been printed independently. Unfortunately it was not; it was clearly set up from a copy of Q1 upon which a large number of corrections, additions, and other alterations had been annotated.[2] The Q2 title-page proclaims it 'Newly perused, augmented, and inlarged': augmented and enlarged it certainly was, and the new perusal, whatever that phrase may mean exactly, resulted not only in the

[1] Donald Gale Stillman, 'A Critical Textual Study of...*The Maid's Tragedy*' (unpub. Michigan diss. 1942), argues that Q1 was printed from the inept copy of authorial papers by an amateur scribe. If this were so, there might be the same textual tangles in Q1, but, one should think, less evidence of misreading and revision.
[2] See 'The Relationship of *The Maid's Tragedy* Q1 and Q2', *Papers of the Bibliographical Society of America*, LI (1957), 322–7.

introduction into the text of over four hundred substantive changes of varying length but also a considerably heavier and more rational system of punctuation. The degree of authority carried by the Q2 changes is, of course, a matter of great importance and one that depends on the nature of the manuscript from which they were drawn.

If the annotator of the Q1 exemplum which served as Q2 copy had made use of a theatrical text, one would expect to find in Q2 some change in the Q1 stage-directions which would indicate theatrical influence. There are about twenty Q1 directions which are materially altered in Q2, but of this number some fifteen probably vary because of changes in the text of the play, errors of the Q2 compositor, or minor alterations of the annotator. Those remaining are

	Q1 Direction	Q2 Direction
I.i.58	Enter Aspatia passing | with attendance.	Enter Aspatia, | passing by.
I.ii.46.1	Enter Calianax.	Enter Calianax to Melantius.
I.ii.262.1	Exeunt Maskers | Descend.	Neptune descends, and | the Sea Gods.
V.iii.107.1	Ent. Evadne.	Enter Evadne. | Her hands | bloudy with | a knife.
V.iii.246.1	Enter Lysip. Melant. Call. Diph. Strato.	Enter Lisip. Melant. Cal. Cleon. Diph. Strato.

The Q2 direction at I.i.58, which strips Aspatia of her attendants, may have been a theatrical change, but there would seem to have been no compelling reason for it. There are about twenty parts in *The Maid's Tragedy*. In performance some parts would doubtless have been doubled, but it is unlikely that the play could have been mounted by a company of fewer than a dozen actors, including four or five boys. When Aspatia enters, there are only five characters on stage, all men; thus several boys should have been available to play her gentlewomen. The Q2 direction at I.ii.46.1 is in phraseology that seems specifically theatrical, but it describes a situation inconsistent with the action. When Calianax enters, Melantius is within, having left the stage to place his lady above. Calianax's first words after his entrance are 'Let him not in' (I.ii.47), and in

Q1 Melantius' entrance is correctly marked after this speech (at I.ii.48.1).[1] The Q2 direction at I.ii.262.1 offers better evidence of theatrical origin. The Q1 version is imprecise: one does not know whether the masquers and Neptune are intended to leave the stage through the trap door or whether Neptune alone descends and the masquers go off at the rear of the stage. The Q2 version clarifies by having Neptune's crew descend, but it is worth noting that its language is perhaps more literary than the language of the Q1 direction and that it does not get the Winds, who should not go with the Sea Gods into the depths, off the stage. The Q2 direction at V.iii.107.1 is like the kind of warning the prompter sometimes gave himself when special make-up or properties were required, but it does not come in advance as such prompt notations often do and it merely reflects Amintor's 'Thy hands are bloudy, and thou hast a knife' (V.iii.126). Although he has no lines to speak, it does seem likely that Cleon should be included in the gathering of characters at the end of the play as specified by the Q2 direction at V.iii.246.1, yet the appearance of his name in Q2 may be no more than the correction of an eyeskip error in Q1. In general, then, the variant stage-directions of Q2 offer little encouragement to the notion that the annotator obtained his materials from a theatrical manuscript. The only one in language that seems specifically theatrical is the entrance of Calianax 'to' Melantius at I.ii.46.1, and that one is wrong.

The additions and corrections which were made to Q1 indicate that the version of the text from which they were drawn was a full one uncontaminated by the factors that had corrupted Q1. Yet if

---

[1] Entrances of one character 'to' another seem to occur only when the second is on stage: e.g. Romeo and Juliet Q2:C3, 7: 'Enter all the guests and gentlewomen to the Maskers' and The Captives, British Museum MS. Egerton 1994, fol. 58b (Malone Society Reprints [1953], p. 40) where 'to ye Clow' was added by the prompter to the author's direction 'Enter Scribonia with an empty pale'. Similar notations are found here and there in The Captives and, indeed, in many other plays of the period, but never, as far as I have been able to discover, does a character enter 'to' another who is within. The special purpose to which the direction was sometimes put is shown by its use in the plot of 2 Seven Deadly Sins, where one finds 'Henry Awaking Enter A Keeper I sincler. to him a seruaunt T Belt'. Here, as Greg suggests, the direction probably means that the servant speaks apart to the keeper, although Henry is also on the stage. See Dramatic Documents from Elizabethan Playhouses, I, 118 and II, plot reproduction, l. 10.

one supposes that untidy and partially illegible foul papers were in the background of Q1, they must also have been in the background of Q2, and the question then arises how in the one instance a degenerate text was produced from them and in the other a text that was reasonably accurate. Possible causes for the corruption of Q1 have already been explored. The most obvious reason for Q2's superiority would seem to be that behind its readings lay a good transcript of the foul papers. It is conceivable that a careful scribe could have produced a better version than the Q1 compositors, yet the general absence of misreading errors from the passages added by Q2 might suggest as the transcriber one of the authors, who of all people could most easily have made sense of the working papers, regardless of their condition. Although there is little direct evidence to show that either Beaumont or Fletcher made a fair copy which lay behind Q2 and even less to indicate which of the two performed the task, an authorial transcript seems the best choice among the possible alternatives; and the failure of Fletcher's linguistic practices to force their way into the passages found only in Q2 allows the inference that Beaumont was the transcriber.

Some features of the text may seem to argue positively for an authorial transcript; yet, when one comes to the point, alternative explanations are often possible. It is difficult to imagine that an author can copy out his own work without making some revisions in it, if only minor rewordings that seem, at the moment, improvements. If one believes an authorial transcript to be in part an ancestor of Q2, one ought to be able to cite variants between Q1 and Q2 that would likely have come into being during transcription, in which case the Q1 reading would be the author's first thought and the Q2 reading his second. The following passages (I.ii.150–7) may serve as an example of the difficulty of showing such revision. Q1 and Q2 read as follows, except that substantive variants are printed in italics and proper nouns, italicized in the originals, in roman:

Q1:   NIGH, Then shine at full *pale* Queen, & by *that* power,   150
      Produce a birth to *fill* this happy houre,
      Of Nimphes and shepheards, *and* let their songs discover,
      Easie and sweete who is a happy lover,
      Of if thou w'oot [   ] thine owne Endimion

From the sweete flowrie *banck* he lies upon,
On Latmus *brow* thy pale beames drawne away,
And of *his* long night let him make *thy* day.   157 ·

Q2:   *Nigh.* Then shine at full *faire* Queene, and by *thy* power   150
       Produce a birth to *crowne* this happy houre,
       Of Nimphes and shepheards, [   ] let their songs discover,
       Easie and sweet who is a happy lover,
       Or if thou w'oot *then call* thine owne Endimion
       From the sweet flowrie *bed* he lies upon,
       On Latmus *top* thy pale beames drawne away,
       And of *this* long night let him make *this* day.   157

Both versions are somewhat defective in placing a comma after
'upon' (l. 155) instead of after 'top' or 'brow' (l. 156). Editors
agree that Q1's 'his' (l. 157) is the correct reading, and most
accept Q2's 'this day' (l. 157), although some reject both Q1 and
Q2 in favour of Q3's 'a day'. Beyond these readings, however,
there is little to choose between the two versions: Cynthia can be
either 'faire' or 'pale' (a pale moon would cast the 'pale beames' of
l. 156); her shining may be either 'that power' or 'thy power'; the
birth of nymphs and shepherds may either 'fill' or 'crowne' the
hour; Endymion may be upon either a 'banck' on Latmus' 'brow'
or a 'bed' on Latmus' 'top', although in the last instance, for
whatever remote value the analogy may have, Drayton has Endymion upon a 'banck' while he watches his flocks and a 'grassy bed'
after his enchantment (*Endimion and Phoebe*, ll. 341 and 983). Q1's
'and' (l. 152) makes the line hypermetrical, but that means little;
and Q2's 'then call' (l. 154) is not decisive—first, because 'Endimion' can be read either with three or with four syllables and,
secondly, because in the Q1 version, as Theobald remarked,
'Endimion' as well as 'birth' can stand as the direct object of
'Produce' (l. 151). The Q2 version could have come about through
authorial tinkering with the language of Q1; yet it is not wholly
beyond belief that the Q1 version grew out of the Q2 through a
combination of misreading ('that' for 'thy' and 'thy' for 'this')
and guessing at nearly illegible words. The ambiguity one finds
here is present in many of the variant passages which one would
like to adduce to prove revision as a cause of the Q2 readings and
hence an authorial transcript behind Q2, but even in instances such

as the one just examined, the odds may seem to favour revision as at least one cause of variation.

Indeed, some differences can best be accounted for on the assumption that the manuscript from which the Q2 readings were drawn was a revision of the foul papers. The following variants from II.ii, one of Fletcher's scenes, may serve as examples:

Lines 66–7	Q1:	Suppose I stand upon the Sea, breach [Sea-beach] now Mine armes thus, and mine haire blowne with the wind,
	Q2:	I stand upon the sea breach now, and thinke Mine armes thus, and mine haire blowne with the wind,
Line 69	Q1:	Be teares [tellers? teachers?] of my story
	Q2:	Tell that I am forsaken
Line 71	Q1:	make me looke good girle
	Q2:	strive to make me looke
Line 86	Q1:	in and whine there
	Q2:	get you in and work
Lines 89–90	Q1:	Good my Lord be not angry, we doe nothing But what my Ladies pleasure is, we are thus in griefe,
	Q2:	My Lord we doe no more then we are charg'd: It is the Ladies pleasure we be thus in griefe,

Some conscious and deliberate change probably took place in these instances, and it is unlikely that anyone but an author would have troubled himself over such minor matters. Thus a fair copy in the background of Q2 seems a probability, and, as has been remarked, the chances are that Beaumont would have been its writer.

There is no particular reason to suspect that the printing of Q2 would have created unusual problems, except perhaps in the incorporation of the manuscript changes into the Q1 exemplum that served as copy. The book seems to have been machined in a routine fashion and to have been set up by a reliable compositor, who made some, but not a great many, mistakes.[1] The added passages are sometimes mislined, but this would seem to indicate only that they

---

[1] The printing of Q2 is described and an evaluation of the proficiency of the compositor made in 'A Textual Study of... *The Maid's Tragedy*' (unpub. Virginia diss. 1958), pp. 326–66.

were written in the margin of the Q2 copy in such space as was available. There is, however, some slight evidence that the annotator did not always work with absolute fidelity to the manuscript from which he obtained the Q2 readings. The accidental or deliberate omission of a passage involving part lines from Q1 is often accompanied by a dislocation of metre, as one can see from the arrangement of Q1 lines, for example, at II.ii.7, II.ii.15, III.i.231–2, III.ii.216, and V.iii.147. Thus when the metre becomes irregular in places where Q2 does not provide a better version—for example, at II.ii.51—one suspects either that the annotator failed to provide a revision or that, if he did, the Q2 compositor failed to note it. As has already been mentioned, the Q2 stage-direction at I.ii.46.1 is clearly wrong and the one at V.iii.246.1 may be. The substitution of 'good heavens' for 'oh God' at V.i.24 and the omission of 'God' at IV.i.1 also look like the annotator's doing, although there is no systematic purging of profanity throughout the text.

The annotator may have been at fault in other ways as well. Mistakes in the rendition of some of the added passages—for example, that at I.ii.234.1–248—indicate that the annotator did not always make his intention clear to the compositor, that the annotator made errors in copying, or that one or both sophisticated material he did not fully grasp. Thus a question arises that is particularly troublesome—the possibility of the annotator's introduction of improvements upon what he found in the authoritative manuscript. If he did make changes according to his own judgement, they would be, except in rare instances, indistinguishable from what one might think to be authorial revisions. Q2 seems, for example, at pains to mend irregularities in the verse of Q1. By and large, Q2 is better metrically than Q1, and one has little choice but to accept the more regular version as authoritative. Yet occasionally what could be the improving hand of the annotator may appear, for example, at I.i.33, where Q1 reads

> Can witnesse with me.
> Tis most true *Melantius*,

which can pass as Beaumont and Fletcher pentameter. Q2 omits 'most', which, while not achieving perfect regularity, at least converts the last part of the line to regular trimeter. Similar occurrences are found at I.i.150, where Q2 again may be attempting to cure a hypermetrical Q1 line by omission (leaving the line a foot short); at II.i.31, where Q2's addition of 'Why' is suspicious, as Beaumont and Fletcher often omit the first unaccented syllable of a pentameter; at III.i.22, where Q2's omission of 'have' makes perfectly regular a line that was regular in Q1 provided that 'We have' was read as 'We've'. A different kind of sophistication is found in the Q2 stage-direction at I.ii.46.1. It should not be an authorial change, nor is it likely to have been an error of the Q2 compositor. The annotator would seem to be the culprit, although what he may actually have been guilty of was the incomplete rendition of a more extensive change in the manuscript. Generally, faults of the annotator are impossible to identify precisely, but the chance that he or the Q2 compositor may not have performed his duties impeccably works against the absolute validity of every Q2 reading.

Ambiguous though it often is, the evidence points toward a history of the text which may be recapitulated as follows: Q1 was printed from late-stage foul papers in Beaumont's hand, including Beaumont's rewriting of Fletcher's scenes. It is considerably corrupt because of several factors, among them the ineptness of Okes's Compositor A and the condition of the manuscript itself, which seems to have been roughly and irregularly written and which contained cancellations and interlineations. Q2 was printed from a copy of Q1 into which had been introduced readings from a fair copy of the foul papers, probably also written out by Beaumont, who made some changes in the process. The annotator or the Q2 compositor, or both, imposed a heavier system of punctuation on the Q1 text, and the annotator may have failed occasionally to record material, may have recorded it incorrectly or illegibly, or may have sophisticated some readings.

After considering much the same evidence as examined here, Howard B. Norland reaches conclusions which tend to degrade the authenticity of Q2 variants, though not Q2 additions.[1] Dr Norland

[1] 'The Text of *The Maid's Tragedy*', *Papers of the Bibliographical Society of America*, LXI (1967), 173–200.

24

believes sheets B–G of Q1 to have been printed from heavily revised foul papers and sheets H–L from a scribal copy of the same. Q2 was printed from a copy of Q1 annotated from the prompt-book, which in its turn was based on an authorial revision of the text represented in Q1. The theatrical scribe who prepared the prompt-book (and possibly others connected with the theatre) improved readings, regularized punctuation, and revised and added stage-directions; and these unauthoritative changes made their way into Q2, through the agency of the annotator, along with genuine authorial changes. Because Q2 readings were exposed to a greater possibility of tampering, the editor should follow Q1 when no clear choice of readings exists.

I agree that foul papers underlay sheets B–G (though I do not think Fletcher's manuscript among them), but I believe the rest of Dr Norland's argument open to the following objections: (1) That the copy underlying B–G was different from that underlying H–L is suggested by the difference in the rate of occurrence of variants between the two sections, but this difference could have arisen from Beaumont's greater satisfaction with the last two acts, the failure of the annotator to work with the same diligence throughout, or greater care on the part of the H–L compositor. Moreover, one does not like to think that only a portion of the play would have been transcribed; if vile copy was good enough for Okes, it should also have been good enough for the second printer. (2) Dr Norland believes the following details indicate the dependence of Q2 on a prompt-book (pp. 194–6): the language of Q2 is regularized and flattened by comparison with that of Q1; Q2 supplies three speech-prefixes omitted by Q1, corrects one of three misassigned speeches in Q1, and misassigns two speeches correctly tagged in Q1; Q2 introduces at I.i.58 a superfluous speech-prefix 'for clarity'; Q2 introduces the messenger to speak part of I.i.140, this change being 'more appropriate and more effective from the production stand-point'; Q2 corrects the mistaken Q1 *Exeunt* at I.i.141; and Q2 reassigns speeches at II.i.14 and II.ii.56 for reasons that would seem 'appropriate to a man of the theater'. An examination of the variations in stage-directions between the two texts leads to the conclusion that 'all of the new stage directions in Q2 are the type that would be added by a theatrical scribe or bookholder in the prompt-copy to make the action or dialogue clearer on the stage', particularly Q2's addition to the direction at V.iii.107.1, which is 'almost surely a production note from the theater prompt-book'. There should, of course, be many more directions of this kind in Q2; they are not found there because 'the scribe annotating Q1 prior to reprinting probably ignored the production notes generally, because they would have no relevance to a reader's edition of the play' (p. 196). There is, in my opinion, not one bit of evidence in this accumulation that conclusively shows the Q2 changes to have been taken from a prompt-book and much that goes against the hypothesis: even allowing for errors on the part of the annotator and the Q2 compositor, one still would not expect to find incorrect speech-prefixes among the Q2 changes if they had such a source and certainly not an incorrect stage-direction (as at I.ii.46.1). Dr Norland himself, for that matter, now regards his article as only exploratory. In his edition of *The Maid's Tragedy*, he generally followed Q2 rather than Q1 in indifferent readings.

For the present critical edition, Q1 has served as the copy-text; its archaic spelling and light punctuation have been retained except in places where the punctuation seriously misleads. The Q2 additions to the text have been accepted as, in general, authoritative, but their punctuation and spelling have been altered when these practices conflict with the system of Q1. In the case of less extensive variations where readings are supplied both by Q1 and Q2, Q1 has been followed when Q2 is obviously wrong, when Q2 modernizes or normalizes by making minor linguistic changes (*e.g.* altering Q1's 'infortunate' to 'unfortunate' at I.i.79 and 'a' to 'he' at I.i.82), and when an argument can be made for the correctness of the Q1 reading, which argument is given in the textual notes unless the desirability of the Q1 reading is obvious because of its better accord with metre, sense, or both. Otherwise, Q2 variants have been received into the text. Q2 variants in Fletcher's scenes as well as in Beaumont's are accepted on the assumption that the manuscript behind the Q2 changes represented, insofar as it can be known, the mutual intention of the two writers. And because Q2 has been accorded such high authority throughout, the usual form of the footnotes, ordinarily concerned with substantive emendations of the copy-text and their sources, has been modified to show any Q 2 reading, as well as any Q 1 reading, which has been rejected.

All extant copies of Q 1 and Q 2 have been collated, and readings from the later seventeenth-century editions and from a selection of subsequent editions are recorded in the Historical Collation. Several well-known editions are omitted from the Collation: Felix E. Schelling's (*Masterpieces of the English Drama*: New York, Cincinnati, and Chicago, 1912) because it follows the text of Bullen's Variorum; the edition introduced by Christopher Morley (New York, 1932) because examination of I.i indicated that the text of Weber was being reprinted with very minor changes; and A. K. McIlwraith's (in *Five Stuart Tragedies*: Oxford, 1953) because it too reprinted the Variorum text. Included, however, are substantive differences from the present text recommended by J. Monck Mason in his influential *Comments on the Plays of Beaumont and Fletcher* (1798) and by J. LeGay Brereton as collected in *Elizabethan Drama: Notes and Studies* (1909). Because this edition was in press when Andrew Gurr's appeared (Edinburgh, 1969), his contributions to the text could not be taken into account.

SPEAKERS

KING.

LYSIPPUS, brother to the King.

AMINTOR, a noble Gentleman.

EVADNE, wife to Amintor.

MELANTIUS
DIPHILUS } brothers to Evadne.

ASPATIA, troth-plight wife to Amintor.

CALIANAX, an old humorous Lord, and father to Aspatia.

CLEON
STRATO } Gentlemen.   10

DIAGORAS, a servant.

ANTIPHILA
OLIMPIAS } waiting Gentlewomen to Aspatia.

DULA, a Lady.

NIGHT
CINTHIA
NEPTUNE } Maskers.
EOLUS

[OTHER PERSONS

SEA GODS
WINDS } Maskers.   20

Courtiers, Ladies, Servants, etc.]

3 a noble Gentleman.] Q3; *om.* Q1–2
*8 CALIANAX,] Q4; CALLIANAX͆ Q1–3

28

The Maydes Tragedy

Enter Cleon, Strato, Lysippus, Diphilus.

Cleon. The rest are making ready sir.

Strato. So let them, theres time enough.

Diphilus. You are the brother to the King my Lord,
 Wee'le take your word.

Lysippus. *Strato* thou hast some skill in poetrie,
 What think'st thou of a maske, will it be well?

Strato. As well as masks can be.

Lysippus.   As masks can be?

Strato. Yes, they must commend their King, and speake in praise
 Of the assembly, blesse the Bride and Bridegroome,
 In person of some god, there tied to rules   10
 Of flatterie.

Cleon.   See good my Lord who is return'd.

Enter Melantius.

Lysippus. Noble *Melantius*, the land by me
 Welcomes thy vertues home to *Rhodes*,
 Thou that with blood abroad buyest us our peace.
 The breath of Kings is like the breath of gods,
 My brother wisht thee here, and thou art here;
 He will be too kinde, and wearie thee
 With often welcomes, but the time doth give thee
 A welcome, above his, or all the worlds.

Melantius. My Lord, my thankes, but these scratcht limbes of mine, 20
 Have spoke my love and truth unto my friends,

o.1 I.i] *Actus.*I.*Scœn.*I. Q1–2	*2 *Strato.*] Q2; *Lys.* Q1
3 the brother] Q2; *om.* the Q1	6 thou] Q1; *om.* Q2
8 their King] Q2; *om.* Q1	9 Bridegroome] Q2; groome Q1
10 there] *i.e.* they're	13 to *Rhodes*] Q2; *om.* Q1
14 blood...buyest] Q2; blowes...bringst Q1	
14 peace.] Q2; peace at home, Q1	17 too] Q2; *om.* Q1
18 welcomes] Q2; welcome Q1	19 worlds] Q2; world Q1

More then my tongue ere could, my mind's the same
It ever was to you; where I finde worth
I love the keeper, till he let it goe,
And then I follow it.
Diphilus.   Haile worthy brother,
He that rejoyces not at your returne
In safetie, is mine enemy for ever.
Melantius.   I thanke thee *Diphilus*: but thou art faultie,
I sent for thee to exercise thine armes
With me at *Patria*, thou camst not *Diphilus*:   30
Twas ill.
Diphilus.   My noble brother my excuse
Is my Kings strict command, which you my Lord
Can witnesse with me.
Lysippus.   Tis most true *Melantius*,
He might not come till the solemnities
Of this great match were past.
Diphilus.   Have you heard of it?
Melantius.   Yes, I have given cause to those, that here
Envy my deeds abroad, to call me gamesome,
I have no other busines here at *Rhodes*.
Lysippus.   We have a maske to night, and you must tread
A souldiers measure.   40
Melantius.   These soft and silken warres are not for me,
The musicke must be shrill and all confus'd
That stirs my blood, and then I daunce with armes:
But is *Amintor* wed?
Diphilus.   This day?
Melantius.   All joyes upon him, for he is my friend,
Wonder not that I call a man so young my friend;
His worth is great, valiant he is and temperate,
And one that never thinkes his life his owne,
If his friend neede it: when he was a boy,

32 strict] Q2; straight Q1   33 most] Q1; *om.* Q2
34 solemnities] Q1; solemnitie Q2   36 I] Q2; and Q1
36 here] Q1; *om.* Q2
43 daunce with armes:] Q2 (Armes); daunce, Q1
46 my friend] Q2; *om.* Q1   47 and temperate] Q2; *om.* Q1

As oft as I return'd (as without boast, 50
I brought home conquest) he would gaze upon me,
And view me round, to finde in what one limbe
The vertue lay to doe those things he heard:
Then would he wish to see my sword, and feele
The quicknesse of the edge, and in his hand
Weigh it, he oft would make me smile at this;
His youth did promise much, and his ripe yeares
Will see it all perform'd.

Enter Aspatia *passing by.*

     Haile Maide and Wife.
Thou faire *Aspatia*, may the holy knot,
That thou hast tied to day, last till the hand 60
Of age undoe't, mayst thou bring a race
Unto *Amintor*, that may fill the world
Successively with souldiers.
Aspatia.   My hard fortunes
Deserve not scorne, for I was never proud
When they were good.   *Exit* Aspatia.
Melantius.   Howes this?
Lysippus.   You are mistaken,
For she is not married.
Melantius.   You said *Amintor* was.
Diphilus. Tis true, but——
Melantius.   Pardon me, I did receive
Letters at *Patria* from my *Amintor*
That he should marie her.
Diphilus.   And so it stood,
In all opinion long, but your arrivall 70
Made me imagine you had heard the change.
Melantius. Who hath he taken then?
Lysippus.   A Ladie sir,
That beares the light about her, and strikes dead

56 Weigh] Q2; Weighes Q1   58 *by*] Q2; *with attendance* Q1
65–6 mistaken, | For‸] Q2 (for); mistaken‸ sir, Q1
72 hath] Q2; has Q1   *73 about] Q2; above Q1

31

With flashes of her eye, the faire *Evadne*
Your vertuous sister.

Melantius.　　　　Peace of heart betwixt them,
But this is strange.

Lysippus.　　　　The King my brother did it
To honour you, and these solemnities
Are at his charge.

Melantius.　　　　Tis royall like himselfe,
But I am sad, my speech beares so infortunate a sound
To beautifull *Aspatia*, there is rage　　　　　80
Hid in her fathers breast, *Calianax*,
Bent long against me and 'a should not thinke,
If I could call it backe, that I would take
So base revenges as to scorne the state
Of his neglected daughter: holds he still
His greatnesse with the King?

Lysippus.　　　　Yes, but this Lady
Walkes discontented with her watrie eyes
Bent on the earth: the unfrequented woods
Are her delight, and when she sees a bancke
Stucke full of flowers, she with a sigh will tell　　90
Her servants, what a prittie place it were
To burie lovers in, and make her maides
Pluck'em, and strow her over like a corse.
She carries with her an infectious griefe,
That strikes all her beholders, she will sing
The mournfulst things that ever eare hath heard,
And sigh, and sing againe, and when the rest
Of our young Ladyes in their wanton blood,
Tell mirthfull tales in course that fill the roome

79 infortunate] Q1; unfortunate Q2　　82 'a] Q1; he Q2
83 If I could] Q2; Could I but Q1　　84 So] Q2; Such Q1
85–6 holds...King?] Q2 (king); *om.* Q1
86–90 Yes...tell] Q2; O t'were pittie, for this Lady sir, | Sits discontented with her watrie eyes bent on the earth, | In unfrequented woods are her delight, | Where when she sees a bancke stucke full of flowers, | Then she will sit, and sigh, and tell Q1
88 earth:] Q1 (c) (~,); ear‸ Q1 (u)　　93 her over] Q2; them over her Q1
97 sigh] Q2; swound Q1　　98 our] Q2; your Q1
99 fill] Q2; fils Q1

With laughter, she will with so sad a looke
Bring forth a storie of the silent death
Of some forsaken virgin, which her griefe
Will put in such a phrase, that ere she end
Shee'le send them weeping one by one away.
Melantius.   She has a brother under my command
  Like her, a face as womanish as hers,
  But with a spirit that hath much outgrowne
  The number of his yeares.

Enter Amintor.

Cleon.   My Lord the Bridegroome.
Melantius.   I might run fiercely, not more hastily   110
  Upon my foe: I love thee well *Amintor*,
  My mouth is much too narrow for my heart,
  I joy to looke upon those eyes of thine,
  Thou art my friend,———but my disordred speech
  Cuts off my love.
Amintor.   Thou art *Melantius*,
  All love is spoke in that, a sacrifice
  To thanke the gods, *Melantius* is return'd
  In safty, victory sits on his sword
  As she was wont, may she build there, and dwell,
  And may thy armour be as it hath beene,
  Onely thy valour and thine innocence.   120
  What endlesse treasures would our enemies give,
  That I might hold thee still thus.
Melantius.   I am poore
  In words, but credit me young man thy mother
  Could do no more but weep, for joy to see thee
  After long absence, all the wounds I have,
  Fetcht not so much away, nor all the cries
  Of widdowed mothers: But this is peace
  And that was warre.
Amintor.   Pardon thou holy god
  Of marriage bed, and frowne not, I am for'st

124 do] Q1; *om.* Q2

In answere of such noble teares as those,   130
To weepe upon my wedding day.
Melantius.   I feare thou art growne too fickle, for I heare
A Lady mournes for thee, men say to death,
Forsaken of thee, on what tearmes I know not.
Amintor.   She had my promise, but the King forbad it,
And made me make this worthy change, thy sister,
Accompanied with graces about her,
With whom I long to loose my lusty youth,
And grow olde in her armes.
Melantius.   Be prosperous.

Enter Messenger.

Messenger.   My Lord the maskers rage for you.
Lysippus.   We are gone,—— 140
Cleon, Strato, Diphilus.
Amintor.   Weele all attend you,——we shall trouble you
With our solemnities.
Melantius.   Not so *Amintor.*
But if you laugh at my rude carriage
In peace, il'e doe as much for you in warre
When you come thither, but I have a mistresse
To bring to your delights, rough though I am,
I have a mistresse and she has a heart
She saies, but trust me, it is stone, no better,
There is no place that I can challenge gentlemen,   150
But you stand still, and here my way lies.

                                        Exeunt.

130 those] Q2; these Q1   132 fickle] Q2; cruell Q1
139.1 *Enter* Messenger.] Q2; *om.* Q1   140 *Messenger.*] Q2; *Amint.* Q1
141 *Diphilus.*] Q2; *Diphilus.* | *Exeunt Lysippus, Cleon, Strato, Diphilus.* Q1
145 peace] Q2; sports Q1   150 gentlemen] Q1; *om.* Q2

Enter Calianax, *with* Diagoras.   [I. ii]

Calianax.   *Diagoras* looke to the dores better for shame, you let
in all the world, and anon the King will raile at me: why very well
said, by *Jove* the King wil have the show i'th Court.

Diagoras.   Why doe you sweare so my Lord? you know heele
have it here.

Calianax.   By this light if he be wise, he will not.

Diagoras.   And if he will not be wise, you are forsworne.

Calianax.   One may swear his heart out, and get thankes on no
side, ile be gone, looke too't who will.

Diagoras.   My Lord I shall never keepe them out. Pray stay, your 10
lookes will terrifie them.

Calianax.   My lookes terrifie them? you coxcomely asse you, ile be
judgd by all the company, whether thou hast not a worse face
then I.

Diagoras.   I meane because they know you, and your office.

Calianax.   Office, I would I could put it off, I am sure I sweat
quite through my office, I might have made room at my daughters
wedding, they ha neere kild her amongst them. And now I must
doe service for him that hath forsaken her, serve that will.

                                           Exit Calianax.

Diagoras.   Hee's so humerous since his daughter was forsaken? 20
hark, hark, there, there, so, so, codes, codes, (*knock within*)——
what now?

Melantius (*within*).   Open the dore.

Diagoras.   Whose there?

Melantius [*within*].   *Melantius.*

Diagoras.   I hope your Lord-ship brings no troope with you, for
if you doe, I must returne them.

0.1 *with*] Q2; *and* Q1   2 raile at] Q2; be angry with Q1
3 i'th] Q3; i'th the Q1–2
*8 may...out] must sweat out his heart with swearing Q1; may sweare his heart
out with swearing Q2–8; may wear his heart out with swearing F2
10 Pray stay,] Q2; *om.* Q1   12 asse you] Q2; asse Q1
13 judgd] Q3 (judgde); judge Q1–2   17 through my] Q2; through in my Q1
18 And] Q2; But Q1
*21 there, there,...codes] Q2; whose﹏ there,   codes Q1
24 Whose there?] Q2 (Who's); Who i'st. Q1   26 with you] Q2; *om.* Q1

Enter Melantius *and a* Lady.

Melantius.   None but this Lady sir.

Diagoras.   The Ladies are all plac'd above, save those that come
in the Kings troope, the best of *Rhodes* sit there, and theres roome. 30

Melantius.   I thanke you sir,——when I have seene you placed
madam, I must attend the King, but the maske done, ile waite on
you againe.   *Exeunt* Melantius, Lady *other dore.*

Diagoras.   Stand backe there, roome for my Lord *Melantius,* pray
beare back, this is no place for such youthes and their truls, let the
dores shut agen: I, do your heads itch? ile scratch them for you,
so now thrust and hang: [*knock within*] againe,——who i'st now?
I cannot blame my Lord *Calianax* for going away, would he were
here, he would run raging amongst them, and breake a dozen
wiser heads than his own in the twinckling of an eye: what's the 40
newes now?

Within.   I pray you can you helpe mee to the speech of the maister
Cooke?

Diagoras.   If I open the dore ile cooke some of your calves heads.
Peace rogues?——[*knock within*] againe,——who i'st?

Melantius (within).   *Melantius?*

Enter Calianax.

Calianax.   Let him not in.

Diagoras.   O my Lord a must,——make roome there for my Lord.

Enter Melantius.

Is your Lady plast?

Melantius.   Yes sir, I thanke you:——
My Lord *Calianax,* well met,   50
Your causelesse hate to me I hope is buried.

30 and theres roome] Q2; there is no roome Q1
33 *Exeunt...dore.*] Dyce; *Exit Melantius Lady other dore.* Q1; *om.* Q2–8, F2
36 agen: I,] Q2; agen, no; Q1   36 for you] Q2; *om.* Q1
38 going away] Q2; giving way Q1
39–40 dozen...own] Q2; dozen heads Q1
46.1–48.1 *Enter...Melantius.*] Q1; *Enter Calianax to Melantius.* at l. 46.1 Q2

36

Calianax.   Yes I doe service for your sister here,
  That brings mine owne poore child to timelesse death,
  She loves your friend *Amintor*, such another
  False hearted Lord as you.
Melantius.   You doe me wrong,
  A most unmanly one, and I am slow
  In taking vengeance, but be well advis'd.
Calianax.   It may be so,——who plac'd the Lady there
  So neere the presence of the King?
Melantius.   I did.
Calianax.   My Lord she must not sit there.
Melantius.   Why?   60
Calianax.   The place is kept for women of more worth.
Melantius.   More worth then she? it misbecomes your age,
  And place to be thus womanish, forbeare,
  What you have spoke I am content to thinke
  The palsey shooke your tongue to.
Calianax.   Why tis well if I stand here to place mens wenches.
Melantius.   I shall forget this place, thy age, my safety,
  And through all cut that poore sickly weeke
  Thou hast to live, away from thee.
Calianax.   Nay I know you can fight for your whore.   70
Melantius.   Bate me the King, and be he flesh and blood
  A lies that sayes it, thy mother at fifteene
  Was black and sinfull to her.
Diagoras.   Good my Lord——
Melantius.   Some god pluck threescore yeares from that fond man,
  That I may kill him, and not staine mine honor;
  It is the curse of souldiers, that in peace
  They shall be braved by such ignoble men,
  As (if the land were troubled,) would with teares
  And knees beg succor from 'em: would that blood
  (That sea of blood) that I have lost in fight,   80

57 but] Q2; *om.* Q1   58–59 there₍ₐ₎ |So...King?] Q2; there. Q1
63 thus] Q2; so Q1   66 Why] Q2; *om.* Q1
67 shall forget] Q2; shall quite forget Q1
71 me] Q1; *om.* Q2   71 he] Q2 (hee); of Q1
79 that] Q2; the Q1

Were running in thy veines, that it might make thee
Apt to say lesse, or able to maintaine,
Shouldst thou say more,——This *Rhodes* I see is nought
But a place priviledg'd to doe men wrong.
Calianax.   I, you may say your pleasure.

Enter Amintor.

Amintor.   What vilde injurie
Has sturd my worthy friend, who is as slow
To fight with words as he is quick of hande?
Melantius.   That heape of age, which I should reverence,
If it were temperate, but testie yeares
Are most contemptible.
Amintor.   Good sir forbeare.   90
Calianax.   There is just such another as your selfe.
Amintor.   He will wrong you, or me, or any man,
And talke as if he had no life to loose
Since this our match: the King is comming in,
I would not for more wealth then I enjoy
He should perceive you raging, he did heare
You were at difference now, which hastned him.
Calianax.   Make roome there.   *Hoboyes play within.*

Enter King, Evadne, Aspatia, *Lords and Ladies.*

King.   *Melantius* thou art welcome, and my love
Is with thee still; but this is not a place   100
To brable in,——*Calianax*, joyne hands.
Calianax.   He shall not have mine hand.
King.   This is no time
To force you too't, I doe love you both,
Calianax you looke well to your office,
And you *Melantius* are welcome home,——
Begin the maske.

82 or] Q2; and Q1
85 say] Q2; talke Q1   85 injurie] Q2; wrong Q1
87 hande] Q2 (hand); hands Q1   88 *Melantius.*] Q2; CAL. Q1
94 comming] Q1(c); come Q1(u)   99 *King.*] Q2; *om.* Q1
99 my] Q2; thy Q1   100 thee] Q2; me Q1

38

Melantius.   Sister I joy to see you, and your choyce,
   You lookt with my eies when you tooke that man,
   Be happy in him.   *Recorders* [*play within.*]
Evadne.   O my deerest brother,
   Your presence is more joyfull then this day,   110
   Can be unto me.

                    The Maske.

                    Night *rises in mists.*

Night.   Our raigne is come, for in the quenching sea
   The Sun is drownd, and with him fell the day:
   Bright *Cinthia* heare my voyce, I am the *Night*
   For whom thou bearst about, thy borrowed light.
   Appeare, no longer thy pale visage shrowde,
   But strike thy silver hornes quite through a cloud,
   And send a beame upon my swarthie face,
   By which I may discover all the place
   And persons and how many longing eies,   120
   Are come to waite on our solemnities.

                    Enter Cinthia.

How dull and black am I? I could not finde
This beautie without thee, I am so blinde,
Me thinkes they shew like to those easterne streaks,
That warne us hence before the morning breaks;
Back my pale servant, for these eies know how,
To shoote farre more and quicker rayes then thou.
Cinthia.   Great Queen they be a troop for whom alone,
   One of my clearest moones I have put on,
   A troope that lookes as if thy selfe and I,   130
   Had pluckt our reines in, and our whips laid by
   To gaze upon these mortals, that appeare
   Brighter then we.

111 Can...me.] Q2; *om.* Q1
112 come] Q2; now Q1
120 and how] Q2; that have Q1
123 I am] Q2; am I Q1

111.1 *The*] Q2; *om.* Q1
*112 quenching] Q1; raging Q2
122 I could] Q2; can I Q1
132 these mortals] Q2; those Q1

Night.   Then let us keepe 'em here,
And never more our chariots drive away,
But hold our places and out-shine the day.
Cinthia.   Great Queene of shaddowes you are pleasd to speake,
Of more then may be done, we may not breake
The gods decrees, but when our time is come,
Must drive away and give the day our roome.
Yet whil'st our raigne lasts, let us stretch our power   140
To give our servants one contented houre,
With such unwonted solemne grace and state
As may for ever after force them hate
Our brothers glorious beames, and wish the night,
Crown'd with a thousand starres, and our cold light:
For almost all the world their service bend
To *Phœbus*, and in vaine my light I lend,
Gaz'd on unto my setting from my rise
Almost of none, but of unquiet eyes.
Night.   Then shine at full faire Queen, and by thy power,   150
Produce a birth to crowne this happy houre,
Of Nimphes and shepheards, let their songs discover,
Easie and sweete who is a happy lover,
Or if thou w'oot then call thine owne *Endimion*
From the sweete flowrie bed he lies upon
On *Latmus* top, thy pale beames drawne away,
And of his long night let him make this day.
Cinthia.   Thou dreamst darke Queene, that faire boy was not
    mine,
Nor went I downe to kisse him, ease and wine,
Have bred these bold tales, poets when they rage   160
Turne gods to men, and make an houre an age,

*135 hold] Q1; keepe Q2   140–149 Yet...eyes.] Q2; *om.* Q1
144 wish] Q3; with Q2; *om.* Q1
150 faire...thy] Q2; pale...that Q1
151 crowne] Q2; fill Q1
152 shepheards, let] Q2; shepheards, and let Q1
154 then call] Q2; *om.* Q1   155 bed] Q2; banck Q1
156 top] Q2; brow Q1   *157 his] Q1; this Q2
157 this] Q2; thy Q1   158 Queene] Q2; power Q1
159 wine] Q2; winde Q1   161 Turne] Q2; Turnes Q1

40

But I will give a greater state and glory,
And raise to time a nobler memory
Of what these lovers are,——rise, rise, I say,
Thou power of deepes, thy surges laid away,
Neptune great King of waters, and by me
Be proud to be commanded.

Neptune *rises.*

Neptune.   *Cinthia* see,
Thy word hath fetcht me hither, let me know
Why I ascend.
Cinthia.   Doth this majestick show
Give thee no knowledge yet?
Neptune.   Yes, now I see,   170
Something entended *Cinthia* worthy thee,
Go on, ile be a helper.
Cinthia.   Hie thee then,
And charge the Winde goe from his rockie den,
Let loose his subjects, onely *Boreas*
Too foule for our intensions as he was,
Still keepe him fast chain'd, we must have none here
But vernall blasts and gentle winds appeare,
Such as blow flowers, and through the glad bowes sing,
Many soft welcomes to the lusty spring.
These are our musique: next thy watrie race   180
Bring on in couples, we are pleas'd to grace
This noble night, each in their richest things
Your owne deepes or the broken vessell brings,
Be prodigall and I shall be as kinde,
And shine at full upon you.
Neptune.   Oh the Winde!

*163 nobler] Q1; noble Q2   168 fetcht] Q2; force Q1
174 his] Q1; thy Q2   179 welcomes] Q2; welcome Q1
180 These...next] Q2 (musicke); Bid them draw neere to have Q1
181 Bring] Q2; Led Q1   183 vessell] Q2; vessels Q1
185 Oh] Q2; See Q1
*185 Winde!] Langbaine; winde_Λ Q1-8, F2

41

Enter Eolus *out of a Rock.*

Commanding *Eolus.*

Eolus.   Great *Neptune.*

Neptune.   He.

Eolus.   What is thy will?

Neptune.   We doe command thee free,
    Favonius and thy milder winds to waite
    Upon our *Cinthia,* but tie *Boreas* straight,
    Hee's too rebellious.

Eolus.   I shall doe it.

Neptune.   Doe. [*Exit* Eolus *into the Rock.*] 190
    Eolus [*within*].   Great maister of the floud, and all below,
    Thy full command has taken——O! the Maine,
    Neptune.

Neptune.   Here.
                    [*Enter* Eolus *and Winds.*]

Eolus.   *Boreas* has broke his chaine,
    And strugling with the rest has got away.

Neptune.   Let him alone, ile take him up at sea,
    He will not long be thence, goe once againe
    And call out of the bottomes of the Maine,
    Blew *Proteus,* and the rest, charge them put on
    Their greatest pearles and the most sparkling stone
    The beaten rock breeds, tell this night is done   200
    By me a solemne honor to the Moone,
    Flie like a full saile.

Eolus.   I am gone.   [*Exit.*]

Cinthia.   Darke *Night,*
    Strike a full scilence, doe a thorow right

188 *Favonius*] Q3; *Fanonius* Q1–2   189 straight] *i.e.* strait
190 too] Q2; *om.* Q1
*190–192 *Neptune.* Doe....Maine,] Theobald; NEPT. Doe_∧ great maister of the
floud, and all below_∧|Thy...taken_∧| EOL. O! the Maine_∧ Q1–8, F2
    191 Great] Q2; *om.* Q1   196 He] Q2; I Q1
    196 long be] Q2; be long Q1   196 once] Q2; hence Q1
    197 call...bottomes] Q2; bid the other call out Q1
    200 tell] Dyce (Mason's suggestion); till Q1–8, F2

To this great *Chorus*, that our musique may
Touch high as heaven, and make the East breake day
At mid-night.   *Musique.*

[*Enter* Proteus *and Sea Gods.*]

Song.

Cinthia *to thy power and thee*
we obey,
Joy to this great company,
and no day   210
Come to steale this night away
Till the rights of love are ended,
And the lusty Bridegroome say,
Welcome light of all befriended.

Pace out you waterie powers below,
let your feete
Like the gallies when they row
even beate.
Let your unknowne measures, set
To the still winds, tell to all,   220
That gods are come immortall great,
To honour this great Nuptuall.

The Measure.

Second Song.

Hold back thy houres darke Night *till we have done,*
The day will come too soone,
Young Maydes will curse thee if thou steal'st away,
And leav'st their blushes open to the day,
Stay, Stay, and hide
the blushes of the Bride.

Stay gentle Night *and with thy darkenesse cover*
the kisses of her lover.   230

212 rights] *i.e.* rites   223 darke] Q2; old Q1
226 blushes] Q2; losses Q1

43

Stay and confound her teares and her shrill cryings,
Her weake denials, vowes and often dyings,
Stay and hide all,
but helpe not though she call.

Another Measure.

Neptune.   Great Queene of us and heaven, heare what I bring
To make this houre a full one.
Cinthia.   Speake Seas King.
Neptune.   The tunes my *Amphitrite* joyes to have,
When she will daunce upon the rising wave,
And court me as she sayles; my *Tritons* play
Musique to lay a storme, ile lead the way.   240

[Third] Song. Measure.

To bed, to bed, come Hymen *lead the Bride,*
And lay her by her husbands side:
Bring in the virgins every one
That greeve to lie alone;
That they may kisse, while they may say a maid,
To morrow t'will be other kist and said:
Hesperus *be long a shining,*
Whilst these lovers are a twining.

[*Enter* Eolus.]

Eolus.   Ho *Neptune.*
Neptune.   *Eolus.*
Eolus.   The sea goes hie,
Boreas hath rais'd a storme, goe and apply   250

231 *shrill*] Q2; *loud* Q1   234 *though*] Q2; *if* Q1
234.1–248 Another...*twining.*] Q2; *om.* Q1
*234.1 Another Measure.] Daniel (Fleay's suggestion); If not her measure *following*
one, *l.* 236 Q2–8, F2; Maskers daunce, *Neptune* leads it‸ Q1
*237–239 The...she...she] Theobald; Thy...they...the Q2–8, F2; *om.* Q1
237 *Amphitrite*] Q3; *Amphitrites* Q2; *om.* Q1
240 lay] Dyce (Heath's suggestion); lead Q2–8, F2; *om.* Q1
250 hath] Q2; has Q1

44

Thy trident, else I prophesie, ere day
Many a tall ship will be cast away,
Desend with all the gods and all their powre,
To strike a calme.

Cinthia.   A thanks to every one,
My favour to you all; to gratulate
So great a service done at my desire,
Ye shall have many floods fuller and higher
Then you have wisht for, and no eb shall dare,
To let the day see where your dwellings are.
Now back unto your government in hast,   260
Least your proud charge should swell above the wast,
And win upon the Iland.

Neptune.   We obey.
                    Neptune *descends, and the Sea Gods.*
                    [*Exeunt* Eolus *and* Winds *into the Rock.*]

Cinthia.   Hold up thy head dead *Night* seest thou not day?
The East begins to lighten, I must downe
And give my brother place.

Night.   Oh I could frowne
To see the day, the day that flings his light
Upon my kingdome, and contems olde *Night*,
Let him goe on, and flame, I hope to see
Another wild fire in his axeltree,
And all fall drencht, but I forget,——speake Queene,   270
The day growes on, I must no more be seene.

Cinthia.   Heave up thy drowsie head agen and see
A greater light, a greater Majestie,
Betweene our sect and us, whip up thy teame,

*254 A...one] Q2; We thanke you for this houre Q1
255 My...gratulate] Q1; and to gratulate Q2
258 and] Q1; *om.* Q2   259 dwellings] Q1; dwelling Q2
260 government] Q2; governments Q1
261 charge] Q2; waters Q1
262.1 Neptune...Gods.] Q2; *Exeunt Maskers*ₐ| *Descend.* following Iland Q1
*267 kingdome] Q1; Kingdomes Q2
271 must] Q2; dare Q1
272 Heave up] Q2; Once heave Q1   *274 sect] *stet* Q1–2
274 whip] Q2; lash Q1

45

The day breaks here, and yon same flashing streame
Shot from the south: say which way wilt thou goe?
Night.   Ile vanish into mists.
Cinthia.   I into day.   *Exeunt.*

Finis Maske.

King.   Take lights their Ladyes, get the Bride to bed,——
We will not see you laid, good night *Amintor*,
Weele ease you of that tedious ceremony,   280
Were it my case I should thinke time runne slow:
If thou beest noble youth, get me a boy
That may defend my Kingdomes from my foes.
Amintor.   All happinesse to you.
King.   Good night *Melantius*.

                                                          Exeunt.

Enter Evadne, Aspatia, Dula, *and other Ladyes.*   II. i

Dula.   Madame shall we undresse you for this fight?
The wars are nak't that you must make to night.
Evadne.   You are very merry *Dula*.
Dula.   I should be
Far merrier Madame, if it were with me
As it is with you.
Evadne.   Howes that?
Dula.   That I might goe
To bed with him with credit that you doe.
Evadne.   Why how now wench?
Dula.   Come Ladyes, will you helpe?
Evadne.   I am soone undone.
Dula.   And as soone done,
Good store of clothes will trouble you at both.

275 same flashing] Q2; sun flaring Q1
277 I into day] Q2; Adew Q1   277.1 *Finis Maske.*] Q2; *om.* Q1
278 lights] Q2; light Q1   278 their] *i.e.* there
*283 Kingdomes] *stet* Q1–2
0.1 II.i] *Actus Secundus.* Q1–2
5–6 *Evadne.* Howes...doe.] Q1; *om.* Q2   3 very] Q2; *om.* Q1
                                               6 with credit] *i.e.* wi'th' credit

Evadne.   Art thou drunke *Dula?*
Dula.   Why heres none but we.   10
Evadne.   Thou thinkst belike there is no modesty
  When we'are alone.
Dula.   I by my troth, you hit my thoughts aright.
Evadne.   You prick me Lady.
1. Lady.   Tis against my will.
Dula.   Anon you must indure more and lie still,
  You're best to practise.
Evadne.   Sure this wench is mad.
Dula.   No faith, this is a trick that I have had
  Since I was foureteene.
Evadne.   Tis high time to leave it.
Dula.   Nay now ile keepe it till the trick leave me,
  A dozen wanton words put in your head,   20
  Will make you livelier in your husbands bed.
Evadne.   Nay faith then take it.
Dula.   Take it Madame, where?
  We all I hope will take it that are here.
Evadne.   Nay then ile give you ore.
Dula.   So will I make
  The ablest man in *Rhodes* or his heart ake.
Evadne.   Wilt take my place to night?
Dula.   Ile hold your cards
  Against any two I know.
Evadne.   What wilt thou doe?
Dula.   Madame weele doo't and make'm leave play too.
Evadne.   *Aspatia* take her part.
Dula.   I will refuse it,
  She will pluck downe a side, she does not use it.   30
Evadne.   Why doe I prethee.

12 we'are] Q1; we are Q2
13 aright] Q2; right Q1   14 Lady] Q2; Madame Q1
*14–15 *1. Lady.* Tis...| *Dula.* Anon] Q1; *Dula.* Tis...| Anon Q2
16 You're] Q2; Tis Q1   18 high] Q2; *om.* Q1
23 I...it] Q2; will take it I hope Q1
26 take] Q2; lie in Q1
31 Why] Q2; *om.* Q1   31 I prethee] Q1; *om.* Q2

Dula.   You will finde the play
  Quickly, because your head lies well that way.
Evadne.   I thanke thee *Dula*, would thou couldst instill
  Some of thy mirth into *Aspatia*,
  Nothing but sad thoughts in her brest doe dwell,
  Me thinkes a meane betwixt you would doe well.
Dula.   She is in love, hang me if I were so,
  But I could run my Countrey, I love too
  To doe those things that people in love doe.
Aspatia.   It were a timelesse smile should prove my cheeke,   40
  It were a fitter houre for me to laugh,
  When at the Alter the religious Priest,
  Were passifying the offended powers,
  With sacrifice, then now; this should have beene
  My right, and all your hands have bin imployd,
  In giving me a spotlesse offering
  To young *Amintors* bed, as we are now,
  For you: pardon *Evadne*, would my worth
  Were great as yours, or that the King or he
  Or both thought so; perhaps he found me worthlesse,   50
  But till he did so, in these eares of mine,
  These credulous eares, he powred the sweetest words
  That art or love could frame; if he were false
  Pardon it heaven, and if I did want ‌ᵃᶜᵏ
  Vertue, you safely may forgive that too,
  For I have lost none that I had from you.
Evadne.   Nay leave this sad talke Madame.
Aspatia.   Would I could, then I should leave the cause.
Evadne.   See if you have not spoild all *Dulas* mirth.
Aspatia.   Thou thinkst thy heart hard, but if thou beest caught   60
  Remember me; thou shalt perceive a fire
  Shot suddenly into thee.
Dula.   Thats not so good,
  Let'em shoot any thing but fire, I feare'm not.

---

40 cheeke] Q 1; checke Q 2   *45 right] Q 1 (*i.e.* rite); night Q 2
59 See] Q 2; Loe Q 1   62 into] Q 2; unto Q 1
63 fire, I] Q 2; fire, and I Q 1

Aspatia.   Well wench thou maist be taken.
Evadne.   Ladies good night, Ile doe the rest my selfe.
Dula.   Nay let your Lord doe some.
Aspatia.   *Lay a garland on my hearse*
                         Of the dismall Yew———
Evadne.   Thats one of your sad songs Madame.
Aspatia.   Beleeve me tis a very pretty one.   70
Evadne.   How is it Madame?

                         Song.

Aspatia.   *Lay a garland on my hearse*
                         Of the dismall Yew,
                    Maidens willow branches beare,
                         Say I died true,
                    My love was false, but I was firme,
                         From my houre of birth,
                    Upon my buried body lay
                         Lightly gently earth.

Evadne.   Fie ont Madame, the words are so strange,   80
   They are able to make one dreame of hobgoblines.
   I could never have the power, sing that *Dula.*

                         [Song.]

Dula.   *I could never have the power*
                    To love one above an houre,
                    But my heart would prompt mine eie
                    On some other man to flie,
                         Venus *fix mine eies fast,*
                         Or if not, give me all that I shall see at last.

Evadne.   So leave me now.
Dula.   Nay we must see you laid.
Aspatia.   Madame good night, may all the mariage joyes   90
   That longing maides imagine in their beds

   64 maist] Q2; must Q1   67–89 *Aspatia. Lay* . . . laid.] Q2; *om.* Q1

4   49   B D W

Prove so unto you, may no discontent
Grow twixt your love and you, but if there doe,
Enquire of me and I will guide your mone,
And teach you an artificiall way to grieve,
To keepe your sorrow waking: love your Lord
No worse then I, but if you love so well,
Alas you may displease him, so did I.——
This is the last time you shall looke on me:
Ladies farewell, as soone as I am dead,   100
Come all and watch one night about my hearse.
Bring each a mournefull storie and a teare,
To offer at it when I goe to earth;
With flattering Ivy claspe my coffin round,
Write on my brow my fortune, let my beere
Be borne by Virgins that shall sing by course,
The truth of maides, and perjuries of men.
Evadne.   Alas I pittie thee.
Omnes.   Madame good night.   *Exit* Evadne.
1. Lady.   Come weele let in the Bridegroome.
Dula.   Where's my Lord?

                    Enter Amintor.

1. Lady.   Here take this light.
Dula.   Youle finde her in the darke.   110
1. Lady.   Your Ladye's scarse a bed yet, you must helpe her.
Aspatia.   Goe and be happy in your Ladyes love,
  May all the wrongs that you have done to me,
  Be utterly forgotten in my death,
  Ile trouble you no more, yet I will take
  A parting kisse, and will not be denied.   [*Kisses* Amintor.]
  You'le come my Lord and see the virgins weepe,
  When I am laid in earth, though you your selfe
  Can know no pittie; thus I winde my selfe
  Into this willow garland, and am prouder   120
  That I was once your love, (though now refus'd)
  Then to have had another true to me.

        92 no] Q2; not Q1   110 Youle] Q2 (You'le); Heele Q1
        111 yet] Q2; *om.* Q1

So with praiers I leave you, and must trie
Some yet unpractis'd way to grieve and die.   *Exit* Aspatia.
Dula.   Come Ladies will you goe?
Omnes.   Good night my Lord.
Amintor.   Much happinesse unto you all.   *Exeunt Ladies.*
I did that Lady wrong, me thinkes I feele
Her griefe shoot suddenly through all my veines,
Mine eyes runne, this is strange at such a time.
It was the King first mov'd me too't, but he   130
Has not my will in keeping,——why doe I
Perplex my selfe thus? something whispers me,
Goe not to bed: my guilt is not so great
As mine owne conscience, too sencible,
Would make me thinke, I onely breake a promise,
And twas the King that forst me: timerous flesh,
Why shakst thou so?
                         Enter Evadne.

                         Away my idle feares,
Yonder she is, the luster of whose eie,
Can blot away the sad remembrance
Of all these things:——oh my *Evadne* spare   140
That tender body, let it not take cold,
The vapors of the night shall not fall here,
To bed my love, *Hymen* will punish us,
For being slack performers of his rights,
Camst thou to call me?
Evadne.   No.
Amintor.   Come, come, my love,
And let us loose our selves to one another,
Why art thou up so long?
Evadne.   I am not well.
Amintor.   To bed, then let me winde thee in these armes,
Till I have banisht sicknesse.

125 *Omnes.*] Q2; 1. LAD. Q1
128 Her] Q2; A Q1   129 runne] Q2; raine Q1
131 doe] Q2; did Q1   136 that forst] Q2; inforst Q1
138 she is] Q2; is she Q1   *142 shall] Q1; will Q2

Evadne.   Good my Lord
I cannot sleepe.
Amintor.   *Evadne* weele watch,   150
I meane no sleeping.
Evadne.   Ile not goe to bed.
Amintor.   I prethee doe.
Evadne.   I will not for the world.
Amintor.   Why my deere love?
Evadne.   Why? I have sworne I will not.
Amintor.   Sworne!
Evadne.   I?
Amintor.   How? sworne *Evadne*?
Evadne.   Yes, sworne *Amintor*, and will sweare againe
If you will wish to heare me.
Amintor.   To whom have you sworne this?
Evadne.   If I should name him the matter were not great.
Amintor.   Come, this is but the coynesse of a bride.
Evadne.   The coynesse of a bride?
Amintor.   How pretilie
That frowne becomes thee.
Evadne.   Doe you like it so?   160
Amintor.   Thou canst not dresse thy face in such a looke,
But I shall like it.
Evadne.   What looke likes you best?
Amintor.   Why doe you aske?
Evadne.   That I may shew you one lesse pleasing to you.
Amintor.   Howes that?
Evadne.   That I may shew you one lesse pleasing to you.
Amintor.   I prethee put thy jests in milder lookes,
It shewes as thou wert angry.
Evadne.   So perhaps
I am indeede.
Amintor.   Why, who has done thee wrong?
Name me the man, and by thy selfe I sweare,   170
Thy yet unconquered selfe, I will revenge thee.

162 likes] Q2; will like Q1   170 I sweare] Q2; sweete love Q1
171 thee] Q2; it Q1

Evadne.   Now I shall trie thy truth. If thou doest love me,
Thou waighst not any thing compar'd with me,
Life, honour, joyes eternall, all delights
This world can yeeld, or hopefull people faine,
Or in the life to come, are light as aire
To a true lover when his Lady frownes,
And bids him doe this: wilt thou kill this man?
Sweare my *Amintor*, and ile kisse the sin
Off from thy lips.
Amintor.   I wonnot swear sweet love,   180
Till I doe know the cause.
Evadne.   I wood thou wouldst,
Why, it is thou that wrongst me, I hate thee,
Thou should'st have kild thy selfe.
Amintor.   If I should know that, I should quickly kill
The man you hated.
Evadne.   Know it then, and doo't.
Amintor.   Oh no, what looke so ere thou shalt put on,
To trie my faith, I shall not thinke thee false,
I cannot finde one blemish in thy face
Where falsehood should abide: leave, and to bed;
If you have sworne to any of the virgins   190
That were your olde companions to preserve
Your maidenhead a night, it may be done
Without this meanes.
Evadne.   A maidenhead *Amintor*
At my yeares?
Amintor.   Sure she raves,——this cannot be
Thy naturall temper, shall I call thy maides?
Either thy healthfull sleepe hath left thee long,
Or else some feaver rages in thy blood.

173 with] Q2; to Q1
175 This] Q2; The Q1
175–176 or. . .come,] Q2; *om.* Q1
179–180 sin | Off from] Q2; sun | Of Q1
181 doe] Q2 (do); *om.* Q1   185 then] Q2; *om.* Q1
186 shalt] Q2; should'st Q1   187 shall not] Q2; cannot Q1
195 Thy] Q2; Her Q1

Evadne.　Neither *Amintor*, thinke you I am mad,
　Because I speake the truth?
Amintor.　　　　　　　Wil you not lie
　With me to night?
Evadne.　　　　　To night? you talke as if　　　　200
　I would hereafter.
Amintor.　　　　Hereafter, yes I doe.
Evadne.　You are deceiv'd,
　Put off amazement and with patience mark
　What I shall utter, for the Oracle
　Knowes nothing truer, tis not for a night
　Or two that I forbeare thy bed, but ever.
Amintor.　I dreame,——awake *Amintor.*
Evadne.　　　　　　　　　You heare right,
　I sooner will finde out the beds of Snakes,
　And with my youthfull blood warme their cold flesh,
　Letting them curle themselves about my limbes,　　210
　Then sleepe one night with thee; this is not faind,
　Nor sounds it like the coynesse of a bride.
Amintor.　Is flesh so earthly to endure all this?
　Are these the joyes of mariage? *Hymen* keepe
　This story (that will make succeeding youth
　Neglect thy ceremonies) from all eares.
　Let it not rise up for thy shame and mine
　To after ages, we will scorne thy lawes,
　If thou no better blesse them; touch the heart
　Of her that thou hast sent me, or the world　　　220
　Shall know: ther'es not an altar that will smoake
　In praise of thee; we will adopt us sonnes,
　Then vertue shall inherit and not blood;
　If we doe lust, we'le take the next we meet,
　Serving our selves as other creatures doe,

198 *Amintor*] Q2; of these, what Q1
199 *Amintor.* Wil] Q2 (Will); AMIN. Is this the truth, wil Q1
200 To night?] Q2; *om.* Q1　　　200–201 if | I] Q2; if you thought I Q1
206 thy] Q2; your Q1　　　208 will] Q2; would Q1
212 coynesse] Q2; kisses Q1　　　220 that] Q2; whom Q1
221 ther'es_A...that] Q2; this,...then Q1

And never take note of the female more,
Nor of her issue: I doe rage in vaine,
She can but jest;——Oh pardon me my love,
So deare the thoughts are that I hold of thee,
That I must breake forth; satisfie my feare,   230
It is a paine beyond the hand of death,
To be in doubt; confirme it with an oath,
If this be true.
Evadne.   Doe you invent the forme,
Let there be in it all the binding wordes
Divels and conjurers can put together,
And I will take it; I have sworne before,
And here by all things holy doe againe,
Never to be acquainted with thy bed.
Is your doubt over now?
Amintor.   I know too much, would I had doubted still,   240
Was ever such a mariage night as this?
You powers above, if you did ever meane
Man should be us'd thus, you have thought a way
How he may beare himselfe, and save his honour:
Instruct me in it, for to my dull eyes
There is no meane, no moderate course to runne,
I must live scorn'd or be a murderer:
Is there a third? why is this night so calme?
Why does not heaven speake in thunder to us,
And drowne her voyce?
Evadne.   This rage will doe no good.   250
Amintor.   *Evadne,* heare me, thou hast tane an oath,
But such a rash one, that to keepe it were
Worse then to sweare it, call it backe to thee,
Such vowes as those never ascend the heaven,
A teare or two will wash it quite away:
Have mercy on my youth, my hopefull youth,
If thou be pittifull, for without boast

228 can but] Q2; cannot Q1   229 that] Q2; which Q1
231 hand] Q2; paine Q1   245 Instruct me in] Q2; Instant me with Q1
250 her] Q2; their Q1   254 those] Q2; that Q1

This land was proud of me: what Lady was there
That men cald faire, and vertuous in this Isle
That would have shund my love? it is in thee   260
To make me hold this worth——Oh we vaine men
That trust all our reputation
To rest upon the weake and yeelding hand
Of feeble woman,——but thou art not stone,
Thy flesh is soft, and in thine eyes doe dwell
The spirit of love, thy heart cannot be hard.
Come leade me from the bottome of dispaire,
To all the joyes thou hast, I know thou wilt,
And make me carefull least the sudden change
Ore-come my spirits.
Evadne.   When I call back this oath,   270
The paines of hell inviron me.
Amintor.   I sleepe and am to temporate, come to bed,
Or by those haires, which if thou hast a soule
Like to thy locks, were threads for Kings to weare
About their armes——
Evadne.   Why so perhaps they are.
Amintor.   Ile dragge thee to my bed, and make thy tongue
Undoe this wicked oath, or on thy flesh
Ile print a thousand wounds to let out life.
Evadne.   I feare thee not, doe what thou darst to me,
Every ill sounding word, or threatning looke   280
Thou shewest to me, will be reveng'd at full.
Amintor.   It will not sure *Evadne.*
Evadne.   Doe not you hazard that.
Amintor.   Ha ye your Champions?
Evadne.   Alas *Amintor* thinkst thou I forbeare
To sleepe with thee, because I have put on
A maidens strictnesse? looke upon these cheekes,
And thou shalt finde the hot and rising blood
Unapt for such a vow; no, in this heart
There dwels as much desire, and as much will,
To put that wished act in practise, as ever yet   290

290 in practise] Q2; *om.* Q1

56

Was knowne to woman, and they have been showne both.
But it was the folly of thy youth,
To thinke this beauty, to what hand soe're
It shall be cald, shall stoope to any second.
I doe enjoy the best, and in that height
Have sworne to stand or die, you guesse the man.
Amintor.　No, let me know the man that wrongs me so,
That I may cut his body into motes,
And scatter it before the Northren winde.
Evadne.　You dare not strike him.
Amintor.　　　　　　　　Doe not wrong me so,　　300
Yes, if his body were a poysonous plant,
That it were death to touch, I have a soule
Will throw me on him.
Evadne.　　　　　Why tis the King.
Amintor.　　　　　　　　　The King.
Evadne.　What will you doe now?
Amintor.　　　　　　　Tis not the King.
Evadne.　What did he make this match for dull *Amintor?*
Amintor.　Oh thou hast nam'd a word that wipes away
All thoughts revengefull, in that sacred name,
The King, there lies a terror, what fraile man
Dares lift his hand against it? let the Gods
Speake to him when they please, till when let us　　310
Suffer, and waite.
Evadne.　Why should you fill your selfe so full of heate,
And haste so to my bed? I am no virgin.
Amintor.　What Divell hath put it in thy fancy then
To mary mee?
Evadne.　　　Alas, I must have one
To father children, and to beare the name
Of husband to me, that my sinne may be
More honorable.
Amintor.　　　What a strange thing am I?

293 hand] Daniel; land Q1–8, F2
304 Tis] Q2; It is Q1　　　　307 name] Q2; word Q1
318 a] Q2; *om.* Q1

Evadne.   A miserable one, one that my selfe
Am sory for.
Amintor.   Why shew it then in this,   320
If thou hast pittie, though thy love be none,
Kill me, and all true lovers that shall live
In after ages crost in their desires,
Shall blesse thy memorie, and call thee good,
Because such mercy in thy heart was found,
To rid a lingring wretch.
Evadne.   I must have one
To fill thy roome againe if thou wert dead,
Else by this night I would, I pitty thee.
Amintor.   These strange and sudden injuries have falne
So thick upon me, that I lose all sense   330
Of what they are, me thinkes I am not wrong'd,
Nor is it ought, if from the censuring world
I can but hide it——reputation
Thou art a word, no more,——but thou hast showne
An impudence so high, that to the world
I feare thou wilt betray or shame thy selfe.
Evadne.   To cover shame I tooke thee, never feare
That I would blaze my selfe.
Amintor.   Nor let the King
Know I conceive he wrongs me, then mine honour
Will thrust me into action, that my flesh   340
Could beare with patience, and it is some ease
To me in these extreames, that I know this
Before I toucht thee; else had all the sinnes
Of mankinde stood betwixt me and the King,
I had gone through 'em, to his hart and thine.
I have lost one desire, tis not his crowne
Shall buy me to thy bed, now I resolve
He has dishonour'd thee: give me thy hand,
Be carefull of thy credit, and sinne close,

319 *Evadne.*] Q2; *om.* Q1   322 live] Q2; love Q1
325 heart] Q2; breast Q1   328 would] Q2; could Q1
345 through‸'em,] Q2 (~‸~‸); through, e'ne‸ Q1
346 lost] Q2; left Q1

58

Tis all I wish; upon thy chamber floure   350
Ile rest to night, that morning visiters
May thinke we did as married people use,
And prethee smile upon me when they come,
And seeme to toy as if thou hadst beene pleas'd
With what we did.
Evadne.   Feare not, I will doe this.
Amintor.   Come let us practise, and as wantonly
As ever loving bride and bridegroome met,
Lets laugh and enter here.
Evadne.   I am content.
Amintor.   Downe all the swellings of my troubled heart,
When we walke thus intwind let all eyes see,   360
If ever lovers better did agree.
                                        Exeunt.

                Enter Aspatia, Antiphila, Olimpias.   [II. ii]

Aspatia.   Away, you are not sad, force it no further,
Good gods, how well you looke, such a full colour
Young bashfull brides put on, sure you are new maried.
Antiphila.   Yes Madame to your griefe.
Aspatia.   Alas poore wentches
Goe learne to love first, learne to lose your selves,
Learne to be flattered, and beleeve and blesse
The double tongue that did it, make a faith
Out of the miracles of ancient lovers,
Such as speake truth and di'd in't, and like me
Beleeve all faithfull, and be miserable.   10
Did you nere love yet wenches? speake *Olimpias*,
Thou hast an easie temper, fit for stamp.

355 we] Q2; I Q1
357 loving] Q2; longing Q1
1 sad] Q2; *om.* Q1
                  359 *Amintor.*] Q2; *om.* Q1
                  2 Good_A gods,] Q2; Good, good, Q1
7–11 The...*Olimpias*,] Theobald; Q1 *prints* The double tongue that did it, | Did you ere love yet wenches, speake *Olimpas, omitting* make a faith...miserable. Q2–8, F2 *print* The ...it, | Make...lovers, | Did...*Olimpias*, [l. 11] | Such...in't, [l. 9] | And...miserable, [ll. 9–10]
   11 nere] Q2; ere Q1   12 an easie] Q2; a metled Q1

59

Olimpias.   Never.
Aspatia.   Nor you *Antiphila?*
Antiphila.   Nor I.
Aspatia.   Then my good girles be more then women, wise,
At least, be more then I was, and be sure
You credit any thing the light gives life to,
Before a man; rather beleeve the sea
Weepes for the ruin'd marchant when he rores,
Rather the wind but courts the pregnant sailes
When the strong cordage crackes, rather the sunne   20
Comes but to kisse the fruit in wealthy Autumme,
When all falles blasted; if you needs must love
(Forc'd by ill fate) take to your maiden bosomes
Two dead-cold Aspicks, and of them make lovers,
They cannot flatter nor forsweare; one kisse
Makes a long peace for all; but man,
Oh that beast man: come lets be sad my girles,
That downe cast of thine eye *Olimpias,*
Showes a fine sorrow;——marke *Antiphila,*
Just such another was the Nymph *Oenones,*   30
When *Paris* brought home *Hellen,*——now a teare,
And then thou art a peece expressing fully
The *Carthage* Queene when from a cold Sea rock,
Full with her sorrow, she tyed fast her eyes,
To the faire *Trojan* ships, and having lost them,
Just as thine does, downe stole a teare!——*Antiphila,*
What would this wench doe if she were *Aspatia?*
Here she would stand, till some more pittying god
Turnd her to Marble,——tis enough my wench,
Show me the peece of needle worke you wrought.   40
Antiphila.   Of *Ariadne* Madame?
Aspatia.   Yes that peece:

13 Nor I] Q1(c)–Q2; Nere I Q1(u)
15–27 and...man:] Q2; *om.* Q1
19 but courts] courts but Q2–8, F2; *om.* Q1
24 dead-cold] Theobald; dead‸cold Q2–8, F2; *om.* Q1
29 fine] Q2; faind Q1   32 fully‸] Q2; furie, Q1
35 and] Q2; *om.* Q1

This should be *Theseus*, has a cousening face,
You ment him for a man.
Antiphila.   He was so Madame.
Aspatia.   Why then tis well enough,——never looke back,
You have a full winde, and a false heart *Theseus*:——
Does not the story say, his Keele was split,
Or his masts spent, or some kind rock or other
Met with his vessell?
Antiphila.   Not as I remember.
Aspatia.   It should ha been so, could the Gods know this,
And not of all their number raise a storme?   50
But they are all as ill. This false smile was well exprest,
Just such another caught me,——you shall not goe so——
Antiphila, in this place worke a quick-sand,
And over it a shallow smiling water,
And his ship plowing it, and then a feare,
Doe that feare to the life wench.
Antiphila.   Twill wrong the storie.
Aspatia.   Twill make the story, wrong'd by wanton Poets,
Live long and be beleev'd, but wheres the Lady?
Antiphila.   There Madame.
Aspatia.   Fie, you have mist it here *Antiphila*,
You are much mistaken wench: 60
These colours are not dull and pale enough,
To show a soule so full of miserie
As this sad Ladies was, doe it by me,
Doe it againe, by me the lost *Aspatia*,
And you shall find all true but the wilde Iland;
I stand upon the Sea-beach now, and thinke
Mine armes thus, and mine haire blowne with the wind,

42 has] *i.e.* h'as   44 back] Q2 (backe); black Q1
50 not] Q2; none Q1   51 well exprest] Q2; exprest well Q1
52 You...so——] *addressed to Theseus in the tapestry*
52–53 so—— | *Antiphila*,] Dyce; ~ˌ~, Q1–5, F2; ~ˌ~ ; Q6–8
54 And...water] Q2; *line repeated* Q1   56 to the life] Q2; bravely Q1
56 *Antiphila*.] Q2; OLIM. Q1   59 here] Q2 (heere); there Q1
63 sad] Q2; poore Q1   65 shall] Q2; will Q1
66 I...thinke] Q2; Suppose I stand upon the Sea, breach now Q1
*66 Sea-beach] Langbaine; Sea, breach Q1; sea ˌ breach Q2–8, F2

61

Wilde as that desart, and let all about me
Tell that I am forsaken; doe my face,
If thou hadst ever feeling of a sorrow,   70
Thus, thus, *Antiphila*: strive to make me looke
Like sorrowes monument, and the trees about me
Let them be dry and leavelesse, let the rocks
Groane with continuall surges, and behind me
Make all a desolation,——looke, looke wenches,
A miserable life of this poore picture.
Olimpias.   Deare Madame.
Aspatia.   I have done, sit downe, and let us
Upon that point fixe all our eyes, that point there;
Make a dumbe silence till you feele a sudden sadnesse
Give us new soules.   80

Enter Calianax.

Calianax.   The King may doe this, and he may not doe it,
My childe is wrongd, disgrac'd,——well, how now huswives,
What at your ease, is this a time to sit still?
Up you young lazie whores, up or ile swenge you.
Olimpias.   Nay good my Lord——
Calianax.   You'l lie downe shortly, get you in and worke,
What are you growne so restie? you want heates,
We shall have some of the Court boyes doe that office.
Antiphila.   My Lord we doe no more then we are charg'd:
It is the Ladies pleasure we be thus in griefe,   90
She is forsaken.
Calianax.   Theres a rogue too,
A young dissembling slave,——well? get you in,——
Ile have a bout with that boy, tis hie time

68 that desart, and] Q2; the place she was in, Q1
69 Tell...forsaken] Q2; Be teares of my story Q1
71 strive...looke] Q2; make me looke good girle Q1
72 monument] Q2; mount Q1   75 looke, looke] Q2; see, see Q1
86 get...worke] Q2; in and whine there Q1
87 restie] Q2 (reasty); rustie Q1
88 doe that office] Q2; heat you shortly Q1
89–90 My...be] Q2; Good my Lord be not angry, we doe nothing | But what
my Ladies pleasure is, we are Q1
92 young] Q2; slie Q1   93 a bout] Q2; about Q1

62

Now to be valiant, I confesse my youth
Was never prone that way: what made an asse,
A Court stale? well I will be valiant,
And beate some dozen of these whelps, and theres
Another of 'em, a trim cheating souldier,
Ile maule that raschall, has out-brav'd me twice,
But now I thanke the Gods I am valiant,——   100
Goe, get you in,——ile take a course with all.

Exeunt omnes.

Enter Cleon, Strato, Diphilus.   III.i

Cleon.   Your sister is not up yet.
Diphilus.   Oh brides must take their mornings rest, the night is
troublesome.
Strato.   But not tedious.
Diphilus.   What ods, hee has not my sisters maiden-head to night?
Strato.   None, its ods against any bridegrome living, he nere gets it
while he lives.
Diphilus.   Y'are merry with my sister, you'le please to allow me
the same freedome with your mother.
Strato.   Shees at your service.   10
Diphilus.   Then shees merry enough of herselfe, shee needs no
tickling: knock at the dore.
Strato.   We shall interrupt them.
Diphilus.   No matter, they have the yeare before them,——
Good morrow sister, spare your selfe to day,
The night will come againe.

Enter Amintor.

Amintor.   Whose there, my brother? I am no readier yet,
Your sister is but now up.
Diphilus.   You looke as you had lost your eyes to night,
I thinke you ha not slept.

95 what...asse,] Q2; *om.* Q1   96 will] Q2; must Q1
*97 whelps, and] Q1; whelps I will, and Q2
99 has] *i.e.* h'as   0.1 III.i] *Actus Tertius.* Q1–2
2 Oh] Q2; Our Q1   6 None] Q1; No Q2

Amintor.   Ifaith I have not.   20
Diphilus.   You have done better then.
Amintor.   We ventured for a boy, when hee is twelve,
A shall command against the foes of *Rhodes*,
Shall we be merry?
Strato.   You cannot, you want sleepe.
Amintor.   Tis true,——(*aside*) but she
As if she had drunke *Lethe*, or had made
Even with heaven, did fetch so still a sleepe,
So sweet and sound——
Diphilus.   Whats that?
Amintor.   Your sister frets
This morning, and does turne her eyes upon mee,
As people on their headsman, she does chafe,   30
And kisse and chafe againe, and clap my cheeks,
Shees in another world.
Diphilus.   Then I had lost, I was about to lay,
You had not got her maidenhead to night.
Amintor [*aside*].   Ha, does hee not mocke mee?——
                                   Y'ad lost indeed,
I doe not use to bungle.
Cleon.   You doe deserve her.
Amintor.   I laid my lips to hers, and that wilde breath
That was so rude and rough to me, last night
Was sweete as Aprill,——(*aside*) ile be guilty too,
If these be the effects.   40

                    Enter Melantius.

Melantius.   Good day *Amintor*, for to me the name
Of brother is too distant, we are friends,
And that is nearer.
Amintor.   Deare *Melantius*,
Let me behold thee. Is it possible?

20 have] Q2; did Q1
22 We ventured] Q2; We have ventured Q1
29 does] Q2; doth Q1
30 their] Q2; the Q1   31 againe] Q2; *om.* Q1
*35 does hee] Q1; he does Q2   36 use to] Q2; *om.* Q1
37 breath] Q2; breach Q1   39 *aside*] Q2 (*following l.* 38); *om.* Q1

Melantius.   What sudden gaze is this?
Amintor.   Tis wondrous strange.
Melantius.   Why does thine eye desire so strict a view
  Of that it knowes so well? theres nothing here
  That is not thine.
Amintor.   I wonder much *Melantius*,
  To see those noble lookes that make me thinke,
  How vertuous thou art, and on the sudden   50
  Tis strange to me, thou shouldst have worth and honour,
  Or not be base and false, and treacherous,
  And every ill. But——
Melantius.   Stay, stay my friend,
  I feare this sound will not become our loves,
  No more embrace me.
Amintor.   Oh mistake me not,
  I know thee to be full of all those deeds,
  That we fraile men call good, but by the course
  Of nature thou shouldst be as quickly chang'd
  As are the windes, dissembling as the Sea,
  That now weares browes as smooth as virgins be,   60
  Tempting the Merchant to invade his face,
  And in an houre cals his billowes up,
  And shoots em at the Sun, destroying all
  A carries on him.——(*Aside*) Oh how neare am I
  To utter my sicke thoughts.
Melantius.   But why, my friend, should I be so by nature?
Amintor.   I have wed thy sister, who hath vertuous thoughts
  Enow for one whole familie, and it is strange,
  That you should feele no want.
Melantius.   Beleeve me this
  Is complement too cunning for me.   70
Diphilus.   What should I be then by the course of nature,
  They having both robd me of so much vertue?
Strato.   Oh call the bride my Lord *Amintor*, that

50 the] Q2; this Q1   53 But] Q2; *om.* Q1
53 Stay] Q2; Say Q1   62 cals] Q2; call Q1
63 shoots] Q2; shoot Q1   66 But] Q2; *om.* Q1

5   65   B D W

Wee may see her blush, and turne her eyes downe,
It is the prittiest sport.
Amintor.   *Evadne.*
Evadne (*within*).   My Lord.
Amintor.   Come forth my love,
Your brothers doe attend to wish you joy.
Evadne [*within*].   I am not ready yet.
Amintor.   Enough, enough.
Evadne [*within*].   They'le mocke me.
Amintor.   Faith thou shalt come in.

Enter Evadne.

Melantius.   Good morrow sister, he that understands   80
Whom you have wed, need not to wish you joy,
You have enough, take heed you be not proud.
Diphilus.   O sister what have you done?
Evadne.   I done? why what have I done?
Strato.   My Lord *Amintor* sweares you are no maid now.
Evadne.   Push.
Strato.   Ifaith he does.
Evadne.   I knew I should be mockt.
Diphilus.   With a truth.
Evadne.   If twere to do againe,
In faith I would not mary.
Amintor (*aside*).   Nor I by heaven.
Diphilus.   Sister, *Dula* sweares   90
She heard you cry two roomes off.
Evadne.   Fie how you talke.
Diphilus.   Lets see you walke, by my troth y'are spoild.
Melantius.   *Amintor.*
Amintor.   Ha?
Melantius.   Thou art sad.
Amintor.   Who I? I thanke you for that,
Shall *Diphilus* thou and I sing a catch?
Melantius.   How?

84 I done?] Q2; *om.* Q1   90 *aside*] Q2; *om.* Q1
*92 *Diphilus.* Lets...spoild] DIPH. Lets...walke. | EVAD. By...spoild Q1–8 ,F2

66

Amintor.   Prethee lets.

Melantius.   Nay thats too much the other way.

Amintor.   I am so lightned with my happinesse,———   100

How dost thou, love? kisse me.

Evadne.   I cannot love you, you tell tales of me.

Amintor.   Nothing but what becomes us,———Gentlemen

Would you had all such wives, and all the world,

That I might be no wonder; y'are all sad,

What doe you envie me? I walke me thinkes

On water, and nere sinke I am so light.

Melantius.   Tis well you are so.

Amintor.   Well? how can I be other

When shee lookes thus? Is there no musicke there?

Lets dance.   110

Melantius.   Why? this is strange *Amintor.*

Amintor.   I do not know my selfe,———[*aside*] yet I could wish

My joy were lesse.

Diphilus.   Ile marrie too if it will make one thus.

Evadne (*aside*).   *Amintor*, harke.

Amintor.   What sayes my love? I must obey.

Evadne [*aside*].   You doe it scurvily, twill be perceiv'd.

Cleon.   My Lord the King is here.

Enter King *and* Lysippus.

Amintor.   Where?

Strato.   And his brother.

King.   Good morrow all.———

Amintor joy on joy fall thicke upon thee,———   120

And Madame you are alterd since I saw you,

I must salute you, you are now anothers,   [*Kisses her.*]

How lik't you your nights rest?

Evadne.   Ill sir.

Amintor.   Indeede

She tooke but little.

---

100 lightned] Q 2; heighned Q 1   108 how can I] Q 2; can you Q 1
111 *Amintor*] Q 2; *om.* Q 1   114 too] Q 2; *om.* Q 1
121 And] Q 2; But Q 1

67   5-2

Lysippus.   You'le let her take more,
And thanke her too shortly.
King.   *Amintor* wert
Thou truely honest till thou wert married?
Amintor. Yes sir.
King.   Tell me then, how shewes the sport
Unto thee?
Amintor. Why well?
King.   What did you doe?
Amintor. No more nor lesse then other couples use,
You know what tis, it has but a course name.   130
King.   But prethee I should thinke by her black eie
And her red cheeke, she should be quick and stirring
In this same businesse, ha?
Amintor.   I cannot tell
I nere tried other sir, but I perceive
She is as quick as you delivered.
King.   Well youle trust me then *Amintor*, to choose
A wife for you agen?
Amintor.   No never sir.
King.   Why? like you this so ill?
Amintor.   So well I like her,
For this I bow my knee in thanks to you,
And unto heaven will pay my gratefull tribute   140
Hourely, and doe hope we shall draw out,
A long contented life together here,
And die both full of gray haires in one day,
For which the thanks is yours, but if the powers
That rule us, please to call her first away,
Without pride spoke, this world holds not a wife
Worthy to take her roome.
King (aside).   I doe not like this;——
All forbeare the roome but you *Amintor*
And your Lady, I have some speech with you

127 then, how] Q2; how ∧ then Q1
128 Unto thee?] Q2; to you. Q1   147 *aside*] Q1; *om.* Q2
149 with you] Q2; *om.* Q1

68

That may concerne your after living well.   150
       [*Exeunt omnes. Manent* King, Evadne *and* Amintor.]
Amintor [*aside*]. A will not tell me that he lies with her,
  If he doe, something heavenly stay my heart,
  For I shall be apt to thrust this arme of mine
  To acts unlawfull.
King.   You will suffer me
  To talke with her *Amintor*, and not have
  A jealous pang?
Amintor.   Sir, I dare trust my wife,
  With whom she dares to talke, and not be jealous.   [*Withdraws.*]
King. How doe you like *Amintor*?
Evadne.   As I did sir.
King. Howes that?
Evadne. As one that to fulfill your will and pleasure,   160
  I have given leave to call me wife and love.
King. I see there is no lasting faith in sin,
  They that breake word with heaven, will breake agen
  With all the world, and so doest thou with me.
Evadne. How sir?
King.   This subtle womans ignorance
  Will not excuse you, thou hast taken oathes
  So great, that me thought they did misbecome
  A womans mouth, that thou wouldst nere injoy
  A man but me.
Evadne.   I never did sweare so,
  You doe me wrong.
King.   Day and night have heard it.   170
Evadne. I swore indeede that I would never love
  A man of lower place, but if your fortune
  Should throw you from this hight, I bad you trust
  I would forsake you, and would bend to him
  That won your throne, I love with my ambition,
  Not with my eies, but if I ever yet

152–153 something...be] Q2; For it is Q1
156 A jealous pang] Q2; jealous pangs Q1
157 With whom] Q2; When Q1   160 will and] Q2; *om.* Q1

Toucht any other, Leprosie light here
Upon my face, which for your royaltie
I would not staine.
King.   Why thou dissemblest, and it is in me   180
To punish thee.
Evadne.   Why, it is in me then,
Not to love you, which will more afflict
Your bodie, then your punishment can mine.
King.   But thou hast let *Amintor* lie with thee.
Evadne.   I hannot.
King.   Impudence, he saies himselfe so.
Evadne.   A lies.
King.   A does not.
Evadne.   By this light he does,
Strangely and basely, and ile proove it so,
I did not onely shun him for a night,
But told him I would never close with him.
King.   Speake lower, tis false.
Evadne.   I am no man   190
To answer with a blow, or if I were,
You are the King, but urge not, tis most true.
King.   Doe not I know the uncontrouled thoughts,
That youth brings with him, when his blood is high,
With expectation and desire of that
He long hath waited for? is not his spirit
Though he be temperate, of a valiant straine
As this our age hath knowne? what could he doe
If such a suddaine speech had met his blood,
But ruine thee for ever? if he had not kild thee   200
He could not beare it thus, he is as we
Or any other wrong'd man.
Evadne.   It is dissembling.
King.   Take him, farewell, henceforth I am thy foe,
And what disgraces I can blot thee with, looke for.

*200 ever?...thee,] *stet* Q1 (~ ?...~ , Q2)
202 It] Q2; This Q1
203–206 *King.* Take...love?] Q2; *om.* Q1

Evadne. Stay sir;——*Amintor*,——you shall heare——*Amintor.*
Amintor. What my love?
Evadne. *Amintor*, thou hast an ingenious looke,
  And should'st be vertuous, it amazeth me
  That thou can'st make such base malicious lies.
Amintor. What my deere wife?
Evadne.   Deere wife? I doe despise thee,   210
  Why nothing can be baser then to sow
  Discention amongst lovers.
Amintor.   Lovers? who?
Evadne. The King and me——
Amintor. Oh God.
Evadne. ——Who should live long and love without distast,
  Were it not for such pickthanks as thy selfe,
  Did you lie with me? sweare now, and be punisht
  In hell for this.
Amintor [*aside*].   The faithlesse sin I made
  To faire *Aspatia*, is not yet reveng'd,
  It followes me,——I will not loose a word   220
  To this vilde woman, but to you my King,
  The anguish of my soule thrusts out this truth,
  Y'are a tirant, and not so much to wrong
  An honest man thus, as to take a pride
  In talking with him of it.
Evadne. Now sir, see how loud this fellow lied.
Amintor. You that can know to wrong, shold know how men
  Must right themselves: what punishment is due,
  From me to him that shall abuse my bed?
  Is it not death? nor can that satisfie,   230
  Unlesse I send your lives through all the land
  To show how nobly I have freed my selfe.
King. Draw not thy sword, thou knowst I cannot feare
  A subjects hand, but thou shalt feele the weight
  Of this if thou doest rage.

209 can'st] Q2; should'st Q1   213 me] Q2; I Q1
221 vilde] Colman; wilde Q1–8, F2   226 lied] Q2; lies Q1
228–229 themselves:...bed?] Q2; ~ ,...~ , Q1
230 Is it] Colman; It is Q1–8, F2   231–232 send...To] Q2; *om.* Q1

Amintor. The waite of that?
If you have any worth, for heavens sake thinke
I feare not swords, for as you are meere man,
I dare as easily kill you for this deede,
As you dare thinke to doe it, but there is
Divinitie about you, that strikes dead   240
My rising passions; as you are my King,
I fall before you and present my sword,
To cut mine owne flesh if it be your will,
Alas! I am nothing but a multitude
Of waking griefes, yet should I murder you,
I might before the world take the excuse
Of madnesse, for compare my injuries,
And they will well appeare too sad a weight
For reason to endure, but fall I first
Amongst my sorrowes, ere my treacherous hand   250
Touch holy things, but why?——I know not what
I have to say,——why did you choose out me
To make thus wretched? there were thousands, fooles,
Easie to worke on, and of state enough
Within the Iland.
Evadne. I wold not have a foole,
It were no credit for me.
Amintor. Worse and worse,
Thou that darst talke unto thy husband thus,
Professe thy selfe a whore, and more then so,
Resolve to be so still. It is my fate,
To beare and bow beneath a thousand griefes,   260
To keepe that little credit with the world——
But there were wise ones to, you might have tane
Another.
King. No, for I beleeve thee honest,
As thou wert valiant.
Amintor. All the happinesse

*245 waking] Q2; walking Q1   250 hand] Q2; sword Q1
253 were] Q2; are Q1   253 fooles] Q2; *om.* Q1
255 Iland] Q2; Land Q1   259 It is] Q2 (it); is it Q1
259 fate] Q2; fault Q1

72

Bestowd upon me turnes into disgrace,
Gods, take your honesty againe, for I
Am loaden with it,——good my Lord the King
Be private in it.
King.   Thou maist live *Amintor*,
Free as thy King, if thou wilt winke at this,
And be a meanes that we may meet in secret.   270
Amintor.   A baud, hold, hold my breast, a bitter curse
Ceaze me, if I forget not all respects
That are religious, on another word
Sounded like that, and through a Sea of sinnes
Will wade to my revenge, though I should call
Paines here, and after life, upon my soule.
King.   Well, I am resolute, you lay not with her,
And so I leave you.   *Exit* King.
Evadne.   You must needs be prating,
And see what follows.
Amintor.   Prethee vex me not,
Leave me, I am afraid some sudden start   280
Will pull a murther on me.
Evadne.   I am gone,
I love my life well.   *Exit* Evadne.
Amintor.   I hate mine as much,
This tis to breake a troth, I should be glad,
If all this tide of griefe would make me mad.

                                        Exit.

                    Enter Melantius.   [III. ii]

Melantius.   Ile know the cause of all *Amintors* griefes,
Or friendship shall be idle.

                    Enter Calianax.

Calianax.   O *Melantius*,
My daughter will die.

---

273 another] Q2; an other Q1   274 Sounded] Q2; Seconded Q1
276 Paines] Q2; Plagues Q1   277 not] Q2; *om.* Q1

Melantius.   Trust me I am sory,
Would thou hadst tane her roome.
Calianax.   Thou art a slave,
A cut-throat slave, a bloody treacherous slave.
Melantius.   Take heed old man, thou wilt be heard to rave,
And lose thine offices.
Calianax.   I am valiant growne,
At all these yeares, and thou art but a slave.
Melantius.   Leave,
Some companie will come, and I respect   10
Thy yeares, not thee so much, that I could wish
To laugh at thee alone.
Calianax.   Ile spoile your mirth,
I meane to fight with thee, there lie my cloake,
This was my fathers sword, and he durst fight,
Are you prepar'd?
Melantius.   Why? wilt thou doate thy selfe
Out of thy life? hence get thee to bed,
Have carefull looking to, and eate warme things,
And trouble not mee: my head is full of thoughts,
More waighty then thy life or death can be.
Calianax.   You have a name in warre, where you stand safe   20
Amongst a multitude, but I will try,
What you dare doe unto a weake old man
In single fight, you'l give ground I feare,
Come draw.
Melantius.   I will not draw, unlesse thou pulst thy death
Upon thee with a stroke; theres no one blow
That thou canst give hath strength enough to kill me.
Tempt me not so far then, the power of earth
Shall not redeeme thee.
Calianax [*aside*].   I must let him alone,
Hees stout, and able, and to say the truth,   30

4 roome] Q2; part Q1
5 bloody treacherous slave.] Q2; bloody——— Q1
7 offices] Q2; office Q1   9 Leave,] Q2; *om.* Q1
22–23 man‸...fight,] Q2; ~ , ...~ ‸ Q1
27 hath] Q2; hast Q1   27 to] Q2; can Q1

74

How ever I may set a face and talke,
I am not valiant: when I was a youth
I kept my credit with a testie tricke
I had, mongst cowards, but durst never fight.
Melantius.   I will not promise to preserve your life
  If you doe stay.
Calianax [*aside*].   I would give halfe my land
  That I durst fight with that proud man alittle,
  If I had men to holde him, I would beate him,
  Till hee askt mee mercie.
Melantius.   Sir will you begone?
Calianax [*aside*].   I dare not stay,   40
  But I will go home and beate my servants all
  Over for this.   *Exit* Calianax.
Melantius.   This old fellow haunts me,
  But the distracted carriage of mine *Amintor*
  Takes deeply on me, I will find the cause,
  I feare his conscience cries, he wrongd *Aspatia.*

                Enter Amintor.

Amintor [*aside*].   Mens eyes are not so subtile to perceive
  My inward miserie, I beare my griefe
  Hid from the world, how art thou wretched then?
  For ought I know all husbands are like me,
  And every one I talke with of his wife,   50
  Is but a well dissembler of his woes
  As I am: would I knew it, for the rarenesse
  Afflicts me now.
Melantius.   *Amintor*, we have not enjoy'd our friendship of late,
  for we were wont to charge our soules in talke.
Amintor.   *Melantius*, I can tell the a good jest of *Strato* and a Lady
  the last day.
Melantius.   How wast?
Amintor.   Why such an odde one.

34 mongst] Q1; amongst Q2   39 askt] Q1; aske Q2
41 go home and] Q2; *om.* Q1   46 Mens] Q2; Mans Q1
46 so] Q2; *om.* Q1   *55 charge] *stet* Q1-2
56 the] *i.e.* thee

75

Melantius. I have longd to speake with you, not of an idle jest 60
thats forst, but of matter you are bound to utter to me.
Amintor. What is that my friend?
Melantius. I have observ'd your wordes fall from your tongue
Wildely, and all your carriage
Like one that strove to shew his merry moode,
When he were ill dispos'd: you were not wont
To put such scorne into your speech or weare
Upon your face ridiculous jollity,
Some sadnesse sits heere, which your cunning would
Cover ore with smiles, and twill not be, 70
What is it?
Amintor. A sadnesse here? what cause
Can Fate provide for me to make me so?
Am I not lov'd through all this Isle? the King
Raines greatnesse on me: have I not received
A Lady to my bed, that in her eye
Keepes mounting fire, and on her tender cheekes
Inevitable colour, in her heart
A prison for all vertue? are not you,
Which is above all joyes, my constant friend?
What saddnesse can I have? no, I am light, 80
And feele the courses of my blood more warme
And stirring then they were; faith marry too,
And you will feele so unexprest a joy
In chaste embraces, that you will indeed
Appeare another.
Melantius. You may shape *Amintor*
Causes to cozen the whole world withall,
And your selfe too, but tis not like a friend,
To hide your soule from me, tis not your nature
To be thus idle: I have seene you stand,
As you were blasted midst of all your mirth, 90
Call thrice aloud, and then start, fayning joy

65 strove] Q2; strives Q1   67 ∧ or] Q2; ——yow Q1
69 cunning] Q2; tongue Q1   *77 Inevitable] Q2; Immutable Q1
87 but] Q2; and Q1   90 blasted∧] Q1; ~, Q2

So coldly: world? what doe I here? a friend
Is nothing: heaven? I would ha told that man
My secret sinnes: ile search an unknowne land,
And there plant friendship, all is withered here:
Come, with a complement? I would have fought,
Or told my friend a lied, ere soothd him so;
Out of my bosome.

Amintor.   But there is nothing.

Melantius.   Worse and worse, farewell;
From this time have acquaintance, but no friend.   100

Amintor.   Melantius, stay, you shall know what that is.

Melantius.   See how you plaid with friendship, be advis'd
How you give cause unto your selfe to say,
You ha lost a friend.

Amintor.   Forgive what I ha done,
For I am so ore-gon with injuries
Unheard of, that I lose consideration
Of what I ought to do,——oh——oh.

Melantius.   Doe not weepe,
What ist? May I once but know the man
Hath turnd my friend thus.

Amintor.   I had spoke at first,
But that——

Melantius.   But what?

Amintor.   ——I held it most unfit   110
For you to know, faith doe not know it yet.

Melantius.   Thou seest my love, that will keep company
With thee in teares, hide nothing then from me,
For when I know the cause of thy distemper,
With mine old armour ile adorne my selfe,
My resolution, and cut through thy foes
Unto thy quiet, till I place thy heart
As peaceable as spotlesse innocence.
What is it?

97 friend] Q2; friends Q1
102 plaid] Q2; plead Q1
105 injuries‸] Q2; miseries, Q1

Amintor.   Why tis this,——it is too bigge
  To get out, let my teares make way awhile.   120
Melantius.   Punish me strangly heaven, if he scape
  Of life or fame, that brought this youth to this.
Amintor.   Your sister——
Melantius.   Well sayd.
Amintor.   You'l wisht unknowne
  When you have heard it.
Melantius.   No.
Amintor.   ——Is much to blame,
  And to the King has given her honour up,
  And lives in whoredome with him.
Melantius.   How's this?
  Thou art run mad with injury indeed,
  Thou couldst not utter this else, speake againe,
  For I forgive it freely, tell thy griefes.
Amintor.   Shees wanton, I am loth to say a whore,   130
  Though it be true.
Melantius.   Speake yet againe, before mine anger grow
  Up beyond throwing downe, what are thy griefes?
Amintor.   By all our friendship, these.
Melantius.   What, am I tame?
  After mine actions, shall the name of friend
  Blot all our family, and strike the brand
  Of whore upon my sister unreveng'd?
  My shaking flesh be thou a witnesse for me,
  With what unwillingnesse I goe to scourge
  This rayler, whom my folly hath cald friend;   140
  I will not take thee basely, thy sword
  Hangs neere thy hand, draw it, that I may whip
  Thy rashnesse to repentance, draw thy sword.
Amintor.   Not on thee, did thine anger goe as high
  As troubled waters: thou shoulds doe me ease,
  Heere, and eternally, if thy noble hand,
  Would cut me from my sorrowes.

128 this‸else,] Q2; ~ , ~‸ Q1   134 tame] Q2; tane Q1
136 strike] Q2; stick Q1   145 shoulds] Q1; shouldst Q2

Melantius.   This is base,
  And fearefull, they that use to utter lies,
  Provide not blowes, but wordes to qualifie
  The men they wrong'd, thou hast a guilty cause.   150
Amintor.   Thou pleasest me, for so much more like this,
  Will raise my anger up above my griefes,
  Which is a passion easier to be borne,
  And I shall then be happy.
Melantius.   Take then more,
  To raise thine anger, tis meere cowardise
  Makes thee not draw, and I will leave thee dead
  How ever: but if thou art so much prest,
  With guilt and feare, as not to dare to fight,
  Ile make thy memory loath'd, and fix a scandall
  Upon thy name for ever.
Amintor.   Then I draw,   160
  As justly as our Magistrates their swords,
  To cut offenders off; I knew before,
  Twould grate your eares, but it was base in you
  To urge a waighty secret from your friend,
  And then rage at it; I shall be at ease
  If I be kild, and if you fall by me,
  I shall not long out live you.
Melantius.   Stay a while,
  The name of friend, is more then familie,
  Or all the world besides; I was a foole.
  Thou searching humane nature, that didst wake   170
  To doe me wrong, thou art inquisitive,
  And thrusts me upon questions that will take
  My sleepe away, would I had died ere knowne
  This sad dishonor; pardon me my friend,
  If thou wilt strike, here is a faithfull heart,
  Pearce it, for I will never heave my hand
  To thine; behold the power thou hast in me,

        153 borne] Q2; knowne Q1
        154 happy] Q2; blessed Q1
        159 scandall] Q2; farewell Q1   170 wake] Q2; make Q1

I doe beleeve my sister is a whore,
A leprous one, put up thy sword young man.
Amintor.   How should I beare it then she being so?   180
I feare my friend that you will loose me shortly,
And I shall doe a foule act on my selfe
Through these disgraces.
Melantius.   Better halfe the land
  Were buried quick together, no *Amintor*,
  Thou shalt have ease: oh this adulterous King
  That drew her too't, where got he the spirit
  To wrong me so?
Amintor.   What is it then to me,
  If it be wrong to you?
Melantius.   Why not so much,
  The credit of our house is throwne away:
  But from his iron den ile waken death,   190
  And hurle him on this King, my honestie
  Shall steele my sword, and on my horrid point
  Ile weare my cause, that shall amaze the eyes
  Of this proud man, and be to glittring
  For him to looke on.
Amintor.   I have quite undone my fame.
Melantius.   Drie up thy watrie eyes,
  And cast a manly looke upon my face,
  For nothing is so wilde as I thy friend
  Till I have freed thee; still this swelling brest,   200
  I goe thus from thee, and will never cease
  My vengeance till I finde thy heart at peace.
Amintor.   It must not be so, stay, mine eyes would tell
  How loath I am to this, but love and teares
  Leave me a while, for I have hazarded
  All that this world calls happy, thou hast wrought
  A secret from me under name of friend,
  Which art could nere have found, nor torture wrong
  From out my bosome: give it me agen,

185 ease: oh] Q2 (Oh); ~ʌ of Q1   194 to] *i.e.* too
202 thy] Q1; my Q2   209 my] Q2; this Q1

For I will finde it where so ere it lies 210
Hid in the mortal'st part, invent a way
To give it backe.
Melantius.   Why would you have it backe?
I will to death persue him with revenge.
Amintor.   Therefore I call it from thee, for I know
Thy blood so high, that thou wilt stir in this,
And shame me to posterity, take to thy weapon.
Melantius.   Heare thy friend that bears more yeares then thou.
Amintor.   I will not heare, but draw, or I——
Melantius.   *Amintor?*
Amintor.   Draw then, for I am full as resolute
As fame, and honor can inforce me be, 220
I cannot linger, draw?
Melantius.   I doe,——but is not
My share of credit equall with thine
If I doe stir?
Amintor.   No? for it will be cald
Honor in thee to spill thy sisters blood,
If she her birth abuse, and on the King
A brave revenge, but on me that have walkt
With patience in it, it will fixe the name
Of fearefull cuckold,——O that word? be quick.
Melantius.   Then joyne with me.
Amintor.   I dare not doe a sinne, or else I would: 230
Be speedy.
Melantius.   Then dare not fight with me, for that's a sin,——
His griefe distracts him,——call thy thoughts agen,
And to thy selfe pronounce the name of friend,
And see what that will worke, I will not fight.
Amintor.   You must?
Melantius.   I will be kild first, though my passions
Offered the like to you, tis not this earth
Shall by my reason to it, thinke awhile

212 Why$_\wedge$...backe?] Q2; ~ ? ... ~, Q1
*214 it from] Q1; it backe from Q2   216 And...posterity] Q2; *om.* Q1
220 be] Q2; *om.* Q1   230 would:] Q2; ~ $_\wedge$ Q1
238 by] *i.e.* buy

For you are, (I must weepe when I speake that,)
All most besides your selfe.
Amintor.   Oh my soft temper,   240
So many sweete words from thy sisters mouth,
I am afraid would make me take her,
To embrace and pardon her, I am mad indeede,
And know not what I doe, yet have a care
Of me in what thou doest.
Melantius.   Why thinks my friend
I will forget his honor, or to save
The braverie of our house, will loose his fame
And feare to touch the throne of Majestie?
Amintor.   A curse will follow that, but rather live
And suffer with me.   250
Melantius.   I will doe what worth shall bid me, and no more.
Amintor.   Faith I am sicke, and desperately I hope,
Yet leaning thus I feele a kinde of ease.
Melantius.   Come take agen your mirth about you.
Amintor.   I shall never doo't.
Melantius.   I warrant you, looke up, weele walke together,
Put thine arme here, all shall be well agen.
Amintor.   Thy love, o wretched I, thy love *Melantius*,
Why I have nothing else.
Melantius.   Be merry then.   *Exeunt.*

Enter Melantius *agen.*

Melantius.   This worthie yong man may doe violence   260
Upon himselfe, but I have cherisht him
As well as I could, and sent him smiling from me
To counterfeit againe, sword hold thine edge,
My heart will never fail me?

239 that] Q2; it Q1   244 yet] Q2; but Q1
247 our] Q2; your Q1   251 and no more] Q2; *om.* Q1
258 wretched‸I,]~ , ~‸ Q1–8, F2

82

Enter Diphilus.

Diphilus,

Thou comst as sent.
Diphilus.   Yonder has bin such laughing.
Melantius.   Betwixt whom?
Diphilus.   Why our sister and the King,
  I thought their spleenes would breake, they laught us all
  Out of the roome.
Melantius.   They must weepe *Diphilus.*
Diphilus.   Must they?
Melantius.   They must?   270
  Thou art my brother, and if I did beleeve,
  Thou hadst a base thought, I would rip it out,
  Lie where it durst.
Diphilus.   You should not, I would first
  Mangle my selfe and finde it.
Melantius.   That was spoke according to our strain:
  Come joyne thy hands to mine, and sweare a firmenesse
  To what project I shall lay before thee.
Diphilus.   You doe wrong us both,
  People hereafter shall not say there past
  A bond more then our loves to tie our lives
  And deathes together.   280
Melantius.   It is as nobly said as I would wish,
  Anon ile tell you wonders, we are wrong'd.
Diphilus.   But I will tell you now, weele right our selves.
Melantius.   Stay not, prepare the armour in my house,
  And what friends you can draw unto our side,
  Not knowing of the cause, make ready too:
  Hast *Diphilus*, the time requires it, hast.   *Exit* Diphilus.
  I hope my cause is just, I know my blood
  Tels me it is, and I will credit it:
  To take revenge and loose my selfe withall,   290
  Were idle, and to scape, impossible,
  Without I had the fort, which (miserie)

275 to mine] Q2; *om.* Q1

83   6-2

Remaining in the hands of my olde enemy
Calianax,——but I must have it.

Enter Calianax.

                                        See
Where he comes shaking by me,——good my Lord
Forget your spleene to me, I never wrong'd you,
But would have peace with every man.
Calianax.   Tis well?
If I durst fight, your tongue would lie at quiet.
Melantius.   Y'are touchie without all cause.
Calianax.   Doe? mock me.
Melantius.   By mine honor I speake truth.
Calianax.   Honor? where ist?   300
Melantius.   See what starts you make into your idle hatred,
To my love and freedome to you. I am come
With resolution to obtaine a sute
Of you.
Calianax.   A sute of me, tis very like
It should be granted sir.
Melantius.   Nay, goe not hence,
Tis this, you have the keeping of the fort,
And I would wish you by the love you ought
To beare unto me to deliver it
Into my hands.
Calianax.   I am in hope thou art mad, to talke to me thus.   310
Melantius.   But there is a reason to move you to it,
I would kill the King, that wrong'd you and your daughter.
Calianax.   Out traitor.
Melantius.   Nay but stay, I cannot scape
The deede once done without I have this fort.
Calianax.   And should I help thee? now thy treacherous mind
Betraies it selfe.
Melantius.   Come delay me not,

*301 idle] Q1; *om.* Q2
302 To...you.] Q2; *om.* Q1 (*which prints* I am come...sute [*l.* 303] *as one line*)
302 am] Q1; *om.* Q2

Give me a suddaine answere, or already,
Thy last is spoke, refuse not offerd love,
When it comes clad in secrets.
Calianax [*aside*].   If I say
I will not, he will kill me, I doe see't   320
Writ in his lookes, and should I say I will,
Heele run and tell the King:——I doe not shun
Your friendship deere *Melantius*, but this cause
Is weightie, give me but an houre to thinke.
Melantius.   Take it,——[*aside*] I know this goes unto the King,
But I am arm'd.   *Exit* Melantius.
Calianax.   Me thinkes I feele my selfe
But twenty now agen, this fighting foole
Wants policie, I shall revenge my girle,
And make her red againe: I pray, my legges
Will last that pace that I will carrie them,   330
I shall want breath before I finde the King.

                                        [*Exit.*]

                Enter Melantius, Evadne, *and Ladyes*.   IV.i

Melantius.   God save you.
Evadne.   Save you sweete brother.
Melantius.   In my blunt eye me thinkes you looke *Evadne*——
Evadne.   Come, you would make me blush.
Melantius.   I would *Evadne*, I shall displease my ends els.
Evadne.   You shall if you commend me, I am bashfull,
  Come sir, how doe I looke?
Melantius.   I would not have your women heare me breake
  Into a commendation of you,
  Tis not seemely.

317 or] Q2; *om.* Q1
318 not] Q2; my Q1
0.1 *Ladyes*] Weber; *a Lady* Q1–8, F2
*2 *Evadne*——] Theobald; ~ . Q1–8, F2
*5 commend] Theobald; command Q1–8, F2
*8 Into a commendation] into a commendations Q1; into commendations Q2;
into commendation Q3–8, F2

318 Thy] Q2; The Q1
0.1 IV.i] *Actus Quartus.* Q1–2
1 God] Q1; *om.* Q2
9 Tis] Q2; it is Q1

85

Evadne.   Goe waite me in the gallerie,——

                                        Exeunt Ladyes.

Now speake.

Melantius.   Ile lock the dore first.

Evadne.   Why?   10

Melantius.   I will not have your guilded things that daunce
In visitation with their millan skins
Choake up my businesse.

Evadne.   You are strangely dispos'd sir.

Melantius.   Good Madame, not to make you merry.

Evadne.   No, if you praise me twill make me sad.

Melantius.   Such a sad commendation I have for you.

Evadne.   Brother,
The Court has made you wittie, and learne to riddle.

Melantius.   I praise the Court for't, has it learnd you nothing?

Evadne.   Me?

Melantius.   I *Evadne*, thou art yong and hansome,   20
A Lady of a sweete complexion,
And such a flowing carriage, that it cannot
Chuse but inflame a Kingdome.

Evadne.   Gentle brother.

Melantius.   Tis yet in thy repentance, foolish woman,
To make me gentle.

Evadne.   How is this?

Melantius.   Tis base,
And I could blush at these yeares, through all
My honord scars, to come to such a parlie.

Evadne.   I understand ye not.

Melantius.   You dare not, foole,
They that commit thy faults flie the remembrance.

Evadne.   My faults sir, I would have you know I care not   30
If they were written here, here in my forehead.

Melantius.   Thy body is to little for the story,

10 the dore] Q2; your dores Q1
16 commendation] Q6; commendations Q1–5
19 it] Q2; *om.* Q1   28 not,] F2; ~ᴧ Q1–7
32 to] *i.e.* too

The lusts of which would fill another woman,
Though she had twins within her.
Evadne.   This is saucie,
Looke you intrude no more, theres your way.
Melantius.   Thou art my way, and I will tread upon thee,
Till I finde truth out.
Evadne.   What truth is that you looke for?
Melantius.   Thy long lost honor: would the gods had set me
Rather to grapple with the plague, or stand
One of their loudest bolts, come tell me quickly,   40
Doe it without inforcement, and take heede
You swell me not above my temper.
Evadne.   How sir?
Where got you this report?
Melantius.   Where there was people
In every place.
Evadne.   They and the seconds of it
Are base people, beleeve them not, they lied.
Melantius.   Doe not play with mine anger, doe not wretch,
                                                    [*Seizes her.*]

I come to know that desperate foole, that drew thee
From thy faire life, be wise and lay him open.
Evadne.   Unhand me and learne manners, such another
Forgetfulnesse forfits your life.   50
Melantius.   Quench me this mighty humor, and then tell me
Whose whore you are, for you are one, I know it,
Let all mine honors perish but ile finde him,
Though he lie lockt up in thy blood, be sudden,
There is no facing it, and be not flattered;
The burnt aire when the dog raines, is not fouler
Then thy contagious name, till thy repentance,
If the gods grant thee any, purge thy sicknesse.
Evadne.   Begon, you are my brother, thats your safty.
Melantius.   Ile be a woulfe first, tis to be thy brother   60
An infamy below the sin of coward,

45 they lied] Q2; theile lie Q1   54 be sudden] Q2; come tell me Q1
60–61 tis...coward] *i.e.* to be thy brother—tis an infamy...

I am as far from being part of thee,
As thou art from thy vertue, seeke a kindred
Mongst sensuall beasts, and make a goate thy brother,
A goate is cooler, will you tell me yet?
Evadne. If you stay here and raile thus, I shall tell you,
Ile ha you whipt, get you to your command,
And there preach to your Centinels, and tell them
What a brave man you are, I shal laugh at you.
Melantius. Y'are growne a glorious whore, where bee your fighters? 70
What mortall foole durst raise thee to this daring,
And I alive? by my just sword, h'ad safer
Bestride a billow when the angry North
Plowes up the sea, or made heavens fire his food;
Worke me no hier, will you discover yet?
Evadne. The fellowes mad, sleepe and speake sence.
Melantius. Force my swolne heart no further, I would save thee,
Your great maintainers are not here, they dare not,
Would they were al, and armed, I would speake loud,
Heres one should thunder to'em, will you tell me? 80
Thou hast no hope to scape, he that dares most,
And dams away his soule to doe thee service,
Will sooner snatch meat from a hungry Lyon
Then come to rescue thee; thou hast death about thee:
Has undone thine honor, poyson'd thy vertue,
And of a lovely rose, left thee a canker.
Evadne. Let me consider.
Melantius. Doe, whose child thou wert,
Whose honor thou hast murdered, whose grave opened,
And so pul'd on the gods, that in their justice
They must restore him flesh agen and life, 90
And raise his drie bones to revenge this scandall.
Evadne. The gods are not of my minde, they had better
Let'em lie sweete still in the earth, theile stinke here.
Melantius. Doe you raise mirth out of my easinesse?
Forsake me then all weaknesses of nature,

64 brother] Q2; father Q1   *74 food] Q2; foe Q1
81–86 Thou...canker.] Q2; *om.* Q1

That make men women, speake you whore, speake truth,
Or by the deare soule of thy sleeping father,
This sword shall be thy lover, tell or ile kill thee,
And when thou hast told all, thou wilt deserve it.
Evadne.   You will not murther me.   100
Melantius.   No, tis a justice and a noble one,
To put the light out of such base offenders.
Evadne.   Helpe?
Melantius.   By thy foule selfe, no humaine help shall help thee
If thou criest: when I have kild thee, as I
Have vow'd to doe, if thou confesse not, naked
As thou hast left thine honor, will I leave thee,
That on thy branded flesh the world may reade
Thy blacke shame and my justice, wilt thou bend yet?
Evadne.   Yes.   110
Melantius.   Up and beginne your storie.
Evadne.   Oh I am miserable.
Melantius.   Tis true, thou art, speake truth still.
Evadne.   I have offended, noble Sir forgive me.
Melantius.   With what secure slave?
Evadne.   Doe not aske me Sir,
Mine owne remembrance is a miserie
Too mightie for me.
Melantius.   Doe not fall backe agen,
My sword's unsheathed yet.
Evadne.   What shall I doe?
Melantius.   Be true, and make your fault lesse.
Evadne.   I dare not tell.
Melantius.   Tell, or ile be this day a killing thee.   120
Evadne.   Will you forgive me then?
Melantius.   Stay I must aske
Mine honour first: I have too much foolish nature
In me, speake.
Evadne.   Is there none else here?
Melantius.   None but a fearfull conscience, that's too many.
Who ist?

123 none else] Q2; no more Q1

89

Evadne.   Oh heare me gently, it was the King.

Melantius.   No more, my worthy fathers and my services
Are liberally rewarded, King I thanke thee:
For all my dangers and my wounds thou hast paid me
In my owne metall, these are souldiers thankes.
How long have you lived thus *Evadne?*

Evadne.   Too long.   130

Melantius.   Too late you finde it, can you be sorry?

Evadne.   Would I were halfe as blamelesse.

Melantius.   *Evadne*, thou wilt to thy trade againe.

Evadne.   First to my grave.

Melantius.   Would gods thou hadst beene so blest.
Dost thou not hate this King now? prethee hate him.
Couldst thou not curse him? I command thee curse him,
Curse till the gods heare and deliver him
To thy just wishes, yet I feare *Evadne*
You had rather play your game out.

Evadne.   No I feele
Too many sad confusions here to let in   140
Any loose flame hereafter.

Melantius.   Dost thou not feele amongst al those one brave anger
That breakes out nobly, and directs thine arme
To kill this base King?

Evadne.   All the gods forbid it.

Melantius.   No al the gods require it,
They are dishonored in him.

Evadne.   Tis too fearfull.

Melantius.   Y'are valiant in his bed, and bold enough
To be a stale whore, and have your Madams name
Discourse for groomes and pages, and hereafter
When his coole Majestie hath laid you by   150

125 Oh...was] Q2; *om.* Q1   126 No more,] Q2 (more.); *om.* Q1
130–131 *Evadne.* Too...can] Q2; *Evad.* Too long, too late I finde it. | *Mel.*
Can Q1
    131 be sorry] Q2; be very sorry Q1
    133 *Evadne,...* againe.] Q2; Woman ˄ thou wilt not to thy trade againe. Q1
    136 Couldst thou not curse him] Q2 (Could'st); Has sunke thy faire soule Q1
    136 thou] Q3; thee Q2

90

To be at pension with some needie Sir
For meat and courser cloathes, thus farre you knew
No feare. Come you shall kill him.

Evadne.   Good Sir——

Melantius.   And twere to kisse him dead, thoudst smother him.
Be wise and kill him, canst thou live and know
What noble minds shall make thee, see thy selfe
Found out with every finger, made the shame
Of all successions, and in this great ruine
Thy brother and thy noble husband broken?
Thou shalt not live thus, kneele and sweare to helpe me   160
When I shall call thee to it, or by all
Holy in heaven and earth thou shalt not live
To breathe a full houre longer, not a thought.
Come tis a righteous oath, give me thy hand,
And both to heaven held up, sweare by that wealth
This lustfull theefe stole from thee, when I say it,
To let his foule soule out.

Evadne.   Here I sweare it,
And all you spirits of abused Ladies,
Helpe me in this performance.

Melantius.   Enough, this must be knowne to none   170
But you and I *Evadne*, not to your Lord,
Though he be wise and noble, and a fellow
Dare step as farre into a worthy action,
As the most daring, I, as farre as justice.
Aske me not why. Farewell.   *Exit* Melantius.

Evadne.   Would I could say so to my blacke disgrace;
Gods where have I beene all this time, how friended,
That I should lose my selfe thus desperately,
And none for pittie shew me how I wandred?
There is not in the compasse of the light   180
A more unhappy creature, sure I am monstrous,
For I have done those follies, those mad mischiefes
Would dare a woman. O my loaden soule,

152 knew] Q2; had Q1   158 great] Q2; thy Q1
162 shalt] Q1; shall Q2   163 full] Q2; foule Q1

Be not so cruell to me, choake not up
The way to my repentance.

Enter Amintor.

O my Lord.
Amintor.   How now?
Evadne.   My much abused Lord.   *Kneele.*
Amintor.   This cannot be.
Evadne.   I doe not kneele to live, I dare not hope it,
    The wrongs I did are greater, looke upon me
    Though I appeare with all my faults.
Amintor.   Stand up.
    This is a new way to beget more sorrowes,   190
    Heaven knowes I have too many, doe not mocke me,
    Though I am tame and bred up with my wrongs,
    Which are my foster-brothers, I may leape
    Like a hand-wolfe into my naturall wildnesse,
    And doe an outrage, prethee doe not mocke me.
Evadne.   My whole life is so leaprous it infects
    All my repentance, I would buy your pardon
    Though at the highest set, even with my life,
    That sleight contrition, that no sacrifice
    For what I have committed.
Amintor.   Sure I dazle.   200
    There cannot be a faith in that foule woman
    That knowes no God more mighty then her mischiefes;
    Thou doest still worse, still number on thy faults,
    To presse my poore heart thus. Can I beleeve
    Theres any seed of vertue in that woman
    Left to shoot up, that dares goe on in sinne
    Knowne and so knowne as thine is? O *Evadne*,
    Would there were any safetie in thy sex,
    That I might put a thousand sorrowes off,
    And credit thy repentance, but I must not,   210
    Thou hast brought me to that dull calamitie,

190 a...sorrowes] Q1; no...sorrow Q2
*199 that₄] Brereton's suggestion; that; Q1–2; thats; Q3–4; thats ₄ Q5–8, F2

92

To that strange misbeleefe of all the world,
And all things that are in it, that I feare
I shall fall like a tree, and finde my grave,
Only remembring that I grieve.
Evadne.   My Lord,
Give me your griefes, you are an innocent,
A soule as white as heaven, let not my sinnes
Perish your noble youth, I doe not fall here
To shadow by dissembling with my teares
As all say women can, or to make lesse   220
What my hot will hath done, which heaven and you
Knowes to be tougher then the hand of time
Can cut from mans remembrance, no I doe not,
I doe appeare the same, the same *Evadne*,
Drest in the shames I liv'd in, the same monster.
But these are names of honour to what I am,
I doe present my selfe the foulest creature,
Most poisonous, dangerous, and despisde of men
Lerna ere bred or *Nilus*: I am hell,
Till you my deare Lord shoot your light into me,   230
The beames of your forgivenesse: I am soule sicke,
And wither with the feare of one condemnd,
Till I have got your pardon.
Amintor.   Rise *Evadne.*
Those heavenly powers that put this good into thee
Grant a continuance of it: I forgive thee,
Make thy selfe worthy of it, and take heed
Take heed *Evadne* this be serious,
Mocke not the powers above that can, and dare
Give thee a great example of their justice
To all insuing eies, if thou plai'st   240
With thy repentance, the best sacrifice.
Evadne.   I have done nothing good to win beleife,
My life hath beene so faithlesse, all the Creatures
Made for heavens honors have their ends, and good ones,

223 Can] Q2; Shall Q1   *240 eies] *stet* Q1-2
242 win] Q2; get Q1

Al but the cousening *Crocodiles*, false women.
They raigne here like those plagues, those killing soares
Men pray against, and when they die, like tales
Ill told and unbeleiv'd, they passe away,
And go to dust forgotten: But my Lord
Those short daies I shall number to my rest,   250
(As many must not see me,) shall though too late,
Though in my evening, yet perceive I will,
Since I can doe no good because a woman,
Reach constantly at something that is neere it;
I will redeeme one minute of my age,
Or like another *Niobe* ile weepe
Till I am water.
Amintor.   I am now dissolved.
My frozen soule melts, may each sin thou hast,
Finde a new mercy, rise, I am at peace: [Evadne *rises*.]
Hadst thou beene thus, thus excellently good   260
Before that devill King tempted thy frailty
Sure thou hadst made a Star: give me thy hand,
From this time I will know thee, and as far
As honour gives me leave, be thy *Amintor*:
When we meete next I will salute thee fairely,
And pray the gods to give thee happy daies,
My Charity shall go along with thee
Though my embraces must be far from thee,
I should ha' kild thee, but this sweete repentance
Lockes up my vengeance, for which, thus I kisse thee,   270
The last kisse we must take, and would to heaven
The holy Preist that gave our hands together,
Had given us equall virtues, go *Evadne*
The gods thus part our bodies, have a care
My honour falles no further, I am well then.
Evadne.   All the deare joyes here, and above hereafter
Crowne thy faire soule, thus I take leave my Lord,
And never shall you see the foule *Evadne*

252 I] Q7; a Q1–6
257 now] Q2; *om.* Q1

Till she have tried all honoured meanes that may
Set her in rest, and wash her staines away.   280

Exeunt.

Hoboies play within.   [IV. ii]
Banquet.   Enter King, Calianax.

King.   I cannot tell how I should credit this
From you that are his enemie.
Calianax.   I am sure
He said it to me, and ile justifie it
What way he dares oppose, but with my sword.
King.   But did he breake without all circumstance
To you his Foe, that he would have the fort
To kill me, and then scape?
Calianax.   If he deny it,
Ile make him blush.
King.   It sounds incredibly.
Calianax.   I so does every thing I say of late.
King.   Not so *Calianax.*
Calianax.   Yes I should sit   10
Mute whilst a Rogue with strong armes cuts your throate.
King.   Well I will trie him, and if this be true
Ile pawne my life ile finde it, ift be false
And that you cloath your hate in such a lie
You shall hereafter doate in your owne house,
Not in the Court.
Calianax.   Why if it be a lie
Mine eares are false, for ile besworne I heard it:
Old men are good for nothing, you were best
Put me to death for hearing, and free him
For meaning it, you would a trusted me   20
Once, but the time is altered.
King.   And will still
Where I may doe with justice to the world,
You have no witnesse?

9 I so] *i.e.* Aye, so   16 Why₍ₐ₎] Q1; ~ ? Q2   17 ile] Q2 (Ile); I Q1

95

Calianax.   Yes my selfe.
King.   No more
I meane there were that heard it?
Calianax.   How no more?
Would you have more? why am not I enough
To hang a thousand Rogues?
King.   But so you may
Hang honest men too if you please.
Calianax.   I may,
Tis like I will doe so, there are a hundred
Will sweare it for a need too, if I say it.
King.   Such witnesses we need not.
Calianax.   And tis hard   30
If my word cannot hang a boisterous knave.
King.   Enough,——where's *Strato?*

                    Enter Strato.

Strato.   Sir.
King.   Why wheres all the Company? call *Amintor* and
Evadne, wheres my brother, and *Melantius?*
Bid him come too, and *Diphilus,* call all
That are without there: *Exit* Strato.
                    If he should desire
The combat of you, tis not in the power
Of all our lawes to hinder it, unlesse
We meane to quit 'em.
Calianax.   Why if you doe thinke
Tis fit an old man, and a Counsellor   40
To fight for what he saies, then you may grant it.

          Enter Amintor, Evadne, Melantius, Diphilus, Lysippus,
                        Cleon, Strato, Diagoras.

King.   Come sirs, *Amintor* thou art yet a Bridegroome,
And I will use thee so, thou shalt sit downe,
Evadne sit, and you *Amintor* too,
This banquet is for you sir: who has brought

          33 and∧] in∧ Q1–3; in. Q4–8, F2   41.2 Diagoras] Q2; *om.* Q1
                              96

A merry tale about him, to raise laughter
Amongst our wine, why *Strato* where art thou?
Thou wilt chop out with them unseasonably
When I desire 'em not.
Strato.   Tis my ill lucke Sir, so to spend them then.   50
King.   Reach me a boule of wine,——*Melantius*
Thou art sad.
Amintor.   I should be Sir the merriest here,
But I ha nere a story of mine owne
Worth telling at this time.
King.   Give me the wine.
Melantius I am now considering
How easie twere for any man we trust
To poyson one of us in such a boule.
Melantius.   I thinke it were not hard Sir, for a Knave.
Calianax [*aside*].   Such as you are.
King.   Ifaith twere easie, it becomes us well   60
To get plaine dealing men about our selves,
Such as you all are here,——*Amintor* to thee
And to thy faire *Evadne*.   [*Drinks.*]
Melantius.   Have you thought   *Aside* [*to* Calianax].
Of this *Calianax?*
Calianax.   Yes marry have I.
Melantius.   And whats your resolution?
Calianax.   Ye shall have it
——Soundly I warrant you.
King.   Reach to *Amintor*, *Strato*.
Amintor.   Here my love,
            [*Drinks, and hands boule to* Evadne.]
This wine will doe thee wrong, for it will set
Blushes upon thy cheekes, and till thou dost
A fault twere pitty.
King.   Yet I wonder much   70
Of the strange desperation of these men

48 chop] Q2; chopt Q1
*52 *Amintor*.] Q2; *Mel.* Q1   63 *Aside*] Q2; *om.* Q1
65–66 it | ——Soundly] Colman (~ , ~); ~ ˄ ~ Q1–8, F2

That dare attempt such acts here in our state,
He could not scape that did it.
Melantius.   Were he knowne,
Unpossible.
King.   It would be knowne *Melantius.*
Melantius.   It ought to be: if he got then away
He must weare all our lives upon his sword,
He need not flie the Iland, he must leave
No one alive.
King.   No, I should thinke no man
Could kill me and scape cleare but that old man.
Calianax.   But I? heaven blesse me, I, should I my liege?   80
King.   I doe not thinke thou wouldst but yet thou mightst,
For thou hast in thy hands the meanes to scape,
By keeping of the fort,——he has *Melantius*,
And he has kept it well.
Melantius.   From Cobwebs Sir,
Tis cleane swept, I can finde no other Art
In keeping of it now, twas nere beseiged
Since he commaunded.
Calianax.   I shall be sure
Of your good word, but I have kept it safe
From such as you.
Melantius.   Keepe your ill temper in,
I speake no malice, had my brother kept it   90
I should ha sed as much.
King.   You are not merry,
Brother drinke wine, sit you all still,——*Calianax*
                                    [*They rise and speake*] *aside.*
I cannot trust thus, I have throwne out words,
That would have fetcht warme bloud upon the cheekes
Of guilty men, and he is never mov'd,
He knowes no such thing.
Calianax.   Impudence may scape,
When feeble virtue is accus'd.
King.   A must

86 beseiged] Q2 (besieg'd); beseidge Q1

If he were guilty feele an alteration
At this our whisper, whilst we point at him,
You see he does not.
Calianax.   Let him hang himselfe,   100
What care I what he does, this he did say.
King.   *Melantius* you can easily conceive
What I have meant, for men that are in fault
Can subtly apprehend when others aime
At what they doe amisse, but I forgive
Freely before this man, heaven doe so too;
I will not touch thee so much as with shame
Of telling it, let it be so no more.
Calianax [*aside*].   Why this is very fine.
Melantius.   I cannot tell
What tis you meane, but I am apt enough   110
Rudely to thrust into ignorant fault,
But let me know it, happily tis naught
But misconstruction, and where I am cleare
I will not take forgivenesse of the gods,
Much lesse of you.
King.   Nay if you stand so stiffe,
I shall call back my mercy.
Melantius.   I want smoothnes
To thanke a man for pardoning of a crime
I never knew.
King.   Not to instruct your knowledge, but to show you
My eares are every where, you meant to kill me,   120
And get the fort to scape.
Melantius.   Pardon me Sir,
My bluntnesse will be pardoned, you preserve
A race of idle people here about you,
Eaters, and talkers to defame the worth
Of those that doe things worthy, the man that uttered this
Had perisht without food, bee't who it will,
But for this arme that fenst him from the Foe.

103 fault] Q2; faults Q1   *124 Eaters] Q2; Facers Q1
124 worth] Q2; world Q1

And if I thought you gave a faith to this,
The plainenesse of my nature would speake more,
Give me a pardon, for you ought to doo't,   130
To kill him that spake this.
Calianax [*aside*].   I that will be
The end of all, then I am fairely paide
For all my care and service.
Melantius.   That old man,
Who calls me enemy, and of whom I
(Though I will never match my hate so low,)
Have no good thought, would yet I thinke excuse me,
And sweare he thought me wrong'd in this.
Calianax.   Who I?
Thou shamelesse Fellow, didst thou not speake to me
Of it thy selfe?
Melantius.   O then it came from him.
Calianax.   From me, who should it come from but from me?   140
Melantius.   Nay I beleeve your malice is enough,
But I ha lost my anger,——Sir I hope
You are well satisfied.
King.   *Lysippus* cheare
Amintor and his Lady,——theres no sound
Comes from you, I will come and doo't my selfe.
Amintor.   You have done all ready Sir for me I thanke you.
King.   *Melantius* I doe credit this from him,
How sleight so ere you mak't.
Melantius.   Tis strange you should.
Calianax.   Tis strang a should beleeve an old mans word,
That never lied ins life.
Melantius.   I talke not to thee,——   150
Shall the wilde words of this distempered man,
Frantique with age and sorrow, make a breach
Betwixt your Majestie and me? twas wrong
To harken to him, but to credit him
As much, at least, as I have power to beare.

138–139 Fellow, . . .selfe?] Q2 (*as prose*); Fellow ‸ that hast spoke to me | Of it
thy selfe. Q1

But pardon me, whilst I speake onely truth,
I may commend my selfe——I have bestowd
My carelesse bloud with you, and should be loath
To thinke an action that would make me loose
That, and my thankes too: when I was a boy   160
I thrust my selfe into my Countries cause,
And did a deed, that pluckt five yeares from time
And stil'd me man then, and for you my king
Your Subjects all have fed by vertue of
My arme, this sword of mine hath plowd the ground,
And reapt the fruit in peace,
And you your selfe have liv'd at home in ease:
So terrible I grew that without swords
My name hath fetcht you conquest, and my heart
And limmes are still the same, my will as great   170
To doe you service: let me not be paid
With such a strange distrust.
  King.   *Melantius*
I held it great injustice to beleeve
Thine enemie, and did not; if I did,
I doe not, let that satisfie,——what strooke
With sadnesse all? more wine.
Calianax.   A few fine words
Have overthrowne my truth, a th'art a Villaine.
Melantius (aside).   Why, thou wert better let me have the fort,
Dotard, I wil disgrace thee thus for ever,
There shall no credit lie upon thy words,   180
Thinke better and deliver it.
Calianax.   My leige,
Hees at me now agen to doe it,——speake,
Denie it if thou canst,——examine him
Whilst he is hot, for if hee coole agen,
He will forsweare it.
King.   This is lunacie
I hope, *Melantius.*

165–166 this...peace,] Q2 (peace;); *om.* Q1   174 not] Q2; *om.* Q1
177 a] *i.e.* ah   178 *aside*] Q2; *om.* Q1

Melantius.   He hath lost himselfe
  Much since his daughter mist the happinesse
  My sister gaind, and though he call me Foe,
  I pittie him.
Calianax.   A pittie a pox upon you.
Melantius.   Marke his disordered words, and at the Maske   190
  Diagoras knowes he rag'd, and raild at me,
  And cald a Ladie Whore so innocent
  She understood him not, but it becomes
  Both you and me to forgive distraction,
  Pardon him as I doe.
Calianax.   Ile not speake for thee,
  For all thy cunning:——if you will be safe
  Chop off his head, for there was never knowne
  So impudent a Rascall.
King.   Some that love him
  Get him to bed: why? pittie should not let
  Age make it selfe contemptible, we must be   200
  All old, have him away.
Melantius.   *Calianax*
  The King beleeves you, come, you shall go home,
  And rest, you ha done well,——[*aside to him*] youle give it up
  When I have usd you thus a month, I hope.
Calianax.   Now, now, tis plaine Sir, he does move me still,
  He saies he knowes ile give him up the fort
  When he has usd me thus a month, I am mad
  Am I not still?
Omnes.   Ha ha ha.
Calianax.   I shall be mad indeed if you doe thus,
  Why should you trust a sturdie fellow there,   210
  (That has no virtue in him, alls in his sword)
  Before me? doe but take his weapons from him
  And hees an Asse, and I am a very foole
  Both with em, and without em, as you use me.
Omnes.   Ha ha ha.
King.   Tis well, *Calianax*, but if you use

214 em...em] Dyce; him...him Q1–8, F2   216 Tis] Q2; Too Q1

This once agen I shall intreat some other
To see your offices be well dischargd.——
Be merry Gentlemen it growes somewhat late,——
Amintor thou wouldst be a bed agen.   220
Amintor.   Yes Sir.
King.   And you *Evadne*,——let me take
Thee in my arms, *Melantius* and beleeve
Thou art as thou deservest to be, my freind,
Still, and for ever,——good *Calianax*
Sleepe soundly, it will bring thee to thy selfe.
                    Exeunt omnes. Manent Melantius *and* Calianax.
Calianax.   Sleepe soundly! I sleepe soundly now I hope,
I could not be thus else. How dar'st thou stay
Alone with me, knowing how thou hast used me?
Melantius.   You cannot blast me with your tongue,
And thats the strongest part you have about ye.   230
Calianax.   I doe looke for some great punishment for this,
For I beginne to forget all my hate,
And tak't unkindly that mine enemy
Should use me so extraordinarily scurvily.
Melantius.   I shall melt too, if you begin to take
Unkindnesses, I never meant you hurt.
Calianax.   Thoult anger me agen; thou wretched roague,
Meant me no hurt! disgrace me with the King,
Lose all my offices, this is no hurt
Is it, I prethee what dost thou call hurt?   240
Melantius.   To poison men because they love me not,
To call the credit of mens wives in question,
To murder children, betwixt me and Land,
This I call hurt.
Calianax.   All this thou thinkst is sport,

222 arms] Q2 (armes); arme Q1
222 and beleeve] Q2; *om.* Q1   230 ye] Q1; you Q2
231 I doe...this,] Q2; Dost not thou...this? Q1
232 For I] Q2; I feele | My selfe Q1   234 extraordinarily] Q2; extremely Q1
235 melt] Q2; meet Q1
236 Unkindnesses] Q2; Unkindnesse Q1
238 hurt] Q2; wrong Q1

For mine is worse, but use thy will with me,
For betwixt griefe and anger I could crie.
Melantius.   Be wise then and be safe, thou maist revenge.
Calianax.   I oth' King, I would revenge of thee.
Melantius.   That you must plot your selfe.
Calianax.   I am a fine plotter.
Melantius.   The short is, I will hold thee with the King   250
In this perplexitie till peevishnesse
And thy disgrace have laid thee in thy grave.
But if thou wilt deliver up the fort,
Ile take thy trembling body in my armes,
And beare thee over dangers, thou shalt hold
Thy wonted state.
Calianax.   If I should tell the King,
Canst thou deni't agen?
Melantius.   Trie and beleeve.
Calianax.   Nay then thou canst bring any thing about,
Melantius, thou shalt have the fort.
Melantius.   Why well,
Here let our hate be buried, and this hand   260
Shall right us both, give me thy aged brest
To compasse.
Calianax.   Nay I doe not love thee yet,
I cannot well endure to looke on thee,
And if I thought it were a curtesie,
Thou shouldst not have it, but I am disgrac't,
My offices are to be tane away,
And if I did but hold this fort a day,
I doe beleeve the King would take it from me,
And give it thee, things are so strangely carried:
Nere thanke me fort, but yet the King shall know   270
There was some such thing int I told him of,
And that I was an honest man.
Melantius.   Heele buy
That knowledge very deerely:

248 oth' King] Q5; oth' the King Q1–4
252 thy disgrace] Q2; his disgrace Q1   259 *Melantius*] Q1; om. Q2

104

Enter Diphilus.

Diphilus

What newes with thee?

Diphilus.　　　　　　This were a night indeed
To doe it in, the King hath sent for her.

Melantius.　She shall performe it then, goe *Diphilus*
And take from this good man my worthy friend
The fort, heele give it thee.

Diphilus.　　　　　　Ha you got that?

Calianax.　Art thou of the same breed? canst thou denie
This to the King too?

Diphilus.　　　　　With a confidence　　　　　　280
As great as his.

Calianax.　　　Faith like enough.

Melantius.　Away and use him kindly.

Calianax.　　　　　　　Touch not me,
I hate the whole straine, if thou follow me
A great way off, Ile give thee up the fort,
And hang your selves.

Melantius.　　　　Be gone.

Diphilus.　　　　　　Hees finely wrought.

　　　　　　　　　　Exeunt Calianax, Diphilus.

Melantius.　This is a night spight of Astronomers
To doe the deed in, I will wash the staine
That rests upon our house, off with his bloud.

Enter Amintor.

Amintor.　*Melantius* now assist me if thou beest
That which thou saist, assist me, I have lost　　　　290
All my distempers, and have found a rage
So pleasing, helpe me.

Melantius [*aside*].　　　Who can see him thus,
And not sweare vengeance?——whats the matter friend?

Amintor.　Out with thy sword, and hand in hand with me
Rush to the chamber of this hated King,
And sinke him with the weight of all his sins
To hell for ever.

Melantius.   Twere a rash attempt,
Not to be done with safetie, let your reason
Plot your revenge, and not your passion.
Amintor.   If thou refusest me in these extremes,   300
Thou art no friend: he sent for her to me,
By heaven to me, my selfe, and I must tell ye
I love her as a stranger, there is worth
In that vild woman, worthy things *Melantius*,
And she repents. Ile doo't my selfe alone,
Though I be slaine, farewell.
Melantius [*aside*].   Heele overthrow
My whole designe with madnes.——*Amintor*,
Thinke what thou doest, I dare as much as valour,
But tis the King, the King, the King, *Amintor*,
With whom thou fightest.——(*Aside*) I know hees honest,   310
And this will worke with him.
Amintor.   I cannot tell
What thou hast said, but thou hast charmd my sword
Out of my hand, and left me shaking here
Defencelesse.
Melantius.   I will take it up for thee.
Amintor.   What a wilde beast is uncollected man!
The thing that we call honour beares us all
Headlong unto sinne, and yet it selfe is nothing.
Melantius.   Alas how variable are thy thoughts?
Amintor.   Just like my fortunes, I was run to that
I purposd to have chid thee for. Some plot   320
I did distrust thou hadst against the King
By that old fellowes carriage, but take heed,
Theres not the least limbe growing to a King
But carries thunder in't.
Melantius.   I have none
Against him.
Amintor.   Why come then, and still remember
Wee may not thinke revenge.
Melantius.   I will remember.

                                                    Exeunt.

Enter Evadne *and a* Gentleman.   V. i

Evadne.   Sir is the King abed?
Gentleman.   Madam an houre agoe.
Evadne.   Give me the key then, and let none be neere.
  Tis the Kings pleasure.
Gentleman.   I understand you Madam, would twere mine,
  I must not wish good rest unto your Ladiship.
Evadne.   You talke, you talke.
Gentleman.   Tis all I dare doe Madam, but the King
  Will wake, and then——
Evadne.   Saving your imagination, pray good night Sir.
Gentleman.   A good night be it then, and a long one Madam,   10
  I am gone.   *Exit.*
Evadne.   The night growes horrible, and all about me
  Like my blacke purpose, O the conscience
                                 King [*discovered*] *a bed.*
Of a lost virgin, whither wilt thou pull me?
To what things dismall, as the depth of hell,
Wilt thou provoke me? Let no woman dare
From this houre be disloyall, if her heart be flesh;
If she have bloud and can feare, tis a daring
Above that desperate fooles that left his peace,
And went to sea to fight, tis so many sins,   20
An age cannot repent'em, and so great,
The gods want mercy for, yet I must through 'em,
I have begun a slaughter on my honour,
And I must end it there,——a sleepes, oh God,
Why give you peace to this untemperate beast,
That hath so long transgrest you? I must kill him,
And I will doo't bravely: the meere joy
Tels me I merit in it, yet I must not

0.1 V.i] *Actus* 5. Q 1–2   2 and let] Q 2; and Sir let Q 1
8 then] Q 2; then methinkes Q 1   14 virgin] Q 2; virtue Q 1
18 daring] Q 2; madnesse Q 1   19 fooles] Q 2; mans Q 1
21 repent'em] Q 1; prevent'm Q 2   24 oh God] Q 1; good heavens Q 2
26 hath so long] Q 2; has so farre Q 1
28 Tels...it] Q 2; Confirmes me that I merit Q 1

107

Thus tamely doe it as he sleepes, that were
To rock him to another world, my vengeance   30
Shall take him waking, and then lay before him
The number of his wrongs and punishments.
Ile shape his sins like furies till I waken
His evill Angell, his sicke conscience,
And then Ile strike him dead. King by your leave, *Ties his armes*
I dare not trust your strength, your Grace and I   *to the bed.*
Must grapple upon even tearmes no more.
So, if he raile me not from my resolution,
I shall be strong enough.——
My Lord the King, my Lord,——a sleepes   40
As if he meant to wake no more,——my Lord,——
Is he not dead already?——Sir, my Lord.
King.   Whose that?
Evadne.   O you sleepe soundly Sir.
King.   My deare *Evadne*,
I have beene dreaming of thee, come to bed.
Evadne.   I am come at length Sir, but how welcome?
King.   What prettie new device is this *Evadne*?
What, doe you tie me to you? by my love
This is a queint one: come my deare and kisse me,
Ile be thy *Mars*, to bed my Queene of love,   50
Let us be caught together, that the gods may see,
And envie our embraces.
Evadne.   Stay Sir, stay,
You are too hot, and I have brought you physicke,
To temper your high veines.
King.   Prethee to bed then, let me take it warme,
Here thou shalt know the state of my body better.
Evadne.   I know you have a surfeited foule body,
And you must bleed.

30 rock] Q2; rake Q1   31 take] Q2; seaze Q1
35 Ile] Q2; I Q1   35 strike] Q1; strick Q2
36 your Grace] Q1; you Grace Q2
39 I...enough] Q2; As I beleeve I shall not, I shall fit him Q1
48 you?...love‸] Theobald; ~‸ ... ~ ? Q1, 5–8, F2; ~, ... ~, Q2–3;
~, ... ~ ? Q4   51 see] Q2; looke Q1   56 Here] Q1; There Q2

King.   Bleed!
Evadne.   I, you shall bleed, lie still, and if the devill
   Your lust will give you leave, repent: this steele   60
   Comes to redeeme the honour that you stole
   King, my faire name, which nothing but thy death
   Can answer to the world.
King.   How's this *Evadne?*
Evadne.   I am not she, nor beare I in this breast
   So much cold spirit to be cald a woman,
   I am a Tiger, I am any thing
   That knowes not pittie, stirre not, if thou doest,
   Ile take thee unprepar'd, thy feares upon thee,
   That make thy sins looke double, and so send thee
   (By my revenge I will) to looke those torments   70
   Prepar'd for such blacke soules.
King.   Thou doest not meane this, tis impossible,
   Thou art too sweet and gentle.
Evadne.   No I am not,
   I am as foule as thou art, and can number
   As many such hels here: I was once faire,
   Once I was lovely, not a blowing rose
   More chastly sweet, till thou, thou, thou foule canker,
   (Stirre not) didst poison me: I was a world of vertue,
   Till your curst Court and you (hell blesse you for't)
   With your temptations on temptations   80
   Made me give up mine honour, for which (King)
   I am come to kill thee.
King.   No.
Evadne.   I am.
King.   Thou art not.
   I prethee speake not these things, thou art gentle,
   And wert not meant thus rugged.
Evadne.   Peace and heare me.
   Stirre nothing but your tongue, and that for mercy
   To those above us, by whose lights I vow,
   Those blessed fires, that shot to see our sinne,

63 How's this] Q2; How Q1

109

If thy hot soule had substance with thy bloud,
I would kill that too, which being past my steele,
My tongue shall reach: Thou art a shamelesse villaine,   90
A thing out of the overcharge of nature,
Sent like a thicke cloud to disperse a plague
Upon weake catching women, such a tyrant,
That for his lust would sell away his subjects,
I, all his heaven hereafter.

King.   Heare *Evadne,*
Thou soule of sweetnesse, heare, I am thy King.

Evadne.   Thou art my shame, lie still, theres none about you
Within your cries, all promises of safetie
Are but deluding dreames: thus, thus thou foule man, *Stabs him.*
Thus I begin my vengeance.

King.   Hold *Evadne,*   100
I doe command thee, hold.

Evadne.   I doe not meane Sir
To part so fairely with you, we must change
More of these love-trickes yet.

King.   What bloudie villaine
Provok't thee to this murther?

Evadne.   Thou, thou monster.   *Stabs him.*

King.   Oh.

Evadne.   Thou keptst me brave at Court, and whorde me, King,
Then married me to a young noble Gentleman,
And whorde me still.

King.   *Evadne,* pittie me.

Evadne.   Hell take me then, this for my Lord *Amintor,*
This for my noble brother, and this stroke   110
For the most wrongd of women.   *Kils him.*

King.   Oh I die.

Evadne.   Die all our faults together, I forgive thee.   *Exit.*

99 *Stabs him.*] Q2; *om.* Q1
103 villaine] Q2; villanie Q1   104 *Stabs him.*] Q1; *om.* Q2

Enter two [Gentlemen] of the Bed-chamber.

1. Gentleman.   Come now shees gone, lets enter, the King expects
it, and will be angry.

2. Gentleman.   Tis a fine wench, weele have a snap at her one of
these nights as she goes from him.

1. Gentleman.   Content: how quickly he had done with her, I see
Kings can doe no more that way then other mortall people.

2. Gentleman.   How fast he is! I cannot heare him breathe.

1. Gentleman.   Either the tapers give a feeble light,   120
Or he lookes very pale.

2. Gentleman.   And so he does,
Pray heaven he be well. Lets looke: Alas,
Hees stiffe, wounded and dead. Treason, treason.

1. Gentleman.   Run forth and call.   *Exit [2.] Gentleman.*

2. Gentleman [within].   Treason, treason.

1. Gentleman.   This will be laid on us:
Who can beleeve a woman could doe this?

Enter Cleon *and* Lysippus.

Cleon.   How now? wheres the traitor?

1. Gentleman.   Fled, fled away, but there her wofull act
Lies still.

Cleon.   Her act! a woman!

Lysippus.   Wheres the body?

1. Gentleman.   There.   130

Lysippus.   Farewell thou worthy man, there were two bonds
That tied our loves, a brother and a King,
The least of which might fetch a floud of teares:
But such the miserie of greatnesse is,
They have no time to mourne, then pardon me.
Sirs, which way went she?

113, 115 *1. Gentleman.... 2. Gentleman.*] 1.... 2. Q1–8, F2 (*and so for Gentlemen through l.* 130)
    121–122 And...well.] Q2; *om.* Q1
    123 Treason, treason] Q2 (Treason, Treason); Treason Q1

Enter Strato.

Strato.   Never follow her,
For she alas was but the instrument.
Newes is now brought in that *Melantius*
Has got the Fort, and stands upon the wall,
And with a loud voice cals those few that passe   140
At this dead time of night, delivering
The innocence of this act.
Lysippus.   Gentlemen,
I am your King.
Strato.   We doe acknowledge it.
Lysippus.   I would I were not: follow all, for this
Must have a sudden stop.

                                        Exeunt.

            Enter Melantius, Diphilus, Calianax *on the walls.*   [V. ii]

Melantius.   If the dull people can beleeve, I am arm'd.
Be constant *Diphilus*, now we have time,
Either to bring our banisht honours home,
Or to create new ones in our ends.
Diphilus.   I feare not,
My spirit lies not that way. Courage *Calianax.*
Calianax.   Would I had any, you should quickly know it.
Melantius.   Speake to the people, thou art eloquent.
Calianax.   Tis a fine eloquence to come to the gallowes,
You were borne to be my end, the devill take you,
Now must I hang for company, tis strange   10
I should be old, and neither wise, nor valiant.

            Enter Lysippus, Diagoras, Cleon, Strato, *Guard.*

Lysippus.   See where he stands as boldly confident,
As if he had his full command about him.
Strato.   He lookes as if he had the better cause, Sir,
Under your gracious pardon let me speake it,

                140 cals those] Q2; cals to those Q1

Though he be mightie spirited and forward
To all great things, to all things of that danger
Worse men shake at the telling of, yet certainly
I doe beleeve him noble, and this action
Rather puld on then sought, his minde was ever   20
As worthy as his hand.

Lysippus.   Tis my feare too,
Heaven forgive all: summon him Lord *Cleon.*

Cleon.   Ho from the walls there.

Melantius.   Worthy *Cleon* welcome,
We could a wisht you here Lord, you are honest.

Calianax (aside).   Well thou art as flattering a knave, though I
dare not tell thee so.

Lysippus.   *Melantius.*

Melantius.   Sir.

Lysippus.   I am sorrie that we meet thus, our old love
Never requir'd such distance, pray to heaven   30
You have not left your selfe, and sought this safetie
More out of feare then honour: you have lost
A noble master, which your faith, *Melantius,*
Some thinke might have preserved, yet you know best.

Calianax [aside].   When time was I was mad; some that dares fight,
I hope will pay this rascall.

Melantius.   Royall young man, those teares looke lovely on thee,
Had they beene shed for a deserving one,
They had beene lasting monuments. Thy brother,
Whilst he was good, I cald him King, and serv'd him,   40
With that strong faith, that most unwearied valour,
Puld people from the farthest sunne to seeke him,
And buy his friendship, I was then his souldier:
But since his hot pride drew him to disgrace me,
And brand my noble actions with his lust,
(That never-cur'd dishonour of my sister,
Base staine of whore, and which is worse,

18 certainly] Q2; certaine Q1   30 to] Q1; *om.* Q2
34 Some thinke] Q2; I'm sure Q1
34-36 preserved, yet...rascall.] Q2; preserved. Q1
43 buy] Q2; begge Q1

The joy to make it still so) like my selfe,
Thus I have flung him off with my allegeance,
And stand here mine owne justice to revenge   50
What I have suffred in him, and this old man
Wrongd almost to lunacie.
Calianax.   Who I?
You wud draw me in, I have had no wrong,
I doe disclaime ye all.
Melantius.   The short is this,
Tis no ambition to lift up my selfe
Urgeth me thus, I doe desire againe
To be a subject, so I may be free;
If not, I know my strength, and will unbuild
This goodly towne; be speedie, and be wise,
In a replie.
Strato.   Be sudden Sir to tie   60
All up againe, what's done is past recall,
And past you to revenge, and there are thousands
That wait for such a troubled houre as this.
Throw him the blanke.
Lysippus.   *Melantius,* write in that
Thy choice, my seale is at it.
Melantius.   It was our honours drew us to this act,
Not gaine, and we will only worke our pardons.
Calianax.   Put my name in too.
Diphilus.   You disclaim'd us all but now *Calianax.*
Calianax.   Thats all one,   70
Ile not be hangd hereafter by a tricke,
Ile have it in.
Melantius.   You shall, you shall:——
Come to the backe gate, and weele call you King,
And give you up the Fort.
Lysippus.   Away, away.

                              Exeunt omnes.

48 so)...selfe,] Q2; ~ , ... ~) Q1   50 to revenge͵] Q2; for revenge, Q1
67 Not] Q6; No Q1–5   74 you] Q2; the Q1

114

Enter Aspatia *in mans apparell.*   [V.iii]

Aspatia.   This is my fatall houre, heaven may forgive
My rash attempt that causelesly hath laid
Griefes on me that will never let me rest,
And put a womans heart into my breast:
It is more honour for you that I die,
For she that can endure the miserie
That I have on me, and be patient too,
May live and laugh at all that you can doe.

Enter Servant.

God save you Sir.
Servant.   And you Sir, whats your businesse?
Aspatia.   With you Sir now, to doe me the faire office   10
To helpe me to your Lord.
Servant.   What, would you serve him?
Aspatia.   Ile doe him any service, but to haste,
For my affaires are earnest, I desire
To speake with him.
Servant.   Sir because you are in such haste, I would be loth to
delay you longer: you cannot.
Aspatia.   It shall become you though to tell your Lord.
Servant.   Sir he will speake with no body, but in particular, I
have in charge about no waightie matters.
Aspatia.   This is most strange: 20
Art thou gold proofe? theres for thee, helpe me to him.
Servant.   Pray be not angry Sir, Ile doe my best.   *Exit.*
Aspatia.   How stubbornly this fellow answer'd me!
There is a vild dishonest tricke in man,
More then in women: all the men I meet
Appeare thus to me, are harsh and rude,
And have a subtletie in every thing,
Which love could never know; but we fond women
Harbour the easiest and the smoothest thoughts,

5 die] Q2; doe Q1   9 God] Q1; Cod Q2
18–19 body, but...matters.] Q1; body. Q2

And thinke all shall goe so, it is unjust   30
That men and women should be matcht together.

Enter Amintor *and his* Man.

Amintor.   Where is he?
Servant.   There my Lord.
Amintor.   What would you Sir?
Aspatia.   Please it your Lordship to command your man
   Out of the roome, I shall deliver things
   Worthy your hearing.
Amintor.   Leave us.   [*Exit* Servant.]
Aspatia (*aside*).   O that that shape
   Should burie falshood in it.
Amintor.   Now your will Sir.
Aspatia.   When you know me, my Lord, you needs must ghesse
   My businesse, and I am not hard to know.
   For till the chance of warre markt this smooth face
   With these few blemishes, people would call me   40
   My sisters picture, and her mine: in short,
   I am the brother to the wrong'd *Aspatia.*
Amintor.   The wrong'd *Aspatia,* would thou wert so too
   Unto the wrong'd *Amintor,* let me kisse
   That hand of thine in honour that I beare
   Unto the wrong'd *Aspatia,* here I stand
   That did it, would I could not: gentle youth
   Leave me, for there is something in thy lookes
   That cals my sins in a most hideous forme
   Into my minde, and I have griefe enough   50
   Without thy helpe.
Aspatia.   I would I could with credit.
   Since I was twelve yeeres old I had not seene
   My sister till this houre I now arriv'd:
   She sent for me to see her marriage,
   A wofull one, but they that are above
   Have ends in every thing: she usd few words,
   But yet enough to make me understand

*47 I] he Q 1–8, F 2   49 hideous] Q 2; odious Q 1

116

The basenesse of the injuries you did her:
That little trayning I have had, is war,
I may behave my selfe rudely in peace,   60
I would not though, I shall not need to tell you
I am but young, and would be loth to loose
Honour that is not easily gaind againe,
Fairely I meane to deale, the age is strict
For single combats, and we shall be stopt
If it be publisht, if you like your sword
Use it, if mine appeare a better to you,
Change, for the ground is this, and this the time
To end our difference.
Amintor.   Charitable youth,
If thou beest such, thinke not I will maintaine   70
So strange a wrong, and for thy sisters sake,
Know, that I could not thinke that desperate thing
I durst not doe, yet to injoy this world
I would not see her, for beholding thee,
I am I know not what: if I have ought
That may content thee, take it, and be gone,
For death is not so terrible as thou,
Thine eies shoote guilt into me.
Aspatia.   Thus she swore,
Thou wouldst behave thy selfe and give me words
That would fetch teares into my eies, and so   80
Thou doest indeed, but yet she bad me watch,
Least I were cossend, and be sure to fight
Ere I returnd.
Amintor.   That must not be with me,
For her ile die directly, but against her
Will never hazard it.
Aspatia.   You must be urgd,
I doe not deale uncivilly with those
That dare to fight, but such a one as you
Must be usd thus.   *She strikes him.*
Amintor.   I prethee youth take heed,
Thy sister is a thing to me so much

Above mine honour, that I can indure   90
All this,——good gods, a blow I can indure,
But stay not, least thou draw a timelesse death
Upon thy selfe.
Aspatia.   Thou art some prating Fellow,
One that has studied out a tricke to talke
And move soft harted people; to be kickt,   *She kickes him.*
Thus to be kickt——(*aside*) why should he be so slow
In giving me my death?
Amintor.   A man can beare
No more and keepe his flesh, forgive me then,
I would indure yet if I could; now show   [*Draws.*]
The spirit thou pretendest, and understand   100
Thou hast no houre to live:——   *They fight.*
                    what dost thou meane,
Thou canst not fight, the blowes thou makst at me
Are quite besides, and those I offer at thee
Thou spreadst thine armes, and takst upon thy brest
Alas defencelesse.
Aspatia.   I have got enough,
And my desire, there is no place so fit
For me to die as here.   [*Falls.*]

          Enter Evadne, *her hands bloudy with a knife.*

Evadne.   *Amintor* I am loaden with events
That flie to make thee happy, I have joyes
That in a moment can call backe thy wrongs   110
And settle thee in thy free state againe,
It is *Evadne* still that followes thee
But not her mischiefes.
Amintor.   Thou canst not foole me to beleeve agen,
But thou hast lookes and things so full of newes
That I am staid.
Evadne.   Noble *Amintor* put off thy amaze,

        104 thy] Q2; thine Q1
        107.1 Evadne, *her...knife.*] Q2 (*Evadne. Her*); *Evadne.* Q1
        115 lookes] Q1(c)–2; bookes Q1(u)   116 staid] Q2; stald Q1

Let thine eies loose, and speake, am I not faire?
Lookes not *Evadne* beautious with these rites now?
Were those houres halfe so lovely in thine eyes   120
When our hands met before the holy man?
I was too foule within, to looke faire then,
Since I knew ill I was not free till now.
Amintor.   There is presage of some important thing
About thee which it seemes thy tongue hath lost,
Thy hands are bloudy, and thou hast a knife.
Evadne.   In this consists thy happinesse and mine,
Joy to *Amintor* for the King is dead.
Amintor.   Those have most power to hurt us, that we love,
We lay our sleeping lives within their armes.   130
Why thou hast raisd up mischiefe to his height
And found one, to out-name thy other faults,
Thou hast no intermission of thy sinnes,
But all thy life is a continued ill,
Blacke is thy coulor now, disease thy nature.
Joy to *Amintor?* thou hast toucht a life
The very name of which had power to chaine
Up all my rage, and calme my wildest wrongs.
Evadne.   Tis done, and since I could not finde a way
To meete thy love so cleare, as through his life   140
I cannot now repent it.
Amintor.   Cudst thou procure the gods to speake to me,
To bid me love this woman, and forgive,
I thinke I should fall out with them, behold
Here lies a youth whose wounds bleed in my breast,
Sent by his violent Fate to fetch his death
From my slow hand, and to augment my woe
You now are present, stain'd with a Kings bloud
Violently shed: this keepes night here
And throwes an unknowne Wildernesse about me.   150

                    [*Offers to go.* Evadne *followes.*]

Aspatia.   Oh oh oh.

138 calme] Q2; tame Q1   139 a way] Q1(c)–2; away Q1(u)
147–149 and...shed:] Q2; *om.* Q1

Amintor.   No more, persue me not.
Evadne.   Forgive me then
And take me to thy bed, we may not part.   [*Kneeles.*]
Amintor.   Forbeare, be wise, and let my rage go this way.
Evadne.   Tis you that I would stay, not it.
Amintor.   Take heed,
It will returne with me.
Evadne.   If it must be
I shall not feare to meete it, take me home.
Amintor.   Thou Monster of crueltie, forbeare.
Evadne.   For heavens sake looke more calme, thine eies are sharper,
Then thou canst make thy sword.
Amintor.   Away, away   160
Thy knees are more to me then violence,
I am worse then sicke to see knees follow me,
For that I must not grant, for Gods sake stand.
Evadne.   Receive me then.
Amintor.   I dare not stay thy language,
In midst of all my anger, and my griefe,
Thou doest awake some thing that troubles me,
And saies I lov'd thee once, I dare not stay,
There is no end of womans reasoning.   *Leaves her.*
Evadne.   *Amintor* thou shalt love me now againe,   [*Rises.*]
Go I am calme, farwell, and peace for ever.   170
Evadne whom thou hatst will die for thee.   *Kills herselfe.*
Amintor.   I have a little humane nature yet
Thats left for thee, that bids me stay thy hand.   *Returnes.*
Evadne.   Thy hand was welcome but it came too late,
Oh I am lost, the heavie sleepe makes hast.   *She dies.*
Aspatia.   Oh oh oh.
Amintor.   This earth of mine doth tremble, and I feele
A starke affrighted motion in my bloud,
My soule growes weary of her house, and I
All over am a trouble to my selfe,   180
There is some hidden power in these dead things

159 sharper] Q2; crueller Q1
175 *She dies.*] Q2; *om.* Q1

120

That calls my flesh unto 'em, I am cold,
Be resolute, and beare'em company;
Theres something yet which I am loath to leave,
Theres man enough in me to meete the feares
That death can bring, and yet would it were done;
I can finde nothing in the whole discourse
Of death I durst not meete the bouldest way,
Yet still betwixt the reason and the act
The wrong I to *Aspatia* did stands up,   190
I have not such another fault to answer,
Though she may justly arme her selfe with scorne
And hate of me, my soule will part lesse troubled,
When I have paid to her in teares my sorrow,
I will not leave this act unsatisfied,
If all thats left in me can answer it.
Aspatia.   Was it a dreame? There stands *Amintor* still,
Or I dreame still.
Amintor.   How doest thou? speake, receive my love and helpe:
Thy bloud climbes up to his old place againe,   200
Theres hope of thy recoverie.
Aspatia.   Did you not name *Aspatia?*
Amintor.   I did.
Aspatia.   And talkt of teares and sorrow unto her?
Amintor.   Tis true, and till these happie signes in thee
Staid my course, it was thither I was going.
Aspatia.   Thou art there already, and these wounds are hers:
Those threats I brought with me, sought not revenge,
But came to fetch this blessing from thy hand.
I am *Aspatia* yet.
Amintor.   Dare my soule ever looke abroad agen?   210
Aspatia.   I shall sure live *Amintor*, I am well,
A kinde of healthfull joy wanders within me.
Amintor.   The world wants lives to excuse thy losse,
Come let me beare thee to some place of helpe.
Aspatia.   *Amintor* thou must stay, I must rest here,

---

182 flesh] Q2; selfe Q1   182 unto] Q1; into Q2
213 lives] Theobald; lines Q1–8, F2

My strength begins to disobey my will.
How dost thou my best soule? I would faine live
Now if I could, wouldst thou have loved me then?
Amintor.   Alas,
All that I ams not worth a haire from thee.   220
Aspatia.   Give me thine hand, mine hands grope up and downe,
And cannot finde thee, I am wondrous sicke.
Have I thy hand, *Amintor?*
Amintor.   Thou greatest blessing of the world, thou hast.
Aspatia.   I doe beleeve thee better then my sense,
Oh I must goe, farewell.   [*Dies.*]
Amintor.   She sounds:——*Aspatia.*——Helpe, for Gods sake:
    water,
Such as may chaine life ever to this frame.——
Aspatia, speake:——what no helpe? yet I foole,
Ile chafe her temples, yet there nothing stirs.   230
Some hidden power tell her *Amintor* cals,
And let her answer me:——*Aspatia* speake.——
I have heard, if there be any life, but bow
The body thus, and it will shew it selfe.
Oh she is gone, I will not leave her yet.
Since out of justice we must challenge nothing,
Ile call it mercy if youle pittie me,
You heavenly powers, and lend forth some few yeeres
The blessed soule to this faire seat againe.
No comfort comes, the gods denie me too.   240
Ile bow the body once againe:——*Aspatia.*——
The soule is fled for ever, and I wrong
My selfe, so long to loose her companie.
Must I talke now? Heres to be with thee love.   *Kils himselfe.*

Enter Servant.

Servant.   This is a great grace to my Lord to have the new King
come to him, I must tell him he is entring. Oh God, helpe, helpe.

229 hands grope] Q2; eyes grow Q1

Enter Lysippus, Melantius, Calianax, Cleon, Diphilus, Strato.

Lysippus.   Wheres *Amintor?*
Strato.   O there, there.
Lysippus.   How strange is this?
Calianax.   What should we doe here?   250
Melantius.   These deaths are such acquainted things with me,
  That yet my heart dissolves not. May I stand
  Stiffe here for ever: eyes call up your teares,
  This is *Amintor*: heart, he was my friend,
  Melt, now it flowes. *Amintor* give a word
  To call me to thee.
Amintor.   Oh.
Melantius.   *Melantius* cals his friend *Amintor*, oh
  Thy armes are kinder to me then thy tongue,
  Speake, speake.   260
Amintor.   What?
Melantius.   That little word was worth all the sounds
  That ever I shall heare againe.
Diphilus.   Oh brother
  Here lies your sister slaine, you loose your selfe
  In sorrow there.
Melantius.   Why *Diphilus* it is
  A thing to laugh at in respect of this,
  Here was my Sister, Father, Brother, Sonne,
  All that I had,——speake once againe, what youth
  Lies slaine there by thee?
Amintor.   Tis *Aspatia*,
  My last is said, let me give up my soule
  Into thy bosome.   [*Dies.*] 270
Calianax.   Whats that, whats that? *Aspatia?*
Melantius.   I never did repent the greatnesse of
  My heart till now, it will not burst at need.
Calianax.   My daughter, dead here too, and you have all fine new
  trickes to greive, but I nere knew any but direct crying.
Melantius.   I am a Pratler, but no more. [*Offers to kill him selfe.*]

246.1 Cleon] Q2; *om.* Q1   273 My] Q2; *om.* Q1

Diphilus.   Hold Brother.
Lysippus.   Stop him.
Diphilus.   Fie how unmanly was this offer in you,
Does this become our straine?
Calianax.   I know not what the matter is, but I am growne very 280
kinde, and am friends with you all now. You have given me that
among you will kill me quickly, but Ile go home and live as long
as I can.   *Exit.*
Melantius.   His spirit is but poore, that can be kept
From death for want of weapons,
Is not my hands a weapon sharpe enough
To stop my breath? or if you tie downe those,
I vow *Amintor* I will never eate
Or drinke, or sleepe, or have to doe with that
That may preserve life, this I sweare to keepe.   290
Lysippus.   Looke to him tho, and beare those bodies in.
May this a faire example be to me,
To rule with temper, for on lustfull Kings
Unlookt for suddaine deaths from God are sent,
But curst is he that is their instrument.
                                                [Exeunt.]

FINIS.

*281 all now] Q1; *om.* Q2   283 *Exit.*] Q1; *om.* Q2

124

TEXTUAL NOTES

Speakers

8 CALIANAX] The name appears as 'Calianax' throughout Okes's part of
Q1 and occasionally in the second part. In the latter, however, the spelling
'Callianax' predominates, possibly because the compositor often substi-
tuted an *ll* ligature for *l* since many *l*'s were needed for the speech-prefix
Mel.

I.i

2 *Strato*.] Modern editors follow Q1 in giving this speech to *Lysippus*,
whom Cleon is addressing; but it is perfectly characteristic of Strato to
break in, and the tone is distinctly his.

73 about] Q3, followed by subsequent early editions, returned to Q1's
'above', a reading that has attracted most modern editors. Dyce argued
that the 'her' refers to Aspatia and supported 'above' by claiming an
analogy with I.i.137, which in Q3+ reads 'graces above her'. In I.i.137,
however, 'above' is clearly without authority; hence the argument must
run the other way and 'about' in I.i.137 must sanction 'about' in this line
as well. Mason's suggestion (*Comments*, pp. 1–2) that 'the light about her'
be altered to 'the lightning's power' has gained no support.

I.ii

8 may...out] The Q1 version appears to confound a revision with fragments of a rejected, but imperfectly cancelled, manuscript reading. 'Sweat'
may be merely a misreading of 'swear' or a remnant of the idea subsequently developed in ll. 16–18; 'with swearing' looks like part of an
abandoned first thought. Q2 nearly set the matter right, but incorrectly
carried over 'with swearing' from Q1, perhaps because the annotator did
did not delete it.

21 there, there,...codes] Q1 prints the passage from l. 20 through l. 24 as
follows:

> DIAG. Hee's so humerous since his daughter was forsa-
> ken? hark, hark, whose there, codes, codes,
> What now?   *within*   *Knock within*
> MEL. Open the dore.
> DIAG. Who i'st.

125

Q2's version is

> *Diag.* Hee's so humorous since his daughter was forsa-
> ken: harke, harke,   there, there,   so, so, codes, codes.
> What now?   *within*   *Knocke within.*
> *Mel.* Open the doore.
> *Diag.* Who's there?

Several matters are involved here. First, the *within* in the midst of l. 22, which describes Melantius' speech, was misplaced by Q1, and the error remained uncorrected in Q2. Secondly, the two texts offer different interpretations of when the *Knock within* is heard. In Q1 it is evidently understood to follow 'forsaken', and Diagoras' 'hark, hark' must be taken to mean 'Listen!' or something similar. The words 'whose there' naturally follow. In Q2, however, *Knock within* must precede 'what now?', and Diagoras' 'hark, hark' refers to the commotion outside the door as Melantius and his lady make their way through the crowd. The question of which version is right leads to another point, the meaning of 'codes' and the significance of the space in Q1 between 'there' and 'codes'. Although some modern editors have read 'codes' as a vulgar exclamation related to 'cod', scrotum, Mason (*Comments*, p. 2) was doubtless right in supposing 'it to be used instead of Gods, Gods! to avoid impiety', like 'cocks', 'cuds', and so on (*cf. OED*, 'God', 13 and 14, where 'Cods' is given as a form of the possessive). But whether or not he understood these words, the Q1 compositor evidently was at a loss regarding the words just before, either because he could not read them or, if he could make them out, because they did not seem to follow 'whose there'. There is no reason to suspect the 'so, so' provided by Q2 to fill the blank left by Q1 or to suspect Q2's correction of 'whose' to 'there', which accords with the other doublets in the line. Q1's 'Who i'st' (l. 24) may be correct, since Diagoras later responds so to a second and a third knock (ll. 37, 45), but the acceptance of Q2's other changes predisposes one to follow Q2 here as well. Thus it would appear that Diagoras, musing over Calianax's eccentric behaviour, is recalled to his door-keeping as he says 'hark, hark', either tries to calm the crowd with 'there, there' and 'so, so' or, if the door has been forced, shoves it to with these words, and then, with rising exasperation or resignation, exclaims 'codes, codes'. He then hears the knock and rather despairingly asks, 'What now?'.

112 quenching]   In comparison with Q1's 'quenching', which more nearly fits the sense of 'the Sun is drownd' (l. 113), Q2's 'raging' seems facile, perhaps a memorial error of the Q2 compositor. Boreas has not yet broken his chain, and it is he who makes the sea to rage.

135 hold]   Q2's 'keepe' seems to be a mistaken repetition of the same word in l. 133, probably a memorial error of the Q2 compositor.

157 his]   See the Textual Introduction, p. 21. The Q2 changes in Night's
speech all seem to be acceptable but this one, Q2's 'this' having been set
for 'his' through confusion arising from the correct change of 'thy' to
'this' later in the line. 'Thy pale beames drawne away' (l. 156) probably
signifies that Endimion is sleeping in darkness, as Cynthia's beams are now
shining here rather than there. His eternal slumber, of course, makes a
'long night'.

163 nobler]   Cf. 'greater', l. 162.

185 Winde!]   Theobald introduced a hyphen after 'Winde', an attractive
emendation in view of the lack of punctuation in both Q1 and Q2, but to
adopt his reading is to force the supposition that the stage-direction is
misplaced, which is unnecessary if Langbaine's stop is accepted. Q2 sometimes follows Q1's occasional omission of punctuation, and Dyce notes
that Eolus is referred to as 'the Winde' at l. 173.

190–192 Neptune. Doe....Maine,]   Q2 follows Q1 in omitting Eolus' exit
(l. 190) and his re-entry (l. 193), and in printing 'great maister...taken' as
a continuation of Neptune's 'Doe' (l. 190). Because Neptune would not
address another character with an epithet proper only to himself to report
the execution of his own order, it is clear that the early editions misassign
these words. Theobald's arrangement has been generally accepted, although
Dyce reports that Heath's ms. notes give the speech to Cinthia, ' "she
perceiving the approach of the milder winds set at liberty by Æolus" '.
Perhaps after 'taken' (i.e. 'been effected'), we are to imagine a pause during
which sounds of the struggle between Boreas and the other winds are heard,
but Q1's omission of punctuation after the word may indicate that Eolus'
'O! the Maine' is an interruption, 'The...taken' being left incomplete.

234.1 Another Measure.]   Q1 follows the Second Song with the direction
'Maskers daunce, Neptune leads it', omitting ll. 234.1–248. Q2 supplies
these lines but with several corruptions. Its version of them begins:

> Nep. Great Queene of us and heaven,
> Heare what I bring to make this houre a full one,
> If not her measure.
> Cinth. Speake Seas King.

In spite of its disturbance of the couplet ('bring'-'King') 'If not her
measure' has been retained as a part of Neptune's speech by several editors.
Seward, followed by the editors of 1778 and Weber, suggested 'If not
o'er-measure', justifying the intercalation by analogy with these lines from
The Faithful Shepherdess:

> ...we have perform'd a work
> Worthy the gods themselves.
> Sat. Come forward, maiden; do not lurk...   (V.v)

Dyce retained the Q2 reading, explaining, 'The meaning of Neptune's speech is clearly this:—Great queen of us and heaven, hear what I bring, endeavoring to make this hour a full one, though perhaps what I bring may not completely fill up her measure. The pronoun *her* is frequently applied to *hour* by our early writers.' Another approach was indicated by Theobald, who rejected the line on the grounds that it was a marginal query in the ms.—'Is this measure [which he took to mean 'song'] Cynthia's?'. Dyce, who also considered this solution ('...If we suppose that the words in question are not a portion of the text, the probability would be that they are a corruption of "If not here, measure," i.e. If the present speech and the next two speeches...be omitted by the actors, let the measure be danced here'), decided against it. F. G. Fleay (*Chronicles of the English Drama* [1891], I, 193) followed this line of argument, but held, more simply, that the line was an error for the direction *Another measure*, misplaced by two lines.

237–239 The...she...she] Seward's change of 'they...the' to 'she... she' is undoubtedly right, the readings of the early editions being consequent upon Q2's taking *Amphitrite* to be plural (in spite of the singular 'joyes'). The emendation of Q2's 'Thy' to 'The' depends on the assumption that the first part of Neptune's speech is addressed to Cinthia rather than to the tritons.

254 A...one] Q1 here reads 'We thanke you for this houre, | My favor to you all to gratulate...'. Because of Q2's defective metre, many editions follow Q1, yet it seems most unlikely that the Q2 reading could have come into being except in response to an annotation. 'My favor to you all' was probably meant to stand, but was omitted by the Q2 compositor, who may have inserted Q2's 'and' because he did not grasp the syntax.

267 kingdome] There is nothing in the text to show whether Night rules a kingdom or, as in Q2, 'Kingdomes'. She could well be thought of as dominating, at one time or another, all the kingdoms of the earth, but the 's' may have been incorrectly added in Q2 by attraction from the nearby 'flings' and 'contems'.

274 sect] Most editors have adopted Seward's (Theobald's) emendation 'set'. The idea is not very appropriate to Night; moreover, the king's luminous majesty is in the South (l. 276) rather than the West, where it should be if it were interposed between Cynthia and her setting, although the rays which emanate from it are 'shot', perhaps across Cynthia's path. 'Sect', however, probably means the courtly audience, servants of Night and Cynthia (l. 141), before whom the king is placed. Norland returned to 'sect', glossing it 'gods and goddesses', but Night and Cynthia are not accompanied.

283 Kingdomes] Because Melantius' conquests have been so extensive (IV.ii.168–9), the King probably holds sway over more than one kingdom. Q3 and most later editions make the word singular.

II.i

14 *1. Lady*.] Because she is elsewhere addressed by name or as 'wench', 'You prick me Lady' cannot be intended for Dula. Q2 may have assigned this short speech to her because of an eyeskip error on the part of the compositor.

45 right] The imagery of Aspatia's speech indicates that she is thinking of the bedding of the bride as a religious ceremony, Hymen's rites (*cf.* II.i. 143–4). Q2's 'night' is probably a compositor's error.

142 shall] Q2's 'will' seems to be a memorial error caused by 'will' in l. 143.

II.ii

66 Sea-beach] The reading of the early editions seems impossible. A 'breach' may be 'the breaking of waves on a coast' (*OED*); the 'breach of the sea' to which Sebastian refers (*Twelfth Night*, I.i.23) is clearly the surf, not the strand. 'Beach', which may have meant 'shingle' rather than 'shore', was in common use in the early 17th century. The Q1 compositor may have set the comma for a hyphen.

97 whelps, and] Disruption of the metre suggests that Q2's 'I will' after 'whelps' is an error, probably brought about by some confusion with the change of Q1's 'I must' to 'I will' in l. 96.

III.i

35 does hee] The Q2 reading is possible if the gentlemen have been mocking Amintor in the less serious sense of that word. If so, Amintor is saying, 'He is not trifling with me as I had thought; he knows about Evadne's depravity'. But since he replies to Diphilus in much the same tone as before, Amintor is probably in doubt about the matter, and the question seems more appropriate.

92 *Diphilus*. Lets...spoild] Colman remarked of the reading of the early editions, '...It is impossible the words thus given to Evadne should be spoken by her...' and rendered the line as 'Lets...walk, Evadne. By... spoil'd'. Dyce, however, apparently taking 'spoild' as 'injured in character by excessive indulgence, lenience, or deference' (*OED*), restored 'By... spoil'd' to Evadne. Spencer followed Dyce in giving the words to Evadne,

but printed ll. 92–3 as one verse line, commenting that such an arrangement 'confirms the reading of the old texts'. Diphilus, however, is speaking as though he were examining a mare whose gait has been ruined by too
hard riding, and 'spoild' is no doubt also intended to mean 'ravished' or
'violated' (*OED*, *v.*¹ 11 c), returning us to something like Colman's interpretation. But there is no need to incorporate 'Evadne' into the speech as
Colman did, since the prefix in Q 1 is an error.

200 ever?...thee₍ₐ₎] Brereton notes, 'The meaning of the latter sentence
["if...thus"] is obviously: He could not shew such cheerful equanimity
if he had not taken vengeance for such an injury'.

245 waking] All editors have adopted the reading of Q 1 and Q 3, though
none has glossed 'walking'. Presumably the word may serve to add the
force of personification to Amintor's griefs or to make them a ghostly
company into which his own identity is fading. 'Waking', however, seems
equally or more suitable, for Amintor sees himself as awakening to new
griefs, some of which had kept him awake while Evadne slept.

III.ii

55 charge] Although usually emended to 'change' (*i.e.* 'exchange') on
analogy with such usages as 'to interchange my bosom' (*A King and
No King*, I.i.369), the quarto reading means 'load' or 'fill' (*OED*). *Cf.*
'The meanest subject | Can find a freedom to discharge his soul...' (*A
King and No King*, I.i.255).

77 Inevitable] Q 2's 'immutable' yields good sense, but Q 2's change is
difficult to explain unless it was introduced from the Q 2 ms. 'Inevitable'
seems to glance at the root *vitare*, to shun, and to mean 'irresistible'. Colman noted an analogue found by Mason (*Comments*, p. 14) in Dryden's
Palamon and Arcite:

> But ev'n that glimmering serv'd him to descry
> Th'inevitable charms of Emily. (ll. 231–2)

214 it from] Q 2's 'backe', which makes the line hypermetrical, was probably
introduced as a result of recollection of the same word in l. 212.

301 idle] Neither Q 1 nor Q 2 seems to render Melantius' speech correctly,
Q 2 being defective perhaps because the compositor failed to understand
the annotator's markings. Q 1 prints 'See...hatred, | I am come...sute',
omitting 'to my love and freedome to you'. Q 2 adds this phrase, but omits
'idle' and 'am' (l. 302), lining 'See...freedome to you' as prose and then
'I come...sute | Of you'.

IV.i

2 *Evadne*——] Dyce here restored the period of the old editions, so that the sense becomes 'you seem to be Evadne'. Evadne's 'Come', however, indicates that she interrupts, thinking that Melantius is going to tease her as Diphilus had done in III.i.

5 commend] 'Command' is an archaic form of 'commend' (*OED*, IV.17, where the last citation is *c.* 1500), but the spelling of 'commendation' in ll. 8 and 16 indicates that here the 'a' is simply an error.

8 Into a commendation] Q1's 'a commendations' may possibly be acceptable, particularly if Melantius is alluding ironically to The Commendations, a liturgical office; but in view of the many terminal misreadings in Q1 there is little point in straining to retain it. Q2 had the choice of 'a commendation' or 'commendations', and, as shown by the survival in Q2 of 'a sad commendations' (l. 16), probably chose the latter alternative incorrectly.

74 food] Dyce returned to the Q1 reading, indicating that 'food' makes no sense. The 'his', however, refers to the angry North, who hurls his billows toward the sky as if to make them swallow the lightning.

199 that_A_] All modern editions follow Q5's 'thats_A_', although Daniel suggests '*That*'s slight contrition, *that*;'. The idea that the second 'that' is a repetition for emphasis (presumably uttered with contempt) is equally applicable to the Q1–Q2 reading; but Brereton's emendation, which makes the two 'that' clauses parallel, seems less awkward and requires the least change in the copy-text.

240 eies] Weber reasonably suggested the emendation 'ages', which makes better metre and which might be defended on palaeographical grounds had Q1 only printed 'eyes'.

IV.ii

52 *Amintor.*] Theobald followed Q1 in giving this speech to Melantius, noting 'The King address'd himself to *Melantius*; and what Impertinence it is in *Amintor* to take his Friend's Answer out of his Mouth?'. All modern editors but Spencer have agreed. It does not seem very likely, however, that the Q2 change could have occurred as the result of an error, whereas in Q1 the prefix *Mel.* could easily have been caught from the *Melantius* of l. 51. Moreover, Amintor, not Melantius, 'should be...the merriest here'.

124 Eaters] Q1's 'Facers', braggarts, is consistent with the context, though it duplicates the meaning of 'talkers', in which Q1 and Q2 concur. It

could be a misreading of 'Eaters', particularly as Q1 also mistook 'worth' for 'world' later in the line. For 'eaters' in the sense of idle servants or hangers-on, see *Epicoene*, III.v.34.

V.iii

47 I] The 'would he could not' of the early editions has provoked many explanations, perhaps the most satisfactory being Spencer's, that the antecedent of 'he' is 'that did it' in the same line. Yet this seems so strained that emendation is preferable, particularly as 'I' and 'he' may resemble one another in the secretary hand.

281 all now] Q2 follows Q1 in lining Calianax's entire speech as verse, although the metre in all lines but the first ('I...am') is defective. Q2's omission of 'all now', if not merely an eyeskip error, may have been an attempt on the part of the annotator or compositor to regularize the line.

PRESS-VARIANTS IN Q1 (1619)

[Copies collated (all that are extant): Bodl (Bodleian Library Mal. 233[1]), Dyce (Victoria and Albert Museum), CSmH (Henry E. Huntington Library), DFo (Folger Shakespeare Library), MB (Boston Public Library), and MH (Harvard University Library).]

SHEET A (*inner forme*)

Sig. A2.
  Variant imprints (*no positive indication as to order*):
    Printed for *Francis Conſtable* and are to be ſold | at the white Lyon ouer againſt the great North | doore of *Pauls Church*. 1619. Bodl, DFo, Dyce, MB

    Printed for *Richard Higgenbotham* and | are to beſold at the Angell in PAVLS | Church-yard. 1619. CSmH, MH

SHEET B (*outer forme*)

Uncorrected: CSmH
1st stage corrected: Bodl

Sig. B2ᵛ.
  I.i.88 earth,]   ear_∧

2nd stage corrected: DFo

Sig. B3.
  I.i.131 wedding]   weding
      141 *Strato*]   Steat

3rd stage corrected: Dyce, MB, MH

Sig. B4ᵛ.
  I.ii.68–9 all, ...liue_∧]   ∼_∧ ···∼,
      94 comming in]   come in

SHEET C (*outer forme*)

Corrected: Bodl, CSmH, Dyce, MB, MH
Uncorrected: DFo

Sig. C1.
  I.ii.128 alone]   a lone

Sig. C2ᵛ.
  I.ii.201 ſolemne] ſo lemne
     202 Darke night‸] Darke night,
    222.2 Second] ſecond
     231 *teares*] *teaɹes*
Sig. C3.
  running-title The] *T he*
  I.ii.261 aboue] aboae
     267 contemnes] contems
Sig. C4ᵛ.
  II.i.95 teach you] teachyou

SHEET E (*outer forme*)

    Corrected: DFo, MB, MH
    Uncorrected: Bodl, Dyce, CSmH

Sig. E1.
  II.ii.13 Nor I] Nere I

SHEET L (*inner forme*)

    Corrected: Bodl, Dyce, DFo, MB, MH
    Uncorrected: CSmH

Sig. L1ᵛ.
  V.iii.115 lookes] bookes
Sig. L2.
  V.iii.139 a way] away

[DFo *shows* Thihe *for the correct L2 catchword* Thine. *Since this variant does not accord with any rational scheme of press correction, it would seem to have arisen from the mistaken replacement of a pulled type.*]

PRESS-VARIANTS IN Q2 (1622)

[Copies collated (all that are extant): BM (British Museum 644.d.6), Bodl (Bodleian Library Mal. 242[3]), Dyce (Victoria and Albert Museum), Worc (Worcester College, Oxford [wants A1]), CtY (Yale University [a made-up copy consisting of sheets A and L of Q2 and B through K of Q3]), DFo (Folger Shakespeare Library), DLC (Library of Congress), ICN (Newberry Library), MB (Boston Public Library), and MH (Harvard University Library).]

SHEET A (*inner forme*)

Corrected: Bodl, Dyce, Worc, DFo, DLC, ICN, MB, MH
Uncorrected: BM, CtY

Sig. A3^v.
   I.i.85–86 ſtill his greatnesse$_\wedge$] ſtil his greatnes?

Sig. A4.
   I.i.140 you.] ~ $_\wedge$
      142 you$_\wedge$] ~.

SHEET B (*outer forme*)

Corrected: BM, Bodl, DFo, DLC, Dyce, MH
Uncorrected: MB, ICN, Worc

Sig. B1.
   I.ii.39 amongſt$_\wedge$ them,] ~ , ~ $_\wedge$
      49 you:] ~ ,

EMENDATIONS OF ACCIDENTALS

I.i

3–4 You...word.] *prose in* Q 1–8,
F 2
7 be?] Q 2; ~ . Q 1
8–11 Yes...flatterie.] *prose in*
Q 1–8, F 2
12–19 Noble...worlds.] Q 1–8, F 2
line Noble *Melantius,* | *and the*
rest as prose.
16–17 here;...kinde,] Q 2 (here:);
~ ,...~ ; Q 1
20–23 My...e[ver]] *prose in* Q 1–8,
F 2
35 it?] Q 2; ~ . Q 1
39–40 We...measure.] Q 1–8, F 2
line We...night, | And...
measure.
49 it:] Q 2; ~ , Q 1
50–51 boast,...conquest)] ~)...
~ , Q 1–8, F 2
53 heard:] Q 4; ~ , Q 1–3
65 this?] Q 2; ~ . Q 1
65–66 You...married.] *one line in*
Q 1–8, F 2

67 but——] Q 8; ~ ‸ Q 1–7, F 2
81 breast,] Q 2; ~ ‸ Q 1
85 daughter:] Q 2; ~ . Q 1
85–86 holds...King?] *one line in*
Q 2–8, F 2; *om.* Q 1
86–90 Yes...tell] Q 3; Q 2 *lines*
Yes...walkes | Discontented
...earth: | The...delight, |
And...flowers, | She...tell;
Q 1 *lines* O...Lady sir, | Sits
...earth, | *etc.*
88 earth:] Q 2; ~ , Q 1
93 corse.] Q 2; ~ , Q 1
110 foe:] Q 2; ~ , Q 1
113 friend,——] ~ , ‸ Q 1–8, F 2
120 innocence.] Q 2; ~ , Q 1
122–124 I...thee] Q 1–8, F 2 *line* I
...man | Thy...thee
135 forbad] Q 2 (forbade); fotbad
Q 1
136 sister,] Q 2; ~ ‸ Q 1
140 gone,——] ~ , ‸ Q 1–8, F 2±
142 you,——] ~ , ‸ Q 1–8, F 2

I.ii

2 me:] Q 2; ~ , Q 1
4–5 Why...here] Q 1–8, F 2 *line*
Why...Lord? | You...here
4 Lord?] Q 2; ~ , Q 1
8–9 One...will] Q 2; Q 1 *lines*
One...get | Thankes...will
10–11 My...them] Q 2–8, F 2 *line*
My...out. | Pray...them (Q 1
om. Pray stay,)
10 out.] Q 2; ~ , Q 1
12 them?] ~ , Q 1–8, F 2
21 codes,——]~ , ‸ Q 1–8, F 2±

21–22 codes,——what] Q 1–8, F 2
line codes, | What
23 *within.*] *following* now?, l. 22
Q 1–8, F 2
31 sir,——] ~ , ‸ Q 1–8, F 2±
33 *Exeunt*] *Exit* Q 1; *om.* Q 2–8, F 2
35 this] Q 2; rhis Q 1
36 itch?] Q 2; ~ , Q 1
37 hang:] Q 2; ~ , Q 1
37 againe,——] ~ , ‸ Q 1–8, F 2
37 now?] Q 6; ~ , Q 1–5
40 eye:] Q 2; ~ , Q 1

42 *Within*] *following l.* 41 *as stage-
direction* Q1–8, F2
48–49 O...plast] *prose in* Q1–8,
F2
48 must,——] ~ , ∧ Q1–8, F2±
49 plast?] Q2; ~ . Q1
49–50 Yes...met] *one line in* Q1–
8, F2
49 you:——] ~ , ∧ Q1–8, F2±
54–55 She...you] Q1–5, F2 *line*
She...hearted | Lord as you;
prose in Q6–8
58 so,——] ~ , ∧ Q1–8, F2±
62 she?] F2; ~ , Q1–7
67–69 I...thee] *prose in* Q1–8, F2
68–69 all ∧...live,] Q1(u); ~ , ...
~ ∧ Q1(c)
73 Lord——] ~ . Q1–5; ~ ! Q6–
8, F2
75 honor;] Q6; ~, Q1–5
76 souldiers,...peace∧] Q2; ~ ∧
...~ , Q1
79 'em:] F2; ~ , Q1–7
87 hande?] Q2; ~ , Q1
98.1 King,] Q2; ~ ∧ Q1
101 in,——] ~ , ∧ Q1–8, F2±
103 too't,] Q2; ~ ∧ Q1
105 home,——] ~ , ∧ Q1–8, F2±
113 day:] Q2; ~ , Q1
114 *Night*] F2; night Q1–7
115 light.] ~ , Q1–5; ~ ; Q6–8,
F2
122 I?] Q2; ~ , Q1
125 breaks;] Q6; ~ , Q1–5
128 alone] Q1(c); a lone Q1(u)
155 upon∧] ~ , Q1–8, F2
156 top,] Q3; ~ ∧ Q1–2
164 are,——] ~ , ∧ Q1–8, F2±
170 yet?] Q2; ~ . Q1
173 Winde] Q8; winde Q1–7, F2
177 vernall] Q2; veranll Q1
182 night,] Q3; ~ ∧ Q1–2
182 things∧] Q2; ~ , Q1

187 will?] Q2; ~ . Q1
191 floud] Q2; flould Q1
195 alone,] Q4; ~ ∧ Q1–3
200 done∧] Q2; ~ , Q1
202 *Night*] night Q1–8, F2
203 Strike] Q2; Srike Q1
209–210 *company,*...*day∧*] Q2; ~
∧...~ , Q1
219 *measures,*] ~ ∧ Q1–8, F2
223 Night] Q8; *night* Q1–7, F2
229 Night] Q8; *night* Q1–7, F2
229 *cover∧*] Q2; ~ . Q1
232 denials,] Q2; ~ ∧ Q1
235–236 Great...one] Q2–8, F2
line Great...heaven, | Heare
...one; *om.* Q1
238 daunce] dance Q2–8, F2; *om.*
Q1
239 sayles;] ~ , Q2–8, F2; *om.* Q1
240 Musique] Musick(e) Q2–8, F2;
om. Q1
240 ile] Ile Q2–8, F2±; *om.* Q1
251 prophesie,...day∧] Q2; ~ ∧
... ~ , Q1
253 gods ∧...powre,] ~ , ... ~ ∧
Q1–8, F2
255 all;] ~ ∧ Q1; *reading differs* Q2–
8, F2
263 *Night*] Q8; night Q1–7, F2
263 day?] Q2; ~ , Q1
264 lighten,] Q2; ~ ∧ Q1
267 contems] Q1(u); contemnes
Q1(c)
267 *Night*] Q3; night Q1–2
270 forget,——] ~ , ∧ Q1–8, F2
273 light,] Q2; ~ ∧ Q1
273 Majestie,] Q3; ~ ∧ Q1–2
274 teame,] ~ ∧ Q1–3
276 south:] ~ , Q1–5; ~ ; Q6–8,
F2
276 goe?] Q2; ~ . Q1
278 bed,——] ~ , ∧ Q1–8, F2
281 slow:] Q2; ~ ∧ Q1

II.i

1 fight?] Q2; ~ , Q1
3–4 I...me] *one line in* Q1–5;
  prose in Q6–8, F2
5–6 That...doe] *one line in* Q1;
  om. Q2–8, F2
7 wench?] Q2; ~ . Q1
7 helpe?] Q2; ~ . Q1
10 *Dula?*] Q2; ~ . Q1
22 where?] Q2; ~ , Q1
26 night?] Q2; ~ . Q1
26–27 Ile...know] *one line in* Q1–
  8, F2
27 doe?] Q2; ~ . Q1
30 a side] Q2; aside Q1
33 couldst] Q2; coulst Q1
38 Countrey,...too₄] Q4; ~ ₄
  ...~ , Q1–3
44 now;] ~ , Q1–8, F2
48 you:] Q2; ~ ₄ Q1
50 so;] ~ , Q1–8, F2
53 frame;] F2; ~ , Q1–7
62–63 Thats...not] Q1–5 *line*
  Thats...thing | but...not;
  lined as prose in Q6–8, F2
67–68 *Lay...Yew*] *one line in* Q2–
  8, F2; *om.* Q1
68 *Yew*——] ~ . Q2–8, F2; *om.*
  Q1
72–79 *Lay...earth*] Q2–8, F2 *line*
  Lay...Yew, | Maidens...true, |
  My...birth, | Upon...earth;
  om. Q1
80–82 Fie...*Dula*] *prose in* Q2–8,
  F2; *om.* Q1
96 waking:] ~ , Q1–5; ~ ; Q6–8,
  F2
98 I.——] ~ , ₄ Q1–5; ~ . ₄ Q6–
  8, F2
116 denied.] Q2; ~ , Q1
118–119 earth,...pittie;] ~ ;...
  ~ , Q1; ~ ;...~ : Q2–8, F2±
125 goe?] Q2; ~ . Q1

129 time.] Q2; ~ , Q1
132 thus?] Q2; ~ ; Q1
133 bed:] Q2; ~ , Q1
134 conscience] Q2; conscienee Q1
134 conscience,...sencible,] ~ ,...
  ~ ₄ Q1; ~ (...~) Q2–8, F2
136 me:] Q2; ~ , Q1
137 so?] Q2; ~ , Q1
145 me?...No.] Q2; ~....~ ? Q1
147 long?] Q2; ~ . Q1
149–151 Good...sleeping] Q1–8,
  F2 *line* Good...sleepe. | *Evadne*
  ...sleeping
153 love?] Q2; ~ . Q1
154 How? sworne *Evadne?*] Q3;
  ~ ? ~ ~ . Q1; ~ ₄ ~ ~ ? Q2
155 againe₄] Q2; ~ . Q1
156 this?] Q2; ~ . Q1
159 bride?] Q2; ~ . Q1
159–160 How...thee] *one line in*
  Q1–8, F2
160 so?] Q2; ~ . Q1
162 best?] Q2; ~ . Q1
163 aske?] Q2; ~ . Q1
165 that?] Q2; ~ . Q1
168–169 So...indeede] *one line in*
  Q1–8, F2
169 wrong?] Q2; ~ , Q1
172 truth. If...me,] ~ , if...~ .
  Q1, 5; ~ , if...~ , Q2–4, 8;
  ~ ; if...~ , Q6–7, F2
178 this:] Q2; ~ , Q1
178 man?] Q2; ~ , Q1
180–181 I...cause] Q2; *one line in*
  Q1
189 abide:...bed;] Q6; ~ ,...~ ,
  Q1–5
193–194 A...yeares] *one line in*
  Q1–8, F2
194 yeares?] Q2; ~ . Q1
194 raves,——] ~ , ₄ Q1 (*possibly*
  ~ . ₄); ~ , ₄ Q2–8, F2

194 be₍ₐ₎] Q2; ~ , Q1
195 maides?] Q2; ~, Q1
198 *Amintor*,] Q3; ~ ₍ₐ₎ Q2; *reading differs* Q1
199 truth?] Q4; ~ . Q1–3
199–200 Wil...night] *one line in* Q1–8, F2
200 to night?] Q2; ~ . Q1
200–201 To...hereafter] *one line in* Q1–8, F2
202–203 You...mark] *one line in* Q1–8, F2
203 mark₍ₐ₎] Q2; ~ , Q1
213 this?] Q2; ~ , Q1
214 mariage?] Q2; ~ , Q1
219 them;] Q6; ~ , Q1–5
221 know:] ~ ₍ₐ₎ Q2–8, F2; *reading differs* Q1
222 thee;] Q6; ~ , Q1–5
223–224 blood;...meet,] Q2 (~ : ...~ ,); ~ ,...~ ; Q1
228 jest;——] ~ ; ₍ₐ₎ Q1–8, F2
236 it;] Q4; ~ , Q1–3
238 bed.] Q2; ~ , Q1
239 now?] Q2; ~ . Q1
241 this?] Q2; ~ : Q1
248 third?] Q2; ~ , Q1
248 calme?] Q2; ~ , Q1
249 thunder] Q2; thundet Q1
250 voyce?] Q2; ~ . Q1
255 away:] Q2; ~ , Q1
258 me:] Q2; ~ , Q1
259 cald] Q2; eald Q1
260 love?] Q2; ~ , Q1
264 woman,——] ~ , ₍ₐ₎ Q1–8, F2
266 hard.] Q4; ~ , Q1–3

270–271 When...me] *lined as prose* Q1–8, F2
272–275 I...armes] Q1–4 *line* I... bed, | Or...locks, | Were... weare | About...armes; Q5 *lines* I...by | Those...locks, | *etc.*; Q6–8, F2 *line* I...by | Those...locks, | Were...arms
273 haires,...soule₍ₐ₎] Q2; ~ ₍ₐ₎... ~ ; Q1
275 armes——] ~ . Q1–2, 4–5, 8, F2; ~ , Q3; ~ ; Q6–7
283 Champions?] Q2; ~ . Q1
286 strictnesse?] Q2; ~ , Q1
288 vow;] Q6; ~ , Q1–5
291–292 Was...youth] Q1–8, F2 *line* Was...showne | Both... youth
291 both.] ~ , Q1–5; ~ ; Q6–8, F2
294 second.] Q2; ~ , Q1
299 Northren] Q2; Northen Q1
305 *Amintor*?] Q2; ~ . Q1
309 it?] Q2; ~ , Q1
313 bed?] Q2; ~ , Q1
315 mee?] Q2; ~ . Q1
329 falne] Q2; falen Q1
334 more,——] ~ , ₍ₐ₎ Q1–8, F2±
337 shame ₍ₐ₎...thee,...feare₍ₐ₎] Q2; ~ ,...~ ₍ₐ₎...~, Q1
343 thee;] Q2; ~ , Q1
345 thine.] Q2; ~ ₍ₐ₎ Q1
348 thee:] ~ , Q1–5; ~ ; Q6–8, F2
349 close,] Q2; ~ ₍ₐ₎ Q1
350 wish;] Q6; ~, Q1–5
361.1 *Exeunt*] *Exit* Q1–8, F2

II.ii

1 Away,] Q2; ~ ₍ₐ₎ Q1
7–11 make...*Olimpias*] Q2–8, F2 *line* Make...lovers, | Did ...*Olimpias*, | Such...in't, |
And...miserable; Q1 *omits all but* Did...*Olimpias*
11 wenches?] Q2; ~ , Q1
11 *Olimpias*] Q2; *Olimpas* Q1

13 *Antiphila?*] Q 2; ~ . Q 1
14 women,] Q 2; ~ ∧ Q 1
14–27 Then. . .girles] Q 2–5 *line*
Then. . .wise, | *then as prose*
through man, *l.* 27, *beginning*
verse again with Come. . .girles;
Q 1 *lines* Then. . .wise, | At. . .
was, come. . .girles *omitting all*
between was, *l.* 15 *and* come, *l.* 27;
Q 6–8, F 2 *line entirely as prose*
15 be sure] Q 5; bee sure Q 2–4;
om. Q 1
29 sorrow;——] ~ ; ∧ Q 1–8, F 2±
30 *Oenones*] Q 2 (*Ænones*); *Oenes*
Q 1
31 *Hellen,*——] ~ , ∧ Q 1–8, F 2±
36 teare!——*Antiphila,*] ~ ! ∧ ~ ,
Q 1; ~ ∧ ∧ ~ : Q 2–8, F 2
37 *Aspatia?*] Q 2; ~ , Q 1
38 more∧] Q 2; ~ , Q 1
39 Marble,——] ~ , ∧ Q 1–8, F 2±
41 peece:] ~ , Q 1–5; ~ . Q 6–8,
F 2
44 enough,——] ~ , ∧ Q 1–8, F 2
45 *Theseus:*——] ~ , ∧ Q 1–5; ~ ; ∧
Q 6–8, F 2
48 vessell?] Q 2; ~ . Q 1
50 storme?] Q 6; ~ , Q 1–4; ~ .
Q 5 (*possibly* ~ ,)
51–53 But. . .sand] Q 1 *lines* But
. . .well, | Just. . .so | *Antiphila*

. . .-sand; Q 2–8, F 2 *line* But
. . .well exprest, | Just. . .*Anti-*
phila, | In. . .-sand
51 ill. This] Q 2; ~ , this Q 1
52 me,——] ~ , ∧ Q 1–8, F 2±
58 Lady?] Q 2; ~ . Q 1
59 *Antiphila*] Q 2; *Antipila* Q 1
65 Iland;] Q 6; ~ , Q 1–5
66 now,] Q 2; ~ ∧ Q 1
69 forsaken;] ~ , Q 1–8, F 2
71 *Antiphila:*] ~ , ∧ Q 1–7, F 2; ~ ,
Q 8
74 continuall] Q 2; contiunall Q 1
75 desolation,——] ~ , ∧ Q 1–8,
F 2±
80.1 Calianax] Q 2; *Calainax* Q 1
82 disgrac'd,——] ~ , ∧ Q 1–8,
F 2±
83–84 What. . .you] Q 1–8, F 2
line What. . .young | Lazie. . .
you
83 still?] Q 2; ~ , Q 1
85 Lord——] ~ . Q 1–8, F 2
87 restie?] Q 2; ~ ∧ Q 1
92 slave,——. . .in,——] ~ , ∧. . .
~ , ∧ Q 1–8, F 2±
95 way:] Q 2; ~ , Q 1
95 asse,] ~ ? Q 2–8, F 2; *om.* Q 1
96 stale?] Q 2; ~ , Q 1
100 valiant,——] ~ , ∧ Q 1–8, F 2±
101 in,——] ~ , ∧ Q 1–8, F 2

III.i

2–3 Our. . .troublesome] Q 1–8,
F 2 *line* Our. . .rest, | The. . .
troublesome
5 night?] Q 2; ~ . Q 1
12 tickling:] ~ , Q 1–5; ~ ; Q 6–8,
F 2
14 matter,] Q 2; ~ ∧ Q 1
14 them,——] ~ , ∧ Q 1–8, F 2±
15–20 Good. . .slept] Q 1 *lines* good
. . .night | will. . .againe. |

Whose. . .yet, | your. . .up. |
You. . .I | thinke. . .slept; *prose*
in Q 2–8, F 2
17 there, my brother?] Q 2; ~ ∧
~ ~ , Q 1
24 merry?] Q 2; ~ . Q 1
25 true,——] ~ , ∧ Q 1–8, F 2±
25 *aside*] *following l.* 27 Q 1; *follow-*
ing l. 25 Q 2–5; *following* sleepe,
l. 25 Q 6–8, F 2

28 sound——] ~ . Q 1–8, F 2

28–32 Your...world] *prose in* Q 1–8, F 2 (*set to short measure in* Q 1)

33–34 Then...night] *prose in* Q 1–8, F 2

35 mee?——] ~ , ∧ Q 1–5; ~ ; ∧ Q 6–8, F 2

35 indeed,] Q 2; ~ ∧ Q 1

39 Aprill,——] ~ , ∧ Q 1–8, F 2±

44 thee. Is] ~ , is Q 1–5; ~ ; is Q 6–8, F 2

44 possible?] Q 2; ~ . Q 1

45 this?] Q 2; ~ . Q 1

48 *Melantius,*] Q 2; ~ . Q 1

53 But——] ~ ∧ Q 2; *om.* Q 1

54–55 I...me] *one line in* Q 1–8, F 2

58 chang'd∧] Q 4; ~ , Q 1–3

59 windes, dissembling∧] Q 6; ~ ∧ ~ , Q 1; ~ , ~ , Q 2–5

64 him.——Oh] ~ , ∧ Oh Q 1–3; ~ . ∧ Oh Q 4–8, F 2

69–70 Beleeve...me] *one line in* Q 1–8, F 2

72 vertue?] Q 2; ~ . Q 1

73–75 Oh...sport] Q 1–8, F 2 *line as prose*

75 prittiest] Q 2 (pritiest); prtitiest Q 1

83 done?] Q 2; ~ . Q 1

88–89 If...mary] *one line in* Q 1–8, F 2

90–91 Sister...off] *one line in* Q 1–8, F 2

94 Ha?] ~ . Q 1–5; ~ ! Q 6–8, F 2

95–96 Who...catch] *prose in* Q 1, 4–8, F 2; Who...*Diphilus* | thou...catch Q 2–3

95 I?] Q 2; ~ , Q 1

96 catch?] Q 2; ~ . Q 1

100–101 I...me] *prose in* Q 1–8, F 2

100 happinesse,——] ~ , ∧ Q 1; ~ : ∧ Q 2–8, F 2

101 thou,] Q 8; ~ ∧ Q 1–7, F 2

101 love?] Q 2; ~ , Q 1

102 cannot] Q 2; connot Q 1

103 us,——] ~ , ∧ Q 1; ~ : ∧ Q 2–8, F 2

105 wonder;] Q 6; ~ , Q 1–5

106 me?] Q 2; ~ , Q 1

108–110 Well...dance] Q 1–8, F 2 *line* Well...thus, | Is...dance

109 thus?...there?] Q 2; ~ , ... ~ , Q 1

112–113 I...lesse] *one line in* Q 1–8; I...selfe; | Yet...less F 2

112 selfe,——] ~ , ∧ Q 1–8, F 2±

116 love?] Q 2; ~ ∧ Q 1

118 Lysippus.] Q 2 (*Lisip.*); *Lisip:* Q 1

118 Where?] Q 2; ~ . Q 1

119–120 all.——...thee,——] ~ . ∧ ... ~ , ∧ Q 1–8, F 2±

123 rest?] Q 2; ~ . Q 1

123–124 Indeede...little] *one line in* Q 1–8, F 2

124–125 You'le...shortly] *one line in* Q 1–8, F 2

125–126 *Amintor*...married] *one line in* Q 1–8; *Amintor*...honest | Till...Married F 2

126 honest] Q 2; honost Q 1

126 married?] Q 2; ~ . Q 1

127–128 Tell...thee] *one line in* Q 1–8, F 2

128 doe?] Q 2; ~ . Q 1

133 businesse,] Q 3; ~ ; Q 1–2

133–134 I cannot...perceive] *one line in* Q 1–8, F 2

136–137 Well...agen] Q 1–8, F 2 *line* Well...*Amintor,* | To...agen

137 agen?] Q 6; ~ . Q 1–5

138 ill?] Q 2; ~ . Q 1

147–150 I...well] Q 1 *lines* I...roome | But...may | Concerne ...well (*omitting* with you); Q 2 *lines* I...roome | *and the rest prose*; Q 3–8, F 2 *line* I...roome | But...with | You...well

147 this;——] ~ ; ∧ Q 1–8, F 2

141

151–156 A...pang] Q1 *lines* A...
doe, | For...unlawfull. | You
...*Amintor,* | And...pang
(*omitting* something...heart);
Q2–8, F2 *line* A...doe, | Some-
thing...apt | To...unlawfull
etc.

156 pang?] Q8; ~ . Q1–5; ~ !
Q6–7, F2

158 *Amintor?*] Q2; ~ . Q1

165 sir?] Q2; ~ . Q1

169–170 I...wrong] *one line in* Q1–
8, F2

178 royaltie] Q2 (royalty); rioyaltie
Q1

181–183 Why...mine] Q1–8, F2
line Why...will | More...mine

186–188 By...night] Q1–8, F2 *line*
By...and | Ile...night

187 ile] Ile Q1–8, F2

190–192 I...true] Q1–8, F2 *line* I
...blow, | Or...true

196 for?] Q2; ~ , Q1

198 knowne?] Q2; ~ , Q1

200 ever?] Q2; ~ , Q1

202 dissembling.] Q2; ~ , Q1

205 sir;——*Amintor,*——...heare
——] ~ ; ∧ ~ , ∧...~ ∧ Q2–8,
F2±; *om.* Q1

210 wife?...wife?] Q2; ~ ....~ ,
Q1

212 who?] Q2; ~ . Q1

213 me——] ~ . Q1–8, F2

215 ——Who]∧ ~ Q1–8, F2

217 me?] Q2; ~ , Q1

217–218 Did...this] Q1–8, F2 *line*
Did...hell | For this

220 me,——] ~ , ∧ Q1–8, F2±

227–228 You...due] Q1–8, F2 *line*
You...how | Men...due

230 death?] ~ , Q1–8, F2 ±

235 that?] Q2; ~ , Q1

241 passions;] Q2; ~ , Q1

244–245 Alas!...you] Q3; Q1–2
line Alas!...of | waking...you

251–252 why?——...say,——] ~
?∧...~ , ∧ Q1–8, F2±

253 wretched?] Q2; ~ , Q1

253 thousands, fooles,] ~ ∧ ~ ∧ Q2–
8, F2 (*om.* fooles, Q1)

255–256 I...me] *one line in* Q1–8, F2

259 Resolve] Q2; Resoule Q1

259 still. It] ~ , it Q1–5; ~ ; it
Q6–8, F2

261 world——] ~ . Q2–8, F2; ~ ,
Q1

262–263 But...Another] *one line in*
Q1–8, F2

263–264 No...valiant] *one line in*
Q1–8, F2

266 Gods,] ~ ∧ Q1–8, F2

267 it,——] ~ , ∧ Q1–8, F2±

278–279 You...follows] *one line in*
Q1–8, F2

281–282 I...well] *one line in* Q1–8,
F2

III.ii

2–3 O...die] *one line in* Q1–8, F2

3–4 Trust...roome] *one line in*
Q1–8, F2

4–5 Thou...slave] *one line in* Q1;
prose in Q2–8, F2

12–15 Ile...prepar'd] Q1–8, F2
line Ile...thee, | There...
sword, | And...prepar'd

15–19 Why...be] *prose in* Q1;
Q2–8, F2 *line* Why...life? |
and the rest as prose

16 life?] Q2; ~ , Q1

18 mee:] Q2; ~ , Q1

26 stroke;] Q6; ~ , Q1–5

27 me.] Q2; ~ , Q1

32 valiant:] Q2; ~ , Q1

33–34 tricke∧ | I had,] Q2; ~ , |
　　~ ~ ∧ Q1
35–39 I...mercie] Q1–3 *line* I...
　　you | *and the rest as prose*; Q4–8,
　　F2 *line entirely as prose*
40–42 I...this] *prose in* Q1–8,
　　F2
43 *Amintor*∧] Q2; ~ , Q1
48 then?] Q2; ~ , Q1
52 am:] ~ , Q1–5; ~ ; Q6–8, F2
52 it,] Q2; ~ ∧ Q1
56 *Strato*∧] Q2; ~ , Q1
58 wast?] Q2; ~ ; Q1
66 dispos'd:] Q2; ~ , Q1
71 here?] Q2; ~ , Q1
72 so?] Q2; ~ , Q1
73 Isle?] Q2; ~ , Q1
74 me:] Q2; ~ , Q1
78 vertue?] Q6; ~ , Q1–5
79 friend?] Q2; ~ : Q1
80 have?] Q2; ~ , Q1
89 idle:] ~ , Q1–5; ~ ; Q6–8, F2
92 coldly:] Q2; ~ , Q1
92 here?] Q2; ~ , Q1
93 nothing:] Q2; ~ ∧ Q1
93 heaven?] Q2 (!); ~ , Q1
94 sinnes:] ~ , Q1–5; ~ ; Q6–8,
　　F2
95 here:] ~ , Q1–5; ~ ; Q6–8, F2
96 Come,...complement?]~ ∧...
　　~ , Q1–8, F2
107–108 Doe...man] Q1–8, F2
　　line Doe...ist? | May...man
109–110 I...that] *one line in* Q1–8,
　　F2
110 that——] ~ , Q1; ~ . Q2–8,
　　F2
110 ——I]∧ ~ Q1–8, F2
123 sister——] ~ . Q1–8, F2
123–124 You'l...it] *one line in* Q1–
　　8, F2
124 ——Is]∧ ~ Q1–8, F2
134 tame?] Q2; ~ , Q1
137 unreveng'd?] Q2; ~ , Q1
140 friend;] Q2; ~ , Q1

145 waters:] Q2; ~ , Q1
154–156 Take...dead] Q1–8, F2
　　line Take...meere | Cowardise
　　...dead
157 ever:] ~ , Q1–5; ~ ; Q6–8, F2
165 it;] Q6; ~ , Q1–5
169 foole.] Q2; ~ , Q1
171 wrong,] Q2; ~ ∧ Q1
174 dishonor;] Q6; ~ , Q1–5
177 thine;] Q6; ~ , Q1–5
180 so?] Q2; ~ , Q1
187–188 so?...me,...you?] Q2;
　　~ ....~ ?...~ . Q1
188–189 Why...away] Q1–8, F2
　　line Why...house | Is...away
189 away:] ~ , Q1–5; ~ ; Q6–8,
　　F2
200 thee;] Q6; ~ , Q1–5
209 bosome:] ~ , Q1–5; ~ ; Q6–8,
　　F2
215–216 Thy...weapon] Q1 *omits*
　　And...posterity, *prints* take...
　　weapon ∧ *continuously with l.* 215;
　　Q2–5 *line as prose* (...pos-
　　terity:...); Q6–8, F2 *line* Thy
　　...me | To...Weapon
223 stir?] Q2; ~ . Q1
228 Of...quick] Q2; Q1 *lines* Of
　　...word, | Be quick
230–231 I...speedy] *one line in*
　　Q1–8, F2
232–233 sin,——...him,——] ~ ,
　　∧...~ , ∧ Q1–8, F2±
245–246 Why...save] *one line in*
　　Q1–8, F2
248 Majestie?] Q2; ~ . Q1
258–259 Thy...else] Q1 *lines* Thy
　　...I | Have...else; Q2–7, F2
　　line Thy...why | I...else; Q8
　　lines as prose
267–268 I...roome] Q1–8, F2 *line*
　　I...breake, | They...roome
269–270 They must?...beleeve] *one
　　line in* Q1–8, F2
272–273 You...it] *prose in* Q1–8, F2

274–276 That...thee] Q1 *lines* That
...hands, | And...I | Shall...
thee; Q2–8, F2 *line* That...
come | joyne...mine, | And *etc.*
274 strain:] ~ , Q1, 3–5; ~ ; Q6–
8, F2; ~ ∧ Q2
275 firmenesse] Q2; fiermenesse Q1
286 too:] ~ , Q1–5; ~ ; Q6–8, F2
287 *Diphilus,*] Q4; *Diph:* Q1–2;
Diphilus ∧ Q3
289 it:] Q2; ~ , Q1
292 which (miserie)] ~ ∧ ~ ∧ Q1–8,
F2
294 *Calianax,*——] ~ , ∧ Q1–8, F2
294 it. See] ~ , see Q1–8, F2
295 me,——] ~ , ∧ Q1–8, F2±

300 ist?] Q2; ~ . Q1
304–305 A...sir] *one line in* Q1–8,
F2
311–312 But...daughter] Q1–3 *line*
But...would | Kill...daugh-
ter; Q4–8, F2 *line as prose*
313–314 Nay...fort] Q1–8, F2 *line*
Nay...done | Without fort
315 thee?] Q2; ~ , Q1
319–324 If...thinke] Q1–8, F2 *line*
If...writ | In...the | King...
Melantius, | But...thinke
322 King:——] ~ : ∧ Q1–8, F2
329 againe:] ~ , Q1–5; ~ ; Q6–8,
F2

IV.i

3 make∧] Q2; ~ , Q1
6 looke?] Q2; ~ . Q1
7–9 I...seemely] Q1–8, F2 *line*
I...me | Breake...seemely
9–10 Goe...speake] *one line in*
Q1–8, F2
9.1 *Exeunt Ladyes.*] Q2; *Exit
Ladyes* ∧ Q1
17–18 Brother...riddle] Q1–8, F2
line Brother...wittie, | And...
riddle
19 nothing?] Q2; ~ . Q1
25 this?] Q2; ~ . Q1
27 scars,] Q2; ~ : Q1
38 honor:] Q2; ~ , Q1
42–43 How...report] *one line in*
Q1–8, F2
43 report?] Q2; ~ . Q1
43–44 Where...place] *one line in*
Q1–8, F2
44–45 They...lied] Q1–8, F2 *line*
They...people, | Beleeve...
lied
55 flattered;] Q6; ~ , Q1–5
59 brother,] Q2; ~ ∧ Q1

65 yet?] Q2; ~ . Q1
68–69 And...you] Q1–8, F2 *line*
And...Centinels, | And...
you
70–71 Y'are...daring] Q1–8, F2
line Y'are...your | Fighters...
daring
70 fighters?] Q2; ~ , Q1
72 alive?] Q2; ~ , Q1
72 safer] Q2; *Safer* Q1
74 food;] Q2; ~ , Q1
75 yet?] Q2; ~ . Q1
77–80 Force...me] *prose in* Q1–8,
F2
80 me?] Q2; ~ . Q1
81–86 Thou...canker] *prose in*
Q2–8, F2; *om.* Q1
85 honor] honour Q2–8, F2; *om.*
Q1
94 easinesse?] Q2; ~ , Q1
104 thee∧] ~ , Q1–2, 4–8, F2; ~ .
Q3
105–107 If...thee] Q1–8, F2 *line*
If...have | Vow'd...left |
Thine...thee

105 criest:] F2; ~ , Q1–5; ~ ; Q6–7

117–118 Doe...yet] *one line in* Q1–8, F2

121–123 Stay...speake] *prose in* Q1–8, F2

122 first:] ~ , Q1–8, F2

136 him?] Q3; ~ , Q1–2

145–146 No...him] *one line in* Q1–8, F2

148 name∧] Q2; ~ , Q1

152–153 For...him] Q1–8, F2 *line* For...feare. | Come...him

153 Sir———] ~ . Q1–5; ~ ! Q6–8, F2

156 thee,...selfe∧] ~ ∧...~ , Q1–3; ~ ∧...~ ∧ Q4–8, F2

174 I,] ~ ∧ Q1–8, F2

176–177 disgrace;...time,] ~ ,... ~ ; Q1–8, F2±

179 wandred?] Q2; ~ . Q1

182 follies,] Q2; ~ ∧ Q1

202 mischiefes;] Q6; ~ , Q1–5

207 is?] Q2; ~ , Q1

229 *Nilus:*] ~ , Q1–5; ~ ; Q6–8, F2

231 forgivenesse:] F2; ~ , Q1–5; ~ ; Q6–7

235 it:] F2; ~ , Q1–5; ~ ; Q6–7

235 thee,] Q2; ~ ∧ Q1

237 serious,] Q2; ~ ∧ Q1

244 ones,] Q2; ~ ∧ Q1

245 *Crocodiles,*] Q2; ~ ∧ Q1

247 die,] Q2; ~ ; Q1

248 told ∧ and unbeleiv'd,] ~ , ~ ~ ∧ Q1–5; ~ , ~ ~ , Q6–8, F2

252 will,] Q6; ~ ∧ Q1–5

254 it;] Q6; ~ , Q1–5

262 Star:] F2; ~ , Q1–5; ~ ; Q6–7

262 hand,] Q2; ~ ∧ Q1

264 *Amintor:*] F2; ~ , Q1–5; ~ ; Q6; ~ . Q7

270 thee,] Q2; ~ ∧ Q1

IV.ii

2–3 I...it] *one line in* Q1–8, F2

7 scape?] Q2; ~ . Q1

7–8 If...blush] *one line in* Q1–8, F2

10 *Calianax*] Q2; *Callianax* Q1 (*and subsequently in text, except as noted*)

15 doate∧] Q2; ~ , Q1

17 it:] Q2; ~ , Q1

21–23 And...witnesse] *prose in* Q1–5; Q6–8, F2 *line* And... world; | You...witness

23 witnesse?] ~ . Q1–8, F2

23–24 No...it] *one line in* Q1–8, F2

24 it?] ~ . Q1–8, F2

24–26 How...Rogues] Q1–8 *line* How...not | I...Rogues; F2 *lines* How...am | Not... Rogues

26 Rogues?] Q2; ~. Q1

26–27 But...please] *one line in* Q1–8, F2

27–29 I...say it] *prose in* Q1–8, F2

30– 31 And...knave] *one line in* Q1–8, F2

32 Enough,———] ~ , ∧ Q1–8, F2±

32 *Strato?*] Q2; ~ . Q1

34 *Melantius?*] Q2; ~ , Q1

36 there: If] Q2 (if); ~ , if Q1

44 too,] Q2; ~ ∧ Q1

45 sir:] Q2; ~ , Q1

47 thou?] Q2; ~ ∧ Q1

51–52 Reach...sad] *one line in* Q1–8, F2

51 wine,———] ~ , ∧ Q1–8, F2±

62 here,———] ~ , ∧ Q1–8, F2±

63–64 Have...*Calianax*] *one line in* Q1–8, F2

64 *Calianax?*] Q2; ~ . Q1

65–66 Ye...you] *one line in* Q1–8, F2

73–74 Were...Unpossible] *one line in* Q1–8, F2

75 be:] ~ , Q1–8, F2

78 No,] Q2; ~ ‸ Q1

83 fort,——] ~ , ‸ Q1–8, F2±

87–89 I...you] Q1–8, F2 *line* I ...word, | But...you

91–92 You...*Calianax*] Q1–8, F2 *line* You...wine, | Sit... *Calianax*

92 still,——] ~ , ‸ Q1–8, F2±

96–97 Impudence...accus'd] *one line in* Q1–8, F2

97–98 A...alteration] *one line in* Q1–8, F2

115–116 Nay...mercy] *one line in* Q1–8, F2

119–121 Not...scape] *prose in* Q1–8, F2

121–122 Pardon...preserve] *prose in* Q1; Q2–8, F2 *line* Pardon ...pardoned, | You preserve

130 pardon, for...doo't,] ~ , ~ ...~ ‸ Q1; ~ (~ ...~) Q2–8, F2

131–132 I...all] *one line in* Q1–8, F2

132–133 then...service] *one line in* Q1–8, F2

133–134 That...I] *one line in* Q1–8, F2

137–139 Who...selfe] Q1 *lines* Who ...me | Of...selfe; *prose in* Q2–8, F2

137 I?] ~ , Q1–8, F2

142 anger,——] ~ , ‸ Q1–8, F2±

143–144 *Lysippus*...sound] *one line in* Q1–8, F2

143 *Lysippus*‸] Licip: Q1–8, F2±

144 Lady,——] ~ , ‸ Q1–8, F2±

150 thee,——] ~ , ‸ Q1–8, F2±

151 man,] Q2; ~ ; Q1

152 sorrow,] Q2; ~ ‸ Q1

153 me?] Q2; ~ ; Q1

164–165 Your...ground] Q1 *lines* Your...arme,(*omitting the rest*); Q2–8, F2 *line* Your...arme, | This...ground

167 ease:] Q2; ~ , Q1

172–173 *Melantius*...beleeve] *one line in* Q1–8, F2

174 did not;] Q5; ~ , Q1 (*omitting* not); ~ ~ , Q2–4

175 satisfie,——] ~ , ‸ Q1–8, F2±

176–177 A...Villaine] *prose in* Q1; Q2–8, F2 *line* A...truth, | A ...Villaine

181–182 My...speake] *one line in* Q1–8, F2

182–183 it,——...canst,——] ~ , ‸...~ , ‸ Q1–8, F2

182 speake,] Q2; ~ ‸ Q1

185–186 This...*Melantius*] *one line in* Q1–8, F2

191 *Diagoras*] *Mel. Diagoras* Q1–8, F2

195–203 Ile...up] *prose in* Q1–2; *prose in* Q3–8, F2 *through* go, *l.* 202, *then* Home...up

196 cunning:——] ~ , ‸ Q1–5, F2; ~ ; ‸ Q6–8

199 bed:] Q2; ~ , Q1

203 well,——] ~ , ‸ Q1–8, F2±

212 me?] Q2; ~ ; Q1

216 *Calianax*,] Q4; *Cal:* Q1–2; ~ ‸ Q3

218–219 discharged.——...late, ——] ~ . ‸...~ , ‸ Q1–8, F2±

221–224 And...*Calianax*] Q1–3 *line as prose through* freind, *l.* 223, *then* Still... *Calianax*; Q4–8, F2 *line entirely as prose*

221 *Evadne*,——] ~ ‸‸ Q1, 7; ~ , ‸ Q2–5; ~ ; ‸ Q6, 8, F2

224 ever,——] ~ ‸‸ Q 1; ~ · ‸
   Q 2–8, F 2
224 *Calianax*‸] Q 3; *Call:* Q 1–2
225.1 Melantius‸] *Mel.* Q 1–8, F 2
229–230 You...ye] Q 2; Q 1 *lines*
   You...thats | the strongest |
   Part...ye
256–257 If...agen] *one line in* Q 1–
   8, F 2
259–262 Why...compasse] Q 1–8
   line Why...and | This...
   brest | To compasse; F 2 *lines*
   Why...and | This *and the rest*
   as prose
269 carried:] Q 2; ~ , Q 1
272–273 Heele...*Diphilus*] *one line*
   in Q 1–8, F 2 (Q 6–8, F 2 *om.*
   Diphilus)
273 *Diphilus*‸] *Diph.* Q 1–5; *om.*
   Q 6–8, F 2
274–275 This...her] Q 1–8, F 2 *line*
   This...in, | The...her
276 *Diphilus*‸] Q 3; *Diph.* Q 1–2

280–281 With...his] *one line in*
   Q 1–8, F 2
282–285 Touch...selves] *prose in*
   Q 1–8, F 2
285.1 Calianax,] *Call.* Q 1–8, F 2±
293 vengeance?——] ~ ? ‸ Q 1–8,
   F 2
301 friend:] Q 2; ~ , Q 1
305 repents.] Q 5; ~ , Q 1–4
306–307 Heele...*Amintor*] *one line*
   in Q 1; Q 2–8, F 2 *line* Heele...
   madnes *as one line with* Amintor
   beginning l. 308
307 madnes.——*Amintor*,] ~ , ‸ ~ ·
   Q 1; ~ , ‸ ~ , Q 2–8, F 2±
310 fightest.——...honest,] ~ , ‸
   ...~ · Q 1; ~ ·‸...~ , Q 2–
   8, F 2±
319 that‸] Q 2; ~ , Q 1
320 for. Some] Q 2; ~ ‸ some Q 1
324–325 I...him] *one line in* Q 1–8,
   F 2
325–326 Why...revenge] *prose in*
   Q 1–8, F 2

V.i

7–8 Tis...then——] *prose in*
   Q 1, 5–7, F 2; Q 2–4 *line* Tis...
   will | Wake...then; Q 8 *lines*
   Tis...wake, | And then
8 then——] ~ · Q 1–8, F 2 (then
   methinkes. Q 1)
10–11 A...gone] Q 2; *prose in*
   Q 1
13.1 King‸] Q 2; *K.* Q 1
17–18 From...daring] Q 1–8, F 2
   line From...heart | Be...
   daring
24 there,——] ~ , ‸ Q 1–8, F 2±
39 enough.——] ~ · ‸ Q 2–8, F 2;
   reading differs Q 1
40 Lord,——] ~ , ‸ Q 1–8, F 2±
41 more,——] ~ , ‸ Q 1–8, F 2

41 Lord,——] ~ , ‸ Q 1–8, F 2±
42 already?——] ~ ? ‸ Q 1–8, F 2
59 I,] Q 6; ~ ‸ Q 1–5
60 repent:] F 2; ~ , Q 1–5; ~ ;
   Q 6–7
78 me:] F 2; ~ , Q 1–6; ~ ; Q 7
85 mercy‸] F 2; ~ , Q 1–7
95 I,] Q 7; ~ ‸ Q 1–6
99 dreames:] F 2; ~ , Q 1–5; ~ ;
   Q 6–7
112 *Exit*] F 2; *Exeunt* Q 1–7
120–121 Either...pale] *prose in* Q 1–
   8, F 2
121–122 And...well] *one line in*
   Q 2–8, F 2; *om.* Q 1
122–123 Lets...dead] *one line in*
   Q 1–8, F 2

147   10-2

125–126 This...this] Q 1–8, F 2 *line*
        This...beleeve | A...this
142–143 Gentlemen...King] *one line*
        in Q 1–8, F 2

144–145 I...stop] *prose in* Q 1–8,
        F 2

V.ii

1 beleeve,...arm'd.] ∼ ∧...∼ ,
  Q 1–8, F 2
2 *Diphilus*,] Q 4 ; *Diph.* Q 1–2; ∼ ∧
  Q 3
32 honour:] ∼ , Q 1–5; ∼ ; Q 6–8,
   F 2
35–36 When...rascall] Q 2–8, F 2
   line When...dares | Fight...
   rascall; *om.* Q 1
35 mad;] Q 6; ∼ , Q 2–5; *om.* Q 1

43 souldier:] ∼ , Q 1–5; ∼ ; Q 6–8,
   F 2
52–53 Who...wrong] *one line in*
   Q 1–8, F 2
59–60 This...replie] *one line in*
   Q 1–8, F 2
59 towne;] Q 6; ∼ , Q 1–5
64–65 *Melantius*...it] Q 1–8, F 2
   line Melantius...choice, | My
   ...it
73 shall:——] ∼ : ∧ Q 1–8, F 2±

V.iii

4 breast:] ∼ , Q 1–5; ∼ ; Q 6–8,
  F 2
11 What,] Q 6; ∼ ∧ Q 1–5
20–21 This...him] *prose in* Q 1–8,
   F 2
35– 36 O...it] *one line in* Q 1–8,
   F 2
47 not:] ∼ , Q 1–5; ∼ ; Q 6–8, F 2
53 houre ∧...arriv'd:] ∼ ,...∼ ,
   Q 1–5; ∼ ;...∼ ; Q 6–8, F 2
56 thing:] ∼ , Q 1–5; ∼ ; Q 6–8, F 2
58 her:] ∼ , Q 1–5; ∼ ; Q 6–8, F 2
75 what:] ∼ , Q 1–5; ∼ ; Q 6–8, F 2
85–87 You...you] *prose in* Q 1;
   Q 2–5 *line* You...with | Those
   ...you; Q 6–8, F 2 *line* You...
   that | Dare...you
91 this,——good gods,] ∼ , ∧ ∼
   ∼ —— Q 1–5; ∼ ; ∧ ∼ ∼ ——
   Q 6–8, F 2
95 kickt,] Q 6; ∼ ∧ Q 1–5
97 death?] Q 2; ∼ . Q 1
99 could;] Q 6; ∼ , Q 1–5

101 live:——] ∼ , ∧ Q 1; ∼ : ∧ Q 2–
    8, F 2
118 faire?] Q 2; ∼ , Q 1
119 *Evadne* ∧] Q 2; *Evad:* Q 1
119 beautious] Q 2; beatious Q 1
119 now?] Q 2; ∼ ∧ Q 1
121 man?] Q 2; ∼ , Q 1
128 King] Q 5; *King* Q 1–4
129 love,] Q 2; ∼ ∧ Q 1
130 armes.] Q 2; ∼ , Q 1
135 nature.] Q 6; ∼ ∧ Q 1; ∼ , Q 2–5
136 *Amintor?*] Q 2; ∼ , Q 1
152 more,] Q 2; ∼ ∧ Q 1
152–153 Forgive...part] Q 1–8, F 2
    line Forgive...bed, | We...
    part
154 Forbeare,] Q 2; ∼ ∧ Q 1
155–156 Take...me] *one line in*
    Q 1–8, F 2
155 heed,] Q 2; ∼ ∧ Q 1
156–157 If...home] Q 1–5 *line* If
    ...it, | Take...home; *one line*
    in Q 6–8, F 2

159–160 For...sword] Q 1–8, F 2
  line For...calme, | Thine...
  sword
160–161 Away...violence] *one line*
  in Q 1–8, F 2
164 stay‸] Q 3; ~ , Q 1–2
175 lost,] Q 2; ~ ‸ Q 1
183 company;] Q 6; ~ , Q 1–5
186 done;] Q 6; ~ , Q 1–5
203 her?] F 2; ~ . Q 1–7
217 live‸] Q 8; ~ , Q 1–7, F 2
219–220 Alas...thee] Q 1–5 *line*
  Alas...haire | From thee; *one*
  line in Q 6–8, F 2
227 ——*Aspatia.*——] ‸ ~ · ‸ Q 1–
  8, F 2±
228 frame.——] ~ · ‸ Q 1–8, F 2
229 speake:——] ~ : ‸ Q 1–8, F 2
232 me:——] ~ : ‸ Q 1–8, F 2
232 speake.——] ~ · ‸ Q 1–8, F 2
241 ——*Aspatia.*——]‸ ~ · ‸Q 1–8,
  F 2±
255 flowes.] ~ , Q 1–5; ~ ; Q 6–8,
  F 2
258–259 *Melantius*...tongue] Q 1–

8, F 2 *line Melantius*...armes |
  Are...tongue
262–264 Oh...there] Q 1–8, F 2
  line Oh...slaine, | You...
  there
264 *Diphilus*‸] *Dip.* Q 1–2; ~ , Q 3–
  8, F 2
267 had,——] ~ , ‸ Q 1–8, F 2±
267–268 All...thee] Q 1–8, F 2 *line*
  All...againe | What...thee
267 againe,] Q 2; ~ ‸ Q 1
268 thee?] Q 2; ~ . Q 1
271 that?] Q 6; ~ ‸ Q 1–5
272–273 I...need] Q 1–8, F 2 *line* I
  ...now, | It...need
279 straine?] Q 2; ~ . Q 1
280–283 I...can] Q 1–8, F 2 *line* I
  ...am | Growne...now | You
  ...me | Quickly...can (Q 2+
  om. all now)
281 now.] Q 2; ~ ‸ Q 1
284 kept‸] Q 2; ~ . Q 1
287 breath?] Q 6; ~ , Q 1; ~ ; Q 2–5
291–292 in....me,] Q 4; ~ ‸...
  ~ . Q 1; ~ ,...~ , Q 2–3

HISTORICAL COLLATION

[This collation includes substantive and semi-substantive differences from the present text appearing in the eight quartos, the folio of 1679, eleven later editions, and the commentaries of Mason and Brereton. Sigla are as follows:

B   *Select Plays by Francis Beaumont and John Fletcher*, with an introduction by G. P. Baker. London and Toronto, 1911. (Everyman's Library.)

Br   J. Le Gay Brereton, 'Notes on Some Plays of Beaumont and Fletcher', *Elizabethan Drama: Notes and Studies*. Sydney, 1909.

C   *The Dramatic Works*, ed. George Colman the Younger. London, 1778. 10 vols.

D   *Works*, ed. Alexander Dyce. London, 1843–6. 11 vols.

F2   The folio of 1679.

L   *Works*, ed. Gerard Langbaine the Younger. London, 1711. 7 vols.

M   *Works*, ed. J. St Loe Strachey. London, 1887. 2 vols. (The Mermaid Series.)

Ma   J. Monck Mason, *Comments on the Plays of Beaumont and Fletcher*. London, 1798.

N   *The Maid's Tragedy*, ed. Howard B. Norland. Lincoln, Nebraska, 1968.

Q1–8   The quartos of (1) 1619, (2) 1622, (3) 1630, (4) 1638, (5) 1641, (6) 1660?, (7) 1661?, (8) 1686.

S   *Elizabethan Plays*, ed. Hazelton Spencer. Boston, 1933.

T   *Works*, ed. Theobald, Seward, and Sympson. London, 1750. 10 vols.

Th   '*The Maid's Tragedy' and 'Philaster'*, ed. Ashley H. Thorndike. Boston, 1906. (The Belles-Lettres Series.)

V   *Works*. London, 1904–12. 4 vols. (Bullen's Variorum. *The Maid's Tragedy*, ed. P. A. Daniel.)

W   *Works*, ed. Henry Weber. Edinburgh, 1812. 14 vols.]

SPEAKERS

3 a noble Gentleman.] *om.* Q1–2   5 brothers] brother Q4–8

I.i

2 *Strato*.] *Lys.* Q1, C+   6 a] the T+(−S, N)
3 the brother] *om.* the Q1   7 masks...masks]   maske...
6 thou] *om.* Q2–4   maske Q3–8, F2, L, T, C, W, B

8 Yes] Why, yes T
8 their King] *om.* Q 1
9 Bridegroome] groome Q 1, N
10 there] they are Q 8, W, B
13 to *Rhodes*] *om.* Q 1
14 blood...buyest] blowes... bringst Q 1
14 us] *om.* Th, S
14 peace.] peace at home, Q 1
17 will...kinde] will be kinde Q 1; will be e'en too kind T; will be too-too kind V; too will be kind Br
18 welcomes] welcome Q 1
19 his] this Q 6–8, F 2, L
19 worlds] world Q 1
32 strict] straight Q 1, T, C, V
33 most] *om.* Q 2–8, F 2, L, W, B
34 solemnities] solemnitie Q 2–8, F 2, L, T, C, W, B
35 were] was T, C, W, B
36 I] and Q 1, D, V, M, Th, S, N
36 here] *om.* Q 2–8, F 2, L, C, W, B
43 with armes] *om.* Q 1
46 Wonder...friend;] *om.* L
46 that] *om.* T
46 my friend] *om.* Q 1
47 and temperate] *om.* Q 1
50 oft] often Q 7
53 those] these Th
56 Weigh] Weighes Q 1
58 *passing by*] *passing with attendance* Q 1, V; *passing with Attendants* T; *om.* W, B; *passing over the Stage* D, M
66 For] sir Q 1, D, V, M, Th
69 he] *om.* Q 7
72 hath] has Q 1, V, N
73 light about her] lightning's power Ma
73 about] above Q 1+(−Q 2, W)
74 the faire] *om.* Q 7
79 infortunate] unfortunate Q 2+ (−N)
82 'a] he Q 2+ (−N)

83 If I could] Could I but Q 1, V
84 So] Such Q 1
85–86 holds... King?] *om.* Q 1
86 Yes...Lady] O t'were pittie, for this Lady sir, Q 1
86 Yes] *om.* B
87 Walkes] Sits Q 1
88 earth;] ear ‸ Q 1(u)
88 the unfrequented] In unfrequented Q 1
89 and] Where Q 1, T, D, V, M, Th
90 she...tell] Then she will sit, and sigh, and tell Q 1
93 strow] strew W, B
93 her over] them over her Q 1
96 things] *om.* Q 8
97 sigh] swound Q 1
98 our] your Q 1
99 fill] fils Q 1
111 much] *om.* Q 7
120 thine] thy Q 4–8, F 2, L, T, C
122 am poore] am but poore Q 4–8, F 2, L, T, C, W, B
124 Could...weep] could no more but weep Q 2–6, 8, F 2, L; could no more weep Q 7
125 have] gave V
126 Fetcht] Fetch F 2, L
127 mothers] mothers too T
128 that] what Q 3–8, F 2, L
130 those] these Q 1
132 fickle] cruell Q 1; sicke Q 3–8, F 2, L
135 *Amintor.*] *Evad.* Q 3
137 about] above Q 3–8, F 2, L, D, V, S; far above T, C, W, M, Th, B
139.1 *Enter* Messenger.] *om.* Q 1
140 *Messenger.*] AMINT. Q 1
141 *Diphilus.*] *Diphilus.* | *Exeunt Lysippus, Cleon, Strato, Diphilus.* Q 1, T, W, B; *Exeunt* [etc.] following *you, l.* 142 D, V, M, Th, S
145 peace] sports Q 1

146 but] yet Q3+ (−N)
150 gentlemen] *om.* Q2; in't Q3+
(−T, N); gentle in't T

151.1 *Exeunt] Exit* Q2–8, F2;
Exeunt severally T; *om.* C

I.ii

0.1 *with] and* Q1, M
2 raile at] be angry with Q1
3 i'th] i'th the Q1–2
8 may] must Q1, V
8 swear] sweat Q1, S, N; wear F2+
8 his heart out] out his heart with
swearing Q1, L, T, C, W, V, B;
his heart out with swearing
Q2–8, F2, D, M, Th, S, N
10 shall] will Q3–8, F2
10 Pray stay] *om.* Q1
12 asse you] asse Q1
13 judgd] judge Q1–2
17 through my] through in my Q1
18 ha] had Q5–8, F2, L; have C,
W, B
18 amongst] among F2+(−V, Th,
S, N)
18 And] But Q1
21 there, there,...codes] whose ∧
there, codes Q1
21 codes, codes] *om.* T
24 Whose there] Who i'st Q1
26 with you] *om.* Q1
30 and theres roome] there is no
roome Q1
32 attend the] attend upon the T
33 *Exeunt...dore.] Exit Melantius
Lady other dore.* Q1; *om.* Q2–8,
F2, L, T, C
36 dores shut] Doors be shut L, T
36 agen: I,] agen, no; Q1, T+
(−S, N)
36 for you] *om.* Q1
38 going away] giving way Q1
39 amongst] among Q4+(−V,
Th, S, N)
39–40 dozen...own] dozen heads
Q1

42 pray you] pray F2, L, T
46 *Melantius?] Melantius* within.
(within *as part of dialogue*) Q8
46.1–48.1 *Enter...*Melantius.] *Enter
Calianax to Melantius* at l. 46.1
Q2–8, F2, L, Th, S
48 a] I F2+(−V, Th, S, N)
49–50 you:...*Calianax,*] ∼ , ...
∼ , Q1–5; ∼ ∧...∼ : Q6–8,
F2, L±
53 mine] my Q3+(−V, Th, S, N)
57 but] *om.* Q1
59 So...King?] *om.* Q1
61 women] a woman Q7
63 thus] so Q1
66 Why] *om.* Q1
66 wenches] Wenches for them T
67 shall forget] shall quite forget
Q1, D, V, M, Th, S, N
71 me] *om.* Q2–8, F2, L, C, W, B
71 he] of Q1
72 A lies] Alyes Q7; He lyes F2+
(−V, Th, S, N)
74 pluck] pluck't Q4–5
77 braved] bran'd Q3–8; brain'd
F2, L
79 that] the Q1, D, V, M
82 or] and Q1
85 say] talke Q1
85 injurie] wrong Q1, T
87 hande] hands Q1, V
88 *Melantius.*] CAL. Q1
94 comming] come Q1(u)
99 *King.*] *om.* Q1
99 my] thy Q1
100 thee] me Q1
102 mine] my Q5+(−V, Th, S, N)
108 lookt...tooke∧] look's...too,
N

111 Can...me.] *om.* Q1
111.1 *The*] *om.* Q1
112 come] now Q1, T
112 quenching] raging Q2+(−T, V)
117 hornes] horne Q5–8, F2, L
117 quite] *om.* Q6–8, F2, L
120 and how] that have Q1
122–127 How...thou.] How... find | This...blind. | Back... how | To...thou: | Methinks ...streaks | That...breaks. *or* beauties *for* beautie, l. 123 Ma
122 I could] can I Q1, T
123 I am] am I Q1, T
124 streaks] stroaks Q8
125 breaks] break Q6–8
131 reines] raines Q3–7, F2
132 these mortals] those Q1
135 hold] keepe Q2
138 but] *om.* Q7
139 Must] Most Q5–6
140–149 Yet...eyes.] *om.* Q1, C
140 whil'st] while L, T, W, B
144 wish] with Q2; *om.* Q1
145 cold] could Q7
150 faire...thy] pale...that Q1
151 crowne] fill Q1
152 shepheards, let] shepheards, and let Q1
154 then call] *om.* Q1, T, V
155 bed] banck Q1, T, V
156 top] brow Q1, V
157 his] this Q2–8, F2, L, T, C, W, B
157 this] thy Q1; a Q3+(−V, S, N)
158 Queene] power Q1
159 wine] winde Q1
161 Turne] Turnes Q1
163 nobler] noble Q2–8, F2, L, C, W, B
165 laid] lade T, C
168 fetcht] force Q1
173 goe] flie Q3+(−S, N)
174 his] thy Q2–8, F2, L, T, C, W, B

175 intensions] intention Q3+(−Th, S, N)
179 welcomes] welcome Q1
180 These...next] Bid them draw neere to have Q1
180 watrie] warrie Q4
181 Bring] Led Q1
183 vessell] vessels Q1, N
185 Oh] See Q1; Hoe Q3+(−Th, S, N)
185 Winde!] winde ∧ Q1–8, F2; Wind- (*i.e.* wind-commanding) T, C, W, V, B, N
188 *Favonius*] *Fanonius* Q1–2
190 too] *om.* Q1
190–192 *Neptune. Doe....Maine,*] NEPT. Doe ∧ great maister of the floud, and all below ∧ | Thy... taken ∧ | EOL. O! the Maine ∧ Q1–8, F2, L±
190 *Exit...Rock.*] *Exit...rock, and re-enters.* W, B
191 Great] *om.* Q1
192 command] commands Q7
192 O] Hoe Q3+(−Th, S, N)
194 And ∧ strugling∧] ~ , ~ , C, W, D, M, B
196 He] I Q1, T, D, V, M
196 long be] be long Q1
196 once] hence Q1
197 call...bottomes] bid the other call out Q1
200 beaten] beating Q5; bearing Q6–8, F2, L
200 tell] till Q1–8, F2, L, T, C, W, B
207 *thee*] them Q3–8, F2, L
209 *this*] *his* L
215 *you*] *your* Q8
223 *darke*] *old* Q1, T
225 *curse*] *cause* Q3
226 blushes] *losses* Q1, T+(−C, N)
231 *shrill*] *loud* Q1
234 *though*] *if* Q1

234.1–248 Another Measure... *twin-ing.*] *om.* Q 1

234.1 Another Measure.] If not her measure *following* one, *l.* 236 Q 2–8, F 2, L, D, M, Th, N; If not o'ermeasure *following* one C, W, B; Maskers daunce, *Nep-tune* leads it ⌃ *following* way, *l.* 240 Q 1 (*following* call, *l.* 234), T, D, M, S

237–239 The...she...she] Thy... they...the Q 2–8, F 2, L; The ...they...the C; The... they ...she W, B; Thy...she... she S; *om.* Q 1

237 *Amphitrite*] *Amphitrites* Q 2; *om.* Q 1

240 lay] lead Q 2–8, F 2, L, T, C, W, B; *om.* Q 1

246 *kist*] *kiss* Q 8

249 sea goes] Seas goe Q 5–8, F 2, L, T, C

250 hath] has Q 1, N

253 the] thy T

254 calme] call F 2, L

254 A...one] We thanke you for this houre Q 1, T, D, V, M, Th, S

255 My...gratulate] and to gratu-late Q 2–8, F 2, L, C, W, B, N

257 many] may Q 7

258 and] *om.* Q 2–8, F 2, L, T, C, W, B

259 dwellings] dwelling Q 2

260 government] governments Q 1, D, V, M

261 charge] waters Q 1

262.1 Neptune...*Gods.*] *Exeunt Maskers* ⌃ | *Descend.* following Iland Q 1

267 kingdome] Kingdomes Q 2–8, F 2, L, Th, S

268 goe ⌃ on,] ~ , ~ ⌃ Q 3

270 fall...forget] false...forgot Q 5–8, F 2, L; fall...forgot C, W, B

271 must] dare Q 1

272 Heave up] Once heave Q 1

274 sect] set T + (− C, N)

274 whip] lash Q 1

275 day breaks] day-break's C, W, B

275 yon same] you some Q 6–8, F 2; yon some L

275 same flashing] sun flaring Q 1, C, W, D, V, M, B, N

275 streame] beam C, W, B

276 say...goe?] Say, wilt thou go? which way? T; *Which way wilt thou go? say.* D, V, M

277 I into day] Adew Q 1

277.1 *Finis Maske.*] *om.* Q 1

278 lights] light Q 1

278 their ⌃ Ladyes,] ~ , ~ , L; ~ ; ~ , T, C, W, D, V, M, B, S, N ±

281 my] may F 2, L

283 my Kingdomes] my Kingdome Q 3 + (− Q 8, Th, S, N); me Q 8

II.i

2 that] *om.* T, C

3 very] *om.* Q 1, T

3–5, 5–6 I...you...That... doe.] *in italics with stage-direction* Singing T, C, W, B

4 Far merrier] *merrier far* T, C, W, B

4 Madame] *om.* T, C, W, B

4 it were] t'were Q 7, T, C, W, B

5–6 *Evadne.* Howes...doe.] *om.* Q 2–8, F 2, L

12 we'are] we are Q 2–7, F 2, L, T, C, W, S

13 aright] right Q 1

14 Lady] Madame Q1
14–15 *1. Lady. Tis...* | *Dula.*
   Anon] *Dula. Tis...* | Anon
   Q2–8, F2, L, T, C, W, B, N
16 You're] Tis Q1
18 high] *om.* Q1
19 *Dula.*] *om.* Q4
21 livelier] lively Q4–8, F2, L
23 I...it] will take it I hope Q1
24 you] thee V
25 heart ake] heart to ake Q6–8,
   F2, L
26 take] lie in Q1
30 does] will M
30 a side] aside T, C
31 Why] *om.* Q1
31 I prethee] *om.* Q2–8, F2, L, C,
   W, B
31 play_∧] ~ . Q3
40 cheeke] checke Q2
45 right] night Q2–8, F2, L, C, W,
   B
49 Were great] Were as great Q7
53 false_∧] ~ , Q4–5; ~ ; Q6–8
56 lost] left Q5–8, F2, L
58 I should] should I Q3+(−V,
   Th, S, N)
58 leave] leane Q3
59 See] Loe Q1
61 shalt] shall Q7
62 into] unto Q1
63 fire, I] fire, and I Q1, V, N
64 maist] must Q1
67–89 *Aspatia. Lay...laid.*] *om.*
   Q1
78 *lay*] lye T+(−S, N)
79 *gently*] gentle Q4+
80 ont] out Q3
87 *eies*] *Eyen* T
89 laid] *om.* Q8
92 no] not Q1
95 And] *om.* Q3+(−S, N)
99 shall] should Q7
106 borne] born F2, L
110 Youle] Heele Q1, T, D, V, M

111 yet] *om.* Q1
122 had] *om.* Q7
122 another] any other Q7
123 with praiers] with my prayers
   Q3+(−N)
125 *Omnes.*] 1. LAD. Q1
128 Her] A Q1, T, D, V, Th
129 runne] raine Q1, T, D, V, M,
   Th
131 doe] did Q1
134 mine] my C
136 that forst] inforst Q1, T, D, V,
   M
138 she is] is she Q1, T
142 shall] will Q2+(−T, D, V,
   N)
146 loose] lose F2+ *including* Ma
   (−C, N)
148 bed, then_∧] ~ ~ _∧ F2, L; ~ _∧
   ~ ; T+(−N)
162 likes] will like Q1, T, V; like L
169 has] hath Q7
170 I sweare] sweete love Q1
171 thee] it Q1
173 with] to Q1
175 This] The Q1
175–176 or...come,] *om.* Q1
176 Or] Are L, T
179–180 sin | Off from] sun | Of Q1
180 wonnot] will not Q4+(−V,
   Th, S, N)
181 doe] *om.* Q1
185 then] *om.* Q1
186 shalt] should'st Q1; shall Q7
187 shall not] cannot Q1
195 Thy] Her Q1, D, V, M, S
198 *Amintor*] of these, what Q1
199 truth? | *Amintor.* Wil] truth. |
   Amintor. Is this the truth, wil
   Q1, T, D, V, M, Th, S, N
200 To night?] *om.* Q1
200–201 if | I] if you thought I Q1
   T, D, V, M, Th, S, N
205 truer] true Q8
206 thy] your Q1

206 but ever] but for ever Q4–8, F2,
  L, C, W, B
208 will] would Q1
212 coynesse] kisses Q1
213 earthly] earthy T
220 that] whom Q1
220 the] thee Q5
221 know: ther'es ∧...that] know ∧
  this,...then Q1, T, D, V, M
228 can but] cannot Q1
229 that] which Q1
231 hand] paine Q1, T
242 You] Ye C, W, B
245 Instruct me in] Instant me with
  Q1
248 this] the Q7
250 drowne] drownd Q7
250 her] their Q1
254 those] that Q1, T, D, V, M
259 men] man Q7
262 trust all] trust out all Q3+(−S,
  N)
264 woman] women Q5–8, F2, L
265 doe] doth Q3+
273 hast] had'st T+(−N)
274 weare] were Q3
283 Ha ye] Ha' you T; Have you
  C, W, D, M, B

290 in practise] om. Q1
290 that] th' T
293 hand] land Q1+(−V, S, N)
304 Tis] It is Q1, T, D, V, B
305 What ∧ did] What, did Q6–8,
  F2, L
307 name] word Q1, T, D, V, M
309 his] up Q7
314 hath...in] put in it Q3; put it
  in Q4+(−N)
318 a] om. Q1, 7, D, V, M, N
319 Evadne.] om. Q1
322 live] love Q1
325 heart] breast Q1
328 would] could Q1
332 is it] it is L, T
340 that] tho' C, W, M, B
342 know] knew Q4+(−Th, S, N)
345 through ∧ 'em,] through, e'ne ∧
  Q1
346 lost] left Q1, T, W, D, V, M,
  B, N
347–348 bed,...thee:] ∼ :... ∼ ,
  Q4–5; ∼ :...∼ ; Q6–8, F2, L
347 bed, now∧] ∼ ∧ ∼ , C
355 we] I Q1
357 loving] longing Q1, D, V, M
359 Amintor.] om. Q1

II.ii

0.1 Antiphila, Olimpias] Antiphila
  and Olimpias F2+(−N)
1 sad] om. Q1
2 Good ∧ gods,] Good, good, Q1
7–10 make...miserable] om. Q1
9 speake] spake T, C, D, V, M, S
9–11 Such...me | Beleeve...
  miserable. | Did...Olimpias,]
  Did...Olimpias, | Such...in't,
  | And...miserable, Q2–8, F2,
  L; ll. 9–10 om. Q1
11 nere] ere Q1
12 an easie] a metled Q1

12 for] to V
13 Nor I] Nere I Q1(u)
15–27 and...man:] om. Q1
16 life] light Q3–8, F2, L, T, C,
  W, B
19 but courts] courts but Q2+(−
  Q8); courts Q8
24 dead-cold] dead ∧ cold Q2–8,
  F2, L; om. Q1
26 man,] Man, base Man T
29 fine] faind Q1
30 Oenones] Oenone Q6–8, F2, L,
  T, C, W, D, M, B

31 *Hellen*] *Ellen* Q7
32 fully‿] furie, Q1
35 and] *om.* Q1
36 thine does] thine eyes does Q3;
    thine eyes doe Q4+(−Th, S,
    N)
44 back] black Q1
49 ha] have Q8, C, W, D, M, B
50 not] none Q1, T, N
51 ill] ill. Ay T; evil D, V, M, Th
51 well exprest] exprest well Q1
52 goe so] goe on so T, C, W, B
52–53 so———| *Antiphila,*] ∼ ‿ ∼ ,
    Q1–5, F2; ∼ ‿ ∼ ; Q6–8; ∼ ,
    ∼ , L; ∼ , ∼ ; T, C, W, B±
    (−N)
54 And...water,] *line repeated* Q1
56 to the life] bravely Q1, T, D, V,
    M
56 *Antiphila*] Olim. Q1
59 Fie] Oh fie T
59 here] there Q1
63 sad] poore Q1
65 shall] will Q1
66 I...thinke] Suppose I stand
    upon the Sea, breach now Q1,
    N; Suppose, I stand upon the
    Sea-beach now T+(−Th, S)
66 Sea-beach] Sea, breach Q1; sea‿
    breach Q2–8, F2, Th, S, N
67 haire] air (Ma *attributes this*
    reading to C, *which actually reads*
    hair *in the copy examined.*)

68 that desart, and] the place she
    was in, Q1
69 Tell...forsaken] Be teares of
    my story Q1; Be teachers of my
    story T, Ma, W, B
71 strive...looke] make me looke
    good girle Q1
72 monument] mount Q1
73 them] me Q7
75 looke, looke] see, see Q1, T, D,
    V, M
79 dumbe] dull Q3+(−S, N)
79 sudden] *om.* T
86 get...worke] in and whine
    there Q1
87 restie] rustie Q1, V
87 heates] heares Q3–5; eares Q6–
    7, F2, L; tears Q8
88 doe that office] heat you shortly
    Q1, T+(−Th, S, N)
89–90 My...be] Good my Lord
    be not angry, we doe nothing |
    But what my Ladies pleasure is,
    we are Q1
90 thus‿ in griefe,] ∼ ‿ ∼ ∼ ‿D;
    ∼ ; ∼ ∼ ‿ Ma, V, M
92 young] slie Q1
93 a bout] about Q1, 3–4, 8
95 what...asse,] *om.* Q1
96 will] must Q1
97 whelps, and] whelps I will, and
    Q2+(−T)
101 with all] withall Q3–7

III.i

2 Oh] Our Q1
6 None] No Q2+(−T, D, V, M,
    Th, N)
20 ha] have Q8, C, W, D, M,
    B
20 have] did Q1
22 We ventured] We have ven-
    tured Q1

23 A] He F2+(−V, Th, S, N)
24 Shall...merry?] *om.* Q5–8, F2,
    L
26 drunke] drank C, W, M, B
29 does] doth Q1
30 does chafe] does so chafe T
30 their] the Q1
31 againe] *om.* Q1

35 does hee] he does Q2+(−D, V, M, N)
36 use to] *om.* Q1
37 that] what Q3–8, F2
37 breath] breach Q1
38 so] *om.* F2, L
39 aside] *om.* Q1; *entire speech aside* D, V, M, Th, S, N
40 be] by L
49 make] made Th
50 the] this Q1
53 But——] *om.* Q1
53 Stay] Say Q1
55 more ₐ] ~ , F2, L, C, W, V, Th, B, S ±
62 cals] call Q1
63 shoots] shoot Q1
64 A] He F2+(−V, Th, S, N)
66 But] *om.* Q1
68 Enow] Enough Q4+ (−Th, S, N)
70 Is complement] complement Q5; complement's Q6+(−V, Th, S, N)
74 Wee] she Q7
84 I done?] *om.* Q1
86 Push] Pish C, W, M, B
90 aside] *om.* Q1, M
90 Nor] Not Q5–8, F2
92 *Diphilus.* Lets...spoild] DIPH. Lets...walke. | EVAD. By... spoild Q1–8, F2, L, T, D, M, Th, S; *Diph.* Let's...walk, Evadne. By...spoil'd C, W, V, B, N
100 lightned] heighned Q1
103 becomes] become C
108 how can I] can you Q1
111 *Amintor.*] *om.* Q1
114 too] *om.* Q1
115 aside] *om.* T, D, V, M, B
120 *Amintor* ₐ] ~ , *(indented like speech-prefix)* Q7
120 on ₐ] ~ , Q5–8, F2, L
121 And] But Q1

123 Indeede] I. deed Q4–5; I! deed Q6–8, F2; Ay! 'deed L+(−V, Th, S, N)
127 then, how] how ₐ then Q1
128 Unto thee?] to you. Q1
135 is...as] is quick, as Ma
139 knee] knees Q7
141 doe] to F2, L
144 is] are C, W, B
147 aside] *om.* Q2+(−V, S, N)
149 with you] *om.* Q1, T
151 A] He F2+(−V, Th, S, N)
151 that] *om.* T
152–153 something...be] For it is Q1
156 A jealous pang] jealous pangs Q1, T
157 With whom] When Q1
160 will and] *om.* Q1, T, D, M
163 breake agen] break word agen Q7
167 that] *om.* Q3+(−S, N)
167 misbecome] not well become Q3+(−Th, S, N)
170 Day] The Day T
176 my] mine F2, L, T
177 Toucht] Touch Q7
186 A...A] He...He F2+(−V, Th, S, N)
188 onely] *om.* Q5–8, F2, L, C, W, B
190 I am] I Q5; I'm Q6–8, F2, L
192 urge not] urge mee not Q3+(−T, N)
195 desire] desires F2, L
200 ever?...thee ₐ] ~ ,...~ ? Ma+ (−Br)
202 It] This Q1
203–206 *King.* Take...love?] *om.* Q1
204 with] *om.* Q5–8, F2, L, C
205 heare——*Amintor*] ~ , ~ Q6–8, F2; ~ ₐ ~ L
207 ingenious] ingenuous Q8, L, T, C, W, B

209 can'st] should'st Q1
213 me] I Q1
214 God] Heaven Q3–8, F2, L, T,
      C, D, M
215 should] shall Q7
221 vilde] wilde Q1–8, F2, L, T
226 lied] lies Q1
228–229 themselves:...bed?] ~ ,
      ...~ , Q1
230 Is it] It is Q1–8, F2, L, T, N
231 lives] Limbs T, Ma, W, D, M,
      B, S
231–232 send...To] om. Q1
233 I] thou Q7
238 easily] easie Q7
245 waking] walking Q1, Q3+
250 hand] sword Q1
253 were] are Q1

253 thousands,] thousand ∧ Q7+
      (−Q8, V, Th, S, N)
253 fooles] om. Q1
255 Iland] Land Q1
256 no] not S
259 It is] is it Q1
259 fate] fault Q1
263 beleeve] believ'd D, V, M, Th, S
264 wert] art T
271 hold, hold] hold F2, L
273 another] an other Q1
274 Sounded] Seconded Q1
276 Paines] Plagues Q1
277 lay] lie T, C
277 not] om. Q1
278 I] om. Q5–8, F2, L
278 needs] om. Q4–8, F2, L
281 pull] put Q8

III.ii

3 daughter will] Daughter——
      she will T
4 roome] part Q1
5 bloody   treacherous   slave.]
      bloody—— Q1
7 offices] office Q1, T
9 Leave,] om. Q1, T
16 to bed] to thy bed T
18 And] om. T
20 where] when Q5–8, F2, L
22–23 man ∧...fight,] ~ ,...~ ∧
      Q1, T
23 give] om. Q5–8, F2, L
27 hath] hast Q1
27 to] can Q1
34 mongst] amongst Q2–8, F2, C,
      Th, S; among L
38 holde him] hold Q5–8, F2, L
39 askt] aske Q2–8, F2, L, Th, S
41 go home and] om. Q1, T
43 the] this Th
43 mine] my C, W, B
46 Mens] Mans Q1

46 so] om. Q1
52 As] A Q6
55 charge] change T+(−N)
55 soules] soule Q3–4
61 matter you] matter that you Th
64 carriage] Carriage has appear'd
      T
65 strove] strives Q1
67 ∧ or] ——yow Q1
69 cunning] tongue Q1
77 Inevitable] Immutable Q1, C;
      Inimitable T
87 And your selfe] And you your-
      self Th, S
87 but] and Q1
90 blasted∧] ~ , Q2–5; ~ ; Q6–8,
      F2, L
92 here] hear Q7
94 an] om. Q7
97 friend] friends Q1
97 a] he F2+(−V, Th, S, N)
101 that] it T, C, W, Br, B
102 plaid] plead Q1

104 I ha] I have Q4+(−V, Th, S, N)
105 injuries‸] miseries, Q1
109 friend] friends Q7
115 old] owne Q3–8, F2, L
116 thy] my W, B
121 scape] escape Q6+(−W, V, B, S, N)
124 to] too Q6–8
126 How's‸] How, Q5–8, F2, L; How is‸ T+(−Th, S, N)
128 this‸ else,] ~ , ~ ‸ Q1
134 tame] tane Q1
136 strike] stick Q1, T+(−Th,S,N)
141 basely] basely tho' T
144 thine] thy Th
144 goe] swell Q3+(−Th, S, N)
145 troubled waters] the wilde surges Q3+(−Th, S, N)
145 shoulds] shouldst Q2+
153 borne] knowne Q1
154 happy] blessed Q1
159 scandall] farewell Q1
170 wake] make Q1
182 act on] action F2
185 ease: oh] ~ ‸ of Q1
192 my] its Q3+(−S, N)
197 eyes] Eyes awhile T
202 thy] my Q2–8, F2, L
206 that] om. Q6–8, F2, L
206 hast] has Q8
208 nor] not Q8
209 my] this Q1
212 Why ‸...backe?] ~ ?...~ , Q1; ~ ,...~ ? Q6–8, F2, L, T
214 it from] it backe from Q2+(−T, S)
216 And...posterity] om. Q1

217 Heare thy] Hear thou thy T
220 me be] me to be Q8
220 be] om. Q1
222 equall with] equal then with T
230 would:] ~ ‸ Q1
239 weepe] weeps Q4
239 that] it Q1, N
242 her] her to me T
244 yet] but Q1
247 our] your Q1
251 and no more] om. Q1
258 love, o wretched‸ I,] ~ , ~ ~ , ~ ‸ Q1–8, F2, L; ~ , (O wretched!) Ay, T+
262 As...could] To my best power Q3+(−N)
263 thine] thy Th
275 to mine] om. Q1, T, V
291 scape] escape Q7
293 in] om. L
299 all] om. M
299 Doe? mock] Do you mock M
301 See] om. T
301 starts] starrs Q7
301 idle] om. Q2–8, F2, L, C, W, B
302 To...you.] om. Q1
302 my love] my good Love T
302 am] om. Q2+
309 Into] to T
310 hope thou] hope that thou Q6–7, F2, L; hopes that thou Q8
316 Come] Come, come T
317 or] om. Q1
318 Thy] The Q1
318 not] my Q1
322 run] tun Q6
330 I] om. L

IV.i

0.1 *Ladyes*] a *Lady* Q1–8, F2, L, T, C, Th
1 God] om. Q2+(−N)

2 *Evadne——*] ~ . Q1–8, F2, L, D, V, N
3 would] will W, B

5 commend] command Q 1–8, F 2,
　　L, N
8 Into a commendation] into a
　　commendations Q 1; into com-
　　mendations Q 2, Th, S, N; into
　　commendation Q 3+(– Th, S,
　　N)
9 Tis] it is Q 1
9 me] *om.* B
10 the dore] your dores Q 1, V
12–13 In...skins | Choake...
　　businesse] Choke...business |
　　In...Skins L
16 commendation] commendations
　　Q 1–5, N
18 has] hath Q 6+(– V, Th, S, N)
19 it] *om.* Q 1
24 repentance] remembrance Q 3–8,
　　F 2, L
28 ye] you Q 3+(– V, Th, S, N)
28 not,] ∼ ∧ Q 1–7
30 you] ye Q 7
34 Though she had] As though
　　sh'ad T
35 Looke∧] ∼ , T
35 theres] there lies Q 3+(– S)
39 Rather...stand] *om.* F 2, L
43 was] were L, T, C, W, B
45 they lied] theile lie Q 1
48 open] upon Q 7
54 be sudden] come tell me Q 1
56 when] where Th
57 thy] they Q 7
61 of coward] of a coward Q 6–8,
　　F 2, L
64 brother] father Q 1
73 Bestride] Bestrid T+(– W, B)
74 food] foe Q 1, D, V, M, Th, S,
　　N
76 fellowes] fellow's is Q 7
81–86 Thou...canker.] *om.* Q 1
83 snatch] fetch Q 3–8, F 2, L, T, C
84 thou] that Q 7
85–86 Has...canker.] Who has
　　...canker? C, W, B

89–90 And...justice | They...
　　life] They...life, | And...jus-
　　tice Q 8
91 this] his Q 6–8, F 2, L, T
93 the] thee Q 7
94 mirth] much Q 3–8
95 weaknesses] weakness Q 4–5
99 wilt] will Q 6–8
101 a noble] a most noble T
114 offended,...Sir ∧] ∼ ,...∼ ,
　　Q 2–5; ∼ ,...∼ ; Q 6–8, F 2,
　　L ±
123 none else] no more Q 1
125 Oh...was] *om.* Q 1
126 No more,] *om.* Q 1
129 owne] one Q 6–7
130–131 *Evadne.* Too...can] *Evad.*
　　Too long, too late I finde it. |
　　Mel. Can Q 1
131 be sorry] be very sorry Q 1, D,
　　M
133 *Evadne,*...againe.]　Woman ∧
　　thou wilt not to thy trade
　　againe. Q 1
134 thou hadst] th'adst Q 3–6, 8, F 2,
　　L, T, C
136 Couldst...him] Has sunke thy
　　faire soule Q 1
136 thou not] thee not Q 2; not thou
　　Q 7
149 for] foe Q 5
152 knew] had Q 1; know Q 4+(–
　　S, N)
154 thoudst] thou'd Q 6–8, F 2, L;
　　thou shouldst W, B
158 great] thy Q 1
161 shall] *om.* M
162 shalt] shall Q 2
163 full] foule Q 1
164 hand] hands C+
167 his] this Q 6–8
167 Here] Heare Q 3
167 I sweare] I do swear T
173 Dare] Dares Q 4+
177 Gods] O Q 3+(– S, N)

178 desperately] disperately Q7
183 loaden] loaded V
186 *Kneele*] *Kneels* Q6+(−S)
189 Stand] Sand Q6
190 a...sorrowes]   no...sorrow
    Q2–8, F2, L; a... Sorrow T+
    (−D, V, M, N)
194 wildnesse] wilderness Q6–8, F2
195 prethee] pray thee F2, L, T
199 that_∧] that; Q1–2; thats; Q3–4;
    thats_∧ Q5+
203 worse] worst Q6–8, F2, L
207 is? O *Evadne,*] ∼ , ∼ ∼ ?
    Q4–5; ∼ _∧ ∼ ∼ ! Q6–8, F2,
    L±
211 that] the Q6–8, F2, L
222 Knowes] Know Q8, T, C, W,
    D, M, B

223 Can] Shall Q1
223 remembrance] remembrances M
232 wither] whether Q6–8; whither
    F2
236 thy selfe] my selfe Q6–8
240 eies] ages D, V, M
240 if thou] if that thou T
242 win] get Q1
244 honors] honour Ma
251 see me] seeme Q7
251 too] *om.* T
252 I] a Q1+(−Q7)
257 now] *om.* Q1
260 thus, thus] thus Q7
275 further] farther Q6, 8, F2+(−
    S, N)
279 she have] sh'ave Q4–8, F2

IV.ii

5 did he] he did Q7
7 scape] escape Q5–8, F2, L, T
16 Why_∧ if] Why? if Q2–3
17 ile] I Q1
20 meaning it] meaning of it Q5–8,
    F2, L, T
22 doe] do't T
25 have more] have no more Q6–8
29 too] to Q7
33 and_∧] in_∧ Q1–3; in. Q4+(±)
41 To] Do T, C, W, B
41.2 Diagoras] *om.* Q1, T, C
46 raise laughter] raise a laughter
    F2, L, T
48 chop] chopt Q1
49 'em] them Q7, C, W, B
52 *Amintor.*] *Mel.* Q1, T+(*includ-
    ing* Ma; −S)
53 mine] my C, W, B
56 we] to Q7
63 *Aside*] *om.* Q1
65 Ye] You C+(−Th, S, N)
65–66 it|——Soundly] ∼ _∧ ∼ Q1–
    8, F2, L, T, N

66 I warrant you] *om.* Q5–8, F2,
    L, T
71 Of] At T+(−S, N)
73 scape] escape Q6–8, F2, L
74 Unpossible] impossible Q8, T,
    C, W, M, B
86 beseiged] beseidge Q1
87 commaunded] commanded it T,
    C, W, Th, B
90 malice] male Q5
92 Brother_∧] ∼ ; Q6–8, F2, L
93 thus] this D, V, Th, S, N
96 scape] escape Q8
97 A] He F2+(−V, Th, S, N)
102 can] can not Q5–8, F2, L
103 fault] faults Q1
110 I] *om.* Q8
111 into ignorant] into an ignorant
    T+(−S, N)
124 Eaters] Facers Q1, T+
124 worth] world Q1
126 perisht] perish Q5
127 the] his V
132 The] *om.* Q5–7

138–139 Fellow,...selfe?] Fellow ∧ that hast spoke to me | Of it thy selfe. Q 1
145 Comes] Come Q 5–8
148 *Melantius.*] *Cal.* Q 3–8
149 *Calianax.*] *Mel.* Q 3–8
149 a] he Q 4+(−Th, S, N)
150 ins] in his Q 4–8, F 2, L, T
155 beare] beat Q 7
164 have] are L
165–166 this...peace,] *om.* Q 1
166 And...peace] And They have reapt the Fruit of it in Peace T
167 you] *om.* F 2, L
169 fetcht] fetch Q 5
170 as] is Q 6–8, F 2, L
174 not] *om.* Q 1
178 aside] *om.* Q 1
178 better] *om.* Q 7
181 deliver] belive Q 7
183 examine] example Q 7
184 Whilst] While T, C, W, B
184 he is] he Q 5; he's Q 6–8, F 2, L
184 if hee] he Q 5; he'l Q 6–8, F 2, L
189 A] *om.* Q 3+(−N)
190 *Melantius.*] *Kin.* Q 3–8, F 2, L
194 me to] me too, to Q 3+(−S, N)
201 away] way Q 7
203 *aside to him*] *Apart to him.* following *Calianax,* l. 201 W, D, M, Th, B
204 have] has Q 6–7; ha' Q 8
204 month] months Q 8
207 thus a] this Q 7
210 should] would Q 4–8, F 2, L, T
211 alls] alas Q 4–5
214 em...em] him...him Q 1–8, F 2, L, T, C, W, B

216 Tis] Too Q 1
216 well] we Q 7
222 arms] arme Q 1
222 and beleeve] *om.* Q 1
230 ye] you Q 2+(−N)
231 I doe...this,] Dost not thou... this? Q 1; Ay, | Do...this: C
232 For I] I feele | My selfe Q 1
234 extraordinarily] extremely Q 1, T
235 melt] meet Q 1
236 Unkindnesses] Unkindnesse Q 1
238 hurt] wrong Q 1
244 I call] is all Q 3+(−D, V, Th, S, N)
248 oth' King] oth' the King Q 1–4
252 thy] his Q 1
259 *Melantius,*] *om.* Q 2–8, F 2, L, C, W, B
265 not have] not not have Q 6
273 *Diphilus*] *Diph.* (*set out to rt. margin like stage-direction*) Q 3–5; *om.* Q 6–8, F 2, L
283 straine, if] Strain of you: if T
286 night spight] night in spight Q 5–8, F 2, L
300 refusest] refused Q 7
302 ye] you C, W, D, M, B
308 what thou] What 'tis thou T
310 *Aside*] *om.* Q 8
310 know hees] know, that he is T
314 up] *om.* Q 7
317 unto...nothing] to...not one T, Ma; to...nothing C, W, B
323 Theres] There is Q 6–8, F 2, L
324 in't] in it Q 6+(−Th, S, N)
326 will] *om.* Q 7
326.1 *Exeunt.*] *om.* Q 3–8, F 2, L

V.i

2 and let] and Sir let Q 1
8 then——] then methinkes. Q 1, D, V, M, Th, S, N

10 a long] along Q 7
11 *Exit.*] *om.* Q 5–8, F 2, L, T
14 virgin] virtue Q 1, V

16 woman] man Q6–8, F2, L
18 daring] madnesse Q1, N
19 fooles] mans Q1; foole Q4–8, F2, L, T
21 repent'em] prevent'm Q2–8, F2, L
24 a] he F2+(−V, Th, S, N)
24 oh God] good heavens Q2+ (−V, N)
26 hath] has Q1, N
26 long] farre Q1
27 And] *om.* Q7
28 Tels...it] Confirmes me that I merit Q1
30 rock] rake Q1
31 take] seaze Q1
32 punishments] punishment Q7
33 shape] shake Q3+(−D, V, M, Th, S, N)
35 Ile] I Q1
35 strike] strick Q2–3
36 not] hot Q8
36 your Grace] you Grace Q2
39 I...enough] As I beleeve I shall not, I shall fit him Q1
40 a] he F2+(−V, Th, S, N)
42 Sir,] *om.* T
48 you?...love₊] ~ ₊...~ ? Q1, 5–8, F2, L, N; ~ , ...~ , Q2–3; ~ ,...~ ? Q4
48 love] Life T

51 see] looke Q1
52 Stay] Say Q6–7
56 Here] There Q2+
56 thou shalt] you shalt Q4; you shall Q5–8, F2, L, T
63 How's this] How Q1
66 I am a] I a Q8
69 looke] seek T
73 too] two Q8
77 More] Most Q6
90 reach] teach Q5–8, F2, L
91 overcharge] overchange Q6–8, F2, L
95 his] is Q4
95 Heare] Here Q6–7
99 *Stabs him.*] *om.* Q1
103 villaine] villanie Q1
104 *Stabs him.*] *om.* Q2+(−N)
106 me, King] me, | King (*with* King *hanging below* me *in normal fashion for turned-over line*) Q1–6, 8; King (*set out to rt. margin as stage-direction following l.* 107) Q7; *om.* King F2, L
121–122 And...well.] *om.* Q1
123 dead. Treason] dead: Ho, Treason T
123 Treason, treason] Treason Q1
140 cals those] cals to those Q1
142 innocence] innocent Q6–8, F2, L

V.ii

0.1 *walls*] *Wall* Q5–8, F2, L
1 beleeve I] believe that I Q7
3 to] *om.* Q7
4 to] *om.* Q3+
14 cause,] ~ ; Q6–8, F2, L
18 certainly] certaine Q1, N
24 a] have Q6+(−V, N)
26 thee] you F2, L, T
29 that] *om.* Q7

30 to] *om.* Q2–8, F2, L, T, C, W, B, N
32 then honour] then of honor Q5
34 Some thinke] I'm sure Q1
34–36 yet...rascall.] *om.* Q1
37 those] whose Q3–8, F2, L, T, C, W, B
40 Whilst] While T, C, B

43 buy] begge Q 1, T, W, D, V, M,
   B; by Q 4–8, F 2, L
47 whore, and] Whore in her; and
   T
48 so)...selfe,] ~ ,...~) Q 1
49 I have] have I Q 6–8, F 2, L, T
50 to revenge∧] for revenge, Q 1
53 You wud] you'd F 2, L, T

57 free] freed Q 5–8, F 2, L, T
61 up] om. Q 6–8, F 2, L
66 honours] honour Q 6–8, F 2, L
67 Not] No Q 1–5, 8, N
67 pardons] pardon Q 5–8, F 2, L, T
69 all] om. Q 5–8, F 2, L, T
74 you] the Q 1

V.iii

4 a] om. Q 7
5 die] doe Q 1
8.1 Enter Servant.] om. Q 7
9 God] Cod Q 2
10 Sir ∧ now,] ~ ; ~ , Q 7
10 faire] om. Q 6–8, F 2, L
11 your] you F 2
15 I] om. Th
15 to] om. Q 3+(−Q 8, Th, S,
   N)
16 you longer] you any longer
   Q 5–8, F 2, L, T, C, W, B
18 will speake] will not speake Q 5
18–19 body, but...matters.] body.
   Q 2–8, F 2, L
25 women] woman Q 7, D, V, M, B
26 are harsh] are all harsh T, C, W,
   M, B
28 fond] found Q 5
29 and the] and Q 6–8, F 2, L
35 that that] that Q 7
39 chance] change Q 6–8, F 2, L
39 markt] marke Q 4–5
42 am the brother] am brother M
47 I] he Q 1+
49 hideous] odious Q 1
58 injuries] injurie Q 6–8, F 2, L, T,
   D, M
62 and would] and you would
   Q 6–8, F 2, L
80 my] mine Q 4+(−C, Th, S, N)
84 For her] For here L
88 I] om. Q 6–8, F 2, L

92 a timelesse] a timely Q 6–7, F 2,
   L; timely Q 8
94 has] hath F 2+(−V, S, N)
101 houre] honour Q 5–8, F 2, L
104 thy] thine Q 1
106 there is] ther's Q 5–8, F 2, L
107.1 her...knife] om. Q 1
115 lookes] bookes Q 1 (u)
116 staid] stald Q 1
122 within] inside M
123 now] how N
125 it] is L
131 his] this Q 6–8, F 2, L, T
132 found one] found out one Q 6–8,
   F 2, L, T, W, B
134 continued] continuall Q 5–8, F 2,
   L
138 calme] tame Q 1
139 a way] away Q 1 (u), 5
146 by his] by a Th, S
147–149 and...shed:] om. Q 1
149 Violently] Most violently T
158 of crueltie] of all Cruelty T, V
159 sharper] crueller Q 1
163 not] om. Q 7
163 Gods] heavens Q 3+(−Th, S,
   N)
165 In] Ith' T
168 womans] womens Q 7, F 2, L, T
169 now] once Q 5–8, F 2, L, T
171 Evadne∧] ~ . (indented like
   speech-prefix) Q 7
174 it] om. Q 6–8, F 2

175 *She dies.*] *om.* Q1
182 flesh] selfe Q1
182 unto] into Q2–4, 6–8, F2, L
191 another] *om.* Q6–8, F2, L
192 her selfe] *om.* Q6–8, F2, L
205 Staid...it was] Did stay... t'was Q3+(−S, N)
206 Thou art] Th'art Q3–8, F2, L, T, C
211 sure] surely Q3–4, C, W, B; *om.* Q5–8, F2, L
213 lives] lines Q1–8, F2, L
213 excuse] expiate T, Ma, V
221 thine] thy Q4+(−V, Th, N)
221 mine] my C, W, B
221 hand...hands] hands...hand Q7
221 hands grope] eyes grow Q1
224 *Amintor.*] *om.* Q7
227 sounds] swounds Q6–8, F2, D; swoons L+(−D, Th, V, N)
227 Gods] heavens Q3+(−Th, S, N)
228 life ever] life for ever Q6–8, F2, L
229 helpe? yet‸] ~ ‸ ~ ? C+(−S, N)
230 there] theres Q4+(−Q7, N); theirs Q7

231 her *Amintor*] her that *Amintor* Q6–8, F2, L
233 any] *om.* Q5–8, F2, L
238 You] Ye C, W, B
238 forth] for Q3+(−V, N)
242 The] Thy Q8
246 God] heaven Q3–8, F2, L, T, C, D, M
246.1 Cleon] *om.* Q1
248 *Strato.*] *Serv.* C+(−Th, S, N)
261 was worth] was more worth T
263 your sister] our sister T
265 of] to Th
268 there] *om.* Q8
269 last is said] senses fade Q3–8, F2, L
273 My] *om.* Q1
281 all now] *om.* Q2–8, F2, L, T, C, W, B
282 live] line Q3
283 *Exit.*] *om.* Q2–8, F2, L, T, C, W, B
286 hands] hand Q6–8, F2, L, T, C, W, B
286 sharpe] good Q4–8, F2, L, T, D, V, M
294 God] heaven Q3+(−Th, S, N)

A KING AND
NO KING

edited by

GEORGE WALTON WILLIAMS

TEXTUAL INTRODUCTION

A King and No King (Greg, *Bibliography*, no. 360) was entered to Edward Blount in the Stationers' Register on 7 August 1618. So far as is now known, Blount did not exercise his licence to publish the play. Greg has suggested that Blount's entry was a blocking entry (*Shakespeare First Folio* [1955], p. 154, n. 1), and the actors may have thought that for a play of proven popularity, such a safeguard was necessary. Whatever the purpose of the entry, Blount evidently transferred or relinquished his privilege (without record) to Thomas Walkley who issued a quarto of the play in 1619. This is the earliest quarto extant.

The printer of this 1619 edition is not named, but, on the basis of the ornaments, Greg has suggested that the quarto was from the shop of John Beale. Mr Turner has analysed the printing of the quarto in detail.[1] He finds that sheets B through (half-sheet) M were composed *seriatim*, and that sheet A was cast off and set after M. The composition was the work of two compositors, one setting sheets B–G, the other sheets H–M and A. No distinguishing features between the two compositors (other than mechanical) were discovered. 'No particular difficulties', he notes, 'were encountered in setting up the text.'

The copy for Q1 appears to have been a scribal transcript, presumably made for a person of quality. Walkley writes in dedicating the play to Sir Henry Nevill: 'I present, or rather returne unto your view, that which formerly hath beene received from you, hereby effecting what you did desire.' Such language strongly suggests that Nevill desired Walkley to print the play, that Walkley received from Nevill the copy of the play, and that, in printing the play, Walkley was returning unto Nevill the copy of the play— now in a printed form. Such a reconstruction may be too exact, but the general impression remains that Nevill owned a transcript of the play which he made available to Walkley. (It is possible that

---

[1] Robert K. Turner, Jr., 'The Printing of *A King and No King* Q1', *Studies in Bibliography*, XVIII (1965), 255–61. See Addendum, page 181 below.

Walkley's threat to publish this copy of the play provoked the blocking entry by Blount.)

Six years after the publication of Q 1 appeared the second quarto, published by Walkley in 1625. Once again no printer is mentioned, but the ornaments indicate that the volume was printed with the stock of Thomas Snodham.[1] The normal expectation is that the second quarto would have been printed from the first; it is indeed a line-for-line reprint. Miss Berta Sturman has demonstrated bibliographical links between the two quartos in ten prose passages throughout the play.[2] Because Q 2 exhibits additions to Q 1 that would seem to stem from the theatrical prompt-book, Miss Sturman has ingeniously argued that the copy for Q 2 was an exemplar of Q 1 that had been annotated for use as a prompt-book by the King's Men. The title-page of Q 2 advertises the play as *'And now the second time Printed, according to the true Copie.'*, and Miss Sturman conjectures that the '*true Copie*' is this prompt-book. This theory accounts neatly for the many theatrical directions that appear in Q 2, but, as Mr Turner has observed, it must be modified to account for the considerable number of literary variants that also appear in Q 2. His modification supposes that an exemplar of Q 1 was compared 'with some authoritative manuscript—the foul papers, the fair copy, or, most likely, the manuscript promptbook itself'.[3] On the

[1] I am indebted to Mr Thomas L. Berger for this identification. He has found the four ornaments in Q 2 (1625) in the following prints by Snodham also: title page ornament (on A 1) in *S.T.C.* 7328 (1624), headpiece (on A 3) in *S.T.C.* 18280 (1623), initial (on A 3) in *S.T.C.* 7466 (1624), tailpiece (on M 3) in *S.T.C.* 16691 (1621). (Strangely, the woodcut of the hand from heaven withdrawing the crown from the King's head does not reappear in any of the later editions of the play [Greg, *Bibliography*, Plate LXVII].) Two difficulties to the attribution of the actual printing to Snodham present themselves: Snodham died in the autumn of 1625; his products were chiefly theological, and he had printed no plays since 1613. Snodham's stock was transferred after his death, but the details are not now clear. Mr Berger has not found Snodham ornaments in 1626 and 1627; they reappear in work from Thomas Harper in 1628. Attempts to identify what appears to be the single compositor of Q 2 elsewhere in Snodham's work have not been successful.

[2] Berta Sturman, 'The Second Quarto of *A King and No King*, 1625', *Studies in Bibliography*, IV (1951–2), 166–70. That Q 2 was indeed printed from Q 1 can be demonstrated also by the high degree of analogy in capitalization in verse passages throughout the play.

[3] Robert K. Turner, Jr., ed. *A King and No King* (Lincoln: University of Nebraska Press, 1963), p. xxviii.

assumption that the actors would be unwilling to give up a prompt-book to the printer, and on the basis of the actual variants, Mr Turner's hypothesis is perhaps the sounder of the two.

The nature and treatment of the copy for Q2 are indeed the most important problems in establishing the text of *A King and No King*; something can be determined about that copy by comparison with Q1. To Miss Sturman the most striking feature of the copy for Q2 is its theatrical quality: 'the additions which have been made to Q1 consist of marginalia which seem to be all of a prompt nature' (p. 169). She finds in Q2 not present in Q1[1] one descriptive direction ('*Beates him.*' at V.i.90) and sixteen entry or exit directions. (Four of these contain '*Flourishes*' to announce the arrival and departure of the Kings; there are none in Q1.) Twenty-eight other directions are expanded, often by the addition of the name of the character (*e.g.* Q1 '*Exit.*', Q2 '*Exit Bessus.*'). More significant expansions are exemplified by these (the Q2 addition is here printed in italics):

I.i.o.1	Enter Mardonius and Bessus, *two Captaines*.
III.i.38.1	Ent. *1 Gent. and* Tigranes.
IV.ii.o.1	Enter Tigranes *in prison*.
IV.ii.238.1	Exeunt *all*.
IV.iv.163.1	Exeunt *cleere*.
V.ii.93.1	Exeunt *all*.
V.iii.108.1	Exeunt *cleere*.
V.iv.326	Enter Pan*thæa and 1 Gent*.

Three other directions offer little improvement on the Q1 forms. At II.ii.21.1, for Q1 'Philip' Q2 reads 'a man'. At II.ii.151.1, Q2 provides exit direction for only two of the three Men who must leave. At III.i.319.1, the Latin form of Q1 is discarded, and the names of those remaining are replaced by the names of those leaving.

Though not all of these additions are of a prompt nature, most of them are clearly designed to provide greater accuracy in

---

[1] Berta Sturman, 'Renaissance Prompt] Copies' (unpublished doctoral dissertation, University of Chicago, 1947), pp. 90–1.

performance and thus may be taken to suggest a theatrical provenience. Three, at least, would seem to support the theory well,
the two '*Exeunt cleere.*' forms and the added direction at V.iii.81
'*Enter Servant, Will. Adkinson:*'.[1]

More remarkable than this situation is the very considerable
degree of linguistic and textual variance between the two quartos.
Mr Hoy has shown that Q 1 exhibits an exclusive preference for the
um spelling over the *em* spelling of the contracted form of *them*; it
also greatly favours the contracted form over the full form.[2] The
distribution is as follows:[3]

48	*um* forms in Q 1 appear in Q 2 as:	them (3)	
		'em (44)	
		um (1)	
19	*them* forms in Q 1 appear in Q 2 as:	them (11)	
		'em (8)	
		um (0)	

Nearly all of the *um* forms are changed to *em* forms in Q 2. It is a
safe assumption that this linguistic change is due to the compositor
of Q 2 and not to the scribe annotating Q 1, and support for this
assumption can be found in the identical pattern of normalization
by other compositors of reprints in the canon.[4] Furthermore, there
is in Q 2 a high degree of fidelity to the Q 1 contracted form (93%);
in the light of this evidence, it is significant that one Q 1 *um* form
was expanded in Q 2 to *them* in order to justify the line (IV.ii.156)
in the line-for-line reprint:

Q 1   *Arb.* Take um away both, and together let um be priso-|ners
Q 2   *Arb.* Take 'em away both, and together let them priso-|ners bee

[1] Adkinson was presumably one of the hired men in the company (T. W. Baldwin,
Organization and Personnel of the Shakespearean Company [Princeton, 1927], p. 142).
[2] Cyrus Hoy, 'The Shares of Fletcher and his Collaborators in the Beaumont and
Fletcher Canon (III)', *Studies in Bibliography*, XI (1958), 85–106.
[3] Mr Hoy's count for Q 1 is 49 *um* forms and 21 *them* forms; I have found 22 *them*
forms (the extra one in III.i). Of these totals, Q 2 omits one *um* form and 3 *them* forms.
These figures do not include the *um* forms that are not abbreviations of *them* (I.i.33,
III.ii.51–3).
[4] Mr Hoy has pointed to this normalization in other reprints ('Shares (III)', *SB*,
XI [1958], 98–9).

Finally, there is only moderate fidelity to the Q 1 long form (58%). One contraction from Q 1 *them* to Q 2 *'em* was presumably also made for justification (III.ii.13–14):

Q 1 monstrous stomacke to abuse them againe, and did it. In this
Q 2 monstrous stomacke to abuse 'em againe, and did it. I' this

Two other contractions to *'em* (I.i.10, 42) can probably be traced to the same cause. The need for justification is compositorial (not scribal), and these four changes can be attributed with some confidence to the compositor of Q 2 and not to the scribe preparing the copy for him. In support of this attribution it is to be noted that the length of the line is three millimetres shorter in Q 2 than in Q 1.[1] One can then tentatively argue that the compositor of Q 2 took upon himself to normalize the spelling of *um*; he also assumed that he had the authority to contract *them* or to expand *um* as he saw fit, and he made such changes eleven times. One might suggest more tentatively that having made this assumption, the compositor assumed further that he had the authority to contract (and therefore to expand) other forms. In the example quoted above, a case can be made for a compositorial origin of *I' this* at the end of the line; another example of contraction discloses the same liberty taken (I.i.219):

Q 1   *Mar.* By my Troth thou wouldst have sunke um both
Q 2   *Mar.* By my troth, thou would'st ha stuncke 'em both

In order to preserve the line-for-line reprint, when the two new letters of the authorial *stuncke* had to be fitted in, two letters of the verb *have* had to be dropped. The same change occurs again also for justification at II.ii.65.

Many changes in the linguistic pattern were, however, not made for reasons of justification; in the line immediately preceding that just quoted (I.i.218) Q 1 *with you* is contracted in Q 2 to *wi' you* in

[1] Sturman, 'Second Quarto', p. 166. An examination of the prose lines in Q 1 and Q 2 suggests that the Q 2 compositor found a loose line in Q 1 readily accommodated to the smaller measure of Q 2; a tighter Q 1 line called for a little adjustment, often the dropping of an *e* from a double *ee* pronoun. It is worth noting the priority in this matter in the line below (I.i.219): to this compositor the *c* and *e* (from *stuncke*) were more important than *ve* (from *have*).

spite of plenty of blank space in the line. At V.iii.93 Q1 *ha* is expanded to Q2 *have* for no apparent reason. Q2 has a much higher proportion of contracted forms than does Q1, and it is clear that many of the contractions are not directly related to the need for justification. I would argue, however, that the general need for reducing the number of characters in a line of type and the presence of occasional contractions made by the scribe in annotating Q1 encouraged the compositor of Q2 to adopt the position that contractions were at his command; I would therefore argue further that most of the Q2 contractions of linguistic forms are without authority.[1] I would then hazard the guess that some textual variants of little importance, such as *no/Nay* (I.i.133), *Enough/I'now* (I.i.458), *laden/loden* (I.i.484), are also his responsibility. Where the limits of compositorial innovation are to be defined is a matter of editorial judgment. Many substantive variants in Q2 are certainly authoritative and essential to the text; others, I am satisfied, derive from the compositor of Q2.

The first quarto is thus the copy-text. The scribe who made the transcript behind it copied the Fletcherian *um* spelling (it was perhaps his own preference as it appears also in the Beaumont scenes), tended to reduce the number of *ye* spellings (reduced even further, from seven to one, by Q2), but reproduced the general quality of contractions in his copy.[2] The annotator of Q1, preparing an exemplar for a new edition, introduced many theatrical matters (he was perhaps not a man of the theatre) and corrected many of the errors of Q2; he seems not to have transferred the linguistic pattern of the manuscript prompt-book to his exemplar. The compositor of Q2 followed his own preferences in linguistic distinctions, allowing his casual attitude to the minute details of his copy to influence his fidelity in more significant substantive matters.

From the first substantive and authoritative quarto and thence

---

[1] This judgment differs from that reached by Mr Hoy ('Shares (I)', *SB*, VIII, [1956], 137–8), but the alternative hypothesis—that the annotator of Q1 changed these minute linguistic details—is hardly to be believed.

[2] The ascriptions of authorship made by Mr Hoy and by earlier critics I have found no evidence to change: Beaumont, I, II, III, IV.iv, V.ii, iv; Fletcher, IV.i, ii, iii, V.i, iii.

the second quarto, in part authoritative, depend all the subsequent editions of the play—six quarto editions and an edition in the second folio (1679). As may be seen from the diagram, the stemma of these printed editions is less straightforward than is usual in these matters.[1]

Q 1
|
Q 2
/   \
Q 3   Q 7
| |
Q 4   Q 8
|
Q 5
/   \
Q 6   F 2

The deterioration of text has been abnormally aggravated in the printing history of *A King and No King* by the pinch-penny attitude of the printer of Q 5 (1655) to run speeches together and to print all as prose after V.i.43 and much as prose before then. This attitude was given currency and prestige by the fact that the second folio decided to print the play from Q 5, giving thereby to the many errors of Q 5 a specious authority that persisted through the eighteenth century. This decision was the more unfortunate because the most recent quarto, Q 7 1676, had with intelligence and sensi-tivity rejected all of the 'modern' reprints and had returned to Q 2 for its copy.

For the present edition the copy-text (Q 1) has been collated historically with the subsequent quartos, with the second folio, and with the editions of Langbaine (1711), Theobald–Seward–

---

[1] But see the transmission of *Philaster*, Vol. I, p. 370.

Sympson (1750), Colman (1778), Weber (1812),[1] Dyce (1843), the Mermaid Series (ed. J. St Loe Strachey, 1887), the Bullen Variorum (ed. R. Warwick Bond, 1904), the Belles-Lettres Series (ed. Raymond M. Alden, 1910), *Early Seventeenth-Century Plays* (ed. H. R. Walley and J. H. Wilson; New York, 1930), and the Regents Renaissance Drama (ed. E. K. Turner, Jr., 1963).

The present text is based on the Folger Shakespeare Library exemplar of Q1 collated with the six other copies of Q1, all that are known to exist: British Museum, Dyce Collection—Victoria and Albert Museum, Bodleian Library, Boston Public Library, Harvard University Library, Henry E. Huntington Library.

A special comment should be given to the exemplar of Q1 in the Dyce Collection in the Victoria and Albert Museum, on which Dyce based his edition. (This exemplar is reproduced in the University Microfilms series, *English Books 1475–1640*.) This exemplar contains about 60 substantive corrections in a seventeenth-century hand; the authority for them is unknown, but they are evidently very early and independent of any printed text. It is possible that they derive from a now lost manuscript or from the recollection of a performance (in such a case they would probably be merely actors' interpolations); a few seem beyond the sensitive correction that an intelligent reader might make to his copy of a popular play that he had admired and enjoyed.

The following manuscript corrections agree with seventeenth-century editions (Q2 except where noted): I.i.111 Tigr. (speech-prefix), 268 too, 420 hast, 507.1 Exeunt; ii.9 high, 18 thee; II.i.223 him, 303 my; III.i.117–18 (five speech prefixes), 206 rage, 270.1 Exit; ii.58 Bess., 77 refer'd, 80 these fi[ve] ye[ars] (Q4); iii.32 a fall, 85 haires; IV.i.16 gainst; ii.64 Spa., 167 Sutlers, 181 till, 212 of (*omit*); iii.100 againe (*omit*), 110 kicker, 119 foote; iv.81 even; V.i.10 Offices, 94 Bes., 129 Bes.; iii.36 Bac.; iv.21 Mar., 93 I (*omit*), 103 Ar. Q1(c), 191 Ara. Q1(c), 349 you (F2).

Of the remaining corrections the following have independently been advanced by later editors:

[1] Weber's edition of the play was based on the copy of the first quarto now in the Boston Public Library. As Mr Turner has noted, that exemplar contains only sheets A–D from Q1; the remainder of the volume consists of sheets from Q3. Weber's textual judgments after II.ii.95 are thus bibliographically misinformed.

I.i.260   I am growne To talke but idlie,] There is an extensive note by
Theobald on this 'beautiful' emendation by Seward (edition pp. 187–8, but
cf. pp. 375–6); Dyce accepts Seward's emendation, supported by the manuscript (p. 246), as does Bond, though Bond has misgivings. Mr Turner
argues for the rejected Q1 reading. The misreading of 'idelie' as 'i desir' is
by no means impossible. It may be noted that the construction 'I am growne'
appears also in line 248 above, and the phrase 'talk idlie' appears in V.ii.71
(see also II.i.264).

I.i.352–3   then As much as now] Langbaine was the first to introduce 'then'
for Q1 'though'. Dyce followed Q1 reluctantly (p. 249); Bond also printed
'though', glossing it to mean 'then'. The error in Q1 can be explained thus:
manuscript 'then', misread (easily) as 'thou', misprinted in Q1 'though'
(followed by all seventeenth-century editions). The same variant occurs
also at V.iv.163.

II.i.o.1–2 *and waiting women*] The manuscript has deleted the name of Mandane
in the direction, as she is evidently a ghost character. Dyce was the first to
delete the character (p. 236). Bond notes that the name appears in Herodotus'
Cyropaedia, and Mr Turner suggests that Mandane may have been intended
as the confidante to Panthæa, but that 'her role was suppressed in favor of
Spaconia's' (p. xxix).

II.i.252   That will not talke] This fairly obvious emendation for the 'take'
of the early editions was first made by Theobald and has been generally
accepted (Dyce, p. 266).

IV.ii.179–80   rock't Into a dead sleepe] Seward's emendation of 'rott' has
been accepted by all editors except Alden. Theobald points out that the
'finely imagin'd' emendation 'is sufficiently confirm'd by the three Verses
that follow'.

V.i.8   You seeme a worthy person] Though Mason advanced the emendation of 'seeme' from 'serve' in 1798, Dyce was the first to print it (p. 322).
He has been followed by most editors. In support of the emendation, it
may be noted that Q1 contains several *v/m* misreadings from its manuscript
copy. The following Q1 readings (to the left of the virgule) are all corrected
in Q2: I.i.179 times/lives, III.ii.80 time/five, IV.i.67 have/tame, IV.ii.200
have/tame.

V.iii.14   one whose dull bodie will require a lamming] For Q1 'launcing'
or Q2 'laming', Weber substituted the emendation 'lamming', 'a phrase
still usual for a *beating*', and noticed the word in the *Honest Man's Fortune*,
V.ii. Dyce followed Weber, supported by the manuscript correction 'lam-
myng' in his quarto (p. 330). Subsequent editors have not concurred on a
single reading. If 'launcing' is the correct reading, then it must follow that
the scribe annotating Q1 as copy for Q2 misread his manuscript with the

correct word printed before him in Q1. Such an hypothesis is untenable. If 'laming' is the correct reading, then it must follow that the compositor of Q1 misread the three minims of 'm', expanding them into the five minims of 'unc'. Such an error is not likely. If 'lamming' is correct, the Q1 compositor misread six minims as five, the annotator corrected with insufficient clarity, and the Q2 compositor misread or misprinted. On the whole, the last hypothesis seems the most reasonable. The passage at V.i.66–7 ('if a laming of him. . . may doe you pleasure') seemed to Dyce to be comparable, and he suggested that here too 'lamming' was intended; Bond and Walley-Wilson adopted Dyce's conjecture. There is hardly textual justification for this emendation.

In addition to these seven emendations, several others seemed to Dyce worthy of particular notice:

III.ii.68–9   I thinke there will be more after him, then before him, I thinke so: pray ye commend me. . .] The annotator has deleted the second 'I thinke'; Dyce (p. 288) queried: 'did these words creep into the text by a mistake of the original compositor, his eye having caught them from the preceding line?' Bond replied: 'this feigned hesitation about accuracy is Bessus' usual cover for a lie' (p. 298).

III.iii.53   but I can onlie see her then] Dyce observed that the annotator's 'shall' 'seems to be the better reading' (p. 292).

IV.iii.104   musted my dear brother?] Dyce observed: *Musted* 'may, perhaps, be right; but I have felt strongly inclined to alter it to "must,"—as the early possessor of my copy of the first 4to. has done' (p. 314).

V.i.31   the sinne of coward] Dyce called attention to the fact that the annotator had emended 'sinne' to 'name'. The *s/n* misreading is not a very likely one.

Two emendations appear to the present editor of interest and merit:

V.i.99–100 (Q1, Q2)
    Ile beat your Captaines braines out,
    Wash um, and put um in againe, that will I.

The annotator reads:

    Ile beat your Captaines braines out,
    Wash um, and put um in againe who will.

V.i.131–2 (Q1, Q2)
    Now let him come, and say he was not sorry,
    and he sleepes for it.

The annotator reads:

> Now let him come, and say he was not sorry,
> and he sleepes for it. heer's poppie for him.

Neither of these emendations gives the impression of having been invented by an intelligent reader and added to the text whimsically; they both point to some external source of unknown authority.

The remaining readings are less interesting or more disputable (the MS reading is given following the Q1 text):

III.i.4   Why *Gobrius* let her;
             Why *Gobrius* tel her;

III.i.46   Too safe I am Sir.
             Too safe I am sure.

III.i.55   As white as innocence her selfe.
             As white as innocence it selfe.

III.i.141   (Q1) Is a long life of yet I hope:
             (MS) Is yet a long life of I hope:
             (Q2) Is a long life off, I hope:

III.ii.122   Ile beate thee into spunge
             Ile beate thee into a spunge

IV.i.20   How farre he has beene asunder
             How farre h's beene asunder

IV.i.52   For that is all the businesse of my life now:
             For that is all my unhappy stars have left me.

IV.ii.32–3   So strong and violent, that should I see her
             Againe, the griefe, and that would kill me Ladie.

             So strong and violent, that should I see Spaconia
                the griefe of that would kill me.

[Evidently in this passage, 'Spaconia' was intended as part of line 33, though written at the end of 32. 'Ladie' which Q2 attributes rightly to the following speech is here deleted.]

V.i.52   Since hee was first a slave
                         Since [I fi]rst knewe him

V.iii.74   (Q1) Whats that in your pocket slave, my key
             (MS) Whats that in your pocket slave,
             (Q2) What's that in your potcket slave, my toe

12-2

V.iv.277–8   (Q1)   Is it to me? in good faith it must not be:
           (MS)   Is it to me? good faith it must not be:
           (Q2)   Is it to me? I sweare it must not be:
                   Nay, trust me, in good faith it must not be;

The final example of this list demonstrates conclusively that the annotator was not consulting any printed text subsequent to Q1, because all such prints contain at this passage two half-lines omitted from Q1 by the compositor's eyeskip. I assume, therefore, that the annotator of the Dyce exemplar compared his copy of the first quarto with a manuscript differing from the transcript belonging to Nevill and from the prompt-book belonging to the company. I posit a third early seventeenth-century manuscript behind this exemplar, and I attribute to it some authority. Where the Dyce annotator agrees with the seventeenth-century editions or with later editors (independent of influence from this manuscript), I have regarded such agreement as sufficient cause to emend the copy-text.

The list of 'Personated Persons', given first in Q3, is reprinted in all subsequent seventeenth-century editions, including Q7 and Q8. (The fact that Q7 contains the list demonstrates that the printer had not only Q2 at hand, but one of quartos 3–6 also.) Q7 (1676) adds the names of the actors 'As it is now Acted at the Theatre Royal, by His Majesties Servants' (Q8 (1693) reprints the list but reads 'Their Majesties Servants'): *Arbaces* Mr Hart., *Tigranes* Mr Kynaston, *Gobrius* Mr Wintershall, *Bacurius* Mr Lydall, *Mardonius* Mr Mohun, *Bessus* Mr Lacy or Mr Shottrell, *Ligones* Mr Cartwright, *Two Sword-men* Mr Watson and Mr Haynes, *Arane* Mrs Corey, *Panthæa* Mrs Cox, *Spaconia* Mrs Marshall.

ADDENDUM

Since these pages were set in type, Dr. Hans Walter Gabler has kindly shown me his notes refining the compositor analysis referred to here (page 169). He supports Mr. Turner's argument that a new compositor began to set in sheet H, and, on the basis of the different spellings of *shee* and *she*, he marks the beginning of the stint at H2^v. He distinguishes, furthermore, three different workmen in the section B-H2. One compositor set sheet B; he is identified by the *bee* spelling of the verb (*be*) and by his preference for the *-y* ending for nouns and adjectives. A second compositor set sheet C and signature D1; he is identified by the *be* spelling and by his preference for the *-ie* ending for nouns and adjectives. A third compositor set signature D1^v through H2; he is identified by the *be* spelling and by a mixture of *-y* and *-ie* endings for nouns and adjectives. Signatures L4^v through A4^v may have been composed by a collaborative effort of the several workmen. As the changes following B4^v, D1, and H2 are clearly related to bibliographical divisions and not to authorial or, one supposes, scribal, Dr. Gabler's thesis is persuasive; but it could be wished that the distinguishing characteristics of these three men were more numerous.

[The Personated Persons

ARBACES, King of Iberia
TIGRANES, King of Armenia
GOBRIUS, Lord Protector of Iberia, father of Arbaces
BACURIUS, a lord
MARDONIUS
BESSUS } Captains in the Iberian army
LIGONES, an Armenian statesman, father of Spaconia
PHILIP, servant of a Citizen's Wife
TWO SWORD-MEN
THREE MEN
A BOY, servant of Bessus
ARANE, the Iberian Queen Mother
PANTHÆA, her daughter
SPACONIA, an Armenian lady, daughter of Ligones
TWO CITIZENS' WIVES
A WOMAN
GENTLEMEN, ATTENDANTS, SERVANTS, MESSENGERS, CITIZENS, WAITING WOMEN

Scene: Armenia, Iberia.]

The Personated Persons] *based on the list in* Q3; *om.* Q1–2

To the right worshipfull, and worthie Knight,
SIR HENRIE NEVILL

WORTHY SIR,
I present, or rather returne unto your view, that which formerly hath beene received from you, hereby effecting what you did desire. To commend the worke in my unlearned method, were rather to detract from it, then to give it any luster. It sufficeth it hath your Worships approbation and patronage, to the commendation of the Authors, and incouragement of their further labours: and thus wholy committing my selfe and it to your Worships dispose I rest, ever readie to doe you service, not onely in the like, but in what I may.

Thomas Walkley.

A King and
no King

Enter Mardonius *and* Bessus.   [I. i]

Mardonius.   *Bessus*, the KING has made a fayre hand on't, has ended the warres at a blow: would my sword had a close basket hilt to hold wine, and the blade would make knives, for we shall have nothing but eating and drinking.

Bessus.   We that are commanders shall doe well enough.

Mardonius.   Faith *Bessus*, such commanders as thou may, I had as live set thee *Perdue* for a pudding yth darke, as *Alexander* the great.

Bessus.   I love these jests exceedingly.

Mardonius.   I thinke thou lov'st them better then quarrelling 10 *Bessus*, Ile say so much ythy behalfe, and yet thou art valiant enough upon a retreate, I thinke thou wouldst kill any man that stopt thee, and thou couldst.

Bessus.   But was not this a brave combate *Mardonius*?

Mardonius.   Why, didst thou see't?

Bessus. You stood with me.

Mardonius. I did so, but me thought thou winkst every blowe they strake.

Bessus. Well, I beleeve there are better Souldiers then I, that never saw two Princes fight in lists.   20

Mardonius. By my troth I thinke so too *Bessus*, many a thousand, but certenly all that are worse then thou have seene as much.

Bessus. Twas bravely done of our King.

Mardonius. Yes, if he had not ended the warres: I am glad thou darst talke of such dangerous businesses.

Bessus. To take a Prince prisoner in the heart of his owne Countrey in single combate.

Mardonius. See how thy bloud cruddles at this, I thinke thou wouldst be contented to be beaten in this passion.

Bessus. Shall I tell you trulie?   30

Mardonius. I.

Bessus. I could willingly venter for it.

Mardonius. Um, no venter neither good *Bessus*.

Bessus. Let me not live, if I doe not thinke it is a braver peece of service, then that Ime so fam'd for.

Mardonius. Why, art thou fam'd for any valour?

Bessus. I fam'd? I, I warrant you.

Mardonius. I am verie heartily glad on't, I have beene with thee ever since thou cam'st ath' warres, and this is the first word that ever I heard on't, prethee who fames thee?   40

Bessus. The Christian world.

Mardonius. Tis heathenishly done of them, in my conscience thou deserv'st it not.

Bessus. Yes, I ha done good service.

Mardonius. I doe not know how thou maist waite of a man in's Chamber, or thy agilitie in shifting a trencher, but otherwise no service good *Bessus*.

Bessus. You saw me doe the service your selfe.

Mardonius. Not so hastie sweet *Bessus*, where was it, is the place vanisht?   50

Bessus. At *Bessus* desperate redemption.

Mardonius. *Bessus* desperate redemption, wher's that?

184

Bessus.   There where I redeemd the day, the place beares my name.

Mardonius.   Prethee who christned it?

Bessus.   The Souldier.

Mardonius.   If I were not a very merrily dispos'd man, what would become of thee: one that had but a graine of coller in the whole composition of his body, would send thee of an arrand to the wormes, for putting thy name upon that field: did not I beat 60 thee there yth head a'th troupes with a trunchion, because thou wouldst needs run away with thy company, when we should charge the enemie?

Bessus.   True, but I did not runne.

Mardonius.   Right *Bessus*, I beat thee out on't.

Bessus.   But came not I up when the day was gone, and redeem'd all?

Mardonius.   Thou knowst, and so doe I, thou meant'st to flie, and thy feare making thee mistake, thou ranst upon the enemie, and a hot charge thou gav'st, as Ile doe thee right, thou art furious in 70 running away, and I thinke we owe thy feare for our victorie. If I were the King, and were sure thou wouldst mistake alwayes, and runne away uppon the enemie, thou shouldst be Generall by this light.

Bessus.   Youle never leave this till I fall foule.

Mardonius.   No more such words deare *Bessus*: for though I have ever knowne thee a coward, and therefore durst never strike thee; yet if thou proceedst, I will allow thee valiant, and beate thee.

Bessus.   Come, come, our King's a brave fellow.

Mardonius.   He is so *Bessus*, I wonder how thou com'st to know 80 it: But if thou wert a man of understanding, I would tell thee he is vain-glorious, and humble, and angrie, and patient, and merrie, and dull, and joyfull, and sorrowfull, in extreamities in an houre: Doe not thinke mee thy friend for this, for if I car'd who knew it, thou shouldst not heare it *Bessus*: here hee is with the prey in his foote.

57   merrily] Q2 (merily); meerely Q1
68   meant'st] Q2; mean'st Q1

185

Senet. Flourish.

Enter Arbaces *and* Tigranes, *with* [*two* Gentlemen *and*] *attendants.*

Arbaces.   Thy sadnesse (brave *Tigranes*) takes away
  From my full victorie; am I become
  Of so small fame, that any man should grieve
  When I orecome him? They that plac't me here,   90
  Intended it an honour large enough
  For the most valiant living, but to dare
  Oppose me single, though he lost the day.
  What should afflict you, you are free as I:
  To be my prisoner, is to be more free
  Then you were formerlie; and never thinke
  The man I held worthy to combat me,
  Shall be us'd servilly: Thy ransome is
  To take my onely sister to thy wife;
  A heavy one *Tigranes*: for shee is   100
  A Ladie that the neighbour Princes send
  Blanks to fetch home: I have beene too unkind
  To her *Tigranes*: shee but nine yeere old,
  I left her, and nere saw her since: your warres
  Have held me long, and taught me, though a youth,
  The way to victorie: shee was a pretty childe
  Then, I was little better; but now fame
  Cries loudly on her, and my Messengers
  Make me beleeve shee is a miracle;
  Sheele make you shrinke as I did, with a stroke   110
  But of her eye *Tigranes*.
Tigranes.   Is it the course of
Iberia, to use their prisoners thus?
  Had Fortune throwne my name above *Arbaces,*
  I should not thus have talkt; for in *Armenia*
  We hold it base: you should have kept your temper,

86.1 *Senet. Flourish.*] Q2; *om.* Q1
88 full] Q2; fall Q1
111 S.P. *Tigranes.*] Q2 (*Tigr.*); *om.* Q1

186

Till you saw home agen; where tis the fashion
Perhaps to brag.
Arbaces.   Bee you my witnesse Earth:
Neede I to brag, doth not this captive Prince
Speake me sufficiently, and all the Acts
That I have wrought upon his suffering Land?   120
Should I then boast? Where lies that foot of ground
Within his whole Realme, that I have not past
Fighting, and Conquering? Farre then from mee
Be ostentation: I could tell the World
How I have laid his Kingdome desolate
With this sole arme, propt by Divinity,
Stript him out of his glories, and have sent
The pride of all his youth to people graves,
And made his Virgins languish for their loves;
If I would brag. Should I that have the power   130
To teach the Neighbour world humility,
Mix with vaine glory?
Mardonius [*aside*].   In deede this is none?
Arbaces.   *Tigranes*, no; did I but take delight
To stretch my deedes as others doe on words,
I could amaze my hearers.
Mardonius [*aside*].   So you doe.
Arbaces.   But he shall wrong his, and my modesty
That thinkes me apt to boast: After an Act
Fit for a God to doe upon his foe,
A little glory in a Souldiers mouth,
Is well becomming, bee it farre from vaine.   140
Mardonius [*aside*].   Its pitty that valour should be thus
      drunke.
Arbaces.   I offer you my Sister, and you answere,
I doe insult: A Lady that no suit
Nor treasure, nor thy Crowne could purchase thee,
But that thou faughtst with mee.
Tigranes.   Though this bee worse
Then that you spoke before, it strikes not mee:

185 faughtst] Q2; faughst Q1

187

But that you thinke to over-grace mee with
The marriage of your Sister, troubles mee;
I would give worlds for ransomes were they mine,
Rather then have her.

Arbaces.   See if I insult   150
That am the Conqueror, and for a ransome
Offer rich treasure to the conquered,
Which he refuses, and I beare his scorne.
It cannot be selfe flattery to say,
The daughters of your Country set by her
Would see their shame; runne home, and blush to death
At their owne foulenesse: yet shee is not faire,
Nor beautifull, those words expresse her not,
They say her lookes are something excellent,
That wants a name: yet were shee odious   160
Her birth deserves the Empire of the world,
Sister to such a Brother, that hath tane
Victorie prisoner, and throughout the Earth
Carries her bound; and should hee let her loose,
Shee durst not leave him: Nature did her wrong
To print continuall conquest on her cheekes,
And make no man worthy for her to take,
But mee that am too neare her; and as strangely
Shee did for mee: But you will thinke I brag.

Mardonius [*aside*].   I doe Ile be sworne. Thy Valour and thy 170
passions severd, would have made two excellent fellowes in their
kindes: I know not whether I should be sorry thou art so valiant,
or so passionate: would one of um were away.

Tigranes.   Doe I refuse her that I doubt her worth?
Were shee as vertuous as shee would be thought,
So perfect, that no one of her owne sex
Would finde a want, had shee so tempting faire,
That shee could wish it off for damning soules,
I would pay any Ransome, twenty lives,

176 no one] Q2; no owne Q1
178 for] Q2; her Q1
179 lives] Q2; times Q1

Rather then meet her married in my bed: 180
Perhaps I have a Love, where I have fixt
Mine eies, not to bee moov'd, and shee on mee:
I am not fickle.
Arbaces.   Is that all the cause?
  Thinke you, you can so knit your selfe in love
  To any other, that her searching sight
  Cannot dissolve it? So before you tride
  You thought your selfe a match for mee in fight:
  Trust mee *Tigranes* shee can doe as much
  In peace, as I in Warre; sheele conquer too
  You shall see, if you have the power to stand   190
  The force of her swift lookes; if you dislike,
  Ile send you home with love, and name your ransome
  Some other way: but if shee bee your choise
  Shee frees you: to *Iberia* you must.
Tigranes.   Sir, I have learnt a Prisoners sufferance,
  And will obey, but give mee leave to talke
  In private with some friends before I goe.
Arbaces.   Some two await him forth, and see him safe,
  But let him freely send for whom he please,
  And none dare to disturbe his conference: 200
  I will not have him know what bondage is
  Till he be free from mee.   *Exeunt* Tigranes [*and two attendants*].
                    This Prince, *Mardonius,*
  Is full of wisdome, Valour, all the graces
  Man can receive.
Mardonius.   And yet you Conquered him?
Arbaces.   And yet I conquered him, and could have don
  Hadst thou joynd with him, thogh thy name in Armes
  Bee great; Must all men that are vertuous
  Thinke suddenly to match themselves with mee:
  I conquered him, and bravely; did I not?
Bessus.   And please your Majesty I was afraid at first.   210
Mardonius.   When wert thou other?
Arbaces.   Of what?
Bessus.   That you would not have spide your best advantages,

for your Majesty in my opinion lay too high; me thinkes, under
favour, you should have laine thus.

Mardonius. Like a Taylor at a wake.

Bessus. And then, ift please your Majesty to remember, at one
time, by my Troth, I wisht my selfe with you.

Mardonius. By my Troth thou wouldst have stunke um both out
oth lists.   220

Arbaces. What to doe?

Bessus. To put your Majesty in mind of an occasion; you lay
thus and *Tigranes* falsified a blow at your leg, which you by
doing thus avoided; but if you had whipt up your leg thus, and
reacht him on th'eare, you had made the bloud-royall runne
abouts head.

Mardonius. What contry fence-schoole didst thou learn that at?

Arbaces. Puft, did I not take him nobly?

Mardonius.   Why you did,
And you have talkt enough on't.

Arbaces.   Talkt enough?
While you confine my words, by Heaven and Earth,   230
I were much better bee a King of Beasts
Then such a people: If I had not patience
Above a god, I should be cald a Tyrant
Throughout the World. They will offend to death
Each minute: Let me heare thee speake againe
And thou art earth againe: why this is like
Tigranes speech, that needs would say, I brag'd.
Bessus hee said I brag'd.

Bessus.   Ha ha ha.

Arbaces.   Why dost thou laugh?——
By all the world Ime growne ridiculous
To my owne subjects: Tye me to a chaire   240
And jest at mee, but I shall make a start
And punish some, that other will take heede

219 stunke] Q2 (stuncke); sunke Q1
225 bloud-royall] Q2 (bloud-Royall); bloud Q1
227 contry fence-schoole] *i.e.* rustic fencing school
229 Talkt] Q7, F2; Talke Q1–6

How they are haughty.——Who will answere mee?
He said I boasted, speak *Mardonius*,
Did I?——He will not answer: O my Temper!
I give you thankes above, that taught my heart
Patience, I can indure his silence.——What will none
Vouchsafe to give mee answer, am I growne
To such a poore respect, or doe you meane
To breake my wind? speake, speak soone one of you,   250
Or else by Heaven——
1. Gentleman.   So please your——
Arbaces.   Monstrous,
  I cannot bee heard out, they cut me off
As if I were too sawcy; I will live
In woods, and talke to Trees, they will allow mee
To end what I begin. The meanest Subject
Can finde a freedome to discharge his soule,
And not I.——Now it is a time to speake,
I harken.
1. Gentleman.   May it please——
Arbaces.   I meane not you,
  Did not I stop you once? but I am growne
To talke but idlie, let another speake.   260
2. Gentleman.   I hope your Majesty——
Arbaces.   Thou drawest thy words
  That I must waite an hower, where other men
Can heare in instants; throw your words away
Quicke, and to purpose, I have told you this.
Bessus.   An't please your Majesty——
Arbaces.   Wilt thou devoure me? this is such a rudenes
  As yet you never shewed mee, and I want
Power to command too, else *Mardonius*
Would speake at my request.——Were you my King,
I would have answered at your word *Mardonius*,   270
I pray you speake, and truely, did I boast?

---

248 answer] Q2 (answere); audience Q1
*260 To talke but idlie,] Seward; To balke, but I desire Q1; To balke, but I defie
Q2–6, F2; *om.* Q7–8
  268 too] Q2; mee Q1

Mardonius.   Truth will offend you.

Arbaces.   You take all great care what will offend me,
When you dare to utter such things as these.

Mardonius.   You told *Tigranes,* you had won his Land
With that sole arme propt by Divinity:
Was not that bragging, and a wrong to us
That daily venturde lives?

Arbaces.   O that thy name
Were great as mine, would I had paid my wealth,
It were as great, that I might combate thee;   280
I would through all the Regions habitable
Search thee, and having found thee, with my Sword
Drive thee about the world, till I had met
Some place that yet mans curiosity
Hath mist of; there, there would I strike thee dead:
Forgotten of Mankind, such Funerall Rites
As Beasts would give thee thou shouldst have.

Bessus [*apart*].   The King
Rages extreamly, shall wee slinke away?
Heele strike us.

2. Gentleman [*apart*].   Content.   290

Arbaces.   There I would make you know t'was this sole arme:
I grant you were my Instruments, and did
As I commanded you, but t'was this Arme
Mov'd you like wheeles, it mov'd you as it pleas'd:——
Whither slip you now? what, are you too good
To waite on mee?——Puff! I had neede have temper
That rule such people; I have nothing left
At my owne choise. I would I might be private:
Meane men enjoy themselves, but tis our curse,
To have a tumult that out of their loves   300
Will waite on us whether we will or no.——
Will you be gone?——Why heere they stand like death,
My word mooves nothing.

1. Gentleman [*apart*].   Must we goe?

Bessus [*apart*].   I know not.

296 Puff!] Q2 (puffe,); *om.* Q1   303 *1.*] Q2; *2.* Q1

192

Arbaces.   I pray you leave me Sirs:———I'me proud of this,
That they will be intreated from my sight:

Exeunt all but Arbaces *and* Mardonius.

Why now they leave mee all:———*Mardonius*!
Mardonius. Sir.
Arbaces.   Will you leave me quite alone? me thinks
Civility should teach you more then this,
If I were but your friend: stay heere, and waite.
Mardonius.   Sir, shall I speake?
Arbaces.   Why you would now thinke much 310
To bee denide, but I can scarce intreat
What I would have: doe, speake.
Mardonius.   But will you heare mee out?
Arbaces.   With me you article to talke thus? well
I will heare you out.
Mardonius.   Sir, that I have ever loved you, my sword hath
spoken for me, that I doe, if it bee doubted, I dare call an oath, a
great one to my witnesse: and were you not my King, from
amongst men, I should have chose you out to love above the
rest: nor can this challenge thanks: for my own sake I should 320
have doted, because I would have lov'd the most deserving man,
for so you are.
Arbaces.   Alas *Mardonius*, rise, you shall not kneele;
We all are Souldiers, and all venter lives:
And where there is no difference in mens worths,
Titles are jests: who can out vallew thee?
Mardonius thou hast lov'd me, and hast wrong,
Thy love is not rewarded, but beleeve
It shall be better, more then friend in armes,
My Father, and my Tutor, good *Mardonius.*   330
Mardonius.   Sir, you did promise you would heare me out.
Arbaces.   And so I will; speake freely, for from thee
Nothing can come but worthy things and true.
Mardonius.   Though you have al this worth, you hold som
qualities that doe eclipse your vertues.

305.1 S.D. Q2; *om.* Q1

Arbaces.　Eclipse my vertues?

Mardonius.　Yes, your passions, which are so manifold, that they
appeare even in this: when I commend you, you hug mee for
that truth: when I speak of your faults, you make a start, and
flie the hearing: but——　　　　　　　　　　　　　　　340

Arbaces.　When you commend me? O that I should live
To neede such commendations: If my deedes
Blew not my praise themselves above the earth,
I were most wretched: spare your idle praise:
If thou didst meane to flatter, and should'st utter
Words in my praise, that thou thoughtst impudence,
My deedes should make um modest: when you praise,
I hug you; 'tis so false, that wert thou worthy
Thou should'st receive a death, a glorious death
From me: but thou shalt understand thy lies,　　　　350
For shouldst thou praise mee into Heaven, and there
Leave me inthron'd, I would despise thee then
As much as now, which is as much as dust,
Because I see thy envy.

Mardonius.　How ever you will use me after, yet for your owne
promise sake heare me the rest.

Arbaces.　I will, and after call unto the windes,
For they shall lend as large an eare as I
To what you utter: speake.

Mardonius.　Would you but leave these hasty tempers, which I 360
doe not say take from you all your worth, but darken um, then
you would shine indeede.

Arbaces.　Well.

Mardonius.　Yet I would have you keepe some passions, least
men should take you for a god, your vertues are such.

Arbaces.　Why now you flatter.

Mardonius.　I never understood the word. Were you no King, and
free from these wilde moodes, should I chuse a companion for
wit and pleasure, it should bee you; or for honesty to enterchange
my bosome with, it would be you; or wisdome to give me counsel, 370

*352 then] Langbaine; though Q1–8, F2
369 honesty] Q2 (honestie); honest, Q1　　　　370 to] Q2; to | to Q1

I would pick out you; or vallor to defend my reputation, still I
would find out you; for you are fit to fight for all the world, if it
could come in question: Now I have spoke, consider to your
selfe, finde out a use: if so, then what shall fall to mee is not
materiall.

Arbaces.   Is not materiall? more then ten such lives
As mine *Mardonius*: it was Nobly said,
Thou hast spoake truth, and boldly, such a truth
As might offend another. I have bin
Too passionate, and idle, thou shalt see   380
A swift amendment: But I want those parts
You praise me for: I fight for all the world:
Give thee a Sword, and thou wilt goe as farre
Beyond mee, as thou art beyond in yeares,
I know thou dar'st, and wilt; It troubles mee
That I should use so rough a phrase to thee,
Impute it to my folly, what thou wilt,
So thou wilt pardon mee; that thou and I
Should differ thus.

Mardonius.   Why 'tis no matter Sir.

Arbaces.   Faith but tis, but thou dost ever take   390
All things I doe thus patiently, for which
I never can requite thee but with love,
And that thou shalt bee sure of. Thou and I
Have not bin merry lately: pray thee tell mee
Where hadst thou that same Jewell in thine eare?

Mardonius.   Why at the taking of a Towne.

Arbaces.   A wench upon my life, a wench *Mardonius*
Gave thee that Jewell.

Mardonius.   Wench, they respect not mee, Ime old and rough,
and every limbe about mee, but that which should, growes 400
stiffer: I' those businesses I may sweare I am truely honest: for I
pay justly for what I take, and would bee glad to be at a certainty.

Arbaces.   Why, doe the wenches incroch upon thee?

Mardonius.   I by this light doe they.

Arbaces.   Didst thou sit at an old rent with um?

401 I' those] Q2; Ith those Q1

Mardonius.   Yes faith.

Arbaces.   And doe they improove themselves?

Mardonius.   I, ten shillings to mee, every new yong fellow they come acquainted with.

Arbaces.   How canst live on't? 410

Mardonius.   Why I thinke I must petition to you.

Arbaces.   Thou shalt take um up at my price.

Enter two Gentlemen *and* Bessus.

Mardonius.   Your price?

Arbaces.   I at the Kings price.

Mardonius.   That may be more then I am worth.

1. Gentleman.   Is he not merry now?

2. Gentleman.   I thinke not.

Bessus.   He is, he is, weele shew our selves.

Arbaces.   *Bessus* I thought you had beene in *Iberia* by this, I bad you haste; *Gobrius* will want entertainment for me. 420

Bessus.   An't please your Majestie I have a sute.

Arbaces.   Ist not lowsie *Bessus*, what ist?

Bessus.   I am to carrie a Lady with me.

Arbaces.   Then thou hast two sutes.

Bessus.   And if I can preferre her to the Ladie *Panthæa* your Majesties sister, to learne fashions as her friends terme it, it will be worth something to me.

Arbaces.   So many nights lodgings as tis thither, will't not?

Bessus.   I know not that, Sir, but gold I shall be sure of.

Arbaces.   Why thou shalt bid her entertaine her from mee, so 430 thou wilt resolve me one thing.

Bessus.   If I can.

Arbaces.   Faith tis a very disputable question, and yet I thinke thou canst decide it.

Bessus.   Your Majestie has a good opinion of my understanding.

Arbaces.   I have so good an opinion of it: 'tis whether thou be valiant.

412.1 S.D. Q2; *om.* Q1
420 you haste] Q2 (You hast); you; halfe Q1
428 will't] Q2 (wilt); will Q1   429 Sir,] Q2 (sir); *om.* Q1
433 and] Q2; *om.* Q1

Bessus.   Some bodie has tradust me to you: doe you see this
sword Sir?
Arbaces.   Yes.   440
Bessus.   If I doe not make my back-biters eate it to a knife within
this weeke, say I am not valiant.

Enter Messenger.

Messenger.   Health to your Majestie.
Arbaces.   From *Gobrius?*
Messenger.   Yes Sir.
Arbaces.   How does he, is he well?
Messenger.   In perfect health.
Arbaces.   Thanke thee for thy good newes,
A trustier servant to his Prince there lives not
Then is good *Gobrius.*   [Arbaces *reads.*] 450
1. Gentleman.   The King starts backe.
Mardonius.   His blood goes backe as fast.
2. Gentleman.   And now it comes againe.
Mardonius.   He alters strangely.
Arbaces.   The hand of Heaven is on me, be it farre
From me to struggle; if my secret sinnes
Have pul'd this curse upon me, lend me teares
Enough to wash me white, that I may feele
A childlike innocence within my brest;
Which once perform'd, O give me leave to stand   460
As fixt as constancie her selfe, my eyes
Set here unmov'd, regardlesse of the World,
Though thousand miseries incompasse me.
Mardonius [aside].   This is strange.——Sir, how doe you?
Arbaces.   *Mardonius* my mother——
Mardonius.   Is shee dead?
Arbaces.   Alas, shees not so happie; thou dost know
How shee hath labour'd since my Father died
To take by treason hence this loathed life,
That would but be to serve her, I have pardon'd   470
And pardon'd, and by that have made her fit
To practise new sinnes, not repent the olde;

197

Shee now has hir'd a slave to come from thence
And strike me here, whom *Gobrius* sifting out,
Tooke, and condemn'd, and executed there,
The carefulst servant: Heaven let me but live
To pay that man; Nature is poore to me,
That will not let me have as many deathes
As are the times that he hath sav'd my life,
That I might die um over all for him.   480
Mardonius.   Sir, let her beare her sins on her owne head,
Vex not your selfe.
Arbaces.   What will the world
Conceive of me? with what unnaturall sinnes
Will they suppose me laden, when my life
Is sought by her that gave it to the world?
But yet he writes me comfort here, my sister
He sayes is growne in beautie, and in grace,
In all the innocent vertues that become
A tender spotlesse maide: shee staines her cheekes
With mourning teares to purge her Mothers ill,   490
And mongst that sacred dew shee mingles prayers,
Her pure oblations for my safe returne.
If I have lost the dutie of a sonne,
If any pompe or vanitie of state
Made me forget my naturall offices;
Nay farther, if I have not everie night
Expostulated with my wandring thoughts,
If ought unto my Parent they have err'd,
And cald um backe: doe you direct her arme
Unto this foule dissembling heart of mine: 500
But if I have beene just to her, send out
Your power to compasse me, and hold me safe
From searching treason; I will use no meanes
But prayers: for rather suffer me to see
From mine own veines issue a deadly floud,
Then wash my dangers off with Mothers bloud.
Mardonius.   I nere saw such sudden extremities.
                                                          Exeunt.

491 that] Q2; her Q1   507.1 S.D. Q2; *om.* Q1

Enter Tigranes, *and* Spaconia.

Tigranes.   Why, wilt thou have me die *Spaconia*,
  What should I doe?
Spaconia.   Nay, let me stay alone,
  And when you see *Armenia* againe,
  You shall behold a Toombe more worth then I;
  Some friend that either loves me, or my cause,
  Will build me something to distinguish me
  From other women: Many a weeping verse
  He will lay on, and much lament those maides
  That place their loves unfortunately high,
  As I have done, where they can never reach: 10
  But why should you goe to *Iberia*?
Tigranes.   Alas, that thou wilt aske me; Aske the man
  That rages in a feaver, why hee lies
  Distemper'd there, when all the other youths
  Are coursing ore the Meadowes with their loves?
  Can I resist it? am I not a slave
  To him that conquer'd me?
Spaconia.   That conquer'd thee?
  Tigranes he has won but halfe of thee,
  Thy bodie; but thy minde may be as free
  As his, his will did never combate thine,   20
  And take it prisoner.
Tigranes.   But if hee by force
  Convey my bodie hence, what helpes it me
  Or thee to be unwilling?
Spaconia.   O *Tigranes*,
  I know you are to see a Ladie there,
  To see, and like I feare: perhaps the hope
  Of her makes you forget me ere we part;
  Be happier then you know to wish: farewell.
Tigranes.   *Spaconia* stay, and heare me what I say:
  In short, destruction meete me, that I may
  See it, and not avoid it when I leave   30

    9 high] Q2; too light Q1   18 thee] Q2 (Thee); *om.* Q1

To be thy faithfull Lover: part with me
Thou shalt not: there are none that know our love;
And I have given gold to a Captaine
That goes unto *Iberia* from the King,
That he would place a Ladie of our Land
With the Kings sister that is offer'd me;
Thither shall you, and being once got in,
Perswade her by what subtile meanes you can
To be as backward in her love as I.

Spaconia.   Can you imagine that a longing maide   40
When shee beholds you, can be puld away
With words from loving you?

Tigranes.   Dispraise my health,
My honestie, and tell her I am jealous.

Spaconia.   Why, I had rather loose you: Can my heart
Consent to let my tongue throw out such words?
And I that ever yet spoke what I thought,
Shall find it such a thing at first to lie.

Tigranes.   Yet doe thy best.

Enter Bessus.

Bessus.   What is your Majestie readie?

Tigranes.   There is the Ladie Captaine.   50

Bessus.   Sweet Ladie by your leave, I could wish my selfe more
full of Courtship for your faire sake.

Spaconia.   Sir I shall find no want of that.

Bessus.   Lady, you must haste, I have received new letters from
the King, that requires more speed then I expected. He will follow
me suddenly himselfe, and beginnes to call for your Majestie
alreadie.

Tigranes.   He shall not doe so long.

Bessus.   Sweet Ladie shall I call you my charge hereafter?

Spaconia.   I will not take upon me to governe your tongue Sir, 60
you shall call me what you please.

[*Exeunt.*]

Enter Gobrius, Bacurius, Arane, Panthæa, *and*
waiting women, with attendance.

Gobrius.   My Lord *Bacurius*, you must have regard
Unto the Queene, shee is your prisoner,
Tis at your perill if shee make escape.
Bacurius.   My Lord I know't, shee is my prisoner
From you committed; yet shee is a woman,
And so I keepe her safe, you will not urge me
To keepe her close; I shall not shame to say
I sorrow for her.
Gobrius.   So doe I my Lord.
I sorrow for her that so little grace
Doth governe her, that shee should stretch her arme   10
Against her King, so little womanhood
And naturall goodnesse, as to thinke the death
Of her owne Sonne.
Arane.   Thou know'st the reason why,
Dissembling as thou art, and wilt not speake.
Gobrius.   There is a Ladie takes not after you,
Her Father is within her, that good man
Whose teares paid downe his sinnes, marke how shee weeps,
How well it does become her; and if you
Can find no disposition in your selfe
To sorrow, yet by gracefulnesse in her   20
Find out the way, and by your reason weepe:
All this shee does for you, and more shee needes,
When for your selfe you will not lose a teare;
Thinke how this want of griefe discredits you,
And you will weepe, because you cannot weepe.
Arane.   You talke to me as having got a time
Fit for your purpose; but you know I know
You speake not what you thinke.
Panthæa.   I would my heart
Were stone, before my softnesse should be urg'd

II.i] *Finis Actus Primi.* Actus Secundus Scena Prima.
0.1 and] Dyce; *and Mandane.* Q 1–8, F 2

Against my Mother, a more troubled thought 30
No Virgin beares about her; should I excuse
My Mothers fault, I should set light a life,
In loosing which, a brother and a King
Were taken from me; If I seeke to save
That life so lov'd, 1 loose another life
That gave me being, I shall loose a Mother,
A word of such a sound in a childes eare,
That it strikes reverence through it: May the will
Of Heaven be done, and if one needes must fall,
Take a poore Virgins life to answere all. 40
Arane. But *Gobrius* let us talke; you know this fault
Is not in me as in another woman.
Gobrius. I know it is not.
Arane. Yet you make it so.
Gobrius. Why, is not all that's past beyond your helpe?
Arane. I know it is.
Gobrius. Nay, should you publish it
Before the world, thinke you twill be believ'd?
Arane. I know it would not.
Gobrius. Nay, should I joine with you,
Should we not both be torne? and yet both die
Uncredited?
Arane. I thinke we should.
Gobrius. Why then
Take you such violent courses? as for me, 50
I doe but right in saving of the King
From all your plots.
Arane. The King?
Gobrius. I bad you rest
With patience, and a time would come for me
To reconcile all to your owne content:
But by this way you take away my power.
And what was done unknowne, was not by me,
But you: your urging being done,

32 set] Q2; let Q1

202

I must preserve mine owne; but time may bring
All this to light, and happily for all.

Arane.   Accursed be this overcurious braine,   60
That gave that plot a birth; accurst this wombe,
That after did conceive to my disgrace.

Bacurius.   My Lord Protector, they say there are divers Letters
come from *Armenia* that *Bessus* has done good service, and
brought againe a day by his particular valour: receiv'd you any
to that effect?

Gobrius.   Yes, tis most certaine.

Bacurius.   Ime sorrie fort, not that the day was wonne, but that
twas wonne by him; wee held him here a coward, hee did me
wrong once, at which I laught, and so did all the world: for, 70
nor I, nor any other held him worth my Sword.

Enter Bessus, *and* Spaconia.

Bessus.   Health to my Lord Protector, from the King these
Letters, and to your grace Madam these.

Gobrius.   How does his Majestie?

Bessus.   As well as conquest by his owne meanes, and his valiant
commanders can make him: your letters will tel you all.

Panthæa.   I will not open mine till I doe know
My brothers health; good Captaine is he well?

Bessus.   As the rest of us that fought are.

Panthæa.   But howes that, is he hurt?   80

Bessus.   Hees a strange Souldier that gets not a knock.

Panthæa.   I doe not aske how strange that Souldier is
That gets no hurt; but whether he have one?

Bessus.   He had divers.

Panthæa.   And is he well againe?

Bessus.   Well againe, ant please your grace? why I was run twice
through the bodie, and shot ith head with a crosse arrow, and yet
am well againe.

Panthæa.   I doe not care how thou dost, is he well?

Bessus.   Not care how I doe, let a man out of the mightinesse 90
of his spirit fructifie forraigne Countries with his bloud for the

71 him] Q2; time Q1

203

good of his owne, and thus he shall be answered: why, I may
live to relieve with speare and shield such a Ladie as you distressed.
Panthæa.   Why, I will care, I am glad that thou art well;
I prethee is he so?
Gobrius.   The King is well, and will be here to morrow.
Panthæa. My prayers are heard; now I will open mine.
Gobrius.   *Bacurius*, I must ease you of your charge:
Madam, the wonted mercie of the King
That overtakes your faults, has met with this,   100
And strucke it out; he has forgiven you freelie,
Your owne will is your Law, be where you please.
Arane.   I thanke him.
Gobrius.   You will be readie to waite
Upon his Majestie to morrow?
Arane.   I will.
Bacurius.   Madam, be wise hereafter.——
I am glad I have lost this Office.   *Exit* Arane.
Gobrius.   Good Captaine *Bessus*, tell us the discourse
Betweene *Tigranes* and our King, and how
We got the victorie.
Panthæa.   I prethee doe,
And if my brother were in any danger,   110
Let not thy tale make him abide there long,
Before thou bring him off, for all that while
My heart will beate.
Bessus.   Madam, let what will beate, I must tell truth, and thus it
was: They fought single in lists but one to one, as for my own
part I was dangerouslie hurt but three dayes before, else perhaps
wee had beene two to two; I cannot tell, some thought wee had;
and the occasion of my hurt was this, the enemie had made
trenches——
Gobrius.   Captaine, without the manner of your hurt be much 120
materiall to this businesse, weele heare it some other time.
Panthæa.   I, I prethee leave it, and goe on with my brother.
Bessus.   I will, but 'twould be worth your hearing: To the lists
they came, and single sword and gauntlet was their fight.

93 as you] Q2; *om.* Q1   106 Arane] Q2; *om.* Q1

Panthæa.   Alas.

Bessus.   Without the lists there stood some dozen Captaines of either side mingled, all which were sworne, and one of those was I: and twas my chance to stand neere a Captaine of the Enemies side, called *Tiribasus*; valiant they said he was: whilst these two Kings were stretching themselves, this *Tiribasus* cast something 130 a scornefull looke on mee, and askt mee whom I thought would overcome: I smilde, and told him, if hee would fight with me, he should perceive by the event of that whose King would winne; something hee answered, and a scuffle was like to grow, when one *Zipetus* offerd to helpe him: I——

Panthæa.   All this is of thy selfe, I prethee *Bessus*
Tell something of my brother, did he nothing?

Bessus.   Why yes, Ile tell your Grace; they were not to fight till the word given, which for my owne part by my troth I confesse I was not to give.   140

Panthæa.   See, for his owne part.

Bacurius.   I feare yet this fellowe's abusd with a good report.

Bessus.   I, but I——

Panthæa.   Still of himselfe.

Bessus.   Cride, give the word, when as some of them saide *Tigranes* was stooping, but the word was not given then: yet one *Cosroes* of the enemies part held up his finger to me, which is as much with us Marshallists, as I will fight with you: I said not a word, nor made signe during the combate; but that once done——   150

Panthæa.   He slips ore all the fight.

Bessus.   I cald him to me, *Cosros* said I——

Panthæa.   I will heare no more.

Bessus.   No, no, I lie——

Bacurius.   I dare be sworne thou dost.

Bessus.   Captaine said I, twas so.

Panthæa.   I tell thee, I will heare no further.

Bessus.   No? your Grace will wish you had.

Panthæa.   I will not wish it: what, is this the Ladie My Brother writes to me to take?   160

139 I confesse] Q2; *om.* Q1   146 yet] Q2; when Q1

Bessus. An't please your Grace this is shee:——Charge will
you come neerer the Princes?

Panthæa. Y'are welcome from your Countrey, and this Land
Shall shew unto you all the kindnesses
That I can make it; what's your name?

Spaconia.   *Thalestris.*

Panthæa. Y'are verie welcome, you have got a letter
To put you to me, that has power enough
To place mine Enemy here; then much more you,
That are so farre from being so to me,
That you nere saw me.   170

Bessus. Madam, I dare passe my word for her truth.

Spaconia. My truth?

Panthæa. Why Captaine, doe you thinke I am afraid sheele steale?

Bessus. I cannot tell, servants are slipperie; but I dare give my
word for her, and for her honestie: shee came along with me,
and many favours shee did me by the way; but by this light none
but what shee might doe with modestie, to a man of my ranke.

Panthæa. Why Captaine, heres no body thinkes otherwise.

Bessus. Nay, if you should, your Grace may thinke your pleasure;
but I am sure I brought her from *Armenia*, and in all that way if 180
ever I toucht any bare on her above her knee, I pray God I may
sinke where I stand.

Spaconia. Above my knee?

Bessus. No, you know I did not, and if any man will say I did,
this Sword shall answere: Nay, Ile defend the reputation of my
charge whilst I live; your Grace shall understand I am secret
in these businesses, and know how to defend a Ladies honour.

Spaconia. I hope your Grace knowes him so well already,
I shall not neede to tell you hee's vaine and foolish.

Bessus. I, you may call mee what you please, but Ile defend your 190
good name against the World; and so I take my leave of your
Grace, and of you my Lord Protector, I am likewise glad to see
your Lordship well.

Bacurius. O Captaine *Bessus*, I thanke you, I would speake with
you anon.

Bessus. When you please, I will attend your Lordship. *Exit.*

206

Bacurius.   Madam, Ile take my leave too.
Panthæa.   Good *Bacurius.*   *Exit* [Bacurius].
Gobrius.   Madam, what writes his Majesty to you?
Panthæa.   O my Lord,   200
  The kindest words, Ile keepe um whilst I live
  Here in my bosome; theres no art in um,
  They lie disordred in this paper, Just
  As hearty Nature speakes um.
Gobrius.   And to mee
  He writes, what teares of joy he shed to heare
  How you were growne in every vertuous way,
  And yeilds all thankes to me, for that deare care
  Which I was bound to have in training you:
  There is no Princes living that enjoyes
  A Brother of that worth.
Panthæa.   My Lord, no Maide   210
  Longs more for any thing, or feeles more heate
  And cold within her brest, then I doe now,
  In hope to see him.
Gobrius.   Yet I wonder much
  At this, hee writes he brings along with him
  A husband for you, that same Captive Prince;
  And if he love you as he makes a shew,
  He will allow you freedome in your choise.
Panthæa.   And so he will my Lord, I warrant you
  He will but offer, and give me the power
  To take, or leave.
Gobrius.   Trust me, were I a Ladie,   220
  I could not like that man were bargain'd with
  Before I chuse him.
Panthæa.   But I am not built
  On such wild humors, if I find him worthy,
  He is not lesse, because hee's offerd.
Spaconia [*aside*].   Tis true, he is not, would he would seem lesse.
Gobrius.   I thinke there is no Ladie can affect

223 him] Q2; time Q1

Another Prince, your Brother standing by;
He does eclipse mens vertues so with his.
Spaconia [*aside*].   I know a Lady may, and more I feare
Another Lady will.
Panthæa.   Would I might see him.   230
Gobrius.   Why so you shall: my businesses are great,
I will attend you when it is his pleasure
To see you Madam.
Panthæa.   I thanke you good my Lord.
Gobrius.   You will be ready Madam?
Panthæa.   Yes.   *Exit* Gobrius [*with attendants*].
Spaconia.   I doe beseech you Madam send away
Your other women, and receive from me
A few sad words, which set against your joyes,
May make um shine the more.
Panthæa.   Sirs leave me all.   *Exeunt women.*
Spaconia.   I kneele a stranger here to beg a thing   240
Unfit for me to aske, and you to grant,
Tis such another strange ill laid request,
As if a beggar should intreat a King
To leave his Scepter and his Throne to him,
And take his rags to wander ore the World
Hungry and cold.
Panthæa.   That were a strange request.
Spaconia.   As ill is mine.
Panthæa.   Then doe not utter it.
Spaconia.   Alas, tis of that nature, that it must
Be utterd, I, and granted, or I die:
I am asham'd to speake it; but where life   250
Lies at the stake, I cannot thinke her woman,
That will not talke something unreasonably
To hazard saving of it: I shall seeme
A strange petitioner, that wish all ill
To them I beg of, ere they give mee ought,

228 his] Q2; this Q1   235 Gobrius] Q2; *om.* Q1
239 *Exeunt women.*] Q2; *om.* Q1
*252 talke] Seward (talk); take Q1-8, F2

Yet so I must: I would you were not faire,
Nor wise, for in your ill consists my good:
If you were foolish, you would heare my prayer;
If foule, you had not power to hinder me:
He would not love you.
Panthæa.   Whats the meaning of it?   260
Spaconia.   Nay, my request is more without the bounds
Of reason yet; for tis not in the power
Of you to doe what I would have you grant.
Panthæa.   Why then tis idle, prethee speake it out.
Spaconia.   Your brother brings a Prince into this Land
Of such a noble shape, so sweete a grace,
So full of worth withall, that every maide
That lookes upon him, gives away her selfe
To him for ever; and for you to have
He brings him: and so mad is my demand,   270
That I desire you not to have this man,
This excellent man, for whom you needs must die,
If you should misse him. I doe now expect
You should laugh at me.
Panthæa.   Trust me, I could weepe
Rather, for I have found in all thy words
A strange disjointed sorrow.
Spaconia.   Tis by me,
His owne desire too, that you would not love him.
Panthæa.   His owne desire? why credit me *Thalestris*
I am no common wooer: If he shall wooe me,
His worth may be such, that I dare not sweare   280
I will not love him; but if he will stay
To have me wooe him, I will promise thee
He may keepe all his graces to himselfe,
And feare no ravishing from me.
Spaconia.   Tis yet
His owne desire, but when he sees your face,
I feare it will not be; therefore I charge you
As you have pitty, stop those tender eares
From his inchanting voice, close up those eyes,

That you may neither catch a dart from him,
Nor he from you: I charge you as you hope   290
To live in quiet, for when I am dead
For certaine I shall walke to visit him,
If he breake promise with me: for as fast
As oathes without a formall ceremony
Can make me, I am to him.
Panthæa.   Then be fearelesse,
For if he were a thing twixt God and man,
I could gaze on him; (if I knew it sinne,
To love him) without passion: Dry your eyes,
I sweare you shall enjoy him still for me,
I will not hinder you; but I perceive   300
You are not what you seeme: Rise, rise, *Thalestris,*
If your right name be so.
Spaconia.   Indeed it is not.
Spaconia is my name; but I desire
Not to be knowne to others.
Panthæa.   Why, by me
You shall not, I will never doe you wrong,
What good I can, I will; thinke not my birth,
Or education such, that I should injure
A stranger Virgin: you are welcome hither.
In company you wish to be commanded,
But when we are alone, I shall be ready   310
To be your servant.

                                          Exeunt.

                    Enter three Men, *and a* Woman.   [II. ii]

1. Man.   Come, come, run, run, runne.
2. Man.   We shall out-goe her.
3. Man.   One were better be hang'd, then carry women out
fidling to these shewes.
Woman.   Is the King hard by?

                    303 my] Q2; *om.* Q1

                              210

1. Man.　You heard hee with the bottles say, hee thought wee should come too late: what abundance of people here is.

Woman.　But what had he in those bottles?

3. Man.　I know not.

2. Man.　Why, Inke good man foole.　　　　　　　　　　10

3. Man.　Inke, what to doe?

1. Man.　Why, the King looke you, will many times call for those bottles, and breake his minde to his friends.

Woman.　Lets take our places quickly, we shall have no roome else.

2. Man.　The man told us hee would walke a foote through the people.

3. Man.　I marry did he.

1. Man.　Our shops are well lookt to now.

2. Man.　S'life yonders my Master I thinke.　　　　　　　20

1. Man.　No, tis not he.

Enter two Citizens Wives, *and* Philip.

1. Citizens Wife.　Lord, how fine the fields be, what sweete living tis in the Countrey.

2. Citizens Wife.　I, poore soules, God helpe um; they live as contentedly as one of us.

1. Citizens Wife.　My Husbands cousen would have had me gone into the Countrey last yeere, wert thou ever there?

2. Citizens Wife.　I, poore soules, I was amongst um once.

1. Citizens Wife.　And what kinde of creatures are they for love of God?　　　　　　　　　　30

2. Citizens Wife.　Very good people, God helpe um.

1. Citizens Wife.　Wilt thou goe with me downe this summer, when I am brought abed?

2. Citizens Wife.　Alas, tis no place for us.

1. Citizens Wife.　Why prethee?

2. Citizens Wife.　Why, you can have nothing there; theres no body cries broomes.

1. Citizens Wife.　No?

2. Citizens Wife.　No truly, nor milke.

19 lookt] Q2; looke Q1

1. Citizens Wife.   Nor milke, how doe they?   40

2. Citizens Wife.   They are faine to milke themselves ith Countrey.

1. Citizens Wife.   Good Lord: but the people there I thinke will bee very dutifull to one of us?

2. Citizens Wife.   I, God knowes will they, and yet they doe not greatly care for our Husbands.

1. Citizens Wife.   Doe they not, alas? In good faith I cannot blame them: for we doe not greatly care for them our selves.——— *Philip* I pray choose us a place.

Philip.   Theres the best forsooth.

1. Citizens Wife.   By your leave good people a little.   50

1. Man.   Whats the matter?

Philip.   I pray you my friend doe not thrust my Mistris so, shees with childe.

2. Man.   Let her looke to her selfe then, has shee not had shroving enough yet? if shee stay shouldring here, shee may hap to goe home with a Cake in her bellie.

3. Man.   How now goodman squitterbreech, why doe you leane so on me?

Philip.   Because I will.

3. Man.   Will you sir sawce-box?   60

1. Citizens Wife.   Looke if one have not strucke *Philip.*———Come hither *Philip*, why did he strike thee?

Philip.   For leaning on him.

1. Citizens Wife.   Why didst thou leane on him?

Philip.   I did not thinke he would have strucke me.

1. Citizens Wife.   As God save me law, thou art as wilde as a Bucke, there is no quarrell, but thou art at one end or other of it.

3. Man.   Its at the first end then; for he will never stay the last.

1. Citizens Wife.   Well slipstring, I shall meete with you.

3. Man.   When you will.   70

1. Citizens Wife.   Ile give a crowne to meete with you.

3. Man.   At a bawdy house.

1. Citizens Wife.   I, you are full of your rogery; ———[*aside*] but if I doe meete you it shall cost me a fall.

52 you] Q2; *om.* Q1
54 shroving] Turner; thrusting Q1; showing Q2–6, F2; shoving Q7–8
69 slipstring] Q2; stripling Q1

Enter one [Man] *running.*

Man.   The King, the King, the King, the King:
Now, now, now, now.

Flourish: Enter Arbaces, Tigranes, Mardonius, *and others.*

All.   God preserve your Majestie.
Arbaces.   I thanke you all: Now are my joyes at full,
When I behold you safe my loving Subjects;
By you I grow, tis your united love   80
That lifts me to this height:
All the account that I can render you
For all the love you have bestowed on me,
All your expences to maintaine my warre,
Is but a little word: you will imagine
Tis slender payment; yet tis such a word
As is not to be bought without our blouds;
Tis peace.
All.   God preserve your Majestie.
Arbaces.   Now you may live securely in your Townes,   90
Your Children round about you; you may sit
Under your vines, and make the miseries
Of other Kingdomes a discourse for you,
And lend them sorrowes: For your selves you may
Safely forget there are such things as teares;
And may you all whose good thoughts I have gain'd,
Hold me unworthy, when I thinke my life
A sacrifice too great to keepe you thus
In such a calme estate.
All.   God blesse your Majestie.   100
Arbaces.   See all good people, I have brought the man,
Whose very name you fear'd, a captive home:
Behold him, tis *Tigranes*; in your hearts
Sing songs of gladnesse, and deliverance.

74.1 *Enter . . . running.*] *Flourish. Enter . . . running.* Q 2; *om.* Q 1
75 *Man.*] Dyce; 3. Q 1; 4. Q 2–8, F 2
76.1 *Flourish:*] Q 2; *om.* Q 1

213

1. Citizens Wife.   Out upon him.

2. Citizens Wife.   How he looks.

Woman.   Hang him, hang him, hang him.

Mardonius.   These are sweete people.

Tigranes.   Sir, you doe me wrong,
   To render me a scorned spectacle
   To common people.

Arbaces.   It was farre from me   110
   To meane it so:——
                         If I have ought deserv'd,
   My loving Subjects let me beg of you
   Not to revile this Prince, in whom their dwels
   All worth of which the nature of a man
   Is capable; valour beyond compare,
   The terror of his name has stretcht it selfe
   Where ever there is sunne: and yet for you,
   I fought with him single, and won him too;
   I made his valour stoope, and brought that name
   Soar'd to so unbeliev'd a height, to fall   120
   Beneath mine: This inspir'd with all your loves,
   I did performe, and will for your content
   Be ever ready for a greater worke.

All.   The Lord blesse your Majestie.

Tigranes [*aside*].   So, hee has made me amends now, with a speech
   in commendation of himselfe: I would not be so vaine-glorious.

Arbaces.   If there be any thing in which I may
   Doe good to any creature, here speake out;
   For I must leave you: and it troubles me,
   That my occasions for the good of you,   130
   Are such as calles me from you; else my joy
   Would be to spend my dayes amongst you all.
   You shew your loves in these large multitudes
   That come to meete me: I will pray for you,
   Heaven prosper you, that you may know old yeeres,
   And live to see your Childrens Children

---

119 brought] Q2; made Q1
126 commendation] Q2; commendations Q1   130 That] Q2; Thus Q1

Eate at your boards with plenty: when there is
A want of any thing, let it be knowne
To me, and I will be a Father to you:
God keepe you all.   140

All.   God blesse your Majestie. God blesse your Majestie.

> *Flourish. Exeunt kings and their traine.*

1. Man.   Come, shall we goe? all's done.

Woman.   I, for Gods sake, I have not made a fire yet.

2. Man.   Away, away, all's done.

3. Man.   Content:——Farewell *Philip.*

1. Citizens Wife.   Away, you haltersack you.

1. Man.   *Philip* will not fight, hee's afraid on's face.

Philip.   I marry am I, afraid of my face.

3. Man.   Thou wouldst be *Philip*, if thou saw'st it in a glasse; it
lookes so like a visor.   150

1. Citizens Wife.   Youle be hang'd sirra.——

> *Exeunt the three* Men, *and the* Woman.

Come *Philip*, walke afore us homeward:——did not his Majestie
say, he had brought us home Peaes for all our money?

2. Citizens Wife.   Yes marry did he.

1. Citizens Wife.   They are the first I heard on this yeere by my
troth, I long'd for some of um; did he not say we should have
some?

2. Citizens Wife.   Yes, and so we shall anon I warrant you, have
every one a pecke brought home to our houses.

> [*Exeunt.*]

Enter Arbaces, *and* Gobrius.   III.i

Arbaces.   My Sister take it ill?

Gobrius.   Not very ill,
Something unkindly shee doth take it Sir,
To have her Husband chosen to her hands.

---

141 God...Majestie.] Q2; *repetition not in* Q1
141.1 S.D. Q2; *Exeunt.* Q1   150 so] Q2; *om.* Q1
153 all] Q2; *om.* Q1
III.i] *Finis Actus Secundi.* | *Actus Tertii Scæna Prima.*

Arbaces. Why *Gobrius* let her; I must have her know
My will, and not her owne must governe her:
What, will shee marrie with some slave at home?
Gobrius. O shee is farre from any stubbornnesse,
You much mistake her, and no doubt will like
Where you wil have her; but when you behold her,
You will be loath to part with such a Jewell.   10
Arbaces. To part with her, why *Gobrius* art thou mad?
Shee is my sister.
Gobrius.   Sir, I know shee is:
But it were pitty to make poore our Land
With such a beauty, to inrich another.
Arbaces. Pish, will shee have him?
Gobrius [*aside*].   I doe hope she will not.——
I thinke shee will Sir.
Arbaces. Were shee my Father and my Mother too;
And all the names for which we think folkes friends,
Shee should be forcst to have him, when I know
Tis fit: I will not heare her say shee's loth.   20
Gobrius [*aside*]. Heaven bring my purpose luckily to passe,
You know tis just.——
                    Sir, sheele not neede constraint,
Shee loves you so.
Arbaces.   How does shee love me, speake?
Gobrius. Shee loves you more then people love their health
That live by labour; more then I could love
A man that died for me, if he could live
Againe.
Arbaces. Shee is not like her Mother then?
Gobrius. O no, when you were in *Armenia*,
I durst not let her know when you were hurt:
For at the first on every little scratch,   30
Shee kept her chamber, wept, and would not eate,
Till you were well; and many times the newes
Was so long comming, that before we heard,
Shee was as neare her death, as you your health.

15 I doe...not.——] Q2; *om.* Q1

216

Arbaces.   Alas poore soule, but yet shee must be rul'd;
I know not how I shall requite her well,
I long to see her; have you sent for her,
To tell her I am ready?
Gobrius.   Sir, I have.

       Enter 1. Gentleman *and* Tigranes.

1. Gentleman.   Sir, here's the Armenian King.
Arbaces.   Hees welcome.   40
1. Gentleman.   And the Queene Mother, and the Princes waite
without.
Arbaces.   Good *Gobrius* bring them in.——   *Exit* Gobrius.
                                Tigranes you
Will thinke you are arriv'd in a strange Land,
Where Mothers cast to poyson their onely sonnes;
Thinke you you shall be safe?
Tigranes.   Too safe I am Sir.

    Enter Gobrius, Arane, Panthæa, Spaconia, Bacurius,
        Mardonius, *and* Bessus, *and* 2. Gentleman.

Arane.   As low as this I bow to you, and would
As low as is my grave, to shew a mind
Thankefull for all your mercies.
Arbaces.   O stand up,
And let me kneele, the light will be asham'd   50
To see observance done to me by you.
Arane.   You are my King.
Arbaces.   You are my Mother, rise;
As farre be all your faults from your owne soule,
As from my memory; then you shall be
As white as innocence her selfe.
Arane.   I came
Onely to shew my dutie, and acknowledge
My sorrow for my sinnes; longer to stay
Were but to draw eyes more attentively

38.1 1. Gentleman *and*] Q2; *om.* Q1   43 S.D. Q2; *om.* Q1
46.2 *and* 2. Gentleman] Turner; *and two Gentlemen* Q2–8, F2; *om.* Q1
48 is] Q2; to Q1

Upon my shame: That power that kept you safe
From me, preserve you still.   60
Arbaces.   Your owne desires shall be your guard.   *Exit* Arane.
Panthæa.   Now let me die:
  Since I have seene my Lord the King returne
  In safety, I have seene all good that life
  Can shew me; I have nere another wish
  For Heaven to grant, nor were it fit I should:
  For I am bound to spend my age to come
  In giving thankes that this was granted me.
Gobrius.   Why does not your Majestie speake?
Arbaces.   To whom?
Gobrius.   To the Princesse.   70
Panthæa.   Alas Sir, I am fearefull, you doe looke
  On me, as if I were some loathed thing
  That you were finding out a way to shunne.
Gobrius.   Sir, you should speake to her.
Arbaces.   Ha?
Panthæa.   I know I am unworthy, yet not ill
  Arm'd, with which innocence here I will kneele,
  Till I am one with earth: but I will gaine
  Some words, and kindnesse from you.
Tigranes.   Will you speake, Sir?
Arbaces [*aside*].   Speake, am I what I was?   80
  What art thou that dost creepe into my breast,
  And darst not see my face? shew forth thy selfe:
  I feele a paire of fierie wings displaide
  Hither, from thence; you shall not tarrie there,
  Up, and be gone, if thou beest love, be gone,
  Or I will teare thee from my wounded flesh,
  Pull thy lov'd downe away, and with a quill
  By this right arme drawne from thy wanton wing,
  Write to thy laughing Mother in thy bloud,
  That you are Powers belied, and all your darts   90
  Are to be blowne away by men resolv'd
  Like dust; I know thou fear'st my words, away.

61 Arane] Q2; *om.* Q1

Tigranes [*aside*].   O miserie, why should he be so slow?
There can no falshood come of loving her;
Though I have given my faith, shee is a thing
Both to be lov'd and serv'd beyond my faith:
I would he would present me to her quicklie.
Panthæa.   Will you not speake at all, are you so farre
From kind words? yet to save my modesty
That must talke till you answer: doe not stand   100
As you were dumbe, say something, though it be
Poyson'd with anger that may strike me dead.
Mardonius.   Have you no life at all? for manhood sake
Let her not kneele, and talke neglected thus;
A tree would find a tongue to answer her,
Did shee but give it such a lou'd respect.
Arbaces.   You meane this Lady? lift her from the earth;
Why doe you let her kneele so long? alas,
Madam your beauty uses to command,
And not to beg; what is your sute to me?   110
It shall be granted, yet the time is short,
And my affaires are great: but wheres my sister?
I bad shee should be brought.
Mardonius [*aside*].   What, is he mad?
Arbaces.   *Gobrius,* where is shee?
Gobrius.   Sir?
Arbaces.   Where is shee man?
Gobrius.   Who Sir?
Arbaces.   Who, hast thou forgot? my Sister.
Gobrius.   Your Sister Sir?
Arbaces.   Your Sister Sir?——
Some one that has a wit, answere; where is shee?
Gobrius.   Doe you not see her there?
Arbaces.   Where?
Gobrius.   There.
Arbaces.   There? where?

117 Some] Q2; *Gob.* Some Q1
118 Sp. Prefixes: *Gobrius....Arbaces....Gobrius....Arbaces.*] Q2; *Arbaces....*
Gobrius.... Arbaces.... Gobrius. Q1

Mardonius.   S'light there, are you blind?
Arbaces.   Which doe you meane, that little one?
Gobrius.   No Sir.   120
Arbaces.   No Sir, why doe you mocke me? I can see
  No other here, but that petitioning Ladie.
Gobrius.   Thats shee.
Arbaces.   Away.
Gobrius.   Sir it is shee.
Arbaces.   Tis false.
Gobrius.   Is it?
Arbaces.   As hell, by Heaven as false as hell,
  My sister: Is shee dead? if it be so,
  Speake boldly to me: for I am a man,
  And dare not quarrell with divinity;
  But doe not thinke to cosen me with this:
  I see you all are mute, and stand amas'd,
  Fearefull to answere me; it is too true   130
  A decreed instant cuts off every life,
  For which to mourne, is to repine; shee died
  A Virgin though, more innocent then sleepe,
  As cleere as her owne eyes, and blessednesse
  Eternall waites upon her where shee is:
  I know shee could not make a wish to change
  Her state for new, and you shall see me beare
  My crosses like a man; we all must die,
  And shee hath taught us how.
Gobrius.   Doe not mistake,
  And vex your selfe for nothing; for her death   140
  Is a long life of yet I hope: Tis shee,
  And if my speech deserve not faith, lay death
  Upon me, and my latest words shall force
  A credit from you.
Arbaces.   Which good *Gobrius*,
  That Ladie dost thou meane?
Gobrius.   That Lady Sir.
  She is your sister, and she is your sister

146–148 She is...thus.] Q2; *om.* Q1

220

That loves you so; 'tis she for whom I weepe
To see you use her thus.
Arbaces.   It cannot be.
Tigranes [*aside*].   Pish, this is tedious,   150
I cannot hold, I must present my selfe;
And yet the sight of my *Spaconia*,
Touches me, as a sudden thunderclap
Does one that is about to sinne.
Arbaces.   Away,
No more of this; here I pronounce him Traytor,
The direct plotter of my death, that names,
Or thinkes her for my Sister: Tis a lie,
The most malicious of the World, invented
To mad your King; he that will say so next,
Let him draw out his Sword, and sheath it here,
It is a sinne fully as pardonable: 160
Shee is no kinne to me, nor shall shee be;
If shee were any, I create her none,
And which of you can question this? my power
Is like the Sea, that is to be obey'd,
And not disputed with: I have decreed her
As farre from having part of bloud with me,
As the nak'd Indians: Come, and answer me,
He that is boldest now; Is that my Sister?
Mardonius [*aside*].   O this is fine.
Bessus.   No marry is shee not an't please your Majestie: 170
I never thought shee was, shees nothing like you.
Arbaces.   No, tis true, shee is not.
Mardonius [*to Bessus*].   Thou shouldst be hang'd.
Panthæa.   Sir, I will speake but once: By the same power
You make my bloud a stranger unto yours
You may command me dead; and so much love
A stranger may importune: pray you doe.
If this request appeare too much to grant,
Adopt me of some other Family
By your unquestion'd word; else I shall live   180
Like sinfull issues that are left in streetes

221

By their regardlesse Mothers, and no name
Will be found for me.
Arbaces.   I will heare no more.——
[*Aside*] Why should there be such musicke in a voice,
And sinne for me to heare it? All the world
May take delight in this, and tis damnation
For me to doe so.——[*To her*] You are faire, and wise,
And vertuous I thinke, and he is blest
That is so neere you as your brother is.——
[*Aside*] But you are naught to me but a disease,   190
Continuall torment without hope of ease;
Such an ungodly sicknesse I have got,
That he that undertakes my cure, must first
Orethrow Divinity, all morall Lawes,
And leave mankinde as unconfinde as beasts,
Allowing them to doe all actions
As freely as they drinke, when they desire.——
[*To her*] Let me not heare you speake againe.——[*Aside*] Yet
    so
I shall but languish for the want of that,
The having which would kill me.——[*To them*] No man here   200
Offer to speake for her; for I consider
As much as you can say.——[*Aside*] I will not toyle
My body, and my mind too, rest thou there,   [*Sits.*]
Heres one within will labour for you both.
Panthæa.   I would I were past speaking.
Gobrius.   Feare not Madam,
The King will alter, tis some sudden rage,
And you shall see it end some other way.
Panthæa.   Pray God it doe.
Tigranes [*aside*].   Though shee to whom I swore be here, I can-
    not
Stifle my passion longer: If my Father   210
Should rise againe disquieted with this,
And charge me to forbeare, yet it would out.——
[*Apart to Panthæa*] Madam, a stranger, and a prisoner begs

206 rage] Q2; change Q1

To be bid welcome.
Panthæa.   You are welcome Sir
I thinke, but if you be not, tis past me
To make you so: for I am here a stranger,
Greater then you: we know from whence you come,
But I appeare a lost thing, and by whom
Is yet uncertaine; found here in the Court,
And onely sufferd to walke up and downe,   220
As one not worth the owning.
Spaconia [*aside*].   O, I feare
Tigranes will be caught, he lookes me thinkes
As he would change his eyes with her; some helpe
There is above for me I hope.
Tigranes. Why doe you turne away, and weepe so fast,
And utter things that misbecome your lookes,
Can you want owning?
Spaconia [*aside*].   O, tis certaine so.
Tigranes. Acknowledge your selfe mine——
Arbaces.   How now?
Tigranes.   And then
See if you want an owner.
Arbaces.   They are talking.
Tigranes. Nations shall owne you for their Queene.   230
Arbaces. *Tigranes*, art not thou my prisoner?
Tigranes. I am.
Arbaces.   And who is this?
Tigranes.   Shee is your Sister.
Arbaces. Shee is so.
Mardonius [*aside*].   Is shee so againe? thats well.
Arbaces. And how dare you then offer to change words with her?
Tigranes. Dare doe it? why you brought me hither Sir
To that intent.
Arbaces.   Perhaps I told you so:
If I had sworne it, had you so much follie
To credit it? The least word that shee speakes
Is worth a life: rule your disorderd tongue,
Or I will temper it.

Spaconia [*aside*].   Blest be that breath.   240

Tigranes.   Temper my tongue? such incivilities
As these, no barbarous people ever knew:
You breake the law of Nature, and of Nations;
You talke to me, as if I were a prisoner
For theft: my tongue be temperd? I must speake
If thunder checke me, and I will.

Arbaces.   You will?

Spaconia [*aside*].   Alas my Fortune.

Tigranes.   Doe not feare his frowne, deare Madam heare me.

Arbaces.   Feare not my frowne? but that 'twere base in me
To fight with one I know I can orecome,   250
Againe thou shouldst be conquered by me.

Mardonius [*aside*].   He has one ransome with him already, me
thinkes twere good to fight double, or quit.

Arbaces.   Away with him to prison.——Now Sir see
If my frowne be regardlesse.——Why delay you?
Seize him *Bacurius*.——You shall know my word
Sweepes like a wind, and all it grapples with,
Are as the chaffe before it.

Tigranes.   Touch me not.

Arbaces.   Helpe there.

Tigranes.   Away.

1. Gentleman.   It is in vaine to struggle.

2. Gentleman.   You must be forc't.

Bacurius.   Sir, you must pardon us,   260
We must obey.

Arbaces.   Why doe you dally there?
Drag him away by any thing.

Bacurius.   Come Sir.

Tigranes.   Justice, thou oughtst to give me strength enough
To shake all these off:——This is tyrannie
Arbaces, subtiller then the burning Buls,
Or that fam'd Tyrants bed. Thou mightst as well
Search in the depth of winter through the Snow
For halfe starv'd people, to bring home with thee
To shew um fire, and send um backe againe,

224

As use me thus.

Arbaces.   Let him be close *Bacurius.*   270

    Exeunt Tigranes [*guarded by the two* Gentlemen] *and* Bacurius.

Spaconia [*aside*].   I nere rejoyc'd at any ill to him,
  But this imprisonment: what shall become
  Of me forsaken?

Gobrius.   You will not let your sister
  Depart thus discontented from you Sir?

Arbaces.   By no meanes *Gobrius*, I have done her wrong,
  And made my selfe beleeve much of my selfe,
  That is not in me.——
                    You did kneele to me,
  Whilst I stood stubborne and regardlesse by;
  And like a god incensed, gave no eare
  To all your prayers: behold, I kneele to you;   280
  Shew a contempt as large as was my owne,
  And I will suffer it; yet at the last
  Forgive me.

Panthæa.   O you wrong me more in this,
  Then in your rage you did: you mocke me now.

Arbaces.   Never forgive me then, which is the worst
  Can happen to me.

Panthæa.   If you be in earnest,
  Stand up, and give me but a gentle looke,
  And two kind words, and I shall be in Heaven.

Arbaces.   Rise you then to; here I acknowledge thee
  My hope, the onely Jewell of my life,   290
  The best of sisters, dearer then my breath,
  A happinesse as high as I could thinke;
  And when my actions call thee otherwise,
  Perdition light upon me.

Panthæa.   This is better
  Then if you had not frown'd, it comes to me
  Like mercy at the blocke; and when I leave
  To serve you with my life, your curse be with me.

Arbaces.   Then thus I doe salute thee, and againe   [*Kisses her.*]

270.1 S.D. Q2; *om.* Q1

To make this knot the stronger.——[*Aside*] Paradice
Is there.——[*To Panthæa*] It may be you are still in doubt,   300
This third kisse blots it out.——[*Aside*] I wade in sinne,
And foolishly intice my selfe along.——
Take her away, see her a prisoner
In her owne chamber, closely *Gobrius*.
Panthæa.   Alas Sir, why?
Arbaces.   I must not stay the answere,
Doe it.
Gobrius.   Good Sir.
Arbaces.   No more, doe it I say.
Mardonius [*aside*].   This is better and better.
Panthæa.   Yet heare me speake.
Arbaces.   I will not heare you speake:——
Away with her, let no man thinke to speake
For such a creature: for shee is a witch,   310
A poysoner, and a Traytor.
Gobrius.   Madam, this Office grieves me.
Panthæa.   Nay, tis well; the King is pleas'd with it.
Arbaces.   *Bessus*, goe you along too with her; I will prove
All this that I have said, if I may live
So long: but I am desperately sicke,
For shee has given me poyson in a kisse;
Shee had it twixt her lips, and with her eyes
Shee witches people: go without a word.——
                    Exeunt omnes, præter Arbaces, Mardonius.
Why should you that have made me stand in war   320
Like fate it selfe, cutting what threds I pleas'd,
Decree such an unworthy end of me,
And all my glories? what am I alas,
That you oppose me? If my secret thoughts
Have ever harbour'd swellings against you,
They could not hurt you, and it is in you
To give me sorrow, that will render me
Apt to receive your mercy; rather so,

301 This] Q2; This, this Q1   306 *Gobrius.*] Q2; *Panthæa.* Q1
312 *Gobrius.*] Q2; *Bacurius.* Q1   313 *Panthæa.*] Q2; *Gobrius.* Q1

Let it be rather so, then punish me
With such unmanly sinnes: Incest is in me   330
Dwelling alreadie, and it must be holie
That pulles it thence.——
                          Where art *Mardonius?*
Mardonius.   Here Sir.
Arbaces.   I prethee beare me, if thou canst;
  Am I not growne a strange weight?
Mardonius.   As you were.
Arbaces.   No heavier?
Mardonius.   No Sir.
Arbaces.   Why, my legs refuse
  To beare my bodie; O *Mardonius,*
  Thou hast in field beheld me, when thou know'st
  I could have gone, though I could never runne.
Mardonius.   And so I shall againe.
Arbaces.   O no, tis past.
Mardonius.   Pray ye goe, rest your selfe.   340
Arbaces.   Wilt thou hereafter when they talke of me,
  As thou shalt heare nothing but infamie;
  Remember some of those things.
Mardonius.   Yes, I will.
Arbaces.   I prethee doe: for thou shalt never see
  Me so again.
Mardonius.   I warrant ye.
                                              Exeunt.

                          Enter Bessus.   [III. ii]

Bessus.   They talke of fame, I have gotten it in the warres, and
will affoord any man a reasonable penny-worth: some will say
they could be content to have it, but that it is to be atchieved with
danger; but my opinion is otherwise: for if I might stand still in
Canon proofe, and have fame fall upon me, I would refuse it:
My reputation came principally by thinking to runne away,
which no bodie knowes but *Mardonius,* and I think he conceales
it to anger me. Before I went to the warres, I came to the Towne a

young fellow without meanes, or parts, to deserve friends; and
my emptie guts perswaded me to lie, and abuse people for my 10
meate, which I did, and they beate me: then would I fast two
dayes, till my hunger cride out on me, raile still; then me thought
I had a monstrous stomacke to abuse them againe, and did it. In
this state I continued till they hung me up by th' heeles, and beate
me with hasle sticks, as if they would have baked mee, and have
cosen'd some bodie with mee for Venison: After this I rail'd,
and eate quietlie: for the whole Kingdome tooke notice of me for
a baffel'd whipt fellow, and what I said, was remembred in mirth,
but never in anger; of which I was glad. I would it were at that
passe againe: After this, God cald an Ant of mine, that left two 20
hundred pounds in a Cosens hand for me, who taking me to be a
gallant young spirit, rais'd a company for mee with the money,
and sent me into *Armenia* with um: Away I would have runne
from them, but that I could get no company, and alone I durst
not run. I was never at battle but once, and there I was running,
but *Mardonius* cudgel'd me; yet I got loose at last, but was so
afraid, that I saw no more then my shoulders doe, but fled with
my whole company amongst my enemies, and overthrew um:
Now the report of my valor is come over before mee, and they say
I was a raw young fellow, but now I am improv'd. A plague 30
of their eloquence, twill cost me many a beating: And *Mardonius*
might helpe this to if he would; for now they thinke to get
honour of me, and all the men I have abus'd, call me freshly to
account, worthily as they call it, by the way of challenge.

Enter a Gentleman.

Gentleman. Good morrow Captaine *Bessus.*
Bessus. Good morrow Sir.
Gentleman. I come to speake with you.
Bessus. You are very welcome.
Gentleman. From one that holds himselfe wronged by you some
  three yeers since: your worth he sayes is fam'd, and he nothing 40
  doubts but you will doe him right, as beseemes a Souldier.
Bessus [*aside*]. A pox on um, so they crie all.

34.1 *a*] Q2; *om.* Q1

228

Gentleman. And a slight note I have about me for you, for the deliverie of which, you must excuse me; it is an office that friendship calles upon mee to doe, and no way offensive to you, since I desire but right on both sides.

Bessus. Tis a challenge Sir, is it not?

Gentleman. Tis an inviting to the field.

Bessus. An inviting? O crie you mercie:——[*aside*] what a complement he delivers it with? he might as agreeablie to my nature 50 present mee poyson with such a speech:——[*reads*] um reputation, um call you to an account, um forst to this, um with my sword, um like a gentleman, um deare to me, um satisfaction.——Tis verie well Sir, I doe accept it, but he must awaite an answere this thirteene weekes.

Gentleman. Why Sir, he would be glad to wipe off his staine as soone as hee can.

Bessus. Sir upon my credit I am already ingag'd to two hundred and twelve, all which must have their staines wipt off, if that be the word, before him.   60

Gentleman. Sir, if you be truly ingaged but to one, he shall stay a competent time.

Bessus. Upon my faith Sir, to two hundred and twelve, and I have a spent bodie too much bruis'd in battle, so that I cannot fight, I must be plaine with you, above three combates a day: All the kindnesse I can doe him, is to set him resolutely in my rowle the two hundred and thirteenth man, which is something: for I tell you, I thinke there will be more after him, then before him, I thinke so: pray ye commend me to him, and tell him this.

Gentleman. I will Sir, good morow to you.   70

Bessus. Good morow good Sir.——   *Exit* Gentleman.
Certenly my safest way were to print my selfe a coward, with a discoverie how I came by my credit, and clap it up on every post: I have received above thirty challenges within this two houres, marry all but the first I put off with ingagement, and by good fortune the first is no madder of fighting then I, so that that's referr'd. The place where it must be ended, is foure dayes journey

58 *Bessus.*] Q2; *om.* Q1   71 Gentleman] Q2; *om.* Q1
77 referr'd] Q2 (referd); reserv'd Q1

of, and our arbytrators are these: He has chosen a gentleman
in travell, and I have a speciall friend, with a quarterne ague
likely to hold him this five yeare for mine; and when his man 80
comes home, wee are to expect my friends health: If they would
send me challenges thus thicke, as long as I liv'd I would have no
other living; I can make seauen shillings a day o'th paper to the
Grocers: yet I learne nothing by all these but a little skill in
comparing of stiles. I doe find evidently that there is some one
Scrivener in this Towne, that has a great hand in writing of
challenges, for they are all of a cut, and six of um in a hand;
and they all end, my reputation is deare to me, and I must require
satisfaction:———whose there? more paper I hope; no, tis my
Lord *Bacurius*, I feare all is not well betwixt us.   90

Enter Bacurius.

Bacurius.   Now Captaine *Bessus*, I come about a frivilous matter,
caus'd by as idle a report: you know you were a coward.
Bessus.   Very right.
Bacurius.   And wrong'd me.
Bessus.   True my Lord.
Bacurius.   But now people will call you valiant, desertlesly I
thinke, yet for their satisfaction, I wil have you fight with me.
Bessus.   O my good Lord, my deepe ingagements———
Bacurius.   Tell not me of your ingagements, Captaine *Bessus*;
it is not to be put off with an excuse: for my owne part, I am none 100
of the multitude that beleeve your conversion from coward.
Bessus.   My Lord, I seeke not quarrels, and this belongs not to
me, I am not to maintaine it.
Bacurius.   Who then pray?
Bessus.   *Bessus* the coward wrong'd you.
Bacurius.   Right.
Bessus.   And shall *Bessus* the valiant, maintaine what *Bessus* the
coward did?
Bacurius.   I prethee leave these cheating trickes, I sweare thou
shalt fight with mee, or thou shalt be beate extreamely, and kickt. 110
Bessus.   Since you provoke me thus farre my Lord, I will fight

78 these] Q2; there Q1   80 five yeare] Q2; time here Q1

with you; and by my Sword it shall cost me twenty pounds,
but I will have my legge well a weeke sooner purposely.

Bacurius.   Your legge, why what ailes your legge? Ile doe a cure
on you, stand up.

Bessus.   My Lord, this is not noble in you.

Bacurius.   What dost thou with such a phrase in thy mouth? I will
kicke thee out of all good words before I leave thee. [*Kicks him.*]

Bessus.   My Lord, I take this as a punishment for the offence I did
when I was a coward.   120

Bacurius.   When thou wert? confesse thy selfe a coward still, or
by this light, Ile beate thee into spunge.

Bessus.   Why I am one.

Bacurius.   Are you so Sir, and why doe you weare a sword then?
Come, unbuckle, quicke.

Bessus.   My Lord——

Bacurius.   Unbuckle I say, and give it mee, or as I live, thy head
will ake extreamely.

Bessus.   It is a pretty hilt, and if your Lordship take an affection
to it, with all my heart, I present it to you for a new-yeers gift.   130

Bacurius.   I thanke you very heartily, sweete Captaine farewell.

Bessus.   One word more, I beseech your Lordship to render me
my knife againe.

Bacurius.   Marry by all meanes Captaine, cherish your selfe
with it, and eate hard good Captaine; we cannot tell whether we
shall have any more such: Adue deare Captaine.   *Exit.*

Bessus.   I will make better use of this, then of my sword: A base
spirit has this vantage of a brave one; it keepes alwayes at a stay,
nothing brings it downe, not beating. I remember I promist the
King in a great audience, that I would make my back-byters eate   140
my sword to a knife, how to get another sword I know not, nor
know any meanes left for me to maintaine my credit but impudence:
Therefore will I outsweare him and all his followers, that this
is all is left uneaten of my sword.

                                                              Exit.

113 well] Q2; *om.* Q1

Enter Mardonius.   [III. iii]

Mardonius.   Ile move the King, hee is most strangely alter'd; I
guesse the cause I feare too right, Heaven has some secret end
in't, and tis a scourge no question justly laid upon him: Hee
has followed mee through twenty roomes, and ever when I
stay to await his command, he blushes like a girle, and lookes
upon me, as if modestie kept in his businesse: so turnes away
from me, but if I goe on, hee followes me againe.

Enter Arbaces.

See, here he is, I doe not use this, yet I know not how, I cannot
chuse but weepe to see him: his very enemies I thinke, whose
wounds have bred his fame, if they should see him now, would 10
find teares in their eyes.

Arbaces [*aside*].   I cannot utter it: why should I keepe
A breast to harbour thoughts I dare not speake?
Darkenesse is in my bosome, and there lies
A thousand thoughts that cannot brooke the light;
How wilt thou vex me when this deede is done
Conscience, that art afraid to let me name it?

Mardonius.   How doe you Sir?

Arbaces.   Why very well *Mardonius*;
How dost thou doe?

Mardonius.   Better then you I feare.

Arbaces.   I hope thou art; for to be plaine with thee,   20
Thou art in hell else: secret scorching flames
That farre transcend earthly materiall fiers,
Are crept into me, and there is no cure;
Is not that strange *Mardonius*, theres no cure?

Mardonius.   Sir, either I mistake, or there is something hid that
you would utter to me.

Arbaces.   So there is, but yet I cannot doe it.

Mardonius.   Out with it Sir: if it be dangerous I shall not shrinke
to doe you service, I shal not esteeme my life a waightier matter

---

7.1 S.D. Q2; *om.* Q1   8 do not use] *i.e.* am not accustomed to
19 doe] Q2; *om.* Q1   23 Are] Q2; Art Q1

then indeed it is, I know tis subject to more chances then it 30
hath houres, and I were better loose it in my Kings cause, then
with an ague, or a fall, or sleeping to a thiefe; as all these are
probable enough: let me but know what I shal do for you.
Arbaces [*aside*].   It will not out.———
                                    Were you with *Gobrius*,
And bad him give my sister all content
The place affoords, and give her leave to send
And speake to whom shee please?
Mardonius.   Yes Sir, I was.
Arbaces.   And did you to *Bacurius* say as much
  About *Tigranes*?
Mardonius.   Yes.
Arbaces.   Thats all my businesse.
Mardonius.   O say not so,   40
  You had an answere of all this before,
  Besides, I thinke this businesse might be utterd
  More careleslie.
Arbaces.   Come, thou shalt have it out; I doe beseech thee
  By all the love thou hast profest to me,
  To see my Sister from me.
Mardonius.   Well, and what?
Arbaces.   Thats all.
Mardonius.   That's strange, shall I say nothing to her?
Arbaces.   Not a word;
  But if thou lovest me, find some subtill way
  To make her understand by signes.
Mardonius.   But what?   50
  What should I make her understand?
Arbaces.   O *Mardonius*, for that I must be pardon'd.
Mardonius.   You may, but I can onelie see her then.
Arbaces.   Tis true;
  Beare her this ring then, and on more advice
  Thou shalt speake to her: Tell her I doe love
  My kindred all; wilt thou?
Mardonius.   Is there no more?

32 a fall] Q2; fall Q1

233

Arbaces. O yes, and her the best;
Better then any brother loves his sister:
That's all.
Mardonius. Me thinkes this   60
Neede not have beene delivered with such caution;
Ile doe it.
Arbaces. There is more yet: Wilt thou be faithfull to me?
Mardonius. Sir, if I take upon me to deliver it,
After I heare it, Ile passe through fire to doe it.
Arbaces. I love her better then a brother ought;
Dost thou conceive me?
Mardonius. I hope I doe not Sir.
Arbaces.   No? thou art dull,
Kneele downe before her, and nere rise againe,
Till shee will love me.
Mardonius.   Why, I thinke shee does.   70
Arbaces. But better then shee does, another way;
As wives love Husbands.
Mardonius.   Why, I thinke there are few wives
That love their husbands better then shee does you.
Arbaces. Thou wilt not understand me: is it fit
This should bee utterd plainlie? take it then
Naked as it is: I would desire her love
Lasciviouslie, leudlie, incestuouslie,
To doe a sinne that needs must damne us both;
And thee to: Dost thou understand me now?
Mardonius. Yes, there's your Ring againe; what have I done   80
Dishonestlie in my whole life, name it,
That you should put so base a businesse to me?
Arbaces. Didst thou not tell mee thou wouldst doe it?
Mardonius. Yes, if I undertooke it; but if all
My heires were lives, I would not be ingag'd
In such a cause to save my last life.
Arbaces. O guilt, how poore, and weake a thing art thou?
This man that is my servant, whom my breath
Might blow about the world, might beate me here
Having his cause, whilst I prest downe with sinne   90

234

Could not resist him.——

　　　　　　　　　　Deare *Mardonius*
It was a motion misbeseeming man.
And I am sorrie for it.

Mardonius.　Pray God you may be so: you must understand,
nothing that you can utter, can remoove my love and service
from my Prince. But otherwise, I thinke I shall not love you
more. For you are sinnefull, and if you doe this crime, you
ought to have no lawes; For after this it will bee great injustice
in you to punish any offendor for any crime: For my selfe I
find my heart too bigge, I feele I have not patience to looke on 100
whilst you runne these forbidden courses: Meanes I have none
but your Favour, and I am rather glad, that I shall loose um both
together, then keepe um with such conditions: I shall find a
dwelling amongst some people, where though our garments
perhaps be courser, we shall be richer farre within, and harbor
no such vices in um. God preserve you, and mend you.

Arbaces.　*Mardonius*, stay *Mardonius*, For though
My present state require nothing but knaves
To be about me, such as are prepar'd
For every wicked act, yet who does know　　　　　　　　　110
But that my loathed Fate may turne about,
And I have use of honest men againe:
I hope I may, I prethy leave me not.

　　　　　　　　Enter Bessus *to them.*

Bessus.　Where is the King?
Mardonius.　There.
Bessus.　An't please your Majestie, ther's the knife.
Arbaces.　What knife?
Bessus.　The Sword is eaten.
Mardonius.　Away you Foole, the King is serious,
And cannot now admit your vanities.　　　　　　　　　120
Bessus.　Vanities? I am no honest man if my enemies have not
brought it to this: what, doe you thinke I lie?
Arbaces.　No, no, tis well *Bessus*, tis very well,
I am glad ont'.

124 I am] Q2; *Mar.* I am Q1

Mardonius.   If your enemies brought it to that, your enemies are cutlers: Come, leave the King.

Bessus.   Why, may not valour approach him?

Mardonius.   Yes, but he has affaires; depart, or I shall be something unmannerly with you.

Arbaces.   No, let him stay *Mardonius*, let him stay,   130
I have occasions with him very weightie,
And I can spare you now.

Mardonius.   Sir?

Arbaces.   Why I can spare you now.

Bessus.   *Mardonius* give way to the state affayres.

Mardonius.   Indeed you are fitter for his present purpose.   *Exit.*

Arbaces.   *Bessus* I should imploy thee; wilt thou do't?

Bessus.   Do't for you? by this ayre I will doe any thing without exception, be it a good, bad, or indifferent thing.

Arbaces.   Do not sweare.   140

Bessus.   By this light but I will, any thing whatsoever.

Arbaces.   But I shall name a thing
Thy conscience will not suffer thee to doe.

Bessus.   I would faine heare that thing.

Arbaces.   Why I would have thee get my Sister for me:
(Thou understands me?) in a wicked manner.

Bessus.   O you would have a bout with her? Ile do't, Ile do't Ifaith.

Arbaces.   Wilt thou, dost make no more ant?

Bessus.   More? no, why is there any thing else? if there be tell me, 150
it shall be done too.

Arbaces.   Hast thou no greater sence of such a sinne?
Thou art too wicked for my company,
Though I have hell within me, and mayst yet
Corrupt me further: pray thee answere me
How doe I shew to thee after this motion?

125 *Mardonius.*] Q2; *om.* Q1
127–129 Q2; *om.* Q1
138 Do't] Q2; Doe Q1
147 a bout] Q7; about Q1–6, F2
151 too] Q2; *om.* Q1

Bessus.   Why your Majestie lookes as well in my opinion as ever
you did since you were borne.

Arbaces.   But thou appearest to me after thy grant
The ugliest, loathed, detestable thing   160
That I have ever met with. Thou hast eyes
Like flames of *Sulphur*, which me thinkes doe dart
Infection on me, and thou hast a mouth
Enough to take me in, where there doe stand
Fower rowes of Iron teeth.

Bessus.   I feele no such thing, but tis no matter how I looke, Ile
doe your businesse as well as they that looke better, and when this
is dispatcht, if you have a minde to your Mother tell me, and
you shall see Ile set it hard.

Arbaces.   My Mother? Heaven forgive me to heare this,   170
I am inspir'd with horror: I hate thee
Worse then my sinne, which if I could come by,
Should suffer death eternall, nere to rise
In any breast againe. Know I will die
Languishing mad, as I resolve I shall,
Ere I will deale by such an Instrument:
Thou art too sinfull to imploy in this;
Out of the world, away.   [*Beats him.*]

Bessus.   What doe you meane Sir?

Arbaces.   Hung round with curses, take thy fearefull flight
Into the desarts, where mongst all the monsters,   180
If thou findst one so beastly as thy selfe,
Thou shalt be held as innocent.

Bessus.   Good Sir.

Arbaces.   If there were no such Instruments as thou,
We Kings could never act such wicked deeds:
Seeke out a man that mockes Divinitie,
That breakes each precept both of Gods and Mans,
And Natures too, and does it without lust;
Meerely because it is a law, and good,
And live with him: for him thou canst not spoile.

Away I say.——   *Exit* Bessus.
                    I will not doe this sinne.   190

237

Ile presse it here till it doe breake my breast;
It heaves to get out: but thou art a sinne
And spight of torture, I wil keep thee in.

                                              [*Exit.*]

                Enter Gobrius, Panthæa, Spaconia.   IV. i

Gobrius.   Have you written, Madam?
Panthæa.   Yes, good *Gobrius.*
Gobrius.   And with a kindnesse, and such winning words
As may provoke him at one instant feele
His double fault, your wrong, and his owne rashnesse?
Panthæa.   I have sent words enough, if words may winne him
From his displeasure, and such words I hope
As shall gaine much upon his goodnesse, *Gobrius*:
Yet fearing since th'are many, and a womans,
A poore beliefe may follow, I have woven
As many truthes within um to speake for me,   10
That if he be but gracious, and receive um——
Gobrius.   Good Ladie, be not fearefull; though he should not
Give you your present end in this, beleeve it
You shall feele (if your vertue can induce you
To labour out this tempest, which I know
Is but a poore proofe 'gainst your patience)
All those contents your spirit will arrive at
Newer, and sweeter to you; your royall brother
(When he shall once collect himselfe, and see
How farre he has beene asunder from himselfe,   20
What a meere stranger to his golden temper)
Must from those rootes of vertue, (never dying
Though somewhat stopt with humour) shoote againe
Into a thousand glories, bearing his faire branches
Hie as our hopes can looke at, straight as Justice,
Loden with ripe contents: he loves you dearely,
I know it, and I hope I neede not further

        IV.i] *Finis Actus Tertii.* | Actus Quarti Scæna Prima.
        12 though] Q2; if Q1   16 'gainst] Q2; against Q1

Winne you to understand it.

Panthæa.   I beleeve it:
But howsoever I am sure I love him dearely,
So dearely, that if any thing I write   30
For my inlarging, should beget his anger,
Heaven be a witnesse with mee, and my faith,
I had rather live intomb'd here.

Gobrius.   You shall not feele a worse stroke then your griefe,
I am sorrie tis so sharpe: I kisse your hand,
And this night will deliver this true storie
With this hand to your brother.

Panthæa.   Peace goe with you,
You are a good man.——   *Exit* Gobrius.
                              My *Spaconia*
Why are you ever sad thus?

Spaconia.   O deere Ladie.

Panthæa.   Prethee discover not a way to sadnesse   40
Neerer then I have in me: our two sorrowes
Worke like two eager Hawkes, who shall get highest;
How shall I lessen thine? for mine I feare
Is easier knowne then cur'd.

Spaconia.   Heaven comfort both,
And give yours happy ends; how ever I
Fall in my stubborne fortunes.

Panthæa.   This but teaches
How to be more familiar with our sorrowes,
That are too much our Masters. Good *Spaconia*,
How shall I doe you service?

Spaconia.   Noblest Ladie,
You make me more a slave still to your goodnesse,   50
And onely live to purchase thankes to pay you;
For that is all the business of my life now:
I will be bold, since you will have it so,
To aske a noble favour of you.

Panthæa.   Speake it, tis yours; for from so sweet a vertue
No ill demand has issue.

Spaconia.   Then ever vertuous, let me beg your will
In helping me to see the Prince *Tigranes*,
With whom I am equall prisoner; if not more.
Panthæa.   Reserve me to a greater end *Spaconia*;   60
Bacurius cannot want so much good manners,
As to denie your gentle visitation,
Though you came only with your owne command.
Spaconia.   I know they will denie me gracious Madam,
Being a stranger, and so little fam'd,
So utter emptie of those excellencies,
That tame authority: But in you sweete Ladie
All these are naturall, beside a power
Deriv'd immediat from your royal brother,
Whose least word in you may command the Kingdome.   70
Panthæa.   More then my word *Spaconia*, you shall carrie,
For feare it faile you.
Spaconia.   Dare you trust a token?
Madam, I feare Ime growne too bold a beggar.
Panthæa.   You are a pretty one, and trust me Ladie
It joyes me I shall doe a good to you,
Though to my selfe I never shall be happie:
Here take this Ring, and from me as a token
Deliver it; I thinke they will not stay you:
So all your owne desires goe with you Ladie.
Spaconia.   And sweete peace to your grace.
Panthæa.   Pray God I find it.   80
                                    Exeunt [severally].

                    Enter Tigranes *in prison.*   [IV.ii]

Tigranes.   Foole that I am, I have undone my selfe,
And with mine owne hand turnd my fortune round,
That was a faire one: I have childishly
Plaied with my hope so long, till I have broke it,

        59 not] Q2; no Q1   67 tame] Q2; have Q1
        71 word] Q2; words Q1
        0.1 *in prison*] Q2; *om.* Q1   2 turnd] Q2 (turn'd); turne Q1

And now too late I mourne for't: O *Spaconia*
Thou hast found an even way to thy revenge now,
Why didst thou follow me like a faint shadow,
To wither my desires? But wretched foole,
Why did I plant thee twixt the Sunne and me,
To make me freeze thus? why did I preferre her   10
To the faire Princes? O thou foole, thou foole,
Thou Family of Fooles, live like a slave still,
And in thee beare thine owne hell, and thy torment;
Thou hast deserv'd it: Couldst thou find no Ladie
But shee that has thy hopes to put her to,
And hazard all thy peace? None to abuse
But shee that lov'd thee ever, poore *Spaconia*,
And so much lov'd thee, that in honestie
And honour thou art bound to meete her vertues;
Shee that forgot the greatnesse of her griefes   20
And miseries, that must follow such mad passions,
Endlesse and wilde as womans: Shee that for thee,
And with thee lost her libertie, her name,
And Countrey; you have paid me, equall Heavens,
And sent my owne rod to correct me with:
A woman; for inconstancie Ile suffer,
Lay it on, Justice, till my soule melt in me
For my unmanly, beastly, sudden doting
Upon a new face; after all my oathes,
Many, and strange ones.   30
I feele my olde fire flame againe, and burne
So strong and violent, that should I see her
Againe, the griefe, and that would kill me.

Enter Bacurius *and* Spaconia.

Bacurius.   Ladie,
Your token I acknowledge, you may passe;
There is the King.

*24 me, equall] Seward; me equall, Q 2–8, F 2; me equall Q 1
33 *Bacurius.* Ladie,] Q 2; *Tigranes*....Ladie. Q 1

Spaconia.   I thanke your Lordship for it. *Exit* Bacurius.
Tigranes [*aside*].   Shee comes, shee comes, shame hide me ever
     from her;
   Would I were buried, or so farre remov'd
   Light might not find me out: I dare not see her.
Spaconia.   Nay, never hide your selfe; for were you hid
   Where earth hides all her riches, nere her center;   40
   My wrongs without more day would light me to you:
   I must speake ere I die; were all your greatnesse
   Doubled upon you, y'are a perjur'd man,
   And onely mighty in the wickednesse
   Of wronging women. Thou art false, false Prince,
   I live to see it: poore *Spaconia* lives
   To tell thee thou art false; and then no more:
   Shee lives to tell thee thou art more unconstant
   Then all ill women ever were together;
   Thy faith as firme as raging overflowes,   50
   That no banke can command; and as lasting
   As boyes gay bubbles blowne in the aire, and broken:
   The wind is fixt to thee, and sooner shall
   The beaten Marriner with his shrill whistle,
   Calme the loude murmurs of the troubled maine,
   And strike it smooth againe; then thy soule fall
   To have peace in love with any: Thou art all
   That all good men must hate, and if thy storie
   Shall tell succeeding ages what thou wert,
   O let it spare me in it, lest true Lovers   60
   In pitty of my wrongs burne thy blacke legend,
   And with their curses shake thy sleeping ashes.
Tigranes.   Oh, oh!
Spaconia.   The destinies I hope have pointed out
   Our ends alike, that thou maist die for love,
   Though not for me: for this assure thy selfe,
   The Princesse hates thee deadly, and will sooner
   Be wonne to marrie with a Bull, and safer,
   Then such a beast as thou art:——[*aside*] I have strucke

64 *Spaconia.*] Q2; *om.* Q1

242

I feare too deepe; beshrow me fort:——Sir,   70
This sorrow workes me like a cunning friendship,
Into the same piece with it:——[*aside*] hee's asham'd,
Alas, I have beene too rugged:——Deare my Lord,
I am sorrie I have spoken any thing,
Indeed I am, that may adde more restraint
To that too much you have: Good Sir be pleas'd
To thinke it was a fault of love, not malice;
And doe as I will doe: forgive it Prince,
I doe, and can forgive the greatest sinnes
To me you can repent of; pray believe me.   80
Tigranes.   O my *Spaconia*! O thou vertuous woman!
Spaconia.   No more, the King Sir.

          Enter Arbaces, Bacurius, *and* Mardonius.

Arbaces.   Have you beene carefull of our noble Prisoner
   That he want nothing fitting for his greatnesse?
Bacurius.   I hope his grace will quit me, for my care Sir.
Arbaces.   Tis well.——
                    Royall *Tigranes*, health.
Tigranes.   More then the stricktnesse of this place can give Sir
   I offer backe againe to great *Arbaces*.
Arbaces.   We thanke you worthy Prince, and pray excuse us,
   We have not seene you since your being here;   90
   I hope your noble usage has beene equall
   With your owne Person: your imprisonment
   If it be any, I dare say is easie,
   And shall not outlast two dayes.
Tigranes.   I thanke you:
   My usage here has beene the same it was
   Worthy a royall Conquerour. For my restraint
   It came unkindly, because much unlookt for;
   But I must beare it.
Arbaces.   What Lady is that *Bacurius*?
Bacurius.   One of the Princesse women Sir.   100
Arbaces.   I feard it: why comes shee hether?
Bacurius.   To speake with the Prince *Tigranes*.

Arbaces.   From whom *Bacurius?*

Bacurius.   From the Princesse Sir.

Arbaces.   I knew I had seene her.

Mardonius [*aside*].   His fit beginnes to take him now againe: tis a strange Feaver, and twill shake us all anone I feare; would he were well cur'd of this raging folly: Give me the warres, where men are mad, and may talke what they list, and held the bravest Fellowes; This pelting pratling peace is good for nothing: drinking's a 110 vertue to it.

Arbaces.   I see theres truth in no man, nor obedience,
But for his owne ends, why did you let her in?

Bacurius.   It was your owne command to barre none from him,
Beside the Princesse sent her Ring Sir, for my warrant.

Arbaces.   A token to *Tigranes,* did she not?
Sirra tell truth.

Bacurius.   I doe not use to lye Sir,
Tis no way I eate or live by, and I thinke
This is no token Sir.

Mardonius [*aside*].   This combat has undone him: If he had beene 120 well beaten, he had beene temperate: I shal never see him hansome againe, till he have a Horse-mans staffe poak't through his shoulders, or an arme broke with a Bullet.

Arbaces.   I am trifled with.

Bacurius.   Sir?

Arbaces.   I know it, as I know thee to be false.

Mardonius [*aside*].   Now the clap comes.

Bacurius.   You never knew me so Sir, I dare speake it,
And durst a worse man tell me though my better.

Mardonius [*aside*].   Tis well said, by my Soule.   130

Arbaces.   Sirra you answere as you had no life.

Bacurius.   That I feare Sir to loose nobly.

Arbaces.   I say Sir once againe——

Bacurius.   You may say Sir what you please.

Mardonius [*aside*].   Would I might doe so.

Arbaces.   I will Sir, and say openly this woman carries letters, by my life I know she carries letters, this woman does it.

105 knew] Q2; know Q1

244

Mardonius   Would *Bessus* were here to take her aside and search
her, he would quickly tell you what she carried Sir.
Arbaces.   I have found it out, this woman carries letters.   140
Mardonius [*aside*].   If this hold, twill be an ill world for Bauds,
   Chamber-maids, and post-boyes, I thanke God I have none but
   his letters pattents, things of his owne inditing.
Arbaces.   Prince this cunning cannot doe it.
Tigranes.   Doe what Sir? I reach you not.
Arbaces.   It shall not serve your turne Prince.
Tigranes.   Serve my turne Sir?
Arbaces.   I Sir, it shall not serve your turne.
Tigranes.   Be plainer good Sir.
Arbaces.   This woman shall carry no more letters backe to your 150
   love *Panthæa*, by heaven she shall not, I say she shall not.
Mardonius [*aside*].   This would make a Saint sweare like a Souldier,
   and a Souldier like termogant.
Tigranes.   This beates me more, King, then the blowes you gave
   me.
Arbaces.   Take um away both, and together let um be prisoners,
   strictly and closely kept, or Sirra your life shall answere it; and
   let no bodie speake with um hereafter.
Bacurius.   Well, I am subject to you, and must endure these
   passions.   160
Spaconia [*aside*].   This is the imprisonment I have lookt
   For alwayes, and the deare place I would chuse.
                    Exit Bacurius *with* Tigranes *and* Spaconia.
Mardonius.   Sir, have you done well now?
Arbaces.   Dare you reprove it?
Mardonius.   No.
Arbaces.   You must be crossing me.
Mardonius.   I have no letters Sir to anger you,
   But a dry sonnet of my Corporals
   To an old Sutlers wife, and that Ile burne Sir:
   Tis like to prove a fine age for the Ignorant.
Arbaces.   How darest thou so often forfeit thy life?
   Thou knowest tis in my power to take it.   170

Mardonius.   Yes, and I know you wonnot,
  Or if you doe, youle misse it quicklie.
Arbaces.   Why?
Mardonius.   Who shall then tell you of these childish follies
  When I am dead? Who shall put to his power
  To draw those vertues out of a floud of humours
  Where they are drownd, and make um shine againe?
  No cut my head off: doe, kill me:
  Then you may talke, and be beleevd, and grow,
  And have your too selfe-glorious temper rock't
  Into a dead sleepe, and the kingdome with you,   180
  Till forraigne swords be in your throats, and slaughter
  Be every where about you like your flatterers.
  Doe, kill me.
Arbaces.   Prethee be tamer good *Mardonius,*
  Thou knowst I love thee, nay I honour thee:
  Beleeve it good old Souldier I am all thine:
  But I am rackt cleane from my selfe: beare with me;
  Woot thou beare with me my *Mardonius?*

                    Enter Gobrius.

Mardonius.   There comes a good man, love him too, hees temperate,
  You may live to have need of such a vertue,   190
  Rage is not still in fashion.
Arbaces.   Welcome good *Gobrius.*
Gobrius.   My service, and this letter to your grace.
Arbaces.   From whom?
Gobrius.   From the rich mine of vertue, and all beautie,
  Your mournefull Sister.
Arbaces.   She is in prison *Gobrius,* is shee not?
Gobrius.   She is Sir till your pleasure doe enlarge her,
  Which on my knees I beg; O tis not fit
  That all the sweetnesse of the world in one;
  The youth, and vertue, that would tame wilde Tygers   200

          *179 rock't] Seward (rock'd); rott Q 1–8, F 2
          181 Till] Q 2; Like Q 1   188 my] Q 2; good Q 1
          200 tame] Q 2; have Q 1

                    246

And wilder people, that have knowne no manners
Should live thus Cloysterd up. For your loves sake
(If there be any in that Noble heart)
To her a wretched Ladie, and forlorne,
Or for her love to you, (which is as much
As Nature, and obedience ever gave)
Have pittie on her beauties.
Arbaces.   Prethee stand up, tis true she is too Faire,
And all these commendations but her owne:
Would thou hadst never so commended her,   210
Or I nere liv'd to have heard it, *Gobrius*;
If thou but knew'st the wrong her beautie does her,
Thou wouldst in pittie of her be a lyar:
Thy ignorance has drawne me wretched man
Whether my selfe nor thou canst well tell. O my Fate,
I thinke shee loves me; but I feare another
Is deeper in her heart: how thinkst thou *Gobrius*?
Gobrius.   I doe beseech your Grace beleeve it not,
For let me perish if it be not false:
Good Sir reade her letter.   220
Mardonius [aside].   This love, or what a divell is it, I know not,
begets more mischiefe then a wake. I had rather be well beaten,
starv'd, or lowsie, then live within the aire ont. He that had seene
this brave fellow charge through a grove of pykes but tother day,
and looke upon him now, will nere beleeve his eyes againe; If
he continue thus but two daies more, a Taylor may beat him
with one hand tyed behind him.
Arbaces.   Alas she would be at libertie,
And there be thousand reasons *Gobrius*,
Thousands that will denie it: 230
Which if she knew, she would contentedly
Be where she is, and blesse her vertue for it,
And me though she were closer. She would *Gobrius*,
Good man indeed she would.
Gobrius.   Then good Sir for her satisfaction

212 knew'st] Q2; knew of Q1
230 Thousands] Q2; *om.* Q1

247

Send for her, and with reason make her know
Why she must live thus from you.
Arbaces.   I will: goe bring her to me.

Exeunt [severally].

[IV. iii]

Enter Bessus, *and two* Sword-men, *and a Boy.*

Bessus.   Y'are verie welcome both:——some stooles there boy,
And reach a Table:——Gentlemen oth' Sword,
Pray sit without more complement:——be gone childe.——

[*Exit Boy.*]

I have beene curious in the searching of you,
Because I understood you wise, and valiant persons.
1. Sword-man.   We understand our selves Sir.
Bessus.   Nay Gentlemen, and my deare friends oth' Sword,
No complement I pray; but to the cause
I hang upon, which in few, is my honour.
2. Sword-man.   You cannot hang too much Sir for your honour,   10
But to your cause, be wise, and speake truth.
Bessus.   My first doubt is my beating by my Prince.
1. Sword-man.   Stay there a little Sir, doe you doubt a beating,
Or have you had a beating by your Prince?
Bessus.   Gentlemen ath' sword, my Prince has beaten me.
2. Sword-man.   Brother what thinke you of this case?
1. Sword-man.   If he have beaten him, the case is cleare.
2. Sword-man.   If he have beaten him I grant the case;
But how? We cannot be too subtill in this businesse:
I say, but how?
Bessus.   Even with his royall hand.   20
1. Sword-man.   Was it a blow of love or indignation?
Bessus.   Twas twentie blowes of indignation gentlemen,
Besides two blowes ath' face.
2. Sword-man.   Those blowes ath' face have made a new case ont',
The rest were but an honourable rudenesse.
1. Sword-man.   Two blowes oth' face, and given by a worse man, I
must confesse as we Sword-men say, had turnd the businesse:
Marke me brother, by a worse man; but being by his Prince,

248

had they beene ten, and those ten drawne ten teeth, beside the
hazard of his nose for ever; all these had beene but favours: 30
This is my flat opinion, which Ile die in.

2. *Sword-man.*   The King may doe much Captaine beleeve it, for
had hee crackt your skull through like a bottle, or broke a rib or
two with tossing of you, yet you had lost no honour: This is
strange you may imagin; but this is truth now Captaine.

Bessus.   I will be glad to imbrace it gentlemen;
But how farre may he strike me?

1. *Sword-man.*   Theres another,
A new cause rising from the time, and distance,
In which I will deliver my opinion:
He may strike, beate, or cause to be beaten; for these are naturall 40
to man: your Prince I say may beate you so farre forth as his
dominion reacheth; that's for the distance: the time, ten mile a
day, I take it.

2. *Sword-man.*   Brother you erre, tis fifteene mile a day,
His stage is ten, his beatings are fifteene.

Bessus.   Tis a the longest, but we subjects must——

1. *Sword-man.*   Be subject to it: you are wise, and vertuous.

Bessus.   Obedience ever makes that noble use ont,
To which I dedicate my beaten bodie;
I must trouble you a little further Gentlemen oth' Sword.   50

2. *Sword-man.*   No trouble at all to us Sir, if we may
Profit your understanding; we are bound
By vertue of our calling, to utter our opinions
Shortly, and discreetly.

Bessus.   My sorest businesse is, I have beene kickt.

2. *Sword-man.*   How farre Sir?

Bessus.   Not to flatter my selfe in it, all over:
My sword lost, but not forst; for discreetely
I renderd it to save that imputation.

34 tossing] Q2; crossing Q1
36 gentlemen] Q2 (Gentlemen); gentleman Q1
47 1. *Sword-man.*] Q2 (1); *om.* Q1
48 *Bessus.*] Q2; 1. Q1
58 lost] Seward; forst Q1–8, F2
58 forst] Seward (forc'd); lost Q1–8, F2

1. Sword-man.   It shewed discretion, the best part of valour.   60

2. Sword-man.   Brother, this is a pretty case, pray ponder on't,
Our friend here has beene kickt.

1. Sword-man.   He has so brother.

2. Sword-man.   Sorely he sayes: Now had he sit downe here
Upon the meere kicke, it had beene cowardly.

1. Sword-man.   I thinke it had beene cowardly indeed.

2. Sword-man.   But our friend has redeem'd it, in delivering
His sword without compulsion; and that man
That tooke it of him, I pronounce a weake one,
And his kicks nullities.
He should have kickt him after the deliverie,   70
Which is the confirmation of a coward.

1. Sword-man.   Brother, I take it you mistake the question:
For say that I were kickt——

2. Sword-man.   I must not say so;
Nor I must not heare it spoke byth' tongue of man:
You kickt deare brother? you are merrie.

1. Sword-man.   But put the case I were kickt?

2. Sword-man.   Let them put it that are things wearie of their lives,
and know not honour: put the case you were kickt?

1. Sword-man.   I doe not say I was kickt.

2. Sword-man.   Nor no silly creature, that weares his head without 80
a case, his soule in a skin-coate: you kickt deare brother?

Bessus.   Nay Gentlemen, let us doe what we shall doe
Truly and honestly; good Sir toth' question.

1. Sword-man.   Why then I say, suppose your boy kickt, Captaine?

2. Sword-man.   The boy may be suppos'd, hee's lyable;
But kicke my brother?

1. Sword-man.   A foolish forward zeale Sir in my friend:——
But to the boy, suppose the boy were kickt?

Bessus.   I doe suppose it.

1. Sword-man.   Has your boy a sword?

Bessus.   Surely no: I pray suppose a sword too.   90

1. Sword-man.   I doe suppose it: you grant your boy was kickt
then.

78 the] Q2; *om.* Q1

250

2. Sword-man.   By no meanes Captaine, let it be suppos'd still;
this word grant, makes not for us.

1. Sword-man.   I say this must be granted.

2. Sword-man.   This must be granted brother?

1. Sword-man.   I, this must be granted.

2. Sword-man.   Still the must.

1. Sword-man.   I say this must be granted.

2. Sword-man.   Give me the must againe; brother you palter.   100

1. Sword-man.   I will not heare you, waspe.

2. Sword-man.   Brother, I say
You palter, the must three times together?
I weare as sharpe steele as another man,
And my Foxe bites as deepe, musted my deare brother?
But to the cause againe.

Bessus.   Nay, looke you Gentlemen——

2. Sword-man.   In a word I ha done.

1. Sword-man.   A tall man, but untemperate; tis great pittie:——
Once more suppose the boy kickt.

2. Sword-man.   Forward.

1. Sword-man.   And being throughly kickt, laughes at the kicker.   110

2. Sword-man.   So much for us; proceede.

1. Sword-man.   And in this beaten scorne, as I may call it,
Delivers up his weapon: where lies the error?

Bessus.   It lies ith beating Sir, I found it
Foure dayes since.

2. Sword-man.   The error, and a sore one,
As I take it; lies in the thing kicking.

Bessus.   I understand that well, tis sore indeed Sir.

1. Sword-man.   That is according to the man that did it.

2. Sword-man.   There springs a new branch: whose was the foote?

Bessus.   A Lords.   120

1. Sword-man.   The cause is mightie, but had it beene two Lords,
And both had kickt you, if you laught, tis cleere.

Bessus.   I did laugh,
But how will that helpe me Gentlemen?

---

100 againe;] Q2; againe, againe; Q1   110 kicker] Q2; kicke Q1
119 foote] Q2; foole Q1   120 A] Q2; Ah Q1

1. Sword-man.   Yes, it shall helpe you, if you laught alowd.

Bessus.   As lowd as a kickt man could laugh, I laught Sir.

1. Sword-man.   My reason now; the valiant man is knowne
  By suffering and contemning, you have
  Enough of both, and you are valiant.

2. Sword-man.   If he be sure he has beene kickt enough: 130
  For that brave sufferance you speake of brother,
  Consists not in a beating, and away,
  But in a cudgeld bodie, from eighteene
  To eight and thirtie: in a head rebuk't
  With pots of all Size, daggers, stooles, and bedstaves,
  This shewes a valiant man.

Bessus.   Then I am valiant, as valiant, as the proudest,
  For these are all familiar things to me:
  Familiar as my sleepe, or want of money.
  All my whole bodi's but one bruize with beating,   140
  I thinke I have beene cudgeld with all nations,
  And almost all Religions.

2. Sword-man.   Imbrace him brother, this man is valiant,
  I know it by my selfe, hees valiant.

1. Sword-man.   Captaine thou art a valiant Gentleman
  To abide upon't, a very valiant man.

Bessus.   My equall friends ath' sword, I must request
  Your hands to this.

2. Sword-man.   Tis fit it should be.

Bessus [*calling*].   Boy, get some wine, and pen and inke within:—— 150
  Am I cleare Gentlemen?

1. Sword-man.   Sir when the world
  Has taken notice what we have done,
  Make much of your bodie, for Ile pawne my steele,
  Men will be coyer of their legs hereafter.

Bessus.   I must request you goe along,
  And testifie to the Lord *Bacurius*,
  Whose foot has strucke me, how you find my cause.

2. Sword-man.   We will, and tell that Lord he must be rul'd,
  Or there be those abroad will rule his Lordship.

                                        Exeunt.

Enter Arbaces *at one doore,* Gobrius *and* Panthæa *at another.*   [IV. iv]

Gobrius.   Sir her's the Princesse.

Arbaces.   Leave us then alone.
For the maine cause of her imprisonment
Must not be heard by any but her selfe.——   *Exit* Gobrius.
You are welcome Sister, and I would to God
I could so bid you by another name.——
[*Aside*] If you above love not such sinnes as these,
Circle my heart with thoughts as cold as snow
To quench these rising flames that harbour here.

Panthæa.   Sir, does it please you, I should speake?

Arbaces.   Please me?
I, more then all the art of Musicke can,   10
Thy speech does please me, for it ever sounds
As thou broughts joyfull unexpected newes:
And yet it is not fit thou shouldst be heard,
I prethee thinke so.

Panthæa.   Be it so, I will.
I am the first that ever had a wrong
So farre from being fit to have redresse,
That twas unfit to heare it; I will backe
To prison rather then disquiet you,
And waite till it be fit.

Arbaces.   No, doe not goe,
For I will heare thee with a serious thought: 20
I have collected all thats man about me
Together strongly, and I am resolvd
To heare thee largely, but I doe beseech thee
Doe not come neerer to me, for there is
Something in that that will undoe us both.

Panthæa.   Alas Sir am I venom?

Arbaces.   Yes to me.
Though of thy selfe I thinke thee to be in
As equall a degree of heate, or cold
As Nature can make, yet as unsound men

3 S.D. Q2; *om.* Q1

Convert the sweetest, and the nourishingst meates   30
Into diseases, so shall I distemperd,
Doe thee, I prethee draw no neerer to me.
Panthæa.   Sir this is that I would: I am of late,
Shut from the world, and why it should be thus
Is all I wish to know.
Arbaces.   Why credit me
Panthæa, credit me that am thy brother,
Thy loving brother, that there is a cause
Sufficient, yet unfit for thee to knowe,
That might undoe thee everlastingly
Onely to heare: wilt thou but credit this?   40
By heaven tis true, beleeve it if thou canst.
Panthæa.   Children and fooles are ever credulous;
And I am both I thinke, for I beleeve:
If you dissemble be it on your head,
Ile backe unto my prison, yet me thinkes
I might be kept in some place where you are:
For in my selfe I finde, I know not what
To call it, but it is a great desire
To see you often.
Arbaces.   Fie, you come in a step, what doe you meane   50
Deare Sister? doe not so: Alas *Panthæa*,
Where I am, would you be? why thats the cause
You are imprisond, that you may not be
Where I am.
Panthæa.   Then I must endure it Sir, God keepe you.
Arbaces.   Nay, you shall heare the cause in short *Panthæa*;
And when thou hearst it, thou wilt blush for me,
And hang thy head downe like a Violet
Full of the mornings dew: There is a way
To gaine thy freedome, but tis such a one   60
As puts thee in worse bondage, and I know,
Thou wouldst encounter fire, and make a proofe
Whether the Gods have care of Innocents,
Rather then follow it; know I have lost
The onely difference betwixt man, and beast,

My reason.

Panthæa.   Heaven forbid.

Arbaces.   Nay it is gone,
And I am left as farre without a bound,
As the wild Ocean that obeyes the winds;
Each suddaine passion throwes me as it lists,
And overwhelmes all that oppose my will: 70
I have beheld thee with a lustfull eye:
My heart is set on wickednesse, to act
Such sinnes with thee, as I have beene afraid
To thinke off: If thou dar'st consent to this,
(Which I beseech thee doe not) thou maist gaine
Thy libertie, and yeeld me a content:
If not, thy dwelling must be darke, and close
Where I may never see thee; For God knowes
That layd this punishment upon my pride,
Thy sight at some time will enforce my madnesse   80
To make a start ene to thy ravishing:
Now spit upon me, and call all reproaches
Thou canst devise together; and at once
Hurle um against me: for I am a sicknesse
As killing as the plague, ready to seize thee.

Panthæa.   Farre be it from me to revile the King:
But it is true, that I should rather chuse
To search out death, that else would search out me,
And in a grave sleepe with my innocence,
Then welcome such a sinne: It is my fate,   90
To these crosse accidents I was ordaind,
And must have patience; and but that my eyes
Have more of woman in um then my heart,
I would not weepe: peace enter you againe.

Arbaces.   Farewell, and good *Panthæa* pray for me;
Thy prayers are pure, that I may find a death,
How ever soone before my passions grow,
That they forget, what I desire, is sinne;
For thether they are tending: If that happen,

81 ene] Q2 (eene); eye Q1

255

Then I shall force thee, though thou wert a Virgin   100
By vow to Heaven, and shall pull a heape
Of strange, yet uninvented sinnes upon me.
Panthæa.   Sir, I will pray for you; yet you shall know
It is a sullen fate that governes us.
For I could wish as heartilie as you
I were no Sister to you, I should then
Imbrace your lawfull love sooner then health.
Arbaces.   Couldst thou affect me then?
Panthæa.   So perfectly
That as it is, I nere shall sway my heart
To like another.
Arbaces.   Then I curse my birth: 110
Must this be added to my miseries
That thou art willing too? Is there no stoppe
To our full happinesse, but these meere sounds,
Brother and Sister?
Panthæa.   There is nothing else:
But these alas will seperate us more
Then twentie worlds betwixt us.
Arbaces.   I have liv'd
To conquer men, and now am overthrowne
Onely by words, Brother and Sister: where
Have those words dwelling? I will find um out
And utterly destroy them, but they are   120
Not to be grasp't: let um be men or beasts,
And I will cut um from the earth, or townes,
And I will rase um, and then blow um up:
Let um be Seas, and I will drinke them off,
And yet have unquencht fire left in my breast:
Let um be any thing but meerely voice.
Panthæa.   But tis not in the power of any Force
Or pollicie to conquer them.
Arbaces.   *Panthæa,*
What shall wee doe? shall we stand firmely here,
And gaze our eyes out?

112 stoppe] Q2 (stop); steppe Q1

256

Panthæa.   Would I could doe so;   130
But I shall weepe out mine.
Arbaces.   Accursed man,
Thou boughtst thy reason at too deare a rate;
For thou hast all thy actions bounded in
With curious rules, when everie Beast is free:
What is there that acknowledges a kindred
But wretched Man? Who ever saw the Bull
Fearefully leave the Heifer that he likt,
Because they had one Dam?
Panthæa.   Sir, I disturbe you,
And my selfe too; twere better I were gone:
I will not be so foolish as I was.   140
Arbaces.   Stay, we will love just as becomes our birthes,
No otherwise: Brothers and Sisters may
Walke hand in hand together; so will we:
Come neerer: Is there any hurt in this?
Panthæa.   I hope not.
Arbaces.   Faith theres none at all:
And tell me truly now, is there not one
You love above me?
Panthæa.   No by Heaven.
Arbaces.   Why yet
You sent unto *Tigranes*, Sister.
Panthæa.   True,
But for another: for the truth——
Arbaces.   No more,
Ile credit thee; I know thou canst not lie,   150
Thou art all truth.
Panthæa.   But is there nothing else
That we may doe, but onely walke; me thinkes
Brothers and sisters lawfully may kisse.
Arbaces.   And so they may *Panthæa*, so will we: [*They kiss.*]
And kisse againe too; we were scrupulous
And foolish, but we will be so no more.   [*They kiss.*]
Panthæa.   If you have any mercy, let me goe

147 Why] Q2; *om.* Q1

17   257   B D W

To prison, to my death, to any thing:
I feele a sinne growing upon my bloud,
Worse then all these, hotter I feare then yours.   160
Arbaces.   That is impossible, what should we doe?
Panthæa.   Flie Sir for Gods sake.
Arbaces.   So we must, away;
Sin growes upon us more by this delay.

                                        Exeunt severall ways.

                    Enter Mardonius, *and* Ligones.   V. i

Mardonius.   Sir, the King has seene your Commission, and
        beleeves it,
And freely by this warrant gives you leave
To visit Prince *Tigranes,* your noble Master.
Ligones.   I thanke his Grace, and kisse his hands.
Mardonius.   But is the maine of all your businesse
Ended in this?
Ligones.   I have another, but a worse;
I am asham'd: it is a businesse——
Mardonius.   You seeme a worthy person, and a stranger
I am sure you are; you may imploy mee if
You please, without your purse, such Offices   10
Should ever be their owne rewards.
Ligones.   I am bound to your noblenesse.
Mardonius.   I may have neede of you, and then this curtesie,
If it be any, is not ill bestowed:
But may I civilly desire the rest?
I shall not be a hurter, if no helper.
Ligones.   Sir, you shall know I have lost a foolish daughter,
And with her all my patience; pilferd away
By a meane Captaine of your Kings.
Mardonius.   Stay there Sir:
If he have reacht the noble worth of Captaine,   20

    163.1 S.D. Q4; *Exeunt.* Q2–3; *om.* Q1
    V.i] *Finis Actus Quarti.* | Actus Quinti Scæna Prima.
    *8 seeme] Dyce (seem); serve Q1–8, F2   10 Offices] Q2 (offices); Officers Q1

                                    258

He may well claime a worthy gentlewoman,
Though shee were yours, and noble.

Ligones.   I grant all that too: but this wretched fellow
Reaches no further then the emptie name,
That serves to feede him; were he valiant,
Or had but in him any noble nature,
That might hereafter promise him a good man;
My cares were something lighter, and my grave
A span yet from me.

Mardonius.   I confesse such fellowes
Be in all royall Campes, and have, and must be   30
To make the sinne of coward more detested
In the meane Souldier, that with such a foyle
Sets of much valour: By description
I should now guesse him to you. It was *Bessus*,
I dare almost with confidence pronounce it.

Ligones.   Tis such a scurvy name as *Bessus*, and now
I thinke tis hee.

Mardonius.   Captaine, doe you call him?
Beleeve me Sir, you have a miserie
Too mighty for your age: A pox upon him,
For that must be the end of all his service: 40
Your daughter was not mad Sir?

Ligones.   No, would shee had beene,
The fault had had more credit: I would doe something.

Mardonius.   I would faine counsell you; but to what I know not:
Hee's so below a beating, that the women
Find him not worthy of their distaves; and
To hang him, were to cast away a rope,
Hee's such an ayrie thin unbodied coward,
That no revenge can catch him:
Ile tell you Sir, and tell you truth; this rascall
Feares neither God nor man: has beene so beaten,   50
Sufferance has made him wanscote;
He has had since hee was first a slave,
At least three hundred daggers set in his head,
As little boyes doe new knives in hot meat;

Ther's not a rib in's bodie a my conscience,
That has not beene thrice broken with drie beating;
And now his sides looke like to wicker targets,
Everie way bended:
Children will shortly take him for a wall,
And set their stone-bowes in his forhead: He   60
Is of so low a sence, I cannot in
A weeke imagine what should be done to him.
Ligones.   Sure I have committed some great sinne,
That this strange fellow should be made my rod:
I would see him, but I shall have no patience.
Mardonius.   Tis no great matter if you have not, if a laming of
him, or such a toy may doe you pleasure Sir, he has it for you,
and Ile helpe you to him: tis no newes to him to have a leg broke,
or a shoulder out, with being turnd ath' stones like a Tanzie:
Draw not your sword, if you love it; for of my conscience his 70
head will breake it: we use him ith' warres like a Ramme to shake
a wall withall; here comes the verie person of him, doe as you
shall find your temper, I must leave you: but if you doe not
breake him like a bisket, you are much too blame Sir.

                                            Exit Mardonius.

                Enter Bessus *and* Sword-men.

Ligones.   Is your name *Bessus?*
Bessus.   Men call me Captaine *Bessus.*
Ligones.   Then Captaine *Bessus* you are a ranke rascall, without
more exordiums, a durty frozen slave; and with the favour of
your friends here, I will beate you.
2. Sword-man.   Pray use your pleasure Sir, you seem to be a 80
gentleman.
Ligones.   Thus Captaine *Bessus,* thus;
Thus twinge your nose, thus kicke you, and thus tread you.
Bessus.   I doe beseech you yeeld your cause Sir quickly.
Ligones.   Indeed I should have told you that first.
Bessus.   I take it so.
1. Sword-man.   Captaine, a should indeed, he is mistaken.

Ligones.   Sir you shall have it quickly, and more beating,
You have stolne away a Lady, Captaine Coward,
And such a one——   *Beates him.*
Bessus.   Hold, I beseech you, hold Sir,   90
I never yet stole any living thing
That had a tooth about it.
Ligones.   Sir I know you dare lie——
Bessus.   With none but Summer Whores upon my life Sir.
My meanes and manners never could attempt
Above a hedge or hey-cocke.
Ligones.   Sirra that quits not me, where is this Ladie?
Doe that you doe not use to doe, tell truth,
Or by my hand Ile beat your Captaines braines out,
Wash um, and put um in againe, that will I.   100
Bessus.   There was a Ladie Sir, I must confesse
Once in my charge: the Prince *Tigranes* gave her
To my guard for her safetie, how I usd her
She may her selfe report, shee's with the Prince now:
I did but waite upon her like a Groome,
Which she will testifie I am sure: If not,
My braines are at your service when you please Sir,
And glad I have um for you.
Ligones.   This is most likely, Sir I aske your pardon,
And am sorrie I was so intemperate.   110
Bessus.   Well, I can aske no more, you would thinke it strange
Now to have me beat you at first sight?
Ligones.   Indeed I would, but I know your goodnes can
Forget twentie beatings. You must forgive me.
Bessus.   Yes, ther's my hand, goe where you will, I shall
Thinke you a valiant fellow for all this.
Ligones [*aside*].   My daughter is a Whore,
I feele it now too sencible; yet I will see her,
Discharge my selfe of being Father to her,
And then backe to my Countrie, and there die.——   120
Farewell Captaine.

90 *Beates him.*] Q2; *om.* Q1   94 *Bessus.*] Q2; *om.* Q1
95 My] Q2; *Bessus.* My Q1

Bessus.   Farewell Sir, farewell,
Commend me to the Gentlewoman I praia.   *Exit* Ligones.
1. Sword-man.   How now Captaine, beare up man.
Bessus.   Gentlemen ath' sword your hands once more, I have
beene kickt againe, but the foolish fellow is penitent, has ask't
me mercy, and my honor's safe.
2. Sword-man.   We knew that, or the foolish fellow had better a
kick't his Grandsire.
Bessus.   Confirme, confirme I pray.
1. Sword-man.   There be our hands againe.   130
2. Sword-man.   Now let him come, and say he was not sorry,
and he sleepes for it.
Bessus.   Alas good ignorant old man, let him goe, let him goe,
these courses will undoe him.

                                                        Exeunt.

                Enter Ligones, *and* Bacurius.   [V. ii]

Bacurius.   My Lord your authoritie is good, and I am glad it is
so, for my consent would never hinder you from seeing your
owne King. I am a Minister, but not a governour of this state;
yonder is your King, Ile leave you.   *Exit.*

                Enter Tigranes, *and* Spaconia.

Ligones [*aside*].   There he is indeed,
And with him my disloyall childe.
Tigranes.   I doe perceive my fault so much, that yet
Me thinkes thou shouldst not have forgiven me.
Ligones.   Health to your Majestie.
Tigranes.   What? good *Ligones*, welcome; what businesse   10
Brought thee hether?
Ligones.   Severall Businesses.
My publique businesse will appeare by this: [*Gives a paper.*]
I have a message to deliver, which
If it please you so to authorise, is
An embassage from the Armenian state,

Unto *Arbaces* for your libertie:
The offer's there set downe, please you to read it.
Tigranes.　There is no alteration happened
Since I came thence?
Ligones.　　　　　None Sir, all is as it was.
Tigranes.　And all our friends are well?
Ligones.　　　　　　　All verie well.　　　　20
Spaconia [*aside*].　Though I have done nothing but what was good,
I dare not see my Father: It was fault
Enough not to acquaint him with that good.
Ligones.　Madam I should have seene you.
Spaconia.　O good Sir forgive me.
Ligones.　Forgive you, why I am no kin to you, am I?
Spaconia.　Should it be measur'd by my meane deserts,
Indeed you are not.
Ligones.　　　　　Thou couldst prate unhappily
Ere thou couldst goe, would thou couldst doe as well.
And how does your custome hold out here?
Spaconia.　　　　　　　Sir?　　　　30
Ligones.　Are you in private still, or how?
Spaconia.　　　　　　What doe you meane?
Ligones.　Doe you take money? are you come to sell sinne yet?
perhaps I can helpe you to liberall Clients: or has not the King
cast you off yet? O thou vild creature, whose best commendation
is, that thou art a young Whore. I would thy Mother had liv'd
to see this: or rather would I had dyed ere I had seene it: why
did'st not make me acquainted when thou wert first resolv'd to
be a Whore? I would have seene thy hot lust satisfied more
privately. I would have kept a dancer, and a whole consort of
Musitions in mine owne house, onely to fiddle thee.　　　　40
Spaconia.　Sir I was never whore.
Ligones.　If thou couldst not say so much for thy selfe thou
shouldst be Carted.
Tigranes.　*Ligones* I have read it, and like it,
You shall deliver it.
Ligones.　　　　　Well Sir I will:
But I have private busines with you.

263

Tigranes.   Speake, what ist?

Ligones.   How has my age deserv'd so ill of you,
That you can picke no strumpets in the Land,
But out of my breed?

Tigranes.   Strumpets good *Ligones*?   50

Ligones.   Yes, and I wish to have you know, I scorne
To get a Whore for any Prince alive,
And yet scorne will not helpe me thinkes: My daughter
Might have beene spar'd, there were enough beside.

Tigranes.   May I not prosper, but Shee's innocent
As morning light for me, and I dare sweare
For all the world.

Ligones.   Why is she with you then?
Can she waite on you better then your men,
Has she a gift in plucking off your stockings,
Can she make Cawdles well, or cut your Cornes,   60
Why doe you keepe her with you? For your Queene
I know you doe contemne her, so should I
And every Subject else thinke much at it.

Tigranes.   Let um thinke much, but tis more firme then earth
Thou seest thy Queene there.

Ligones.   Then have I made a faire hand, I cald her Whore, if I
shall speake now as her Father, I cannot chuse but greatly rejoyce
that she shall be a Queene: but if I should speake to you as a
Statesman shee were more fit to be your Whore.

Tigranes.   Get you about your businesse to *Arbaces*,   70
Now you talke idlie.

Ligones.   Yes Sir, I will goe.
And shall she be a Queene? she had more wit
Then her old Father when she ranne away:
Shall shee be a Queene? now by my troth tis fine,
Ile dance out of all measure at her wedding:
Shall I not Sir?

Tigranes.   Yes marrie shalt thou.

Ligones.   Ile make these witherd Kexes beare my bodie
Two houres together above ground.

Tigranes.   Nay, goe, my businesse requires haste.

Ligones.   Good God preserve you, you are an excellent King.   80
Spaconia.   Farewell good Father.
Ligones.   Farewell sweete vertuous Daughter;
I never was so joyfull in my life,
That I remember: shall shee be a Queene?
Now I perceive a man may weepe for joy,
I had thought they had lied that said so.   *Exit.*
Tigranes.   Come my deare love.
Spaconia.   But you may see another
May alter that againe.
Tigranes.   Urge it no more;
I have made up a new strong constancie,
Not to be shooke with eyes; I know I have
The passions of a man, but if I meete   90
With any subject that shall hold my eyes
More firmely then is fit; Ile thinke of thee,
And runne away from it: let that suffice.

                                            Exeunt.

                Enter Bacurius, *and a* Servant.   [V. iii]

Bacurius.   Three gentlemen without to speake with me?
Servant.   Yes Sir.
Bacurius.   Let them come in.
Servant.   They are enterd Sir already.

                Enter Bessus, *and* Swordmen.

Bacurius.   Now fellowes, your busines.——[*To Servant*] Are these
the Gentlemen?
Bessus.   My Lord I have made bold to bring these Gentlemen my
Friends ath' sword along with me.
Bacurius.   I am afraid youle fight then.
Bessus.   My good Lord I will not, your Lordship is mistaken,
feare not Lord.
Bacurius.   Sir I am sorrie fort.   10
Bessus.   I can aske no more in honor.——Gentlemen you heare
my Lord is sorrie.

Bacurius.   Not that I have beaten you, but beaten one that will be beaten: one whose dull bodie will require a lamming: as surfeits doe the diet, spring and fall.

Now to your swordmen, what come they for good Captaine Stock-fish?

Bessus.   It seemes your Lordship has forgot my name.

Bacurius.   No, nor your nature neither, though they are things fitter I confesse for any thing, then my remembrance, or anie honest mans: what shall these billets doe, be pilde up in my Wood-yard?

Bessus.   Your Lordship holds your mirth still, God continue it: but for these Gentlemen they come——

Bacurius.   To sweare you are a Coward, spare your Booke, I doe beleeve it.

Bessus.   Your Lordship still drawes wide, they come to vouch under their valiant hands, I am no Coward.

Bacurius.   That would be a shew indeed worth seeing: sirra be wise and take money for this motion, travell with it, and where the name of *Bessus* has been knowne, or a good Coward stirring, twill yeeld more then a tilting. This will prove more beneficiall to you, if you be thriftie, then your Captaineship, and more naturall. ——Men of most valiant hands is this true?

2. Sword-man.   It is so most renowned.

Bacurius.   Tis somewhat strange.

1. Sword-man.   Lord, it is strange, yet true; wee have examined from your Lordships foote there to this mans head, the nature of the beatings; and we doe find his honour is come off cleane, and sufficient: This as our swords shall helpe us.

Bacurius.   You are much bound to your bilbow-men, I am glad you are straight again Captaine: twere good you would thinke some way to gratifie them, they have undergone a labour for you *Bessus,* would have puzzeld *Hercules,* with all his valour.

2. Sword-man.   Your Lordship must understand we are no men ath' Law, that take pay for our opinions: it is sufficient wee have cleer'd our friend.

14 a] Q2; *om.* Q1   *14 lamming] Weber; launcing Q1; laming Q2–8, F2
15 fall] Q2; full Q1   36 *Bacurius.*] Q2; *om.* Q1

Bacurius.   Yet here is something due, which I as toucht in conscience will discharge Captaine; Ile pay this rent for you.

Bessus.   Spare your selfe my good Lord; my brave friends aime 50 at nothing but the vertue.

Bacurius.   Thats but a cold discharge Sir for their paines.

2. Sword-man.   O Lord, my good Lord.

Bacurius.   Be not so modest, I will give you something.

Bessus.   They shall dine with your Lordship, that's sufficient.

Bacurius.   Something in hand the while.——Ye rogues, ye apple-squiers: doe you come hether with your botled valour, your windie frothe, to limit out my beatings?   [*Kicks them.*]

1. Sword-man.   I doe beseech your Lordship——

2. Sword-man.   O good Lord——   60

Bacurius.   Sfoote, what a many of beaten slaves are here?—— Get me a cudgell sirra, and a tough one.   [*Exit* Servant.]

2. Sword-man.   More of your foot, I doe beseech your Lordship.

Bacurius.   You shall, you shall dog, and your fellow beagle.

1. Sword-man.   A this side good my Lord.

Bacurius.   Off with your swords, for if you hurt my foote, Ile have you fleade you rascals.

1. Sword-man.   Mines off my Lord.

2. Sword-man.   I beseech your Lordship stay a little, my strap's tied to my codpiece point: Now when you please.   70

Bacurius.   Captaine, these are your valiant friends, you long for a little too?

Bessus.   I am verie well, I humblie thanke your Lordship.

Bacurius.   Whats that in your pocket, slave; my key you mungrell? thy buttocks cannot be so hard, out with't quicklie.

2. Sword-man.   Here tis Sir, a small piece of Artillerie, that a gentleman a deare friend of your Lordships sent me with to get it mended Sir; for if you marke, the nose is somewhat loose.

Bacurius.   A friend of mine you rascall?——I was never wearier of doing nothing, then kicking these two foote-bals.   80

Enter Servant.

Servant.   Heres a good cudgell Sir.

67 fleade] *i.e.* flayed
80.1 *Enter* Servant.] Q3; *Enter* Servant, *Will. Adkinson:* Q2; *om.* Q1

Bacurius.   It comes too late; I am wearie, prethee doe thou beate um.

2. Sword-man.   My Lord this is foule play ifaith, to put a fresh man upon us; Men, are but men.

Bacurius.   That jest shall save your bones.——Captaine, rally up your rotten regiment, and be gone:——I had rather thresh, then be bound to kicke these raskals, till they cride hold:—— *Bessus* you may put your hand to them now, and then you are quit.——Farewell, as you like this, pray visit mee againe, twill 90 keepe me in good breath.   *Exit* Bacurius.

2. Sword-man.   Has a divellish hard foote, I never felt the like.

1. Sword-man.   Nor I, and yet Ime sure I ha felt a hundred.

2. Sword-man.   If he kicke thus ith dog-daies, he will be drie founderd:——what cure now Captaine, besides oyle of bayes?

Bessus.   Why well enough I warrant you, you can goe?

2. Sword-man.   Yes, God be thanked; but I feele a shrewd ach, sure he has sprang my huckle bone.

1. Sword-man.   I ha lost a haunch.

Bessus.   A little butter friend, a little butter; butter and parselie 100 is a soveraigne matter: *probatum est.*

2. Sword-man.   Captaine, we must request your hands now to our honours.

Bessus.   Yes marrie shall ye, and then let all the world come, we are valiant to our selves, and theres an end.

1. Sword-man.   Nay, then we must be valiant; O my ribbes.

2. Sword-man.   O my small guts, a plague upon these sharpe toe'd shooes, they are murderers.

                                                      Exeunt.

Enter Arbaces *with his Sword drawne.*   [V. iv]

Arbaces.   It is resolv'd, I bore it whilst I could,
I can no more, Hell open all thy gates,
And I will thorough them; if they be shut,
Ile batter um, but I will find the place
Where the most damn'd have dwelling; ere I end,

86–87 Captaine,...up] Q2; Up with Q1   91 S.D. Q2; *om.* Q1

Amongst them all they shall not have a sinne,
But I may call it mine: I must beginne
With murder of my friend, and so goe on
To an incestuous ravishing, and end
My life and sinnes with a forbidden blow   10
Upon my selfe.
                    Enter Mardonius.

Mardonius.   What Tragedie is nere?
That hand was never wont to draw a Sword,
But it cride dead to something.
Arbaces.   *Mardonius,*
Have you bid *Gobrius* come?
Mardonius.   How doe you Sir?
Arbaces.   Well, is he comming?
Mardonius.   Why Sir are you thus?
Why does your hand proclaime a lawlesse warre
Against your selfe?
Arbaces.   Thou answerest me one question with another,
Is *Gobrius* comming?
Mardonius.   Sir he is.
Arbaces.   Tis well.
I can forbeare your questions then, be gone.   20
Mardonius. Sir, I have markt——
Arbaces.   Marke lesse, it troubles you and me.
Mardonius.   You are more variable then you were.
Arbaces.   It may be so.
Mardonius.   To day no Hermit could be humblier
Then you were to us all.
Arbaces.   And what of this?
Mardonius.   And now you take new rage into your eies,
As you would looke us all out of the Land.
Arbaces.   I doe confesse it, will that satisfie?
I prethee get thee gone.
Mardonius.   Sir I will speake.
Arbaces.   Will ye?
Mardonius.   It is my dutie: 30

20 I can] Q2; *Mardonius.* I can Q1   21 *Mardonius.*] Q2; *om.* Q1

I feare you will kill your selfe: I am a subject,
And you shall doe me wrong in't: tis my cause,
And I may speake.
Arbaces.   Thou art not traind in sinne,
It seemes *Mardonius*: kill my selfe? by heaven
I will not doe it yet; and when I will,
Ile tell thee: then I shall be such a creature,
That thou wilt give me leave without a word.
There is a method in mans wickednesse,
It growes up by degrees; I am not come
So high as killing of my selfe, there are   40
A hundred thousand sinnes twixt me and it,
Which I must doe; I shall come toot at last,
But take my oath not now, be satisfied,
And get thee hence.
Mardonius.   I am sorrie tis so ill.
Arbaces.   Be sorrie then,
True sorrow is alone, grieve by thy selfe.
Mardonius.   I pray you let mee see your sword put up
Before I goe; Ile leave you then.
Arbaces.   Why, so!   [*Puts up sword.*]
What follie is this in thee? is it not
As apt to mischiefe as it was before?   50
Can I not reach it thinkest thou? these are toyes
For children to be pleas'd with, and not men;
Now I am safe you thinke: I would the booke
Of Fate were here, my sword is not so sure,
But I should get it out, and mangle that
That all the destinies should quite forget
Their fix't decrees, and hast to make us new
Farre other Fortunes, mine could not be worse,
Wilt thou now leave me?
Mardonius.   God put into your bosome temperate thoughts,   60
Ile leave you though I feare.
Arbaces.   Goe, thou art honest.——
                              Exit Mardonius.

61.1 Mardonius] Q 2; *om.* Q 1

270

Why should the hastie errors of my youth
Be so unpardonable, to draw a sinne
Helpelesse upon me?

Enter Gobrius.

Gobrius [*aside*].   There is the King,
   Now it is ripe.
Arbaces.   Draw neere thou guiltie man,
   That art the author of the loathedst crime
   Five ages have brought forth, and heare me speake
   Curses incurable; and all the evils
   Mans bodie or his spirit can receive
   Be with thee.
Gobrius.   Why Sir doe you curse me thus?   70
Arbaces.   Why doe I curse thee? if there be a man
   Subtill in curses, that exceedes the rest,
   His worst wish on thee. Thou hast broke my hart.
Gobrius.   How Sir? Have I preserv'd you from a childe,
   From all the arrowes, malice or ambition
   Could shoot at you, and have I this for pay?
Arbaces.   Tis true thou didst preserve me, and in that
   Wert crueller then hardned murderers
   Of Infants and their mothers; thou didst save me
   Onely till thou hadst studdied out a way   80
   How to destroy me cunningly thy selfe:
   This was a curious way of torturing.
Gobrius.   What doe you meane?
Arbaces.   Thou knowst the evils thou hast done to me:
   Dost thou remember all those witching letters
   Thou sentst unto me to *Armenia*,
   Fild with the praise of my beloved Sister,
   Where thou extolst her beautie? what had I
   To doe with that, what could her beautie be
   To me? and thou didst write how well shee lov'd me,   90
   Doest thou remember this? so that I doated
   Something before I saw her.
Gobrius.   This is true.

271

Arbaces.   Is it? and when I was returnd thou knowst
Thou didst pursue it, till thou woundst mee in
To such a strange, and unbeleev'd affection,
As good men cannot thinke on.
Gobrius.   This I grant,
I thinke I was the cause.
Arbaces.   Wert thou? Nay more,
I thinke thou meantst it.
Gobrius.   Sir I hate a lie
As I love God, and honestie, I did:
It was my meaning.
Arbaces.   Be thine owne sad Judge,   100
A further condemnation will not need:
Prepare thy selfe to die.
Gobrius.   Why Sir to die?
Arbaces.   Why wouldst thou live, was ever yet offendor
So impudent, that had a thought of mercy
After confession of a crime like this?
Get out I cannot, where thou hurlst me in,
But I can take revenge, that's all the sweetnesse
Left for me.
Gobrius [*aside*].   Now is the time.——Heare me but speake.
Arbaces.   No, yet I will be farre more mercifull
Then thou wert to me; thou didst steale into me,   110
And never gavest me warning: so much time
As I give thee now, had prevented thee
For ever. Notwithstanding all thy sinnes,
If thou hast hope, that there is yet a prayer
To save thee, turne, and speake it to your selfe.
                                        [*Draws his sword.*]
Gobrius.   Sir, you shall know your sinnes before you doe um:
If you kill me——
Arbaces.   I will not stay then.
Gobrius.   Know
You kill your Father.

Arbaces.   How?

Gobrius.   You kill your Father.

Arbaces.   My Father? though I know it for a lie
Made out of feare to save thy stained life: 120
The verie reverence of the word comes crosse me,
And ties mine arme downe.

Gobrius.   I will tell you that
Shall heighten you againe, I am thy Father,
I charge thee heare me.

Arbaces.   If it should be so,
As tis most false, and that I should be found
A bastard issue, the dispised fruite
Of lawlesse lust, I should no more admire
All my wilde passions: but another truth
Shall be wrung from thee: If I could come by
The spirit of paine, it should be powr'd on thee,   130
Till thou allowest thy selfe more full of lies
Then he that teaches thee.

Enter Arane.

Arane.   Turne thee about,
I come to speake to thee, thou wicked man,
Heare me thou Tyrant.

Arbaces.   I will turne to thee,
Heare me thou Strumpet: I have blotted out
The name of mother, as thou hast thy shame.

Arane.   My shame? thou hast lesse shame then any thing:
Why dost thou keepe my daughter in a prison?
Why dost thou call her Sister, and doe this?

Arbaces.   Cease thou strange impudence, and answere quickly,   140
If thou contemn'st me, this will aske an answere,
And have it.   *Points to his sword.*

Arane.   Helpe me gentle *Gobrius.*

Arbaces.   Guilt dare not helpe guilt, though they grow together
In doing ill, yet at the punishment
They sever, and each flies the noyse of other,

142 S.D. Q8; *om.* Q1–7, F2

Thinke not of helpe, answere.

Arane.   I will, to what?

Arbaces.   To such a thing as if it be a truth,
Thinke what a creature thou hast made thy selfe,
That didst not shame to doe, what I must blush
Onely to ask thee: tell me who I am,   150
Whose sonne I am, without all circumstance;
Be thou as hastie, as my Sword will be
If thou refusest.

Arane.   Why you are his sonne.

Arbaces.   His sonne? Sweare, sweare, thou worse then woman
      damn'd.

Arane.   By all thats good you are.

Arbaces.   Then art thou all
That ever was knowne bad. Now is the cause
Of all my strange misfortunes come to light:
What reverence expects thou from a childe
To bring forth which thou hast offended Heaven,
Thy husband and the Land? Adulterous witch   160
I know now why thou wouldst have poyson'd me,
I was thy lust which thou wouldst have forgot:
Then wicked mother of my sinnes, and me,
Shew me the way to the inheritance
I have by thee: which is a spacious world
Of impious acts, that I may soone possesse it:
Plagues rott thee, as thou liv'st, and such diseases
As use to pay lust, recompence thy deed.

Gobrius.   You doe not know why you curse thus.

Arbaces.   Too well:
You are a paire of Vipers, and behold   170
The Serpent you have got; there is no beast
But if he knew it, has a pedigree
As brave as mine, for they have more discents,
And I am every way as beastly got,
As farre without the compasse of a law,
As they.

163 Then] Q 2; Thou Q 1

Arane.   You spend your rage, and words in vaine,
And raile upon a guesse: heare us a little.
Arbaces.   No I will never heare, but talke away
My breath, and die.
Gobrius.   Why but you are no Bastard.
Arbaces.   Howe's that?
Arane.   Nor childe of mine.
Arbaces.   Still you goe on   180
In wonders to me.
Gobrius.   Pray you be more patient,
I may bring comfort to you.
Arbaces.   I will kneele,
And heare with the obedience of a childe;   [*Puts up sword.*]
Good Father speake, I doe acknowledge you,
So you bring comfort.
Gobrius.   First know our last King your supposed Father
Was olde and feeble when he marryed her,
And almost all the Land as shee past hope
Of issue from him.
Arbaces.   Therefore shee tooke leave
To play the whoore, because the King was old: 190
Is this the comfort?
Arane.   What will you find out
To give me satisfaction, when you find
How you have injur'd me: let fire consume mee,
If ever I were whore.
Gobrius.   Forbeare these starts,
Or I will leave you wedded to despaire,
As you are now: if you can find a temper,
My breath shall be a pleasant westerne wind,
That cooles, and blastes not.
Arbaces.   Bring it out good Father,
Ile lie, and listen here as reverentlie
As to an Angell: If I breathe too loude,   200
Tell me; for I would be as still as night.
Gobrius.   Our King I say was old, and this our Queene

Desired to bring an heire; but yet her husband
Shee thought was past it, and to be dishonest
I thinke shee would not; if shee would have beene,
The truth is, shee was watcht so narrowlie,
And had so slender opportunitie,
Shee hardly could have beene: But yet her cunning
Found out this way; shee fain'd her selfe with child,
And postes were sent in haste throughout the Land,   210
And God was humbly thankt in every Church,
That so had blest the Queen, and prayers were made
For her safe going, and deliverie:
Shee fain'd now to grow bigger, and perceiv'd
This hope of issue made her feard, and brought
A farre more large respect from everie man.
And saw her power increase, and was resolv'd,
Since shee believ'd shee could not have't indeede;
At least shee would be thought to have a child.

Arbaces.   Doe I not heare it well; nay, I will make   220
No noise at all; but pray you to the point,
Quicke as you can.

Gobrius.   Now when the time was full,
Shee should be brought abed; I had a sonne
Borne, which was you: This the Queene hearing of,
Mov'd me to let her have you, and such reasons
Shee shewed me, as shee knew would tie
My secresie: she sware you should be King;
And to be short, I did deliver you
Unto her, and pretended you were dead;
And in mine owne house kept a Funerall,   230
And had an emptie coffin put in earth:
That night the Queene fain'd hastilie to labour,
And by a paire of women of her owne,
Which shee had charm'd, shee made the world believe
Shee was deliver'd of you: you grew up
As the Kings sonne, till you were six yeere olde;
Then did the King die, and did leave to me
Protection of the Realme; and contrarie

To his owne expectation, left this Queene
Truly with childe indeed of the faire Princesse   240
Panthæa: Then shee could have torne her heire,
And did alone to me, yet durst not speake
In publike; for shee knew shee should be found
A Traytor, and her talke would have beene thought
Madnesse, or any thing rather then truth:
This was the onely cause why shee did seeke
To poyson you, and I to keepe you safe:
And this the reason why I sought to kindle
Some sparke of love in you to faire *Panthæa*,
That shee might get part of her right agen.   250
Arbaces.   And have you made an end now, is this all?
If not, I will be still till I am aged,
Till all my heires are silver.
Gobrius.   This is all.
Arbaces.   And is it true say you too Maddam?
Arane.   Yes, God knowes it is most true.
Arbaces.   *Panthæa* then is not my Sister?
Gobrius.   No.
Arbaces.   But can you prove this?
Gobrius.   If you will give consent:
Else who dare goe about it?
Arbaces.   Give consent?
Why I will have them all that know it rackt
To get this from um.——All that waites without   260
Come in, what ere you be come in, and be
Partakers of my Joy.

                Enter Mardonius, Bessus, *and others.*

                O you are welcome.
Mardonius the best newes——nay, draw no neerer
They all shall heare it:——I am found no King.
Mardonius.   Is that so good newes?
Arbaces.   Yes, the happiest newes
That ere was heard.

          254 too] Q2; *om.* Q1   257 *Gobrius.*] Q2; *om.* Q1

Mardonius.   Indeed twere well for you,
 If you might be a little lesse obey'd.
Arbaces.   One call the Queene.
Mardonius.   Why she is there.
Arbaces.   The Queene
 Mardonius, *Panthæa* is the Queene,
 And I am plaine *Arbaces*:——goe some one,   270
 She is in *Gobrius* house.——   *Exit* 1. Gentleman.
                              Since I saw you
 There are a thousand things deliverd to me
 You little dreame of.
Mardonius.   So it should seeme: My Lord,
 What furi's this?
Gobrius.   Beleeve me tis no fury,
 All that he sayes is truth.
Mardonius.   Tis verie strange.
Arbaces.   Why doe you keepe your hats off Gentlemen,
 Is it to me? I sweare it must not be:
 Nay, trust me, in good faith it must not be;
 I cannot now command you, but I pray you
 For the respect you bare me, when you tooke   280
 Me for your King, each man clap on his hat
 At my desire.
Mardonius.   We will: but you are not found
 So meane a man but that you may be cover'd
 As well as we, may you not?
Arbaces.   O not here,
 You may, but not I, for here is my Father
 In presence.
Mardonius.   Where?
Arbaces.   Why there: O the whole storie
 Would be a wildernesse to loose thy selfe
 For ever.——O pardon me deare Father,
 For all the idle, and unreverent words

---

268 One] Q2; On, Q1
271 *Exit* 1. Gentleman.] Dyce; *Exit a Gentleman.* Q2–8, F2; *om.* Q1
277–278 I sweare...me,] Q2; *om.* Q1

That I have spoke in idle moodes to you.

I am *Arbaces*, we all fellow subjects,

Nor is the Queene *Panthæa* now my Sister.

Bessus.   Why if you remember fellow subject *Arbaces*, I tolde
you once she was not your sister, I and she look't nothing like you.

Arbaces.   I thinke you did good Captaine *Bessus*.

Bessus.   Here will arise another question now amongst the
Swordmen, whether I be to call him to account for beating me,
now he's prov'd no King.

Enter Ligones.

Mardonius.   Sir, heres *Ligones*

The Agent for the Armenian state.   300

Arbaces.   Where is he?——I know your businesse good *Ligones*.

Ligones.   We must have our King againe, and will.

Arbaces.   I knew that was your businesse, you shall have

Your King againe, and have him so againe

As never King was had.——Goe one of you

And bid *Bacurius* bring *Tigranes* hither,

And bring the Ladie with him, that *Panthæa*

The Queene *Panthæa* sent me word this morning

Was brave *Tigranes* mistresse.   *Exit* 2. Gentleman.

Ligones.   Tis *Spaconia*.

Arbaces.   I, I, *Spaconia*.

Ligones.   She is my daughter.   310

Arbaces.   Shee is so, I could now tell any thing

I never heard; your King shall goe so home

As never man went.

Mardonius.   Shall he goe on's head?

Arbaces.   He shall have Chariots easier then ayre

That I will have invented; and nere thinke

He shall pay any ransome; and thy selfe

That art the Messenger shall ride before him

On a Horse cut out of an entire Diamond,

That shall be made to goe with golden wheeles,

294 and] Q 2; say Q 1   300 state] Q 2; King Q 1
309 *Exit* 2. Gentleman.] Dyce; *Exit two Gent.* Q 2–8, F 2; *om.* Q 1

I know not how yet.

Ligones.   Why I shall be made   320
For ever, they belied this King with us
And sayd he was unkind.

Arbaces.   And then thy daughter,
She shall have some strange thinge, wele have the kingdome
Sold utterly, and put into a toy,
Which she shall weare about her carelesly
Some where or other.———

Enter Panthæa *and* 1. Gentleman.

                              See the vertuous Queene.
Behold the humblest subject that you have
Kneele here before you.

Panthæa.   Why kneele you to me
That am your vassall?

Arbaces.   Grant me one request.

Panthæa.   Alas, what can I grant you? What I can   330
I will.

Arbaces.   That you will please to marry me,
If I can prove it lawfull.

Panthæa.   Is that all?
More willingly, then I would draw this ayre.

Arbaces.   Ile kisse this hand in earnest.

[*Enter* 2. Gentleman.]

2. *Gentleman.*   Sir, *Tigranes*
Is comming though he made it strange at first
To see the Princesse any more.

Arbaces.   The Queene,
Thou meanest.———

323 thinge] Q2 (thing); thinke Q1
326 S.D. *Enter*...Gentleman.] Q2; *Enter Panthæa.* Q1
334 S.P. 2. Gentleman.] Q2; *Mardonius* Q1
335 at first] Q2 (At first); *om.* Q1

Enter [Bacurius *with*] Tigranes *and* Spaconia.

          O my *Tigranes* pardon me,
Tread on my necke I freely offer it,
And if thou beest so given; take revenge,
For I have injur'd thee.
Tigranes.   No, I forgive,   340
And rejoice more that you have found repentance,
Then I my libertie.
Arbaces.   Maist thou be happie
In thy faire choice; for thou art temperate:
You owe no ransome to the state, know that;
I have a thousand joyes to tell you of,
Which yet I dare not utter, till I pay
My thankes to Heaven for um: will you goe
With me, and helpe me; pray you doe.
Tigranes.   I will.
Arbaces.   Take then your faire one with you.——And you Queene
Of goodnesse, and of us, O give me leave   350
To take your arme in mine:——Come every one
That takes delight in goodnesse, helpe to sing
Loude thankes for me, that I am prov'd no King.
                           [*Exeunt.*]

FINIS.

*337 S.D. *Enter*...Spaconia.
349 you Queene] F2 (you Queen); your Queene Q1–8

TEXTUAL NOTES

I.i

260 talke but idlie]   See Textual Introduction, p. 177.

352 then]   See Textual Introduction, p. 177.

II.i

0.1–2 *and waiting women*]   See Textual Introduction, p. 177.

252 talke]   See Textual Introduction, p. 177.

IV.ii

24 me, equall]   The Q2 punctuation, 'paide me equall,', followed by all seventeenth-century editions and by Langbaine, reflects a common idiom of the period, but Seward's correction reflects what may be a private idiom of Fletcher's. A comparable passage occurs in *The Woman Hater*, III.i.6–9: 'heare me equall heavens, | Let not your furious rodd, that must afflict me, | Be that imperfect peece of nature, | . . . woman, unsatiate woman.'

179 rock't]   See Textual Introduction, p. 177.

V.i

8 seeme]   See Textual Introduction, p. 177.

V.iii

14 lamming]   See Textual Introduction, p. 177.

V.iv

337 *Enter . . . Spaconia.*]   The sequence of events from line 270 is not clear in Q1, but Q2 offers directions that supply some of the inadequacies. At line 270 Arbaces requests 'some one' to call Panthæa, and Q2 supplies an exit direction for the attendant. At line 326 a Q2 direction brings Panthæa and the attendant back on stage. Before their return, at line 305 Arbaces requests 'one of you' to carry a message to Bacurius. Again Q2 supplies an exit direction for this second attendant. The speech beginning 'Sir, *Tigranes*' at line 334 is evidently the report of this attendant. Q1 gives

it to Mardonius, plainly in error because Mardonius does not have the information delivered in the speech; Q2 gives the speech to the attendant (*2 Gent.*), though it provides no re-entry direction for him. Editors since Dyce have provided that entry, and Mr Turner has further accepted Dyce's conjecture that Bacurius enters here instead and delivers the speech. The present edition (following Dyce) provides the entry for the attendant and (following Q2) gives him the speech; and it brings Bacurius on stage with Tigranes and Spaconia (line 337). Such a direction conforms strictly with Arbaces' order and includes Bacurius in 'the gathering of all the courtly characters at the end of the play' (Turner, p. 132).

PRESS-VARIANTS IN Q1 (1619)

[Copies collated: BM (British Museum 643.h.8; lacks half-sheet M), Bodl (Bodleian Library Malone 242 (8)), Dyce (Victoria and Albert Museum); CSmH (Henry E. Huntington Library), DFo (Folger Shakespeare Library), MB (Boston Public Library, lacks A2 and sheets E–M), MH (Harvard University). These comprise the known extant copies.]

SHEET L (*outer forme*)

Corrected: BM, Bodl, DFo, MH
Uncorrected: Dyce, CSmH

L3 V.iv.103 *Arb.*] *omitted*
L4ᵛ V.v.191 *Ara.*] *Arb.*

EMENDATIONS OF ACCIDENTALS

Dedication

5 desire.] ~ : Q1; *om.* Q2+

I.i

2 blow:] ~ , Q1+
6 *Bessus*,] Q4+ ; *Bes.*ₐ Q1–3
24 warres:] Q2+ ; ~ , Q1
30 trulie?] Q4+ ; ~ . Q1–3
36 Why,] Q2+ ; ~ ₐ Q1
37 fam'd?] ~ , Q1–8; ~ ! F2
50 vanisht?] Q4, 7–8, F2; ~ . Q1–3, 5–6
52 that?] Q4+ ; ~ . Q1–3
55 it?] Q4–6, 8, F2; ~ . Q1–3, 7
61 headₐ] Q7–8, F2; ~ , Q1–6
63 enemie?] F2; ~ . Q1–8
90 him?] Q4–6, F2; ~ : Q1; ~ ; Q2–3, 7–8
92 living,] Q6, F2; ~ ; Q1–5, 7–8
93 day.] Q7–8, F2; ~ , Q1–6
94 I:] ~ , Q1–6, F2; ~ . Q7–8
103 *Tigranes*:] ~ , Q1–6, F2; ~ . Q7–8
114 talkt;] ~ : Q1; ~ ₐ Q2–6, F2; ~ , Q7–8
115 base:] ~ ; Q1; ~ , Q2+
130 brag.] ~ , Q1+
132 glory?] Q2, 7–8, F2; ~ . Q1; ~ : Q3–6
146 not mee:] ~ ₐ Q1; me not; Q2+
148 mee;] ~ , Q1+ ; ~ . F2
157 foulenesse:] ~ ; Q2+ ; ~ , Q1
160 name: yetₐ] Q2+ ; ~ ₐ ~ : Q1
161 world,] Q2, 4–7, F2; ~ . Q1, 3; ~ ; Q8
173 passionate:] ~ , Q1+
174 worth?] Q7–8, F2; ~ , Q1–6

194 *Iberia*] Q2+ ; *Ileria* Q1
202 S.D. *after line* 201 *in* Q1
202 Prince, *Mardonius*,] Q3+ ; ~ ₐ ~ ₐ Q1–2
214 high;] ~ ₐ Q1; ~ , Q2+
227 contryₐ fence] Q2+ ; ~ -~ Q1
228–229 Why...on't.] *one line in* Q1+
229 enough?] F2; ~ , Q1–5; ~ ! Q7–8; ~ . Q6
238 laugh?——] ~ ? ₐ Q1+
243 haughty.——Who] ~ ; ₐ who Q1+
245 I?——] ~ ? ₐ Q1+
247 silence.——What] ~ ; ₐ what Q1+
250 wind?] Q2+ ; ~ , Q1
251 Heaven——] ~ , Q1–3, 7–8; ~ . Q4–6, F2
251 your——] ~ , Q1; ~ . Q2+
257 I.——Now] ~ , ₐ now Q1–6, F2; ~ . ₐ Now Q7–8
258 please——] ~ , Q1; ~ . Q2+
260 talke] ~ , Q1–6, F2; *om.* Q7–8
261 Majesty——] ~ , Q1; ~ . Q2+
265 Majesty——] ~ : Q1; ~ . Q2+
269 request.——Were] ~ ; ₐ were Q1–4, 7–8, F2; ~ , ₐ were Q5–6
274 utter] Q2+ ; uttter Q1
288 away?] Q2+ ; ~ ; Q1
291 arme:] ~ , Q1–8; ~ . F2

294 pleas'd:———] ~ : ‸ Q1–3, 7–8;
　　~ , ‸ Q4–6; ~ . ‸ F2
295 what,] ~ ‸ Q1+
296 mee?———] ~ ? ‸ Q1–3, 7–8;
　　~ ‸‸ Q4–6, F2
298 choise.] ~ , Q1+
301 no.———] ~ ; ‸ Q1+
302 gone?———Why] ~ ? ‸ why
　　Q1+
304 Sirs:———] ~ , ‸ Q1+
306 all:———] ~ : ‸ Q1+
306 *Mardonius* !] ~ , Q1±
314 thus?] ~ : Q1+
317 oath,] Q3+; ~ ‸ Q1–2
317–318 a great] Q2–8, F2; a-|
　　great Q1
332 will;] Q3–6, F2; ~ , Q1, 7–8;
　　~ ‸ Q2
337 Yes,] Q3, 7–8, F2; ~ ‸ Q1–2,
　　4–6
340 but———] ~ , Q1–2, 7–8; ~ .
　　Q3–6, F2
342 commendations] Q2+; com-
　　mandations Q1
367 word. Were] word, were Q1±

369 you;] Q3–5, F2; ~ , Q1–2;
　　~ : Q6–8
371 you;] Q4–6, F2; ~ : Q1–3, 7–8
372 out you;] F2; out you, Q1;
　　you out; Q2–8
374 use:]~ ? Q1–2; ~ ; Q3+
376 materiall?] F2; ~ : Q1, 3; ~ .
　　Q2, 4–8
400 should,] Q3–6, F2; ~ ‸ Q1–2,
　　7–8
403 Why,] Q4, F2; ~ ‸ Q1–3, 5–8
420 *Gobrius*] *Gobrias* Q1+
425 *Panthæa*] Q2–4, 7–8; *Panthan*
　　Q1; *Pentha* Q5–6, F2
432 If] Q2+; Jf Q1
444 *Gobrius*] *Gobrias* Q1+
450 *Gobrius*] *Gobrias* Q1+
464 strange.———] ~ , ‸ Q1+
465 mother———] ~ : Q1–2, 7–8;
　　~ . Q3–6, F2
474 *Gobrius*] *Gobrias* Q1+
475 there,] Q4–6, F2; ~ ‸ Q1–3;
　　~ . Q7–8
492 returne.] Q3; ~ : Q1–2, 4+

I.ii

4 I;] F2; ~ , Q1–8
17–18 That...halfe of thee,] *one
line in* Q1; Q2–4 *line:* That...
but halfe | Of thee,; Q7–8 *line:*
That...halfe of | Thee,; F2
lines: That...has won | But
half of thee,; *prose in* Q5–6
17 thee?] ~ , Q1–3, 7–8; ~ ‸ Q4–
5, F2; ~ . Q6

26 me‸] me; Q1±
26 part;] ~ , Q4–6, F2; ~ ‸ Q1–
3, 7–8
29 short,] Q2+; ~ ‸ Q1
32 not:] ~ , Q1+
45 words?] Q7–8; ~ , Q1–6, F2
55 expected. He] ~ ‸ he Q1; ~ ,
he Q2+

II.i

0.1 Gobrius] Gobrias Q1+
6 safe,] Q2+; ~ : Q1
7 close;] ~ , Q1+
23 teare;] ~ , Q1+
41 *Gobrius*] *Gobrias* Q1+

52–57 I bad...done,] Q1–4, 7–8
line: I...time | Would...me |
To...content: | But...power.
| And...me, | But...done, ;
prose in Q5–6; F2 *lines:* I...

time | Would...all to | Your
...take | Away...unknown, |
Was...done
55 power.] ~ , Q1, 4–8, F2; ~ ∧
Q2–3
57 you:] Q2+; ~ , Q1
57 urging∧] Q2+; ~ , Q1
86 grace?] ~ ; Q1; ~ , Q2–8; ~ :
F2
103–104 You...morrow?] Q1±
line: You...readie | To waite
...morrow?; prose in Q5–6,
F2
105 hereafter.——] ~ : ∧ Q1–8; ~ ;
∧ F2
119 trenches——] ~ . Q1+
143 I——] F2; ~ : Q1, 4–6; ~ .
Q2–3, 7–8
150 done——] ~ . Q1–2, 4–8, F2;
~ , Q3
152 I——] ~ : Q1–7; ~ ? Q8; ~ .
F2
154 lie——] ~ . Q1±
158 No?] Q3–6, F2; ~ , Q1–2, 7–8
159 what,] ~ ∧ Q1+

161 shee:——] ~ : ∧ Q1+
172 truth?] Q2+; ~ . Q1
198 Exit] after line 197 in Q1–2, 7–8;
Exeunt Bessus and Bacurius.
F2; om. Q3–6
210–215 My...Prince;] prose in Q1–
8; F2 lines: My...anything |
And feels...her breast. | Than
...him. | Gob. Yet...much |
At...with him | A husband...
Prince,
214 along] a-|long Q1–2
220–224 Trust...offerd.] Q1–4, 7–
8 line: Trust...like | That...
him. | But...humors, | If...
lesse, | Because...offerd.; prose
in Q5–6, F2
234 Madam?] Q8; ~ : Q1; ~ .
Q2–7, F2
235 Exit] after line 234 in Q1+
278 desire?] Q7–8; ~ , Q1–6; ~ !
F2
302 not.] ~ , Q2±; ~ ∧ Q1
311.1 Exeunt.] Q2–4, 6–8, F2;
Exit. Q1; Exeunt ∧ Q5

II.ii

*In this scene the prefixes for the three Men are simple numerals in Q1–8, F2;
for the Woman 'Weo.' Q1±.*

7 late:] Q2+; ~ , Q1
47 selves.—— | Philip] ~ . ∧∧
Philip Q1, 5–6; ~ . ∧ | Philip
Q2–4, 7–8; ~ . ∧ Phi-|lip F2
55 yet?] Q7–8, F2; ~ ; Q1–4; ~ ,
Q5–6
61 Philip.——Come] ~ , ∧ come
Q1+
73 rogery;——] ~ ; ∧ Q1+
107 Woman.] 3 Weo. Q1±
111 so:—— | If] ~ : ∧∧ if Q1±
141.1 S.D. location] Dyce; after line
140 Q1±
142 goe?] Q2+; ~ , Q1

145 Content:——] ~ : ∧ Q1±
148 am I,] ~ ∧ Q1+
151.1 Exeunt...Woman.] Langbaine (except 'and Woman');
Exeunt 1, 2, 3, and Women. Q1;
Exeunt 2.3. and Women. Q2–4,
7–8; Exeunt 2.3. and woman.
Q5–6, F2
151.1 S.D. location] Dyce; after line
150 Q1±
151–152 sirra.—— | Come] ~ : ∧∧
~ Q1+
152 homeward:——] ~ ; ∧ Q1+

III.i

15 will not.——] ~ . ‸ Q2; ~ , ‸
   Q3–8, F2; *om.* Q1

22 just.—— |] ~ : ‸‸ Q1; ~ , ‸
   Q2+

26–27 A man...Againe.] *one line*
   in Q1–4, 7–8; *prose in* Q5–6, F2

39, 41 *1. Gentleman.*] Q2+; *Gent.*
   Q1

43 in.——] ~ , ‸ Q1; ~ · ‸ Q2±

43–46 *Tigranes*...safe?] Q1+ *line:*
   Tigranes...arriv'd | In...poy-
   son | Their...safe?

61 S.D. *location*] Q2+; *after line*
   60 Q1

62 die:] ~ , Q1+

80 you‸] Q2+; ~ , Q1

80 speake,] Q7–8; ~ ‸ Q1–6, F2

82 face?] Q2+; ~ , Q1

93 slow?] Q4–6, F2; ~ , Q1–3;
   ~ ! Q7–8

94 her;] F2; ~ , Q1–8

95 faith,] ~ ; Q1±

107 Lady?] ~ , Q1; ~ : Q2–8, F2

113 What,] F2; ~ ‸ Q1–8

114 Sir?] ~ . Q1+

116 Sir?——] ~ ? ‸ Q1+

118 There?] ~ , Q1+

147 so;] ~ , Q2+; *om.* Q1

163 this?] Q2+; ~ , Q1

175 yours‸] ~ ; Q1–8; ~ , F2

176 dead;] ~ , Q1+

177 importune:] ~ , Q1+

177 doe.] ~ ; Q1±

183 more:——] ~ ; ‸ Q1; ~ , ‸
   Q2+

185 it?] Q2+; ~ : Q1

187 so.——You] ~ ; ‸ you Q1±

189 is.——] ~ : ‸ Q1±

197 desire.——] ~ · ‸ Q1±

198 againe.——Yet] ~ ; ‸ yet Q1±

200 me.——] ~ : ‸ Q1±

202 say.——] ~ : ‸ Q1±

212 out.——] ~ : ‸ Q1–2, 7–8; ~ ,
   ‸ Q3–4; ~ · ‸ Q5–6, F2

228 mine——] ~ . Q1+

228–229 And...owner.] *one line in*
   Q1+

233 againe?] Q2+; ~ , Q1

234 And...her?] *prose in* Q1±

235 it?] ~ , Q1–8; ~ ! F2

236 so:] ~ , Q1+

238 it?] Q2–5, 7–8, F2; ~ : Q1; ~ .
   Q6

241 tongue?] Q7–8; ~ ; Q1–6; ~ !
   F2

246 will?] F2; ~ . Q1–8

249 frowne?] Q2+; ~ : Q1

251 conquered] conquerd Q1; conquer'd Q2–8, F2

254 prison.——] ~ ; ‸ Q1; ~ : ‸
   Q2–8, F2

255 regardlesse.——Why] ~ : ‸
   why Q1–3, 7–8; ~ ; ‸ Why
   Q4–6, F2

256 *Bacurius.*——You] ~ , ‸ you
   Q1+

260–262 Sir...thing.] Q1+ *line:*
   Sir...obey. | Why...away |
   By...thing.

264 off:——] ~ : ‸ Q1±

270.1 *Exeunt*] F2; *Exit* Q2–8; *om.*
   Q1

277 me.—— | You] ~ : ‸‸ you
   Q1+

280 you;] ~ , Q1+

282–283 And...Forgive me.] *one*
   line in Q1+

299 stronger.——] ~ ; ‸ Q1–2,
   7–8; ~ , ‸ Q3–6, F2

300 there.——] ~ : ‸ Q1+

301 This] Q2+; ~ , Q1

301 kisse] Q2+; ~ , Q1

301 out.——] ~ . ‸ Q1–2, 7–8;
   ~ , ‸ Q3–6, F2

302 along.——] ~ : ∧ Q1–2, 7–8; ~ ; ∧ Q3–6, F2
305–306 I...Doe it.] *one line in* Q1+
308 you speake:——] ~ ; ∧ Q1; ~ . ∧ Q2, 7–8; ~ , ∧ Q3–6, F2
313 well;] ~ ∧ Q1+
319 word.——] ~ . ∧ Q1+

332 thence.—— | Where] ~ ; ∧∧ where Q1–2, 7–8; ~ , ∧∧ where Q3–6, F2
335–336 refuse...*Mardonius*,] *one line in* Q1+
344–345 I prethee...again.] *prose in* Q1+

III.ii

19 glad.] ~ , Q1–4, 7–8; ~ ; Q5–6, F2
49 mercie:——] ~ , ∧ Q1+
51 speech:——] ~ : ∧ Q1+
53 satisfaction.——] ~ : ∧ Q1+
57 can.] ~ , Q1; could. Q2–4, 6–8, F2; could ∧ Q5
60 word,] Q7–8, F2; ~ ∧ Q1–6
63 Sir,] Q3–8, F2; ~ ∧ Q1–2
64 cannot] Q4+; can-|not Q1–3
69 so:] ~ , Q1–6; ~ . Q7–8; ~ ; F2

71–72 Sir.—— | Certenly] ~ . ∧∧ ~ Q1+
71 S.D. *location*] Dyce; *after line* 70 Q1+
73 up on] upon Q1+
89 satisfaction:——] ~ : ∧ Q1–7, F2; ~ . ∧ Q8
97 thinke,] Q2+; ~ ∧ Q1
98 ingagements——] ~ . Q1+
126 Lord——] ~ . ∧Q1+

III.iii

7–8 againe. | See] Q2–4, 7–8, F2; ~ . ∧ ~ Q1, 5–6
12 it:] ~ , Q1+
13 thoughts∧] ~ ? Q1–3, F2; ~ , Q4–8
13 speake?] Q4–8; ~ : Q1–3; ~ . F2
17 Conscience,] Q2+; ~ ? Q1
17 it?] F2; ~ . Q1–8
18–19 Why...doe?] *one line in* Q1+
25–26 Sir,...me.] Q1–8, F2 *line*: Sir,...hid | That...me.
28 Sir:] ~ , Q1+
34 out.—— | Were] ~ : ∧ were Q1–5, 7–8, F2; ~ . ∧ ~ Q6
50–51 But...understand?] *one line in* Q1+
50 But what?] ~ , Q1; ~ ∧ Q2–8, F2

59–60 Better...all.] *one line in* Q1+
63 There...me?] Q1+ *line*: There ...yet, | Wilt...me?
63 yet:] ~ , Q1+
68–70 No?...me.] Q1+ *line*: No, ...her, | And...me.
68 No?] ~ , Q1+
72–73 Why,...you.] Q1+ *line*: Why...their | Husbands... you.
75 plainlie?] Q7, F2; ~ ; Q1–6, 8
81 it,] Q4+; ~ ∧ Q1–3
91 him.—— | Deare] ~ , ∧∧ deare Q1; ~ , ∧∧ hear Q2–6; ~ . ∧∧ hear Q7–8; ~ : ∧∧ hear F2
98 lawes;] ~ . Q1+
99 my selfe] my | selfe Q1–2
103 conditions:] ~ , Q1; ~ ; Q2+
117 knife?] Q2+; ~ : Q1

121 Vanities?] ~ , Q 1–6; ~ ! Q 7–
   8, F 2
122 this:] ~ , Q 1–6, F 2; ~ . Q 7–8
126 cutlers:] ~ , Q 1+
133 Sir?] F 2; ~ . Q 1–8
136 *Exit.*] Q 2+; *exit.* Q 1
137 do't?] Q 4–6, 8, F 2; ~ ⌃ Q 1;
   ~ . Q 2–3, 7
138 you?] Q 7–8, F 2; ~ , Q 1–6
141 By...whatsoever.] *lined as in*
   Q 2–8, F 2; Q 1 *lines:* By...
   will, | Any...whatsoever.
146 (Thou...me?)] ⌃ ~ ...~ ⌃⌃
   Q 1–2 ⌃ ~ ...~ , ⌃ Q 3 ±

147–148 O   you...Ifaith.]   Q 1+
   line: O you...her? | Ile...
   Ifaith.
150 More?] Q 3+; ~ , Q 1–2
150 else?] Q 2+; ~, Q 1
153 company,] Q 2+; ~ ⌃ Q 1
170 Mother?] ~ , Q 1–3, 6; ~ !
   Q 4–5, 7–8, F 2
179–180 Hung...monsters,] *lined as*
   in Q 2–8, F 2; *prose in* Q 1
190 say.——— | I] ~ ; ⌃⌃ I Q 1; ~ ,
   ⌃⌃ I Q 2–8, F 2
190 S.D. *after* sinne Q 1+

IV.i

1 written,] Q 7–8; ~ ⌃ Q 1–6, F 2
1 *Gobrius*] *Gobrias* Q 1+
4 rashnesse?] Q 2+; ~ . Q 1
9 follow,] Q 2+; ~ ; Q 1
11 um———] F 2; ~ . Q 1–8
16 patience)] ~ , Q 1; ~ : Q 2–8,
   F 2
28 it:] ~ , Q 1; ~ . Q 2+
31 anger,] Q 2+; ~ ; Q 1

32 faith,] Q 2+; ~ ⌃ Q 1
34–37 You...brother.] *lined as in*
   Q 2+; *prose in* Q 1
38 man.——— | My] ~ ; ⌃⌃ my Q 1;
   ~ . ⌃ | ~ Q 2+
38 S.D. *location*] Q 2–7, F 2; *after*
   brother. *line* 37 *in* Q 1, 8
43 thine?] Q 4+; ~ : Q 1; ~ , Q 2–3

IV.ii

17 ever,] ~ : Q 1; ~ ? Q 2+
27 on,] Q 7–8; ~ ⌃ Q 1–6, F 2
30 ones.] ~ , Q 1–8, F 2
33 me. | Ladie,] Q 2+; ~ ⌃⌃ ~ . Q 1
36–37 Shee...remov'd] *lined as in*
   Q 3+; *prose in* Q 1–2
63 oh!] Q 2+; ~ : Q 1
69 art:———] ~ : ⌃ Q 1, 3–6, F 2;
   ~ . ⌃ Q 2, 7–8
70 fort:———] ~ : ⌃ Q 1; ~ ⌃⌃ Q 2–
   3; ~ ; ⌃ Q 5–6, F 2; ~ , ⌃ Q 4,
   7–8
72 it:———] ~ ; ⌃ Q 1+
73 rugged:———] ~ : ⌃ Q 1+
86 well.——— | Royall] ~ , ⌃⌃
   royall Q 1, 4–6, F 2; ~ : ⌃⌃ ~
   Q 2–3, 7–8

86 *Tigranes,*] Q 4+; ~ ⌃ Q 1–3
90 here;] ~ , Q 1+
106–108 His...folly:] Q 1 *lines:*
   His...againe | Tis...all |
   Anone...folly:; Q 2+ *line:*
   His...againe | Tis...feare; |
   Would...folly:
115 Beside...warrant.] *lined as in*
   Q 2+; Q 1 *lines:* Beside...Sir, |
   For...warrant.
115 Sir,] Q 2+; ~ ⌃ Q 1
116 not?] Q 2+; ~ : Q 1
125 Sir?] F 2; ~ . Q 1–8
130 said,] Q 4+; ~ ⌃ Q 1–3
133 againe———] ~ ⌃ Q 1; ~ . Q 2+
145 what] Q 2–3; What Q 1, 4+
145 Sir?] Q 2+; ~ , Q 1

147 Sir?] Q2+; ~ . Q1
148 Sir,] Q2+; ~ ∧ Q1
154 more, King,] Q7–8, F2; ~ ∧ ~ ∧ Q1–3; ~ ∧~ , Q4–6
161–162 This...chuse.]*prose in* Q1; Q2+ *line*: This...alwaies, | And...chuse:
169 life?] Q2+; ~ , Q1
171–172 Yes...quicklie.] *prose in* Q1+

187 selfe:] ~ , Q1+
187 me;] ~ , Q1–8, F2
188 *Mardonius?*] Q2+; ~ . Q1
215 tell.] ~ , Q1; ~ ; Q2, 7; ~ : Q3–6, 8, F2
222 beaten,] Q2+; ~ ∧ Q1
229 *Gobrius,*] Q2+; ~ ∧ Q1
230 that] Q2+; That Q1
238 will:] ~ ∧ Q1; ~ ; Q2, 7–8, F2; ~ , Q3–6

IV.iii

In this scene the prefixes for the Sword-men *are simple numerals in* Q1+.

1 both:——] ~ , ∧ Q1–3, 7–8; ~ ; ∧ Q4–6, F2
2 Table:——] ~ ; ∧ Q1+
3 complement:——] ~ : ∧ Q1–3, 7–8; ~ ; ∧ Q4–6, F2
3 childe.——] ~ , ∧ Q1–8; ~ . ∧ F2
14 Prince?] Q2+; ~ . Q1
16 case?] Q2+; ~ ∧ Q1
19 businesse:] ~ ∧ Q1–4; ~ , Q5–6, F2; ~ ; Q8
21 indignation?] Q4+; ~ . Q1–3
42 distance:] ~ , Q1; ~ ; Q2+
46 must——] F2; ~ ∧ Q1; ~ . ∧ Q2–8
57–59 *prose in* Q1+
57 it,] Q2–3, 5–8, F2; ~ ∧ Q1, 4
57 over:] ~ , Q1+
73 kickt——] ~ . Q1–5, 7–8, F2; ~ ∧ Q6
74 man:] Q8; ~ ∧ Q1; ~ , Q2–7; ~ . F2
75 brother?] Q2–3, 7–8; ~ ; Q1; ~ , Q4–6; ~ ! F2
81 brother?] Q2+; ~ . Q1

84 kickt,] Q2+; ~ ∧ Q1
86 *prose in* Q1; *om.* Q2+
87 friend:——] ~ ; Q1+
101 you,] Q4, F2; ~ ∧ Q1–3, 5–8
101–103 Brother...man,] *prose in* Q1+
102 together?] ~ ; Q1+
104 musted] Q2+; musled Q1
104 brother?] Q2–8; ~ : Q1; ~ . F2
105 Gentlemen——] ~ . Q1–4, 7–8, F2; ~ ∧ Q5–6
107 pittie:——] ~ : ∧ Q1; ~ , ∧ Q2–3, 7–8; ~ ; ∧ Q4–6, F2
114–116 It lies...kicking.] Q1–8 *line*: It...Sir, | I...since. | The ...it; | Lies...kicking.; F2 *lines*: It...since. | The...it, | Lies...kicking.
144 selfe,] Q3+; ~ ∧ Q1–2
147–148 *prose in* Q1+
150 Boy,] Q2+; ~ ∧ Q1
150 within:——] ~ : ∧ Q1+
151–152 Sir...done,] *one line in* Q1+
155–157 *prose in* Q1+

IV.iv

3 selfe.——] ~ : ∧ Q1; ~ . ∧ Q2+
5 name.——] ~ , ∧ Q1; ~ : ∧ Q2+

9 speake?] Q2–5, 7–8, F2; ~ I
   Q6; ~ . Q1
9 me?] Q2+; ~ , Q1
10 I,] Q7–8, F2; ~ ∧ Q1–6
10 can,] Q5, F2; ~ ; Q1–4, 6–8
18 rather∧] Q3+; ~ , Q1–2
33 would:] Q2+; ~ , Q1
40 heare:] ~ , Q1+
40 this?] F2; ~ , Q6; ~ ; Q1–5,
   7–8
51 Sister?] ~ , Q1+
52 be?] Q2+; ~ , Q1
56 *Arbaces*] Q2+; *Abr.* Q1
77 not,] Q5+; ~ ∧ Q1–4
110 birth:] ~ , Q1+
112 too?] Q2+; ~ , Q1

113 sounds,] Q7–8; ~ ∧ Q1–6, F2
114 Sister?] Q2+; ~ . Q1
114 else:] ~ , Q1–7, F2; ~ ; Q8
128–130 Or...out?] Q1 *lines:* Or
   ...them. *Panthæa,* | [*remain-
   der as prose*]; Q2+ *line:* Or...
   them. | *Panthæa,* What...doe? |
   Shall...out?
143 we:] ~ ∧ Q1; ~ ; Q2, 7–8; ~ ,
   Q3–6, F2
147–148 yet...Sister.] *one line in*
   Q1+
148 *Tigranes,*] Q2+; ~ ∧ Q1
148–149 True,...truth——] *one line
   in* Q1+
154 we:] ~ , Q1+

V.i

1–3 Sir...Master.] *prose in* Q1+
3 *Tigranes,*] Q2+; ~ ∧ Q1
6–11 I have...rewards.] *prose in*
   Q1+
7 asham'd:] ~ , Q1+
7 businesse——] Q3–4; ~ . ~
   Q1–2, 7–8; ~ . ∧ Q6, F2
36–37 Tis such...hee.] *prose in*
   Q1+
50 man:] ~ , Q1+
50 beaten,] Q7–8; ~ : Q1–6, F2
51–54 Sufferance...meat;] Q1–4,
   7–8 *line:* Sufferance...had |
   Since...daggers | Set...meat;
   prose in Q5–6, F2
60–62 And set...him.] Q1, 7–8
   line [*possibly prose*]: And...
   sence, | I...him.; *prose in* Q2–
   6, F2
82–83 *prose in* Q1+
89 Lady,] Q3, 5–8, F2; ~ ∧ Q1–2, 4
90 one——] ~ . Q1+
93 lie——] ~ . Q2–4, 7–8, F2; ~
   ∧ Q1, 5–6
97 Ladie?] Q2+; ~ , Q1

99 out,] Q2+; ~ . Q1
108 you.] Q2+; ~ ? Q1
112 sight?] ~ . Q1, 3+; ~ : Q2
113–114 Indeed...me.] Q1–4, 7–8
   line: Indeed...forget | Twentie
   ...me.; *prose in* Q5–6, F2
115–116 Yes...this.] *prose in* Q2+;
   Q1 *lines:* Yes...thinke | You
   ...this.
120 die.——] ~ ; ∧ Q1; ~ . ∧ Q2,
   7–8; ~ , ∧ Q3–6, F2
121–122 Farewell   Sir,...praia.]
   prose in Q1+
122 Gentlewoman] Q5–8; Gentle- |
   woman Q1–3, F2; Gentlewo- |
   man Q4
122 *Exit.*] *after* 'Captaine' *in line*
   121 *in* Q1+
124–126 Gentlemen...safe.] Q1–3,
   7–8 *line:* Gentlemen...have |
   Beene...penitent, | Has...
   safe.; *prose in* Q4–6, F2
127–128 We   knew...Grandsire.]
   Q1 *lines:* We...kick't. | His
   Grandsire.; *prose in* Q2+

131–132 Now...it.] Q1–4, 7–8 *line:*
Now...sorry,|And...it.; *prose*
in Q5–6, F2

133–134 Alas...undoe him.] Q1–4,
7–8 *line:* Alas...goe, | Let...
him.; *prose in* Q5–6, F2

V.ii

4.1 S.D. *location*] Q2+; *after line*
5 Q1
10–11 What...hether?] *lined as in*
Q7–8; *prose in* Q1–6, F2
20 are well?] F2; ~ . Q1–8
30 here?] Q2+; ~ . Q1
30 Sir?] Q2+; ~ . Q1
45–46 Well...you.] *one line in* Q1–
4, 7–8; *prose in* Q5–6, F2

50 breed?] Q2+; ~ . Q1
66–69 Then...Whore.] *prose in*
Q5–6, F2; Q1–4, 7–8 *line:*
Then...Whore, | If...chuse |
But...if | I...fit | To...
Whore.
72 Queene?] Q2+; ~ , Q1
74 Queene?] Q2+; ~ ∧ Q1

V.iii

In this scene the prefixes for the Sword-men *are simple numerals in* Q1+.

3 busines.——Are] ~ , ∧ are Q1;
~ ? ∧ ~ Q2–6, F2; ~ ; ∧ ~
Q7–8
4 Gentlemen?] Q2+; ~ . Q1
8–9 *prose as in* Q5–6, F2; Q1–4,
7–8 *line:* My...mistaken, |
Feare...Lord.
11 honor.——] ~ , ∧ Q1+
14–15 as...fall.] *one line of verse in*
Q1–4, 7–8; *prose in* Q5–6, F2
21 mans:] F2; ~ , Q1–2, 7–8; ~ ?
Q3–6
24 come——] Q7–8, F2; ~ . Q1–
5; *om.* Q6
33–34 naturall.——] ~ ; ∧ Q1–8;
~ : ∧ F2
56 while.——] ~ ; ∧ Q1–3, 7–8;
~ , ∧ Q4–6, F2
56 Ye] ye Q1; you Q2+
56–57 apple-squiers] apple-|squiers
Q1–4, 7–8; applesquires Q5–6;
apple-squires F2

58 beatings?] Q2+; ~ . Q1
59 Lordship——] ~ . Q1+
60 Lord——] ~ . Q1+
61 here?——Get] ~ ? ∧ get Q1±
74 pocket,] Q3+; ~ ∧ Q1–2
74 slave;] ~ , Q1–2, 7–8; *om.*
Q3–6, F2
77 gentleman] Q5–6, F2; gentle-|
man Q1, 4; gen-|tleman Q2–3,
7–8
79 rascall?——] ~ ? ∧ Q4+; ~ , ∧
Q1–3
86 bones.——] ~ , ∧ Q1; ~ ; ∧
Q2+
87 gone:——] ~ ; ∧ Q1–8; ~ : ∧
F2
88 hold:——] ~ : ∧ Q1–3, 7–8;
~ ; ∧ Q4–6, F2
90 quit.——] ~ . ∧ Q1–2, 4–8, F2;
~ , ∧ Q3
95 founderd:——] ~ : ∧ Q1+
96 goe?] Q2–8; ~ . Q1, F2

V.iv

13–14 *Mardonius,...come?*] *one line of verse in* Q1+

13 *Mardonius,*] Q2±; *Mar.* Q1

21 markt——] ~ . Q1+

28 satisfie?] Q2+; ~ , Q1

30 dutie:] ~ , Q1–3, 7–8; ~ . Q4–6, F2

34 selfe?] ~ , Q1–8; ~ ! F2

36 thee:] ~ ∧ Q1+

36 then∧] ~ : Q1+

42 doe;] ~ , Q1+

42 last,] ~ ; Q1+

48 Why,] ~ ∧ Q1+

48 so!] ~ ? Q1, 3–8, F2; ~ . Q2

61 honest.——] ~ , ∧ Q1, 4–6, F2; ~ . ∧ Q2–3, 7–8

61.1 *Exit.*] *after* feare *in line* 61 *in* Q1–2, 7–8; *om.* Q3–6, F2

64–65 There...ripe.] *one line in* Q1+

68 incurable;] ~ , Q1+

71 thee?] Q4–6, F2; ~ , Q1–3, 7–8

84 me:] ~ , Q1–2, 7–8; ~ ; Q3–6, F2

88 beautie?] ~ ; Q1–2, 7–8; ~ , Q3–6, F2

90 To me?] Q2–4, 7–8, F2; ~ , Q1, 6; ~ ∧ Q5

91 this?] Q4+; ~ : Q1; ~ , Q2–3

93 it?] Q7–8, F2; ~ , Q1–6

96–97 This...cause.] *one line in* Q1+

97–98 Wert...it.] *one line in* Q1–4, 7–8, F2; *prose in* Q5–6

108 time.——Heare] ~ , ∧ heare Q1+

115.1 S.D. *om.* Q1+

116 um:] ~ ∧ Q1; ~ . Q2; ~ , Q3+

117 me——] Q7–8; ~ . Q1–6, F2

117–118 Know | You kill your Father.] *one line in* Q1+

122–124 I...me.] Q1–4, 7–8 *line:* I...thy | Father...me.; *prose in* Q5–6, F2

133 thee,] Q7–8; ~ ∧ Q1–6, F2

137 shame?] Q7–8; ~ , Q1–6; ~ ! F2

141.1 S.D. *location*] *after* me, *in line* 141 *in* Q8; *om.* Q1–7, F2

154 His...damn'd.] Q1–4, 7–8 *line:* His sonne? | Sweare...damn'd; *prose in* Q5–6, F2

155–157 Then...light:] *lined as in* Q2–4, 7–8; Q1 *lines:* Then... is | The...light; *prose in* Q5–6, F2

160 Land?] F2; ~ : Q1–8

172 knew it,] Q3+; knew, it ∧ Q1–2

180–181 Still...me.] *one line in* Q1–4, 7–8, F2; *prose in* Q5–6

181–182 Pray...to you.] *one line in* Q1; Q2–4, 7–8 *line:* Pray... comfort to | You.; *prose in* Q5–6, F2

256 Sister?] F2; ~ . Q1–8

257–258 If...it?] *one line in* Q1, 3–4, 7–8, F2; *prose in* Q2, 5–6

258 it?] Q2+; ~ . Q1

260 um.——] ~ : ∧ Q1; ~ , ∧ Q2–6, F2; ~ . ∧ Q7–8

262 Joy.|] ~ : ∧ Q1; ~ ; ∧ Q2–4, 7–8; ~ , ∧ Q5–6, F2

262 S.D. *location*] *after line* 262 *in* Q1+

263 newes——] ~ , Q1–6, F2; ~ ! Q7–8

264 it:——] ~ : ∧ Q1; ~ , ∧ Q2+

265–266 Yes...heard.] *one line in* Q1–4, 7–8, F2; *prose in* Q5–6

268–269 The Queene | *Mardonius,* ...Queene,] *one line in* Q1–4, 7–8; *prose in* Q5–6, F2

270 *Arbaces:*——] ~ : ∧ Q1±

271 house.——— | Since] ~ ; ∧∧ since Q1; ~ , ∧∧ since Q2–3, 5, 7–8; ~ ∧∧∧ since Q4; ~ . ∧∧ since F2; home, ∧∧ since Q6

274 this?] Q2±; ~ . Q1

280–281 Me...desire.] *lined as in Q2–4, 7–8; one line in Q1; prose in Q5–6, F2*

285–286 You...presence.] *lined as in Q2–4, 7–8; prose in Q5–6, F2; one line in Q1*

288 ever.———] ~ ; ∧ Q1; ~ : ∧ Q2+

290 you.] ~ ; ∧ Q1; ~ : ∧ Q2+

301 he?———] ~ ? ∧ Q2+; ~ , ∧ Q1

305 had.———] ~ . ∧ Q1±

309 Exit] *Exeunt* Q7–8; *om.* Q1

326 other.———] ~ . ∧ Q1+

326 S.D. *location*] *after line* 326 *in* Q1; *after* before you *line* 328 *in* Q2+

328–329 Why...vassall?] Q1 *lines:* Why...you | To...vassall?; *one line in* Q2–4, 7–8, F2; *prose in* Q5–6

330–331 Alas...will.] Q1 *lines:* Alas ...you? | What...will.; *one line in* Q2–4, 7–8, F2; *prose in* Q5–6

334 S.D.] Dyce; *om.* Q1+

334–335 Sir...strange] *one line in* Q1–4, 7–8; *prose in* Q5–6, F2

337 meanest.———|] ~ . ∧∧ Q2–4, 7–8; ~ , ∧∧ Q5–6, F2; ~ : ∧∧ Q1

337 S.D. *location*] *after* more *in line* 336 Q2+; *after* Queene, *in line* 336 Q1

349 you.———And] ~ , ∧ and Q1–4, 7–8; ~ ; ∧ and Q5–6, F2

350 us,] Q5–6, F2; ~ ; Q1; ~ . Q2–4, 7–8

351 mine:———] ~ : ∧ Q1+

HISTORICAL COLLATION

[This collation against the present text includes the nine seventeenth-century
texts (Q1 1619, Q2 1625, Q3 1631, Q4 1639, Q5 1655, Q6 1661, Q7 1676,
F2 1679, Q8 1693), and editions of Langbaine (L, 1711), Theobald–Seward–
Sympson (S, 1750), Colman (C, 1778), Weber (W, 1812), Dyce (D, 1843),
Strachey [Mermaid] (M, 1887), Bond [Variorum] (B, 1904), Alden [Belles
Lettres] (A, 1910), Walley-Wilson (WW, 1930), Turner [Regents] (T, 1963).
Omission of a siglum indicates that the text concerned agrees with the reading
of the lemma.]

I.i

0.1 *Enter...Bessus.] Enter Mardonius and Bessus, two Captaines.*
Q2–8, F2

1–2 has ended] he haz ended Q2+
(−A, −T); h'as ended T

6–7 had as] had's Q2

10 them] 'em Q2+ (−A, −T)

11 thou art] thou'rt Q2–8, F2, L,
S, C, W, WW

13 and] if Q2–8, F2, L, S, C; an D,
M, B, WW, T

15 see't] see'r Q6; see it C, W, WW

16 with me] wi' me Q2–8, F2, L,
S, C

17 winkst] winkedst Q7–8, F2+
(−A, −T)

18 strake] strooke Q2–8, F2

24 I am] I'me Q2+ (−A, −T)

26 of his] of's Q2–8, F2, L, S

28 cruddles] curdles Q3–6, F2, L,
S, C

29 wouldst] couldst Q2+ (−A,
−T)

29 in this] i' this Q2+ (−A, −T)

32 for it] for't Q2–8, F2, L, S, D,
M, B

33 good] *om.* Q2–8, F2, L, C

34 it is] t'is Q2+ (−A, −T)

37 I fam'd] Fam'd Q2–8, F2, L,
S, C, D, M

37 I, I warrant] I warrant C

38 I am verie] I'me eene Q2+
(−W, −A, −T)

39 ath'] to' th Q2–8, F2, L, S, C;
to the W, D, M, B, WW; o'th
T; a'th A

39 is] *om.* Q2–8

42 them] 'em Q2+ (−A, −T)

45 of] on Q7–8

46 in shifting a] of shifting of a
Q3–6, F2, L; in shifting of a C

52 *Bessus*] At *Bessus* Q2–8, F2, L,
S, C, W

55 Prethee] Pray thee Q2–8, F2,
L, S

56 Souldier] Souldiers Q3–6, F2,
L, S, C

57 merrily] meerely Q1

59 composition] compasion Q5;
compassion Q6

62 away] a way Q5, 8

66 not I] I not Q3–6, F2, L, S, C

68 meant'st] mean'st Q1, 4–6, 8,
A; meanedst F2, L, S, D, M, B

73 the enemie] th' enemy Q2–6,
F2, L, S, C

79 Come, come] Com, Q2–8, F2, L, C, W

80 com'st] cam'st Q2+ (−W, −A, −T)

83 extreamities] extremity Q2–8, F2, L, S, C

85 the] his Q2–8, F2, L, S, C

86.1–3 Senet...attendants.] *Enter Arbaces and Tigranes, with Attendants.* Q1; *Enter &c. Senet Flourish.* | *Enter* Arbaces *and* Tigranes *two Kings, &c:* | *The two Gentlemen.* Q2, 7–8; *Enter &c. Senet...Kings and two Gentlemen.* Q3–6, F2

88 full] fall Q1

94 free as] as free as F2, L, S, C, W, M

103 yeere] yeeres Q4–6, 8, F2+ (−A, −T)

111 *Tigranes.* Is] Is Q1

111 Is it] Is't Q2–8, F2, L, S, C, D, M, B

112 their] her C, W

113 *Arbaces*] *Arbace* Q5–6, F2

114 for] sir Q2–8, F2, L, S, C

123 Farre] Fare Q5–6

126 With] By Q2+ (−T)

133 no] Nay Q2–8, F2, C

137 an] any Q3–6, F2, L

138 God] good Q2–6; good man F2, L

140 farre] fare Q5–6

141 Its] Tis Q2+ (−A, −T)

145 faughtst] faughst Q1

146 spoke] spake Q2–8, F2, L, S, C, D

146 not mee] me not Q2–8, F2, L, S, C, D, M

159 are] have Q2+ (−T)

160 name: yet] name yet: Q1

167 for her] her for Q2, 7–8

167 take] taste Q3–6, F2, L, C

176 no one] no owne Q1

177 Would] Could Q2+ (−A, −T)

177 had] were Q7–8, S

177 had shee] she had C, W

178 for] her Q1

179 lives] times Q1, A, T

187 fight] sight F2

198 two] to Q2–8, F2, L; do S, C, W

202 *Exeunt Tigranes.*] *Exe:* Q1; *Exit Tigranes.* Q2–8, F2

205 don] *om.* Q2, 7–8; done't Q3, C, D, M, B, WW; don't Q4–6, F2, L, S

210 And] An S, C, W, D, M, B, WW

217 ift] if Q2–8, F2, L

218 with you] wi' you Q2–6, F2+ (−A, −T)

219 have] ha Q2+ (−A, −T)

219 stunke] sunke Q1

220 oth] of o'th Q2

225 on th'] on the Q2+ (−A, −T)

225 -royall] *om.* Q1, A

226 abouts] about his Q2, 7–8, W, D, M, B, WW; downe his Q3–6, F2, L, S, C

227 didst thou learn that] learn'st that Q2–6; learn'st thou that Q7; learn'st thou F2, Q8, L; learn'dst that C

228 Puft] Pish Q2–8, F2, L, S, C; Puff W, D, M, B, WW

228 I not] not I Q2–8, F2, L, S, C, D, M, B

229 Talkt] Talke Q1–6, W, A, WW

230 While] Will Q2+ (−T)

230 words] word F2

240 to] in Q2–8, F2, L, C

242 other] others Q7–8, F2, L+ (−A, −T)

242 will] may Q2+ (−A, −T)

248 mee] *om.* Q7–8

248 answer] audience Q1, W, T

250 speak soone one] speak, some one Q2+ (−T)

259 but...growne] *om.* Q7–8

260 To talke but idlie] To balke;
but I desire Q1, W, T; To
balke, but I defie Q2–6, F2, L;
To talk! But I defy—— C; *om.*
Q7–8

261 drawest] draul'st Q2–4, 7–8, S,
C, D, M, B, A, WW

263 instants] an instant Q7–8

265 An't] And Q2–8, F2, L; An S,
C

267 yet] *om.* Q3–6, F2, L

268 too] mee Q1; ye W

279 great] as great Q4–6, F2, L

280 that] as Q2+ (−A, −T)

282 with] wi' Q2–6, F2, L, S, C

285 Hath] Had M, B, WW

296 Puff!] *om.* Q1, W

297 rule] rules Q4–6

302 Will...gone] Goe get you gone
Q2+ (−S, −A, −T)

303 word] words Q3–6, F2+ (−A,
−T)

303 mooves] move F2+ (−A, −T)

303 *1. Gentleman.*] *2 Gent.* Q1, A

305 they] *om.* Q2; you Q3–6, F2+
(−A, −T)

305.1 *Exeunt...Mardonius.*] *om.* Q1

314 With me you article] You article
with me S

319 chose] chosen Q8

321 doted] done Q2–6; done it
Q7–8, F2+ (−W, −A, −T)

330 good] stood Q8

337 manifold] manifest Q7–8

339 when] but when Q2–8, F2, L,
S, C, B

339 of] *om.* Q2–8, F2+ (−A, −T)

340 hearing: but] Hearing out S;
hearing o' t B

343 above] about Q2–8, F2+ (−A,
−T)

352 then] though Q1–8, F2, W, D,
M, B, WW, T

360 hasty] nasty M

361 worth] worths W, WW

361 um] it S, C

362 would] will Q3–6, F2, L, S, C,
W

368 wilde] *om.* Q2–8, F2, L, S, C

369 honesty] honest, Q1, B, T

370 it] it | it Q7

370 would] should Q3–6, F2+
(−A, −T)

370 to] to | to Q1

371 defend] descend Q6

372 would] should Q2–8, F2, L, S,
C

372 out you] you out Q2–8, F2, L,
C, W

383 thee] me Q4–6, F2, L

390 tis] it is Q2–8, F2+ (−A, −T)

391 I] *om.* Q6

395 in thine] i' thine Q2–4; in thy
Q6

401 I' those] Ith those Q1; In those
Q7–8

403 the] they Q2

405 um] them Q7–8

409 with.] with. Enter *Bessus,* and
the two *Gent.* Q2

411 you] yon Q2

412 um] them Q2–8, F2, L, S, C

412.1 *Enter...Bessus.*] *om.* Q1

415 I am] I'me Q2+ (−A, −T)

416 *1. Gentleman.*] *2 Gent.* Q2–8,
F2, L, S, C, W

417 *2. Gentleman.*] *1 Gent.* Q2–8,
F2, L, S, C, W

420 you haste] you; halfe Q1

421 An't] And Q2–8, F2, L; An S,
C

422 Ist] Is it Q8

424 two] to Q5

425 *Panthæa*] *Panthan* Q1; *Pentha*
Q5–6, F2

426 be] we Q2

428 will't] will Q1

429 Sir] *om.* Q1, W

430 shalt] shall Q 8
433 and] *om.* Q 1, A
442.1 *Enter* Messenger] *Enter a Messenger* Q 2–6, F 2; *Enter a Messenger with a packet*] Q 7–8
448 Thanke thee] Take that Q 2+ (−A, −T)
458 Enough] I'now Q 2–4; I now Q 5–6; Enow Q 7–8, S, C, W, D, M; now F 2, L
462 here] her Q 3–6, 8
473 has hir'd] had stir'd Q 2–8, F 2, L, A; had hired S, C, W, D, M, B, WW

477 to] in Q 7–8
480 um] them Q 6
484 laden] loden Q 2–8, F 2, L, S, C
488 become] come Q 5–6
490 mourning] morning Q 5–6, F 2, L
491 that] her Q 1, A
496 farther] further C, W
502 Your] Our Q 5
504 prayers] praier Q 2+ (−T)
506 dangers] danger Q 2+ (−W, −WW, −T)
507 saw] *om.* Q 4–6
507.1 *Exeunt.*] *om.* Q 1

I.ii

1 die] fly W, D, M, B, A, WW
5 either loves] ever lov'd Q 3–6, F 2, L, C; ever loves W
9 place] plac'd F 2, L, S, C, W
9 high] too light Q 1; too high W, T
16 it] *om.* Q 7–8
18 thee] *om.* Q 1
26 makes] make F 2, L
33 have] gave Q 4
33 given] gin Q 2, 7–8
33 to] unto Q 3–6, F 2+ (−T)

35 would] will Q 2–8, F 2, L, S, C
53 find] feele Q 2–8, F 2+ (−A, −T)
55 requires] require F 2+ (−A, −T)
55 speed] hast Q 2–8, F 2, L, S, C, W
58 long] Lord Q 2
61.1 *Exeunt.*] *Finis Actus Primi.* Q 1; *The end of the First Act.* Q 2–3; *om.* Q 4–8, F 2

II.i

0.1–2 Panthæa, *and waiting women, with attendance.*] *Panthea, and Mandane, waiting women...* Q 1; *Panthea, and Mandane, waiting-women, with Attendants.* Q 2–6, F 2; *Panthea, and Mandane, waiting-women, with Attendants, and Guards.* Q 7–8
4 know't] know it Q 7–8
17 paid] waide Q 2–8, F 2, L, S, C
26 *Arane.*] *Arv.* Q 5; *Arb.* Q 6
31 her] *om.* Q 2–8, F 2, L, S, C
32 set] let Q 1

36 shall] should W, WW
37 eare] ears Q 5–6, F 2, L, S
42 woman] Mother Q 2–8, F 2, L, S, C
46 twill] t'wood Q 2–5, 7–8, F 2+ (−A, −T); 'twould not Q 6
47 not] *om.* Q 6
48 torne] sworn S
57 But you: your urging being] But you, your urging, being Q 1; But you, your urging; being S, W, D, B, WW
58 mine] my Q 2–8, F 2, L, S, C

299

59 this] *om.* Q6
69 hee] a Q2–6
71 nor I] neither I, S; not I, A
71 him] time Q1
72 Lord] *om.* F2
93 as you] *om.* Q1, W
94 I am] I'me Q2–8, F2+ (−A, −T)
97 pryaers are] prayer is Q3–6, F2, L, S, C, W
97 I will] will I Q2+ (−W, −A, −T)
106 Arane.] *om.* Q1
108 Betweene] betwixt Q2+ (−A, −T)
109 We] He Q8
114 truth] the truth Q2–8, F2, L, S, C, A, T
121 heare it] hear't Q2+ (−A, −T)
122 I, I prethee] I prethee Q2+ (−B, −A, −T); Ay, prithee B
124 gauntlet] Target S
128 neere] next Q2+ (−A, −T)
128 of the] oth' Q2–8, F2, L, S, C
131 whom] who F2, L, S, D, M, B, WW
136 prethee] pray thee Q2–8, F2, L, S, C
139 I confesse] *om.* Q1, W, WW
143 I, but] But Q2–8, F2, L, S, C
145 when as] whenas T
145 saide] say Q2+ (−A, −T)
146 yet] when Q1, T
156 twas so] so twas Q2–8, W, D, M, B, WW; so it was F2, L, S, C
161 An't] And Q2–8, F2, L, S
162 neerer] neere Q3–6, F2, L, S, C, W
163 Y'are] Your Q8; You'r Q3–6, F2+ (−W, −A, −T); You're Q7; You are W
164 kindnesses] kindnesse Q2–8, F2, L

165 *Thalestris*] *Thalectris* Q2–6, F2
173 sheele] she' Q8
175 for her honestie] for honesty Q2–8, F2, L, S, C, W, WW
175 along] a long Q2
181 on] of Q2+ (−A, −T)
181 on her] *om.* Q8
196 *Exit.*] *Exit Bessus.* Q2–4, 7–8; *om.* F2
198 *Exit*] Q1–2, 7–8; *om.* Q3–6; *Exeunt Bessus and Bacurius.* F2
199 Majesty] *om.* Q8
201 whilst] while C, W, M
204 um] them Q6
206 vertuous] vertues Q2–8, F2; Virtue's L
211 or] and Q2–8, F2, L, S, C, W
213 hope] hopes F2, L, S
216 love] loves Q5–6, F2, L, S
217 your] a C
218 my Lord] *om.* Q8
221 were] where Q5–6
222 chuse] chose L, S, C, W
223 him] time Q1
226 there is] ther's Q3–6, F2, L
228 does] doeth Q3–6, F2+ (−T)
228 his] this Q1
233 Madam] *om.* Q2–8, F2, L, S, C
235 Gobrius] *om.* Q1
239 *Exeunt women.*] *om.* Q1
251 the] a Q6
252 talke] take Q1–8, F2, L
259 foule] fool Q6
264 prethee] pray thee Q2–8, F2, L, S
266 shape] sharp Q6
277 owne] one Q5–6
277 too] so Q2–8, F2, L, S, C, W
287 those] these Q5–6, F2, L
292 shall] will Q3–6, F2, L, S, C
301 You] Your Q4–5
301 *Thalestris*] *Thalectris* Q2–6
303 my] *om.* Q1
304 others] other Q4–6, F2, L, S
311.1 *Exeunt.*] *Exit.* Q1

300

II.ii

1 run] *om.* Q8

3 women out] out women Q3–6,
F2, L, S, C

4 fidling] sidling Q5

6 say] sayd Q2+ (−A, −T)

12 looke] looks Q6

12 those] these Q5–6, F2, L, S

14 quickly] *om.* Q2–8, F2, L, S, C,
W

16 a foote] afoote Q2–5, 7–8, A,
T; o' foot F2+ (−A, −T)

19 lookt] looke Q1

21.1 *Enter...Philip.*] *Enter a man
with two Citizens wives.* Q2–8,
F2

28 2.] *3.* Q5–6

32 with me downe] downe with me
Q3–6, F2+ (−W, −A, −T)

33 abed] to bed Q2–8, F2+ (−A,
−T)

34 tis] it is Q2–8, F2, L, S, C

35 prethee] pray thee Q2–8, F2, L,
S

41 ith] 'the Q2

44 2.] *1.* Q3

46 In] I' Q2–8, F2, L, S, C, W

51 *1.] 3.* Q2–8, F2, L, S, C, T

52 you] *om.* Q1, D, A

52 friend] friends W

52 thrust] trust Q6

54 shroving] thrusting Q1, S, C,
W, D, M, B, A, WW; showing
Q2–6, F2, L; shoving Q7–8

55 hap to] haps Q2–8, F2, L, S, C

58 so] *om.* Q2–8, F2, L, S, C, W

61 have] ha' Q2+ (−A, −T)

66 law] la Q2+ (−A, −T)

66 thou art] thou'rt Q2+ (−W,
−T)

67 there is] there's Q2+ (−A, −T)

67 thou art] thou'rt Q2+ (−W,
−A, −T)

67 one] one one Q3

67 of it] on't Q2+ (−A, −T)

68 he will] hee'le Q2+ (−A, −T)

68 never] nere Q2–8, F2, S+
(−A, −T); near L

69 slipstring] stripling Q1, W

72 *3. Man.*] *om.* Q6

73 you are] you're Q2+ (−A,
−T)

74 cost] cast Q2–6

74.1 *Enter one running.*] *Flourish,
Enter one running.* Q2–8, F2;
om. Q1

75 *Man.*] *3.* Q1, T; *4.* Q2–8, F2,
L, S, C, W, A

75 *The King*] *three times only* Q5–
6, F2, L, S

76.1 *Enter...others.*] *Flourish: En-
ter Arbaces, Tigranes, the two
Kings, and Mardonius.* Q2–8,
F2

78 thanke] think Q5–6

87 without] but with Q2–8, F2, L,
S, C

87 our] your Q3–6, F2, L, S, C

87 blouds] bloud Q7

90 in] i' Q2–6, F2, L, S, C

91 you may] may Q5–6, F2, L

96 may you] you may Q3–6, F2,
L, C, W

96 all] fall Q6

97 when] where Q3–6, F2

103 Behold] Beheld Q5–6

103 hearts] heart Q2–8, F2, L

107 *Woman.*] *3 Woman.* Q1–8, F2,
L, S, C, W, A

107 hang him,] *om.* Q2+ (−A,
−T)

110 farre] so farre Q3–6, F2, L

113 Not] nor Q5–6

114 nature] name Q5–6, F2, L

118 with] *om.* Q7–8

118 won] I won Q7–8
119 brought] made Q1, A
122 will] well Q3–4
123 worke] word Q3–6
126 commendation] commendations Q1, T
130 That] Thus Q1, T
131 calles] call Q2+ (–T)
132 amongst] among Q4–6, F2, L, S, C
137 Eate] Sit Q2+ (–T)
139 to] so Q4
141 God...Majestie.] *repetition om.* Q1, A
141.1 *Flourish.*] *om.* Q1, T
141.1 *kings and their traine*] *om.* Q1
143 Gods] God Q5–6, F2
146 haltersack] holtersack Q6

147 *1. Man.*] *2.* Q2+ (–D, –M, –B)
150 so] *om.* Q1, A
151.1 *Exeunt...Woman.*] *Exeunt 1, 2, 3, and Women.* Q1; *Exeunt 2. 3. and women.* Q2–4, 7–8; *Exeunt 2. 3. and woman.* Q5–6, F2
152 afore] before F2, L, S, C, W
152 homeward] homewards Q2+ (–A, –T)
153 all] *om.* Q1, A
155 They are] They're F2+(–A, –T); The'are Q2–8
155 on] of F2, L, S, C
159 to] to to Q7
159.1 *Exeunt.*] *Finis Actus Secundi.* Q1; *The end of the Second Act.* Q2–3; *om.* Q4–8, F2

III.i

1 take] takes Q6
2 doth] does Q2–5, 7–8, F2+ (–A, –T)
9 wil] would Q5–6, F2, L, S
15 I doe...not] *om.* Q1
22 Sir, sheele] she will Q2–8, F2, L, S, C, W
30 For] fore Q5
31 would] could Q3–6, F2, L, S, C, W, D, M, B, WW
34 you] *om.* Q3–6
38.1 *1. Gentleman and*] *om.* Q1
39 here's] here is Q2+ (–A, –T)
43 them] 'em Q2+ (–A, –T)
43 S.D. *om.* Q1, 3–6, F2
46.2 *and 2. Gentleman*] *and two Gentlemen* Q2–6, F2; *and two Gentlemen, Attendants, and Guards.* Q7–8; *om.* Q1
48 is] to Q1, D, M, A, WW; *om.* B
55 *Arane.*] *Arb.* Q5–6
57 sorrow] Sorrowes Q3–6, F2, L, S, C, W, WW

61 *Arbaces.*] *Ara.* Q2–6
61 guard] guide Q2+ (–A, –T)
61 Arane] *om.* Q1
79 kindnesse] kind ones Q7–8
80 *Tigranes.*] *Gobrias.* D
82 thy selfe] my selfe Q4
84 thence] hence Q2–6, F2, L
84 there] here Q7–8
85 thou] you WW
86 flesh] breast Q2–8, F2, L, S, C, W
87 a] thy Q3–6, F2, L
88 wanton] wonted Q4–6, F2, L
89 in thy] i' thy Q2–8, F2, L, S, C
102 that may] that it may Q3–6, F2, L, W, WW
103 manhood] manhoods Q8
117 Some] *Gob.* Some Q1
117 has] hath Q2+ (–A, –T)
117 where] *om.* Q8
118 *Gobrius., Arbaces., Gobrius., Arbaces.*] *Arb., Gob., Arb., Gob.* Q1

128 But] And Q2+ (−A, −T)

133 sleepe] sheepe Q2–8, F2, L

141 yet] *om.* Q2–8, F2, L

146–148 She...thus.] *om.* Q1

150 hold] holp Q8

162 any] ever Q2+ (−D, −A, −T)

170 is shee] she is Q3–6, F2+ (−A, −T)

186 and] yet S

189 your] my Q3–6, F2; a L, S, C, W

196 them] 'em Q2–8, F2, L, S, C, W, WW

198 so] see Q2–8, F2, L

206 rage] change Q1, A, T

207 shall] will M, B

208 God] heaven Q3–6, F2+ (−A, −T)

219 in the] i'th Q2–8, F2, L; i'the S, C, W, WW

221 one] own Q6

234 how dare you then] how then dare you Q3–4, C, W, D, M, B, WW; then how dare you Q5–6, F2, L, S

235 doe] *om.* Q8

240 that] the Q3–6, F2, L

243 law] lawes Q2–8, F2, L, S, C, W, WW

266 fam'd] fram'd Q3–6

266 Tyrants] Titans Q3–6, F2, L

267 in the] i' the Q2–8, S+ (−A, −T); i' th' F2, L

267 depth] deepe Q3–8, F2, L, S, C, W, D, M

270.1 *Exeunt...Bacurius.] F2; Exit ...Q2–8; om.* Q1

273 forsaken?] forsaken? *Exit* Spaconia Q7–8

281 was] *om.* Q8

289 to; here] to heare Q3–6, F2, L

298 I doe] do I T

300 still] yet Q2+ (−A, −T)

301 This] This, this Q1, T

306 *Gobrius.] Pan.* Q1

311 poysoner] prisoner Q4–6, F2, L

312 *Gobrius.] Bac.* Q1

313 *Panthæa.] Gob.* Q1

314 along] *om.* M, B, WW

318 had it] had't Q2–8, F2, L

318 twixt] betwixt Q2–8, F2, L

319.1 *Exeunt...Mardonius.] Exeunt Gobrius, Panthea, Bessus, and Spaconia.* Q2–6, F2; *Exeunt Gobrius, Panthea, and Bessus.* Q7–8

333 prethee] pray thee Q2–8, F2, L, S, C, W

334 I not] not I Q2, 7–8

339 no] do Q6

340 ye] you Q2+ (−A, −T)

344 prethee] pray thee Q2–8, F2, L, S, C, W

346 *Mardonius....ye.] om.* Q2–8, F2, L, C, W; *Mar.* I warrant you. S

III.ii

0.1 Bessus.] *Bessus alone.* Q2–8, F2, L, S, C

1 fame] game Q7–8

3 have it] have Q2, 7–8

12 on] o– Q3

13 them] 'em Q2+ (−A, −T)

13–14 In this] I' this Q2–4, 7–8; I, this Q5–6, F2

14 by th'] b' the Q2–6; by the W, D, M, B, WW

15 with] wi' Q2–5, 7–8, F2, L, S, C

15 would have] would ha' Q7–8

16 with] wi' Q2–5, 7–8, F2, L, S, C

20 God] heaven Q3–6, F2+ (−A, −T)

20 cald] cals Q 5–6, F 2, L, S
21 pounds] pound Q 2–8, F 2, L
27 afraid] fraide Q 2–6, F 2
28 my enemies] mine enemies S, C, W, WW
30 plague] pox Q 7–8
31 of] on F 2, L, S, C, W, D, M, WW
33 of] on Q 2+ (– A, – T)
33–34 to account] *om.* Q 2–8, F 2, L
34 the] *om.* Q 2, 7–8
34.1 *a*] *om.* Q 1, A
35–70 *Gentleman.*] *3 Gentleman* Q 2–8, F 2
38 You are] You'r Q 2+ (– A, – T)
40–41 nothing doubts] doth nothing doubt Q 2+ (– A, – T)
44 it is] 'tis Q 7–8
49 crie you] cir you Q 5; Sir your F 2, L, S
50 agreeablie] agreeable Q 4–6, 8, F 2, L, S
51–53 um] um, um, um Q 2+ (– A) [*each time throughout speech*]
52 an] *om.* Q 2+ (– A, – T)
54 awaite] wait W, WW
56 his] this W
57 can] could Q 2+ (– A, – T)
58 *Bessus.*] *om.* Q 1
65 with you] *om.* Q 2–8, F 2, L, S, C, W, WW
66 doe] shew Q 2+ (– A, – T)
66 resolutely] resolvedly Q 2+ (– A, – T)
67 hundred] hundreth Q 2–3; hundredth D, M

69 ye] you Q 2+ (– A, – T)
71 Gentleman.] *om.* Q 1; *3 Gen.* Q 2–8, F 2
74 this] these Q 4
75 by] my Q 8
76 so that that's] so that's Q 6, 8
77 referr'd] reserv'd Q 1, T
78 these] there Q 1
80 likely] like Q 2+ (– A, – T)
80 this] these Q 4, A
80 five yeare] time here Q 1; five yeares Q 4–6, F 2+ (– B, – A, – T)
82 send] finde Q 2–8, F 2, L
87 um] them Q 6
97 with] *om.* C, W
100 owne] one Q 5–6
109 prethee] pray thee Q 2–8, F 2, L, S; pr'ythee W
110 shalt fight] shall fight C, W
110 beate] beaten Q 5–6, F 2+ (– A, – T)
112 pounds] pound Q 2–8, F 2, L
113 legge well a weeke] legge a weeke Q 1; leg well a waeke Q 5; leg well and walk Q 6
114 Ile] I Q 3
120 a] *om.* Q 4–6
124 you weare] your were Q 3
125 quicke] *om.* F 2, L, S
127 I say,] say, Q 3–6
131 very] *om.* Q 7–8
136 *Exit*] *Exit Bacurius.* Q 2–8, F 2; *om.* Q 1
139 beating] beting Q 5–6
143 will I] I will Q 2+ (– A, – T)
144 all is] all that's Q 2–6, F 2+ (– A, – T); all that is Q 7–8
144.1 *Exit.*] *Exit Bessus.* Q 2–8, F 2

III.iii

1 he is] he's Q 7–8
5 await his] wait his Q 3–6, F 2, L, C, W, WW; wait's S

7.1 S.D. *om.* Q 1
11 in their] i' their Q 2–8, F 2, L, S, C, W

14 lies] lie F2+ (−A, −T)
16 me] 'em F2, L
19 doe] *om.* Q1
23 Are] Art Q1
24 not that] it not Q3–6, F2+ (−A, −T)
24 theres] there is Q7–8
28 shall] will Q3–6, F2+ (−A, −T)
29 you] your Q6
30 tis] it is F2, L, S
31 hath] haz Q2–8, F2+ (−A, −T)
31 were] wear Q6
32 a fall] fall Q1, A
32 fall, or] fall, Q6
41 all] *om.* Q2–8, F2, L, C, W
47 shall I] I shall Q3–6, F2, L
50 what] *om.* Q2+ (−A, −T)
51 should] shall Q3–6, F2+ (−B, −A, −T)
55 on] one Q3–6, F2
61 such] such a Q2–8, F2, L, C, W, T
63 There is] There's Q6
65 doe it] do't Q6
68 I doe] you doe Q3–6, F2, C, W
78 doe] *om.* M, B
85 heires] haires Q2+
86 cause] case Q3–6, F2, L
86 life] of life S
87 how] ha how Q4–6, F2, L
89 about] upon Q4–6, F2, L
90 his] this Q3–6, F2, L, S, C, W, D
91 Deare] heare Q2–8, F2, L, C, W
94 Pray God] Heaven grant Q3–6, F2, L, S, C, W, D, M
100 feele I] feele I I Q5; feele? I Q6
106 no] nor Q6
106 God] the Gods Q3–4, F2, L, S, C, W, D, M; thee Gods Q5–6
106 you and] and S, C
106 mend you] mend Q3–6, F2, W

108 require] requires Q3–6, F2, L, S, C, W, M
112 of] for Q3–6, F2+ (−A, −T)
113.1 *to them*] *om.* Q2–8, F2+ (−B, −A, −T)
114 Where is] Where's Q2, 7–8
119 Away] A way Q5
121 I am] I'me Q2+ (−A, −T)
124 I am] *Mar.* I am Q1
124 I am] I'me Q3–5, F2+ (−A, −T)
125 *Mardonius.*] *om.* Q1
125 that] this Q3–6, F2, L, S, C, W
127–129 *Bessus....you.*] *om.* Q1
131 occasions] occasion Q3–6, F2, L, S, C, W
135 the] these Q4–6, F2, L, S
136 his] this Q5–6, F2, L
136 *Exit.*] *Exit Mar.* Q2–8, F2
138 Do't] Doe Q1, A
138 without] out Q3
142 a] the Q3–6, F2, L, S, C, W
145 would] would fain Q7–8
146 understands] understandst Q2+
147 a bout] about Q1–2, 5–6
149 dost] do'st thou Q2+ (−A, −T)
150 be tell me] be me Q3; be Q4–6, F2, L, S
150 tell] trust C, W
151 too] *om.* Q1, A
154 and] thou Q4–8, F2, L, S
157–158 ever you] ever your Q2
161 have] *om.* Q5–6, F2, L
162 Like] Like the Q3–6, F2, L
167 your] my Q4–6, F2, L, S
171 I hate] now I hate Q3–6, F2+ (−T)
186 Gods...mans] God...man Q7–8, F2+ (−A, −T)
187 Natures] nature Q7–8, C, W
193.1 *Exit.*] *Finis Actus Tertii.* Q1; *The end of the Third Act.* Q2–3; *om.* Q4–8, F2

IV.i

0.1 Spaconia] *and* Spaconia F2
8 since] *om.* Q4–6, F2, L
8 th'are] they are Q2–8, F2, L,
    W, M, B, WW; they're S, C, D
10 um] them Q6
11 um] them Q6
12 though] if Q1, A
15 out] on't Q2–8, F2, L
16 'gainst] against Q1, A, T
17 those] these M, B, WW
23 shoote] shot Q4–6
24 his] *om.* S
27 not] no Q6
27 further] farther Q2–8, F2, L, S
29 But] *om.* Q1, D, M, B, A, WW

38 Gobrius] *om.* Q1, A
45 yours] you Q2–8, F2, L
55 *Panthæa.*] *Spaconia.* Q2
59 I am] I'm Q7–8, S, C
59 not] no Q1, B, A, WW
66 those] these Q2–8
66 excellencies] excellences M, B,
    WW
67 tame] have Q1, B
68 beside] besides Q6
71 word] words Q1
73 Ime] I am Q2+ (−A, −T)
73 growne] *om.* Q7–8
80 God] Heaven Q3–6, F2+ (−A,
    −T)

IV.ii

0.1 *in prison*] *om.* Q1
2 mine] my Q2–5, 7–8, F2+
    (−A, −T)
2 turnd] turne Q1
14 it] *om.* Q3–6, F2, L
20 forgot] forgat C
20 griefes] griefe Q2–8, F2, L, S,
    C, W
22 as] in S, C, W
22 womans] women Q2–5, 7–8,
    F2, L, S, C, W; woman Q6
23 lost] left Q2+ (−A, −T)
24 me, equall] me equall Q1; me
    equall, Q2–8, F2, L, W, T
26 inconstancie] unconstancy Q7–8
33–34 me. *Bacurius.* Ladie, | Your]
    me Ladie. | *Bac.* Your Q1
39 for] or Q2–8, F2, L, S, C, W
44 the] your Q2–8, F2, L, S, C, W
46 it] him M, B
47 then no more] tell thee more S
48 unconstant] inconstant C, W,
    WW

50 as firme] is firme Q3–6, F2, L,
    C, W
51 and] *om.* Q2–8, F2, L, S, C, W,
    WW
52 boyes] boys' S, D, M, B, WW,
    A, T; boy's C, W
52 in the aire] in th'ayre Q3; i'th
    air Q4–6, F2, L, S, C, W, WW;
    i'the D, M, B
55 murmurs] murmure Q2–8, F2,
    L, S, C, W, WW
61 wrongs] wrong Q5–6, F2, L, S
61 thy] they A
64 *Spaconia.*] *om.* Q1
65 alike] *om.* Q4–6, F2, L
70 beshrow] beshrew Q3–4, S, C,
    W, M, WW
70 fort] for it M, B, WW
72 hee's] 'tis Q2–8, F2, L, C
74 spoken] spoke, Q8
80 me] *om.* Q2–8, F2, L, S, C, W
82 No] Nay Q3–6, F2
82.1 *and*] *om.* Q2–8, F2

85 quit] quite Q2–4; 'quite Q7–8
94 outlast two] last too F2, L; last
   two S
94 I thanke you] I thank you, Sir S
99 Lady is] Ladie's Q2+ (–A,
   –T)
105 knew] know Q1, T
110 pratling] prating Q2–8, F2, L,
   S, C, W
111 to it] to't Q2+ (–A, –T)
114 barre] bare Q6
115 Beside] Besides F2+ (–A, –T)
117 Sirra] Sir Q2–8, F2, L, S, C, W
117 tell truth] tell the truth S
122 poak't] yoakt Q2–8, F2, L, S,
   C, W
123 broke] broken Q5–6, F2, L, S
124 trifled] stifled Q4–6
134 say Sir what you please] say
   what you please Sir Q2+ (–A,
   –T)
135 Mardonius.] om. Q2–8, F2, L,
   S, C, W
142 God] heaven Q3–6, F2+ (–A,
   –T)
144 doe it] do't Q2–8, F2+ (–A,
   –T)
145 Doe] om. Q1
153 and...termogant] om. Q2–8,
   F2, L
156 let um] let them Q2–8, F2, L,
   S, C, W
156 be prisoners] prisoners bee Q2–
   8, F2, L, S, C, W
158 um] them Q6
159 Bacurius.] Tigranes. Q2+ (–T)
161 Spaconia.] om. Q2–6, F2, L
162 deare] deerer Q4–6, F2, L
162.1 Exit...Spaconia.] Exeunt Tigranes, Spaconia, Bacurius. Q2–
   8, F2
163 have you] you have Q4–6, F2,
   L, S
164 reprove] prove Q6

167 Sutlers] Sadlers Q1, A, T
168 to] no Q5
169 often] oft S
170 tis] it is D, M, B, WW
171 wonnot] will not Q7–8; wo'not
   F2
173 then] om. Q2–8, F2, L, S, C, W,
   A
173 these] this Q2
176 Where] When Q2–8, F2, L, S,
   C, W
176 um] them Q6
177 doe...me] om. Q2+ (–T)
178 grow] grow worse Q2+ (–T)
179 rock't] rott Q1–8, F2, L, A
180 dead] deepe Q4–6, F2, L, S, C
181 Till] Like Q1
186 all] om. Q2–8, F2, L, S, C, W
188 Woot] Wilt Q7–8
188 my] good Q1, D, M, B, A, WW
194 all] om. Q3–6, F2, L, C, W
197 doe] to Q2–8, F2, L
200 tame] have Q1
203 heart] heat Q5–6
204 her] here Q5
204 a] om. Q5–6
208 Prethee] Pray thee Q2–8, F2,
   L, S, C, W
212 knew'st] know'st Q5–6, F2, L;
   knew of Q1, T
221 is it] it is Q2+ (–T)
228 she would] she fain would S
229 be thousand] be a thousand Q6,
   F2, L, S
230 Thousands] om. Q1, A; Thousand Q5–6
230 denie it] deny't Q2–5, 7, F2, L,
   S, C
232 where] were Q8
232 vertue] vertues Q3–6, F2, L, S,
   C, W
236 make] let M, B
238.1 Exeunt.] Exeunt all. Q2–8,
   F2

IV.iii

1 there] *om.* F 2, L
5 understood] understand Q 2+
    (− A, − T)
7 my] *om.* Q 3–6, F 2, L, C, W
8 to the] to' th Q 2–3, 7–8
8 cause] case D, M
10 *2 Sword-man...honour,] om.*
    Q 6
11 cause] case D, M
11 be wise] *Bes.* Be wise Q 2–8, F 2
11 speake truth] speak the truth S,
    M, B, WW
12 *Bessus.*] *om.* Q 2–8, F 2
17 have] haz Q 2–8, F 2, L, S, C, W
81 he] a Q 2–5; I Q 6
24 case] cause Q 2–8, F 2, L, S, C,
    W, A
25 honourable] horrible Q 3–6, F 2,
    L
27 we] the Q 3–6, F 2, L, S, C, W
29 drawne ten] drawen Q 3; drawne
    Q 4–6, F 2, L
29 beside] besides F 2+ (− A, − T)
30 these] this Q 2–8, F 2, L, S, C,
    W
30 had] bad Q 4
33 hee] a Q 2–5
34 tossing] Q 2; crossing Q 1, T
36 gentlemen] gentleman Q 1
37 Theres] There is F 2, L, S, C
38 cause] case D, M
42 reacheth] reaches W, WW
42 mile] miles Q 4–6, F 2+ (− A,
    − T)
44 erre] ere Q 5
44 mile] miles F 2+ (− A, − T)
46 a the] the Q 4–6, F 2, L, M, B;
    of the S, C, W
47 *1. Sword-man.*] *om.* Q 1
48 *Bessus.*] 1. Q 1
53 opinions] opinion C, W, WW
58 sword] swrod Q 5; word Q 6

58 lost...forst] forst...lost Q 1–
    8, F 2, L, A
61 case] cause Q 5–6, F 2, L, S, W
63 sit] set Q 2–6, F 2, L, S, C, W,
    A; sat Q 7–8
64 it had] t'had Q 2+ (− A, − T)
66 delivering] delivery Q 5–6
70 He] A Q 2–5; And Q 6
70 deliverie] delivering Q 5–6, F 2,
    L, S, W, WW
74 byth'] by the Q 2–8, F 2, L, D,
    M, B, WW; by S
75 you are] you'r Q 2–8, F 2, L, S, C
78 the] *om.* Q 1
82 what] that Q 2, 7–8, A
83 Sir] Sirs Q 2+ (− T)
83 toth'] to the Q 2+ (− A, − T)
84 Captaine] the Captaine Q 6
85 hee's] is Q 2–8, F 2, L, C, W
86 But...brother?] *om.* Q 2–8, F 2,
    L
90 Surely] Surly Q 5–6
91 you] your Q 5; You'll Q 6
91 your] you Q 5
94 this] the Q 2+ (− A, − T)
98 the] this Q 2–8, F 2, L, S, C, W
100 Give] I Give Q 5–6; I, give F 2;
    Ay, give L, S, C, W
100 againe;] againe, againe Q 1, T
100 brother] *om.* Q 6
101 I will] will Q 5 ['I' *moved up to
    line* 100.]
104 And my Foxe] and fox Q 6
104 musted] musled Q 1
105 cause] case D, M
107 untemperate] intemperate Q 4–6,
    F 2+ (− A, − T)
110 throughly] thoroughly S, C, W,
    M, B, WW, T; thorowly Q 5,
    F 2, L; throwly Q 6
110 kicker] kicke Q 1, A
112 beaten] baren Q 6

112 may] will Q6
113 error?] error I Q6
115 one] on Q5–6
117 sore] so F2, L, S
119 foote] foole Q1
120 A] Ah Q1
121 cause] case D, M, B, WW
121 mightie] weighty Q6
122 laught] laugh Q4–6, F2, L
125 *1. Sword-man.*] *2.* Q2+
128 contemning, you] contemning it; you S
135 Size] sizes Q6
135 daggers] degrees F2, L

145 *1. Sword-man.*] *2.* Q3
146 To] *om.* D, M
146 abide upon't] bide upon Q2–8, F2, L, C, W
150 Boy] Both Q6
150 get some] get me some Q4–6, F2+ (–C, –T)
151 cleare] clean Q6
151 when] *om.* Q2–8, F2, L
152 we] you Q7–8
157 cause] case D, M, B, WW
158 *2. Sword-man.*] *3.* Q6
158 We] Go Q6
159 be] are Q5–6, F2, L, S

IV.iv

0.1 Gobrius] *and Gobrius* Q2–8, F2
3 *Exit* Gobrius.] *om.* Q1
4 You are] You'r Q2+ (–A, –T)
4 I] *om.* Q4–6, F2, L
4 God] heaven Q3–6, F2, L, S, C, W, D, M
8 these] the Q7–8
9 should] shall Q2–3, 6–8, C, W, WW
9 speake?] speak I Q6
11 does] doth Q2+ (–T)
12 broughts] brought'st Q2+
13 heard] head Q6
14 prethee] pray thee Q2–8, F2, L, S, C, W
15 I am] Am I Q3–6, F2, L, C, W
15 the] she Q5
27 thy selfe] myself B
28 As equall] In equall Q3–6, F2, L; In as equal Q2, Q7–8
28 a] *om.* Q5–6, F2, L
28 cold] could Q6
30 Convert] Gonvert C
32 prethee] pray thee Q2–5, 7–8, F2, L, S, C, W; pray the Q6

37 that there is a cause] and there is a cause Q3–4; and there is no cause Q5; and ther is none can see Q6
42 ever] very W
45 prison] prisoner Q6
50 step] stop Q4–6
55 God] Heaven Q3–6, F2+ (–A, –T)
56 cause] case F2, L
63 Innocents] innocence Q2+ (–W, –T)
64 know I have] Know that I have Q3–6, F2, L, W; Know, that I've S, C
65 beast] best Q6
66 Heaven] God WW
66 it is] tis Q3–6, F2, L
69 as] where Q3–6, F2+ (–B, –A, –T)
78 God] heaven Q3–6, F2, L, S, C, W, D, M
81 ene] eye Q1
84 um] them Q6
86 Farre] Fare Q5
87 should] shall Q2+ (–A, –T)
93 um] them Q6

100 though thou wert] though tho'
 wert Q2–3, 7
102 sinnes] sinne Q3–6, F2, L, S,
 C, W, D, M
112 stoppe] steppe Q1
114 else] elfe Q5
119 um] them Q6
120 them] 'em Q2–8, F2+ (−A,
 −T)
121 um] them C, W
122 um] them Q6
123 rase] raise Q6
123 um...um] them...them Q6
123 then] them F2
124 um] them Q6
124 them] 'em Q2+ (−A, −T)
126 um] them Q6
140 I will] *Arb.* I will Q2+ (−T)
141 *Arbaces.*] *om.* Q2+ (−T)

143 will] shall W
144 in this] i'this Q2
145 theres] there is Q2+ (−A, −T)
147 Why] *om.* Q1
150 I know] *om.* Q3–6, F2, L, S
155 were] were too Q3–6, F2, L, S,
 W
159–160 I...yours] I dare no longer
 stay Q7–8
160 I feare] *om.* Q3–6, F2, L
162 Gods] heavens Q3–6, F2+
 (−A, −T)
163.1 *Exeunt...ways.] Finis Actus
 Quarti.* Q1; *The end of the Fourth
 Act.* Q2; *Exeunt severall wayes.
 The end of the Fourth Act.* Q3;
 Exeunt severall waies. Q4–6, F2;
 Exeunt. Q7–8

V.i

2 leave] power Q2+ (−A, −T)
4 hands] hand Q2+ (−A, −T)
8 seeme] serve Q1–8, F2, L, S, C,
 W, T
10 Offices] Officers Q1
25 he] a Q2–6
28 something] so much Q2+ (−A,
 −T)
33 By] By the T
40 the] an W
41 had] *om.* Q8
50 has] he haz Q5–6, F2, L, S;
 h'has C; h'as Q7–8, T
52 hee] a Q2–6
53 in his] in's Q2–5, 7–8, F2+
 (−A, −T)
55 a my] in my Q6; i'my Q7–8;
 o' F2+ (−A)
57 to] two Q3–6, F2, L, S, C, W,
 D, M
60–61 He | Is] Is Q1; He's Q7–8,
 S

61 low] bace Q2–8, F2, L, S, C, W,
 D, M
62 should] shall Q2–8, F2, L, S,
 C, W
63 Sure] surely S
64 strange] *om.* Q3–6, F2, L; base
 S, C, W
66 laming] lamming B, WW
68 broke] broken Q6, F2, L, S,
 W, D, M, B, WW; broken Q5
70 of] on Q2+ (−A, −T)
74.2 *and] and the* Q2–8, F2
83 kicke you, and thus] kick, and
 thus Q2, 7–8, M; kick, thus
 Q3–6, F2, L, S, C, W
83 tread you] tread upon you S, C,
 W
85 told you that first] told that first
 Q5–6, F2, L, S
87 a] he Q7–8, F2+ (−A, −T)
89 a] an Q4–6, F2, L, S, B
90 *Beates him.*] *om.* Q1

93 Sir] *om.* Q3–6, F2, L, S, C, W
94 *Bessus.*] *om.* Q1
95 My] *Bes.* My Q1
98 use] use not Q3
99 your] your your Q2
100 I] *om.* D, M, B, WW
106 she] I B
106 I am] I'm L, S, C
109 your] you Q2–8, F2, L
111 would] will Q3–6, F2, L, S
112 Now] Not Q4–5, F2, L
118 sencible] sensibly Q7–8
119 of] from Q3–6, F2, L, S, C, W

122 praia] pray Q2+ (–T); pray'ee T
122 Ligones.] *om.* Q1
125 has] H'as Q7–8, S, C, T
126 honor's] honour Q2, 7–8
127 a] have Q2+ (–A, –T)
129 *Bessus.*] *om.* Q1
131 *2. Sword-man.*] *om.* Q2–8, F2, L, S, C, W
131–132 he...he] a...a Q2–6
134.1 *Exeunt.*] *Exeunt cleere.* Q2–6, F2; *Exeunt omnes.* Q7–8

V.ii

12 businesse] businesses Q4–6, F2
14 please] pleases C, W
15 Armenian] Armenia Q 2
34 commendation] commendations Q2–6
36 would] that Q3–6, F2+ (–A, –T)
40 mine] my Q2–5, 7–8, F2+ (–T)
44 and like] and I like Q2+ (–T)
49 in the] i'the Q2–8, C, W, D, M, B, WW; i'th' F2, L
52 any] my Q2
54 enough] enow Q3–6, F2+ (–A, –T)
54 beside] besides Q2+ (–A, –T)

58 men] man Q2+ (–A, –T)
61 your] a Q2–8, F2, L, S, C, W, D, M
68 should] shall Q2–8, F2, L, S, D, M, B, WW
74 a] *om.* Q2–8, F2, L, S, C, W, A, WW
80 God] heaven Q3–6, F2+ (–A, –T)
82 in my] in all my Q3–6, F2, L, S
85 *Exit.*] *Exit Lygones.* Q2–8, F2
91 shall] should Q2–8, F2, L, S, C, W, D, M, A
93.1 *Exeunt.*] *Exeunt all.* Q2–8, F2

V.iii

0.1 a] *his* Q2–8, F2
2.1 *Enter...Swordmen*] *Enter Bessus with the two Sword-men.* Q2–8, F2
8 is mistaken] is much mistaken Q5–6, F2, L
11 can] *om.* Q2+ (–A, –T)
14 a] *om.* Q1
14 lamming] laming Q2–8, F2, L, S, C, A; launcing Q1, T

15 fall] full Q1
20 I confesse] I must confesse Q2+ (–A, –T)
23 God] heaven Q3–6, F2+ (–A, –T)
24 come] tome Q5; to me Q6
29 sirra] Sirs S, C, W
34 most] more Q8
36 *Bacurius.*] *om.* Q1
37 *1. Sword-man.*] *Swordman.* Q6

43 thinke] think on F2, L, S, D,
    M, B, WW
43 some] *om.* M
43 way to] way how to S, C, W
43 they] That Q6
46 ath'] of the WW
48 here] there Q2+ (−A, −T)
52 their] the Q2–8, F2, L, C, W
56 Ye...ye] You...You Q2+
    (−A, −T)
57–58 your windie] You windy T
61 many] beavie Q2–5, 7–8, F2,
    L, S, C, W, D, M, A; beauty
    Q6; meiny B, WW
63 doe] do do Q5
65 *1. Sword-man.*] *2. Swor.* Q8
65 A] O' Q7–8, F2+ (−A)
74 slave; my key] slave, my toe
    Q2, 7–8; hurts my toe Q3–6,
    F2+ (−T)
75 with't] with it Q2–8, F2, L, S,
    C
80 nothing] any thing F2, L, S
80.1 *Enter* Servant.] *Enter Servant,
    Will. Adkinson:* Q2; *om.* Q1
81 Heres] Here is Q5–6, F2, L, S,
    C, W
82 I am] I'me Q2–8, F2, L, S
82 prethee] pray thee Q2–8, F2,
    L, S

83 um] them Q2+ (−A, −T)
85 but men] but men, Sir Q2+
    (−T)
86–87 Captaine, rally up] Up with
    Q1, A, T
87 up] upon Q6
88 hold] ho Q2–8, F2, L, S, C, W,
    D, M
91 breath] health Q3–6, F2, L, S,
    C, W
91 *Exit* Bacurius.] *om.* Q1
92 Has] He has W, WW; H'as Q7–
    8, F2, L, S, C, D, M, B, T;
    'Has A
93 Ime] I am Q2–8, F2, L, S, C,
    W, WW
93 ha] have Q2–8, F2, L, S, C, W,
    WW
94 he...he] a...a Q2–6
95 besides] beside Q3–6
97 God] heaven Q3–6, F2+ (−A,
    −T)
98 he has] haz Q2–6; h'as Q7–8,
    F2, L, S, D, M, B; he's C, W,
    WW
101 is] and Q4–6, F2
102 hands] hand Q2+ (−T)
108 shooes] shows Q5–6
108.1 *Exeunt.*] *Exeunt cleere.* Q2–6,
    F2; *Exeunt omnes.* Q7–8

V.iv

1 bore] bare Q5–6, F2, L, S
2–7 Hell...mine] *om.* Q2–8, F2,
    L
8 With] Wi' th' S, C
8 friend] friends Q5–6, F2, L,
    S
9 an] that Q3–6, F2, L, S, C, W,
    D, M, WW
15 he] a Q2–6
16 does...hand] do...hands F2,
    L, S, C, W

20 I can] *Mar.* I can Q1
21 *Mardonius.*] *om.* Q1
24 humbler] humbler Q2+ (−A,
    −T)
36 thee: then] thee then: Q1–8, F2,
    L, S, C, W
42 doe; I] doe, and I Q3–6, F2, L,
    S, W; do, I Q8
42 at] *om.* S
49 not] now A
51 toyes] tales Q7–8

55 should] would Q5–6, F2+ (–A, –T)
58 Farre] For Q2–8, F2, L, W, D, M
60 God] Heaven Q3–6, F2+ (–A, –T)
69 temperate] temporall Q2, 7
61.1 *Exit* Mardonius.] *Exit.* Q1; *om.* Q3–6, F2
62 errors] error Q5–6, F2, L, S
66 That] Thou Q7–8
68 Curses incurable] Curses more incurable Q3–6, F2, L
76 for pay] for my pay Q5–6, F2, L
88 extolst] extol'dst S, C, W, D, M, B, WW
93 and] and I Q1
94–95 in | To] into Q1, 5–6, F2, L
98 meantst] mean'st Q2, 6
98 a] to Q4–6, F2, L, S
99 God] heaven Q3–6, F2+ (–A, –T)
103 *Arbaces.*] Q1(c); *om.* Q1(u)
103 wouldst] shouldst Q3–6, F2+ (–B, –A, –T)
106 hurlst] hurl'dst C
110 into] in to Q4
112 thee] me S, C, W, D, M, B, A, WW
115 to your selfe] thy selfe Q2, 7–8; to thy selfe Q3–6, F2, S+ (–T); to myself L
119 know it] know't Q2–6, F2, L
129 wrung] wrong Q5–6
140 thou] thy Q5–6, F2, L, S
141.1 S.D. *om.* Q1–7, F2
158 expects] expectst Q4–6, 7–8, F2+ (–A)
163 Then] Thou Q1, S, B, A, WW, T
175 a] *om.* Q4–6, F2, L
181 you] *om.* Q1

182 *Arbaces.*] *Arane.* Q2–4
183 heare] here Q2–3
188 as shee] thought she was F2, L; thought her S
191 *Arane.*] Q1(c); *Arb.* Q1(u)
194 were whore.] were a whore Q5–6, F2, L
207 opportunitie] oportunities Q2+ (–A, –T)
211 God was humbly thankt] humble thankes was given Q3–6, F2, L
212 That...Queen] *om.* Q3–6, F2, L
219 least] lest Q2
222 Quicke] quickly Q5–6, F2, L
223 abed] to bed Q2+ (–A, –T)
226 shewed me] shew'd to me S
226 knew would] knew well would S, C, W, WW
227 sware] swore Q2+ (–A, –T)
232 the] this Q2–8, F2, L, S, C, W
234 Which] whom M, B, WW
236 yeere] years F2+ (–A, –T)
244 talke] tale Q2+ (–A, –T)
249 sparke] sparkes Q2+ (–A, –T)
252 am] be Q3–6, F2+ (–A, –T)
253 are] be Q2+ (–A, –T)
254 too] *om.* Q1
255 God] heaven Q3–6, F2, L, S, C, W, D, M
257 *Gobrius.*] *om.* Q1
258 who] wo Q6
258 dare] dares Q2+ (–A, –T)
259 them] 'em Q2+ (–A, –T)
260 waites] wait F2+ (–A, –T); wait'st T
262 *Enter...others.*] *Enter Bessus, Gentlemen, Mardonius, and other Attendants.* Q2–8, F2
263 *Mardonius*] [*printed as speech prefix* Q2;] *Arb.* Q3–8, F2, L
265 happiest] happie Q5–6
268 One] On, Q1

313

271 house] home Q6
271 *Exit 1. Gentleman.*] *Exit a Gent.*
　Q2–8, F2; *om.* Q1
277–278 I...me,] *om.* Q1
280 bare] beare Q2–3
282 but] *om.* Q2–8, F2, L, C, W
284 here] her Q6
290 spoke] spoken Q6
294 I and] I say Q1; I said T
298 he's] he is Q2+ (−A, −T)
300 state] King Q1
301 *Ligones*] lignes Q6
309 *Exit 2. Gentleman.*] *Exit two*
　Gent. Q2–6, F2; *Exeunt two*
　Gent. Q7–8; *om.* Q1

316 He] A Q2; An Q3; One Q4–6,
　F2, L
317 shall] shalt Q8, F2, L, D, M, B
319 That] *om.* Q6
323 thinge] thinke Q1
326 *Enter...Gentleman.*] *Enter*
　Pan. Q1
334 *2. Gentleman.*] *Mar.* Q1; *Bacu-*
　rius. T
335 at first] *om.* Q1
344–345 state, know that; | I] state,
　know that | I Q2+ (−T)
347 um] them Q6
349 And you] and your Q1–8
354 FINIS.] *om.* F2+ (−B, −A,
　−T)

314

CUPID'S REVENGE

edited by

FREDSON BOWERS

TEXTUAL INTRODUCTION

Cupid's Revenge (Greg, *Bibliography*, no. 328), acted by the Children of Her Majesty's Revels, was first published in 1615, printed by Thomas Creede for Josias Harrison. Entry had been made in the Stationers' Register to Harrison on 24 April, with the notation that the play was licensed by Bucke. On 15 April 1619 Harrison transferred his right to Thomas Jones, who in 1630 published the second edition, printed by Augustine Mathews on the evidence of the ornaments. On 24 October 1633 Jones transferred the play to Mathews, who published the third edition in 1635. On 28 July 1641 Mathews transferred the copy to J. Raworth, whose widow Ruth finally assigned it to Humphrey Moseley on 4 March 1647. Moseley's advertisements list the play (presumably in its third edition) between 1653 and 1660. In 1679 the text was given its fourth edition in the Second Folio, occupying sigs. ²3 E 2ᵛ–3 G 4ᵛ, pp. 404–24. A droll called 'The Loyal Citizens' from material in IV.iii was included in *The Wits*, 1662 and 1672, identified erroneously as from *Philaster*, whereas the droll 'The Club-Men' from *Philaster* is stated to be from *Cupid's Revenge*. Q3 was used as the copy.

The first quarto of 1615 listed Fletcher alone as the author, but the correct attribution to Beaumont and Fletcher was made in Q2 and repeated thereafter. The second quarto also provided a made-up list of characters, wanting in the first, but is otherwise a paginal reprint of the first, often slavish in its adherence to error and with relatively few corrections. The third quarto of 1635 was printed from 1630 and was slightly bolder in venturing a few more alterations of words as well as of faulty punctuation. The 1679 Folio was set up very closely from Q2. The variants of the second, third, and fourth editions show no signs of authority.

The first quarto collates A^2 B–L^4 (L4 blank). Two compositors set the text alternating with each other in irregular stints, but usually of about half a gathering, and so arranged that (exclusive of the preliminaries) Compositor X set 47 pages and Compositor Y

set 29 pages: two pages (sigs. H2ᵛ and I2ᵛ) appear to have been divided between them. The assignment of the pages on spelling and typographical evidence is rarely in doubt.

Compositor *X* never uses a tailed italic *m* to conclude a speech-prefix, but on various occasions in the text he runs short of roman capital I's and P's and substitutes italic *I* and small-capital or italic *P*. He invariably sets 'Sir' and 'sir'; he may use the spelling 'Tellamon' (possibly from copy); in his early pages he always introduces the contraction 'em' for 'them' by an apostrophe though (under influence of copy?) omitting the apostrophe in his later pages; he prefers not to capitalize 'father' and 'heaven', and he italicizes few special words. He never uses the spelling 'bene' and ordinarily he puts an apostrophe in the contractions 'shee's' and 'hee's'. Compositor *X* prefers to set titles like '*Duke*', '*Prince*', '*Duchess*' in italic and he generally capitalizes 'Prince' whether in roman or italic. He prefers to set '*gods*' with a lower-case 'g' although occasionally capitalizing; however, he invariably italicizes the word. He shows a very distinct preference for 'be' as a spelling, and a generally marked preference for 'he', 'she', 'me', and 'we'. Finally, he shows something of a preference for a preterite in -'*d* although he will often set simple -*d*; however, very rarely indeed does he set a preterite in -*de*.

On the other hand, Compositor *Y* often uses the tailed italic *m*, and on occasion he will substitute colons after speech-prefixes when short of full stops. He always spells 'Telamon' and almost invariably 'Syr'. He seems never to prefix an apostrophe to 'em' and he generally prefers to capitalize 'Father' and 'Heaven'. Although he spells 'bene' usually, a few 'beene' spellings creep in, and he will sometimes omit the apostrophe in 'hees' or 'shees'. He has an odd trick of italicizing special words like *Zany*, *Musitions*, *Fortune*, *Eunuch*, *Januarie*, *May*, *Ambition*, *Architect*, *Page*, *Image*, and *Canted*. Compositor *Y* prefers not to capitalize 'prince', which he sets in roman. He usually sets titles like 'Duke' and so on in roman although a few cases of italic appear; he always sets 'gods' or 'Gods' (which he prefers) in roman. He shows a distinct liking for the long forms 'bee', 'hee', 'shee', 'mee', and 'wee'. The preterite in -*de* is something of a favourite although he may set the other forms.

318

Largely on the basis of these distinctions, the following pages of Q1 may be assigned to Compositor X: B1–B4ᵛ, C1–C2ᵛ, D3–D4ᵛ, E1–E2ᵛ, F1–F2ᵛ, G1ᵛ–G2, H1–H2ᵛ(upper half), H4, I2ᵛ(lower half)–I4ᵛ, K1–K4, L1–L3ᵛ.

To Compositor Y may be assigned: C3–C4ᵛ, D1–D2ᵛ, E3–E4ᵛ, F3–F4ᵛ, G1, G2ᵛ–G4ᵛ, H2ᵛ(lower half)–H3ᵛ, H4ᵛ, I1–I2ᵛ(upper half), K4ᵛ.

In terms of the line-numbering of the present edition, Compositor X set: I.i.1–I.iv.96 (to doe.|); II.ii.93–II.iv.71; II.vi.83 (|Beside)–III.ii.82; III.iii.2 (|suffers)–III.iv.34; IV.i.6–115; IV.i.203 (|have your)–IV.ii.8 (actions,|); IV.iii.48–V.iv.14 (goe|); V.iv.46–233.

Compositor Y set: I.iv.96 (|Away)–II.ii.92; II.iv.72–II.vi.83 (rising.|); III.ii.83–III.iii.2 (age|); III.iv.35–IV.i.5; IV.i.116–203 (You|); IV.ii.8 (|and dwell)–IV.iii.47; V.iv.14 (|save)–45.

Sig. H2ᵛ (IV.i.102 [|that all]–134) seems to reflect a page in which Compositor Y relieved X between the fourteenth and fifteenth lines. The upper half of the page has two 'sir' and four 'me' spellings, both characteristic of X. On the other hand, the lower half has two examples of the distinctive tailed m associated with Y, two 'Syr' and one 'Prince' forms, and four 'mee' spellings as against two 'me'. The division seems to have taken place, then, after the exit of Urania, with Y starting at line 116.

Sig. I2ᵛ (IV.iii.31–63 (counsell:|)) may also be a divided page. In favour of the hypothesis that Y set the first nineteen lines is the continuation of heavy capitalization from sig. I2 for the upper half but its abrupt dropping-off in the lower half, especially in the shift from 'Neighbour' to 'neighbour'. Line 20 with its short form 'she' and its italicized *Duke* could define the first line of the setting by X. Above this point appear four 'shee' and one 'mee' as against a single 'she', and there are two 'shees' without the apostrophe. Below, are two 'be', two 'she', one 'he', one 'we', and one 'me' with no long forms at all. Also in the lower part is the spelling 'beleeve', found in X sometimes as against Y's characteristic 'believe'. But a change in the setting of prose (see below) at line 15 or 16 is perhaps the real point of division. Thus IV.iii.44 or 45 seems to mark the beginning of X's relief of Y. On the other hand, I2ᵛ ends with a short line in prose, 'Pray forward with your counsell:', and I3 begins with the new prose line 'I am what I am...'. It is true that between sigs. I2 and I2ᵛ prose is similarly divided, but here the start of a new line on I2ᵛ, 'And lay my Cut-fingred Gantlet ready for mee...', marks a shift from an address to the other citizens to a command to his off-stage servant. Such changes of address are often marked by the start of new lines of prose in the Elizabethan printed drama. It might be possible to speculate that sig. I3 was indeed begun by X, using cast-off copy, simultaneous with some part of Y's stint, and that X then returned to complete Y's page I2ᵛ after finishing the inner forme. But such a mechanical reason, not wholly to be worked out in terms of the respective stints, may not be necessary after all. It is possible, perhaps, to interpret the Second Citizen's 'Pray forward with your counsell' as addressed to the First, and the lines beginning 'I am what I am' as a real change of address directed to the Second Citizen, with whom he has been quarrelling.

It is odd that sig. K4ᵛ, assigned to Y, interrupts a run of X pages, although it is possible to speculate that Y could have taken over while X was busy with imposition or with distribution of type. The page (V.iv.14[|save]–45) does show possible mixed characteristics. Strongly in favour of Y is the spelling 'Syr' and the fact that 'boy' in X's preceding and succeeding pages here becomes 'Boy' four times. Two 'be' and two 'me' forms as against an equal number of 'bee' and 'mee' spellings is no better than neutral. On the whole, there seems to be every reason to assign the page to Y, and the attribution may be confirmed by the peculiarity of the catchword in which, in a manner unique with Compositor Y, the first word of the speech is given as the catchword instead of the speech-prefix (see below).

Sig L2ᵛ (V.iv.141–75) is partly anomalous. In favour of Y is the 'Syr' at line 147, and perhaps the form 'shees'; but otherwise the evidence points exclusively to X. For example, the page has short pronominal spellings—two 'me', three 'she', and one 'we'—against no long forms; even more important, perhaps, are seven 'be' spellings as against only two 'bee'. In addition, 'heaven' is uncapitalized in X's manner three times. The evidence of 'em' without an apostrophe is neutral at this point, for X in the later pages seems to have dropped the initial apostrophe he originally favoured. The clinching evidence for X, however, rests in the form of the catchword, which sets the speech-prefix and also the first word of the speech in a manner almost exclusively favoured by X but never employed by Y (for the details see the Textual Note to V.iv.46). How the 'Syr' wandered into an X page must be left to speculation. Mechanical reasons could be suggested, but they would be sheer guesswork and therefore not worth discussing.

The quarto was printed with two skeleton-formes for each sheet but with the running-titles (the evidence for the quarters) occasionally shifting vis-a-vis each other within the forme as they are transferred and with a rather extraordinary amount of resetting or partial repair. Whether one or two presses were employed is not to be determined from the evidence. The only suggestion that possibly there might have been two is the construction of a third skeleton-forme (involving the once repeated spelling *Kupids* changed back to *Cupids* by press-correction) for the outer forme of C, a sheet in which Compositor Y made his first appearance. But since the former skeleton-forme in B does not reappear as an entity and thereafter the book continues at press with only two, the evidence is susceptible of another explanation if Y (as seems likely) was responsible for the construction of the C outer skeleton. Thus the case is a stand-off, and one press the better probability.

What can be asserted, however, from the pattern of pages as determined by the spelling evidence is that the copy was not cast off and set by formes, but instead that setting was, in general, *seriatim* with one compositor relieving the other at the end, often, of a normal stint but occasionally it would seem to enable his fellow to impose a forme, distribute type, and so on. On the other hand, between sigs. E4^v and F1 when X relieved Y, a break in the type-setting of prose indicates clearly that some copy had been cast off to enable the relieving workman to begin his stint before the completion of setting by his fellow. Nevertheless, the irregularity of some of the stints may appear to preclude copy cast off very far ahead of typesetting, or, indeed, on all occasions; hence the kinds of textual disruption, including difficulty with verse-lining, which may accompany copy cast off by formes cannot be strongly

321

operative in this text and some other explanation for the erratic verse-lining must be sought.

The unusual form of notation for properties in several stage-directions suggests that the copy for this play had had some connexion with the theatre. This notation specifies a property on the entrance of the characters even though it is not to be used until later in the scene. An illustration is at II.vi.7.1, *'Enter Leontius & Timantus, a Jewell and a Ring'*, when, in fact, the jewell and ring are not presented to Bacha by Leontius until line 90. Similar is V.ii.0, *'Enter Bacha and Timantus: Bacha reading a letter'*. In fact, Bacha is not reading on her entrance since the letter is handed to her by Timantus in the second line and she does not read it until the fifth. The clearest example occurs at V.iv.0, which reads, *'Enter Leucippus, Urania,: Leuc. with a bloudy handkercher'*. This is a property that the actor must keep concealed until he uses it to staunch Urania's wound and then exhibit it in line 73 of the scene.[1]

Stage-directions of this nature are evidently the result of a book-keeper's markings. Probably also from the book-keeper are directions such as those about the Guard at IV.ii.83,89, or the misplaced direction given in this text at V.iv.96.1 specifying *'Fight here'* before the properly placed direction for Leucippus to give Timantus a sword. The technical specification for *Cornets* at I.i.24.1, I.iii.0, and V.iii.0 may perhaps reflect a theatrical notation although it could be authorial.

Nevertheless, some reason exists to query whether the manuscript was itself a promptbook or derived from one. A number of errors exist in the directions, including the omission of Ismenus from the entrance at I.i.24.1, of the Priest's singing boy at I.ii.0, of Zoylus at I.v.40.1, of Timantus at III.iv.64.1 and IV.i.13.1, and

---

[1] Other stage-directions specifying properties clearly reflect the copy, not a helpful compositor, because the context would not lead a compositor to add them. For example, at II.ii.0 the stage-direction reads, *'Enter Bacha, & Leucippus, Bacha, A handkercheffe'*. The specification of this property is almost certainly by the same hand that added those above, even though she could enter weeping, as illustrated in lines 11 and 53, in the first of which Leucippus tells her to dry her eyes. Less certain as a special notation is II.iv.26.1, *'Enter Leontine with a staffe and a looking-glasse'*. This may have been a normal authorial direction, for the looking glass is required by Leontius' first words, 'This Feather is not large enough', although the glass itself is not mentioned until line 43, *'Timantus, let me see the glasse againe'*.

of Bacha at V.iii.142.1. Less important are the omission of exits for Leucippus at III.ii.224 and Timantus at III.iii.23. Some signs of literary directions, as against theatrical, are preserved. For instance, in the royal entrance at I.i.24.1 Leontius does not precede the others, as he should do according to protocol. Some directions are permissive, such as I.ii.34.2, '*After the Measure Enter Nilo and others*', although it is true that such a direction is not unknown in promptbooks. Dorialus, Agenor, and Nisus are referred to at I.i.103.1 as '*Exeunt all but these three Lords*', a clearcut authorial direction; at V.ii.40.1 as '*Enter Ismenus and 3. Lords*'; and at V.iv.142.1, '*Enter Ismenus with the Lords*'. Despite the care with properties and with specifying at V.iv.47.1 that Timantus is disguised, Urania at V.i.0 is not noted as dressed in boy's clothes. Finally, the considerable corruption of the text that seems to have its origin in compositorial difficulty with handwriting does not argue for the fair copy that would have formed the promptbook.

The hypothesis that best fits the evidence here, as in other plays, is that the manuscript was authorial papers that had been looked over by the book-keeper, who made various notes in them to be followed when the papers were copied out to make up the promptbook. If this is so, the manuscript provided the company and then used by the printer since it had been superseded by the promptbook may well have been authorial papers. The question then must be asked whether these were holographs by each author or some form of a copy. That the printer manifestly had difficulty with the verse lining and the handwriting does not argue for a scribal fair copy of authorial foul papers. On the other hand, after due allowance is made for the characteristics imposed on the text by each compositor, no distinctive spelling or other variants stand out as demonstrably variant authorial accidentals in the scenes by different hands. Professor Cyrus Hoy, whose linguistic assignment of authorship has guided the editors of this edition, gave to Beaumont I.i, iii; II.i–ii, iv–v; III.i–ii; IV.i, v; V.i; and to Fletcher I.ii, v; II.iii.vi; III.iii–iv; IV.ii, iv; V.ii, iv.[1] However, he remarks, 'The linguistic

---

[1] 'The Shares of Fletcher and his Collaborators in the Beaumont and Fletcher Canon (III)', *Studies in Bibliography*, XI (1958), 90–1. Dr Hoy's study did not treat the present edition's I.iii and V.iii as separate scenes. The authorship of these two speeches of Cupid may perhaps be in doubt, and indeed that at V.iii may be spurious.

evidence that emerges from the play gives no very clear indication of the respective shares of the two dramatists', and he draws the inference that the play had been given its final form by Beaumont. That Beaumont may have copied out the play, revising it in the process from the combined foul papers in order to produce a copy suitable for submission to the theatre company, is a hypothesis that the general uniformity of the accidentals save for the noted compositorial characteristics appears to support, especially since Fletcher's individual linguistic preferences are obscured. If it is true that at III.iv.122 we do not have a missing line but instead an example of revision and of the undeleted original (see the Textual Note), the hypothesis might be supported since this is a Fletcher scene.

The rate of error of the two compositors and the kind of error each perpetrated are not markedly different and, unfortunately, thus fail to support emendation on an analytical basis. Each compositor seems to have had difficulty in lining the manuscript, and if is only by a slight margin that Compositor Y may be thought ot as more adept at following correct lining than Compositor X. How the manuscript was written out is difficult to reconstruct. Only in two Fletcher scenes, III.iv and V.iv, are there large blocks of verse set as prose, but that in III.iv may be instructive. This scene begins almost at the head of sig. G2, set by Compositor X, and its first thirty-four verse lines, as numbered in the present edition, are set as prose. When Compositor Y starts his stint with sig. G2^v and line 35, the dialogue immediately changes to mislined verse until, shortly, correct lineation is restored at line 42. This evidence would suggest that part of the difficulty experienced by the compositors may have come from the inscription of at least some of the verse in a form that could not readily be distinguished from prose. Certainly, the compositors sometimes lined mechanically, starting an ostensible verse line with a capital merely because a sufficient number of words had been set in the preceding line to give the appearance of verse. They were inclined to treat prose and verse in the same manner. For example, although Ismenus speaks prose exclusively until near the end of V.iv when he is about to be made king, his lines are ordinarily chopped into crude verse (and have so been printed by previous editors). The three lords Nisus, Agenor, and Dorialus create similar difficulties since on the whole they are prose-speaking characters. The treatment may vary wildly, moreover, within the work of the same compositor. For example, Compositor *X* begins I.i.1–15 with the lords speaking correctly in prose on sig. B 1. On sig. B 1ᵛ after a few short lines that offer no evidence the same lords become verse speakers in such crude form as

Nis. Shee's twenty yeere old, I wonder
  She aske not a Husband.
Dor. That were a folly in her, having refus'd all the
  Great Princes in one part of the world:
  Sheele dye a Maide. (ll. 18–20)

Then following the royal entrance Leontius, who speaks verse almost exclusively, is given lines printed in such form as

Leon. Come fayre *Hidaspes*, thou art
  Dutchesse to day,
  Art thou prepard to aske, thou knowest
  My oath will force performance.
  And *Leucippus*, if she now aske ought that shall,
  Or would have performance
  After my death, when by the helpe of heaven,
  This Land is thine, accursed be thy race,
  May every one forget thou art my sonne,
  And so their owne obedience. (ll. 25–32)

Here lines 25–8 ending with 'performance' are manifestly lined with no regard for metrics, but starting with 'After my death' and line 29 the correct lineation is inexplicably restored after an incorrect short line. These curious anomalies persist. Still in the work of Compositor *X*, later in the scene, the comments of the lords are chopped into verse that sometimes, as with the speech of Nisus (ll. 156–9), is no more than letterpress filling the prose measure but capitalized at the start of each line. Moreover, in IV.iii, which Compositor *Y* begins on sig. I 2, and continues on I 2ᵛ, various of the early speeches such as lines 1–40 are often little more than prose to the full measure with line capitalization. Interestingly, when X takes over on sig. I2ᵛ (line 44 or 45) he sets the prose correctly.

This general inclination to set prose as verse suggests that one cause of the mislining of verse itself by both compositors may have been inscription in the printer's copy that was confusing in its differentiation. The evidence is sometimes subject to other interpretation but on the whole leans in this direction. For example, the Fletcher scene III.iii starts at the foot of sig. G1 set by Y, and with a line of prose as verse.[1] This verse is continued by Compositor X on sig. G1ᵛ for about half a page, but with the entrance of Timantus at line 16.1 the setting correctly turns to prose, and as prose concludes the scene as the first line on sig. G2. However, when X continues on sig. G2 with III.iv—another Fletcher scene—he sets all of this page in prose (ll. 1–34) although it is unquestionably verse. When at line 35 Compositor Y takes over with sig. G2ᵛ he sets mislined verse in lines 35–41 until at line 42 he starts correct verse-lining which, with a few lapses, is maintained to the end of the scene in his stint. The question arises, then, whether III.iv.1–34 set by X reflects his interpretation of the manuscript whereas Y, taking over, recognized the inscription as verse, or whether X deliberately set verse in the copy as prose but Y chose to follow the verse of the manuscript.

To this question no answer can be given that is satisfactory in all respects. At first sight, Y's faltering mislineation at the head of

---

[1] Although the line nearly fills the measure, the catchword 'Suffers' with a cap indicates that the line was set as verse.

In fact, although the three lords are normally prose-speaking characters, one or more of them may speak verse in a scene. The present speech of Nisus could indeed be regarded as verse in its setting as:

> And a fine Duke, that through his doting age
> Suffers him [selfe] to be a childe againe
> Under his Wives tuition.

But though Agenor's following speech is correctly in prose, the Dorialus response (ll. 6–9) is set in verse although manifestly prose, and Nisus' next speech (ll. 10–13) though set mechanically as verse (the first two lines are no more than capitalized prose) is demonstrably prose as well. Thus Nisus does not seem to be a verse-speaker in this scene, and it follows that his first speech was almost certainly in prose also. Interestingly, however, Y started it as verse in its initial line and then X continued it as verse overpage. Agenor's speech set as prose (ll. 4–5) ought to show how the manuscript was inscribed.

sig. G2ᵛ would seem to favour the hypothesis that the copy was in prose. However, another explanation can be advanced to account, at least in some part, for the mislineation. On occasion part lines beginning speeches are set without error, thus demonstrating by their consistent correctness in a speech, or series of speeches, that the copy was so lined. An interesting example occurs at the start of Beaumont's scene II.ii set by Compositor *Y*, where Bacha's part lines 1, 3, 13, 23, and 35 are properly set, as are those of Leucippus at lines 53 and 58. On the other hand, Leucippus' part lines at 12, 20, 32, 35, and 44 are incorrectly set and cause the mislineation of the speeches. Typical is the mislining at lines 44–6:

Leuc. Why doest thou thinke mee so base to tell?
These limmes of mine shall part
From one another on a wracke,

before resuming correct lining with line 47. That the mislineation would be corrected here—and frequently elsewhere in these same circumstances—suggests that the copy was verse-lined but that the compositor could be confused by initial part lines and for a time adopt his own system of lineation before returning to the manu-script verse. On the other hand, Bacha's lines 33–5, beginning with a part line, are set as prose, and Leucippus' lines 20–3 start with an incorrect line of verse extending the part line but then conclude with two lines set as prose, the first capitalized. Either Compositor *Y* in these cases was uncertain whether the manuscript was written in verse or in prose, or else he was following prose copy here and lining his verse for himself elsewhere. The latter seems less probable in that the frequent lining by both compositors without respect for metrical considerations does not suggest ears so finely tuned as to recover from prose such correct part lines as are set in Bacha's speeches in this scene, despite a lapse in her part, and more lapses in the speeches of Leucippus.

Given such contradictory evidence, the most comprehensive hypothesis would suggest that in the main the manuscript's verse speeches were written out in verse but in such a manner that on various occasions the compositors were uncertain whether it was prose or verse and felt impelled to interpret the evidence in their own manner. That interpretation was felt to be necessary on various occasions is demonstrated by the numerous examples of prose speeches set as crude unmetrical verse, sometimes indeed even as mere capitalized prose. The reverse, of course, ought also to have been true: a compositor could set verse as prose as X did in IV.iii although his fellow, after some preliminary miscalculation, proceeded to continue the scene correctly as verse. This hypothesis is of some small help in the editorial relining of the text that is required from time to time, since it follows that the special areas of misinterpretation are likely to be speeches containing part lines either in initial or medial positions, with the odds favouring the eventual return to correct lineation before the conclusion of the speech. That on occasion copy might be cast off and the relieving compositor start his stint before his fellow had finished is indicated by the break between sigs. E4^v and F1. On this clearcut occasion the setting is not affected in matters of lineation.

On the other hand, such other points where a change of compositors was made as between sigs. G2 and G2^v do appear to result in different interpretations of the copy. That a mechanical reason for setting verse as prose, as on sig. G2, might be present, then, if the cast-off copy proved to be seriously miscalculated and needed compression is always a possibility. But, at least as between sigs. G2 and G2^v, this explanation does not appear to hold, for the characteristics of III.iv.1–34 on G2 do not differ from the latter half of III.iii on G1^v, and this fact is significant since in this case X's stint was confined only to sigs. G1^v–G2. Hence the change on G1^v at line III.iii.17 from prose set as verse to prose set as prose would suggest more a recognition of the true nature of the copy (oddly, following the entrance of Timantus) instead of the beginning of a desperate effort to save space continued on G2 by the setting of all verse as prose. That Compositor X in two adjoining Fletcher scenes was unable to distinguish the verse of III.iv from the prose of III.iii certainly has some bearing on the appearance of the copy at this juncture. But because on G2^v Compositor Y was able to interpret the continued scene III.iv correctly as verse does not encourage any hypothesis that X's portion of III.iv had actually been inscribed as prose in the copy. It would appear, instead, that the manuscript was sometimes so ambiguous as to lead both compositors to feel required to intervene with their own attempts at lineation or else of interpretation of copy as prose or verse. Yet, as remarked above, in some places a sophisticated lineation of the text including part lines could have resulted only from following verse-lined copy.

On the whole a number of cases of verse that has been mislined result, seemingly, from the intervention of the compositors, who misinterpreted initial or medial part lines. That the strong contrasts between misinterpreted passages, or even scenes, and correctly lined verse, or of prose set as prose, may have a physical origin in the varying nature of the manuscript is an attractive hypothesis. However, that it followed on the collection of foul papers as copy seems to be a theory that will not stand up to scrutiny, for the difficulties represented in III.iv do not seem to be circumscribed by individual scenes and certainly not by the work of either author, although in the case of III.iv and of V.iv, with their large blocks of verse set as prose, the temptation exists to relate these unusual blocks to the fact that both scenes are Fletcher's. Dr Hoy's linguistic evidence, and the general evidence against any strong noticeable differences in the accidentals between scenes of different authorship (without regard for compositor), suggest that Beaumont may, indeed, have made a copy of the original foul papers, possibly revising Fletcher's scenes in the process. Whether he copied out again all of his own papers or intercalated some of the original sheets and transcribed others is not to be determined. Yet one way or another, it may be that it was the nature of Beaumont's inscription that caused the compositors the unusual difficulty in recognizing verse or prose and thus in establishing the correct lineation.

One other feature of Q1 suggests that the copy was not in final theatrical form. The use of titles is chaotic in the work of both authors: Leontius is sometimes a duke and sometimes a king; Leucippus may be a marquis or a prince; Hidaspes a duchess or a princess; and Bacha a duchess or a queen. Dr James Savage, in his 1942 unpublished University of Chicago dissertation-edition of the play, after surveying the opinions of older critics for and against the presence of a revising third hand (whether Massinger or Field), suggested that the confusion grew out of the combined use of the New Arcadia and the Old Arcadia as sources for the play (pp. xcviii–cii). That is, in the Old Arcadia Basilius is consistently called 'Duke' and his wife Gynecia is called 'Duchess'. The New Arcadia never uses these titles and on the few occasions when the names are not employed calls them 'King' and 'Queen'. This explanation is much to be preferred to the theory of revision by a third hand, but it does not solve all difficulties, especially since it does not account for the extremely haphazard use of the variant titles in the work of both dramatists. For example, in Beaumont's III.ii.31–2 Timantus addresses Leucippus with, 'Sir, your Highnes is welcome home, the Duke and Queene will presently come foorth to you.' In III.iii, a Fletcher scene, 'Duke' and 'Duchess' are the only titles; but in Fletcher's following scene III.iv although Leontius in line 21 addresses Bacha as 'Queen', in line 30 she is 'Duchess'. In line 65 and thereafter Leucippus is a prince, in line 165 Bacha calls Leontius a duke and again in line 177, although in line 174 Leucippus is prince. In reply to this speech Nisus refers to the king. In V.i.23 (a Beaumont scene) Urania calls Leucippus a prince, which Ismenus repeats in line 42 and Urania again in line 44, but in line 46 he is Urania's brother, 'the good Marquesse'.

Examples as close to each other as these do not encourage a hypothesis that the particular source for a scene dictated the form of the titles. On the other hand, since the confusion exists in the work of both dramatists, a careless partial revision of Fletcher's variant system of titles by Beaumont in making the final copy cannot be blamed. If we may believe the metrics of Fletcher's III.iv.21 and of Beaumont's V.i.44, 'Queen' and 'Prince' respectively were the original forms. It may have been that both dramatists were bemused by their double source, but the evidence of III.ii.31–2 with 'Duke' and 'Queen' in the same phrase does not encourage such a belief. If the confusion is indeed to be rationalized (and presumably it had some basis), one is forced into the perhaps desperate hypothesis that in the original foul papers the characters were royal, as in the New Arcadia; but as a consequence of rereading the Old Arcadia before he wrote out the copy for the theatre Beaumont made a casual and certainly a careless attempt to alter the titles to duke, duchess, marquis, counting on the scribe to straighten all out on this basis (which starts the play) when the promptbook was made up from his manuscript.

The play may have been written about 1607–8, no doubt for the Children of Her Majesty's Revels who are listed on the title-page. The Children, reorganized in 1610, had amalgamated in March, 1613, with the Lady Elizabeth's men under Henslowe. In February of 1615 the company brought articles of grievance against Henslowe, alleging that he had 'broken' the company. A reorganization then seems to have taken place that included Prince Charles's men. Although the Children had joined the Henslowe company in 1613, some form of separate identity seems to have been retained in respect to their wardrobe and play stock. Thus it is a reasonable assumption to relate the difficulties in February 1615 to the sale of the play marked by its registration for printing in April, especially since it was one of the very last of the unpublished plays in the Revels repertory. If so, the publisher secured his copy from the theatre legitimately. ('The Printer to the Reader' remarks that he had no personal acquaintance with the author.) Yet this provenience is very far from establishing the nature of the copy as the promptbook, especially since the play is found in the Cockpit list of 1639 as part of the repertory of the King and Queen's young company.[1] It would seem most probable that the Children had retained the copy presented by the authors as insurance against loss or damage to the promptbook, and it was this authorial manuscript—not the promptbook or a copy of it—that was sold in 1615 to Harrison. As remarked above, the most plausible hypothesis seems to be that this manuscript was a Beaumont copying-out and revision of the original mixed foul papers, marked in a preliminary manner for transcription into the official promptbook.

Given the unauthoritative nature of the succeeding editions, the copy-text for the present critically edited text is the first quarto of 1615 in respect both to the substantives and the accidentals. The following copies (all that are recorded) have been collated in order to establish the form of this Q1 text: British Museum copy 1 (C.71.d.27), copy 2 (Ashley 76), copy 3 (644.d.2; imperfect,

---

[1] G. E. Bentley, *The Jacobean and Caroline Stage*, I (1941), 330–1.

wanting A 1–2); Dyce Collection in the Victoria and Albert Museum; Henry E. Huntington Library, copy 1 (Devonshire), copy 2 (Chew; imperfect, B 4 substituted from Q 3); Harvard University; and the Carl Pforzheimer Library. Press-variants exist in C(o), C(i), D(o), E(o), and K(o). Although a few of these represent necessary corrections, others corrupt the text or substitute conventional for unconventional spellings. None gives clear evidence of reference to copy.

To construct the Historical Collation the Q 1 copy-text has been collated against Q 2 of 1630 in the Trinity College, Cambridge, copy; Q 3 of 1635 in the Folger Shakespeare Library copy; and F 2 of 1679 in the copy at the University of Virginia. Later editions collated are the *Works*, 1711, edited by Langbaine; 1750, edited by Theobald, Seward, and Sympson; 1778, edited by George Colman the Younger; 1812, edited by Henry Weber; and 1843–6, edited by Alexander Dyce. Monck Mason's *Comments on the Plays of Beaumont and Fletcher*, 1797, has also been consulted.

The italic titles, chiefly in the work of Compositor X, have been silently placed in roman, and so has italic *qod*. The other italic words are noted when altered.

NOTE: In *Studies in Bibliography*, XXV (1971), Dr Hans Walter Gabler will publish an article on the printing of Q 1, and another on the work of Compositors X and Y in other plays, which offers more detail and carries on the editor's investigation in the present introduction.

[PERSONS

Cupid.
Leontius, Duke of Licia.
Leucippus, son to Leontius.
Ismenus, nephew to Leontius.
Agenor, }
Dorialus, } Lords.
Nisus, }
Timantus, a venal courtier.
Zoylus, a Dwarf.
Telamon, servant to Leontius.   10
Nilo, an officer.
Four Citizens.
Boy to the First Citizen.
Priest of Cupid.

Bacha, a young widow, later wife to Leontius.
Hidaspes, daughter to Leontius.
Urania, daughter to Bacha by her first marriage.
Cleophila, } attendants on Hidaspes.
Hero, }
Maid, to Bacha.   20
Woman, to Urania.

Gentlemen, Young Men, Maidens, Guards.

Scene: Licia.]

The Printer to the Reader

It is a custome used by some Writers in this Age to Dedicate their Playes to worthy persons, as well as their other works; and there is reason for it, because they are the best Minervaes of their braine, and expresse more puritie of conceit in the ingenious circle of an Act or Scœne, then is to be found in the vast circumference of larger Volumnes; and therefore worthy an answerable Mecœnas, to honour and bee honoured by them. But not having any such Epistle from the Authour (in regard I am not acquainted with him) I have made bolde my selfe, without his consent to dedicate this Play to the Juditious in generall, of what degree soever; not insinuating herein with any, be they never 10 *so great, that want judgement, for to them it belongs not, though they pay for it, more then in this respect, that like Æsops Cocke, having met with a precious Stone by accident, they knew not the true use thereof, but had rather have a Barlie-corne to their humour, then a perfect Diamond. But leaving them to their ignorance, I once againe dedicate this Booke to the Juditious, some whereof I have heard commend it to be excellent, who, because they saw it Acted, and knew what they spake, are the better to be beleeved: and for my part I censure it thus, That I never red a better.*

CUPIDS REVENGE

Enter Dorialus, Agenor, Nisus.

Agenor.   Trust me my Lord *Dorialus*, I had mist of this if you had
not call'd me, I thought the Princesses birth day had beene to
morrow.

Nisus.   Why, did your Lordship sleepe out the day?

Dorialus.   I marvell what the Duke meant to make such an idle
vow.

Nisus.   Idle, why?

Dorialus.   Is't not idle, to sweare to graunt his Daughter any thing
she shall aske on her byrth day? she may aske an impossible thing:
and I pray heaven she doe not aske an unfit thing at one time or   10
other; tis dangerous trusting a mans vow upon the discretion on's
daughter.

Agenor.   I wonder most at the Marquesse her brother, who is
alwaies vehemently forward to have her desires graunted.

Dorialus.   Hee's acquainted with 'em before.

Agenor.   Shee's doubtlesse very chaste and vertuous.

Dorialus.   So is *Leucippus* her Brother.

Nisus.   Shee's twenty yeere old, I wonder she aske not a Husband.

Dorialus.   That were a folly in her, having refus'd all the great
Princes in one part of the world: sheele dye a Maide.   20

Agenor.   Shee may aske but one, may she?

Nisus.   A hundred times this day if shee will; and indeed, every
day is such a day, for though the Duke has vow'd it onely on this
day, he keepes it every day: he can deny her nothing.

Cornets. Enter Hidaspes, Leucippus, Leontius,
[Ismenus,] Timantus, Tellamon.

Leontius.   Come fayre *Hidaspes*, thou art Dutchesse to day,
Art thou prepard to aske? thou knowest my oath
Will force performance. And *Leucippus*, if she

1.i] ¶ *Act. pri. Sceana. pri.* Q1   *21 one] *stet* Q1–F2

Now aske ought that shall, or would have performance
After my death, when by the helpe of heaven,
This Land is thine, accursed be thy race,   30
May every one forget thou art my sonne,
And so their owne obedience——
Leucippus.   Mightie Sir,
I doe not wish to know that fatall houre,
That is to make me King, but if I doe,
I shall most hastily (and like a sonne)
Performe your graunts to all, chiefely to her:——
Remember that you aske what wee agreed upon.   [*Aside to* Hidaspes.]
Leontius.   Are you prepard? then speake.
Hidaspes.   Most Royall Sir,
I am prepard, nor shall my will exceede
A Virgins bounds, what I request shall both   40
At once bring you and me a full content.
Leontius.   So it ever does: thou onely comfort
Of my feeble age, make knowne thy good desire,
For I dare sweare thou lov'st me.
Hidaspes.   This is it I begge,
And on my knees. The people of your Land,
The *Lycians*, are through all the Nations
That know their name, noted to have in use
A vaine and fruitlesse Superstition;
So much more hatefull, that it beares the shew
Of true Religion, and is nothing else   50
But a selfe-pleasing bold lasciviousnes.
Leontius.   What is it?
Hidaspes.   Many Ages before this,
When every man got to himselfe a Trade,
And was laborious in that chosen course,
Hating an idle life, farre worse then death:
Some one that gave himselfe to wine and sloth,
Which breed lascivious thoughts, and found himselfe
Contemnd for that by every painefull man;

*41 you and] *omit* Q 1–F 2; me and you Colman
*58 Contemnd] Seward; conioynd Q 1–F 2

336

To take his staine away, framde to himselfe
A god, whom he pretented to obey.　　　　　　　　60
In being thus dishonest, for a name
He call'd him *Cupid*. This created god,
Mans nature being ever credulous
Of any vice that takes part with his blood,
Had ready followers enow: and since
In every age they grew, especially
Amongst your Subjects, who doe yet remaine
Adorers of that drowsie Deitie:
Which drinke invented: and the winged Boy,
(For so they call him) has his sacrifices　　　　　70
To these loose naked statutes through the Land,
And in every Village, nay the Palace
Is not free from 'em. This is my request,
That these erected obsceane Images
May be pluckt downe and burnt: and every man
That offers to 'em any sacrifice,
May lose his life.
Leontius.　　　　　But be advis'd
My fayrest daughter, if he be a god,
He will expresse it upon thee my childe:
Which heaven avert.
Leucippus.　　　　　　　There is no such power:　　　80
But the opinion of him fills the Land
With lustfull sinnes: every young man and mayd
That feele the least desire to one another,
Dare not suppresse it, for they thinke it is
Blinde *Cupids* motion: and he is a god.
Leontius.　　This makes our youth unchaste. I am resolv'd:
Nephew *Ismenus*, breake the Statues downe
Here in the Palace, and command the Citie
Doe the like, let Proclamations
Be drawne, and hastily sent through the Land　　　90
To the same purpose.

*60 obey.] ~ , Q 1–2, F 2; ~ ; Q 3
*71 To] *omit* Q 1–F 2, L; And S ,C,W, D

Ismenus. Sir, I will breake downe none my selfe, but I will deliver your command: hand I will have none int, for I like it not.

Leontius. Goe and command it.   *Exit* Ismenus.

Pleasure of my life,
Wouldst thou ought else? Make many thousand suits,
They must and shall be graunted.

Hidaspes.   Nothing else.

Leontius.   But goe and meditate on other suites,
Some sixe daies hence Ile give thee audience againe,
And by a new oath binde my selfe to keepe it:
Aske largely for thy selfe, dearer then life,   100
In whom I may be bold to call my selfe
More fortunate then any in my age,
I will deny thee nothing.

Leucippus.   Twas well done Sister.

Exeunt all but these three Lords.

Nisus.   How like you this request my Lords?

Dorialus.   I know not yet, I am so full of wonder; we shall be gods our selves shortly, and we pull 'em out of heaven o' this fashion.

Agenor.   We shall have wenches now when we can catch 'em, and we transgresse thus.

Nisus.   And we abuse the gods once, tis a Justice we should be 110 held at hard meate: for my part, Ile eene make ready for mine owne affection, I know the god incenst, must send a hardnes through all good womens hearts, and then we have brought our eggs and muskadine to a faire market: Would I had gin an hundred pound for a tolleration, that I might but use my conscience in mine owne house.

Dorialus.   The Duke hee's old and past it, he would never have brought such a plague upon the land else, tis worse then Sword and Famine: Yet to say truth, we have deserv'd it, we have liv'd so wickedly, every man at his livery, and wou'd that wou'd 120 have suffis'd us: we murmurd at this blessing, That was nothing; and cryde out to the god for endlesse pleasures: he heard us, and supplyed us, and our women were new still as we needed 'em:

---

*100 selfe,] *stet* Q 1–F 2   *121 That] that Q 1–F 2   123 needed] S; need Q 1–F 2

yet we like beasts still cryde, Poore men can number their whores,
give us abundance: we had it, and this curse with all.

Agenor.   Berlady we are like to have a long Lent ont, flesh will
be flesh now: Gentlemen I had rather have angred all the gods
then that blinde Gunner. I remember once the people did but
slight him in a sacrifice: and what followed? Women kept their
houses, grew good huswives, honest forsooth, was not that fine? 130
wore their owne faces, though they wore gay cloathes, without
survaying: and which was most lamentable, they lov'd their
husbands.

Nisus.   I doe remember it to my griefe. Young Mayds were as
cold as Cowcumbers, and much of that complexion: bawds were
abolisht: and to which misery it must come againe, there were no
Cuckolds. Well, wee had neede pray to keepe these divels from
us, the times grow mischievous.

Enter one with an Image [and exit with it to destruction].

There he goes. Lord! This is a sacriledge I have not heard of:
would I were gelt, that I might not feele what followes.   140

Agenor.   And I too. You shall see within these few yeeres a fine
confusion i'the countrey, marke it: Nay, and we grow for to
depose the Powers, and set up Chastitie againe, well I ha done. A
fine new Goddesse certainely, whose blessings are hunger and
hard bedds.

Nisus.   This comes of fulnes, a sin too frequent with us; I beleeve
now we shall finde shorter commons.

Dorialus.   Would I were married, somwhat has some savour.
The race of Gentry will quite run out, now tis onely left to
husbands: if younger sisters take not the greater charitie, tis 150
lawfull.

Agenor.   Well, let come what will come, I am but one, and as the
plague falles, Ile shape my selfe: If women will be honest, Ile be
sound: if the god be not too unmercifull, Ile take a little still
where I can get it, and thanke him, and say nothing.

124 whores] S; woers Q1–F2   127 flesh now:] flesh: now ‸ Q1–F2
131 wore gay] Dyce; weare gay Q1–F2   *148 savour] *stet* Q1–F2
149 out, now] out ‸ now, Q1–F2   *150 charitie,] Q3; ~ ‸ Q1–2

339   22-2

Nisus. This ill winde yet may blow the Citie good, and let them
(if they can) get their owne children, they have hung long enough
in doubt: but howsoever, the old way was the surer, then they
had 'em.

Dorialus. Farewell my Lords, Ile eene take up what rent I can 160
before the day, I feare the yeere will fall out ill.

Agenor. Weele with you Sir: And *Love* so favour us,
As we are still thy servants. Come my Lords,
Lets to the Duke, and tell him to what folly
His doting now has brought him.

Exeunt.

Enter Priest of Cupid [*and his boy*], *with* [I. ii]
foure young men and Maydes.

Priest. Come my children, let your feete,
In an even Measure meete:
And your cheerefull voyces rise,
For to present this Sacrifice
To great *Cupid*, in whose name,
I his *Priest* begin the same.
Yong men take your Loves and kisse,
Thus our *Cupid* honourd is.
Kisse againe, and in your kissing,
Let no promises be missing: 10
Nor let any Mayden here,
Dare to turne away her eare,
Unto the whisper of her Love,
But give Bracelet, Ring, or Glove,
As a token to her sweeting,
Of an after secret meeting:
Now boy sing, to sticke our hearts
Fuller of great *Cupids* darts.

0.1 *Enter*] Q3; *omit* Q1–2   *5 To] Q3; Lo Q1–2

Song.

Lovers rejoyce, your paines shall be rewarded,
The god of love himselfe grieves at your crying;   20
No more shall frozen honour be regarded,
Nor the coy faces of a maid denying.
No more shall Virgins sigh, and say we dare not,
For men are false, and what they doe they care not.
All shall be well againe, then doe not greeve,
Men shall be true, and women shall beleeve.

Lovers rejoyce, what you shall say henceforth,
When you have caught your Sweet-hearts in your armes,
It shall be accounted Oracle, and worth:
No more faint-hearted Gyrles shall dreame of harmes,   30
And cry they are too young: the god hath said,
Fifteene shall make a Mother of a Mayd:
Then wise men, pull your Roses yet unblowne,
Love hates the too ripe fruite that falles alone.

The Measure.

After the Measure Enter Nilo [*with several Gentlemen*] *and others.*

Nilo.   No more of this: here breake your Rights for ever,
  The Duke commands it so; Priest doe not stare,
  I must deface your temple, though unwilling,
  And your god *Cupid* here must make a Scarcrow
  For any thing I know, or at the best,
  Adorne a Chimney-peece.   40
Priest.   O Sacriledge unheard of!
Nilo.   This will not helpe it,
  Take downe the Images and away with 'em.
  Priest change your coat you had best, all service now
  Is given to men: prayers above their hearing
  Will proove but bablings; learne to lye, and thrive,
  Twill proove your best profession: for the gods,

  21   *regarded*] Q 2; *rewarded* Q 1   35 Rights] *i.e.* rites *as in* Q 3

He that lives by 'em now, must be a begger.
There's better holinesse on earth they say,
Pray God it aske not greater sacrifice.
Goe home,   50
And if your god be not deafe as well as blinde,
He will make some smoake for it.
Gentleman.   Sir——
Nilo.   Gentlemen there is
No talking, this must be done, and speedily;
I have Commission that I must not breake.
Gentleman.   We are gone, to wonder what shall follow.
Nilo.   On to the next Temple.

Exeunt.

Cornets. Descendit Cupid.   [I. iii]

Cupid.   Am I then scornd? is my all-doing will
And power, that knowes no limit, nor admits none,
Now look't into by lesse then gods and weakned?
Am I, whose Bow strooke terror through the earth,
No lesse then Thunder, and in this, exceeding
Even gods themselves, who kneel before my Altars,
Now shooke off and contemd by such, whose lives
Are but my recreation! anger rise,
My sufferance and my selfe are made the subject
Of sinnes against us. Goe thou out displeasure,   10
Displeasure of a great god, flying thy selfe
Through all this Kingdome: sowe what ever evills
Proud flesh is taking of, amongst these Rebels;
And on the first heart that despisd my Greatnesse,
Lay a strange misery, that all may know
Cupids revenge is mightie; with this arrow,

52   make] Q3; *omit* Q1–2
3 gods ˄ and weakned?] ∼ ? ∼ ∼ ˄ Q1–F2
6–7 themselves, who kneel...Altars,...off˄] Dyce; themselves; whose knees...
Altars ˄...off; Q1–F2
*14 despisd] Q3 (despis'd); despise Q1–2
*16 this] Seward; his Q1–F2

Hotter then plagues or mine owne anger, will I
Now nobly right my selfe: nor shall the prayers
Nor sweete smokes on my Altars hold my hand,
Till I have left this a most wretched Land.   20

Exit.

Enter Hidaspes, *and* Cleophila.   [I. iv]

Hidaspes.   *Cleophila*, what was he that went hence?
Cleophila.   Meanes your Grace now?
Hidaspes.   I meane that hansome man,
  That something more then man I met at dore.
Cleophila.   Here was no hansome man.
Hidaspes.   Come, hee's some one
  You would preserve in private, but you want
  Cunning to doe it, and my eyes are sharper
  Then yours, and can with one neglecting glaunce,
  See all the graces of a man. Who was't?
Cleophila.   That went hence now?
Hidaspes.   That went hence now: I he.
Cleophila.   Faith here was no such one as your Grace thinks;   10
  Zoylus your Brothers Dwarfe went out but now.
Hidaspes.   I thinke twas he: how bravely he past by!
  Is he not growne a goodly Gentleman?
Cleophila.   A goodly Gentleman Madame?
  He is the most deformed fellow i'the Land.
Hidaspes.   O blasphemy! he may perhaps to thee
  Appeare deformed, for he is indeed
  Unlike a man: his shape and colours are
  Beyond the Art of Painting; he is like
  Nothing that we have seene, yet doth resemble   20
  Apollo, as I oft have fancied him,
  When rising from his bedde he sturres himselfe,
  And shakes day from his hayre.
Cleophila.   He resembles *Apollos* Recorder.
Hidaspes.   *Cleophila*, goe send a Page for him,
  And thou shalt see thy error, and repent.   *Exit* Cleophila.

343

Alas what doe I feele, my blood rebells,
And I am one of those I us'd to scorne,
My mayden-thoughts are fledde, against my selfe
I harbour Traytors: my Virginitie,   30
That from my child-hood kept me company,
Is heavier then I can endure to beare:
Forgive me *Cupid,* for thou art a god,
And I a wretched creature; I have sinn'd,
But be thou mercifull, and graunt that yet
I may enjoy what thou wilt have me love.

Enter Cleophila.

Cleophila.   *Zoylus* is heere Madame.

Enter Zoylus.

Hidaspes.   Hee's there indeed.
Now be thine owne Judge; see thou worse then mad,
Is he deformed? looke upon those eyes,
That let all pleasure out into the world,   40
Unhappy that they cannot see themselves.
Looke on his hayre, that like so many beames,
Streaking the East, shoote light ore halfe the world.
Looke on him all together, who is made
As if two Natures had contention
About their skill, and one had brought foorth him.
Zoylus.   Ha, ha, ha: Madame, though Nature hath not given mee
So much as others in my outward shew;
I beare a heart as loyall unto you
In this unsightly body (which you please   50
To make your myrth) as many others doe
That are farre more befriended in their births:
Yet I could wish my selfe much more deformed
Then yet I am, so I might make your Grace
More merry then you are, ha, ha, ha.

29 fledde,...selfe₄] ~ ₄...~ , Q1; ~ ₄...~ ? Q2, F2; ~ ₄...~ ; Q3
30 Traytors:] Q1(u); ~ ₄ Q1(c)   30 my] Seward; in my Q1–F2
36 me₄ love] Seward; me, Love Q1–F2

Hidaspes.   Beshrew me then
   If I be merry; but I am content
   Whilst thou art with me: thou that art my Saint,
   By hope of whose milde favour I doe live
   To tell thee so: I pray thee scorne me not;
   Alas, what can it adde unto thy worth   60
   To tryumph over me, that am a Mayd
   Without deceit, whose heart does guide her tongue,
   Drownd in my passions? yet I will take leave
   To call it reason that I dote on thee.
Cleophila.   The Princesse is besides her Grace I thinke,
   To talke thus with a fellow that will hardly
   Serve i'th' darke when one is drunke.
Hidaspes.   What answere wilt thou give me?
Zoylus.   If it please your Grace to jest on, I can abide it.
Hidaspes.   If it be jest, not to esteeme my life,   70
   Compard with thee: If it be jest in me,
   To hang a thousand kisses in an houre
   Upon those lippes, and take 'em off againe:
   If it be jest for me to marry thee,
   And take obedience on me whilst I live:
   Then all I say is jest:
   For every part of this, I sweare by those
   That see my thoughts, I am resolv'd to doe.
   And I beseech thee, by thine owne white hand,
   (Which pardon me, that I am bold to kisse   80
   With so unworthy lippes) that thou wilt sweare
   To marry me, as I doe here to thee,
   Before the face of heaven.
Zoylus.   Marry you! ha, ha, ha.
Hidaspes.   Kill me or graunt: wilt thou not speake at all?
Zoylus.   Why I will doe your will for ever.
Hidaspes.   I aske no more: but let me kisse that mouth
   That is so mercifull, that is my will:
   Next, goe with me before the King in hast,
   That is my will, where I will make our Peeres
   Know, that thou art their better.

Zoylus.   Ha, ha, ha, that is fine, ha, ha, ha. 90
Cleophila.   Madam, what meanes your Grace?
  Consider for the love of heaven to what
  You runne madly; will you take this Viper
  Into your bed?
Hidaspes.   Away, hold off thy hands:
  Strike her sweete *Zoylus*, for it is my will,
  Which thou hast sworne to doe.
Zoylus.   Away for shame,
  Know you no manners: ha, ha, ha.
                    Exeunt [Hidaspes *and* Zoylus].
Cleophila.   Thou knowst none I feare,
  This is just *Cupids* Anger, *Venus* looke
  Downe mildely on us: And commaund thy Sonne
  To spare this Ladie once, and let me be   100
  In love with all: and none in love with mee.
                                        Exit.

                    Enter Ismenus: *and* Timantus.   [I. v]

Timantus.   Is your Lordship for the warres this sommer?
Ismenus.   *Timantus* wilt thou goe with mee?
Timantus.   If I had a companie my Lord——
Ismenus.   Of Fidlers: Thou a Companie?
  No, no, keepe thy company at home, and cause cuckolds: The
  warres will hurt thy face, theres no semsters, Shoemakers, nor
  Taylors, nor almon milk ith morning, nor poacht egges to keepe
  your worship soluble, no man to warme your shyrt, and blow
  your roses: nor none to reverence your round lace breeches:
  If thou wilt needes goe, and goe thus, get a case for thy Captain- 10
  ship, a shower will spoyle thee else. Thus much for thee.
Timantus.   Your Lordships wondrous witty, very pleasant,
  beleeve't.   *Goes apart.*

            13 *Goes apart*] *Exit* Q 1–F 2

                            346

Enter Telamon, Dorialus, Agenor, Nisus, Leontius.

Leontius.   No newes yet of my Sonne?

Telamon.   Syr, there be divers out in search: no doubt theyl bring
the truth where hee is, or the occasion that ledde him hence.

Timantus [aside].   They have good eyes then.

Leontius.   The Gods goe with them:
Who be those that wayte there?

Telamon.   The Lord *Ismenus*, your Generall, for his dispatch.

Leontius.   O nephew; Wee have no use to imploy your vertue   20
In our warre: now the province is well setled:
Heare you ought of the Marquis?

Ismenus.   No Syr.

Leontius.   Tis strange hee should be gone thus: This five dayes
Hee was not seene.

Timantus [aside].   Ile hold my life, I could boult him in an houre.

Leontius.   Wher's my Daughter?

Dorialus.   About the purging of the Temples, Syr.

Leontius.   Shees chast and vertuous; Fetch her to mee,
And tell her I am pleasd to graunt her now   30
Her last request, without repenting mee,
Be it what it will: shee is wise *Dorialus*,   *Exit* Nisus.
And will not presse me farther then a Father.

Dorialus.   I pray the best may follow: yet if your grace
Had taken the opinions of your people,
At least of such, whose wisedomes ever wake
About your safety, I may say it Syr,
Under your noble pardon, that this change
Either had bene more honour to the Gods,
Or I thinke not at all. Syr, the princesse.   40

Enter Hidaspes [, Zoylus] *and* Nisus.

Leontius.   O my Daughter, my health!
And did I say my soule, I lyde not,
Thou art so neere mee; speake, and have what ever

14 of] Q2; *omit* Q1   42–43 not,...mee;] ~ ;...~ , Q1–F2

347

Thy wise will leades thee too: had I a Heaven,
It were too poore a place for such a goodnes.
Dorialus. Whats heere?
Agenor. An Apes skin stufft I thinke, tis so plumpe.
Hidaspes. Syr, you have past your word, still be a prince,
And hold you to it. Wonder not I presse you,
My life lyes in your word, if you break that,   50
You have broke my hart, I must aske thats my shame,
And your will must not deny mee: Now for Heaven
Be not forsworne.
Leontius.   By the Gods I will not,
I cannot, were there no other power
Then my love calld to a witnes of it.
Dorialus. They have much reason to trust: You have forsworn
one of em out oth countrey already.
Hidaspes. Then this is my request: This Gentleman.
Bee not ashamd Syr: you are worth a Kingdome.   [*To* Zoylus.]
Leontius. In what?   60
Hidaspes. In way of marriage.
Leontius. How?
Hidaspes. In way of Marriage, it must be so.
Your Oath is tyde to heaven: as my love to him.
Leontius. I know thou doest but trie my Age,
Come aske againe.
Hidaspes. If I should aske all my life time, this is
All still. Syr I am serious, I must have
This worthy man without enquyring why;
And suddenly, and freely: Doe not looke   70
For reason or obedience in my words:
My Love admits no wisedome, onely hast:
And hope hangs on my furie. Speake Syr, speake,
But not as a Father, I am deafe and dull to counsell:
My inflamed bloud heares nothing but my will,
For Gods sake speake.
Dorialus. Heres a brave alteration.
Nisus. This comes of Chastitie.
Hidaspes. Will not you speake Syr?

348

Agenor.   The God begins his vengeance; what a sweet youth he 80
has sent us here, with a pudding ins belly?

Leontius.   O let me never speake,
Or with my words let me speake out my life;
Thou power abusde, great Love whose vengence now
We feele and feare, have mercie on this Land.

Nisus.   How does your Grace?

Leontius.   Sicke, very sicke I hope.

Dorialus.   Gods comfort you.

Hidaspes.   Will not you speake? Is this your royall word?
Doe not pull perjurie upon your soule.
Syr, you are olde, and neere your punishment;   90
Remember.

Leontius.   Away base woman.

Hidaspes.   Then be no more my Father, but a plague
I am bound to pray against: bee any sinne
May force mee to dispaire, and hang my selfe:
Bee thy name never more remembred King
But in example of a broken Faith,
And curst even to forgetfullnes: may thy Land
Bring forth such Monsters as thy daughter is!
I am weary of my rage. I pray forgive mee,   100
And let mee have him, will you Noble Syr?

Leontius.   Mercie, mercie heaven:
Thou heire of all dishonour, shamest thou not
To draw this little moysture left for life,
Thus rudely from mee? Carry that Slave to death.

Zoylus.   For Heavens sake Syr, it is no fault of mine,
That shee will love mee.

Leontius.   To death with him, I say.

Hidaspes.   Then make hast Tyrant, or Ile be before him;
This is the way to Hell.

Leontius.   Hold fast, I charge you: away with him.   110

                              [*Exit* Zoylus *attended.*]

Hidaspes.   Alas old man, Death hath more dores then one,
And I will meete him.   *Exit* Hidaspes.

108 before] Seward; for Q1–F2   110 you:] ∼ ∧ Q1–F2   112 I] Q2; *omit* Q1

Leontius.   *Dorialus,* Pray see her in her Chamber,
And lay a guard about her: [*Exit* Dorialus.]
The greatest curse the Gods lay on our frailties,
Is will and disobedience in our Issues,
Which wee beget as well as them, to plague us
With our fond loves; Beasts you are onely blest
That have that happy dulnesse to forget
What you have made, your young ones grieve not you,   120
They wander where they list, and have theyr wayes
Without dishonor to you; and their ends,
Fall on em without sorrow of their parents,
Or after ill remembrance: Oh this Woman!
Would I had made my selfe a Sepulcher,
When I made her: Nephew where is the prince?
Pray God hee have not more part of her basenesse
Then of her bloud about him:
                         Gentlemen, where is hee?
Ismenus.   I know not Syr. Has his wayes by him selfe, is too wise
for my companie.   130
Leontius.   I doe not like this hiding of him selfe,
From such societie as fits his person:
Some of it needs must yee know.
Ismenus.   I am sure not I: nor have knowne twice this ten dayes,
which if I were as proude as some of em I should take scurvily:
but hee is a young man, let him have his swinge, twill make
him——   Timantus *whispers to the* Duke.
Theres some good matter now in hand:
How the slave geers and grinnes: the Duke is pleasde: theres
a newe paire of Scarlet Hose now, and as much money to spare, as 140
will fetch the old from pawne, a Hat and a Cloake to goe out to
morrow: garters and stockings come by nature.
Leontius.   Bee sure of this.
Timantus.   I durst not speake else Syr.
                                        [*Exeunt omnes.*]

132 fits] Colman; *omit* Q 1–F 2
133 of it needs must yee] Q 1 (u); of it yee needs must Q 1 (c)
135–136 scurvily:...man,] ~ ,...~ : Q 1–F 2±

Cornetts. Descendit Cupid.   II. i

Cupid.   *Leucippus* thou art shot through with a shaft
  That will not rankle long, yet sharpe enough
  To sowe a world of helpelesse miserie
  In this unhappie Kingdome: doest thou thinke
  Because thou art a prince, to make a part
  Against my power? but it is all the fault
  Of thy ould Father, who believes his Age
  Is colde enough to quench my burning Darts,
  But hee shall know ere long, that my smart loose,
  Can thawe Ice, and inflame the witherd hart   10
  Of *Nestor*: thou thy selfe art lightly stroke,
  But his madde love, shall publish that the rage
  Of *Cupid*, has the power to conquer Age.

                                                    Exit.

Enter Bacha, *and* Leucippus. Bacha, [*with*] *a handkercheffe.*   [II.ii]

Leucippus.   Why, whats the matter?
Bacha.   Have you got the spoyle
  You thirsted for? O tyrannie of men!
Leucippus.   I pray thee leave.
Bacha.   Your envie is Heaven knowes,
  Beyond the reach of all our feeble Sexe:
  What paine alas could it have bene to you,
  If I had kept mine honour? you might still
  Have bene a prince, and still this Countreyes Heyre.
  That innocent Guard, which I till now had kept,
  For my defence, my vertue, did it seeme
  So dangerous in a State, that your selfe came   10
  To suppresse it?
Leucippus.   Drie thine eyes again,
  Ile kisse thy teares away, this is but follie,
  Tis past all helpe.
Bacha.   Now you have wonne the treasure,

II.i] *Actus secundus. Scœna prima.* Q1   4 unhappie] Q3; happie Q1-2

351

Tis my request that you would leave mee thus,
And never see these empty walles againe:
I know you will doe so, and well you may:
For there is nothing in em that is worth
A glaunce. I loath my selfe, and am become
Another woman; One me thinkes with whome
I want acquaintance.

Leucippus.   If I doe offend thee,   20
I can be gone, and though I love thy sight,
So highly do I prize thine owne content,
That I will leave thee.

Bacha.   Nay, you may stay now;
You should have gone before: I know not now
Why I should feare you: All I should have kept
Is stolne: Nor is it in the power of man
To robbe me farther: if you can invent
Spare not; No naked man feares robbing lesse
Then I doe: now you may for ever stay.

Leucippus. Why, I could doe thee farther wrong.   30
Bacha. You have a deeper reach in evill then I:
Tis past my thought.

Leucippus.   And past my will to act:
But trust mee I could doe it.

Bacha.   Good Syr doe,
That I may knowe there is a wrong beyond
What you have done mee.

Leucippus.   I could tell the world
What thou hast done.

Bacha.   Yes you may tell the world:
And doe you thinke I am so vaine to hope
You will not? you can tell the world but this,
That I am a widdow, full of teares in shewe,
My Husband dead (and one that lov'd mee so)   40
Hardly a weeke, forgot my modestie,
And caught with youth and greatnesse, gave my selfe

To live in sinne with you: This you may tell:
And this I doe deserve.
Leucippus.   Why, doest thou
  Thinke mee so base to tell? These limmes of mine
  Shall part from one another on a wracke,
  Ere I disclose; But thou doest utter words
  That much afflict mee: you did seeme as ready
  Sweete *Bacha* as my selfe.
Bacha.   You are right a man:
  When they have witcht us into miserie,   50
  Poore innocent soules, they lay the fault on us:
  But bee it so——For prince *Leucippus* sake
  I will beare any thing.
Leucippus.   Come weepe no more.
  I wrought thee to it, it was my fault:
  Nay, see if thou wilt leave? Here, take this pearle,
  Kisse me sweete *Bacha*, and receive this purse.
Bacha.   What should I doe with these? they will not decke
  My minde.
Leucippus.   Why, keepe em to remember mee.
  I must be gone, I have bene absent long,
  I know the Duke my Father is in rage: 60
  But I will see thee suddenly againe,
  Farewell my *Bacha*.
Bacha.   Gods keepe you:
  Do you heare Syr: pray give me a point to weare.
Leucippus.   Alas good *Bacha*, take one,
  I pray thee where thou wilt.
Bacha.   Comming from you:
  This point is of as high esteeme with mee,
  As all pearle and golde: nothing but good
  Bee ever with or neere you.
Leucippus.   Fare thee well
  Mine owne good *Bacha*; I will make all haste.   *Exit.* 70
Bacha.   Just as you are a Dosen I esteeme you: no more: does he
  thinke I would prostitute my selfe for love? it was the love of
  these pearles and golde that wanne mee.

I confesse
I lust more after him then any other,
And would at any rate if I had store,
Purchase his fellowship: but being poore,
Ile both enjoy his bodie and his purse,
And hee a Prince, nere thinke my selfe the worse.

Enter Leontius, Leucippus, Ismenus, Timantus.

Leontius.   Nay, you must backe and shew us what it is,   80
  That witches you out of your Honour thus.
Bacha.   Whose that?
Timantus.   Looke there Syr.
Leontius.   Lady, never flye,
  You are betrayde.
Bacha.   Leave mee, my teares, a while,
  And to my just rage give a little place:
  What saucy man are you, that without leave,
  Enter upon a Widdowes mournefull house?
  You hinder a dead man from many teares,
  Who did deserve more then the world can shed,
  Though they should weepe themselves to Images:
  If not for love of mee, yet of your selfe,   90
  Away, for you can bring no comfort to mee.
  But you may carry hence, you know not what.
  Nay, sorrow is infectious.
Leontius.   Thou thy selfe
  Art growne infectious: wouldst thou know my name?
  I am the Duke, father to this young man
  Whom thou corruptst.
Bacha [aside].   Has he then told him all?
Leucippus.   You doe her wrong Sir.
Bacha.   O he has not told.——
  Sir I beseech you pardon my wild tongue,
  Directed by a weak distempord head,
  Madded with griefe: Alas I did not know   100
  You were my Soveraigne; but now you may

90 love] Q2; *omit* Q1

354

Command my poore unworthy life, which will
Be none I hope ere long.

Leontius.   All thy dissembling will never hide thy shame:
And wert not more respecting Woman-hood
In generall, then any thing in thee, thou shouldst
Be made such an example, that posteritie,
When they wou'd speake most bitterly, should say,
Thou art as impudent as Bacha *was.*

Bacha.   Sir, though you be my King, whom I will serve   110
In all just causes: yet when wrongfully
You seeke to take mine Honour, I will rise
Thus and defie you; for it is a Jewell
Dearer then you can give, which whilst I keepe,
(Though in this lowly house) I shall esteeme
My selfe above the Princes of the earth
That are without it. If the Prince your sonne,
Whom you accuse me with, know how to speake
Dishonour of me, if he doe not doe it,
The plagues of hell light on him, may he never   120
Governe this Kingdome: here I chalenge him
Before the face of heaven, my Liege, and these,
To speake the worst he can: if he will lye,
To lose a womans fame, Ile say he is
Like you (I thinke I cannot call him worse.)
Hee's dead, that with his life would have defended
My reputation, and I forc't to play
(That which I am) the foolish woman,
And use my liberall tongue.

Leucippus [*aside*].   Is't possible!   130
We men are children in our carriages,
Compard with women: wake thy selfe for shame,
And leave not her whose honour thou shou'dst keepe
Safe as thine own, alone to free her self:
But I am prest I know not how, with guilt,
And feele my conscience (never us'd to lye)
Loth to allow my tongue to adde a lye
To that too much I did: but it is lawfull

To defend her, that onely for my love
Lov'd evill.
Leontius.   Tell me, why did you *Leucippus*
Stay here so long?
Leucippus.   If I can urge ought from me   140
But a truth, hell take me.
Leontius.   Whats the matter,
Why speake you not?
Timantus.   Alas good Sir, forbeare
To urge the Prince, you see his shamefastnes.
Bacha.   What does he say Sir? if you be a Prince
Shew it, and tell the truth.
Ismenus.   If you have layne with her tell your Father, no doubt he
has done as ill before now: The Gentlewoman will be proud ont.
Bacha.   For Gods sake speake.
Leucippus.   Have you done prating yet?
Ismenus.   Who prates?
Leucippus.   Thou knowst I do not speake to thee *Ismenus*:   150
But what said you *Timantus* concerning my shamefastnes?
Timantus.   Nothing I hope that might displease your Highnes.
Leucippus.   If any of thy great, Great-grandmothers
This thousand yeeres, had beene as chaste as she,
It wou'd have made thee honester. I stayd
To heare what you wou'd say: she is by heaven
Of the most strict and blamelesse chastitie
That ever woman was: (good gods forgive me)
Had *Tarquin* met with her, she had beene kild
With a Slave by her ere she had agreed: 160
I lye with her! wou'd I might perish then.
Our Mothers, whom we all must reverence,
Could nere exceede her for her chastitie,
Upon my soule: for by this light
Shee's a most obstinate modest creature.
Leontius.   What did you with her then so long *Leucippus?*
Leucippus.   Ile tell you Sir: You see shee's beautifull.
Leontius.   I see it well.
Leucippus.   Moov'd by her face, I came

356

With lustfull thoughts, which was a fault in me:
But telling truth, something more pardonable,   170
(And for the world I will not lye to you:)
Proud of my selfe, I thought a Princes name
Had power to blow 'em downe flat of their backs;
But here I found a Rocke not to be shooke:
For as I hope for good, Sir, all the battery
That I could lay to her, or of my person,
My greatnes, or my gold, could nothing moove her.
Leontius.   Tis very strange, being so young and fayre.
Leucippus.   Shee's almost thirtie Sir.
Leontius.   How doe you know
Her age so just?
Leucippus.   She told it me her selfe   180
Once when she went about to shew by reason
I should leave wooing her.
Leontius.   She staines the ripest Virgins of the age.
Leucippus.   If I had sinn'd with her, I would be loth
To publish her disgrace: but by my life
I would have told it you, because I thinke
You would have pardond me the rather Sir:
And I will tell you father: By this light,
(But that I never will bestow my selfe
But to your liking) if she now would have me,   190
I now would marry her.
Leontius.   How's that *Leucippus*!
Leucippus.   Sir, will you pardon me one fault, which yet
I have not done, but had a will to doe,
And I will tel it?
Leontius.   Bee't what it will, I pardon thee.
Leucippus.   I offerd marriage to her.
Leentius.   Did she refuse it?
Lcuoippus.   With that earnestnes, and almost scorne, to thinke
Of any other after her lost Mate,
That she made me thinke my selfe unworthy of her.

177 my] *omit* Q 1–F 2
187–188 rather Sir: | And...light,] Dyce; rather: | And...light Sir Q 1–F 2

357

Leontius.   You have stayd too long *Leucippus.*
Leucippus.   Yes Sir.——
    Forgive me heaven, what multitudes of oathes   200
    Have I bestowd on lyes, and yet they were
    Officious lyes, there was no malice in 'em.
Leontius [*aside*].   She is the fayrest creature that ever I beheld;
    And then so chaste, tis wonderfull! the more
    I looke on her, the more I am amaz'd.
    I have long thought of a wife, and one I would have had,
    But that I was afraid to meete a woman
    That might abuse my age: but here she is
    Whom I may trust too; of a chastitie
    Impregnable, and approved so by my sonne: 210
    The meanes of her byrth will still preserve her
    In due obedience; and her beauty is
    Of force enough to pull me backe to youth.
    My sonne once sent away, whose rivall-shippe
    I have just cause to feare, if power, or gold,
    Or wit, can win her to me, she is mine.——
    Nephew *Ismenus,* I have new intelligence,
    Your Province is unquiet still.
Ismenus.   Ime glad ont.
Leontius.   And so dangerously,   220
    That I must send the Prince in person with you.
Ismenus.   Ime glad of that too: Sir will you dispatch us, we shall
    wither heere for ever.
Leontius.   You shall be dispacht within this houre:
    Leucippus, never wonder nor aske,
    It must be thus. Lady I aske your pardon,
    Whose vertue I have slubberd with my tongue,
    And you shall ever be chaste in my memory hereafter:
    But we old men often dote: to make
    Amends for my great fault, receive that Ring: 230
    Ime sorry for your griefe, may it soone leave you.
    Come my Lords lets goe.   *Exeunt.* [*Manet* Bacha.]
Bacha.   Heaven blesse your Grace.——

209 too] *i.e.* to *as in* II.iv.40   211 meanes] *i.e.* meanness *as in* F 2

One that had but so much modestie left, as to blush,
Or shrinke a little at his first encounter,
Had beene undone; where I come off with honour,
And gayne too: they that never wou'd be trackt
In any course, by the most suttle sense,
Must beare it through with frontlets impudence.

Exit.

Enter Dorialus, Agenor, Nisus.   [II. iii]

Dorialus.   Gentlemen, this is a strange peece of Justice, to put the
wretched Dwarfe to death because she doted on him. Is she not a
woman, and subject to those mad figaries her whole Sexe is infected
with? Had she lov'd you, or you, or I, or all on's, (as indeed the
more the merryer still with them) must we therefore have our
heads par'd with a Hatchet? So she may love all the Nobility out
ath Dukedome in a month, and let the raskals in.
Nisus.   You will not, or you doe not see the neede that makes this
just to the world?
Dorialus.   I cannot tell, I would be loth to feele it: But the best is, 10
she loves not proper men, we three were in wise cases else: but
make me know this need.
Nisus.   Why yes: Hee being taken away, this base incontinence
dyes presently, and shee must see her shame and sorrow for it.
Dorialus.   Pray God she doe: but was the Sprat beheaded, or did
they swing him about like a chickin, and so breake his necke.
Agenor.   Yes, he was beheaded, and a solemne justice made of it.
Dorialus.   That might have beene deducted.
Agenor.   Why how would you have had him dide?
Dorialus.   Faith I would have had him rosted like a warden in a 20
browne paper, and no more talke ont: or a feather stucke in's head,
like a Quaile: or a hangd him in a Dog-coller: what should hee be
beheaded? wee shall have it grow so base shortly, Gentlemen
will be out of love with it.
Nisus.   I wonder from whence this race of the Dwarfes first
sprung?

25 race] W; *omit* Q 1–F 2

Dorialus.   From an olde leacherous payre of breeches that lay
upon a wench to keepe her warme: for certainely they are no mans
worke: and I am sure a Monkey would get one of the guard to this
fellow, he was no bigger then a small Portmantu, and much about 30
that making, if t'ad legs.

Agenor.   But Gentlemen, what say you to the Prince?

Nisus.   I, concerning his being sent I know not whither.

Dorialus.   Why then hee will come home I know not when: you
shall pardon me, Ile talke no more of this subject, but say, gods
be with him where ere he is, and sende him well home againe:
For why hee is gone, or when he will returne, let them know
that directed him: Onely this, there's mad Moriscoes in the state;
but what they are, Ile tell you when I know. Come, lets goe,
heare all, and say nothing.

Agenor.   Content.   40

Exeunt.

Enter Timantus *and* Telamon.   [II. iv]

Telamon.   *Timantus*, is the Duke ready yet?

Timantus.   Almost.

Telamon.   What ayles him?

Timantus.   Faith I know not, I thinke he has dreamt he's but
eighteene: has been worse since he sent you forth for the frizling-
yron.

Telamon.   That cannot be, he lay in Gloves all night, and this
morning I brought him a new Periwig with a locke at it, and
knockt up a swinge in's chamber.

Timantus.   O but since, his Taylor came, and they have fallen 10
out about the fashion on's cloathes: and yonders a fellow come, has
board a hole in's eare; and he has bespake a Vauting-horse, you
shall see him come foorth presently: hee lookes like Winter,
stucke here and there with fresh flowers.

Telamon.   Will he not Tilt thinke you?

Timantus.   I thinke he will.

Telamon.   What does he meane to doe?

4 *Timantus.*] Q2; *Tela.* Q1   9 swinge] *i.e.* swing *as in* Q2

Timantus.   I know not: but by this light I thinke hee is in love;
he wou'd ha bin shav'd but for me.

Telamon.   In love, with whome?   20

Timantus.   I could guesse, but you shall pardon me: hee will take
me along with him some whither.

Telamon.   I over-heard him aske your opinion of some bodies
beautie.

Timantus.   Yes, there it goes that makes him so youthfull, and
has layd by his Crutch, and halts now with a leading staffe.

Enter Leontius *with a staffe and a looking-glasse.*

Leontius.   *Timantus.*

Timantus.   Sir.

Leontius.   This Feather is not large enough.

Timantus.   Yes faith, tis such a one as the rest of the yong 30
Gallants weare.

Leontius.   *Telamon,* does it doe well?

Telamon.   Sir, it becomes you, or you become it, the rareliest——

Leontius.   Away, dost thinke so?

Telamon.   Thinke sir? I know it. Sir, the Princesse is past all hope
of life since the Dwarfe was put to death.

Leontius.   Let her be so, I have other matters in hand: but this
same Taylor angers me, he has made my dublet so wide: and see,
the knave has put no points at my arme.

Timantus.   Those will be put too quickly Sir, upon any occasion. 40

Leontius.   *Telamon,* have you bid this Dauncer come a mornings?

Telamon.   Yes Sir.

Leontius.   *Timantus,* let me see the glasse againe: looke you how
carelesse you are growne, is this tooth well put in?

Timantus.   Which Sir?

Leontius.   This Sir.

Timantus.   It shall be.

Telamon.   Me thinks that tooth should put him in mind on's yeeres:
and *Timantus* stands as if (seeing the Duke in such a youthfull
habite) he were looking in's mouth how olde he were.   50

Leontius.   So, so.

Telamon.   Will you have your Gowne sir?

Leontius.   My Gowne? why, am I sicke? bring mee my Sword.
                                                    Exit Telamon.
Timantus, Let a couple of the great horses be brought out for us.
Timantus.   Heele kill himselfe.——Why, will you ride sir?
Leontius.   Ride? Dost thou thinke I cannot ride?
Timantus.   O yes sir, I know it: but as I conceive your journey,
you wou'd have it private; and then you were better take a Coach.
Leontius.   These Coaches make mee sicke: yet tis no matter, let
it be so.   60

                Enter Telamon *with a sword.*

Telamon.   Sir, heere's your sword.
Leontius.   O well sed: let me see it, I could me thinkes——Why
    Telamon, bring me another: what, thinkst thou I will weare a
    sword in vaine?
Telamon.   He has not strength enough to draw it, a yoake of
    Fleas tyde to a hayre would have drawne it. Tis out sir now, the
    Scabbert is broke.
Leontius.   O put it up againe, and on with it; me thinks I am not
    drest till I feele my sword on.
    Telamon, if any of my counsell aske for mee, say I am gone to 70
    take the ayre.   [*Exeunt* Leontius *and* Telamon *severally.*]
Timantus.   He has not bene drest this twenty yeares then. If this
    vaine holde but a weeke, hee will learne to play oth base violl and
    sing too't: Hees poeticall alreadie; for I have spyde a Sonnet ons
    making lye by's beddes side. Ile be so unmannerly to reade it.
                                                        Exit.

    Enter Hidaspes, Cleophila, *and* Hero: Hidaspes *in a Bedde.*   [II. v]

Hidaspes.   Hees dead, hees dead, and I am following.
Cleophila.   Aske *Cupid* mercie Madame.
Hidaspes.   O my hart!
Cleophila.   Helpe! stirre her, *Hero*!
Hidaspes.   O, ô.

    4-5 her, *Hero*! | *Hidaspes.* O, ô.] her: *Hero, Hida, ô, ô* Q 1 (u); her: *Hero: Hida: ô, ô*
Q 1 (c)

                            362

Cleophila.   Shees going, wretched women that wee are:
    Looke to her, and Ile pray the while.   *Shee kneeles.*
Hero.   Why, Maddame?
Cleophila.   *Cupid* pardon what is past,
                    And forgive our sinnes at last,   10
                    Then we will be coye no more,
                    But thy Deitie Adore,
                    Troths at fifteene wee will plight,
                    And will tread a Dance each night,
                    In the Fields, or by the Fire,
                    With the youths that have desire.

    How does shee yet?
Hero.   O ill——
Cleophila.   Given Eare-rings we will weare,
                    Bracelets of our Lovers haire,   20
                    Which they on our Armes shall twist,
                    With theyr names carv'd, on the wrist.
                    All the Money that wee owe,
                    Wee in Tokens will bestowe:
                    And learne to write, that when tis sent,
                    Onely our Loves know what it meant:
                    O then pardon what is past,
                    And forgive our sinnes at last.

    What, mends shee?
Hero.   Nothing, you do it not wantonly, you shuld sing.   30
    Leave, leave, tis now too late.
Cleophila.   Why, shee is dead?
Hero.   Her last is breathed.
Cleophila.   What shall we doe.
Hero.   Goe runne,
    And tell the Duke; and whilst Ile close her eyes.
                                            [*Exit* Cleophila.]

17 *How...yet?*] Q 1–3 *print, braced, in two lines to the right of ll.* 15–16 (F 2 *opposite*
l. 16)
    22 the] *omit* Q 1; *our* Q 2–F 2
    29 *What, mends shee?*] Q 1–3 *print, braced, in two lines to the right of ll.* 27–28
(F 2 *opposite l.* 28)
    31 dead?] ∼ : Q 1–2, F 2; *omit* Q 3   *33 whilst] *stet* Q 1–F 2

Thus I shutte thy faded light,
And put it in eternall night.
Where is shee can boldly say
Though shee be as fresh as May
She shall not by this Corps be laid,
Ere to morrowes light doe fade.
Let us all now living bee,   40
Warnd by thy strict Chastitie,
And marry all fast as we can.
Till then we keepe a piece of man,
Wrongfully from them that owe it:
Soone may every Maide bestow it.

                                        [*Exit.*]

                Enter Bacha *and a* Maide.   [II. vi]

Bacha.   Who is it?
Maid.   Forsooth theres a gallant Coach at the dore, and the brave
old man int, that you said was the Duke.
Bacha.   *Cupid* graunt hee may be taken—away.
Maid.   Hee is comming up, and lookes the swaggeringst, and has
such glorious cloathes.
Bacha.   Let all the house seeme sad, and see all handsome.

        Enter Leontius *and* Timantus, [*with*] *a Jewell, and a Ring.*

Leontius.   Nay widdow flie not back, we come not now to chide,
stand up and bidde me welcome.
Bacha.   To a poore widdows house that knowes no end of her ill   10
fortune: your Highnes is most welcome.
Leontius.   Come kisse me then, this is but manners widdow:
Nere fling your head aside, I have more cause of griefe then you:
my Daughters dead: but what? tis nothing. Is the rough *French*
horse brought to the dore? They say he is a high goer, I shall soone
try his mettall.
Timantus.   Hee will be sir, and the gray *Barbary*, they are fiery
both.

        *4 taken—away.] taken.   *Away.* Q 1–F 2
        7 seeme] Seward (seem); see me Q 1–F 2

Leontius.   They are the better: Before the gods I am lightsome,
very lightsome: How doest thou like mee Widdowe?   20
Bacha.   As a person in whome all graces are.
Leontius.   Come, Come, yee flatter: Ile clappe your cheeke for
that, and you shall not be angry.
Hast no *Musicke*? Now could I cutte three times with ease, and doe
a crosse point, should shame all your gallants.
Bacha.   I doe believe you——and your selfe too:
Lorde what a fine olde *Zany* my Love has made him? 'Is mine,
I am sure: Heaven make mee thankfull for him.
Leontius.   Tell mee how olde thou art, my pretty sweet heart?
Timantus.   Your Grace will not buye her, shee may trippe Syr!   30
Bacha.   My sorrowe showes mee Elder then I am by many
yeares.
Leontius.   Thou art so witty I must kisse agen.
Timantus.   In deed her Age lyes not in her mouth: nere looke it
there Syr, she has a better register, if it be not burnt.
Leontius.   I will kisse thee, I am a fire *Timantus.*
Timantus.   Can you chuse Syr, having such heavenly Fire before
you?
Leontius.   Widdow, guesse why I come, I prethee doe.
Bacha.   I cannot Syr, unles you bee pleasde to make a myrth 40
out of my rudenesse: and that I hope your pittie will not let yee,
the subject is so barren: [*Aside*] Bite King Bite, Ile let you play a
while.
Leontius.   Now as I am an honest man, Ile tell thee truly——
how many foote did I jump yesterday *Timantus*?
Timantus.   Fourteen of your owne, and some three fingers.
Bacha [*aside*].   This Fellow lyes as lightly, as if hee were in cutte
Taffata.
Alas good Almanacke get thee to Bedde, and tell what weather
wee shall have to morrow.   50
Leontius.   Widdow I am come in short to be a Suiter.
Bacha.   For whome?
Leontius.   Why by my troth, I come to woo thee wench: and
winne thee for my selfe: Nay, looke upon mee: I have about mee
that will doe it.

Bacha. Now Heaven defend mee, your whore shall I never bee: I thanke the Gods, I have a little left mee to keepe me warme, and honest: if your grace take not that, I seeke no more.

Leontius. I am so farre from taking any thing, Ile adde unto thee.

Bacha. Such Additions may bee for your ease Syr, not my 60 honestie: I am well in being single, good Syr seeke another, I am no meate for money.

Leontius. Shall I fight for thee?
This Sword shall cut his throte, that dares lay clayme but to a Finger of thee, but to a looke: I would see such a fellow.

Bacha [aside]. It would bee but a cold sight to you:
This is the father of *Saint George* a foote-backe: Can such drie Mummy talke?

Timantus. Before the gods, your grace looks like *Æneas.*

Bacha [aside]. Hee lookes like his olde father upon his backe, 70 crying to get Aboord.

Leontius. How shall I win thy love, I pray thee tell me? Ile marry thee if thou desirest that: That is an honest course, I am in good earnest, and presently within this houre, I am madde for thee: prethee deny me not, for as I live Ile pine thee, but Ile have thee.

Bacha [aside]. Now hees in the Toyle, ile hold him fast.

Timantus [to her]. You doe not know what tis to be a Queene, goe to, you're madde else: what the olde man falls short of, there's others can eche out, when you please to call on em.

Bacha [to him]. I understand you not. [*Aside*] Love I adore thee. 80
——Syr, on my knees I give you harty thanks, for so much honouring your humble Handmayd above her byrth: farre more her weake deservings. I dare not trust the envious tongues of all, that must repine at my unworthy rising. Beside, you have many fayre ones in your kingdome borne to such woorth: ô turne your selfe about and make a Noble choyse.

56–57 whore shall I never bee:] Seward (I shall never be); whore shall never: Q1–F2

*68 Mummy] Seward; Mumming Q1–F2

75 pine] *stet* Q1–2, F2

*78 goe to, you're madde else:] Dyce; Goe to your Maide, else ‸ Q1–2; Goe too you Mayd, (*omit* else) Q3; Go too you Maid, else ‸ F2

80 Love] *i.e.* Cupid, *addressed in an aside*

Leontius.   If I doe, let me famish: I will have thee, or breake up house, and boord heere.

Bacha.   Sir, you may command an unwilling woman to obey yee: but heaven knowes——   90

Leontius.   No more: these halfe a dozen kisses, and this Jewell, and every thing I have, and away with me, and clappe it up; and have a boy by the morning. *Timantus*, let one be sent post for my sonne againe, and for *Ismenus*: they are scarce twentie mile on their way yet, by that time weele be married.

Timantus.   There shall Sir.

Exeunt.

Enter Dorialus, Agenor, Nisus. III. i

Nisus.   Is not this a fine mariage?

Agenor.   Yes, yes, let it alone.

Dorialus.   I, I, the King may marry whom's list, lets talke of other matters.

Nisus.   Is the Prince comming home certainely?

Dorialus.   Yes, yes, hee was sent post for yesterday, lets make haste, weele see how his new Mother-in-law will entertaine him.

Nisus.   Why well I warrant you: did you not marke how humbly she carryed her selfe to us on her mariage day, acknowledging her owne unworthynesse, and that she would be our servant.   10

Dorialus.   But marke whats done.

Nisus.   Regard not shew.

Agenor.   O God! I knew her when I have beene offred her to be brought to my bed for five pound: whether it could have beene performd or no, I know not.

Nisus.   Her daughters a pretty Lady.

Dorialus.   Yes: and having had but meane bringing up, it talks the pretlest and innocentlest, the Queene wilbe so angry to heare her betray her breeding by her language: but I am perswaded shee's well dispos'd.   20

93 morning. *Timantus*, let] F 2; morning ₐ *Timantus.* Let Q 1–3
0.1 III.i] *Actus tertij. Scœn. pri.* Q 1

Agenor.   I thinke better then her mother.

Nisus.   Come, we stay too long.

Exeunt.

Enter Leucippus *and* Ismenus.   [III. ii]

Ismenus.   How now man, strooke dead with a tale?

Leucippus.   No, but with a truth.

Ismenus.   Stand of your selfe: can you endure blowes, and shrinke at words?

Leucippus.   Thou knowst I have told thee all.

Ismenus.   But that all's nothing to make you thus: your Sisters dead.

Leucippus.   Thats much, but not the most.

Ismenus.   Why, for the other let her marry and hang, tis no purpos'd fault of yours: and if your father will needes have your 10 cast whore, you shall shew the duty of a childe better in being contented, and bidding much good doe his good old heart with her, then in repining thus at it: let her goe: what, there are more wenches man, weele have another.

Leucippus.   O thou art vaine, thou knowst I do not love her:
What shall I doe? I would my tongue had led me
To any other thing, but Blasphemy,
So I had mist commending of this woman,
Whom I must reverence now she is my mother;
My sinne *Ismenus* has wrought all this ill: 20
And I beseech thee, to be warnd by me,
And doe not lye, if any man should aske thee
But *How thou dost*, or, *What a clocke tis now*,
Be sure thou doe not lye, make no excuse
For him that is most neere thee: never let
The most officious falsehood scape thy tongue,
For they above (that are intirely truth)
Will make that seede, which thou hast sowne of lyes,
Yeeld miseries a thousand fold
Upon thine head, as they have done of mine.   30

368

Enter Timantus.

Timantus.   Sir, your Highnes is welcome home, the Duke and
Queene will presently come foorth to you.
Leucippus.   Ile waight on them.
Timantus.   Worthy *Ismenus*, I pray how have you sped in your
warres?
Ismenus.   This Rogue mocks me.——
Well *Timantus*, 'pray how have you sped here at home at shovel-
boord?
Timantus.   Faith reasonable. How many Townes have you taken
in this Summer?   40
Ismenus.   How many Stagges have you beene at the death of this
grasse?
Timantus.   A number. 'Pray how is the Province setled?
Ismenus.   Prethee how does the dunne Nagge?
Timantus.   I thinke you mocke me my Lord.
Ismenus.   Mocke thee? Yes by my troth doe I: why what wouldst
thou have me doe with thee? Art good for any thing else?

Enter Leontius, Bacha, Dorialus, Agenor,
Nisus, Telamon.

Leucippus.   My good *Ismenus*, hold me by the wrist:
And if thou see'st me fainting, wring me hard,
For I shall soone againe else——   *Kneeles.* 50
Leontius.   Welcome my sonne; rise, I did send for thee
Backe from the Province, by thy Mothers counsell,
Thy good Mother here, who loves thee well:
She would not let me venture all my Joy
Amongst my enemies: I thanke thee for her,
And none but thee, I tooke her on thy word.
Leucippus [*aside to* Ismenus].   Pinch harder.
Leontius.   And she shall bid thee welcome: I have now
Some neere affayres, but I will drinke a Health
To thee a non: Come *Telamon*, Ime growne   60
Lustier, I thanke thee for't, since I marryed;

50 soone] *i.e.* sound *or* swoon

I can stand now alone, why *Telamon*,
And never stagger.   *Exit* Leontius, Telamon.
Bacha.   Welcome most noble sir, whose fame is come
Hither before you: out alas you scorne me,
And teach me what to doe.
Leucippus.   No, you are my Mother.
Bacha.   Farre unworthy of that name God knowes:
But trust me, here before these Lords,
I am no more but Nurse unto the Duke;
Nor will I breede a faction in the State,   70
It is too much for me that I am rays'd
Unto his bed, and will remaine the servant
Of you that did it.
Leucippus.   Madame I will serve you
As shall become me. [*Aside*] O dissembling woman!
Whom I must reverence though. Take from thy quiver,
Suer-aymd *Apollo*, one of thy swift darts,
Headed with thy consuming golden beames,
And let it melt this body into mist,
That none may finde it.
Bacha.   Shall I begge my Lords
This Roome in private for the Prince and me?   80
                    Exeunt all but Leucippus *and* Bacha.
Leucippus [*aside*].   What will she say now?
Bacha [*aside*].   I must still enjoy him:
Yet there is still left in me a sparke of woman,
That wishes hee would move it, but he stands,
As if hee grewe there with his eyes on earth.——
Syr, you and I when we were last together
Kept not this distance as we were afraide
Of blasting by our selves.
Leucippus.   Madame tis true,
Heaven pardon it.
Bacha.   Amen Syr. You may thinke
That I have done you wrong in this strange marriage.
Leucippus.   Tis past now.
Bacha.   But it was no fault of mine: 90

The world had calld me madde, had I refusde
The King: nor layde I any traine to catch him,
It was your owne Oathes did it.

Leucippus.   Tis a truth
That takes my sleepe away, but woud to Heaven,
If it had so beene pleasde, you had refusde him,
Though I had gratifide that courtesie
With having you my selfe: But since tis thus,
I doe beseech you that you will bee honest
From henceforth, and not abuse his credulous Age,
Which you may easily doe. As for my selfe   100
What I can say you know alas too well
Is tyde within me, here it will sit like lead,
But shall offend no other; it will plucke mee
Backe from my entrance into any myrth,
As if a servant came, and whisperd with mee
Of some Friends death: but I will beare my selfe,
To you, with all the due obedience
A sonne owes to a Mother: more then this,
Is not in mee, but I must leave the rest
To the just gods: who in their blessed time,   110
When they have given me punishment enough,
For my rash sinne, will mercifully finde
As unexpected meanes to ease my griefe
As they did now to bring it.

Bacha [*aside*].   Growne so godly:
This must not bee.——And I wilbe to you,
No other then a natural Mother ought:
And for my honestie, so you will sweare
Never to urge me, I shall keep it safe
From any other.

Leucippus.   Blesse mee, I should urge you?

Bacha.   Nay but sweare then that I may be at peace,   120
For I doe feele a weaknesse in my selfe,
That can denie you nothing; if you tempt me,
I shall embrace sinne as it were a friend,
And runne to meet it.

Leucippus. If you knew how farre
It were from mee, you would not urge an Oath.
But for your satisfaction, when I tempt you——
Bacha. Sweare not:——I cannot move him:——this sad talke
Of things past helpe, does not become us well.
Shall I send one for my Musitions, and weele daunce?
Leucippus. Dance Madame? 130
Bacha. Yes, a *lavalta.*
Leucippus. I cannot dance Madam.
Bacha. Then lets be mery.
Leucippus. I am as my Fortunes bidde me.
Doe not you see mee sowre?
Bacha. Yes. And why thinke you I smile?
Leucippus. I am so farre from any joy my selfe,
I cannot fancie a cause of myrth.
Bacha. Ile tell you, we are alone——
Leucippus. Alone? 140
Bacha. Yes.
Leucippus. Tis true, what then?
Bacha. What then?
You make my smiling now break into laughter:
What think you is to be don then?
Leucippus. We should pray to Heaven for mercie.
Bacha. Pray, that were a way indeede
To passe the time, but I will make you blush,
To see a bashfull woman teach a man
What wee should doe alone,——trye againe 150
If you can finde it out.
Leucippus. I dare not thinke
I understand you.
Bacha. I must teach you then;
Come, kisse me.
Leucippus. Kisse you?
Bacha. Yes, be not ashamde:
You did it not your selfe, I will forgive you.

Leucippus.   Keepe you displeased gods, the due respect
I ought to beare unto this wicked woman,
As shee is now my Mother, fast within mee,
Least I adde sins to sinnes, till no repentance
Will cure mee.
Bacha.   Leave these melancholly moodes,   160
That I may sweare thee welcome on thy lippes
A thousand times.
Leucippus.   Pray leave this wicked talke,
You doe not knowe to what my Fathers wrong
May urge mee.
Bacha.   Ime carelesse, and doe weigh
The world, my life, and all my after hopes
Nothing without thy Love: mistake me not,
Thy Love, as I have had it, free and open
As wedlock is, within it selfe, what say you?
Leucippus.   Nothing.
Bacha.   Pitty me, beholde a Dutchesse
Kneeles for thy mercie, and I sweare to you,
Though I should lye with you, it is no Lust,   170
For it desires no change, I could with you
Content my selfe: what answere will you give?
Leucippus.   They that can answere must be lesse amazde,
Then I am now: you see my teares deliver
My meaning to you.
Bacha.   Shall I be contemd?
Thou art a beast, worse then a savage beast,
To let a Lady kneele, to begge that thing
Which a right man would offer.
Leucippus.   Tis your will Heaven:
But let me beare me like my selfe,
How ever shee does.
Bacha.   Were you made an Eunuch,   180
Since you went hence? yet they have more desire
Then I can finde in you: How fond was I
To beg thy love? Ile force thee to my will.

157 fast] Mason; Hast Q 1–F 2

Doest thou not know that I can make the King
Dote as my list? yeeld quickly, or by Heaven
Ile have thee kept in prison for my purpose,
Where I will make thee serve my turne, and have thee
Fed with such meates as best shall fit my endes
And not thy health, why doest not speake to mee?
And when thou doest displease mee, and art growne   190
Lesse able to performe; then I will have thee
Kill'd and forgotten: Are you striken dumbe?
Leucippus.   All you have nam'de, but making of me sinne
With you, you may commaund, but never that;
Say what you will, Ile heare you as becomes me,
If you speake wickedly, I will not follow
Your counsell, neither will I tell the world
To your disgrace, but give you the just honour
That is due from me to my Fathers wife.
Bacha.   Lord how full of wise formality   200
You are grown of late: but you were telling mee
You could have wisht that I had marry'd you,
If you will sweare so yet, Ile make away
The King.
Leucippus.   You are a strumpet.
Bacha.   Nay, I care not
For all your Raylings: They will Batter walls
And take in Townes, as soone as trouble mee.
Tell him, I care not, I shall undoe you only,
Which is no matter.
Leucippus.   I appeale to you still,
And for ever, that are and cannot be other.
Madame I see tis in your power   210
To worke your will on him: And I desire you
To lay what traines you will for my wished death,
But suffer him to finde his quiet grave
In peace; Alas he never did you wrong:
And further I beseech you pardon mee,
For the ill word I gave you, for how ever

*185 as my list] *stet* Q1–F2   *196 wickedly] Dyce; *omit* Q1–F2

374

You may deserve it, it became not mee
To call you so, but passion urges mee
I know not whether: my heart breake now,
And ease mee ever.

Bacha.　　　　　Pray you get you hence　　　　　　　220
With your goodly humor, I am weary of you extreamly.

Leucippus.　Trust mee, so am I of my selfe too:
Madame, Ile take my leave; gods set all right.

Bacha.　Amen, Syr get you gone;　　　　[Exit Leucippus.]
Am I denyde? it does not trouble mee
That I have mov'd, but that I am refusde:
I have lost my patience: I will make him know
Lust is not Love, for Lust will finde a mate
While there are men, and so will I: and more
Then one, or twenty.

　　　　　　　　Enter Timantus.

　　　　　Yonder is Timantus,　　　　　　　　　230
A fellow voyde of any worth to raise himselfe,
And therfore like to catch at any evill
That will but plucke him uppe; him will I make
Mine owne.——　Timantus.

Timantus.　　　　　Maddame?

Bacha.　　　　　　　　Thou knowest well
Thou wert, by chance, a meanes of this my raising:
Brought the Duke to me, and though t'were but chance
I must reward thee.

Timantus.　　　　I shall bend my service
Unto your Highnes.

Bacha.　　　　　But doe it then entirely,
And in every thing: And tell mee, Couldst thou nowe
Thinke that thing thou wouldst not doe for mee?　　　240

Timantus.　Noe by my soule Maddame.

Bacha.　　　　　　　Then thou art right.
Goe to my Lodging, and Ile follow thee
With my instruction.　　　　　　Exit Timantus.

　　217 deserve it, it] deserve it Q1–F2　　　*221 goodly] stet Q1–F2

I doe see allready,
This prince that did but now contemne mee, dead:
Yet will I never speake an evill word
Unto his Father of him, till I have wonne
A beliefe I love him, but Ile make
His vertues his undoing, and my praises
Shall be so many swords against his brest,
Which once performde, Ile make *Urania*   250
My Daughter, the Kings heyre, and plant my Issue,
In this large Throne: Nor shall it bee withstood,
They that begin in Lust, must end in blood.

Exit.

Enter Dorialus, Agenor, Nisus.   [III. iii]

Dorialus. Wee live to knowe a fine time, Gentlemen.
Nisus. And a fine Duke, that through his doting age suffers him selfe to be a childe againe under his Wives tuition.
Agenor. All the Land holds in that tenor too: in womans service! sure we shall learne to spinne.
Dorialus. No, thats too honest: we shall have other liberall Sciences taught us too soone; Lying, and Flattering, those are the studies now: and Murther shortly I know, wil be humanity. Gentlemen, if we live here we must be knaves, beleeve it.
Nisus. I cannot tell my Lord *Dorialus*, though my owne nature 10 hate it, if all determine to be knaves, Ile try what I can doe upon my selfe, thats certaine, I will not have my throat cut for my goodnes, the vertue will not quit the paine.
Agenor. But pray you tell mee, why is the Prince, now ripe and full experient, not made a doer in the State?
Nisus. Because he is honest.

Enter Timantus.

Timantus. Goodnes attend your Honours.
Dorialus. You must not be amongst us then.

3 selfe] Langbaine; *omit* Q1–F2
4 tenor] *a pun, as well, on* tenure, *which is the reading of* Seward
15 doer] Seward; dore Q1–F2

Timantus.   The Dutchesse, whose humble Servant I am prou'de to
be, would speake with you.   20
Agenor.   Sir we are pleas'd to wayte: when is it?
Timantus.   An houre hence my good Lords, and so I leave my
service.   [*Exit* Timantus.]
Dorialus.   This is one of her Ferrets that shee bolts businesse
out withall: this fellow, if hee were well ript, has all the linings
of a knave within him: how slye he lookes!
Nisus.   Have we nothing about our cloathes that he may catch at?
Agenor.   O' my conscience there's no treason in my dublet, if
there bee, my elboes will discover it, they are out.
Dorialus.   Faith, and all the harme that I can finde in mine is, 30
that they are not payd for, let him make what he can of that, so
he discharge that. Come, lets goe.

                                                        Exeunt.

                   Enter Bacha, Leontius, Telamon.   [III. iv]

Bacha.   And you shall finde sir
  What a blessing heaven gave you in such a sonne.
Leontius.   Pray gods I may. Lets walk and change our subject.
Bacha.   O sir, can any thing come sweeter to you,
  Or strike a deeper joy into your heart
  Then your sons vertue?
Leontius.   I allow his vertues:
  But tis not hansome thus to feed my self
  With such immoderate praises of mine own.
Bacha.   The subject of our commendations
  Is it selfe growne so infinite in goodnes,   10
  That all the glory wee can lay upon it,
  Though we should open volumes of his praises,
  Is a meere modesty in his expression,
  And shewes him lame still, like an ill wrought peece
  Wanting proportion.
Leontius.   Yet still he is a man,
  And subject still to more inordinate vices,

─────────────────────────────────────
  *32 that] *stet* Q1–F2   8 immoderate] Langbaine; moderate Q1–F2

                              377

Then our love can give him blessings.

Bacha.   Else hee were a god:
Yet so neere as he is, hee comes to heaven,
That we may see so farre as flesh can poynt us
Things onely worthy them, and onely these   20
In all his actions.

Leontius.   This is too much my Queene.

Bacha.   Had the gods lov'd mee, that my unworthy wombe
Had bred this brave man.

Leontius.   Still you runne wrong.

Bacha.   I would have liv'd upon the comfort of him,
Fed on his growing hopes.

Leontius.   This touches me.

Bacha.   I know no friends, nor being, but his vertues.

Leontius.   You have layd out words inough upon a subject——

Bacha.   But words cannot expresse him sir:
Why what a shape Heaven has conceiv'd him in,
Oh Nature made him up!

Leontius.   I wonder Dutches——   30

Bacha.   So you must: for lesse then admiration
Loses this god-like man.

Leontius.   Have you done with him?

Bacha.   Done with? ô good gods what qualities
Thus passe by us without reverence!

Leontius.   I see no such perfection.

Bacha.   O deere Syr:
You are a father, and those joyes to you,
Speake in your heart, not in your tongue.

Leontius.   This leaves a tast behind it worse then physick.

Bacha.   Then for his wisedome, valour, good Fortune,
And all those Friends of honour, they are in him   40
As free and naturall as passions in a Woman.

Leontius.   You make me blush at all these yeares
To see how blindely you have flung your praises

---

*17 blessings] Seward; blessing Q1–F2   24 I] Q2; A Q1
33 qualities] Colman; frailties Q1–F2   34 Thus] Q2 (thus); this Q1
*39 for his] Seward; for all his Q1–F2

378

Upon a Boye, a very childe, and worthlesse,
Whilst I live, of these Honours.

Bacha.　I would not have my love Syr make my toung
Show me so much a woman as to praise
Or dispraise, where my will is, without reason
Or generall allowance of the people.

Leontius.　Allowance of the people, what allow they?　　　50

Bacha.　Al I have sed for truth, and they must doe it,
And dote upon him: love him, and admire him.

Leontius.　Howes that?

Bacha.　For in this youth and noble forwardnes
All things are bound together that are kingly,
A fitnesse to bear rule——

Leontius.　No more.

Bacha.　And soveraintie, not made to know command——

Leontius.　I have sed: no more.

Bacha.　I have done Syr though unwilling, and pardon me.　　60

Leontius.　I doe, not a word more.

Bacha [*aside*].　I have gin thee poyson
Of more infection then the Dragons tooth
Or the grosse Ayre ore heated.

Enter Timantus.

Leontius.　*Timantus* when saw you the prince?

Timantus.　I left him now Syr.

Leontius.　Tell me truely,
Out of your free opinion without courting,
How you like him?

Timantus.　How I like him?　　　70

Leontius.　Yes, for you in conversation
May see more then a Father.

Bacha [*aside*].　It workes.

Timantus.　Your grace has chosen out an ill observer.

Leontius.　Yes I meane of his Ill: you take rightly.

54 this youth] *i.e.* this his youth (Dyce)
54 forwardnes] Q2; frowardnes Q1
64.1 *Enter* Timantus.] Q3; *omit* Q1–2

379

Timantus.   But you take me wrong: All I know by him
I dare deliver boldly: He is the store-house
And head of vertue, your great selfe excepted,
That feeds the Kingdome.
Leontius.   These are flatteries:
Speake me his vices, there you doe a service   80
Worth a Fathers thankes.
Timantus.   Syr, I cannot.
If there bee any, sure they are the times
Which I could wish lesse dangerous.
But pardon me, I am too bolde.
Leontius.   You are not:
Forward and open what these dangers are.
Timantus.   Nay good Syr.
Leontius.   Nay fall not off againe, I will have all.
Timantus.   Alas Syr, what am I, you should believe
My eyes or eares so suttle to observe
Faults in a State? all my maine busines   90
Is service to your Grace, and necessaries
For my poore life.
Leontius.   Doe not displease me Syrrha,
But that you know tell mee, and presently.
Timantus.   Since your Grace will have it
Ile speake it freely: Always my obedience
And Love, preserv'd unto the Prince.
Leontius.   Prethee to the matter.
Timantus.   For Syr if you consider
How like a Sunne in all his great employments,
How full of heate——
Leontius.   Make me understand what I desire.   100
Timantus.   And then at his returne——
Leontius.   Doe not anger mee.
Timantus.   Then thus Syr, All mislike yee,
As they would do the gods, if they did dwell with em.
Leontius.   What?

78 vertue,...excepted,] Q3; ~ :...~ ∧ Q1–2
97 *Leontius.*] Q2; *Timan.* Q1

Timantus.   Talke and prate, as their ignorant rages leades em,
   Without Allegeance or Religion.
   For Heavens sake have a care of your owne person,
   I cannot tell, theyr wickednes may leade
   Farther then I dare thinke yet.
Leontius.   O base people.   110
Timantus.   Yet the prince,
   For whom this is pretended may perswade em,
   And no doubt will, vertue is ever watchfull,
   But be you still secur'de and comforted.
Leontius.   Heaven how have I offended, that this rod
   So heavy and unnaturall, should fall upon mee
   When I am olde and helplesse.
Timantus.   Brave Gentleman,
   That such a madding love shuld follow thee,
   To robbe thee of a Father: All the Court
   Is full of dangerous whispers.
Leontius.   I perceive it,   120
   And spight of all theyr strengths will make my safetie:
   Ile cut him shorter.
Bacha.   What a fowle Age is this,
   When Vertue is made a sworde to smite the vertuous?
   Alas, alas!
Leontius.   Ile teach him to flye lower.
Timantus.   By no means Syr, rather make more your love,
   And hold your favour to him: for tis now
   Impossible to yoke him, if his thoughts,
   As I must nere believe, run with their rages:
   Hee never was so innocent, but what reason
   His grace has to with draw his love from mee   130
   And other good men that are neere your person
   I cannot yet finde out: I know my duety
   Has ever bene attending.
Leontius.   Tis too plaine:

115 how] Q2; you Q1
*122 Ile cut him shorter.] Q1+ *then follow with:* Leon. Ile cut him shorter first,
then let him rule. (Q2+ *drop* Leon.)   *129 never] *stet* Q1–F2

He meanes to play the villaine, Ile prevent him,
Not a word more of this, be private.   *Exit* Leontius.
Timantus.   Madame ti's done.
Bacha.   He cannot escape mee. Have you spoken with the noble
men?
Timantus.   Yes Madame they are heere: I waite a further service.
Bacha.   Still let it be the prince, you neede no more instructions. 140
Timantus.   No I have it.   *Exit* Timantus.

Enter Dorialus, Nisus, Agenor.

Bacha [aside].   That foole that willingly provokes a woman,
Has made him selfe another evil Angell,
And a newe Hell, to which all other torments
Are but meere pastime:——Now my Noble Lordes
You must excuse mee that unmannerly
Wee have broke your private businesse.
Agenor.   Your good grace may command us, and that.
Bacha.   Faith my Lord *Agenor*: Tis so good a cause
I am confident, you cannot loose by it.   150
Dorialus [aside].   Which way does shee Fish now? The Divell is
but a Foole to a right woman.
Nisus.   Madame wee must needes winne in doing service
To such a gratious Ladie.
Bacha.   I thanke you, and will let you know the businesse,
So I may have your helpes: never be doubtfull,
For tis so just a cause, and will to you
Upon the knowledge, seeme so honourable,
That I assure my selfe your willing harts
Will strait bee for mee in it.   160
Agenor [aside].   If she should prove good now, what wert like?
Dorialus [aside].   Thunder in Januarie, or a good woman, thats
stranger then all *Affricke*.
Bacha.   It shall not neede your wonder, this it is;
The Duke you know is olde, and rather subject
To ease and prayers now, then all those troubles,
Cares, and continuall watchings, that attend

140 Still let it be] Till yet be Q 1–F 2

A kingdomes safetie: therefore to prevent
The fall of such a flourishing Estate
As this has ever bene, and to put off   170
The murmure of the people that increase
Against my government, which the gods knowe
I onely feele the trouble of: I present
The prince unto your loves, a Gentleman
In whome all Excellencies are knit together,
All peeces of a true man, let your prayers
Winne from the Duke halfe his Vexation,
That he may undertake it, whose discretion
I must confesse, though it be from the Father,
Yet now is stronger, and more apte to governe.   180
Tis not my owne desire, but all the Lands,
I know the weakenesse of it.

Nisus.   Madam, this noble care and love has won us
For ever to your loves, weele to the King,
And since your Grace has put it in our mouthes,
Weele winne him with the cunningst words we can.

Dorialus [*aside*].   I was never cousend in a woman before, for
commonly they are like Apples: If once they bruse they will growe
rotten through, and serve for nothing but to asswage swellings.

Bacha.   Good Lords delay no time since tis your good pleasures 190
To thinke my counsell good, and by no meanes
Let the prince knowe it, whose affections
Will stirre mainely against it; besides his Father,
May hold him dangerous, if it be not carryed
So that his forward will appeare not in it,
Goe, and be happie.

Dorialus.   Well, I would not bee Chronikled as thou wilt be for a
good woman, for all the world.

Nisus.   Madame, wee kisse your hands, and so inspird,
Nothing but hapinesse can crowne our prayers.   200

                                              Exeunt.

172 knowe] Langbaine (know); knowes Q 1–F 2
*181 Lands,] Q 2; ~ ₐ Q 1   184 loves] Q 3; lives Q 1–2
199 inspird,] Seward; inspire. Q 1–F 2

Enter Leucippus, Ismenus.   IV.i

Leucippus.   And thus she has usd me, ist not a good mother?
Ismenus.   Why killed you her not?
Leucippus.   The Gods forbid it.
Ismenus.   S'light, if all the women ithe world were barren, shee
had dyde.
Leucippus.   But tis not reason directs thee thus.
Ismenus.   Then have I none at all, for all I have in mee directs mee:
Your Father's in a pretty Rage.
Leucippus.   Why.
Ismenus.   Nay, tis well, if hee knowe himselfe, but some of the   10
Nobilitie have delivered a petition to him: whats int, I know not,
but it has put him to his trumps: hee has taken a months time to
answere it, and chafes like himselfe.

Enter Leontius, Bacha, [Timantus,] *and* Telamon.

Leucippus.   Hee's here *Ismenus.*
Leontius.   Set me downe *Telamon. Leucippus*——
Leucippus.   Sir.
Bacha.   Nay good sir bee at peace, I dare sweare
Hee knew not of it.
Leontius.   You are foolish: peace.
Bacha.   All will goe ill, deny it boldly sir,
Trust me he cannot proove it by you.
Leucippus.   What!
Bacha.   Youle make all worse too with your facing it.   20
Leucippus.   What is the matter!
Leontius.   Knowst thou that petition?
Looke on it well: wouldst thou be joynd with mee
(Unnaturall childe to be weary of me)
Ere Fate esteeme me fit for other worlds.
Bacha.   May be he knowes not of it.
Leucippus.   O strange carriages!
Sir, As I have hope that there is any thing
To reward doing well, my usages

IV.i] *Actus quarti. Cœna prima* Q1   7 have] Q2; gave Q1

Which have beene (but tis no matter what)
Have put me so farre from the thought of Greatnes,
That I should welcome it like a disease   30
That grew upon me, and I could not cure.
They are my enemies that gave you this,
And yet they call me friend, and are themselves
I feare abus'd. I am weary of my life,
For Gods sake take it from me: it creates
More mischiefe in the State then it is worth.
The usage I have had, I know would make
Wisedome her selfe run frantick through the streetes,
And Patience quarrell with her shaddow.
Sir, this sword——   40
Bacha.   Alas: helpe for the love of heaven,
Make way through me first, for he is your father.
Leontius.   What, would he kill me?
Bacha.   No sir, no.
Leontius.   Thou alwaies mak'st the best ont: but I feare——
Leucippus.   Why doe you use me thus? who ist can thinke
That I would kill my father, that can yet
Forbeare to kill you? Here sir is my sword,
I dare not touch it, lest she say againe
I would have kild you: let me not have mercy   50
When I most neede it, if I would not change
Place with my meanest servant. [*To her*] Let these faults
Be mended Madame: if you saw how ill
They did become you, you would part with them.
Bacha.   I told the Duke as much before.
Leucippus.   What? what did you tell him?
Bacha.   That it was onely an ambition,
Nurst in you by your youth, provokt you thus,
Which age would take away.
Leontius.   It was his doing then: come hither Love.   60
Bacha.   No indeed sir.
Leucippus.   How am I made, that I can beare all this?
If any one had us'd a friend of mine
Nere this, my hand had carryed death about it.

25   385   BDW

Leontius. Lead me hence *Telamon*:
Come my deare *Bacha*, I shall finde time for this.
Ismenus.   Madame, you know I dare not speake before the King;
but you know well, if not Ile tell it you, you are the most wickedst,
and most murderous strumpet that ever was call'd Woman.
Bacha.   My Lord,   70
What I can do for him he shall command me.
Leontius.   I know thou art too kinde; away I say.
                                    Exit Leontius, Bacha, Timantus, Telamon.
Ismenus.   Sir, I am sure we dreame: this cannot be.
Leucippus.   O that we did, my wickednes has brought
All this to passe, else I should beare my selfe——

            Enter Urania, [*passes over the stage*].

Ismenus.   Looke, doe you see whose there? your vertuous Mothers
issue: kill her, yet take some little pidling revenge.
Leucippus.   Away, the whole Court calles her vertuous;
For they say, she is unlike her mother
And if so she can have no vice.   80
Ismenus.   Ile trust none of em that come of such a breed.
Leucippus.   But I have found
A kinde of love in her to me: alas,
Thinke of her death! I dare be sworne for her,
She is as free from any hate to me
As her bad mothers full. She was brought up
Ith Country, as her tongue will let you know
If you but talke with her, with a poore Unkle,
Such as her mother had.

            Enter Urania [*againe*].

Ismenus.   Shees come againe.   90
Urania.   I would fene speake to the good Marquesse
My brother, if I but thought he could abaid me.
Leucippus.   Sister, how doe you.
Urania.   Very well I thanke you.
Ismenus.   How does your good mother?

                    *75 selfe——] ~ . Q1–F2
                            386

Leucippus.   Fye, fye, *Ismenus* for shame,
  Mocke such an innocent soule as this?
Urania.   Feth a she be no good, God may her so.
Leucippus.   I know you wish it with your heart dear sister,
  But she is good I hope.   100
Ismenus.   Are you so simple, to make so much of this? Doe you
  not know that all her wicked mother labours for, is but to rayse
  her to your right, and leave her this Dukedome.
Urania.   I, but nere sir be afred;
  For though she take th'ungainst weas she can,
  Ile nere hat fro you.
Leucippus.   I should hate my selfe *Ismenus*;
  If I should thinke of her simplicity,
  Ought but extreamely well.
Ismenus.   Nay as you will.   110
Urania.   And though she be my Mother,
  If she take any course to doe you wrong,
  If I can seet, youst quickly heare ont sir:
  And so Ile take my leave.
Leucippus.   Farewell good Sister, I thanke you.   *Exit* Urania.
Ismenus.   You believe all this?
Leucippus.   Yes.   *Enter* Timantus.

Ismenus.   A good faith doth well, but mee thinkes it were no harde
  matter now, for her Mother to send her: yonder's one you may
  trust if you will too.   120
Leucippus.   So I will,
  If he can shew me as apparant signes
  Of truth as shee did; Does he weepe *Ismenus*?
Ismenus.   Yes, I think so: some goods happend I warrant; Doe
  you heare you? What honest man has scapd miserie, that you are
  crying thus?
Timantus.   Noble *Ismenus*, wheres the Prince?
Ismenus.   Why there; hast wept thine eyes out?
Timantus.   Syr, I beseech you heare mee.
Leucippus.   Well, speake on.
Ismenus.   Why, will you heare him?   130

Leucippus.   Yes *Ismenus*, why?

Ismenus.   I would heare blasphemy as willingly.

Leucippus.   You are to blame.

Timantus.   No Syr: Hee is not to blame;
   If I were as I was.

Ismenus.   Nor as thou art, yfaith a whit to blame.

Leucippus.   Whats your busines?

Timantus.   Faith Syr, I am ashamed to speake before you,
   My conscience tells me I have injurd you,
   And by the earnest instigation
   Of others have not done you to the King   140
   All wayes the best and friendliest offices,
   Which pardon mee, or I will never speake.

Ismenus.   Never pardon him and silence a knave.

Leucippus.   I pardon thee.

Timantus.   Your mother sure is naught.

Leucippus.   Why shouldst thou thinke so?

Timantus.   O noble Syr, your honest eyes perceive not
   The dangers you are led to; shame upon her,
   And what fell miseries the gods can thinke on
   Showre downe upon her wicked head, she has plotted,
   I know too well your death: would my poore life   150
   Or thousand such as mine is might be offered
   Like sacrifices up for your preserving,
   What free oblations would she have to glut her;
   But shee is mercilesse, and bent to ruine,
   If Heaven and good men steppe not to your reskue,
   And timely, very timely, O this Dukedome!
   I weepe, I weepe for the poore Orphanes ith Countrey
   Left without Friends; or parents.

Leucippus.   Now *Ismenus*, what thinke you of this fellow?
   This was a lying knave, a flatterer,   160
   Does not this love still shew him so?

Ismenus.   This love, this halter: if he prove not yet the cunningst,
   ranckest Rogue that ever canted, Ile never see man againe: I

149 Showre] Q2; Shewe Q1   152 preserving] Q2; presuming Q1
158 without] Weber; With but Q1–F2

know him to bring, and can interpret every new face he makes,
looke how he wrings like a good stoole for a teare: Take heede,
Children and Fooles first feele the smart, then weepe.

Leucippus.   Away, away, such an unkinde distrust,
Is worse then a dissembling, if it be one,
And sooner leades to mischiefe. I believe it,
And him an honest man: he could not carry   170
Under an evill cause so true a sorrow.

Ismenus.   Take heede, this is your Mothers scorpion, that carries
stings even in his teares, whose soule is a rancke poyson through:
Touch not at him, if you doe you are gone, if you had twenty lives:
I knewe him from a Roguish boy, when hee would poyson Dogges,
and keepe tame Toades. Hee lay with his Mother, and infected her,
and now shee begges ith Hospitall, with a patch of velvet, where
her Nose stood, like the queene of spades, and all her Teeth in her
purse. The Divell and this fellow are so neere, tis not yet knowne
which is the eviller Angell.   180

Leucippus.   Nay then I see tis spite: Come hether frend.
Hast thou not heard the cause yet that incensd
My mother to my death, for I protest
I feele none in my selfe.

Timantus.   Her will Syr, and ambition, as I thinke
Are the provokers of it as in women
Those two are ever powerfull to destruction,
Beside a hate of your still growing vertues,
Shee being onely wicked.

Leucippus.   Heavens defend me
As I am innocent, and ever have bin   190
From all immoderate thoughts and actions,
That carrie such rewards along with em.

Timantus.   Syr all I know, my duety must reveale,
My country and my love commaund it from mee,
For whom Ile lay my life downe. This night comming,
A Counsell is appointed by the Duke,
To sit about your apprehension:
If you dare trust my faith: which by all good things
Shall ever watch about you: goe along,

And to a place Ile guide you, where no word,   200
Shall scape without your hearing: Nor, no plot
Without discovering to you, which once known,
You have your answers and prevention.

Ismenus.   You are not so mad to go; shift of this fellow, you shall
bee rul'd once by a wise man: ratsbane get you gone, or——

Leucippus.   Peace, peace for shame, thy love is too suspitious,
Tis a way offered to preserve my life,
And I will take it: be my Guide *Timantus*,
And doe not minde this angry man, thou knowst him:
I may live to requite thee.   210

Timantus.   Sir, this service is done for vertues sake,
Not for reward, how ever he may hold me.

Ismenus.   The great pox on you: but thou hast that curse so much,
twill grow a blessing in thee shortly. Sir, for wisdomes sake court
not your death, I am your friend and subject, and I shall lose in
both: if I lov'd you not, I would laugh at you, and see you run
your neck into the noose, and cry a Woodcocke.

Leucippus.   So much of man, and so much fearefull; fye.
Prethee have peace within thee: I shall live
Yet many a golden day to hold thee heere   220
Deerest and neerest to me: Goe on *Timantus*.
I charge you by your love no more, no more.

                                        Exeunt Leucippus, Timantus.

Ismenus.   Goe, and let your owne rod whip you: I pity you. And
dog, if he miscarry thou shalt pay fort; Ile study for thy punishment,
and it shall last longer and sharper then a tedious Winter, till
thou blasphemst, and then thou diest and dambst.

                                        Exit.

                    Enter Leontius *and* Telamon.   [IV. ii]

Leontius.   I wonder the Dutchesse comes not.
Telamon.   She has heard sir your will to speake with her:
But there is something leaden at her heart
(Pray God it be not mortall) that even keepes her
From conversation with her selfe.

                                        390

Enter [Bacha] *the Dutchesse.*

Bacha.   O whither will yee my crosse affections pull me?
  Fortune, Fate, and you whose powers direct
  Our actions, and dwell within us: you that are Angells
  Guiding to vertue, wherefore have you given
  So strong a hand to evill? wherefore sufferd   10
  A Temple of your owne, you Deities,
  Where your faire selves dwelt onely, and your goodnes,
  Thus to be soyld with sinne?
Leontius.   Heaven blesse us all.
  From whence comes this distemper? speake my faire one.
Bacha.   And have you none, love and obedience,
  You ever faithfull Servants, to imploy
  In this strange story of impietie,
  But mee a Mother? Must I bee your strumpet,
  To lay blacke treason open, and in him
  In whome all sweetnes was: in whom my love   20
  Was prou'de to have a being, in whome Justice,
  And all the gods (for our imaginations)
  Can worke into a man, were more then vertues.
  Ambition downe to Hell, where thou wert fosterd,
  Thou hast poysond the best soule, the purest, whitest,
  And meerest innocentst it selfe that ever
  Mens greedy hopes gave life to.
Leontius.   This is still stranger:
  Lay this treason open to my correction.
Bacha.   O what a combat duety and affection
  Breedes in my bloud.
Leontius.   If thou concealst him may   30
  Beside my death the curses of the Countrey,
  Troubles of conscience, and a wretched ende,
  Bring thee unto a poore forgotten grave.
Bacha.   My being, for another tongue to tell it:
  O ease a mother! some good man that dares

  6 my] Q2; me Q1   *18 strumpet] *stet* Q1–F2   19 open] Seward; upon Q1–F2
  *21 prou'de] Q2; proud'de Q1   *35 O ease‿] Seward; Cease, Q1–F2

Speake for his King and Countrey: I am full
Of too much womans pittie: yet ô Heaven,
Since it concernes the safety of my soveraigne
Let it not be a cruelty in mee
Nor draw a Mothers name in question,   40
Amongst unborne people, to give up that man
To law and Justice that unrighteously
Has sought his fathers death: be deafe, be deafe Syr,
Your Sonne is the Offendor: Now have you all,
Would I might never speake againe.
Leontius.   My Sonne? Heaven helpe mee.
No more: I thought it: and since his life is growne
So dangerous, let them that gave him, take him:
Hee shall dye, and with him all my feares.
Bacha.   O use your mercie: you have a brave subject   50
To bestowe it on. Ile forgive him Syr:
And for his wrong to mee, Ile be before yee.
Leontius.   Durst his villenie extend to thee?
Bacha.   Nothing but heates of youth Syr.
Leontius.   Uppon my life
Hee sought my Bed.
Bacha.   I must confesse he loved mee,
Somewhat beyond a Sonne: and still pursude it
With such a Lust, I will not say Ambition,
That cleane forgetting all obedience,
And onely following his first heate unto mee,
Hee hotely sought your death, and me in Marriage.   60
Leontius.   O Villaine!
Bacha.   But I forget all: and am halfe ashamde
To presse a man so farre.

Enter Timantus.

Timantus.   Where is the Duke? for Gods sake bring me to him.
Leontius.   Here I am; Each corner of the Dukedome
Sends new affrights forth: what wouldst thou? speake.
Timantus.   I cannot Sir, my feare tyes up my tongue.

66 thou? speake.] Q2; ~ ∧ ~ ? Q1

392

Leontius.   Why, whats the matter?
Take thy courage to thee, and boldly speake,
Where are the Guard? In the Gods name, out with it.   70
Timantus.   Treason, treason.
Leontius.   In whome?
Bacha.   Double the Guard.
Timantus.   There is a fellow Syr——
Leontius.   Leave shaking man.
Timantus.   Tis not for feare, but wonder.
Leontius.   Well?
Timantus.   There is a fellow Syr, close ithe Lobby:
You othe Guarde, looke to the dore there.
Leontius.   But let me knowe the businesse.
Timantus.   O that the hearts of men shuld be so hardned
Against so good a Duke: for Gods sake Syr,
Seeke meanes to save your selfe. This wretched slave   80
Has his sword in his hand, I knowe his heart:
Oh it hath almost killd mee with the thought of it.
Leontius.   Where is hee?
                              Enter the Guard, to bring him in.
Timantus.   The Lobby Syr, close in a corner:
Looke to your selves, for Heavens sake,
Mee thinkes hee is here already.
Fellowes of the Guard be valiant.
Leontius.   Goe sirs, and apprehend him;
Treason shall never dare mee in mine owne Gates.
Timantus [*to* Bacha].   Tis done.   *There they bring the Prince in.*
Bacha [*to* Timantus].   And thou shalt finde it to thy best content. 90
Leontius.   Are these the comforts of my Age? theyre happy
That ende theyr dayes contented with a little,
And live aloofe from dangers: to a King
Every content doth a newe perill bring.
O let mee live no longer: shame of Nature,
Bastard to Honour, Traytor, Murderer,
Divell in a humane shape, A way with him,
Hee shall not breath his hote infection here.

                        83.1 *to*] *and* Q 1–F 2
                                 393

Leucippus.   Syr heare mee.

Leontius.   Am I or hee your Duke? away with him   100
 To a close prison: your Highnes now shall know,
 Such branches must be cropt before they growe.

Leucippus.   What ever Fortune comes, I bid it welcome,
 My innocencie is my Armor: Gods preserve you. *Exit [guarded]*.

Bacha.   Fare thee well.
 I shal never see so brave a Gentleman:
 Would I could weepe out his offences.

Timantus.   Or I could weepe out mine eyes.

Leontius.   Come Gentlemen,
 Weele determine presently about his death: 110
 Wee cannot be too forward in our safety:
 I am very sick, leade me unto my Bed.

                                                     Exeunt.

                Enter [first] Cittizen *and his* Boye.   [IV. iii]

1. Cittizen.   Syrrha, go fetch my Foxe from the Cutlers: Theres
money for the scowring: Tell him, I stoppe a Grote since the last
great Muster: Hee had in store Pitch for the bruze he tooke with
the Recoyling of his Gunne.

Boye.   Yes Syr.

1. Cittizen.   And doe you heare? when you come, Take downe my
Buckler, and sweepe the Copwebs off: and grinde the picke ont:
and fetch a Naile or two, and tacke on bracers: your Mistris made
a potlid ont, I thanke her, at her Mayds wedding, and burnt off
the handle.   10

Boye.   I will Syr.   *Exit.*

1. Cittizen.   Whoes within heere, hoe Neighbour, not styrring yet?

                [*Enter* second Cittizen.]

2. Cittizen.   O God morrow, god morrowe: what newes, what
newes?

1. Cittizen.   It holdes, he dyes this morning.

        108 could] Q2; would Q1
        *2 I stoppe a Grote] *stet* Q1–F2   7 ont] Seward; out Q1–F2

                          394

2. Cittizen.   Then happy man be his fortune, I am resolvde.

1. Cittizen.   And so am I, and fortie more good fellowes that wil not give their heads for the washing, I take it.

2. Cittizen.   Sfoote man, who would not hang in such good companie, and such a cause? A Fire, a Wife and Children: Tis 20 such a Jest that men should looke behinde em to the world, and let theyr honours, their honours Neighbour, slip.

1. Cittizen.   Ile give thee a pinte of Bastard and a rolle for that bare word,

2. Cittizen.   They say that we Taylors, are things that laye one another, and our Geese hatche us: Ile make some of um feele they are Geese ath game then.——
Ifack take down my Bill, tis ten to one I use it: [*Calls within.*]
Take a good heart man, all the low ward is ours, with a wett
finger.——   30
[*Calls within.*] And lay my Cut-fingred Gantlet ready for mee, that that I used to worke in, when the Gentlemen were up against us; a beaten out of towne, and almost out a debt to, for a plague on um, they never paid wel since. And take heede sirrah, your mistris heares not of this businesse: shees neere her time: yet if shee doe, I care not, shee may long for Rebellion, for shee has a divellish spirite.

1. Cittizen.   Come, lets call up the new Irenmonger: is as tough as steele, and has a fine wit in these resurrections. Are you stirring Neighbour?   40

3. Cittizen within.   O Good morrowe Neighbours, Ile come to you presently.

2. Cittizen.   Go too, this is his Mothers doing: shees a Polecat.

1. Cittizen.   As any is in the world.

2. Cittizen.   Then say I have hit it, and a vengeance on her, let her be what she will.

1. Cittizen.   Amen say I, shee has brought things to a fine passe with her wisedome, doe you marke it?

2. Cittizen.   One thing I am sure she has, the good old Duke she gives him pappe againe they say, and dandles him, and hangs a 50 corrall and bells about his necke, and makes him beleeve his

*33 a beaten] *stet* Q1

395

teeth will come agen; which if they did, and I he, I would worry
her as never curre was worried: I would neighbour, till my teeth
met I know where, but thats counsell.

Enter third Citizen.

3. Cittizen.   Good morrow neighbours: heare you the sadde
newes?
1. Cittizen.   Yes, would we knew as well how to prevent it.
3. Cittizen.   I cannot tell, me thinks twere no great matter, if men
were men: but——
2. Cittizen.   You do not twit me with my calling neighbor?   60
3. Cittizen.   No surely, for I know your spirit to be tall: pray be
not vext.
2. Cittizen.   Pray forward with your counsell:
I am what I am, and they that prove me, shall finde me to their
cost: do you marke mee neighbour, to their cost I say.
1. Cittizen.   Nay looke how soone you are angry.
2. Cittizen.   They shall neighbours: yes, I say they shall.
3. Cittizen.   I doe beleeve they shall.
1. Cittizen.   I know they shall.
2. Cittizen.   Whether you doe or no I care not two-pence, I am 70
no beast, I know mine owne strength neighbors; God blesse the
King, your companies is fayre.
1. Cittizen.   Nay neighbour now yee erre, I must tell you so and
yee were twentie neighbours.
3. Cittizen.   You had best goe peach, doe, peach.
2. Cittizen.   Peach, I scorne the motion.
3. Cittizen.   Doe, and see what followes: Ile spend an hundred
pound, and be two I care not, but Ile undo thee.
2. Cittizen.   Peach, ô disgrace: peach in thy face, and doe the
worst thou canst: I am a true man, and a free-man: peach!   80
1. Cittizen.   Nay looke, you will spoyle all.
2. Cittizen.   Peach!
1. Cittizen.   Whilst you two brawle together, the Prince will lose
his life.

63 *2. Cittizen.*] Q2; *1.* Q1

396

3. Cittizen.   Come, give me your hand, I love you well, are you for the action?

2. Cittizen.   Yes: but peach provokes me, tis a cold fruit, I feele it cold in my stomacke still.

3. Cittizen.   No more, Ile give you cake to disgest it.

Enter the fourth.

4. Cittizen [calls within].   Shut up my shop, and bee ready at a 90 call boyes, and one of you runne over my olde tucke with a few ashes, tis growne odious with tosting cheese: and burne a little giniper in my murrin, the maide made it her chamber-pot: an houre hence Ile come againe; and as you here from me, send me a cleane shirt.

3. Cittizen.   The Chandler by the wharfe, and it be thy will.

2. Cittizen.   Gossip good morrow.

4. Cittizen.   O good morrow Gossip: good morrow all, I see yee of one minde, you cleave so close together: come tis time, I have prepared a hundred if they stand.   100

1. Cittizen.   Tis well done: shall we sever, and about it?

3. Cittizen.   First lets to the Taverne, and a pynt a peece will make us Dragons.

2. Cittizen.   I will have no mercy, come what will of it.

4. Cittizen.   If my tucke hold Ile spit the Guard like Larks with sage betweene em.

2. Cittizen.   I have a foolish bil to reckon with em, wil make some of their hearts ake, and Ile lay it on: now shall I fight, twill doe you good to see me.

3. Cittizen.   Come Ile do something for the Towne to talke of 110 when I am rotten: pray God there bee enough to kill, thats all.

Exeunt.

Enter Dorialus, Nisus, Agenor.   [IV. iv]

Agenor.   How blacke the day begins!

Dorialus.   Can you blame it, and looke upon such a deed as shall be done this morning?

93 murrin] *i.e.* morion   98 yee] Q2; wee Q1

Nisus. Does the Prince suffer to day?

Dorialus. Within this houre they say.

Agenor. Well, they that are most wicked are most safe: twill be a strange Justice and a lamentable, gods keepe us from the too soone feeling of it.

Dorialus. I care not if my throat were next: for to live still, and live heere, were but to growe fat for the Shambles. 10

Nisus. Yet we must doe it, and thanke em too, that our lives may be accepted.

Agenor. Faith Ile go starve my selfe, or grow diseas'd, to shame the hangman; for I am sure hee shall be my Herald, and quarter me.

Dorialus. I a plague on him, hee's too excellent at armes.

Nisus. Will you goe see this sadde sight my Lord *Agenor*?

Agenor. Ile make a mourner.

Dorialus. If I could doe him any good I would goe,
The bare sight else will but afflict my spirit; 20
My prayers shall be as neere him as your eyes:
As you finde him setled,
Remember my love and service to his Grace.

Nisus. We will weepe for you sir, farewell.

Exeunt [Nisus, Agenor].

Dorialus. Farewel to all our happinesse, a long farewel.
Thou angry power, whether of heaven or hell,
That layst this sharpe correction on our Kingdome
For our offences, infinite and mighty,
O heare me, and at length be pleas'd, be pleas'd
With pitty to draw backe thy vengeance, 30
Too heavy for our weaknesse; and accept,
(Since it is your discretion, heavenly Wisedomes,
To have it so) this sacrifice for all,
That now is flying to your happinesse,
Onely for you most fit: let all our sinnes
Suffer in him. *A shoute within.*
Gods, whats the matter! I hope tis joy.
How now my Lords?

24 you] Q3; ioy Q1   *25 Farewel] stet Q1–F2

Enter Agenor *and* Nisus.

Nisus.   Ile tell you with that little breath I have,
More joy then you dare thinke; The Prince is safe   40
From danger.
Dorialus.   How!
Agenor.   Tis true, and thus it was; His houre was come
To lose his life, he ready for the stroke,
Nobly, and full of Saint-like patience,
Went with his Guard: which when the people saw,
Compassion first went out, mingled with teares,
That bred desires, and whispers to each other,
To doe some worthy kindnes for the Prince.
And ere they understood well how to doe,   50
Fury stept in, and taught them what to doe,
Thrusting on every hand to rescue him,
As a white innocent: then flew the rore
Through all the streetes, of *Save him, save him, save him*;
And as they cryde, they did; for catching up
Such sudden weapons as their madnesse shew them,
In short, they beat the Guard, and tooke him from em,
And now march with him like a royall Army.
Dorialus.   Heaven, heaven I thanke thee. What a slave was I
To have my hand so farre from this brave rescue,   60
'Tad beene a thing to bragge on when I was olde.
Shall we runne for a wager to the next Temple and give
thanks?
Nisus.   As fast as wishes.

                                              [*Exeunt.*]

Enter Leucippus *and* Ismenus: *the people*   [IV.v]
              within stoppes.

Leucippus.   Good friends goe home againe, there's not a man
Shall goe with me.
Ismenus.   Will you not take revenge? Ile call them on.
Leucippus.   All that love me depart:

                         399

I thanke you, and will serve you for your loves:
But I will thanke you more to suffer me
To governe em: once more, I doe beg yee,
For my sake to your houses.
All within.   Gods preserve you.
Ismenus.   And what house will you goe too?   10
Leucippus.   *Ismenus* I will take the wariest courses
That I can thinke of to defend my selfe,
But not offend.
Ismenus.   You may kill your mother, and never offend your
father, an honest man.
Leucippus.   Thou knowst I can scape now, thats all I looke for:
Ile leave.
Ismenus.   *Timantus,* a pox take him, would I had him here, I
would kill him at his owne weapon, single, sithes wee have built
inough on him: plague ont, Ime out of all patience: discharge such 20
an Army as this, that would have followed you without paying,
ô gods!
Leucippus.   To what end should I keepe em? I am free.
Ismenus.   Yes, free o'th Traytors, for you are proclaymed one.
Leucippus.   Should I therefore make my selfe one?
Ismenus.   This is one of your morall Philosophy is it? Heaven
blesse me from subtilties to undo my self with; but I know, if
reason her selfe were here, she would not part with her owne
safetie.
Leucippus.   Well, pardon *Ismenus,* for I know   30
My courses are most just; nor will I staine em
With one bad action: for thy selfe, thou knowst,
That though I may command thee, I shall be
A ready servant to thee if thou needst:
And so Ile take my leave.
Ismenus.   Of whome?
Leucippus.   Of thee.
Ismenus.   Heart, you shall take no leave of me.
Leucippus.   Shall I not?

7 em] *i.e.* their loves
*19 weapon, single, sithes] Q2 (~ ∧ ~ , ~); ~ ∧ ~ ∧ ~ Q1

Ismenus.   No by the gods shall you not: nay if you have no more 40
wit but to goe absolutely alone, Ile bee in a little.

Leucippus.   Nay prethee good *Ismenus* part with me.

Ismenus.   I wonnot yfaith, never move it any more; for by this
good light I wonnot.

Leucippus.   This is an ill time to be thus unruly:
Ismenus you must leave me.

Ismenus.   Yes if you can beat me away: else, the gods refuse me if
I will leave you till I see more reason; you sha'nt undoe your selfe.

Leucippus.   But why wilt not leave me?

Ismenus.   Why Ile tell you, Because when you are gone, then——— 50
life, if I have not forgot my reason——hell take mee: you put
mee out of patience so: O! marry when you are gone, then will
your Mother: a pox confound her, she never comes in my head
but she spoiles my memory to: there are a hundred reasons.

Leucippus.   But shew me one.

Ismenus.   Shew you, what a stirre here is, why I will shew you:
Doe you thinke; well, well, I know what I know, I pray come,
come. Tis in vaine: but I am sure. Divels take em, what doe I
meddle with em? You know your selfe. Soule, I thinke I am: is
there any man ith world? as if you knew not this already better 60
then I. Pish, pish, Ile give no reason.

Leucippus.   But I will tell thee one why thou shouldst stay:
I have not one friend in the Court but thou,
On whom I may be bold to trust to send mee
Any intelligence: and if thou lov'st me
Thou wilt doe this, thou needst not feare to stay,
For there are new-come Proclamations out,
Where all are pardoned but my selfe.

Ismenus.   Tis true, and in the same Proclamation your fine sister
Urania, whome you us'd so kindly, is proclaymd heyre apparant 70
to the Crowne.

Leucippus.   What though, thou mayst stay at home without
danger.

Ismenus.   Danger, hang danger, what tell you mee of danger?

Leucippus.   Why if thou wilt not do't, I think thou dar'st not.

51 hell] Q2; heele Q1

Ismenus.   I dare not: if you speake it in earnest, you are a boy.

Leucippus.   Well sir, if you dare, let me see you do't.

Ismenus.   Why so you shall, I will stay.

Leucippus.   Why God a mercy.

Ismenus.   You know I love you but too well.   80

Leucippus.   Now take these few directions: farewell,

Send to me by the wariest wayes thou canst:

I have a soule tells me we shall meete often.

The gods protect thee.

Ismenus.   Poxe o' me selfe for an Asse, Ime crying now, God be
with you, if I never see you againe: why then pray get you gone,
for griefe and anger wonnot let me know what I say. Ile to the
Court as fast as I can, and see the new heyre apparant.

Exeunt.

Enter Urania [*in boys clothes*] *and her woman.*   V. i

Urania.   What, hast thou found him?

Woman.   Madame he is comming in.

Urania.   Gods blesse my brother where so ere he is:

And I beseech you keepe me fro the bed

Of any naughtie Tyrant whom my mother

Would ha me have to wrong him.

Enter Ismenus.

Ismenus.   What would her new Grace have with me?

Urania.   Leave us a while.   *Exit* Woman.

My Lord *Ismenus,*

I pray for the love of heaven and God,

That you would tell me one thing, which I know   10

You can doe weele.

Ismenus.   Wheres her faine Grace?

Urania.   You know me weel inough, but that you mock,

I am she my sen.

Ismenus.   God blesse him that shall bee thy husband; if thou
wearst breeches thus soone, thoult bee as impudent as thy mother.

V.i] *Actus Quintus. Scœni Primi.* Q 1   8 Woman] Q 3; *M.* Q 1–2

Urania.   But will you tell me this one thing?

Ismenus.   What ist? if it be no great matter whether I doe or no, perhaps I will.

Urania.   Yes faith tis matter.   20

Ismenus.   And what ist?

Urania.   I pray you
Let me know whaire the Prince my brother is.

Ismenus.   Ifaith you shan be hangd first; is your mother so foolish to thinke your good Grace can sift it out of me?

Urania.   If you have any mercy left i'you
To a poore wench tell me.

Ismenus.   Why, wouldst not thou have thy braines beat out for this, to follow thy mothers steps so young?

Urania.   But beleeve me, she knowes none of this.   30

Ismenus.   Beleeve you? why, do you thinke I never had wits? or that I am runne out of them? how should it belong to you to know, if I could tell?

Urania.   Why I will tell you, and if I speake false
Let the Divell ha me: Yonders a bad man,
Come from a Tayrant to my mother, and what name
They ha for him, good faith I cannot tell.

Ismenus.   An Embassador.

Urania.   Thats it: but he would carry me away,
And have me marry his Master; and Ile day   40
Ere I will ha him.

Ismenus.   But whats this to knowing where the Prince is?

Urania.   Yes, for you know all my mother does
Agen the Prince is but to ma me great.

Ismenus.   Pray, I know that too well, what then?

Urania.   Why I would goe to the good Marquesse my Brother,
And put my selfe into his hands, that so
He may preserve himselfe.

Ismenus.   O that thou hadst no seede of thy Mother in thee, and couldst meane this now.   50

Urania. Why feth I do,
Wou'd I might nere stirre more if I doe not.

23 me] Q2; we Q1

Ismenus. I shall prove a ridiculous foole, Ile be damnd else: hang
me if I doe not halfe beleeve thee.

Urania. By my troth you may.

Ismenus. By my troth I doe: I know Ime an Asse fort, but I
cannot helpe it.

Urania. And won you tell me then?

Ismenus. Yes faith will I, or any thing else ith world, for I think
thou art as good a creature as ever was borne. 60

Urania. But aile goe i' this ladst reparrell:
But you mun helpe me to Silver.

Ismenus. Helpe thee: why the Poxe take him that will not helpe
thee to any thing ith world, Ile helpe thee to Mony, and Ile doe't
presently to, and yet soule, if you should play the scurvie Harlotrie
little pockie baggage now and couzen mee, what then?

Urania. Why, an I do, wou'd I might nere see day agen.

Ismenus. Nay by this light I do not thinke thou wilt: Ile presently
provide thee mony and a letter.   *Exit* Ismenus.

Urania. I but Ile nere deliver it. 70
When I have found my Brother, I will begge
To serve him; but he shall never kno who I am;
For he must hate me then for my badde mother:
Ile say I am a countrey Lad that want a service,
And have streid on him by chance, lest he discover me;
I know I must not live long, but that taime
I ha to spend, shall be in serving him.
And though my Mother seeke to take his life away,
In ai day my brother shall be taught
That I was ever good, though she were naught. 80
                                          Exit.

                Enter Bacha *and* Timantus.   [V. ii]

Bacha. Runne away, the divell be her guide.

Timantus. Faith shees gone: theres a Letter, I found it in her
pocket. [*Aside*] Would I were with her, shees a hansome Lady, a
plague upon my bashfulnes, I had bobd her long agoe else.

o.1 Timantus.] Timantus: Bacha *reading a letter.* Q1–F2

Bacha.   What a base Whore is this, that after all   [*Reads.*]
My wayes for her advancement, should so poorely
Make vertue her undoer, and choose this time,
The King being deadly sicke, and I intending
A present marriage with some forraigne Prince,
To strengthen and secure my selfe. She writes here   10
Like a wise Gentlewoman, She will not stay:
And the example of her deare brother, makes her
Feare her selfe, to whome shee meanes to flye.

Timantus.   Why, who can helpe it?

Bacha.   Now povertie and Leacherie which is thy end, rot thee,
where ere thou goest with all thy goodnes.

Timantus.   Berlady theyle bruze her: and shee weare a brasse.
I am sure theyle breake stone walles: I have had experience of
them both, and they have made me desperate: but theres a
Messenger Madam come from the Prince with a Letter to *Ismenus,* 20
who by him returnes an answere.

Bacha.   This comes as pat as wishes: thou shalt presently away
Timantus.

Timantus.   Whither Madame?

Bacha.   To the Prince, and take the Messenger for guide.

Timantus.   What shall I doe there? I have done too much
mischiefe to be beleeved againe, or indeede, to scape with my head
on my backe if I be once knowne.

Bacha.   Thou art a weake shallow foole: get thee a disguise, and
withall, when thou comst before him, have a Letter faind to deliver 30
him; and then, as thou hast ever hope of goodnes by me, or after
me, strike one home stroke that shall not neede another: dar'st
thou? speake, dar'st thou? if thou fal'st off, goe bee a Rogue
againe, and lye and Pander to procure thy meate: darst thou?
speake to me.

Timantus.   Sure I shall never walke when I am dead, I have no
spirit: Madame, Ile bee drunke but Ile doe it, thats all my refuge.
                                                            Exit.

16 thou] Q2; to Q1   17 weare a] *i.e.* were of *as in* Q2+
*32–33 dar'st thou?] ~ ~ ∧ Q1–F2
34 thou?] Q2; ~ ∧ Q1

Bacha. Away, no more, then Ile rayse an Army whilst the King yet lives, if all the meanes and power I have can doe it I cannot tell. 40

Enter Ismenus *and three Lords* [Dorialus, Agenor, Nisus].

Ismenus. Are you inventing still? weele ease your studies.

Bacha. Why how now sawcy Lords?

Ismenus. Nay Ile shake yee, yes divell, I will shake yee.

Bacha. Doe not you know me Lords?

Nisus. Yes deadly sin we know ye, would we did not.

Ismenus. Doe you heare Whore, a plague a God upon thee, the Duke is dead.

Bacha. Dead!

Ismenus. I, wild-fire and brimstone take thee: good man hee is dead, and past those miseries which thou, salt infection-like, like a 50 disease, flungst upon his head. Dost thou heare, and twere not more respect in Woman-hood in generall then in thee, because I had a Mother, who I will not say shee was good, shee liv'd so neere thy time, I would have thee in vengeance of this man, whose peace is made in heaven by this time, tyde to a post, and dryde ith sunne, and after carryed about and shone at fayres for money, with a long storie of the divell thy father that taught thee to be whorish, envious, bloudy.

Bacha. Ha, ha, ha.

Ismenus. You fleering harlot, Ile have a horse to leape thee, and 60 thy base issue shall carry Sumpters. Come Lords, bring her along, weele to the Prince all, where her hell-hood shall waite his censure; and if he spare thee she Goat, may he lye with thee againe; and beside, mayst thou lay upon him some nastie foule disease that hate still followes, and his end, a dry ditch. Leade you corrupted whore, or Ile draw gode shall make you skippe: away to the Prince.

Bacha. Ha, ha, ha, I hope yet I shall come too late to finde him.

[*Exeunt.*]

Cornets. Cupid *from above.*   [V.iii]

The time now of my Revenge drawes neere;
Nor shall it lessen, as I am a god,
With all the cryes and prayers that have beene;
And those that be to come, tho they be infinite,
In neede and number.

[*Exit.*]

Enter Leucippus, Urania [*disguised*].   [V.iv]

Leucippus.   Alas poore boy, why dost thou follow me?
What canst thou hope for? I am poore as thou art.
Urania.   In good feth I shall be weell and rich enough
If you will love me, and not put me from you.
Leucippus.   Why dost thou choose out me boy to undo thee?
Alas for pitty, take another Master,
That may be able to deserve thy love
In breeding thee hereafter: me thou knowst not
More then my misery: and therefore canst not
Looke for rewards at my hands: would I were able,   10
My pretty knave, to doe thee any kindnes:
Truely good boy, I would upon my faith:
Thy harmelesse innocense mooves me at heart,
Wilt thou goe save thy selfe?
Why doest thou weepe? Alas I doe not chide thee.
Urania.   I cannot tell; if I goe from you Syr,
I shall nere dawne day more: Pray if you can
(I will bee true to you) let mee waite on you:
If I were a man, I would fight for you:
Sure you have some ill-willers, I would slay um.   20

1–5 The time...number.] Seward; *printed in* Q1–F2 *following* V.iv *and above the*
FINIS, *headed* Cupids Speech. *The stage-direction for* V.iii *is in its place, however,*
though as if completing V.ii.68 *with a direction.*
0.1 Urania] Colman; Urania: Leucippus *with a bloudy hankercher.* Q1–F2
16 *Urania.* I cannot tell....] *Lines 16–45 may just possibly be prose as printed in*
Q1–F2 (*save for ll.* 28–29 *as verse*) *but enough true pentameters exist to suggest that*
some sort of loose verse is intended

Leucippus.   Such harmelesse soules are ever Prophets——Well
I take thy wish, thou shalt be with mee still:
But prithee eate then, my good Boy:
Thou wilt die my childe if thou fasts one day more.
This foure dayes thou hast tasted nothing:
Goe into the Cave and eate: Thou shalt
Finde something for thee, to bring thy bloud agen,
And thy faire collour.
Urania.   I can not eate God thanke you,
But Ile eate to morrow.
Leucippus.   Thow't bee dead by that time.
Urania.   I should be well then, for you will not love me.   30
Leucippus.   Indeed I will.
(This is the prettiest passion that ere I felt yet:)
Why dost thou looke so earnestly upon me?
Urania.   You have fayre eyes Master.
Leucippus.   Sure the Boy dotes:——
Why dost thou sigh my childe?
Urania.   To thinke that such
A fine man should live, and no gay Lady love him.
Leucippus.   Thou wilt love me?
Urania.   Yes sure till I dye,
And when I am in heaven Ile eene wish for you.
Leucippus.   And Ile come to thee Boy.
(This is a love I never yet heard tell of:)   40
Come, thou art sleepy childe, goe in,
And Ile sit with thee:——heaven what portends this?
Urania.   You are sad, but I am not sleepy, woulde I
Could doe ought to make you merry: shall I sing?
Leucippus.   If thou wilt good boy.

[*Song.*]

Alas my boy, that thou shouldst comfort me,
And art farre worse then I!

33   thou] Q2; you Q1
*46 Alas] Q3; *Leucippus.* Alas Q1-2

408

Enter Timantus *with a letter disguised.*

Urania.   Lawe Master, theres one, looke to your sen.

Leucippus.   What art thou, that in this dismall place,
Which nothing could finde out but misery,   50
Thus boldly steps? Comfort was never here,
Here is nor foode, nor beds, nor any house
Built by a better Architect then beasts;
And ere you get a dwelling from one of them,
You must fight for it: if you conquer him,
He is your meate; if not, you must be his.

Timantus.   I come to you (for if I not mistake,
You are the Prince) from that most Noble Lord
Ismenus with a Letter.

Urania.   Alas, I feare I shall be discovered now.   60

Leucippus.   Now I feele my selfe the poorest of all mortall things.
Where is he that receives such courtesies,
But he has meanes to shew his gratefulnes
Some way or other? I have none at all:
I know not how to speake so much as well
Of thee but to these trees.

Timantus.   His Letters speake him sir——

Urania.   Gods keepe him but fro knowing me till I dye:
Aye me, sure I cannot live a day.

Leucippus *opening the Letter, the whilst* Timantus *runnes at him,*
and Urania *steppes before.*

O thou foule Traytor: How doe you Master?   70

Leucippus.   How dost thou my childe?——alas, looke on this,
It may make thee repentant, to behold
Those innocent drops that thou hast drawne from thence.
                            [Shews bloudy handkercher.]

Urania.   Tis nothing sir and you be well.

Timantus.   O pardon me, know you me now sir?
                            [Kneeles and discovers himselfe.]

51 steps] Q2 (stepst); stept Q1   54 a] Q3; *omit* Q1–2
*67–68 him...me] Mason; me...him Q1–F2
69.1 Leucippus *opening the Letter....]* Q1–F2 *place after l.* 66
71 this] Q3; his Q1–2

Leucippus.   How couldst thou finde me out?
Timantus.   We intercepted a Letter from *Ismenus,*
And the bearer directed me.
Leucippus.   Stand up *Timantus* boldly,
The world conceives that thou art guilty   80
Of divers treasons to the State and me:
But ô farre be it from the innocence
Of a just man to give a traytor death
Without a tryall: here thy Country is not
To purge thee or condemne thee; therefore
(A nobler tryall then thou dost deserve,
Rather then none at all) here I accuse thee
Before the face of heaven, to be a traytor
Both to the Duke my father and to me,
And the whole Land: speake, is it so or no?   90
Timantus.   Tis true sir, pardon me.
Leucippus.   Take heed *Timantus* how thou
Dost cast away thy selfe, I must proceede
To execution hastily if thou
Confesse it: speake once againe, ist so or no?
Timantus.   I am not guilty sir.
                        The Prince gets his sword and gives it him.
Leucippus.   Gods and thy sword acquit thee, here it is.
Timantus.   I will not use any violence against your Highnesse.
Leucippus.   At thy perill then, for this must be thy tryall:
And from henceforth looke to thy selfe.   100
Timantus.   I doe beseech you sir let me not fight.   [*Kneeles.*]
Leucippus.   Up, up againe *Timantus,*
There is no way but this beleeve me. Now if——
                        Timantus drawes his sword, and runnes at him when he
                        turnes aside. Fight here: [Timantus *falles.*]
Fye, fie *Timantus,* is there no usage can
Recover thee from basenesse? Wert thou longer
To converse with men, I would have chidde thee for this:

          *86–87 (A...all)] Weber;ₐ ~ ...~ ,ₐ Q1–F2
          *96.1 The Prince...him.] Fight here: The Prince...him. Q1–F2
          103.2 Fight here] Q1–F2 print before the stage-direction at l. 96.1

Be all thy faults forgiven.

Timantus.   O spare me sir, I am not fit for death.

Leucippus.   I thinke thou art not; yet trust me, fitter then

For life: Yet tell mee ere thy breath be gone,   110

Knowst of any other plots against me?

Timantus.   Of none.

Leucippus.   What course wouldst thou have taken when thou

     hadst kild me?

Timantus.   I would have tane your Page, and maried her.

Leucippus.   What Page?

Timantus.   Your boy there.——   *Dyes.*

               Urania *sounds.*

Leucippus.   Is he falne mad in death, what does he meane?

Some good God help me at the worst: how dost thou?

Let not thy misery vexe me, thou shalt have

What thy poore heart can wish: I am a Prince,   120

And I will keepe thee in the gayest cloathes,

And the finest things, that ever pretty boy

Had given him.

Urania.   I know you well enough.

Feth I am dying, and now you know all too.

Leucippus.   But stir up thy selfe; looke what a Jewell here is,

See how it glisters: what a pretty shew

Will this make in thy little eare? ha, speake,

Eate but a bit, and take it.

Urania.   Doe you not know me?

Leucippus.   I prethee minde thy health:

Why thats well sayd my good boy, smile still.   130

Urania.   I shall smile till death an I see you.

I am *Urania* your sister-in-law.

Leucippus.   How!

Urania.   I am *Urania.*

Leucippus.   Dulnesse did ceaze me, now I know thee well;

Alas why camst thou hither?

Urania.   Feth for love,

I would not let you know till I was dying;

For you could not love mee, my Mother was
So naught.

Leucippus.   I will love thee, or any thing:
What? wilt thou leave me as soone as I know thee?   140
Speake one word to me:
Alas shees past it, she will nere speake more.
What noyse is that?

Enter Ismenus, *with the Lords* [*and* Bacha].

It is no matter who comes on me now.
What worse then mad are you that seeke out sorrowes?
If you love delights be gone from hence.

Ismenus.   Syr, for you we come, as Souldiers to revenge the wrongs
you have suffered under this naughtie Creature: what shall bee
done with her? say, I am ready.

Leucippus.   Leave her to heaven brave Cousen,   150
They shall tell her how she has sind against em,
My hand shall never be staind with such base bloud:
Live wicked Mother,
That reverent title bee your pardon, for
I will use no extremitie against you,
But leave you to heaven.

Bacha.   Hell take you all, or if there be a place
Of torment that exceedes that, get you thither:
And till the divels have you, may your lives
Be one continued plague, and such a one,   160
That knowes no friends nor ending. May all ages
That shall succeede curse you as I doe:
And if it be possible, I aske it heaven,
That your base issues may be ever Monsters,
That must for shame of nature and succession,
Be drownd like dogs.
                              Would I had breath to plague you.

Leucippus.   Would you had love within you, and such griefe
As might become a Mother: looke you there,
Know you that face, that was *Urania*:

157 or] Q2; *omit* Q1   166 plague] please Q1–2, F2; poyson Q3

These are the fruits of those unhappy Mothers,   170
That labour with such horrid byrths as you doe:
If you can weepe, theres cause; poore innocent,
Your wickednes has kild her: Ile weepe for you.
Ismenus.   Monstrous woman,
  Mars would weepe at this, and yet she cannot.
Leucippus.   Here lies your Minion too, slaine by my hand,
  I will not say you are the cause: yet certaine,
  I know you were too blame, the Gods forgive you.
Ismenus.   See, she stands as if she were inventing
Some new destruction for the world.
Leucippus.   *Ismenus,*   180
Thou art welcome yet to my sad companie.
Ismenus.   I come to make you somewhat sadder sir.
Leucippus.   You cannot, I am at the height already.
Ismenus.   Your Fathers dead.
Leucippus.   I thought so, heaven be with him:
  O woman, woman, weepe now or never,
  Thou hast made more sorrowes then we have eyes to utter.
Bacha.   Now let heaven fall, I am at the worst of evils,
  A thing so miserable wretched, that every thing,
  The last of humane comforts hath left me:
  I will not bee so base and colde, to live   190
  And wayte the mercies of these men I hate:
  No, tis just I dye,
  Since Fortune hath left me my steep discent attends me:
  Hand, strike thou home, I have soule enough to guide;
  And let all know, as I stood a Queene,
  The same Ile fall, and one with me.
          She stabs the Prince with a knife [and then her selfe].
Leucippus.   Ho.
Ismenus.   How doe you sir?
Leucippus.   Neerer my health, then I thinke any here.
  My tongue begins to faulter: what is man?   200
  Or who would be one, when he sees a poore
  Weake woman can in an instant make him none.

193 steep] Seward; step Q 1–F 2

Dorialus.   She is dead already.

Ismenus.   Let her be damnd already as she is:
Post all for Surgeants.

Leucippus.   Let not a man sturre, for I am but dead:
I have some few words which I wold have you heare,
And am afrayd I shall want breath to speake em:
First to you my Lords,
You know *Ismenus* is undoubtedly   210
Heyre of *Licia*, I doe beseech you all,
When I am dead to shew your duties to him.

Lords.   We vow to do't.

Leucippus.   I thanke you.

       Next to you Couzen *Ismenus*,
That shall be the Duke, I pray you let
The broken Image of *Cupid* be reedified,
I know all this is done by him.

Ismenus.   It shall be so.

Leucippus.   Last, I beseech you that my Mother-in-Law
May have a buriall according to——   *Dyes.* 220

Ismenus.   To what sir?

Dorialus.   There is a full point.

Ismenus.   I will interpret for him; she shal have buriall
According to her owne deserts, with dogs.

Dorialus.   I would your Majestie would haste for setling of the
people.

Ismenus.   I am ready.
Agenor, goe and let the Trumpets sound
Some mournefull thing, whilst we convey the body
Of this unhappy Prince unto the Court,   230
And of that vertuous Virgin to a grave:
But dragge her to a ditch, where let her lye
Accurst, whilst one man has a memory.

             Exeunt.

FINIS.

TEXTUAL NOTES

I.i

21 aske but one]   Line 22 'A hundred times this day if shee will' doubtless suggested the Q3 variance 'once'; but the Q3 editor, although sometimes clever in emending error, had no recourse except to his own ingenuity, and the Q1 reading 'one' (with 'request' understood) seems sufficiently justified by the language of lines 8–12.

41 bring you and me a full content]   One may compare *Philaster*, I.i.105–107, 'What I have done thus publique, is not onely To adde a comfort in particular, To you or me, but all'.

58 Contemnd]   Seward's emendation of Q1–F2 'conjoynd' appears to be necessary. O.E.D. records two Elizabethan instances of 'conjoin' used erroneously for 'enjoin', but the latter would not work here.

60 obey.]   The Q1–F2 comma after 'obey' joins with that in the same editions after 'man' in line 58 to present such a puzzle in modification as to lead some editors, like Dyce, to the desperate expedient of retaining the original comma after 'obey' but emending the comma after 'dishonest' in the next line to a full stop. Yet an association of 'In being thus dishonest' with the naming of the god seems the more natural ('being' can scarcely be a noun) although it poses a problem in meaning, especially in whether the dishonest one is to be taken as the god or the man. However, the pun seems almost inevitable that the man's cupidity (cupiditatem) led to his assignment of the name Cupid (cupido); and indeed it may well seem preferable to the weak alternative, which is that the man having been dishonest in framing a god had to continue the deception by giving it a name.

71 To these loose naked statutes]   This passage is manifestly corrupt, but the problem is where. It seems evident, in examining the syntax, that 'since' in line 65 must be an adverb meaning 'since then', as in II.iv.10, and not a conjunction introducing a long dependent clause before the independent clause beginning 'This is my request'. The distinction seems to be between the ready followers that clustered in the time of the invention of this god and their growth in following ages accompanied by the system of sacrifice to the naked statues ('statutes' is an acceptable old form). The Q1 colons after 'Deitie' and 'invented' in lines 68–69 present no especial problems since they seem to be inserted to mark off a parenthesis. However, the full stop in Q1–F2 after 'sacrifices' (line 70) can be correct only if a missing line after line 70 or 71 had applied to the remaining text before 'This is my

request'. A missing line is not impossible, but a dropped word may be simpler to conjecture. Seward, followed by other editors, believed that the word was 'And' from the line below, which he transferred to line 70; but he then had to invent the omission of 'self' after 'Palace' in order to fill out the pentameter, an expedient rejected by his followers who were thus left with a metrically deficient line. If a word has been omitted, it may have been 'To' before Q1 'These loose naked statutes', and this emendation has been adopted in the present text, accompanied by the deletion of the full stop after 'sacrifices', as perhaps the best way of mending the syntax. The alternative, which may be right, is to leave the full stop after 'sacrifices' and to confess the next few lines to be corrupt in a manner not to be emended.

100 selfe,] Dyce places a semicolon here so that 'dearer then life', as a vocative, begins a new sentence with 'I' in line 103 as the subject. But the Q1 punctuation is perfectly defensible if 'dearer. . .age' is thought of as a parenthesis.

121 That] The capitalization of Q1 'that' is required to indicate that 'That was nothing' is intended to be reported speech, or what was murmured. Following Mason, both Weber and Dyce instead emend 'was' to 'twas', which spoils the point.

148 savour] Weber emends to 'favour', assuming a confusion of 'f' and 'ſ'; but Dr James Savage notes that the meaning is, in general, 'A little is better than nothing', and he points to a line in Rowley's *Fortune by Land and Sea*, 'You know something hath some savour', where the reference is to a little property.

150 charitie,] Although Q1 has no comma after 'charitie', some syntactical punctuation is required to mark off what appears to be the end of the dependent clause. The general meaning of the passage may be that now that married women will prove chaste, if their unmarried younger sisters do not take their place in charity to men, all sexual intercourse will be confined to the lawful married state. Possibly it is fanciful to observe a surface meaning that in this topsy-turvy world now presented by the new decrees the younger sisters need no longer take upon themselves the 'greater charitie' of chastity while waiting for their elder sisters to marry, but will now hasten into marriage before their elders.

I.ii

5 To great *Cupid*] Although one could rationalize the Q1 reading 'Lo great *Cupid*' by placing a full stop after 'sacrifice', the syntax with the Q3 correction 'To' is certainly superior, and the confusion of 't' and 'I' (especially in the manuscript minuscule) is easy to imagine.

I.iii

14 despisd] Seward and other editors before Dyce retain Q1 'despise' and emend 'heart' to 'hearts'. However, since the first object of the revenge is Hidaspes, who was the first heart to despise Cupid, and the next scene shows the 'strange misery' laid on her, it seems likely that the series of imperative verbs led the compositor to the easy orthographic confusion of d:e in 'despisd:despise' and thus to the Q1 reading. In this sequence Cupid threatens the whole land, then specifies a particular punishment, by his displeasure, for Hidaspes who was the originator of the heresy, and returns finally to a forecast of nationwide destruction, which we may take to include the love-delusions of Leontius and the downfall of Leucippus.

16 this arrow] Seward's emendation of Q1–F2 'his arrow' is surely justified. It would be idle to argue that it was with 'displeasure's' arrow that Cupid proposed to vindicate himself. Cupid's arrows either attracted or repelled.

II.v

33 whilst] The sentence is complete, not suspended. The use of 'whilst' in this passage to signify 'in the meantime' is cited in O.E.D.

II.vi

4 taken—away] According to the Q1 typography, in which '*Away.*' is set in italic, capitalized, and placed against the right margin after the end of the sentence with '...taken.', the word was intended by the compositor to represent a stage-direction. The alternative is that '*Away.*' was thought to be a command by Bacha to her maid, italicized as were Cleophila's asides to Hero in the preceding scene II.v.17, 29, also set by Compositor *Y*. But neither a stage-direction nor a command is possible here in context, and it would seem that some manuscript marking or spacing (represented in this edition by a dash) was confused. Without question the word must end Bacha's line, and as a play on 'captured amorously' as well as 'removed from here'.

68 Mummy] Tempting as it might be to retain Q1–F2 'Mumming' in view of the reference to St George (perhaps the reason why Compositor *Y* mis-set the word), Seward's emendation is necessary in view of the frequent O.E.D. citations of *mummy* as a jocular term for dead flesh or a body in which life is extinct, or for dried or desiccated meat, but the lack of any support for *mumming* in a sense applicable to the passage. Moreover, Dr Savage has provided a parallel reference to St George from *The Woman's Prize*, I.iii, that indicates some pictorial representation, not a mumming:

...we shall have you looke
For all your great words, like St George at Kingston,
Running a foot-back from the furious dragon,
That with her angry tail belabours him
For being lazy.

75 pine] Q3's 'pine for' is wasted ingenuity, in view of O.E.D.'s support for 'pine' as *to torment* (i.e. to pain) or *to wear out*.

78 you're madde else] In support of Dyce's emendation of Q1–F2 'Maide' with other combinations of words, see III.ii.91, 'The world had calld me madde, had I refusde | The King'.

III.ii

153–154 ashamde: You] Mason suggested the removal of the stop after 'ashamde' and its transfer to follow 'your selfe'; *i.e. Don't be ashamed that you did not think of it yourself; I will forgive your bashfulness.* This is ingenious but unnecessary. Bacha means in Q1–F2, *Do not be ashamed of kissing me. You did not initiate it—I ordered you to.*

185 as my list] Langbaine emended to 'at my list', followed by Seward and Colman, whereas Weber preferred 'as me list'. This is a difficult matter. If 'list' is a verb, 'me list' would seem to be required. On the other hand, 'list' as a noun may mean *desire, pleasure, wish*. O.E.D. does not happen to record the idiom 'at my list', although there would appear to be no reason why this construction would not be possible. The present editor, with some diffidence, retains the Q1–F2 reading with 'list' as a noun and conjectures that some such verb as *dictates* is to be understood.

196 wickedly] Dyce's addition of this word (suggested by line 156 but especially by line 161) may make the best of a bad job. Except for the short line of Q1, 'But give you the just honour', the original metre is acceptable granted more elisions or weak syllables than in the preceding lines. Yet if the Q1 wording is to be preserved, the syntax demands a revision of the clause relationship so that the sentence would read (as represented by Weber), 'but never that, say what you will; Ile heare you ...if you speake; I will not follow....' On its side this syntactical reconstitution has such a punctuation reversal (for Q1 that;...will,) as occurs at I.v.42–43, 72, and at II.ii.14–15; but it would also require a further tinkering by the substitution of a heavier stop after 'speake' than the Q1 comma. Even with this, however, it may be thought that the transition beginning 'I will not follow' is unduly abrupt without a qualifying 'but'. The 'tell the world', also, seems to require such a precise referent as is provided by 'speake wickedly'. On the whole, then, Dyce's emendation seems to represent the simplest mending of some form of textual corruption that has affected Q1.

418

221 goodly]　Dyce followed Heath's notes in emending to 'godly', which is possible in view of III.ii.14, 'Growne so godly'. But the emendation is not strictly necessary since 'goodly' and 'godly' are practically interchangeable at this time and hence 'goodly'—though without the sneer—is paralleled at III.iii.13, 17.

III.iii

32 discharge that]　At first sight Seward's emendation 'it' for 'that' is attractive since orthographically 'y^t' for 'that' might be misread. But the original appears to be worth preserving as a calculated, not an accidental, repetition: Let him make what he can of my clothes not being paid for so long as he discharges the debt I owe my tailor.

III.iv

17 blessings]　Seward's emendation of Q1–F2 'blessing' balances the plural 'vices' of line 16.

39 for his wisedome]　Q1–F2 'for all his wisedome' may have resulted from memorial contamination with 'and all those Friends' in the next line of Q1.

122 Ile cut him shorter.]　One of two things seems to have happened: (1) after these words and the Q1 original continuation, Bacha makes some objection that Leucippus is his heir, but the line (or more) is lost; (2) a revision in the manuscript has been made but the original insufficiently deleted. Difficulties exist in either case. The loss of one or more lines (although perhaps only a few words) complete with Bacha's speech-prefix is not impossible although this would be the only known case in the play. On the other hand, if the emended lining of the present edition is correct, Bacha's part-line (line 122) 'What a fowle Age is this' could not complete the full line, '*Leon.* Ile cut him shorter first, then let him rule.' However, this might not be much of an objection since not every short line in this scene requires such completion, although the line in question comes within an extensive passage in which speakers complete their predecessors' lines. Nevertheless, if one or other of Leontius's speeches is to be rejected, the first printed must stand not only for metrical reasons but also because Leontius's promise to cut his son shorter *first* and *then* let him rule may be thought to require some antecedent not present in Q1. Hence, if one must substitute for the other, the first must be the revision; and, if so, the second would have been set only if it had been insufficiently excised (along with some interjection by Bacha) following the insertion of the substitute. On the whole, the most plausible conjecture would seem to be that originally line 121, 'And spight of all theyr strengths will make my safetie', ended Leontius's speech, followed by a pretended objection from Bacha, such as

But he's your heir, to which '*Leon.* Ile cut him shorter first, then let him rule' was the response. However, it was then seen that Leontius's promise to allow Leucippus to succeed him after having been taught a lesson was too mild for his subsequent actions (and perhaps for Bacha's lines 122–123); hence Bacha's objection and Leontius's promise were crossed out, though insufficiently, and the words 'Ile cut him shorter' were added after 'safetie', probably in the same manuscript line. With this revision a dramatically sound progression was secured, with Leontius at first muttering, 'Ile cut him shorter', and then at line 124, 'Ile teach him to flye lower'. If this hypothesis is correct, the nature of the manuscript is, unfortunately, by no means solved. That is, since the evidence appears to run for the whole play against the veiw that the copy for the print was the collected foul papers of both dramatists, Beaumont (if he were the copyist) could have made the revision himself in this Fletcher scene, or he could have mistakenly followed the ambiguous Fletcher papers and so perpetuated the error.

129 Hee never was so innocent] Starting with Seward editors alter 'never' to 'ever' but without improving matters basically. The syntax cannot be divorced from the question of verbal emendation. The comma in Q1 after 'rages' is emended in the present edition to a colon in order to mark off the complex sentence ending with the dependent clause 'if his thoughts... run with their rages'. The alternative is to start a new sentence with this clause, inverted before the independent clause 'he never was so innocent', but this makes nonsense. Indeed, 'yoke' and 'run' must go together in the same sentence. Thus it may seem better to interpret the words as meaning: *He never was so innocent as he is now; nevertheless, what reason....* The comma after 'innocent' takes the place of a full stop, actually.

181 Lands,] Q1, with no punctuation after 'Lands', proceeds, 'I know the weakness of it.' Mason took 'it' to refer to the Duke's discretion. Weber interpreted 'it' as referring to the inadequacy of Bacha's desire as compared with that of the country. Just as likely the 'it' may refer to the weakness of the country under Leontius's rule, which she knows.

IV.i

75 else I should beare my selfe——] The dash to emend Q1's final full stop seems required. The difficulty lies in 'beare'; but it is easier to assume that the word stands for *conduct* and that the speech is interrupted by Urania's entrance than it is to attempt to distort the sense of 'beare' or to emend save by the dash.

IV.ii

18 strumpet] Colman's emendation 'trumpet', followed by Weber and Dyce, is tempting but not wholly necessary. Love and Obedience are to be

taken as corrupting her to this unnatural office. It is not inappropriate for
Bacha to use sexual imagery.

21 prou'de]   Q1 'proud'de' may represent an incompletely realized press-
correction although the outer forme of sheet H (the reading occurs on sig.
H4ᵛ) is not known to be variant. This page was set by Compositor *Y*. For
'prou'de' in Q1 set by Compositor *X* see III.iii.19. This intrusive apostrophe in the word 'proud' may thus be established to represent the copy
in each case.

35 O ease a mother!]   If it were not for the dangling 'some good man . . .
Countrey', a case might be made for the Q1 reading 'Cease, a mother!' as
one of a series of disjointed ejaculations. But such a reference to being a
mother would clash somewhat with lines 39–40, 'Let it not be a cruelty in
mee|Nor draw a Mothers name in question'. Moreover, Seward's emenda-
tion connects with 'I am full of too much womans pittie', and joins the
'good man' and his task of reporting the treason to easing her of the
burden.

IV.iii

2 I stoppe a Grote]   Editors have wisely refrained from commenting on
this phrase since it seems to be irremediably corrupt. A *grot* may mean a
fragment, a particle, or an atom. *Grout* is beer, porridge, sediment or lees,
or a thin fluid mortar. *Groot* is soil, mud, earth. If the latter is intended,
there may be some connection with the need to cleanse the sword. On the
other hand, if 'Grote' is the small coin *groat*, a connection may be established between the phrase and the otherwise inexplicable remark about the
pitch at the cutler's shop which the citizen may be wanting to purchase.
On the whole the latter seems more probable, but we cannot even be sure
that the colon after 'Muster' is accurate since an erroneous colon is present
in Q1 after 'Pitch'. Thus, just possibly, the colon might be moved from its
position after 'Muster' to after 'Grote', but the sense is still obscure. It
would seem that 'stoppe' is the major corruption, but what it represents
this editor cannot determine although it may be that the final letter should
be 'd'.

33 a beaten out of towne]   Although Q2 was suspicious of this phrase and
emended 'a' to 'and', the Q1 reading may be defended as meaning 'a-
beaten' with something like 'they were' understood before, a sense that
may be assisted by changing the Q1 comma after preceding 'us' to a semicolon. Or the 'a beaten . . .' may be taken as introducing a parenthesis:
those gentlemen who were a-beaten out of town. . . . On the other hand, if 'a'
were taken as a pronoun, the auxiliary of the verb 'beaten' has been omitted
in error.

IV.iv

25 Farewel to all our happinesse,] Dyce prints 'Farewell' as the response
to Nisus in line 24 and thus puts a colon after it and begins Dorialus's
soliloquy with the more metrically regular line, 'To all our happinesse, a
long farewel.' However, this treatment destroys the *epanalepsis*, that is, the
repetition of the same word at the beginning and end of a line of verse,
as in *King Lear* III.ii.1.

IV.v

19 sithes] Beginning with Seward editors have taken this word to be
scythes and have punctuated so as to make Ismenus's proposal a challenge
to single fight, or duel, with scythes as weapons. But Timantus is not a
rustic, and in I.v Ismenus's satire has been directed against his courtly
foppishness. It would seem, instead, that 'sithes' is here the old word for
since. If it is used as an adverb in the general sense of past time up to the
present, something of a stronger stop than a comma would be appropriate
before it. But if 'sithes' is a conjunction, the meaning would be ironic:
since we have built enough on him, I will now kill him. The former is perhaps
slightly to be preferred.

V.ii

32–33 dar'st thou? speake,] This emendation of Q1–F2 'dar'st thou speake'
is justified by the terms of the same error in lines 34–35, which read in
Q1–F2, 'darst thou speake to me', this erroneous construction being
corrected in Q2.

V.iv

46 Alas...] The context would suggest that a lost song should be placed
between lines 45 and 46; nevertheless, editors have ignored the hint and
have run-on the verse, lining it: 'If thou wilt good boy. Alas my boy, that
thou | Shouldst comfort me, and art farre worse then I!' In support of the
context, Q1 lines as in the present edition, but 'If thou wilt good boy.'
ends sig. K4ᵛ (set by Compositor *Y*) and—with a repeated speech-prefix
—sig. L1 (set by Compositor *X*) begins, '*Leu.* Alas my boy...' in prose
although line 46, whether by chance or not, begins the second line on the
page, 'and art farre worse then I.' The repeated speech-prefix strongly
suggests some disruption such as a break between two independent
speeches by the same character. On the other hand, the catchword on K4ᵛ
and the following word on L1 do not agree in that the catchword is simply
'Alas' as if Compositor *Y* would have continued with the same speech

without the prefix if he had carried on to set sig. L1. If this evidence were to hold, the setting of the speech-prefix by Compositor X beginning the first line of the continued speech on sig. L1 might be of no particular significance and the omission of a song would be in doubt. However, the evidence does not hold. Although ordinarily the speech-prefix is given as a catchword in this quarto, the practice differs between the two compositors. Compositor X fifteen times sets the speech-prefix and the first word of the speech as the catchword and only twice the speech-prefix alone. He never omits the speech-prefix. On the other hand, Compositor Y three times sets the speech-prefix alone as the catchword, and eight times he omits the speech-prefix and sets the first word of the new speech as the catchword. He never sets both speech-prefix and first word. (This last becomes the decisive feature for assigning to Compositor X the doubtful page L2^v, with its catchword of speech-prefix and first word, just as the lack of the speech–prefix settles the case for Compositor Y's setting of the doubtful page K4^v.) Sig. K4^v with its catchword of 'Alas', then, joins sigs. C3, C4, D2, G4^v, H2^v, I1, and I1^v as exhibiting a special characteristic of Y's setting of catchwords without the speech-prefix. On their example, there is every reason to believe that X's setting of the prefix at the top of L1 followed the manuscript and that Y would also have set the prefix if he had continued to the next page. The nature of the manuscript thus being demonstrated at this point, it follows that the critic may readily conjecture the absence of some material between the speeches, and the context suggests that this missing material was a song.

68 Gods keepe him but fro knowing me till I dye]   The reading of Q1 found favour until Mason made the inevitable suggestion of reversing the pronouns, in which he was followed by Weber and by Dyce, but some residual doubt exists about this emendation of Q1 'keepe me...knowing him'. In its favour is the obvious clarification of the sense and, for what the evidence is worth, a similar case of reversed pronouns in *Philaster* V.ii.40, provided 'no price' means *without value* and not *priceless*, something of a moot point perhaps. (This traditional emendation in *Philaster*, incidentally, was also first made by Mason.) O.E.D. and the Shakespeare Concordance give no examples to encourage the interpretation of 'knowing' as *being known by*. Hence the Q1–F2 reading must stand or fall on its sense. If the original reading is to be retained, Urania can mean one thing only: Gods keep me from revealing the fact that I know Leucippus to be the Prince, for that revelation would expose my disguise. On the face of it, this is not the most natural sense, for at the entrance of Timantus Urania has feared that he would recognize her. The next reference, thus, would normally be that she hopes she will die (and she cannot live more than a day longer in her weakened condition) before Leucippus knows the truth about her. At this point for her to worry that in her weakness she may inadvertently blurt out her knowledge of Leucippus's true identity seems to be anomalous.

Moreover, as the scene continues, 'know' keeps its ordinary signification. At line 75 Timantus doffs his disguise and asks, 'know you me now sir?' When Timantus before his death partly reveals her secret and Leucippus tells her he is a prince, Urania at line 123 responds, 'I know you well enough' (which might be taken as echoing line 68), but at line 128 she asks, 'Doe you not know me?' When she gives her name, at line 135 Leucippus exclaims, 'now I know thee well', to which Urania responds, 'I would not let you know till I was dying'. Finally, Leucippus begs, 'What? wilt thou leave me as soone as I know thee?' Only at line 123 is there the faintest suggestion of an echo of the Q1–F2 version in 'I know you well enough. Feth I am dying, and now you know all too.' Under these circumstances, although there is some possibility of sophisticating the text it would seem that Mason's emendation may hold and that the compositor, or the inscriber of the manuscript, was guilty of memorial confusion in line 68.

70.1 Leucippus *opening the Letter* . . .]   Since Timantus's speech of line 67 must manifestly come before the action described in this stage-direction, the Q1–F2 position of the direction after line 66 is faulty. It would seem, however, that more than a line is involved. Urania's lines 68–69 are an aside and appear to refer to her weakness from lack of food (see above lines 23–29). They fill the interval in which Timantus presents the letter (line 67) and then withdraws, while Leucippus is occupied in reading it, before starting his fatal assault. 'O thou foule Traytor', then, is not an afterthought to an aside delivered after Urania is wounded and lying on the stage, but instead more appropriately they are her words when she steps between them and receives the wound. Seward's placement of the direction after line 69 is perhaps strictly accurate but a trifle inconvenient. Dyce prefers the Q1 position after line 66, which quite alters the circumstances of Urania's aside.

86–87 (A nobler tryall . . . none at all) here]   Conscious of the difficult syntax, and of the limping metre of line 85, Seward added 'receive' after 'therefore', in which he was followed only by Colman. Other editors, including the present, follow Weber in the addition of round brackets to clarify the parenthetical element. Line 85 is not necessarily metrically deficient. In this play, as occasionally in Elizabethan verse, the caesura fortified by a strong mark of punctuation takes the place of a syllable that may even be stressed.

96.1 *The Prince* . . . *him*.]   The Q1 prefatory '*Fight here:*' is another of the stage-directions in this play that are not truly anticipatory in the usual sense but instead detail an action or a prop needed later in the scene. The order of events seems to be as follows. Leucippus presents Timantus with an extra sword, in its scabbard, to prepare him for the judicial combat. The first action of the fight is, then, the base attack of Timantus when the Prince is not looking. The combat itself takes place only after this attack and is terminated when Timantus is fatally wounded. Leucippus then reproves the dying man, 'Fye, fie *Timantus*...' and receives information from him. Superficially a case could be argued for the reproof in lines 104–105 to be made before the combat, but the continuation of line 105, 'Wert thou longer...', cannot come after the fight because it is firmly hitched to lines 104–105, and thereafter no apt place appears. Line 108 is not pre-combat but instead represents Timantus's plea not to be despatched as he lies wounded and helpless.

PRESS-VARIANTS IN Q1 (1615)

[Copies collated: BM¹ (C.71.d.27), BM² (Ashley 76), BM³ (644.d.2), D (Dyce), CSmH¹ (Huntington: Devonshire), CSmH² (Huntington: Chew), MH (Harvard), Pforz (Pforzheimer).]

SHEET C (*outer forme*)

Corrected: BM¹⁻³, D, CSmH², MH, Pforz
Uncorrected: CSmH¹

Sig. C1.
 I.iii.2 nor] not

Sig. C2ᵛ.
 I.iv.94 off] of

Sig. C3.
 r-t *Cupids*] *Kupids*
 I.iv.96 *Zoy.*] *Zilo.*
  96 ſhame.] ſhame,
 I.v.13.1 *Dorialus*] *Porialus*

Sig. C4ᵛ.
 r-t *Cupids*] *Kupids*
 I.v.98 forgetfulnes] forgetfullnes
  112 *Hidaſ.*] *Hidas.*

SHEET C (*inner forme*)

Corrected: BM¹⁻³, D, CSmH², MH, Pforz
Uncorrected: CSmH¹

Sig. C1ᵛ.
 I.iv.2 *Cleo.*] *Cleo*
  14–15 Madame? | He is the moſt] Madame? He is | The moſt
  30 Traytors] Traytors:

Sig. C3ᵛ.
 r-t *Reuen ge*] *Reuenge*
 I.v.51 Thats] That
  52 muſt not deny] muſt deny

Sig. C4.
 I.v.59 aſhamd, Syr:] aſhamd Syr
  67 *Hidaſ:*] *Hidaſ.*

SHEET D (*outer forme*)

Corrected: BM¹⁻³, CSmH¹⁻², Pforz
Uncorrected: D, MH

Sig. D1.
I.v.133 yee needs muſt] needs muſt yee
II.i.7 old] ould

Sig. D2ᵛ.
[II.ii.61 againe.] againe,
    89 Images:] Images

SHEET E (*outer forme*)

Corrected: BM³, D, CSmH¹⁻², MH, Pforz
Uncorrected: BM¹⁻²

Sig. E1.
II.iii.2 *Hero: Hida:*] *Hero, Hida,*
    11 more,] more
    30 ſing.] ſing
    31 Shee is] Sheeis

Sig. E1.
II.iii.2 Is] is

Sig. E4ᵛ.
II.vi.64 looke,] looke
    78 eech] eche
    82 all] all,

SHEET K (*outer forme*)

Corrected: BM¹⁻³, D, CSmH², MH, Pforz
Uncorrected: CSmH¹

Sig. K3.
    K3] K5

WORD-DIVISION

[NOTE: The following words which are hyphenated at the end of a line in
the present edition are true hyphenated compounds in Q1.]
    I.v.10 Captain-|ship
    II.iv.5 frizling-|yron

EMENDATIONS OF ACCIDENTALS

The Printer to the Reader
7 *having*] *baving* Q 1

I.i

HT REVENGE] Q 2; REVENG
   Q 1
18 Q 1–F 2 *line*: wonder | Shee
19–20 Q 1–F 2 *line*: That...the |
   Great...world: | Sheele...
   Maide.
22–24 Q 1–F 2 *line*: A...will; |
   And...though | The...day, |
   He...deny | Her nothing.
24.1 *Cornets*] Q 1–F 2 *print as separate line*
25–28 Q 1–F 2 *line*: Come...art |
   Dutchesse to day, | Art...
   knowest | My...performance. |
   And...shall, | Or...perform-
   ance
26 aske?] Q 3; ~ , Q 1–2
32 obedience ———] ~ 1 Q 1–F 2
36 her:———] ~ : ˄ Q 1–F 2
37 Q 1–F 2 *line*: wee | Agreed
38–43 Q 1–F 2 *line*: Most...pre-
   pard, | Nor...bounds, | What
   ...bring | Me...content. |
   Leontius. So...does: | Thou
   ...age, | Make...desire,
57–58 Q 1–F 2 *line*: Which...
   thoughts; | And...conjoynd |
   For...man,
57 thoughts,] ~ ; Q 1–F 2
58 man;] ~ , Q 1–F 2
70 sacrifices˄] ~ . Q 1–F 2
76–77 *One line in* Q 1–F 2
77–79 Q 1–F 2 *line*: But...be | A
   god...childe:

92–93 Q 1–F 2 *line*: Sir...selfe, |
   But...command: | Hand...
   not.
94 *Exit* Ismenus.] Q 1 (*Exit.*)–F 2
   place at end of l. 96
100 life,] Q 3; ~ ˄ Q 1–2
101 selfe˄] ~ , Q 1–F 2
103 will] Q 1 (*text*); wil Q 1 (*cw*)
105–107 Q 1–F 2 *line*: I...wonder, |
   We...shortly, | And...
   fashion.
105 yet,] F 2; ~ ˄ Q 1–3
105 wonder;] ~ , Q 1–F 2
108–125 Q 1–F 2 *line*: We...can |
   Catch...thus. | *Nisus.* And...
   Justice | We...part, | Ile...
   affection, | I...hardnes |
   Through...have | Brought...
   market: | Would...tolleration,
   | That...mine | Owne house. |
   Dorialus. The...would | Never
   ...else, | Tis...Famine: | Yet
   ...liv'd | Wou'd...this |
   Blessing...the | God...use, |
   And...still | As...cryde, |
   Poore...us | Abundance...all.
122 pleasures:] ~ , Q 1–2, F 2; ~ ;
   Q 3
126–133 Q 1–F 2 *line*: Berlady...
   ont, | Flesh...rather | Have...
   Gunner. | I...him | In...
   followed? | Women...hus-
   wives, | Honest...fine? | Wore
   ...faces, | Though...survay-

428

ing: | And...lamentable, | They...husbands.

131 cloathes,] ~ ∧ Q1–F2

134–159 Q1–F2 *line*: I...griefe, | Young...Cowcumbers, | And ...complexion: | Bawds... misery | It...againe. | These ...Cuckolds. | Well...these | Divels...us, | The...mischievous. | There...Lord! | *Enter ...Image.*|This...of:| Would ...not | Feele...followes. | *Agenor.* And...these | Few... it: | Nay...Powers, | And... done. | A...blessings | Are... bedds. | *Nisus.* This...us; | I ...commons.|*Dorialus.* Would

...savour. | The...now, | Tis ...sisters | Take...lawfull. | *Agenor.* Well...come, | I... falles, | Ile...be | Sound... unmercifull, | Ile...it, | And... nothing. | *Nisus.* This...good, | And...children, | They... 'em.

134 griefe.] ~ , Q1–F2

136 againe,] F2; ~ . Q1–3

138.1 *Enter...*] Q1–F2 *below* 'There he goes, Lord!' *in l.* 139

139 goes.] ~ , Q1–F2

148 savour.] ~ , Q1; ~ ∧ Q2–3; ~ ; F2

154 sound:] ~ , Q1; ~ . Q2–F2

160 rent] | Rent Q1–3; Rent F2

I.ii

41–42 Q1–F2 *line*: This...Images | And...'em.

49–50 *One line in* Q1–F2

53–54 Q1–F2 *line*: Gentlemen... talking, | This...speedily;

I.iii

18 nobly] Q3; Nobly Q1–2

I.iv

12 by!] Q2; ~ ? Q1

17 deformed] Q3; deform'd Q1–2

36.1 *Enter* Cleophila.] F2; Q1–3 *print on l.* 35

37.1 *Enter* Zoylus.] Q1–3 *print on l.* 36; F2 *as part of* 36.1

47–48 Q1–F2 *line*: Ha...Nature | Hath...much | As...shew;

55–57 Q1–F2 *line*: Beshrew...

merry; | But...me: | Thou... Saint,

61–63 Mayd ∧...passions?] ~ ? ...~ ; Q1–F2

95 Zoylus] Q2; Zoylous Q1

97 Exeunt.] Exit. Q1–F2

98–101 *Prose in* Q1–F2

98 Anger] F2; *Anger* Q1–3

I.v

3 Lord——] ~ ∧ Q1; ~ , Q2;
~ . Q3, F2
5–11 Q1–F2 *line*: No...cuck-
olds: | The...semsters, | Shoe-
makers...morning, | Nor...
soluble, | No...roses: | Nor...
breeches: | If...thus, | Get...
thee. (F2: Get...else. | Thus
...thee.)
5 cuckolds:] F2; ~ , Q1–3
20 O nephew] F2; *Onephen* Q1;
O nephew Q2–3
20 vertue] | Vertue Q1–F2
24–25 Q1–F2 *line*: Tis...thus: |
This...seene.
31 mee,] ~ . Q1–F2
32 *Exit* Nisus.] Q1–F2 *print on l.* 31
38 pardon,] ~ : Q1–3; ~ ; F2
40 Syr,] F2; ~ ∧ Q1–3
40.1 Hidaspes] Q2; Hidaspis Q1
48–52 Q1–F2 *line*: Syr...word, |
Wonder...word, | If...aske |
Thats...mee: | Now...for-
sworne.
54 power∧] ~ , Q1–F2
56–57 Q1–F2 *line*: trust: | You
56 trust:] ~ , Q1–F2
58 Gentleman.] Q3; Gent: Q1–2,
F2
59 Q1–F2 *line*: Syr: | You
59 ashamd∧] Q1(u); ~ , Q1(c)
67–76 Q1–F± *line*: If...still. |
Syr...with-|out...freely: |
Doe...words: | My...wise-

dome, | Onely...furie. | Speake
...Father, | I...bloud | Heares
...will, | For...speake.
72 wisedome,...hast:] ~ :...~ ,
Q1–F2
84–85 *Prose in* Q1–F2 *although
lined* in Q1–3 now | we
84 abusde,...Love∧] ~ ∧...~ ,
Q1, 3; ~ ∧...~ ∧ Q2; ~ :...
~ , F2
90–91 *Prose in* Q1–F2
93 plague∧] ~ , Q1–F2
95 selfe:] ~ , Q1–F2
98–99 Q1–F2 *line*: And...forget-
fullness: | May...is!
98 forgetfullnes] Q1(u); forgetful-
nes Q1(c)
99 is!] ~ ? Q1–F2
103–105 Q1–F2 *line*: Thou...draw
|This...mee? | Carry...death.
117 them,...us∧] ~ ∧...~ , Q1–
2, F2; ~ ∧...~ ∧ Q3
120 you,] Q3; ~ ∧ Q1–2
124 Woman!] Q3; ~ ∧ Q1–2
128 him:] ~ , Q1; ~ . Q2–F2
128 Gentlemen,] Q2 (~ :); Gent:
Q1
129–130 Q1–F2 *line*: Syr. | Has
136 Q1–F2 *line*: man, | Let
137 him——] ~ . Q1–F2
139–142 Q1–F2 *line*: How...
pleasde: | Theres...much |
Money...Hat | and...morrow:
| Garters...nature.

II.i

0.1 *Descendit*] *Discend* Q1–2, F2;
Discend. Q3
4 Kingdome:] ~ , Q1–F2
6 power?] ~ , Q1–F2

7 ould] Q1(u); old Q1(c)
10 hart∧] Q2; ~ , Q1
11 *Nestor*:] ~ , Q1–F2

II.ii

0.1 *a*] F2; *A* Q1–3

2 for?] F2; ~ . Q1–3

7 Heyre.] ~ , Q1–F2

10–11 *One line in* Q1–F2

11 it?] F2; ~ . Q1–3

11–13 Q1–F2 *line*: Drie...away, | This...helpe.

14–15 thus,...againe:] ~ :...~ , Q1–F2

18 glaunce.] ~ , Q1–2, F2; ~ ; Q3

20–23 Q1–F2± *line*: If...gone, | And...thine | owne...thee.

32–36 And...done.] *prose in* Q1–F2

36 world:] ~ ∧ Q1–F2

38 not?] F2; ~ : Q1–3

40–41 dead (and...so) | Hardly ∧ a weeke,] dead: And...so ∧ | Hardly, a weeke ∧ Q1–F2 (so. Q3; so, F2)

42–44 Q1–F2 *line*: And...greatnesse, | Gave...you: | This... deserve.

44–45 Q1–F2 *line*: Why...tell? | These...part | From...wracke

44 Why,] ~ ∧ Q1–F2

49–51 Q1–F2± *line*: You... witcht | us...soules, | They... us:

56 receive this] Q2; receive t this Q1

57–58 *One line in* Q2–F2

58 Why,] ~ ∧ Q1–F2

59–60 long,...rage:] ~ :...~ , Q1–F2

61 againe,] Q1(u); ~ . Q1(c)

65–70 Q1–F2± *line*: Alas...wilt. | *Bacha*. Comming...high | Esteeme...but | good...you. | *Leucippus*. Fare...Bacha; | I ...haste.

71–74 Q1–F2 *line*: Just...you: |

No...prostitute | My...pearles | And...confesse

72 more:] ~ , Q1–F2

72 love?] F2; ~ : Q1–3

73 mee.] ~ , Q1–F2

82–83 Lady...betrayde.] *one line in* Q1–F2

82 flye,] ~ ∧ Q1–F2

83 mee,...teares,] ~ ∧...~ ∧ Q1–F2

87 teares,] ~ . Q1–F2

90 selfe,] ~ ∧ Q1–F2

93 Nay,] ~ ∧ Q1–F2

94 wouldst] Q3; woulst Q1; woul'st Q2

96 all?] F2; ~ . Q1–3

97 told.——] ~ . ∧ Q1–F2

97–106 Q1–F2 *line*: O...pardon | My...head, | madded... know | You...may | Command...life, | Which...long. | *Leontius*. All...shame: | And ...in | Generall...shouldst

109 Bacha] *Bacha* Q1–F2

110–111 Q1–F2 *line*: Sir...will | Serve...wrongfully

129–142 Q1–F2 *line*: Is't...our | Carriages...selfe | For...thou | Shou'dst...self: | But... guilt, | And...lye) | Loth... lye | To...lawfull | To... evill. | *Leontius*. Tell...long? | *Leucippus*. If...hell | Take me. | *Leontius*. What's...not? (Q3 truth, | Hell)

146–147 Q1–F2 *line*: If...Father, | No...now: | The...ont.

164–165 Q1–F2 *line*: Upon... shee's | A...creature.

168–169 Q1–F2 *line*: Moov'd... face, | I...thoughts, | Which ...me:

170 truth] Q2; ttuth Q1
175 good,] Q3; ~ ‸ Q1–2
179–180 *One line in* Q1–F2
193–194 *One line in* Q1–F2
196–198 Q1–F2 *line*: With...
    scorne | To...she | Made...
    her.
199–201 *Prose in* Q1–F2 *though
    lines capitalized*
199 Sir.——] ~ , ‸ Q1–F2
204–207 Q1–F2 *line*: And...looke
    | On...amaz'd. | I...have |
    Had...woman

216 mine.——] ~ . ‸ Q1–F2
220–221 *Prose in* Q1–F2
221 Prince] Q2; Pirnce Q1
223–224 Q1–F2 *line*: dispatch | Us
224 houre:] F2; ~ , Q1–3
226–230 Q1–F2 *line*: Lady...have
    | Slubberd...be | Chaste...
    hereafter: | But...for | My
    ...Ring:
228 hereafter:] Q3; ~ ; Q1–2
232 Grace.——] ~ . ‸ Q1–F2

II.iii

1–12 Q1–F2 *line*: Gentlemen...
    Justice, | To...because | She
    ...and | Subject...Sexe | Is
    ...I, | Or...still | With...
    par'd | With...Nobility | Out
    ...in. | *Nisus*. You...neede |

That...world? | *Dorialus*. I...
    it: | But...three | Were...
    need.
2 him.] ~ ; Q1–F2
37 why‸] ~ , Q1–F2

II.iv

26.1 *Leontius*.] Q3; *Leontine*.
    Q1
55 himselfe.——] ~ . ‸ Q1–F2
62 thinkes——] Q3; ~ . Q1–2
65 strength] Q2; strenghth Q1

70 *Telamon*] *Leon*: *Telamon* Q1–F2
70 say] Q3; | Say Q1–2
72 then.] ~ , Q1–F2
74 for] Q3; | For Q1–2
75 side.] ~ , Q1–F2

II.v

0.1 Hidaspes,...Hero:] Q3
    (Hero;); ~ :...~ , Q1–2
1 *Hidaspes*.] Q3; *omit* Q1–2
7 *Shee kneeles*.] Q3; Q1 (*Shee*)–2
    place on l. 8
8 Why,] ~ ‸ Q1–F2
14 night,] ~ . Q1–2, F2; ~ ‸ Q3
18 ill——] ~ : Q1–2, F2; ~ . Q3
22 carv'd,...wrist.]   ~ ‸...~ ,
    Q1–F2±
29 *mends*] Q3; | *Mends* Q1–2

31 Leave] *Hero*. Leave Q1–F2
31 Why,] ~ ‸ Q1–2; ~ . Q3; ~ ?
    F2
31 shee] | Shee Q1–F2
33 and] And Q1–F2
37 May‸] *May*: Q1–2, F2; *May*,
    Q3
41 Chastitie,] Q3; ~ . Q1–2
42 can.] ~ , Q1–F2
44 it:] ~ ‸ Q1–2, F2; ~ , Q3
45.1 [*Exit*.]] *Exeunt*. Q2–F2

432

II.vi

2 and] Q3; | And Q1–2
10 of] Q3; | Of Q1–2
14 tis] Tis Q1–F2
14 nothing. Is] Q3; nothing, is
   Q1; ~ , Is Q2
26 you——] ~ , Q1–F2
27 'Is] Is' Q1–F2
29 *Leontius*.] Q3; *Leu*: Q1–2
30 Syr!] ~ ? Q1–2, F2; ~ . Q3
32 yeares.] Q3; ~ ? Q1–2
36, 37, 45 *Timantus*] *Timanthus* Q1
44 truly——] ~ , Q1–2, F2; ~ ;
   Q3
53–55 Q1–F2 *line*: Why...wench:
   | And...mee: | I...it.
60 not] | Not Q1–F2
64–65 Q1–F2 *line*: This...clayme
   | But...would | See...fellow.
65 looke:] ~ ₐ Q1(u); ~ , Q1(c)
67–68 Q1–F2 *line*: backe: | Can
67 -backe:] ~ , Q1–F2

68 talke?] ~ . Q1–F2
71 crying] | Crying Q1–F2
73 course] Q3; | Course Q1–2
75 for] Q3; | For Q1–2
79 eche] Q1(u); eech Q1(c)
80 not.] ~ , Q1–F2
80 thee.——] ~ , ₐ Q1–2, F2; ~ .
   ₐ Q3
81–88 Q1–F2 *line*: Syr...much |
   Honouring...byrth: | Farre
   ...the | Envious...unwor-|thy
   rising. | Beside...kingdome |
   Borne...about|And...choyse.
   | *Leontius*. If...thee, | Or...
   heere.
83 all,] Q1(u); ~ ₐ Q1(c)
94 againe,...*Ismenus*:] ~ :...~ ,
   Q1–F2
96.1 *Exeunt*.] Exeunt. | *Finis Act.
   secundi*. Q1–3

III.i

12 Regard] Q2; regard Q1

III.ii

19 nowₐ] ~ , Q1–3; ~ : F2
28–29 Q1–F2 *line*: Will...sowne
   | Of...fold
36–37 me.—— | Well] ~ . ₐ ~
   Q1–F2
62 *Telamon*,] Q3; ~ . Q1–2
75–76 Q1–F2 *line*: Whom...thy |
   Quiver...darts,
84 earth.——] ~ , ₐ Q1–2, F2;
   ~ . ₐ Q3
87–89 Q1–F2 *line*: Madame...it.
   | *Bacha*. Amen Syr. | You...
   marriage.

93–96 Q1–F2 *line*: Tis...but |
   Woud...had | Refusde...
   courtesie
93 truthₐ] ~ : Q1–F2
103 other;] ~ , Q1–F2
106 death:] ~ , Q1–F2
109–110 Q1–F2 *line*: Is...the |
   Just...time,
114–116 *Prose in* Q1–F2
115 bee.——] ~ . ₐ Q1–F2
118–119 *One line in* Q1–F2
119 mee,] Q3; ~ ₐ Q1–2
122 nothing;] Q3; ~ , Q1–2

433

123–124 *One line in* Q1–F2
125 Oath.] Q2; ~ , Q1
126 satisfaction] Q2; satistaction Q1
127 not:——...him:——] ~ :_ᴧ_
...~ ,_ᴧ_ Q1–F2±
130 Madame?] Q3; ~ . Q1–2
131 a *lavalta*] *A lavalta* Q1; *Alavalta*
Q2, F2; a Lavalta Q3
134 Fortunes] Q3; *Fortunes* Q1–2
136 Q1–F2 *line*: Yes. | And
139 alone——] ~ : Q1–2, F2; ~ .
Q3
140 Alone?] Q2; ~ . Q1
143–145 Q1–F2 *line*: What...now
| Break...then?
150 alone,——] ~ ,_ᴧ_ Q1–2; ~ :_ᴧ_
Q3, F2
151–153 Q1–F2 *line*: I...you. |
Bacha. I...me.
158–159 *One line in* Q1–F2
165 Love:...not,] ~ ,...~ : Q1–
F2
175–176 *One line in* Q1–F2
175–178 *Prose in* Q3
178–183 Q1–F2 *line*: Tis...like |
My...does. | *Bacha.* Were...
hence? | yet...you: How...
will. (Q3 *prose ll.* 178–179)
187–188 Q1–F2 *line*: Where...fed
| With endes

196–198 Q1–F2 *line*: If...counsell,
| Neither...disgrace, | But...
honour
200–204 Q1–F2 *line*: Lord...
grown | Of...mee | You...
you, | If...King.
207–208 *One line in* Q1–F2
208–211 Q1–F2 *line*: I...are | And
...power | To...you
209 other.] ~ , Q1–F2
214 wrong:] Q3; ~ , Q1–2
219–220 *One line in* Q1–F2
219 whether:] F2; ~ _ᴧ_ Q1; ~ ,
Q2–3
229 more_ᴧ_] ~ . Q1–F2
230 twenty. Yonder] ~ : yonder
Q1–F2
230 *Enter* Timantus.] Q1–F2 *place
between ll.* 229–230
231 worth_ᴧ_...himselfe,] ~ ,...~
_ᴧ_ Q1; ~ ,...~ , Q2–F2
233 uppe;] F2; ~ , Q1–3
234 owne.——] ~ :_ᴧ_ Q1–F2
235 chance,] Q2; ~ _ᴧ_ Q1
237–240 Q1–F2 *line*: I...Highnes.
| *Bacha.* But...thing: | And...
thing | Thou...mee?
239 thing:] ~ , Q1–2, F2; ~ ; Q3
243 instruction.] ~ _ᴧ_ Q1–F2
251 and] Q2; aud Q1

III.iii

1 Gentlemen.] Q3; Gentl. Q1–2
2–3 Q1–F2 *line*: And...age |
Sufferance...againe | Under
...tuition.
4 service!] ~ ? Q1–2, F2; ~ : Q3
6–15 Q1–F2± *line*: No...other
| Liberall...soone; | Lying...
now: | And...Gentlemen, | If
...it. | *Nisus.* I...my | Owne

...knaves, | Ile...certaine, |
I...goodnes, | The...paine. |
Agenor. But...mee, | Why...
experient, | Not...State?
8 humanity.] ~ _ᴧ_ Q1; ~ , Q2–
F2
9 Gentlemen,] Q3; Gent. Q1–2
26 lookes!] ~ ? Q1–F2
28 there's] Q2; rhere's Q1

434

III.iv

1–34 *Prose in* Q1–F2

27 subject——] ~ . Q1–F2

30 Dutches——] *Dutches.* Q1–F2

35–37 Q1–F2 *line:* O...joyes | To...tongue.

39–41 Q1–F2 *line:* Then...valour, | Good...honour, | They...passions | In a Woman.

45 live,] Q2; ~ ∧ Q1

46 Syr make] Q2; Syr: Make Q1

47 woman∧] ~ : Q1–F2

50 they?] Q3; ~ ∧ Q1; ~. Q2

51 Al∧] ~ , Q1–F2

51 sed] Q2; seed Q1

55 kingly,] Q2; ~ ∧ Q1

56 rule——] ~ : Q1–2, F2; ~ . Q3

58 command——] ~ ∧ Q1; ~ . Q2–F2

59 sed:] Q2; ~ ∧ Q1

67–69 *Prose in* Q1–F2

69 him?] Q3; ~ : Q1; ~ . Q2

71–72 Yes...more] *one line in* Q1–2, F2; Q3 *prose ll.* 71–73

79–83 *Prose in* Q1–2, F2; Q3 *lines:*...vices, | There...thankes, | *Timantus.* Sir...are | The...dangerous.

80 vices,] Q2; ~ ∧ Q1

84–85 *One line in* Q1–F2

84 not:] ~ , Q1–F2

89 eares∧] Q3; ~ , Q1–2

90 State?] ~ , Q1–3; ~ : F2

91 Grace] Q2; Gracc Q1

99 heate——] ~ . Q1–F2

101 returne——] ~ ∧ Q1–F2

106–107 Q1–F2 *line:* Talke...rages | leades...Religion

106 ignorant] Q2; ignoant Q1

111–113 Q1–F2 *line:* Yet...may | Perswade...watchfull,

113 watchfull,] Q2; ~ ∧ Q1

117–120 Q1–F2± *line:* Brave...shuld | follow...Father: | All...whispers. (F2 *prose ll.* 117–119 [Father: |])

120–122 *Prose in* Q1–2, F2; Q3 *lines:* strengths | Will

122–124 Q1–2 *line:* What...is | Made...alas! (*prose in* Q3–F2)

128 rages:] ~ , Q1–F2

133–135 Q1–F2 *line:* villaine, | Ile

145 pastime:——] ~ : ∧ Q1–2, F2; ~ ; ∧ Q3

151 Q1–F2 *line:* now? | The

153–154 Q1–2 *line:* Madame...doing | Service...ladie. (*prose in* Q3–F2)

155–156 *Prose in* Q1; Q2–F2 *line:* businesse, | So

155–156 businesse,...helpes:] ~ : ...~ , Q1–2, F2; ~ ,...~ , Q3

162–163 Q1–F2 *line:* woman, | Thats

168 safetie:] ~ , Q1–2, F2; ~ ; Q3

174 Gentleman∧] Q3; Gent. Q1–2

183–189 Q1–F2± *line:* Madam...us | For...King, | And...mouthes, | Weele...can. | *Dorialus.* I...before, | For...bruse | They...no-|thing...swellings.

190–191 Q1–F2 *line:* Good...good | Pleasures...meanes

195 appeare] Q2; apreare Q1

197 wilt] | Wilt Q1–F2

IV.i

4 barren] Q2; | Barren Q1
6 directs] Q2; | Directs Q1
10 the] Q2; thc Q1
13.1, 15, 65, 72.1 Telamon] Tellamon Q1–F2±
15 *Leucippus*———] ~ . Q1–F2
18–19 *Prose in* Q1–F2
28 have] Q2; hane Q1
63–64 Q1–F2 *line*: If. . .this, | My
 . . .it.
65–69 Q1–F2 *line*: Lead. . .deare |
 Bacha. . .this. | *Ismenus.* Ma-
 dame. . .before | The. . .you, |
 You. . .murderous | Strumpet
 . . .Woman.
70–71 *One line in* Q1–F2
73 dreame:] ~ ₐ Q1–2; ~ , Q3, F2
74 did,] Q2; ~ ₐ Q1
79–80 *Prose in* Q1–F2
84 death!] Q2; ~ ; Q1
89.1 *Enter* Urania.] Q3; Q1–2, F2
 place on l. 87
91–92, 96–97, 99–100 *Prose in* Q1–
 F2
97 this?] ~ . Q1–F2
101–103 Q1–F2 *line*: Are. . .this? |
 Doe. . .know | That. . .rayse |
 Her. . .Dukedome.
101 this?] F2; ~ , Q1–3
102 know] Q3; ~ , Q1–2
116 this?] ~ : Q1; ~ . Q2–F2
118–120 Q1–F2± *line*: A. . .thinkes
 | It. . .send | Her. . .too.
121–122 *One line in* Q1–F2
130 Why,] Q3; ~ ₐ Q1; ~ ; Q2
139 instigation] Q2; ~ , Q1
147 to;] Q2; ~ ₐ Q1
153 her;] ~ , Q1–F2
161 so?] ~ . Q1–F2
162–166 Q1–F2 *line*: This. . .yet |
 The. . .canted, | Ile. . .bring, |
 And. . .makes; | Looke. . .

teare. | Take. . .Fooles | First
 . . .weepe.
163 canted] F2 (Canted); *Canted*
 Q1–3
163 againe:] Q2; ~ , Q1
165 teare:] Q2; ~ , Q1
166 smart, then] Q3; ~ : Then
 Q1–2
168 worse] Q2; wosse Q1
169 mischiefe.] ~ ₐ Q1–3; ~ ,
 F2
172–180 Q1–F2± *line*: Take. . .
 scorpion, | That. . .teares, |
 Whose. . .Touch | Not. . .
 twenty | Lives. . .when | Hee
 . . .Toades. | Hee. . .now |
 Shee. . .velvet | Where. . .
 spades, | And. . .this | Fellow
 . . .is | the. . .Angell.
176 Toades.] ~ , Q1–F2
178 stood,] ~ : Q1–F2
178 spades,] ~ . Q1–F2
179 purse. The] ~ , the Q1–F2
179 tis] Q3; Tis Q1–2
182–184 *Prose in* Q1–2, F2; Q3
 lines:. . .friend, | Hast. . .
 mother | To. . .
184 selfe.] ~ ? Q1–F2
189–192 Q1–F2± *line*: Heavens
 . . .innocent, | And. . .and | Ac-
 tions. . .em.
193 reveale,] Q2; ~ ₐ Q1
195 comming,] F2; ~ . Q1–3
199 goe] Q3; Goe Q1–2
200–201 you,. . .hearing:] Q3
 (hearing:); ~ :. . .~ , Q1–2
201 plot] Q3; ~ . Q1–2
202–203 *Prose in* Q1–2, F2; Q3
 lines: knowne, | You
206–212, 218–222 *Prose in* Q1–F2
207 a way] Q2; away Q1
218 fye.] ~ , Q1–F2

223–226 Q1–F2 *line*: Goe...you: |
I...fort; | Ile...last | Longer
...Winter, | Till...dambst.

224 fort;] Q3; ~ , Q1–2

IV.ii

0.1 Telamon] Q2; Tellamon Q1
2 heard] Q2; hard Q1
6–7 Q1–F2 *line*: Fortune...ac-
tions, | And...Angells
11 Deities,] ~ ₐ Q1–F2
12 goodnes,] ~ ₐ Q1–F2
14 comes] Q2; coms Q1
16 Servants,] Q3; ~ ₐ Q1–2
18 Mother?...strumpet,] Q3; ~ ,
...~ ? Q1; ~ ;...? Q2
19 open,] Q3; ~ ₐ Q1–2
22 (for our imaginations)] ₐ ~ ~
~ ₐ Q1–F2
23 vertues.] ~ , Q1–2, F2; ~ : Q3
24 fosterd,] Q2; ~ ₐ Q1
27–28 Q1–F2 *line*: This...treason
| Open...correction.
28 treason ₐ] Q2; ~ , Q1
34 being,...it:] ~ :...~ , Q1–
F2
41 man ₐ] Q2; ~ : Q1
44 Offender:] Q2; ~ , Q1
47–49 Q1–F2 *line*: No...since |
His...that | Gave...dye, |
And...feares.
47 more:] Q3; ~ ₐ Q1; ~ ! Q2
48 dangerous, let] ~ : Let Q1–2,
F2; ~ ; let Q3
51–52 Q1–F2 *line*: To...his |
Wrong...yee.
54–55 *One line in* Q1–F2
55 mee,] ~ ₐ Q1–F2

56 Sonne:] Q2; ~ , Q1
57 Lust,] Q2; ~ : Q1
57 Ambition] *Ambition* Q1–F2
64 *Timantus.*] Q2; *omit* Q1
68–70 Q1–F2   *line*: Why...
courage | To...Guard? | In...
it.
72 Syr——] ~ . Q1–F2
74 Well?] ~ . Q1–F2
75 ithe] ith Q1–2; i'th Q3; i'th' F2
76 to the] Q2; tothe Q1
79 Duke:] ~ , Q1–2, F2; ~ ; Q3
87–88 Q1–2, F2 *line*: Goe...shall
| Never...Gates. (*prose in* Q3)
91–93 Q1–F2 *line*: Are...Age? |
Theyre...Contented | With
...King
91 the] Q2; rhe Q1
92 contented] Q2; Contented Q1
93 dangers:] ~ , Q1–F2
94 content] Q2; coutent Q1
95–96 longer:...Honour,] ~ ,...
~ : Q1–2, F2; ~ ,...~ , Q3
100 him] Q2; im Q1
105–106 *One line in* Q1–2, F2 (Q3
prints ll. 105–107 *as prose*)
106 Gentleman:] Q3; Gentl: Q1;
~ . Q2
108 weepe] Q2; weeepe Q1
109–112 Q1–F2 *line*: Come... pre-
sently | About...our | Safety
...Bed.

IV.iii

1, 6, 12 *1. Cittizen.*] *Cittizen.* Q1–
F2
3 bruze he] Q3; bruze: He Q1–2
7 grinde] Q2; | Grinde Q1

7 ont:] ~ , Q1–F2
8 two,] Q3; ~ : Q1–2
8 tackle] Q2; | Tacke Q1
9 her,] Q3; ~ ₐ Q1–2

10 handle] Q3; | Handle Q1–2
13 newes] Q2; | Newes Q1
17 fortie] Q3 (forty); 40. Q1–2
17 that] Q3; | That Q1–2
19 good] Q2; | Good Q1
20 Fire,] Q2; ~ ₍ Q1
20 Children:] ~ , Q1–3; ~ ; F2
21 world, and] ~ : And Q1–2; ~ ;
    and Q3; ~ : and F2
22 Neighbour,] F2; ~ ₍ Q1–3
23 Bastard] *Bastard* Q1–F2
23 for] Q2; | For Q1
25 laye] Q2; | Laye Q1
27 Geese] Q2; Geefe Q1
27 then.——] ~ , ₍ Q1–2; ~ . ₍
    Q3, F2
28–29 it: | Take] it: Take Q1–
    F2±
28 it:] ~ , Q1–2; ~ ; Q3; ~ . F2
29 good] Q3; | Good Q1–2
30 finger.——] | Finger. ₍ Q1–
    F2±
31–37 Q1–2, F2 *line:* And…mee,
    | That…were | Up…a | Debt

...since. | And…this | Busi-
    nesse…doe, | I…Rebellion, |
    For…spirite, (*prose in* Q3)
32 Gentlemen₍] Q3; Gentl: Q1–2
32 us;] ~ , Q1–F2
34 since.] ~ , Q1–2; ~ : Q3–F2
34 sirrah,] Q3; ~ : Q1–2
35 businesse:] ~ , Q1–F2
38 tough] Q2; | Tough Q1
39 resurrections.] Q3; ~ ; Q1–2
41–42 Q1–2, F2 *line:* Neighbours
    | Ile (*prose in* Q3)
41 *3. Cittizen within.*] *3. Within.*
    (*from this point all citizens are
    given only numerals as speech-
    prefixes*) Q1–F2
43 Polecat] *Polecat* Q1–F2
53 neighbour,] Q3; ~ ₍ Q1–2
61 surely,…tall:] ~ :…~ , Q1–
    F2
86 action?] F2; ~ . Q1–3
93 -pot:] F2; ~ , Q1–3
99 minde,] ~ ₍ Q1–F2

IV.iv

13 diseas'd,] ~ ₍ Q1–F2
20 spirit;] ~ , Q1–2, F2; ~ : Q3
22–23 *One line in* Q1–2, F2 (Q3
    lines: love | And)
24.1 Exeunt] Q2; *Exit* Q1
35–36 *One line in* Q1–F2
36 *shoute*] Q3 (*shout*); shute Q1–2
39 have,] ~ ; Q1–2, F2; ~ ₍ Q3
40 thinke;] Q3; ~ , Q1–2
40–41 Q1–2 *line:* More…from |

Danger. (Q3 *lines:* Prince | Is;
    prose in F2)
55 did;] Q2; ~ ₍ Q1
56 them,] ~ . Q1–F2
59–63 Q1–F2 *line:* Heaven…
    thee. | What…from | This…
    on | When…the | Next…
    thanks?
59 thee.] ~ , Q1–2, F2; ~ ; Q3

IV.v

1–2 *Prose in* Q1–F2
7 em: once₍] ~ ₍…~ : Q1–2,
    F2; ~ ₍…~ ₍ Q3
11–13 *Prose in* Q1–F2
15 father,] Q2; ~ ₍ Q1

16–17 *Prose in* Q1–F2
18 *Timantus,*] Q2; *Tima.* Q1
26–29 Q1–F2 *line:* This…it? |
    Heaven…with; | But…here,
    | She…safetie.

438

27 know, if‸] Q2; ~ ‸ ~ , Q1
34–35 Q1–2 *line*: A...Ile | Take
my leave. (Q3 *lines*: so | Ile;
prose in F2)
36 Of] Q2; of Q1

41 absolutely] Q2; obsolutely Q1
81–84 *Prose in* Q1–F2
88.1 *Exeunt.*] Q1 *follows with* ' *Finis
Actus quartus.*'

V.i

1 What,] Q3; ~ ‸ Q1–2
15 husband;] ~ , Q1–F2
22–23 *One line in* Q1–F2
24 first;] ~ , Q1–F2
25 your] Q2; yonr Q1
26–27 *One line in* Q1–F2
28, 31 Why,] Q3; ~ ‸ Q1–2
33 if] Q2; If Q1
34 you,] Q3; ~ : Q1; ~ ; Q2

35 me:] Q2; ~ , Q1
43 does‸] ~ : Q1–F2
45 then] Q3; ten Q1–2
46–47, 51–52 *Prose in* Q1–F2
56 but] | But Q1–F2
65 if] Q3; | If Q1–2
67 wou'd] Q2; woud Q1
79–80 Q1–2 *line*: In...was | Ever
...naught.

V.ii

2 Letter,] Q3; ~ ‸ Q1–2
3 pocket. Would] ~ , would Q1–
F2
4 agoe] Q2; a goe Q1
7 Make] Q2; make Q1
8 sicke,] F2; ~ : Q1–2; ~ . Q3

18 have] Q2; hane Q1
26 much] Q2; mnch Q1
34 againe] Q2; a againe Q1
36–37 dead,...spirit:] ~ : ... ~ ,
Q1–F2±

V.iv

0.1 Urania.] Q2; Urana,: Q1
6 Alas ‸ ...pitty,] ~ , ... ~ ‸ Q1–
F2
11–15 Q1–F2± *line*: My...truely
| Good...harmelesse | Inno-
cense...goe | Save...not |
chide thee.
12 faith:] Q3; ~ ‸ Q1; ~ , Q2
14 selfe?] ~ , Q1; ~ ; Q2–F2
16–28 *Prose in* Q1–F2
16 tell;] ~ ‸ Q1–2, F2; ~ , Q3
16 you ‸ Syr,] ~ , ~ ‸ Q1; ~ ,
~ ; Q2–F2
18 (I...you) ‸ ~ ... ~ : Q1–F2
18 to...let] Q2; | To...Let
Q1

21 Prophets——] ~ , Q1; ~ :
Q2–F2
23 eate ‸ then] ~ , ~ ‸ Q1–F2
24 if] Q2; | If Q1
31–38 *Prose in* Q1–F2
32 (This...yet:) ‸ ~ ... ~ : ‸ Q1–
F2
34 dotes:——] ~ : ‸ Q1–F2
40–47 *Prose in* Q1–F2
40 (This...of:)] ‸ ~ ... ~ : ‸ Q1–
F2
42 thee:——] ~ : ‸ Q1–F2
46 And] and Q1–F2
49 this] Q2; rhis Q1
57–59 *Prose in* Q1–F2
62 receives] Q2; recives Q1

67 *Timantus*. His...sir——] Q 1–
   F 2 *place after stage-direction*
68–78 *Prose in* Q 1–2
69 day.] ~ , Q 1–F 2
71 childe?——] ~ ?_∧ Q 1–F 2
89–90 Q 1–2, F 2 *line*: Both...the |
   Whole...no? (Q 3 *lines*: and |
   The)
92–95 *Prose in* Q 1–F 2
100 And] | and Q 1–F 2±
103–107 Q 1–F 2 *line*: There...me.
   | Now...no | Usage...thou |
   Longer...chidde | Thee...
   forgiven.
109–111 *Prose in* Q 1–F 2
114 have] Q 2; hane Q 1
114, 115 Page] F 2; *Page* Q 1–3
122–123 *One line in* Q 1–F 2
129–130 *Prose in* Q 1–2, F 2
136–139 *Prose in* Q 1–F 2
139–146 Q 1–F 2 *line*: I...wilt |
   Thou...thee? | Speake...it, |
   She...more. | What...who |

Comes...you | That...de-
   lights | Be...hence.
150–156 *Prose in* Q 1–F 2
153 Mother] F 2; *Mother* Q 1–3
161–162 Q 1–F 2 *line*: That...end-
   ing. | May...doe:
167–168 Q 1–2 *line*: Would...such
   | Griefe...there,
180–181 *One line in* Q 1–F 2
184–205 *Prose in* Q 1–F 2
193 Fortune] F 2 (fortune); *Fortune*
   Q 1–3
199 here.] ~ , Q 1–F 2
209–211 Q 1–F 2 *line*: First...is |
   Undoubtedly...all,
214–217 Q 1–F 2 *line*: I...you. |
   Next...Duke, | I...*Cupid* |
   Be...him.
216 Image] Q 3; *Image* Q 1–2
220 May] | may Q 1–F 2±
224 According] | according Q 1–
   F 2±

440

[NOTE: The following editions are herein collated: Q1 (1615), Q2 (1630), Q3 (1635), F2 (1679), L (*Works*, 1711, ed. Gerard Langbaine the Younger), S (*Works*, 1750, ed. Theobald, Seward, and Sympson), C (*Works*, 1778, ed. George Colman the Younger), W (*Works*, 1812, ed. Henry Weber), D (*Works*, 1843–46, ed. Alexander Dyce). Occasional references to M list readings in Monck Mason's *Comments*, 1797. Only substantive and semi-substantive variants are recorded. Dialect forms originating in Q1–F2 but not in later editors are listed, except for the Q3 substitution of *um* for Q1–2 *em*.]

Printer to the Reader] omit Q2+

I.i

11 on's] of one's S; of his C, W
18 yeere] years C, W
21 one] once Q3, W, D
35 hastily] heartily S, C, W
36 graunts] grant F2, L, S
37 upon] on S
41 you and] *omit* Q1–F2, L, S, C; me and you M, W, D
51 selfe-pleasing] false-pleasing F2, L, S
58 Contemnd] conjoynd Q1–F2, L, W
60 obey.] ~ , Q1–2, F2; ~ ; Q3
71 To these] These Q1–F2, L; And these S, C, W, D
72 And] *omit* S, C, W, D
72 Palace] Palace self S, C
74 erected] erect Q2–F2, L
80 There] Sir, there S
89 Doe] To do S, C, W
104 Lords] Lord Q2–F2, L, S, C, W

110 a] *omit* S
114 gin] giv'n Q3+
121 was] 'twas M, W, D
123 needed] need Q1–F2, L
124 whores] woers Q1–F2, L
126 will] shall Q2+(−D)
127 flesh ‸ now:] ~ : ~ ‸ Q1–F2, L
130 grew] and grew Q3, C
130 fine] five Q3
131 though they wore] Though they weare Q1–F2, L; nay, They let us wear S, C, W; as though they were M
137 pray] to pray W
143 depose] despose Q2–3
143 ha] have Q2+
148 savour] favour W
149 out, now] ~ ‸ ~ , Q1–F2, L, S, C
151 lawfull] awful M

I.ii

0.1 *Enter*] omit Q1–F2
4 For] *omit* C

5 To] Lo Q1–2, F2, L
21 *regarded*] *rewarded* Q1

22 *maid*] *maids* Q 2+ (–D)
29 *It*] *omit* S, M
42 the] their Q 3, C, W

42 Images] Image F 2, L, S
51 your] our F 2, L
52 make] *omit* Q 1–2, F 2

I.iii

3 gods ∧ and weakned?] ~ ? ~ ~
    ∧ Q 1–F 2, L, S
6 who kneel] whose knees Q 1+
    (–D); who've knelt M
6 my] the L, S
11 flying] fly Q 3, C, W; fling S, D
13 of] off F 2, L

14 heart] hearts S, C, W
14 despisd] despise Q 1–2, F 2, L, S,
    C, W
16 this] his Q 1–F 2, L
17 or] of C, W
19 sweete] *omit* F 2, L

I.iv

2 Meanes] What meanes Q 2+
    (Whom means S)
30 Traytors:] ~ ∧ Q 1(c)–F 2, L
30 my] in my Q 1–F 2, L
36 me ∧ love] ~ , Love Q 1–F 2, L
37 *Cleophila.*] *omit* L

47 Ha, ha, ha] Ha, ha S
62 does] doth Q 2+
65 besides] beside S, C, W
93 madly] thus madly S
101 with all] withal F 2

I.v

3 I] *omit* L
6 theres] there are S, C, W
6 nor] *omit* S
14 of] *omit* Q 1
17 have] must have S, C, W
18 be] are C, W
24 This] These F 2+
26 life] hold F 2, L
40.1 *Enter*] *Enter* Hidaspes, Nisus,
    and Zoylous. Q 2+
42–43 not,...mee;] ~ ;...~ ,
    Q 1–F 2, L, S
49 not] not that S
51 thats] that that's S
52 must] *omit* S
52 Heaven] Heav'n's sake S
61, 63 In way] in the way Q 2+
75 My] *omit* Q 2+ (–D)

108 before] for Q 1–F 2, L
110 you:] ~ ∧ Q 1–F 2, L
112 I] *omit* Q 1
129 Has] He has W
132 fits] *omit* Q 1–F 2, L; suits S
133 of it needs must yee] of it yee
    needs must Q 1(c)–2, F 2, L; of
    it ye must needs Q 3; of you
    needs must S, C, W; of ye needs
    must D
134 this] these S, C, W
135–136 scurvily:...man,] ~ ,...
    ~ : Q 1–F 2±
136 let] and let S
136 his] this F 2, L
141 a Cloake...out] Cloke...out
    in S

442

II.i

4 unhappie] happie Q 1–2
5 part] Party S

7 his] this F 2, L
9 smart] dart Q 3, S, C, W

II.ii

10 your] you your S, C, W
17 that is] thats Q 1–F 2, L
23 *Bacha.*] *Leu.* Q 1
29 I] you Q 1
32 thought] thoughts Q 2+ (−D)
35 tell the] tell all the Q 2+ (−D)
49 right a] a right L, S
64 one] on F 2, L
71 Dosen] donor M
71 esteeme] steem F 2, L
90 love] *omit* Q 1
91 comfort] comforts F 2, L, S
112 mine] my F 2, L, S, C
128 am] am indeed D (*conj.*)
141 a] *omit* S
144 you] thou Q 2+

146 doubt] doubt but Q 2+
166 with her then] then With her S
177 my gold] *omit* my Q 1+
183 the age] her age Q 2+ (−M, D)
187 Sir] *omit* Q 1–F 2, L, C, W; for
　　it S
188 you father] your father L; you
　　farther S, M, W, D
192 me] my Q 2–3
200 multitudes] multitude Q 2+
　　(−D)
220 And] *omit* S
232 goe] begone Q 2+
238 frontlets] frontleste Q 2; front-
　　less F 2+

II.iii

1 Gentlemen, this] This, Gentle-
　　men, S
7 ath] o'th Q 2+
19 dide] dye Q 3, C, W, D

22 a hangd] *omit* a Q 3, C, W; ha'
　　hanged D
22 what] why S
25 race] *omit* Q 1–F 2, L; Love of
　　S, C; love, the M

II.iv

4 *Timantus.*] *Tela.* Q 1
11 on's] of his S, C
13 like] just like S
19 ha] have Q 3
26 has] he has S, C
30 a] an F 2+
41 this] the W
44 growne] growe Q 2

54 *Timantus,*] *Leon.* Q 2–F 2, L;
　　omit S, C, W
54 Let] and let S
56 thou] *omit* S
61 Sir] *omit* S
61 sword] sword, Sir S
72 then] thus S, C, W

II.v

4 stirre] *Hero.* Stir Q3+ (−S)
4 *Hero*] *omit* Q3+ (−S)
6 women] woman Q2, F2
14 each] at Q2+ (−D)
22 the] *omit* Q1; our Q2+
26 it] is Q3, C

31–32 late. *Cleophila.* Why...
breathed.] *Cleo.* Why. | *Hero.*
Leave, leave! 'tis now too late:
Shee is dead, | Her last is breathed.
Q3, C, W, D
31 shee is] is she L, S

II.vi

2 theres a] there is a F2, L, S
4 away] *omit* Q3, C, W
7 seeme] see me Q1–F2, L
9 welcome] freely welcome S
22 yee] you C, W, D
27 'Is] He's Q3, C, W, D
30 will] will sure S
41 yee] you C, W, D
44 I am an] I'm S
56–57 whore shall I never bee]
whore shall never: Q1–2, F2,
L; whore I shall be never S;
whore you shall never Q3;
whore! (*or?*) You shall never C,
W, D
60 Such] Sir, such S

60 Syr] *omit* S
60 not] not for S
61 well] well enough S
68 Mummy] Mumming Q1–F2, L
74 I] *fails to ink* Q2; *omit* F2, L, S
75 pine] pine for Q3, C, W, D
78 you're madde else:] your Maide,
else ‿ Q1–2; you Mayd, Q3;
you Maid, else ‿ F2, L; you're
made. What C; you're made!
Else W
93 the] *omit* Q2+
93 morning. *Timantus*, let] morning *Timantus*. Let Q1–3
94 mile] miles Q2+

III.i

14 pound] pounds F2+

III.ii

3 of] off F2, L
6 that all's] that's all S
26 The] Thy L
30 of] on Q2+
31 Sir, your Highnes] Your high-
ness, Sir, S
31 Duke] King Q3, C, D
34 pray how have] pray you, have
Q2, F2, L, S; pray you, how
have Q3, C, W

47 doe] to do W
50 soone] swoone Q2+
53 Thy good Mother] By thy
Mother's S
62 I can stand...] Why, *Telamon*,
I can stand now alone Q3, C,
W, D
83 would] should F2, L, S
93 did] that did Q3, C, W
95 so beene] been so L, S, W

444

108 to a] to his L, S, W
124 knew] know Q1
136 *Bacha.*] *Leu.* Q1
153 ashamde:] ~ ‸ M, W
157 fast] hast Q1–F2, L, S, C
185 as] at L, S, C
185 my] me W
196 wickedly] *omit* Q1+ (−D)

201 You are] you'r F2, L, S, D; are you Q3, C
217 deserve it, it] deserve, it Q1+
221 goodly] godly D
234 owne: —— *Timantus. Timantus.*] ~ : ‸ ~ . Q1–3; ~ : ~ , ~ . F2
240 wouldst] couldst Q3

III.iii

3 selfe] *omit* Q1–F2
4 tenor] Tenure S, C, W, D
11 if] yet if S
15 experient] experienc't Q3, C, W

15 doer] dore Q1–F2, L
19 prou'de] prov'd Q3
28 O'] O Q2–F2, L
32 that] it S

III.iv

2 a] *omit* F2, L
8 immoderate] moderate Q1–F2
10 so] *omit* L
17 blessings] blessing Q1–F2, L, D
20 worthy] worthy of Q3, C
24 I] A Q2
33 with] with him Q3, C, W
33 qualities] frailties Q1–F2, L, W; virtues S
34 Thus] this Q1
39 for his] for all his Q1–F2, L, W
39 good] and good S, C
42 at] for Q3, C
54 this] his S, C, W
54 forwardnes] frowardnes Q1
64.1 *Enter* Timantus.] *omit* Q1–2, F2, L
69 you] do you S
75 take] talke Q2+ (−D)
78 virtue,] ~ : Q1–2, F2, L
97 *Leontius.*] *Timan.* Q1
100 me] me to S
103 yee] you C, W, D
106 prate] prate, Sir, S
106 leades] Lead S+

115 how] you Q1
116 upon] on S
117 Brave] Poor brave S
122 shorter.] shorter. | *Leon.* Ile cut him shorter first, then let him rule. Q2+ (Q3+ *sp. pref. dropped*)
129 never] ever S+ (+M)
140 Still let it be] Till yet be Q1–2, F2, L; Till you see Q3, C, W, D; Still beset S
148 and that] and that—— Q3, C, W; and—— S
163 all *Affricke*] all the monsters in Afric Q3, C, W, D
170 has] hath Q3
170 ever] *omit* Q2+ (−D)
171 murmure] murmurs D
172 knowe] knowes Q1–F2
179 the] a Q3, C, W, D
184 loves] lives Q1–2, F2, L
193 stirre mainely] mainly stir S
199 hands] hand Q3+
199 inspird] inspire Q1–F2, L

445

IV.i

1 And] *omit* Q3, C, W
4 ithe] in the Q3, C, W
7 have] gave Q1
13 chafes] he chafes S
17 knew] knows F2, L, S
31 and] that Q3
42 way] a way W
68 it] *omit* Q2+(−D)
68 wickedst] wicked C, W, D
71 I can...him_∧] can I...him? F2, L, S
112 wrong] wrang Q3, C, W, D
125 you are] thou art Q2+

133 to] too Q2–F2
141 All wayes] Alwayes Q2+
143 Never] Then never S
149 Showre] Shewe Q1
152 preserving] presuming Q1
157 ith] in this S, C, W
158 without] with but Q1–F2, L; without or S, C
158 or] not Q3
163 see] seem S
164 bring] b'a Rogue S; be one M
175 from] for Q2+ (−D)
195 whom] which L, S

IV.ii

2 will] will is Q3, C, W
6 O] *omit* S
6 yee] you Q3, F2, S+; *omit* L
6 my] me Q1
7 Fortune] O Fortune S
8 within] in S
18 strumpet] trumpet C, W, D
19 open] upon Q1–F2, L
22 our] all our L, S
22 imaginations] imitations W
26 innocentst] innocence S+
27 Mens] Mans Q3, C, W, D

30 Breedes] Breed C, W, D
35 O ease] Cease Q1–F2, L
44 have you] you have S
52 yee] you C, W, D
66 thou? speake] ∼ ∧ ∼ ? Q1
69 thy] my L
82 thought] thoughts S
83 The] I'th Q3–F2, C, W, D
89 *There*] *Here* Q3
98 infection] affection F2, L
104 innocencie] innocence S, C, W
108 could] would Q1

IV.iii

3 store] stone Q2+
7 ont] out Q1–F2, L
8 bracers] the bracers Q3, C, W
9 Mayds] Mans F2, L
20 Fire, a] fire o' C, W, D
22 theyr honours] *omit* C, W, D
22 Neighbour] neighbours Q3, C
28 Ifack] *Jacke* Q3, C, W, D
33 a beaten] and beaten Q2+
33 a debt] o' debt S, D; of C, W

38 is] h'is Q2; he's Q3, D; he is S, C
63 2.] *1.* Q1
73 yee] you Q3
73 I] now I F2, L, S
73 you] ye Q3, W
74 were] are F2, L, S
78 and] An't Q3, C, W, D; And't S
98 yee] wee Q1
99 you] ye C, W
100 a] an F2+

IV.iv

2 upon] on S
17 my] *omit* S
20 will] would Q3, C, W, D
22 you] y' S; ye C, W

24 you] ioy Q1
27 That] Thou Q2–F2, L, S
39 that] what W
56 shew] shew'd L+

IV.v

7 yee] of ye S
15 an] or any S
17 leave] leave thee Q3; will leave
   S+ (−D)
19 sithes‸] scythes. S (sithes.), C,
   W, D
19 wee] We've S

23 should] shall Q3, C, W
30 pardon] pardon me D (*conj.*)
34 to] unto C
51 hell] heele Q1
76 it] *omit* W
81 farewell] and farewell S, C, W
85 me] my F2+

V.i

3 Gods] God S, W
16 breeches] the breeches F2, L, S
23 me] we Q1
28 not thou] thou not F2, L, S
31 wits] my wits S
37 faith] feith Q3, C, W; feth D

43 you] y' S; ye C, W
46 would] could F2, L, S
51 feth] ifeth S
61 reparrell] apparel F2, L, S
66 little] the little S
79 ai] a Q3, L

V.ii

0.1 Timantus.] Timantus: Bacha
   reading a Letter. Q1+(−D)
13 Feare] Fear for S
16 thou] to Q1
17 weare a] were of Q2+
32 one home] home one Q3
42 sawcy] you saucy S
43, 45 yee...yee] you...you C,
   W, D

44 you] *omit* L
50 -like] *omit* C, M, W, D
52 in] to Q3+ (−F2)
63 thee] the L
64 upon] to on S
66 gode] a gode Q2+
68 Ha] I la F2, L

V.iii

1 Revenge] full revenge D (*query*)

V.iv

0.1 Urania.] Urania: Leucippus
    with a bloudy handkercher. Q1–
    F2, L
13 innocense] Innocency S
17 dawne] draw L, S, C
22 I] *omit* S
23 then] *omit* Q2+ (−D)
24 fasts] fast F2+
25 This] These S, C, W
27 thee] thee there S
32 that] *omit* S
33 thou] you Q1
38 you] you there S
48 sen] selfe Q2+
49 in] into S, W, D
51 steps] stept Q1; stepst Q2+
52 is nor] is no Q2+
54 a] *omit* Q1–2, F2, L, S
60 discovered now] now discovered
    S
68 fro] from Q3+
68 him...me] me...him Q1–F2,
    L, S, C

71 this] his Q1–2, F2
73 drawne] drawe Q2
84 thy] the Q2+ (−D)
85 therefore] therefore receive S, C
110 thy] my Q1
114 *Timantus.*] *omit* F2
147 for] 'tis for S
151 They] And they S
156 or] *omit* Q1
166 plague] please Q1–F2, L, S;
    poyson Q3, C, W, D
188 miserable] miserably Q2+
189 The] ev'n the S
193 steep] step Q1–F2
195 stood] have stood S
197 Ho] Oh Q3, C, W, D
210 undoubtedly] undoubted S, C,
    W
216 Image] Images S, C, W, D
228 *Agenor,* goe] *Agenor.* Goe Q2+
    (−D)
233 one man] woman D

THE SCORNFUL LADY

edited by

CYRUS HOY

TEXTUAL INTRODUCTION

The Scornful Lady (Greg, *Bibliography*, no. 334) was entered in the Stationers' Register on 19 March 1616 by Miles Partridge: '*Ent. M. Patriche: lic. G. Bucke: a plaie called The Scornefull Ladie, by Fra. Beaumont and Jo. Flecher.*' The text of the first quarto edition, printed for Partridge by (according to Greg) Richard Bradock, duly appeared in that year. On 8 May 1617, the Register records the transfer of Partridge's rights in the play to T. Jones, a transaction that is at some variance with the information set forth on the title-page of the next edition, the quarto of 1625, which declares that text to have been 'Printed for M.P. and are to be sold by Thomas Iones'. 'M.P.' is presumably the same Miles Partridge who published Q1, though, as Greg notes, 'he is not otherwise known to have been in business after 1618'. Greg identifies the printer of Q2 as Augustine Mathewes. Whatever the precise role of Jones (publisher or bookseller) in relation to Q2, his role as the publisher of Q3 (1630) is clear from the title-page of that edition, which was printed by Bernard Alsop and Thomas Fawcet. On 24 October 1633, the Register records the transfer of Jones's rights in copy for the play to A. Mathewes, and in 1635 Mathewes, who ten years before had served as printer for Q2, printed his own edition, the fourth thus far to appear. Q5, which appeared in 1639, was printed by 'M.P.' (Marmaduke Parsons who, according to Greg, 'had taken over the press of Mathewes'); the Robert Wilson for whom, according to the Q5 title-page, the text was printed had, says Greg, 'no apparent interest in the copy: he died this year or the next'. Technically, copy for the play was still the property of Mathewes, and the Register, under date of 28 July 1641, records its transfer to J. Raworth; on 4 March 1647, the Register records its subsequent transfer from Raworth's widow to Humphrey Moseley, and Moseley was the publisher of the next quarto edition, the sixth, which appeared in 1651; the printer was apparently William Wilson. There are in existence, in fact, three separate editions each bearing the date '1651' on its title-page, of which only one (Greg 334f) is the genuine Moseley article, actually printed in that year. The other two (Greg 334g and 334h) are pirated editions, the products of Francis Kirkman's celebrated publishing activities in and around the year 1661. What terms itself 'The Seventh Edition' (appropriately enough, if all the editions dated 1651 are regarded as a single one) appeared in 1677, with a title-page proclaiming the play 'As it was acted with great Applause by the late Kings Majesties Servants, at the Black-Fryers': a piece of information that was up-dated by means of a cancel title-page publicizing the play 'As it is now Acted at the Theater Royal'. The publishers appear to have been Dorman Newman and Thomas Collins. The cancel title-page reveals a change of bookseller, from Langley Curtis to Simon Neale. The play next appeared in the 1679 Folio collection of Beaumont and Fletcher's *Comedies and Tragedies*. An 'Eighth Edition' was printed in quarto in 1691, for Dorman Newman. No ninth edition, proclaimed as such, is known. An undated 'Tenth Edition' (Greg 334l), probably published by Jacob Tonson, cannot, as will later be shown, have been printed earlier than 1710.

The first quarto (1616) is the only substantive edition of the play, each succeeding quarto text being but a reprint of the edition immediately preceding it, through Moseley's Q6. However, though Q6 was printed from Q5, here, for the first and only time in the sequence of the ten seventeenth-century quarto editions, some consultation back to Q1 was made. It was, to be sure, of the slightest, and some of the Q6 restorations of Q1 readings that had come either to be omitted from or corrupted in the intervening five editions may have been fortuitous (as at II.ii.104, II.iii.22, IV.ii.36, V.ii.198, V.iv.52; see Historical Collation). But consultation of a copy of Q1 is demonstrable near the beginning of IV.i, where Q6 recovers four readings (at IV.i.58, 65, 69, 87–88; see Historical Collation) omitted in Qq 2–5.

Concerning the other two editions dated 1651, Greg suggested, though without certainty, that the text which he designated as 334h (and which in the apparatus to the present edition is designated as Q7) was printed from 334f (the true Q6), and a complete collation of the two editions makes it clear that this is so. However, his suggestion that 334h 'may be even later than' 334g cannot be, for

Johan Gerritsen has demonstrated 'that 334g was set from 334f for sheets A–D, [and] from 334h for sheets E–H'.[1] Thus Greg's 334g (designated in the apparatus to the present edition as Q8) derives in part from Q6 and in part from Q7. The 1677 quarto, designated in the present edition as Q9, was printed from Q6. The text of the play in the 1679 Folio was printed from Q3. The quarto of 1691, designated in the present edition as Q10, was printed from Q9. The undated 'Tenth Edition', designated in the present edition as Q11, was printed from Q10.

Regarding this undated quarto, Greg notes that 'the BM catalogue queries 1695 as the date', but the catalogue to which he is referring is that of 1881–1900 (Supplementary Volume 2–B, published in 1900). The 1965 British Museum catalogue (Volume 13) queries 1710 as the date of this edition, and that is certainly very much closer the truth. The edition can in fact be dated with considerable precision by means of a cast list (sig. A3ᵛ) which represents the play as it was being acted during the season 1710–11 by the company at Drury Lane. The Dramatis Personae which the undated quarto sets forth and which seems hitherto to have gone unnoticed is as follows:

Elder Loveless	Mr. Wilks
Young Loveless	Mr. Mills
Savil	Mr. Dogget

[1] 'The Dramatic Piracies of 1661: A Comparative Analysis', *Studies in Bibliography*, xi (1958), 128. I do not understand why, on p. 129, Dr Gerritsen refers to 334h as 'the eighth edition'. His own demonstration that 334g was printed in part from 334h must establish the priority of the latter, which is properly the seventh edition. Elsewhere Gerritsen's description of the three editions dated 1651 is far from clear. He refers on p. 122 to 'the second *Scornful Lady*, Greg's no. 334g' and two lines later to 'the first *Scornful Lady*' which shares with Kirkman's pirated edition of Heywood's *Love's Mistress* a damaged letter N on its title-page (which I have not been able to discover), and a row of fleurs-de-lis enclosed in parentheses above, and a row of dashes below, the Dramatis Personae on sig. A2. The only 1651 edition to which this applies is 334h. Gerritsen is wrong in stating that it was Professor Bowers who noted that the fleuron band on A1ᵛ of *Love's Mistress* recurred on A2 of *The Scornful Lady*; neither play is mentioned in the article by Bowers that Gerritsen cites in footnote 5. In fact, the identification, which first linked the 334h *Scornful Lady* to the Kirkman piracies, seems first to have been made by R. C. Bald (in 'Francis Kirkman, Bookseller and Author', *Modern Philology*, xli (1943–4), 26), though Bald unaccountably calls it 334g. In the passage referred to on p. 122 of Gerritsen's article, he seems to be echoing the language of Strickland Gibson (*A Bibliography of Francis Kirkman*, Oxford Bibliographical Society Publications, New Series, 1 [1947], 59).

Lady	Mrs. Oldfield
Martha	Mrs. Bicknell
Abigail	Mrs. Willis
Welford	Mr. Booth
Roger	Mr. Cibber
Captain	Mr. Cross
Traveller	Mr. Carnaby
Poet	Mr. Norris
Tobacco Man	—
Morecraft	Mr. Bullock
Widow	Mrs. Cox

The point to be noted is that the actors and actresses whose names are given herein could have been assembled together for a performance of *The Scornful Lady* in the season 1710–11, and for at least two seasons thereafter, but not before. Wilks, Mills, Dogget, Mrs Oldfield, Mrs Bicknell, Mrs Willis, Cibber, and Bullock had acted the play at the Queen's theatre during the previous season, 1709–10, but Booth and Norris were members of the Drury Lane company during that season,[1] and in the partial cast that is recorded for the performance of the play on 11 February 1710, no mention is made of the actor who took the part of Welford, while Bowen, not Norris, played the Poet (Avery, p. 212). But with the re-alignment of the Queen's and the Drury Lane companies in November 1710, the actors named in the quarto cast list have been brought together (Avery, pp. 233–4); and the record that has been preserved of the cast which acted the play on 25 January 1711 is the cast of the quarto, so far as it goes (Avery, p. 241). The quarto list goes farther, for it supplies what no other record of this period does: the names of the actors who played the roles of the Captain, the Traveller, and the Widow.

The undated 'Tenth Edition' is not, then, a seventeenth-century edition; it cannot have appeared earlier than the very end of 1710, and more probably dates from 1711.[2] The text has its value to the

[1] Emmett L. Avery, editor, *The London Stage 1660–1800, Part 2: 1700–1729* (Carbondale, Illinois, 1960), p. 198.

[2] It can of course be somewhat later than this. The cast recorded for the performance of 25 January 1711 (which is the cast of the quarto) was still acting together in performances of the play on 11 October 1711, 4 January 1712, and 28 February 1713 (Avery, pp. 260, 266, 296). By the end of that year it has begun to alter; Johnson

historian of the theatre, with its list of actors and its 'Epilogue Spoken by Mr. *Pinkethman*, mounted on an Ass; a long Whig on the Ass's Head' (the same ploy, with the same actor, to which audiences of some six years before had been treated in performances of Henry Norris's revision of Beaumont and Fletcher's *Beggar's Bush*, titled *The Royal Merchant* (Avery, p. 96)). But its value to the textual scholar is distinctly limited. It represents a final deterioration of the textual line, now thoroughly muddied from the accumulated errors of eight reprintings extending over almost a full century, and its numerous substantive departures from its source (the 1691 quarto) have no authority. And while at one point (III.ii.116) I have received an emendation from it into the present edition, I have not thought fit to further swell an already abundant historical collation by including the undated quarto's many variant readings therein.

The most important information about these editions may be summarized as follows:

Edition	Date	Publisher(s)	Printer(s)	Set from
Q1	1616	Partridge	Bradock	MS
Q2	1625	Partridge (?)	Mathewes	Q1
Q3	1630	Jones	Alsop & Fawcet	Q2
Q4	1635	Mathewes	Mathewes	Q3
Q5	1639	Mathewes	Parsons	Q4
Q6 (Greg, 334f)	1651	Moseley	Wilson	Q5
Q7 (Greg, 334h)	c. 1661	Kirkman	Johnson	Q6
Q8 (Greg, 334g)	c. 1661	Kirkman	Johnson (?)	Q6 and Q7
Q9	1677	Newman & Collins	Maxwell & Roberts	Q6
F2	1679	Marriot *et al.*	Macock	Q3
Q10	1691	Newman	?	Q9
Q11 (Greg, 334l)	c. 1711	Tonson	?	Q10

Three scenes from *The Scornful Lady* (III.ii, IV.i.1–99, IV.ii.56–106), strung together under title of 'The False Heire', were reprinted in abridged form in Kirkman's *The Wits, or Sport upon Sport* (1662). The text used there seems in the main to have been

replaces Dogget as Savil in the performance of 18 December 1713 (Avery, p. 313), and in all subsequent performances through the period ending 1729 for which a cast is recorded.

Q5, though at one point (IV.i.58) some one of the editions dated 1651 has been consulted since the word 'royal' (omitted from Q2–5 but restored in Q6–8) is given.

Q1 must be the copy-text for any edition of the play, and on it critical attention will centre. It was printed from a manuscript very nearly related to the authors' own papers. Whether the manuscript behind Q1 was prepared by one of the dramatists (if either, it is more likely to have been Beaumont, in view of the scarcity of Fletcher's famous *ye*'s[1]), or, as seems somewhat more likely, by a scribe, the quarto print exhibits a number of features, specifically with reference to stage-directions, that are more likely to be traceable to an authorial manuscript or a transcript thereof, than to a manuscript that had been prepared for use in the theatre. There are some inconsistencies and errors, notably in the early pages. Abigail's initial speech-prefixes (at I.i.25, 29, 33, 37, 39) are all labelled 'Younglove'; and she continues to be 'Younglove' in stage-directions through II.i.47.1. Thereafter, she is regularly referred to as 'Abigail'. The quarto stage-direction which opens II.i reads: '*Enter Lady, her sister Martha, Welford, Yongloue, and others.*' But in fact only the Lady, Welford, and Sir Roger (who is not named) are on stage when II.i begins. No 'others' are ever to appear in the course of the scene, though Martha and Younglove are brought on in another (correct) entrance forty-seven lines later; here, however, Martha has undergone a change of name: '*Enter Maria the Ladies sister, and Yongloue to them with a posset.*' The quarto abounds with stage-directions that could not have been of much use in a prompt-book: e.g. I.ii.63.1: '*Enter his Comrades. Captaine, Traueller.*' where 'his' refers to Young Loveless, and the Comrades named represent but two of the total four; unnamed are the Poet, who has a speaking part in the scene that follows, and the Tobacco-man, who is a mute throughout. In all their subsequent entrances, the Comrades are simply brought on in a body, and no attempt is made to specify them individually. Characters are regularly introduced in terms of their function: '*Savill the Steward*' (I.i.0.1),

---

[1] For an account of the division of the play's authorship, see my 'The Shares of Fletcher and his Collaborators in the Beaumont and Fletcher Canon (III)', *Studies in Bibliography*, XI (1958), 96.

'*Mistres Yongloue the waiting woman*' (I.i.23.1), '*Sir Roger the Curate*' (I.i.259.1), '*Moorecraft the vsurer*' (II.iii.0.1). Sometimes a stage-direction trails off into a fine authorial imprecision, as at III.ii.0.1–3: '*Enter Yo. Louelesse and Comrades, Moorcraft, Widow, Sauil, and the rest.*' Sometimes a direction has the effect of conveying not so much a sense of the stage business, as an account of what has happened in the plot: '*Enter young Louelesse and Widdow, going to be married*' (IV.ii.0.1–2). And the designation of a character varies as his role alters; after the Widow is married, she becomes Young Loveless' 'Lady' in the stage-direction at V.iv.101.1. The authorial provenance of such textual features as these is familiar; so it is too with the use of such phrases as 'to them' and 'to him' in stage-directions (e.g. at I.i.201.1, II.i.47.2, II.iii.57.2, III.i.312.1), and the Latin stage-direction, '*Exeunt omnes præter*' etc., used at I.i.225, and III.ii.221.

From the evidence of the running-titles, the composition of Q I proceeded as follows: work was begun using a single skeleton-forme, and in this was printed both the outer and inner formes of sheets B and C. But with sheet D a second skeleton-forme was added, and this with the original one was used in the printing of sheets D, E, F, and G (Skeleton-forme 1 used for outer D, E, and F, and inner G; Skeleton-forme 2 used for inner D, E, and F, and outer G). With sheet H a third skeleton-forme was constructed, and this was used in printing both the outer and the inner formes of that sheet; it is readily distinguished by the spelling *Lady* in all four of its running-titles (*Ladie* in all running-titles elsewhere in the text outside sheet H), and by the spelling *Scornfull* in two of them (*Scornefull* in all running-titles elsewhere in the text). Sheet I returns to the pattern of sheet G, with Skeleton-forme 1 printing the inner forme, and forme 2 printing the outer. Running-titles from these two formes were used in printing half-sheet K.

But the most remarkable bibliographical feature of Q I consists in the evidence to be assembled from the printer's measure. Sheets B and C were set by a compositor using a 90 mm. measure. With sheets D and E it is increased to 94 mm., and with sheets F and G the measure goes up to 100 mm. Sheet H, an anomaly as already noted in its running-titles, is set with a 95 mm. measure. The

100 mm. measure of sheets F and G is resumed with sheet I, and continues to the end (sig. K2ᵛ).

Two things are apparent from the foregoing: that as work on the printing of the play progressed, the printer became anxious (1) to save time (and so he adds new skeleton-formes and, in the case of sheet H, a second compositor, to be discussed later), and anxious (2) to save space, with the progressive expansion of the printer's measure, from the 90 mm. with which he began to the 100 mm. with which he ended. The matter of saving space bears directly on the most vexing issue that the editor of *The Scornful Lady* faces: the tendency of his Q1 copy-text to set verse as prose.

Special interest must attach to the tendency of a text to print verse as verse in some instances, and verse as prose in others, when the text in question represents a work of dual authorship. The question naturally arises: does the treatment of verse in the printed text reflect alternative methods of setting it forth (lined and unlined) in the copy? The question is particularly difficult in the case of a play like *The Scornful Lady*, where the alternation of verse and prose is not correspondent to distinctive scenic units; rather, the two are found constantly modulating one into another, rather in the way an operatic *scena* modulates from recitative to aria and back again, within a single scene. The whole of III.i, for instance, framed at beginning and end by the prose exchange between Welford and Abigail, but containing within it an extended sequence of verse dialogue punctuated periodically by prose interjections, is but one of many examples of the practice.

The bibliographical evidence makes it clear that in the copy underlying Q1, verse passages were properly lined, and that the tendency in the quarto to set some of these as prose was dictated solely by the desire to save space, a desire that grew as work on the printing of Q1 went forward. Since the early part of the play is almost entirely in prose, the problem of just how much space would be needed to set verse passages as verse did not immediately present itself; the one passage of verse that had occurred prior to II.ii (at I.i.144–62) is set as such. II.ii opens with sixteen lines of verse, and these too are appropriately lined; but when a bit farther on the compositor came upon the longest verse passage he had yet encountered (at II.ii.85–128) he set it as prose. Again there follows a long prose stretch: the last 46 lines of II.ii, the whole of II.iii, and the first 76 lines of III.i. The long verse passage at III.i.77–246 is printed as verse through line 204, from its beginning on sig. E 3 to near the end of sig. E 4ᵛ. The last four lines on sig. E 4ᵛ (lines 205–7 in the present edition) are printed as prose, and beginning at the top of sig. F 1, the Lady's speech at lines 208–15, as well as her speech a bit farther on at lines 221–31, are printed as prose. But this does not mean that the nature of the quarto copy, as concerns lineation, has changed, nor that a new compositor has come on the job at the beginning of sheet F who is possessed of a tendency to set verse as prose. It simply means that the compositor is doing everything he can at this point to save space. His printer's measure, which has already been widened once, from 90 mm. to 94 mm. at the beginning of sheet D, is now widened again, to 100 mm. And he sets as prose the two longest verse speeches in the copy immediately before him. But he does not set everything as prose in the closing section (lines 208–46) of this verse sequence. The verse context surrounding the Lady's two verse speeches is preserved, even if the verse lineation of the speeches themselves is not; thus the compositor is found setting as verse the Elder Loveless' two-line speech at 216–17, and the Lady's at 232–4, and Welford's at 241–3. In what follows, the compositor can be seen practising similar economies (as in the Lady's speech at 285–90, printed as prose, but certainly verse), though since most of the remainder of the scene is in fact prose, the opportunities are limited. There is a good deal of verse in III.ii (the first 25 lines, Young Loveless' two long speeches to the Widow at 83–101 and 106–22) and it is for the most part set as prose, though here again, shorter verse speeches (such as Young Loveless' at 45–7, the Widow's at 30–1, Savil's at 222–5) are preserved. This is the pattern too of IV.i and of the rest of the play as a whole: all the longer verse speeches are set as prose, but interspersed with these throughout are verse speeches of two or three lines which are clearly verse in intention as well as typographical arrangement. No theory of divided authorship can account for this; nor can we posit a compositor who, from habit, preference, or sheer mindlessness, sets everything he comes on in his copy as prose. The point is, precisely, that the compositor here is not setting *everything* as prose; he is setting verse as prose only when he can effect some worthwhile saving of space. A two-line verse speech, even if it is set as prose, is likely to spill over in to two lines anyway; so the compositor of Q1 tends to leave it as he found it in his copy. An eighteen-line verse speech, such as the Elder Loveless' at IV.i.201–18, can be printed in prose in thirteen lines (sig. G3ᵛ); and it is this sort of economy that the compositor who set the major portion of the Q1 text is found practising throughout.

Sig. G4ᵛ stands out in the last half of the quarto because, for the first time since sig. E4ᵛ, verse is being set as verse. The reason for this is clear from the bibliographical evidence: a new compositor will come on the job to set sheet H, and there has been some casting-off of copy which has left Compositor *A*, after exercising his familiar economies through the seven pages he has set of sheet G, with space to burn on the last page of that sheet. There is evidence that he burnt it a bit too lavishly, for by the time he has reached the end of sig. G4ᵛ, he is back to setting verse as prose (IV.i.307–17).

I have already demonstrated the anomalous nature of sheet H, with its new skeleton-forme, and its setting from a printer's measure of a width (95 mm.) different from any other on exhibit in the text. With it a new compositor (Compositor *B*) appears whose work in the quarto is confined to the two formes of this sheet. His presence is most readily distinguished from that of Compositor *A* by his abbreviations for the Elder Loveless' speech-prefix. This has been overwhelmingly given as *El.Lo.* through sheets B–G; starting with sig. H1, we have *Eld.L.* (which eventually, by sig. H2ᵛ, has become *Eld.lo.*, the form used throughout the rest of the sheet). So too with the abbreviation for the speech-prefix of Young Loveless. Through sheets B–G, this has been given as *Yo.Lo.*; in sheet H it appears as *Yo.L.* In sheet I and half-sheet K, the forms (*El.Lo.* and *Yo.Lo.*) characteristic of Compositor *A* reappear. Compositor *B*, in sheet H, is responsible for four out of the five occurrences of the pronominal contraction *'em* (for *them*) in the text; the prevailing form of this contraction throughout the rest of the text is *'um*. Elsewhere I have discussed the possibility that '*um* may be a form characteristic of Fletcher's language practices (*SB*, XI, 97–8). Compositor *B*'s abilities were not above reproach, and his masters seems to have known it. More press corrections were made in the two formes of the sheet that he set than in any other sheet in the quarto.

A final difference may be noted in the practice of the two workmen. The compositor of sheet H can fairly be said to do what I have argued that Compositor *A* does not do: set *everything* as prose. Nothing escapes in sheet H, where not only the long verse speeches but all the shorter ones (*e.g.* IV.i.360–1, IV.ii.105–8, V.i.26–8) have lost their verse lineation. There is in fact a great deal of verse in Compositor *B*'s section of the play. He begins setting at IV.i.318 in the midst of a verse passage that continues, with minor prose exchanges between the Lady and Abigail, to the end of the scene. IV.ii is entirely verse. So are the first 79 lines of V.i, to the entrance of Abigail. All the Lady's speeches in V.ii through line 61, where Compositor *B*'s stint ends, are in verse. Q1 presents all this as prose. The continuation of V.ii which Compositor *A* begins setting on sig. I1 at line 62 is likewise verse printed as prose through line 141; thereafter there is a good deal of modulation back and forth between the two idioms to the end of the scene. V.iii is entirely prose, and printed as such; and such verse speeches as find their way into the busy action of the final scene, V.iv (notably at the beginning and end), are few and brief. But it is pleasant to watch Compositor *B* on sigs. K2–K2ᵛ, the last pages of the text, now that he is in the home stretch and it is clear that his remaining material will fit comfortably into the space available for it, generously lining as verse two passages (173–4 and 178–83) that are very obviously prose. It is as if he were making up for past offences.

The present edition is based on a collation of the nine extant copies of Q1: Bodleian Library, copy one (Mal. 242[7]; imperfect, wanting leaf K1, which has been supplied from a copy of Q4), copy two (4° T.38.Art[4]); British Museum; the Dyce Collection in the Victoria and Albert Museum; the Bute Collection in the National Library of Scotland; the Boston Public Library (imperfect; wanting leaves G2 and G3); Harvard University Library (imperfect; wanting leaves G2 and G3, which have been supplied from a copy of Q4); the Henry E. Huntington Library; the W. A. Clark Memorial Library.

The copy-text (Q1) has been collated with Q2 (1625), Q3 (1630), Q4 (1635), Q5 (1639), Q6 (1651), Q7 (Greg, 334h), Q8 (Greg, 334g), Q9 (1677), F2 (1679), Q10 (1691), Q11 (Greg, 334l), and the editions of Langbaine, 1711 (L); Sympson, 1750 (S); Colman, 1778 (C); Weber, 1812 (W); Dyce, 1843 (D); and the edition prepared by R. W. Bond for Volume I of the Variorum Edition, 1904 (V).

The Actors are these.

Elder LOVELESSE, *a Suter to the Lady*
Young LOVELESSE, *a Prodigall*
SAVILL, *Steward to the eldest* LOVELESSE
LADY, *and* ⎱ *two Sisters*
MARTHA, ⎰
YONGLOVE, *or* ABIGELL, *a waiting Gentlewoman*
WELFORD, *a Suter to the Lady*
Sir ROGER, *Curate to the Lady*

A ⎰ CAPTAINE,
⎱ TRAVELER,   *hangers on to young*
⎱ POET,   LOVELESSE
⎰ TOBACCO-MAN, ⎰

Wenches
Fidlers
MOORECRAFT, *an Usurer*
A rich Widdow
Attendants

The Actors are these.] Q2; *om.* Q1

464

The Scornful Lady:

A Comedy.

Enter the two Lovelesses, Savill *the Steward, and a Page.*   I. i

Elder Loveless.   Brother, is your last hope past to mollifie *Moorecrafts* heart about your Morgage?

Young Loveless.   Hopelesly past: I have presented the Usurer with a richer draught, then ever *Cleopatra* swallowed; he hath suckt in ten thousand pownds worth of my Land, more then hee paid for at a gulpe, without Trumpets.

Elder Loveless.   I have as hard a task to performe in this house.

Young Loveless.   Faith mine was to make a Userer honest, or to loose my land.

Elder Loveless.   And mine is to perswade a passionate woman, 10 or to leave the Land.

Savill make the boate stay, I feare I shall begin my unfortunate journey this night, though the darkenesse of the night and the roughnes of the waters might easily disswade an unwilling man.
                                                   [*Exit Page.*]

Savil.   Sir, your fathers old friends hold it the sounder course for your body and estate, to stay at home, and marry, and propagate, and governe in your Countrey, then to travell for diseases, and returne following the Court in a nightcap, and die without issue.

Elder Loveless. Savill, you shall gaine the opinion of a better servant, in seeking to execute, not alter my will, howsoever my 20 intents succeede.

Young Loveless.   Yonders Mistres *Yonglove* brother, the grave rubber of your mistres toes.

Enter Mistres [Abigail] Yonglove *the waiting woman.*

Elder Loveless.   Mistres *Yonglove.*

I.i] *Actus primus, Scæna prima.* Q1

30   465   BDW

Abigail.   Master *Lovelesse*, truly wee thought your sailes had beene hoist: my Mistres is perswaded you are Sea-sicke ere this.

Elder Loveless.   Loves she her ill taken up resolution so dearely? Didst thou move her for me?

Abigail.   By this light that shines, thers no removing her, if she get a stiffe opinion by the end. I attempted her to day when they say a woman can deny nothing. 30

Elder Loveless. What criticall minute was that?

Abigail.   When her smock was over her eares: but shee was no more pliant then if it hung about her heeles.

Elder Loveless.   I prethee deliver my service, and say I desire to see the deere cause of my banishment; and then for *France.*

Abigail.   Ile doe't: harke hether, is that your Brother?

Elder Loveless.   Yes, have you lost your memory?

Abigail.   As I live hee's a pretty fellow.   *Exit.*

Young Loveless.   O this is a sweete *Brache.*   40

Elder Loveless.   Why she knows not you.

Young Loveless.   No, but she offered me once to know her: to this day she loves youth of eighteene; she heard a tale how *Cupid* strooke her in love with a great Lord in the Tilt-yard, but he never sawe her; yet shee in kindnesse would needes weare a willow garland at his wedding. She lov'd all the Players in the last Queenes time once over: She was strook when they acted lovers, and forsook some when they plaid murtherers. Shee has nine *Spurroyals*, and the servants say she hords old gold; and she herselfe pronounces angerly, that the Farmers eldest sonne, or her Mistres husbands Clark that shall be, that marries her, shall make her a jointure of fourescore pounds a yeer; she tels tales of the serving-men. 50

Elder Loveless.   Enough, I know her brother. I shall entreate you onely to salute my Mistres, and take leave, wee'l part at the staiers.

                    Enter Lady *and waiting woman* [Abigail].

Lady.   Now Sir, this first part of your will is performed: whats the rest?

                    25, 29, 33, 37, 39 S.P. *Abigail*] Q4; *Yong.* Q1-3

Elder Loveless. First let me beg your notice for this Gentleman
my Brother.   60

Lady. I shall take it as a favour done to me, though the gentleman
hath received but an untimely grace from you; yet my charitable
disposition would have been ready to have done him freer
curtesies as a stranger, then upon those cold commendations.

Young Loveless. Lady, my salutations crave acquaintance and
leave at once.

Lady. Sir I hope you are the master of your owne occasions.

                                  Exeunt Young Loveless, Savil.

Elder Loveless. Would I were so. Mistres, for me to praise over
againe that worth, which all the world, and you your selfe can
see——   70

Lady. Its a cold Rome this; Servant.

Elder Loveless. Mistres——

Lady. What thinke you if I have a chimney fort out heer?

Elder Loveless. Mistres another in my place, that were not tyed
to beleeve all your actions just, would apprehend himselfe
wrongd: But I, whose vertues are constancy and obedience——

Lady. Yonglove, make a good fire above to warme me after my
servants *Exordiums.*

Elder Loveless. I have heard and seene your affability to bee such,
that the servants you give wages to may speake——   80

Lady. Tis true, tis true; but they speake toth' purpose.

Elder Loveless. Mistres your will leades my speeches from the
purpose. But as a man——

Lady. A *Simile* servant? This roome was built for honest meaners,
that deliver themselves hastily and plainely, and are gone. Is this
a time or place for *Exordiums*, and *Similes*, and *metaphors*? If
you have ought to say, breake intoo't; my answers shall very
reasonably meete you.

Elder Loveless. Mistres I came to see you.

Lady. Thats happily dispacht, the next?   90

Elder Loveless. To take leave of you.

Lady. To be gon?

Elder Loveless. Yes.

Lady. You neede not have dispair'd of that, nor have us'd so many circumstances to win me to give you leave to performe my command: Is there a third?

Elder Loveless. Yes, I had a third, had you been apt to heare it.

Lady. I? never apter. Fast (good servant) fast.

Elder Loveless. Twas to intreat you to heare reason.

Lady. Most willingly, have you brought one can speake it? 100

Elder Loveless. Lastly, it is to kindle in that barren heart love and forgivenes.

Lady. You would stay at home?

Elder Loveless. Yes Ladie.

Lady. Why you may, and doubtlesly will, when you have debated that your commander is but your Mistres, a woman, a weake one, wildly overborne with passions: but the thing by her commanded, is to see *Dovers* dreadfull cliffe, passing in a pore waterhouse the dangers of the mercilesse channell twixt that and *Callis*, five long houres saile, with three pore weekes victuals—— 110

Elder Loveless. You wrong me.

Lady. Then to land dumb, unable to enquire for an English hoast, to remove from Citty to Cittie, by most chargeable post-horse, like one that rod in quest of his mother tongue——

Elder Loveless. You wrong me much.

Lady. And all these (almost invincible labours) performed for your mistres, to be in danger to forsake her, and to put on new alleagance to some French Lady, who is content to change language with you for laughter, and after your whole yeare spent in tennis and broken speech, to stand to the hazard of being laught 120 at at your returne, and have tales made on you by the chamber-maids.

Elder Loveless. You wrong me much.

Lady. Lowder yet.

Elder Loveless. You know your least word is of force to make mee seeke out dangers, move mee not with toies: but in this banishment, I must take leave to say, you are unjust: was one kisse forc't from you in publike by me so unpardonable? why all the howers of day and night have seene us kisse.

Lady. Tis true, and so you satisfied the company that heard 130 me chide.

468

Elder Loveless.   Your owne eyes were not dearer to you then I?

Lady.   And so you told um.

Elder Loveless.   I did, yet no signe of disgrace neede to have
staind your cheeke: you your selfe knew your pure and simple
heart to be most unspotted, and free from the least basenesse.

Lady.   I did: But if a Maides heart doth but once thinke that shee
is suspected, her owne face will write her guiltie.

Elder Loveless.   But where lay this disgrace? The world that knew
us, knew our resolutions well: And could it bee hop'd that I 140
should give away my freedome, and venture a perpetuall bondage
with one I never kist? or could I in strict wisdome take too much
love upon me, from her that chose me for her husband?

Lady.   Beleeve me; if my wedding smock were on,
Were the gloves bought and given, the Licence come,
Were the Rosemary branches dipt, and all
The Hipochrists and cakes eate and drunke off,
Were these two armes incompast with the hands
Of Bachelers, to leade me to the Church;
Were my feete in the dore, were *I John*, said,   150
If *John* should boast a favour done by me,
I would not wed that yeare: And you I hope,
When you have spent this yeere commodiously,
In atcheiving Languages, will at your returne
Acknowledge me more coy of parting with mine eies,
Then such a friend: More talke I hold not now,
If you dare goe!

Elder Loveless.   I dare you know; First let me kisse.

Lady.   Farewell sweet servant, your taske perform'd,
On a new ground as a beginning sutor,   160
I shall be apt to heare you.

Elder Loveless.   Farewell cruell Mistres.

Exit Ladie [*and* Abigail].

Enter Yong Lovelesse *and* Savill.

Young Loveless.   Brother youle hazard the loosing your tide to
Gravesend: you have a long halfe mile by land to *Greenewich*.

153 this] Q3; his Q1–2

469

Elder Loveless. I goe: but brother, what yet unheard of course to live, doth your imagination flatter you with? your ordinary meanes are devourd.

Young Loveless. Course? why horse-coursing I thinke. Consume no time in this: I have no estate to bee mended by meditation: hee that busies himselfe about my fortunes, may properly be said 170 to busie himselfe about nothing.

Elder Loveless. Yet some course you must take, which for my satisfaction resolve and open: If you will shape none, I must informe you, that that man but perswades himselfe hee meanes to live, that imagins not the meanes.

Young Loveless. Why live upon others, as others have lived upon mee.

Elder Loveless. I apprehend not that: you have fed others, and consequently disposd of um: and the same measure must you expect from your maintainers, which will be too heavy an 180 alteration for you to beare.

Young Loveless. Why ile purse; if that raise mee not, Ile bet at bowling-alleys, or man whores; I would fain live by others: but Ile live whilst I am unhangd, and after the thoughts taken.

Elder Loveless. I see you are tide to no particular imployment then.

Young Loveless. Faith I may choose my course: they say nature brings foorth none but shee provides for em: Ile trie her liberalitie.

Elder Loveless. Well, to keepe your feete out of base and dangerous paths, I have resolved you shall live as Master of my 190 house. It shall bee your care *Savill* to see him fed and clothed, not according to his present estate, but to his birth and former fortunes.

Young Loveless. If it be referd to him, if I be not found in Carnation Jearsie stockins, blew divels breeches, with three guards downe, and my pocket ith sleeves, ile nere looke you i'th face againe.

Savil. A comlier wear I wusse it is then those dangling slops.

Elder Loveless. To keep you ready to doe him all service peaceably, and him to command you reasonably, I leave these further directions in writing, which at your best leisure together 200 open and reade.

Enter Abigail *to them with a Jewell.*

Abigail.   Sir my Mistres commends her love to you in this token, and these words; It is a Jewell (she saies) which as a favour from her shee would request you to weare till your yeares travell be performed: which once expired, she will hastily expect your happy returne.

Elder Loveless.   Returne my service with such thanks, as she may imagine the heart of a sodenly over-joyed man would willingly utter: and you (I hope) I shall with slender arguments perswade to weare this Diamond, that when my Mistres shall through my 210 long absence, and the approch of new sutors, offer to forget mee; you may call your eie downe to your finger, and remember and speake of me: She will heare thee better then those allyed by birth to her; as we see many men much swaied by the groomes of their chambers, not that they have a greater part of their love or opinion on them, as on others, but for they know their secrets.

Abigail.   A my credit I sweare, I thinke twas made for mee: Feare no other sutors.

Elder Loveless.   I shall not neede to teach you how to discredit their beginnings, you know how to take exception at their 220 shirts at washing, or to make the maids sweare they found plasters in their beds.

Abigail.   I know, I know, and doe not you feare the sutors.

Elder Loveless.   Farewell, be mindefull and be happy: the night cals mee.   *Exeunt omnes præter* Abigail.

Abigail.   The Gods of the winds befriend you Sir: a constant and a liberall lover thou art; more such God send us.

Enter Welforde.

Welford [*to servant within*].   Let um not stand still, we have rid hard.

Abigail [*aside*].   A sutor I know by his riding hard, Ile not be seen. 230

Welford.   A pretty Hall this: No servant in't? I would look freshly.

201.1 Abigail] Q4; *Yongloue* Q1–3
225 S.D. Abigail] Q4; *Yongloue* Q1–3

Abigail [*aside*]. You have delivered your arrand to mee then: ther's no danger in a hansome young fellowe: Ile shew my selfe.

[*Advances.*]

Welford. Lady may it please you to bestowe upon a stranger the ordinary grace of salutation: Are you the Ladie of this house?

Abigail. Sir, I am worthily proud to be a servant of hers.

Welford. Lady I should be as proud to be a servant of yours, did not my so late acquaintance make me dispaire.

Abigail. Sir, it is not so hard to atcheive, but nature may bring it 240 about.

Welford. For these comfortable words I remaine your glad debtor. Is your Ladie at home?

Abigail. She is no stragler Sir.

Welford. May her occasions admit me to speake with her?

Abigail. If you come in the way of a Sutor, No.

Welford. I know your affable vertue will be moved to perswade her, that a Gentleman benighted and straied offers to be bound to her for a nights lodging.

Abigail. I will commend this message to her: but if you aime at 250 her bodie, you will be deluded: other weomen the house holds of good carriage and government; upon any of which if you can cast your affection, they will perhaps bee found as faithfull, and not so coy.   *Exit* Abigail.

Welford. What a skin full of lust is this? I thought I had come awoeing, and I am the courted party. This is right Court fashion: Men, weomen, and all woe; catch that catch may. If this soft hearted woman have infusde any of her tendernesse into her Lady, there is hope she will be pliant. But who's here?

Enter Sir Roger *the Curate.*

Roger. God save you Sir, My Lady lets you know shee desires 260 to be acquainted with your name before she conferre with you.

Welford. Sir my name cals me *Welford.*

Roger. Sir, you are a gentleman of a good name. [*Aside*] I'le trie his wit.

251 house holds] Dyce; housholds Q 1–4; house-hold's Q 5–10; house-hold F
254 S.D. Abigail] Q 4; *Yongloue* Q 1–3

Welford. I will uphold it as good as any of my Ancestors had this two hundred yeares Sir.

Roger. I knew a worshipfull and a religious gentleman of your name in the Bishopricke of *Durham*. Call you him Cosen?

Welford. I am onely allyed to his vertues Sir.

Roger. It is modestly said: I should carry the badge of your 270 Christianity with me to.

Welford. Whats that, a Crosse? there's a tester.

Roger. I meane the name which your Godfathers and Godmothers gave you at the Font.

Welford. Tis *Harry*: but you cannot proceede orderly now in your Catechisme: for you have told mee who gave mee that name. Shal I beg your names.

Roger. Roger.

Welford. What roome fill you in this house?

Roger. More roomes then one.   280

Welford. The more the merrier. But may my boldnesse know, why your Lady hath sent you to discipher my name?

Roger. Her owne words were these; To know whether you were a formerly denied sutor, disguised in this message: For I can assure you shee delights not in *Thalame*: *Himen* and she are at variance, I shall returne with much hast.   *Exit* Roger.

Welford. And much speede Sir I hope: certainely I am arived amongst a Nation of new found fooles: on a Land where no Navigator has yet planted wit. If I had foreseene it, I would have laded my breeches with bels, knives, copper and glasses to trade 290 with the weomen for their virginities: yet I feare I should have betraied my selfe to an needlesse charge then: heres the walking night-cap againe.

Enter Roger.

Roger. Sir, my Ladies pleasure is to see you: who hath commanded mee to acknowledge her sorow, that you must take the paines to come up for so bad entertainement.

Welford. I shall obey your Lady that sent it, and acknowledge you that brought it to be your Arts Master.

Roger. I am but a Bachiler of Art Sir; and I have the mending of

473

all under this roofe, from my Lady on her downe bed, to the 300
maide in the pease strawe.

Welford.   A Cobler Sir?

Roger.   No Sir. I inculcate Divine service within these walles.

Welford.   But the inhabitants of this house doe often imploy you
on errands, without any scruple of conscience.

Roger.   Yes, I doe take the aire many mornings on foote, three or
foure miles for egges: but why move you that?

Welford.   To knowe whether it might become your function to
bid my man to neglect his horse a little, to attend on mee.

Roger.   Most properly Sir.   310

Welford.   I pray ye doe so then: and whilst I will attend your
Lady. You direct all this house in the true way?

Roger.   I doe Sir.

Welford.   And this dore (I hope) conducts to your Lady?

Roger.   Your understanding is ingenious.

Exeunt severally.

Enter Yong Lovelesse *and* Savill *with a writing.*   [I. ii]

Savil.   By your favour Sir you shall pardon me.

Young Loveless.   I shall beate your favour Sir, crosse me no more;
I say they shall come in.

Savil.   Sir you forget one, who I am.

Young Loveless.   Sir I doe not; thou art my brothers Steward,
his cast off mill-money, his Kitchen Arethmatick.

Savil.   Sir I hope you will not make so little of me.

Young Loveless.   I make thee not so little as thou art: for indeed
there goes no more to the making of a Steward, but a faire
Imprimis, and then a reasonable *Item* infus'd into him, and the 10
thing is done.

Savil.   Nay then you stirre my duty, and I must tell you——

Young Loveless.   What wouldst thou tell me, how Hoppes goe, or
hold some rotten discourse of sheepe, or when our Lady day
fals? Prethee farewell, and entertaine my friends, bee drunke, and
burne thy Table-bookes: and my deare sparke of velvet thou and
I——

Savil.   Good Sir remember.

Young Loveless.   I doe remember thee a foolish fellowe, one that did put his trust in Almanacks, and horse-faiers, and rose by 20 hony and pot-butter. Shall they come in yet?

Savil.   Nay then I must unfold your Brothers pleasure, these be the lessons Sir, he left behinde him.

Young Loveless.   Prethee expound the first.

Savil.   I leave to keep my house three hundred pounds a yeare; and my Brother to dispose of it——

Young Loveless.   Marke that my wicked Steward, and I dispose of it.

Savil.   Whilst hee beares himselfe like a Gentleman, and my credit fals not in him. Marke that my good young Sir, marke 30 that.

Young Loveless.   Nay if it be no more I shall fulfill it: whilst my legs will carry mee ile beare my selfe gentleman-like, but when I am drunke, let them beare mee that can. Forward deare steward.

Savil.   Next it is my will, that hee bee furnisht (as my brother) with attendance, apparrell, and the obedience of my people.

Young Loveless.   Steward this is as plaine as your olde minikin breeches. Your wisdome will relent now, will it not? Be mollified or——you understand mee Sir, proceed.   40

Savil.   Next, that my Steward keepe his place, and power, and bound my brothers wildnesse with his care.

Young Loveless.   Ile heare no more this *Apocripha*, binde it by it selfe steward.

Savil.   This is your Brothers will, and as I take it, he makes no mention of such company as you would draw unto you. Captaines of Gallifoists, such as in a cleare day have seene *Callis*, fellows that have no more of God, then their oaths comes to: they weare swords to reach fire at a Play, and get there the oyld end of a pipe for their guerdon: then the remnant of your regiment are 50 wealthy Tobacco merchants, that set up with one ownce, and breake for three; together with a forlorne hope of Poets, and all these looke like Carthusians, things without linnen: Are these fit company for my Masters Brother?

Young Loveless.   I will either convert thee (O thou Pagan steward)
or presently confound thee and thy reckonings, who's there?
call in the Gentlemen.

Savil.   Good Sir.

Young Loveless.   Nay you shall know both who I am, and where I
am.   60

Savil.   Are you my masters Brother?

Young Loveless.   Are you the sage Master Steward, with a face
like an olde *Ephimerides?*

Enter his Comrades: Captaine, Traveller[, Poet, Tobacco-man].

Savil.   Then God helpe all, I say.

Young Loveless.   I, and tis well said my olde peere of *France:*
welcome gentlemen, welcome gentlemen; mine owne deere lads,
y'are richly welcome. Know this old *Harry*-groate.

Captain.   Sir I will take your love——

Savil [*aside*].   Sir you will take my purse.

Captain.   And studie to continue it.   70

Savil.   I doe beleeve you.

Traveller.   Your honourable friend and masters brother, hath
given you to us for a worthy fellow, and so wee hugge you Sir.

Savil [*aside*].   Has given himselfe into the hands of varlets, not to
be carv'd out.——Sir are these the peeces?

Young Loveless.   They are the Morrals of the age, the vertues.
Men made of Gold.

Savil [*aside*].   Of your gold you meane Sir.

Young Loveless.   This is a man of warre, that cries goe on, and
weares his Colours——   80

Savil [*aside*].   In's nose.

Young Loveless.   In the fragrant field. This is a Traveller Sir,
knows men and manners, and has plowd up the Sea so far, till
both the poles have knockt, has seene the Sunne take Coach, and
can distinguish the colour of his horses, and their kindes, and had a
Flanders Mare leapt there.

Savil.   Tis much.

Traveller.   I have seene more Sir.

Savil.   Tis even enough a conscience; sit downe, and rest you,

you are at the end of the world already. Would you had as good a 90
living Sir as this Fellowe could lie you out of: has a notable guift
in't.

Young Loveless.   This ministers the Smoke, and this the Muses.

Savil.   And you the clothes, and meate, and money, you have a
goodly generation of um, praye let um multiply, your Brothers
house is big enough, and to say truth, ha's too much Land, hang
it durt.

Young Loveless.   Why now thou art a loving stinkeard. Fire
off thy annotations and thy rent bookes; thou hast a weake
braine *Savill*, and with the next long Bill thou wilt runne mad. 100
Gentlemen you are once more welcome to three hundred pounds
a yeere; wee will bee freely merry, shall we not?

Captain.   Merry as mirth, and wine my lovely *Lovelesse.*

Poet.   A serious looke shall be a Jury to excommunicate any man
from our company.

Traveller.   We will have nobody talke wisely neither.

Young Loveless.   What thinke you gentlemen by all this Revenew
in drinke?

Captain.   I am all for drinke.

Traveller.   I am drie till it be so.   110

Poet.   He that will not crie Amen to this, let him live sober,
seeme wise, and die ath *Corum.*

Young Loveless.   It shall bee so, wee'l have it all in drinke, let
meate and lodging goe, th'are transitory, and shew men meerely
mortall: then wee'l have wenches, every one his wench, and every
weeke a fresh one: weele keepe no powderd fleshe: all these wee
have by warrant under the Title of things necessarie. Heere upon
this place I ground it: the obedience of my people, and all
necessaries: Your opinions Gentlemen?

Captain.   Tis plaine and evident that he meant wenches.   120

Savil.   Good Sir let me expound it.

Captain.   Heere be as sound men as your selfe Sir.

Poet.   This doe I holde to bee the interpretation of it; In this
word Necessarie, is concluded all that bee helpes to man: woman
was made the first, and therefore heere the chiefest.

Young Loveless.   Beleeve me tis a learned one, and by these words:

The obedience of my people, (you steward being one) are bound
to fetch us wenches.

Captain. He is, he is.

Young Loveless. Steward attend us for instructions. 130

Savil. But will you keepe no house Sir?

Young Loveless. Nothing but drinke, three hundred pounds in
drinke.

Savil. O miserable house, and miserable I that live to see it.
Good Sir keep some meate.

Young Loveless. Get us good whoores, and for your part, Ile
bourd you in an Alehouse, you shall have cheese and onyons.

Savil. What shall become of me, no chimney smoking? Well
prodigall, your brother will come home. *Exit.*

Young Loveless. Come lads Ile warrant you for wenches, three 140
hundred pounds in drinke.

Exeunt omnes.

Enter Lady, Welford, *and* [Sir Roger]. II.i

Lady. Sir now you see your bad lodging, I must bid you
goodnight.

Welford. Lady if there be any want, tis in want of you.

Lady. A little sleepe will ease that complement. Once more good
night.

Welford. Once more deare Lady, and then all sweet nights.

Lady. Deare Sir be short and sweet then.

Welford. Shall the morrow prove better to me, shall I hope my
sute happier by this nights rest?

Lady. Is your sute so sickly that rest will helpe it? Pray ye 10
let it rest then till I call for it. Sir as a stranger you have had all
my welcome: but had I knowne your errand ere you came, your
passage had been straighter: Sir, good night.

Welford. So faire, and cruell, deare unkinde goodnight. *Exit* Lady.
Nay Sir you shall stay with me, Ile presse your zeale so far.

II.i] *Actus 2. Scæna prima.* Q1
.01] Langbaine; *Enter Lady, her sister Martha, Welford, Yongloue, and others.*
Q1+

Roger.   O Lord Sir.

Welford.   Doe you love *Tobacco?*

Roger.   Surely I love it, but it loves not me; yet with your reverence ile be bold.

Welford.   Praye light it Sir. How doe you like it?   20

Roger.   I promise you it is notable stinging geare indeede. It is wet Sir, Lord how it brings downe Reume!

Welford.   Handle it againe Sir; you have a warme text of it.

Roger.   Thanks ever premised for it. I promise you it is very powerfull, and by a Trope, spirituall: for certainely it moves in sundrie places.

Welford.   I, it does so Sir, and me especially to aske Sir, why you weare a night-cap.

Roger.   Assuredly I will speake the truth unto you; you shall understand Sir, that my head is broken, and by whom? even by 30 that visible beast the Butler.

Welford.   The Butler? certainely hee had all his drinke about him when he did it. Strike one of your grave Cassock? The offence Sir?

Roger.   Reproving him at Tra-trip Sir, for swearing: you have the totall surely.

Welford.   You tould him when his rage was set atilt, and so hee cract your Cannons. I hope hee has not hurt your gentle reading: But shall wee see these Gentleweomen to night?

Roger.   Have patience Sir, untill our fellowe *Nicholas* bee deceast, that is, a sleepe: for so the word is taken; to sleepe to die, to die 40 to sleepe: a very Figure Sir.

Welford.   Cannot you cast another for the Gentleweomen?

Roger.   Not till the man bee in his bed, his grave; his grave, his bed; the very same againe Sir. Our Comick Poet gives the reason sweetly; *Plenus rimarum est*, he is full of loopeholes, and will discover to our Patronesse.

Welford.   Your comment Sir has made me understand you.

Enter Martha *the Ladies sister, and* Abigail *to them with a posset.*

Roger.   Sir be addrest, the graces doe salute you with the full bowle of plenty. Is our old enemy entomb'd?

47.1 Martha] Q3; *Maria* Q1–2   47.1 Abigail] Q10; *Yongloue* Q1–9, F

Abigail.   He's fast.   50
Roger.   And does he snore out supinely with the Poet?
Martha.   No, he out-snores the Poet.
Welford.   Gentlewoman, this curtesie shall binde a stranger to
you, ever your servant.
Martha.   Sir, my Sisters strictnesse makes not us forget you are
a stranger and a Gentleman.
Abigail.   In sooth Sir were I chang'd into my Lady, a Gentleman
so well indued with parts, should not be lost.
Welford.   I thanke you Gentlewoman, and rest bound to you.
[*Aside*] See how this fowle familiar chewes the Cudde: From 60
thee and three and fiftie, good love deliver me.
Martha.   Will you sit downe Sir, and take a spoone?
Welford.   I take it kindely Lady.
Martha.   It is our best banquet Sir.
Roger.   Shall we give thankes?
Welford.   I have to the Gentlewoman already Sir.
Martha.   Good Sir *Roger* keepe that breath to coole your part
o'th posset, you may chance have a scalding zeale else: and you
will needes bee doing, pray tell your twenty to your selfe. Would
you could like this Sir!   70
Welford.   I would your Sister would like mee as wel Lady.
Martha.   Sure Sir she would not eate you: but banish that
imagination; she's onely wedded to herselfe, lies with herselfe, and
loves herselfe; and for an other husband then herselfe, he may knock
at the gate, but nere come in: bee wise Sir, she's a woman, and a
trouble, and has her many faults, the least of which is, she cannot
love you.
Abigail.   God pardon her, she'l doe worse, would I were worthy
his least griefe Mistres *Martha.*
Welford [*aside*].   Now I must over-heare her.   80
Martha.   Faith would thou hadst them all withal my heart: I
doe not thinke they would make thee a day older.
Abigail.   Sir will you put in deeper, tis the sweeter.
Martha.   Wel said old sayings.
Welford [*aside*].   She lookes like one indeed.——Gentlewoman

57 into] Q2; into into Q1

480

you keepe your word, your sweete selfe has made the bottom
sweeter.

Abigail.   Sir I begin a frolick, dare you change Sir?

Welford.   My selfe for you, so please you. [*Aside*] That smile has
turnd my stomacke: This is right the old Embleame of the Moyle 90
cropping off thistles: Lord what a hunting head shee carries,
sure she has been ridden with a Martingale. Now love deliver me.

Roger [*aside*].   Doe I dreame, or doe I wake? surely I know not: am I
rub'd off? is this the way of all my mornings prayers? Oh *Roger*,
thou art but grasse, and woman as a flower. Did I for this consume
my quarters in meditation, vowes, and wooed her in *Heroycall
Epistles?* Did I expound *The Owle*, and undertooke, with labour
and expence the recollection of those thousand Peeces, consum'd
in Cellors and Tobacco shops of that our honour'd Englishman
Nicholas Breton? Have I done this, and am I done thus too? I will 100
end with the Wise-man, and say, He that holds a woman, has an
Eele by the tayle.

Martha.   Sir, 'tis so late, and our entertainment (meaning our
posset) by this is growne so cold, that 'twere an unmannerly part
longer to hold you from your rest: let what the house has be at
your command Sir.

Welford.   Sweet rest be with you Lady; and to you what you
desire too.

Abigail.   It should be some such good thing like your self then.

                                        Exeunt [Martha *and* Abigail].

Welford.   Heaven keepe mee from that curse, and all my Issue. 110
Good night Antiquitie.

Roger [*aside*].   *Solamen Miseris socios habuisse doloris*: but I
alone——

Welford.   Learned Sir, will you bid my man come to me? and
requesting a greater measure of your learning, good night, good
Master *Roger.*

Roger.   Good Sir, peace be with you.   *Exit* Roger.

Welford.   Adue deare *Domine*. Halfe a dozen such in a Kingdome
would make a man forsweare confession: for who that had but
halfe his wits about him would commit the counsell of a serious 120
sin to such a cruell nightcap?

Enter Servant [*drunk*].

Why how now, shall we have an Antique? Whose head do you carry upon your shoulders, that you jole it so against the post? Is't for your ease? or have you seene the Sellor? Where are my slippers sir?

Servant. Here Sir.

Welford. Where Sir? have you got the pot verdugo? have you seene the horses Sir?

Servant. Yes Sir.

Welford. Have they any meate? 130

Servant. Faith Sir they have a kinde of wholsome rushes, hay I cannot cal it.

Welford. And no provender?

Servant. Sir so I take it.

Welford. You are merry Sir, and why so?

Servant. Faith Sir, heere are no oates to be got, unlesse youle have um in porredge: the people are so mainely given to spoonemeate: yonders a cast of Coach-mares of the gentlewomans, the strangest Cattell.

Welford. Why? 140

Servant. Why they are transparant sir, you may see through them: and such a house!

Welford. Come Sir, the truth of your discovery.

Servant. Sir they are in tribes like Jewes: the Kitchen and the Dayrie make one tribe, and have their faction and their fornication within themselves; the Buttry and the Laundry are an other, and ther's no love lost; the chambers are intire, and what's done there, is somewhat higher then my knowledge; but this I am sure, betweene these copulations, a stranger is kept vertuous, that is, fasting. But of all this the drinke Sir—— 150

Welford. What of that Sir?

Servant. Faith Sir I will handle it as the time and your patience will give me leave. This drinke, or this cooling Julip, of which three spoonefuls kils the Calenture, a pinte breeds the cold Palsie——

Welford. Sir you bely the house.

482

Servant.   I would I did Sir. But as I am a true man, if twere but
one degree colder, nothing but an asses hoofe would hold it.
Welford.   I am glad on't Sir: for if it had proved stronger, you
had been tongue-tide of these commendations. Light me the 160
candle Sir, Ile heare no more.

Exeunt.

Enter Yong Lovelesse *and his Comrades* [Captain, Traveller,   [II.ii]
Poet, Tobacco-man], *with wenches, and two Fydlers.*

Young Loveless.   Come my brave man of war, trace out thy darling,
And you my learned Councell, set and turne boyes:
Kisse till the Cow come home, kisse close, kisse close knaves.
My moderne Poet, thou shalt kisse in couplets.

Enter with wine.

Strike up you merry varlets, and leave your peeping,
This is no pay for Fidlers.
Captain.   O my deare boy, thy *Hercules*, thy Captaine
Makes thee his *Hilas*, his delight, his solace.
Love thy brave man of war, and let thy bounty
Clap him in *Shamois*:   10
Let ther be deducted out of our maine potation
Five Marks in hatchments to adorne this thigh,
Crampt with this rest of peace, and I will fight
Thy battels.
Young Loveless.   Thou shalt hav't boy, and fly in Fether,
Leade on a march you Michers.

Enter Savill.

Savil.   O my head, O my heart, what a noise and change is heere;
would I had been cold ith mouth before this day, and nere have
livd to see this dissolution. Hee that lives within a mile of this
place, had as good sleepe in the perpetuall noise of an iron mill. 20
Ther's a dead Sea of drinke ith Sellor, in which goodly vessels lie
wract, and in the middle of this deluge appeares the tops of
flagons and blacke jacks, like Churches drownd ith marshes.

11 deducted] Q2; deductedd Q1
23 drownd] Q2; drown Q1

Young Loveless.   What art thou come? My sweet Sir *Amias*
welcome to *Troy*. Come thou shalt kisse my *Hellen*, and court her
in a dance.

Savil.   Good Sir consider.

Young Loveless.   Shall we consider gentlemen. How say you?

Captain.   Consider? that were a simple toy ifaith.
Consider? whose morrals that? The man that cries   30
Consider, is our foe: let my steele know him.

Young Loveless.   Stay thy dead doing hand, he must not die yet:
Prethee be calme my *Hector.*

Captain.   Peasant, slave,
Thou groome, composde of grudgeings, live and thanke
This Gentleman, thou hadst seene *Pluto* else.
The next consider kils thee.

Traveller.   Let him drinke downe his word againe in a gallon of
Sacke.

Poet.   Tis but a snuffe, make it two gallons, and let him doe it
kneeling in repentance.   40

Savil.   Nay rather kill me, theres but a lay-man lost. Good
Captaine doe your office.

Young Loveless.   Thou shalt drinke Steward, drinke and dance my
Steward. Strike him a horne-pipe sqeakers, take thy stiver, and
pace her till shee stew.

Savil.   Sure Sir I cannot daunce with your Gentlewomen, they are
too light for mee, 'pray breake my head, and let me goe.

Captain.   He shall dance, he shall dance.

Young Loveless.   Hee shall daunce, and drinke, and bee drunke
and dance, and bee drunke againe, and shall see no meate in a 50
yeere.

Poet.   And three quarters.

Young Loveless.   And three quarters be it.

Captain.   Who knocks there? let him in.

44 stiver] Sympson; striuer Q 1 +
46 Gentlewomen] Q 3; Gentlewoman Q 1–2

Enter Elder Lovelesse *disguised.*

Savil.   Some to deliver me I hope.

Elder Loveless.   Gentlemen, God save you all, my businesse is to one Master *Lovelesse.*

Captain.   This is the Gentleman you meane; view him, and take his Inventory, hee's a right one.

Elder Loveless.   He promises no lesse Sir.   60

Young Loveless.   Sir your businesse?

Elder Loveless.   Sir, I should let you know, yet I am loath, yet I am sworne too't——would some other tongue would speake it for mee.

Young Loveless.   Out with it a Gods name.

Elder Loveless.   All I desire Sir is, the patience and sufferance of a man, and good Sir be not moov'd more——

Young Loveless.   Then a pottle of Sacke will doe, heere's my hand, prethee thy businesse?

Elder Loveless.   Good Sir excuse mee, and whatsoever you heare, 70 thinke, must have beene knowne unto you, and bee your selfe discreete, and beare it nobly.

Young Loveless.   Prethee dispatch me.

Elder Loveless.   Your brothers dead Sir.

Young Loveless.   Thou dost not meane dead drunke?

Elder Loveless.   No, no, dead and drown'd at sea Sir.

Young Loveless.   Art sure hee's dead?

Elder Loveless.   Too sure Sir.

Young Loveless.   I, but art thou very certainely sure of it?

Elder Loveless.   As sure Sir as I tell it.   80

Young Loveless.   But art thou sure he came not up againe?

Elder Loveless.   He may come up, but nere to call you brother.

Young Loveless.   But art sure he had water enough to drowne him?

Elder Loveless.   Sure Sir he wanted none.

Young Loveless.   I would not have him want, I lov'd him better; Heere I forgive thee: and i'faith bee plaine, How doe I beare it?

Elder Loveless.   Very wisely Sir.

Young Loveless.   Fill him some wine. Thou dost not see me moov'd,

These transitory toyes nere trouble me,
Hee's in a better place my friend, I know't.   90
Some fellowes would have cryed now, and have curst thee,
And falne out with their meat, and kept a pudder;
But all this helps not, he was too good for us,
And let God keepe him: there's the right use on't friend.
Off with thy drinke, thou hast a spice of sorrow
Makes thee dry: fill him another. *Savill,*
Your Masters dead, and who am I now *Savill?*
Nay, let's all beare it well, wipe, *Savill,* wipe,
Teares are but throwne away:
We shall have wenches now, shal we not *Savill?*   100
Drinke to my friend Captaine.
Savil.   Yes Sir.
Young Loveless.   And drinke inumerable.
Savil.   Yes forsooth Sir.
Young Loveless.   And you'le straine cursie and be drunke a little.
Savil.   I would be glad, Sir, to doe my weake indeavour.
Young Loveless.   You may be brought in time to love a wench too.
Savil.   In time the sturdie Oake Sir——
Young Loveless.   Some more wine for my friend there.
Elder Loveless [*aside*].   I shall be drunke anon for my good newes: 110
But I have a loving brother, that's my comfort.
Young Loveless.   Heere's to you sir,
This is the worst I wish you for your newes:
And if I had another elder brother,
And say it were his chance to feede more fishes,
I should bee still the same you see me now,
A poore contented Gentleman.——
More wine for my friend there, hee's dry againe.
Elder Loveless [*aside*].   I shall be if I follow this beginning.
Well, my deare brother, if I scape this drowning,   120
'Tis your turne next to sinke, you shall ducke twice
Before I helpe you.——Sir I cannot drinke more,
'Pray let me have your pardon.
Young Loveless.   O Lord sir, 'tis your modestie: more wine,

*101 Drinke...Captaine.] Q1–2

486

Give him a bigger glasse; hugge him my Captaine,
Thou shalt bee my cheefe mourner.

Captain.   And this my pennon. Sir a ful rouse to you,
And to my Lord of Land heere.

Elder Loveless [aside].   I feele a buzzing in my braines, pray God
they beare this out, and Ile nere trouble them so far againe.——— 130
Heers to you Sir.

Young Loveless.   To my deare Steward, downe a your knees you
infidel, you Pagan; be drunke and penitent.

Savil.   Forgive me Sir and ile be any thing.

Young Loveless.   Then be a Baude: Ile have thee a brave Baud.

Elder Loveless.   Sir I must take my leave of you, my busines is
so urgent.

Young Loveless.   Lets have a bridling cast before you goe. Fils a
new stoupe.

Elder Loveless.   I dare not Sir by no meanes.   140

Young Loveless.   Have you any minde to a wench? I would
faine gratifie you for the paines you tooke Sir.

Elder Loveless.   As little as to the tother.

Young Loveless.   If you finde any stirring, doe but say so.

Elder Loveless.   Sir you are too bounteous, when I finde that
itching, you shall asswage it Sir before another: this onely, and
farewell Sir. Your brother when the storm was most extream,
told all about him, he left a will, which lies close behinde a
chimney in the matted chamber: and so as well Sir, as you have
made me able, I take my leave.   150

Young Loveless.   Let us imbrace him all: if you grow drie before
you end your businesse, praye take a baite heere, I have a fresh
hogshead for you.

Savil.   You shall neither will nor choose sir. My Master is a
wonderfull fine Gentleman, has a fine state, a very fine state Sir,
I am his steward Sir, and his man.

Elder Loveless [aside].   Would you were your owne Sir, as I left
you. Well I must cast about, or all sinks.

Savil.   Farewell Gentleman, Gentleman. Gentleman———

Elder Loveless.   What would you with me Sir?   160

Savil.   Farewell Gentleman.

Elder Loveless.   O sleepe Sir, sleepe.   *Exit* Elder Loveless.

Young Loveless.   Well boies, you see whats falne, lets in and drinke, and give thankes for it.

Savil.   Let's give thanks for't.

Young Loveless.   Drunke as I live.

Savil.   Drunke as I live boyes.

Young Loveless.   Why now thou art able to discharge thine office, and cast up a reckoning of some waight; I will bee knighted, for my state wil beare it, 'tis sixteene hundred boies: off with 170 your husks, Ile skin you all in sattin.

Captain.   O sweet *Lovelesse!*

Savil.   All in sattin? O sweet *Lovelesse.*

Young Loveless.   March in my Noble Compeeres: and this my Countesse shall be led by two: and so proceed we to the will.

                 Exeunt.

    Enter Moorecraft *the usurer, and* Widdow.   [II. iii]

Morecraft.   And Widdow, as I say be your owne friend: your husband left you wealthy, I and wise, continue so sweet duck, continue so. Take heede of young smooth varlets, younger brothers, they are wormes that will eate through your bags: they are very lightning, that with a flash or two will melt your money, and never singe your purse strings: they are colts, wench, colts, headdy and dangerous, till we take um up, and make um fit for bonds; looke upon mee, I have had, and have yet matter of moment gyrle, matter of moment; you may meete with a worse backe, Ile not commend it.   10

Widow.   Nor I neither Sir.

Morecraft.   Yet thus farre by your favour widdow, 'tis tuffe.

Widow.   And therefore not for my dyet, for I love a tender one.

Morecraft.   Sweet widdow leave your frumps, and bee edified: you know my state, I sell no Perspectives, Scarfes, Gloves, nor Hangers, nor put my trust in Shoo-ties: and where your husband in an age was rising by burnt figs, dreg'd with meale and powdered

     165. S.P. *Savil.*] Q6; *Cap.* Q1–5

sugar, saunders and graines, wormeseed and rotten reasons, and
such vile tobacco, that made the foot-men mangie; I in a yeere
have put up hundreds; inclos'd, my widdow, those pleasant 20
meadowes, by a forfeit morgage: for which the poore Knight
takes a lone chamber, owes for his Ale, and dare not beat his
Hostesse: nay more——

Widow.   Good Sir no more, what ere my husband was, I know
what I am, and if you marry mee, you must beare it bravely off
Sir.

Morecraft.   Not with the head, sweet widdow.

Widow.   No, sweet sir, but with your shoulders: I must have you
dubd, for under that I will not stoope a feather. My husband was a
fellow lov'd to toyle, fede ill, made gaine his exercise, and so grew 30
costive, which for I was his wife, I gave way to, and spun mine
owne smocks course, and sir, so little——but let that passe. Time,
that weares all things out, wore out this husband, who in penitence
of such fruitlesse five yeeres marriage, left mee great with his
wealth, which if you'le bee a worthie gossip to, be knighted Sir.

Enter Savill.

Morecraft.   Now sir, from whom come you? whose man are you
Sir?

Savil.   Sir, I come from young Master *Lovelesse.*

Morecraft.   Be silent sir, I have no money, not a penny for you,
hee's sunke, your Master's sunke, a perisht man sir.   40

Savil.   Indeede his brother's sunke Sir, God be with him, a perisht
man indeede, and drown'd at Sea.

Morecraft.   How saidst thou, good my friend, his brother drown'd?

Savil.   Untimely, Sir, at sea.

Morecraft.   And thy young Master left sole heire?

Savil.   Yes, Sir.

Morecraft.   And he wants money?

Savil.   Yes, and sent me to you; for he is now to be knighted.

        22 not] Q2; nor Q1
        29 not] Q4; *om.* Q1-3
        30 fede] Q2 (fed); feede Q1
        31 I gave] F; and gaue Q1-10

Morecraft. Widdow, be wise, there's more land comming, widdow be very wise, and give thanks for me widdow.   50
Widow. Be you very wise, and bee knighted, and then give thanks for me Sir.
Savil. What sayes your Worship to this money?
Morecraft. I say, he may have money if he please.
Savil. A thousand Sir?
Morecraft. A thousand Sir, provided any wise Sir, his land lye for the payment, otherwise——

Enter Young Lovelesse *and Comrades* [Captain, Traveller, Poet, Tobacco-man] *to them.*

Savil. Hee's here himselfe Sir, and can better tell you.
Morecraft. My notable deare friend, and worthy Master *Lovelesse,* and now right worshipfull, all joy and welcome.   60
Young Loveless. Thanks to my deare incloser, Master *Moorecraft;* prethee olde Angell gold, salute my family, Ile doe as much for yours; this, and your owne desires, faire Gentlewoman.
Widow. And yours Sir, if you meane well; [*aside*] 'tis a hansome Gentleman.
Young Loveless. Sirrha, my brothers dead.
Morecraft. Dead?
Young Loveless. Dead, and by this time souc't for Ember weeke.
Morecraft. Dead?
Young Loveless. Drown'd, drown'd at sea: Man, by the next 70 fresh Conger that comes we shall heare more.
Morecraft. Now by the faith of my body it mooves me much.
Young Loveless. What, wil't thou be an Asse, and weepe for the dead? why I thought nothing but a generall inundation would have mov'd thee: prethee be quiet, he hath left his land behind him.
Morecraft. O, ha's he so?
Young Loveless. Yes faith, I thanke him for't, I have all boy, hast any ready money?
Morecraft. Will you sell Sir?   80
Young Loveless. No not outright good Gripe; marry, a morgage, or such a slight securitie.

Morecraft.   I have no money Sir for morgage; If you will sell, and all or none, Ile worke a new Mine for you.

Savil.   Good Sir looke afore you, hee'le worke you out of all else: if you sell all your Land, you have sold your Countrey, and then you must to sea to seeke your brother, and there lye pickled in a poudering tub, and breake your teeth with biskets and hard beefe that must have watering Sir: and where's your three hundred pounds a yeere in drinke then? If you'le tun up the straights you may, for you have no calling for drinke there, but with a Cannon, nor no scoring but on your ships sides, and then if you scape with life, and take a fagot boat, and a bottle of *Usquebaugh*, come home poore men, like a type of Theames Street stinking of pitch and poore John. I cannot tell Sir, I would be loth to see it.

Captain.   Steweard, you are an Asse, a measel'd mungrell, and were it not againe the peace of my soveraigne friend heere, I would breake your forecasting coxcombe, dogge I would, even with thy staffe of office there, thy pen and Inkhorne. Noble boy, the god of gold here has sed thee well, take mony for thy durt: hark and beleeve, thou art cold of constitution, thy seat unhealthful, sell and be wise; we are three that will adorne thee, and live according to thine owne heart childe: mirth shall be onely ours, and onely ours shal be the blacke eyde beauties of the time. Money makes men eternall.

Poet.   Doe what you will, 'tis the noblest course, then you may live without the charge of people, onely wee foure will make a family, I and an age that shall beget new *Annals*, in which Ile write thy life my sonne of pleasure, equall with *Nero* or *Caligula*.

Young Loveless.   What meane they Captaine?

Captain.   Two roring boyes of *Rome* that made all split.

Young Loveless.   Come Sir, what dare you give?

Savil.   You will not sell Sir?

Young Loveless.   Who told you so Sir?

Savil.   Good Sir have a care.

Young Loveless.   Peace, or Ile tacke your tongue up to your roofe. What money? speake.

Morecraft.   Sixe thousand pound Sir.   120

Captain.   Take it, h'as overbidden by the Sunne: binde him to
his bargaine quickly.

Young Loveless.   Come, strike mee lucke with earnest, and draw
the writings.

Morecraft.   There's a Gods penny for thee.

Savil.   Sir, for my old Masters sake let my Farme be excepted,
if I become his tenant I am undone, my children beggers, and my
wife God knowes what: consider me deare Sir.

Morecraft.   Ile have all in or none.

Young Loveless.   All in, all in: dispatch the writings.   130

Exit with Comrades.

Widow.   Goe, thou art a pretty forehanded fellow, would thou
wert wiser.

Savil.   Now doe I sensibly begin to feele my selfe a rascall:
would I could teach a Schoole, or begge, or lye well, I am utterly
undone; now he that taught thee to deceive and cousen, take thee
to his mercy: so be it.   *Exit* Savill.

Morecraft.   Come widow, come, never stand upon a knighthood,
'tis a meere paper honour, and not proofe enough for a Sergeant.
Come, come, Ile make thee——

Widow.   To answere in short, 'tis this Sir, No knight, no widow: 140
if you make mee any thing, it must be a Lady; and so I take my
leave.

Morecraft.   Farewell sweet widdow, and thinke of it.

Widow.   Sir I do more then thinke of it, it makes me dreame sir.

Exit Widow.

Morecraft.   Shee's rich and sober, if this itch were from her: and
say I bee at charge to pay the Footmen, and the Trumpets, I and
the Horsmen too, and be a Knight, and she refuse me then; then
am I hoyst into the Subsidy, and so by consequence should prove
a Coxcombe: Ile have a care of that. Sixe thousand pound, and
then the Land is mine, there's some refreshing yet.   150

Exit.

Enter Abigall, *and drops her Glove.*   III. i

Abigail.   If he but follow mee, as all my hopes tels me hee's man enough, up goes my rest, and I know I shall draw him.

Enter Welford.

Welford [*aside*].   This is the strangest pamperd peece of flesh towards fiftie, that ever frailty cop't withall, what a trim *Lenvoy* heere she has put upon me: these woemen are a proud kinde of cattell, and love this whorson doing so directly, that they wil not sticke to make their very skinnes Bawdes to their flesh. Here's dogskin and storax sufficient to kill a Hauke: what to do with it, beside nayling it up amongst *Irish* heads of Teere, to shew the mightines of her palme, I know not: there she is, I must enter into Dialogue. 10 ——Lady you have lost your glove.

Abigail.   Not Sir if you have found it.

Welford.   It was my meaning Lady to restore it.

Abigail.   'Twill be uncivell in me to take backe a favour, Fortune hath so well bestowed Sir, 'pray weare it for me.

Welford [*aside*].   I had rather weare a Bell.——But harke you Mistrisse, What hidden vertue is there in this glove, that you would have me weare it? Is't good against sore eyes, or wil it charme the toothake? Or these red tops, beeing steept in white wine soluble, wil't kill the itch? or h'as it so conceald a providence to 20 keepe my hand from bonds? If it have none of these, and proove no more but a bare glove of halfe a crowne a payre, twill bee but halfe a courtesie, I weare two alwaies: faith let's draw cuts, one will doe me no pleasure.

Abigail [*aside*].   The tendernesse of his yeeres keepes him as yet in ignorance, hee's a well moulded fellow, and I wonder his bloud should stirre no higher; but tis his want of company: I must grow neerer to him.

III.i] *Finis Actus secundi.* | *Actus* 3. *Scæna prima.* Q1
0.1] *and drops her Glove.*] Q2; *om.* Q1
18 against] Q2; aganst Q1

Enter Elder Lovelesse *disguised.*

Elder Loveless.   God save you both.

Abigail.   And pardon you Sir: this is somewhat rude, how came 30
you hither?

Elder Loveless.   Why through the dores, they are open.

Welford.   What are you? and what businesse have you here?

Elder Loveless.   More I beleeve then you have.

Abigail.   Who would this fellow speake with? Art thou sober?

Elder Loveless.   Yes, I come not here to sleepe.

Welford.   Prethee what art thou?

Elder Loveless.   As much (gay man) as thou art, I am a Gentleman.

Welford.   Art thou no more?

Elder Loveless.   Yes, more then thou dar'st be, a Souldier.   40

Abigail.   Thou dost not come to quarrell?

Elder Loveless.   No, not with weomen; I come to speake here
with a Gentlewoman.

Abigail.   Why I am one.

Elder Loveless.   But not with one so gentle.

Welford.   This is a fine fellow.

Elder Loveless.   Sir I am not fine yet, I am but new come over,
direct mee with your ticket to your Taylor, and then I shall bee
fine Sir. Lady, if there be a better of your sex within this house,
say I would see her.   50

Abigail.   Why am not I good enough for you Sir?

Elder Loveless.   Your way you'le be too good, 'pray end my
busines.——[*Aside*] This is another Suter: O frayle woman.

Welford [*aside*].   This fellow with his bluntnes hopes to doe more
then the long suites of a thousand could: though he be sowre hee's
quicke, I must not trust him.——Sir, this Lady is not to speake
with you, she is more serious: you smell as if you were new
calkt; goe and be hansome, and then you may sit with her
Serving-men.

Elder Loveless.   What are you Sir?   60

Welford.   Guesse by my outside.

Elder Loveless.   Then I take you Sir for some new silken thing

58 calkt] Q2; ralkt Q1

494

wean'd from the countrey, that shall (when you come to keepe
good company) be beaten into better manners. 'Pray good proud
Gentlewoman helpe me to your Mistres.

Abigail.   How many lives hast thou, that thou talk'st thus
rudely?

Elder Loveless.   But one, I am neither cat nor woman.

Welford.   And will that one life Sir maintaine you ever in such
bold sawcinesse?   70

Elder Loveless.   Yes amongst a nation of such men as you are, and
be no worse for wearing: Shall I speake with this Lady?

Abigail.   No by my troth shall not you.

Elder Loveless.   I must stay here then.

Welford.   That you shall not neyther.

Elder Loveless.   Good fine thing tell me why.

Welford.   Good angry thing Ile tell you:
  This is no place for such companions,
  Such lousie Gentlemen shall finde their businesse
  Better i'th Suburbs; there your strong pitch perfume,   80
  Mingled with lees of Ale, shall reeke in fashion:
  This is no Thames street Sir.

Abigail.   This Gentleman informes you truly:
  Prethee be satisfied, and seeke the Suburbs,
  Good Captaine, or whatever title else,
  The warlike Eeleboats have bestow'd upon thee,
  Goe and reforme thy selfe: prethee be sweeter,
  And know my Lady speakes with no such swabbers.

Elder Loveless.   You cannot talke me out with your tradition
  Of wit you picke from plaies, goe too, I have found yee: 90
  And for you, tender Sir, whose gentle bloud
  Runnes in your nose, and makes you snuffe at all
  But three pil'd people, I doe let you know,
  He that begot your worships sattin sute,
  Can make no men Sir: I will see this Lady,
  And with the reverence of your silkenship,
  In these old Ornaments.

Welford.   You will not sure.

Elder Loveless.   Sure Sir I shall.
Abigail.   You would be beaten out.
Elder Loveless.   Indeed I would not, or if I would be beaten,
  Pray who shall beat me? this good Gentleman   100
  Lookes as he were o'th peace.
Welford.   Sir you shall see that: will you get you out?
Elder Loveless.   Yes, that, that shall correct your boyes tongue,
  Dare you fight? I will stay here still.
Abigail.   O their things are out, helpe, helpe for Gods sake,
  Maddam; Jesus they foyne at one another,
  Maddam, why who is within there?

Enter Lady.

Lady.   Who breedes this rudenes?
Welford.   This uncivill fellow:
  He sayes he comes from sea, where I beleeve
  H'as purg'd away his manners.
Lady.   What of him?   110
Welford.   Why he will rudely, without once God blesse you,
  Presse to your privacies, and no deniall
  Must stand betwixt your person and his businesse;
  I let goe his ill language.
Lady.   Sir, have you businesse with me?
Elder Loveless.   Maddame some I have,
  But not so serious to pawne my life for't:
  If you keepe this quarter, and maintaine about you
  Such Knights o'th *Sun* as this is, to defie
  Men of imployment to yee, you may live,   120
  But in what fame?
Lady.   Pray stay Sir, who h'as wrong'd you?
Elder Loveless.   Wrong me he cannot, though uncivilly
  He flung his wilde words at me: But to you
  I thinke he did no honour, to deny
  The haste I come withall, a passage to you,
  Though I seeme course.
Lady.   Excuse me, gentle sir, twas from my knowledge,

99 be] Q2; *om.* Q1

496

And shall have no protection. And to you Sir,
You have shewed more heat then wit, and from your selfe
Have borrowed power, I never gave you here,   130
To doe these wilde unmanly things: my house
Is no blinde streete to swagger in: and my favours
Not doting yet on your unknowne deserts
So farre, that I should make you Master of my businesse:
My credit yet, stands fayrer with the people
Then to be tryed with swords: And they that come
To doe me service, must not thinke to winne me
With hazard of a murther: If your love
Consist in fury, carry it to the Campe,
And there in honour of some common mistres,   140
Shorten your youth. I pray be better temperd,
And give me leave awhile Sir.
Welford.   You must have it.   *Exit* Welford.
Lady.   Now Sir, your businesse?
Elder Loveless.   First I thanke you for schooling this young fellow,
   Whom his owne follies, which 'is prone inough
   Daily to fall into, if you but frowne,
   Shall levell him away to his repentance:
   Next I should rayle at you, but you are a woman,
   And anger lost upon you.
Lady.   Why at me Sir?
   I never did you wrong, for to my knowlege   150
   This is the first sight of you.
Elder Loveless.   You have done that,
   I must confesse I have the least curse in,
   Because the least acquaintance: But there be
   (If there be honour in the mindes of men)
   Thousands, when they shall know what I deliver,
   (As all good men must share in't) will to shame
   Blast your blacke memory.
Lady.   How is this good Sir?
Elder Loveless.   Tis that, that if you have a soule will choake it:
   Y'ave kild a Gentleman.
Lady.   I kild a Gentleman?

32   **497**   B D W

Elder Loveless.   You and your crueltie have kild him woman;   160
And such a man (let me be angry in't)
Whose least worth waighed above all weomens vertues
That are, I spare you all to come too: guesse him now.
Lady.   I am so innocent I cannot Sir.
Elder Loveless.   Repent you meane: you are a perfect woman,
And as the first was, made for mans undoing.
Lady.   Sir you have mist your way, I am not she.
Elder Loveless.   Would he had mist his way too, though hee had
Wandered farther then weomen are ill spoken of,
So he had mist this misery, you Lady.   170
Lady.   How doe you doe Sir?
Elder Loveless.   Well inough I hope,
While I can keepe my selfe from such temptations.
Lady.   Pray leape into this matter, whither would yee?
Elder Loveless.   You had a Servant that your peevishnes
Injoyned to travell.
Lady.   Such a one I have
Still, and should be grieved 'twere otherwise.
Elder Loveless.   Then have your asking, and be griev'd, hee's dead;
How you will answere for his worth I know not,
But this I am sure, eyther he, or you, or both
Were starke mad, else he might have liv'd   180
To have given a stronger testimony toth' world
Of what he might have beene. He was a man
I knew but in his evening: ten Sunnes after,
Forc't by a tyrant storme our beaten barke
Bulg'd under us; in which sad parting blow,
He cal'd upon his Saint, but not for life,
On you unhappy woman; and whilst all
Sought to preserve their soules, he desperately
Imbrac't a wave, crying to all that see it,
If any live, goe to my Fate, that forc't me   190
To this untimely end, and make her happy:
His name was *Lovelesse*: And I scap't the storme.
And now you have my businesse.
Lady.   Tis too much.

498

Would I had beene that storme, he had not perisht.
If you'le raile now I will forgive you Sir,
Or if you'le call in more, if any more
Come from this ruine, I shall justly suffer
What they can say: I doe confesse my selfe
A guilty cause in this. I would say more,
But griefe is growne to great to be delivered.   200
Elder Loveless [*aside*].   I like this well: these weomen are strange
      things.——
Tis somewhat of the latest now to weepe,
You should have wept when he was going from you,
And chain'd him with those teares at home.
Lady.   Would you had told me then so, these two armes
Had beene his Sea.
Elder Loveless.   Trust mee you moove me much:
But say he lived, these were forgotten things againe.
Lady [*aside*].   I, say you so? Sure I should know that voyce:
This is knavery. Ile fit you for it:——
Were he living sir,   210
I would perswade you to be charitable,
I, and confesse we are not all so ill
As your opinion holds us. O my friend,
What penance shall I pull upon my fault,
Upon my most unworthy selfe for this?
Elder Loveless.   Leave to love others, 'twas some jealousie
That turn'd him desperate.
Lady [*aside*].   Ile be with you straight:
Are you wrung there?
Elder Loveless [*aside*].   This works amaine upon her.
Lady.   I doe confesse there is a Gentleman
H'as borne me long good will——
Elder Loveless [*aside*].   I doe not like that.   220
Lady.   And vowed a thousand services to me;
To me, regardlesse of him: But since Fate,
That no power can withstand, h'as taken from me
My first and best Love, and to weepe away
My youth is a meere folly: I will shew you

What I determine sir: you shall know all:
Call Master *Welford* there: That Gentleman
I meane to make the modell of my Fortunes,
And in his chaste imbraces keepe alive
The memory of my lost lovely *Lovelesse*:   230
Hee is somewhat like him too.
Elder Loveless.   Then you can Love?
Lady.   Yes certaine sir.
Though it please you to thinke me hard and cruell,
I hope I shall perswade you otherwise.
Elder Loveless [*aside*].   I have made my selfe a fine foole.

Enter Welford.

Welford.   Would you have spoke with me Maddame?
Lady.   Yes Master *Welford*, and I aske your pardon
Before this gentleman, for being froward:
This kisse, and henceforth more affection.
Elder Loveless [*aside*].   So, 'tis better I were drown'd indeed.   240
Welford [*aside*].   This is a sudden passion, God hold it.
This fellow out of his feare sure ha's
Perswaded her, Ile give him a new suit on't.
Lady.   A parting kisse: and good Sir let me pray you
To waite me in the Gallerie.
Welford.   I am in another world. Maddame where you please.
                                        Exit Welford.
Elder Loveless [*aside*].   I will to Sea, an't shal go hard but Ile be
    drown'd indeed.
Lady.   Now Sir you see I am no such hard creature,
But time may winne me.
Elder Loveless.   You have forgot your lost Love.   250
Lady.   Alas Sir, what would you have me doe? I cannot call him
    backe againe with sorrow; Ile love this man as deerely, and
    beshrow me, Ile keepe him farre inough from sea: and twas told
    me, now I remember me, by an old wise woman, that my first
    Love should be drown'd: and see Tis come about.
Elder Loveless [*aside*].   I would she had told you your second

should be hang'd to, and let that Come about:——but this is
very strange.

Lady.   Faith Sir, consider all, and then I know you'le bee of my
minde: if weeping would redeeme him, I would weepe still.   260

Elder Loveless.   But say that I were *Lovelesse*,
And scap't the storme, how would you answere this?

Lady.   Why for that Gentleman I would leave all the world.

Elder Loveless.   This young thing too?

Lady.   That young thing too,
Or any young thing else: why I would lose my state.

Elder Loveless.   Why then he lives still, I am he, your *Lovelesse*.

Lady.   Alas I knew it Sir, and for that purpose
Prepar'd this Pageant: get you to your taske.
And leave these Players tricks, or I shal leave you,   270
Indeede I shall. Travell, or know me not.

Elder Loveless.   Will you then marry?

Lady.   I will not promise, take your choyse. Farewell.

Elder Loveless.   There is no other Purgatory but a woman.
I must doe something.   *Exit* Lovelesse.

Enter Welford.

Welford.   Mistres I am bold.

Lady.   You are indeed.

Welford.   You have so overjoyed me Lady.

Lady.   Take heed you surfet not, pray fast and welcome.

Welford.   By this light you love me extremely.

Lady.   By this, and tomorrowes light, I care not for you.   280

Welford.   Come, come, you cannot hide it.

Lady.   Indeed I can, where you shall never finde it.

Welford.   I like this mirth well Lady.

Lady.   You shall have more on't.

Welford.   I must kisse you.

Lady.   No sir.

Welford.   Indeed I must.

Lady.   What must be, must be; Ile take my leave,
You have your parting blow: I pray commend me
To those few friends you have, that sent you hither,

And tell them, when you travell next, 'twere fit
You brought lesse bravery with you, and more wit,
You'le never get a wife else.   290
Welford. Are you in earnest?
Lady. Yes faith. Wil you eat sir? your horses wil be ready straight,
you shall have a napkin laid in the buttery for yee.
Welford. Do not you love me then?
Lady. Yes, for that face.
Welford. It is a good one Lady.
Lady. Yes, if it were not warpt, the fire in time may mend it.
Welford. Me thinks yours is none of the best Lady.
Lady. No by my troth Sir: yet o' my conscience,
You could make shift with it.   300
Welford. Come, 'pray no more of this.
Lady. I will not: Fare you well. Ho, who's within there? bring
out the Gentlemans horses, hee's in haste; and set some cold meate
on the table.
Welford. I have too much of that, I thanke you Lady: take your
Chamber when you please, there goes a black one with you Lady.
Lady. Farewell young man.   *Exit* Lady.
Welford. You have made me one. Farewell: and may the curse of
a great house fall upon thee, I meane the Butler. The Divell and
all his works are in these women: would all of my sexe were of 310
my minde, I would make um a new Lent, and a long one, that
flesh might be in more reverence with them.

Enter Abigall *to him.*

Abigail. I am sorry Master *Welford.*
Welford. So am I, that you are here.
Abigail. How do's my Lady use you?
Welford. As I would use you, scurvily.
Abigail. I should have beene more kinde Sir.
Welford. I should have beene undone then. 'Pray leave mee, and
looke to your sweet meats: harke, your Lady calls.
Abigail. Sir I shall borrow so much time without offending.   320
Welford. Y'are nothing but offence: for Gods love leave me.
Abigail. Tis strange my Lady should be such a tyrant.

Welford.   To send you to mee. 'Pray goe stitch, good doe, y'are more trouble to me then a Terme.

Abigail.   I doe not know how my good will, if I said love I lyed not, should any way deserve this.

Welford.   A thousand waies, a thousand waies: sweet creature let me depart in peace.

Abigail.   What creature Sir? I hope I am a woman.

Welford.   A hundred I thinke by your noyse.   330

Abigail.   Since you are angry sir, I am bold to tell you, that I am a woman, and a ribbe.

Welford.   Of a roasted horse.

Abigail.   Conster me that.

Welford.   A Dogge can doe it better. Farewell Countesse, and commend me to your Lady: tell her shee's proud, and scurvy; and so I commit you both to your tempter.

Abigail.   Sweet Master *Welford.*

Welford.   Avoide olde Satanus: Goe daube your ruines, your face lookes fowler then a storme: the footeman staies you in the Lobby   340 Ladie.

Abigail.   If you were a Gentleman I should know it by your gentle conditions! are these fit words to give a gentlewoman?

Welford.   As fit as they were made for yee: Sirrah, my horses. Farewell old Adage, keepe your nose warme, the Reume will make it horne else.   *Exit* Welford.

Abigail.   The blessings of a prodigall young heire be thy companions *Welforde.* Marry come up my gentleman, are your gummes growne so tender they cannot bite? A skittish Filly will be your fortune *Welford,* and faire enough for such a packsaddle. And I   350 doubt not, (if my aime hold) to see her made to amble to your hand.

                                          Exit Abigal.

351 amble] Q2; amable Q1

Enter Young Lovelesse *and Comrades* [Captain, Poet,　　　[III. ii]
Traveller, Tobacco-Man], Moorcraft, Widow, Savil,
and the rest.

Captain.　　Save thy brave shoulder, my young puissant Knight,
And may thy back-sword bite them to the bone,
That love thee not: thou art an errant man,
Goe on. The circumcisde shall fall by thee.
Let land and labour fill the man that tils,
Thy sword must bee thy plough, and *Jove* it speede.
Mecha shall sweate, and *Mahomet* shall fall,
And thy deere name fill up his monument.
Young Loveless.　　It shall Captaine, I meane to be a worthy.
Captain.　　One worthy is too little, thou shalt be all.　　　10
Morecraft.　　Captaine I shall deserve some of your love too.
Captain.　　Thou shalt have heart and hand to noble *Moorcraft*,
If thou wilt lend me money.
I am a man of Garrison, be rulde,
And open to me those infernall gates,
Whence none of thy evill angels passe againe,
And I will stile thee Noble; nay *Don Diego*,
Ile woe thy *Infanta* for thee, and my Knight
Shall feast her with high meats, and make her apt.
Morecraft.　　Pardon me Captaine, y'are beside my meaning.　　20
Young Loveless.　　No Master *Moorecraft*, t'is the Captaines meaning
I should prepare her for yee.
Captain.　　　　　　　　　Or provoke her.
Speake my moderne man, I say provoke her.
Poet.　　Captaine I say so too, or stir her to it.
So saies the Criticks.
Young Loveless.　　But howsoever you expound it Sir, she's very
welcome, and this shall serve for witnesse. And widdow, since
y'are come so happily, you shall deliver up the keys, and free
possession of this house; whilst I stand by to ratifie.
Widow.　　I had rather give it back againe beleeve me,　　　30
'Tis a misery to say you had it. Take heede.
Young Loveless.　　'Tis past that widowe, come, sit downe; some

wine there: there is a scurvy banquet if we had it. All this faire
house is yours Sir. *Savill.*

Savil. Yes Sir.

Young Loveless. Are your keys ready, I must ease your burden.

Savil. I am ready Sir to be undone, when you shall call me to't.

Young Loveless. Come come, thou shalt live better.

Savil [*aside*]. I shall have lesse to doe, thats all, ther's halfe a
dozen of my friends ith fields, sunning against a banke, with halfe 40
a breech among um, I shall bee with um shortly. The care and
continuall vexation of being rich eate up this rascall. What shall
become of my poore familie? they are no sheepe, and they must
keepe themselves.

Young Loveless. Drinke Master *Moorecraft*, praye be merry all:
Nay and you will not drinke ther's no society.

Captaine speake lowd, and drinke: widdow a word.

Captain. Expound her throughly Knight.——
Here God a gold, here's to thy faire possessions:
Bee a Barron, and a bolde one: 50
Leave off your tickling of young heires like trouts,
And let thy chimneys smoke. Feede men of war,
Live and bee honest, and be saved yet.

Morecraft. I thanke you worthy Captain for your counsell. You
keep your chimneys smoking there, your nostrels, and when you
can, you feede a man of war: this makes not you a Barron, but a
bare-one: and how or when you shall be saved, let the clarke
o'th company (you have commanded) have a just care of.

Poet. The man is much moved. Be not angry Sir, but as the Poet
sings; Let your displeasure be a short furie, and goe out. You 60
have spoke home, and bitterly, to him Sir! Captain take truce,
the Miser is a tart and a witty whorson.

Captain. Poet you faine perdie, the wit of this man lies in his
fingers ends, he must tell al: his tongue fils but his mouth like a
neats-tongue, and onely serves to lick his hungry chaps after a
purchase: his braines and brimstone are the Divels diet to a fat
userers head.——To her Knight, to her: clap her abourd and stow
her. Wheres the brave Steward?

Savil.   Heres your poore friend, and *Savil* Sir.

Captain.   Away, th'art rich in ornaments of nature.   70
First in thy face, thou hast a serious face,
A betting, bargaining, and saving face,
A rich face, pawne it to the Usurer;
A face to kindle the compassion
Of the most ignorant and frozen Justice.

Savil.   'Tis such, I dare not shew it shortly sir.

Captain.   Be blithe and bonny Steward: Master *Moorecraft*,
Drinke to this man of reckoning.

Morecraft.   Heere's e'ne to him.

Savil [*aside*].   The Divell guide it downward: would there were 80
in't an acre of the great broome field he bought, to sweepe your
durty conscience, or to choake ye, 'tis all one to me Usurer.

Young Loveless.   Consider what I told you, you are young,
Unapt for worldly busines: Is it fit
One of such tendernes, so delicate,
So contrary to things of care, should stirre
And breake her better meditations,
In the bare brokage of a brace of Angels?
Or a new kirtell, though it be of satten?
Eate by the hope of forfeits, and lie downe   90
Onely in expectation of a morrow,
That may undoe some easie harted foole,
Or reach a widowes curses? Let out money,
Whose use returnes the principall? and get
Out of these troubles, a consuming heire:
For such a one must follow necessary,
You shall die hated, if not old and miserable;
And that possest wealth that you got with pining,
Live to see tumbled to anothers hands,
That is no more akin to you, then you   100
To his cosenage.

Widow.   Sir you speake well, would God that charity
Had first begunne here.

Young Loveless.   Tis yet time.——Be merry,

77 Be] Q3; By Q1–2   90 forfeits] Weber; surfets Q1+

Me thinkes you want wine there, ther's more i'th house:
Captaine, where rests the health?

Captain.   It shall goe round boy!

Young Loveless.   Say you can suffer this, because the end
Points at much profit, can you so farre bow
Below your blood, below your too much bewty,
To be a partner of this fellowes bed,
And lie with his diseases? If you can,   110
I will not presse you further: yet looke upon him:
Ther's nothing in that hide-bound Usurer;
That man of mat, that all decai'd, but aches:
For you to love, unlesse his perisht lungs,
His drie cough, or his scurvy. This is truth,
And so farre I dare speak it: he has yet
Past cure of Phisicke, spaw, or any diet,
A primative pox in his bones; and a' my knowledge
Hee has beene tenne times rowell'd: ye may love him;
He had a bastard, his owne toward issue,   120
Whipt, and then cropt for washing out the roses,
In three farthings to make um pence.

Widow.   I doe not like these Morrals.

Young Loveless.   You must not like him then.

Enter Elder Lovelesse.

Elder Loveless.   By your leave Gentlemen.

Young Loveless.   By my troth Sir you are welcome, welcome
faith: Lord what a stranger you are growne; pray know this
Gentlewoman, and if you please these friends here: We are merry,
you see the worst on's; your house has been kept warme Sir.

Elder Loveless.   I am glad to heare it brother, pray God you are   130
wise too.

Young Loveless.   Pray Master *Moorecraft* know my elder brother,
and Captaine doe your complement. *Savil*, I dare swere is glad
at heart to see you: Lord, we heard Sir you were droun'd at Sea,
and see how luckely things come about!

Morecraft.   This money must be paid againe Sir?

113 decai'd] Q2; dccai'd Q1   116 it] Q11; yet Q1–10

Young Loveless. No Sir, pray keepe the sale, t'wil make good Taylers measures! I am well I thanke you.

Widow. By my troth the Gentleman has stew'd him in his owne sauce, I shal love him fort. 140

Savil. I know not where I am, I am so glad: your worship is the welcom'st man alive; upon my knees I bid you welcome home: here has beene such a hurry, such a din, such dismall drinking, swearing, and whoring, 'thas almost made me mad: We have al liv'd in a continuall *Turneball streete*; Sir blest be Heaven, that sent you safe againe. Now shall I eate, and goe to bed againe.

Elder Loveless. Brother dismisse these people.

Young Loveless. Captaine be gone a while, meet me at my old *Randevouse* in the evening, take your small Poet with you.

[*Exeunt* Captain *and* Poet *and other Comrades.*]

Master *Moorecraft*, you were best goe prattle with your learned 150 Counsell, I shall preserve your money! I was cosen'd when time was, we are quit Sir.

Widow. Better and better still.

Elder Loveless. What is this fellow brother?

Young Loveless. The thirsty Usurer that supt my Land off.

Elder Loveless. What does he tarry for?

Young Loveless. Sir to be Land-lord of your house and state: I was bold to make a little sale Sir.

Morecraft. Am I over-reacht? if there be law, Ile hamper yee.

Elder Loveless. Prethee bee gone, and raile at home, thou art so 160 base a foole I cannot laugh at thee: Sirrha, this comes of cousening, home and spare, eate reddish til you raise your summes againe. If you stir farre in this, Ile have you whipt, your eares nayl'd for intelligencing, o'th pillory, and your goods forfeit: you are a stale Cousener, leave my house: no more.

Morecraft. A poxe upon your house. Come Widow, I shall yet hamper this young gamester.

Widow. Good twelve i'th hundred keepe your way, I am not for your dyet: marry in your owne Tribe *Jew*, and get a Broker.

Young Loveless. Tis well said widdow: will you jogge on Sir? 170

Morecraft. Yes, I will goe, but 'tis no matter whither:

154 S.P. *Elder Loveless.*] Q2; *Yo.Lo.* Q1

But when I trust a wilde foole, and a woman,
May I lend gratis, and build Hospitals.   [*Exit.*]

Young Loveless.   Nay good sir make all even, here's a widdow
wants your good word for me: shee's rich, and may renue me
and my Fortunes.

Elder Loveless.   I am glad you looke before you. Gentlewoman,
here is a poore distressed younger brother.

Widow.   You doe him wrong Sir, hee's a Knight.

Elder Loveless.   I aske your mercy: yet 'tis no matter, his 180
Knighthood is no inheritance I take it: whatsoever he is, hee's
your servant, or would bee Lady. Faith bee not mercilesse, but make
a man; hees young and hansome, though he be my brother, and
his observances may deserve your love: hee shall not fall for
meanes.

Widow.   Sir, you speake like a worthy brother: and so much I doe
credit your faire language, that I shall love your brother: and so
love him, but I shall blush to say more.

Elder Loveless.   Stop her mouth. I hope you shall not live to know
that houre when this shall be repented. Now brother I should 190
chide, but Ile give no distaste to your faire Mistrisse, I wil instruct
her in't, and she shall doo't: you have bin wild, and ignorant,
'pray mend it.

Young Loveless.   Sir every day now spring comes on.

Elder Loveless.   To you, good Master *Savill*, and your Office,
thus much I have to say: Y'are from my Steward become, first
your owne Drunkard, then his Bawde: they say y'are excellent
growne in both, and perfect: give me your keyes Sir *Savill*.

Savil.   Good Sir consider who you left me too.

Elder Loveless.   I left you as a curbe for, not to provoke my 200
brothers follies: Where's the best drinke now? come, tell me
Savill: where's the soundest whores? Ye old he Goat, ye dry'd
Ape, ye lame stallion, must you be leaping in my house? your
whores, like Fayries dance their night rounds, without feare
eyther of King or Constable, within my walles! Are all my
Hangings safe? my sheepe unsold yet? I hope my Plate is currant,

187 credit] Q2; cerdit Q1
203 leaping] Q6; leading Q1–5   206 unsold] Q1(u); unfold Q1(c)

I ha' too much on't. What say you to three hundred pounds in
drinke now?

Savil.   Good Sir forgive me, and but heare me speake.

Elder Loveless.   Me thinks thou shouldst be drunke still, and not 210
speake, 'tis the more pardonable.

Savil.   I will sir, if you will have it so.

Elder Loveless.   I thanke ye; yes e'ne pursue it Sir: doe you
heare? get a whore soone for your recreation: goe looke out
Captaine Brokenbreech your fellow, and quarrell, if you dare:
I shall deliver these keyes to one shall have more honesty, though
not so much fine wit Sir. Yee may walke and gather *Cresses* sir
to coole your liver; there's something for you to begin a dyet,
you'le have the poxe else. Speed you well, Sir *Savill*: you may
eate at my house to preserve life; but keepe no fornications in the 220
stables.   *Exeunt omnes preter* Savill.

Savil.   Now must I hang my selfe, my friends will looke for't.
Eating and sleeping, I doe despise you both now:
I will runne mad first, and if that get not pitty,
Ile drowne my selfe, to a most dismall ditty.

Exit Savill.

Enter Abigall *solus.*   IV. i

Abigail.   Alasse poore Gentlewoman, to what a misery hath age
brought thee? to what scurvy Fortune? thou that hast beene a
companion for Noble men, and at the worst of those times for
Gentlemen: now like a broken Servingman, must begge for
favour to those that would have crawl'd like Pilgrims to my
chamber, but for an apperition of me: you that bee comming on,
make much of fifteene, and so till five and twenty: use your time
with reverence, that your profit may arise: it will not tarry with
you *Ecce signum*: here was a face, but time that like a surfet eates
our youth, (plague of his Iron teeth, and draw um for't), h'as 10
been a little bolder here then welcome: and now to say the truth
I am fit for no man. Old men i'th house, of fiftie, call me Granam;

IV.i] *Finis Actus tertij.* | *Actus 4. Scæna prima.* Q1
2 thee? to] Q1(c); thee to? to Q1(u)   6 apperition] Q1(u); apprition Q1(c)

and when they are drunke, e'ene then, when *Jone* and my Lady
are all one, not one will doe me reason. My little Levite hath
forsaken me, his silver sound of Cytterne quite abolish't, his
dolefull *hymmes* under my chamber window, digested into
tedious learning: well foole, you leap't a Haddock when you
left him: hee's a cleane man, and a good Edifier, and twenty
nobles is his state *de Claro*, besides his pigges in *posse*. To this
good *Homilist* I have beene ever stubborne, which God forgive 20
me for, and mend my manners: and Love, if ever thou hadst
care of fortie, of such a peece of laye ground, heare my prayer,
and fire his zeale so farre forth that my faults, in this renued
impression of my love, may shew corrected to our gentle Reader.

Enter Roger.

See how neglectingly he passes by me: with what an Equipage
Canonicall, as though he had broke the heart of *Bellarmine*, or
added some thing to the singing Brethren. Tis scorne, I know it,
and deserve it. Master *Roger*.

Roger.　　Faire Gentlewoman, my name is *Roger*.

Abigail.　　Then gentle *Roger*.　　　　　　　　　　　　　30

Roger.　　Ungentle *Abigall*.

Abigail.　　Why Master *Roger* will you set your wit to a weak
womans.

Roger.　　You are weake indeed: for so the Poet sings.

Abigail.　　I doe confesse my weaknesse sweet Sir *Roger*.

Roger.　　Good my Ladies Gentlewoman, or my good Ladies
Gentlewoman (this trope is lost to you now) leave your prating,
you have a season of your first Mother in yee: and surely had the
divel beene in love, he had beene abused too: goe *Dalida*, you
make men fooles, and weare figge breeches.　　　　　　40

Abigail.　　Well, well, hard hearted man; dilate upon the weake
infirmities of weomen: these are fit texts: but once there was a
time——would I had never seene those eies, those eies, those
orient eies.

Roger.　　I they were pearles once with you.

Abigail.　　Saving your reverence Sir, so they are still.

Roger. Nay, nay, I doe beseech you leave your cogging, what they are, they are, they serve me without Spectacles I thanke um.

Abigail. O will you kill me?

Roger. I doe not thinke I can, 50
Y'are like a Coppy-hold with nine lives in't.

Abigail. You were wont to beare a Christian feare about you: For your owne Worships sake——

Roger. I was a Christian foole then: Doe you remember what a dance you led me? how I grew qualm'd in love, and was a dunce? could expound but once a quarter, and then was out too: and then at prayers once (out of the stinking stir you put me in) I praid for mine owne royall issue. You doe remember all this?

Abigail. O be as then you were.

Roger. I thanke you for it; surely I wil be wiser *Abigall*: and 60 as the Ethnick Poet sings, I wil not loose my oile and labour too. Y'are for the worshipfull I take it *Abigall*.

Abigail. O take it so, and then I am for thee.

Roger. I like these teares well, and this humbling also, they are Symptomes of contrition, as a Father saith. If I should fall into my fit againe, would you not shake me into a quotidian Coxcombe? Would you not use me scurvily againe, and give me possets with purging comfets in't? I tel thee Gentlewoman, thou hast been harder to me then a long chapter with a pedigree.

Abigail. O Curate cure me: I will love thee better, dearer, longer. 70 I wil doe anything, betray the secrets of the maine household to thy reformation. My Ladie shall looke lovely on thy learning; and when true time shal point thee for a Parson, I will convert thy egs to penny custards, and thy tythe goose shall grase and multiplie.

Roger. I am mollified: as wel shal testifie this faithful kisse: and have a great care Mistres *Abigall*, how you depresse the spirit any more with your rebukes and mockes: for certainely the edge of such a folly cuts it selfe.

Abigail. O sir you have pierst me thorow. Heere I vow a recantation 80 to those malitious faults I ever did against you. Never more will I despise your learning, never more pin cardes and cunny

55 qualm'd] F; quaum'd Q1+   73 convert] Q2; cnnuert Q1

tailes upon your Cassock, never againe reproach your reverend
nightcap, and cal it by the mangie name of murrin, never your
reverend person more, and say, you looke like one of *Baals*
Priests in a hanging; never againe, when you say grace, laugh at
you, nor put you out at prayers: never crampe you more with the
great Booke of Martyrs; nor when you ride, get sope and thistles
for you. No my *Roger*, these faults shall be corrected and amended,
as by the tenor of my teares appeares.   90

Roger.   Now cannot I hold if I should bee hang'd, I must crie to.
Come to thine own beloved, and doe even what thou wilt with me,
sweet, sweet *Abigail.* I am thine own for ever: heers my hand,
when *Roger* proves a recreant, hang him i'th Bel-ropes.

Enter Lady *and* Martha.

Lady.   Why how now Master *Roger*, no prayers downe with you
to night? did you heare the bell ring? You are courting, your
flock shall fat well for it.

Roger.   I humblie aske your pardon: Ile clap up Praiers (but
staie a little) and be with you againe.   *Exit* Roger.

Enter Elder Loveless.

Lady.   How dare you being so unworthie a Fellow,   100
Presume to come to move me anie more?

Elder Loveless.   Ha, ha, ha.

Lady.   What ailes the fellow.

Elder Loveless.   The fellow comes to laugh at you.
I tell you Lady, I would not for your Land,
Be such a Coxecome, such a whining Asse,
As you decreed me for when I was last heere.

Lady.   I joy to heare you are wise Sir, tis a rare Jewell
In an elder Brother: praye be wiser yet.

Elder Loveless.   Me thinks I am very wise: I doe not come a woeing; 110
Indeed Ile move no more love to your Ladiship.

Lady.   What make you heere then?

Elder Loveless.   Onely to see you, and be merry Ladie:

*84–85 never your…more,] *stet* Q1–10, F
86 in] Q2; *om.* Q1

Thats all my businesse. Faith lets be verie merrie.
Wher's little *Roger*? he's a good fellow:
An hower or two well spent in wholsome mirth
Is worth a thousand of these puling passions.
Tis an ill world for Lovers.
Lady.   They were never fewer.
Elder Loveless.   I thanke God ther's one lesse for me Ladie.   120
Lady.   You were never any Sir.
Elder Loveless.   Till now; and now, I am the prettiest fellow.
Lady.   You talke like a Taylor Sir.
Elder Loveless.   Me thinkes your faces are no such fine things now.
Lady.   Why did you tell mee you were wise. Lord what a lying
age is this, where wil you mend these faces?
Elder Loveless.   A hogs face soust is worth a hundred of um.
Lady.   Sure you had some Sow to your Mother.
Elder Loveless.   She brought such fine white pigs as you: fit for
none but Parsons Ladie.   130
Lady.   Tis wel you will alow us our Cleargie yet.
Elder Loveless.   That shall not save you. O that I were in love
againe with a wish.
Lady.   By this light you are a scurvy fellowe, praye be gone.
Elder Loveless.   You know I am a cleane skind man.
Lady.   Do I know it?
Elder Loveless.   Come, come, you would know it; thats as good:
but not a snap, never long for't, not a snap deare Lady.
Lady.   Harke ye Sir, harke ye, get ye to the Suburbs,
There's horseflesh for such hounds: will you goe Sir?   140
Elder Loveless.   Lord, how I lov'd this woman, how I worshipt
This pretty calfe with the white face heere: as I live,
You were the prettiest foole to play withall,
The wittiest little varlet, it would talke:
Lord how it talkt; and when I angred it,
It would cry out, and scratch, and eate no meate,
And it would say, Goe hang——
Lady.   It will say so still, if you anger it.
Elder Loveless.   And when I askt it, if it would be married,

147 it] Q1(c); yet Q1(u)

514

It sent mee of an errant into *France*:
And would abuse me, and be glad it did so——
Lady.   Sir, this is most unmanly, 'pray be gone.
Elder Loveless.   And sweare (even when it twitterd to be at me)
I was unhansome——
Lady.   Have you no manners in you?
Elder Loveless.   And say my backe was melted, when the God
     knowes
I kept it at a charge: Foure Flaunders Mares
Would have beene easier to me, and a Fencer.
Lady.   You thinke all this is true now.
Elder Loveless.   Faith whether it be or no, 'tis too good for you. 160
But so much for our mirth: Now have at you in earnest.
Lady.   There is enough Sir, I desire no more.
Elder Loveless.   Yes faith, weele have a cast at your best parts now,
And then the divell take the worst.
Lady.   Pray Sir no more, I am not much affected
With your commendations; tis almost dinner,
I know they stay you at the Ordinary.
Elder Loveless.   E'ene a short Grace, and then I am gone:
You are a woman,
And the proudest that ever lov'd a Coach: 170
The scornfullest, scurviest, and most scencelesse woman;
The greediest to be prays'd, and never mov'd,
Though it be grosse and open; the most envious,
That at the poore fame of anothers face,
Would eate your owne, and more then is your owne,
The paint belonging to it:
Of such a selfe opinion, that you thinke
None can deserve your glove: and for your malice,
You are so excellent, you might have beene
Your Tempters tutor: Nay, never cry.   180
Lady.   Your owne heart knowes you wrong me: I cry for ye?
Elder Loveless.   You shall before I leave you.
Lady.   Is all this spoke in earnest?
Elder Loveless.   Yes, and more as soone as I can get it out.

156 God] Q 1 (c); gods Q 1 (u)

Lady.   Well, out with't.

Elder Loveless.   You are, let me see——

Lady.   One that has us'd you with too much respect.

Elder Loveless.   One that hath us'd me (since you will have it so)
  The basest, the most Foot-boy like, without respect
  Of what I was, or what you might be by me:
  You have us'd me, as I would use a jade,   190
  Ride him off's legges, then turn him into the Commons:
  You have us'd me with discretion, and I thanke yee.
  If you have many more such prettie Servants,
  Pray build an Hospitall, and when they are old,
  Keepe um for shame.

Lady.   I cannot thinke yet this is serious.

Elder Loveless.   Will you have more on't?

Lady.   No faith, there's inough if it be true:
  Too much by all my part: you are no Lover then?

Elder Loveless.   No, I had rather be a Carrier.   200

Lady.   Why the gods amend all.

Elder Loveless.   Neither doe I thinke
  There can bee such a fellow found i'th world,
  To be in love with such a froward woman:
  If there bee such, th'are madde, *Jove* comfort um.
  Now you have all, and I as new a man,
  As light, and spirited, that I feele my selfe
  Cleane through another creature. O 'tis brave
  To be ones owne man. I can see you now
  As I would see a Picture, sit all day
  By you and never kisse your hand: heare you sing,   210
  And never fall backward; but with as set a temper,
  As I would heare a Fidler, rise and thanke you.
  I can now keepe my money in my purse,
  That still was gadding out for Scarfes and Wastcoats:
  And keepe my hand from Mercers sheepskins finely.
  I can eate Mutton now, and feast my selfe
  With my two shillings, and can see a Play
  For eighteene pence againe: I can my Lady.

Lady [aside].   The carriage of this fellow vexes me.——

516

Sir, pray let mee speake a little private with you,   220
[*Aside*] I must not suffer this.
Elder Loveless.   Ha, ha, ha, what would you with me?
You will not ravish me? Now, your set speech.
Lady.   Thou perjurd man——
Elder Loveless.   Ha, ha, ha, this is a fine *Exordium*:
And why I pray you perjurd?
Lady.   Did you not sweare a thousand thousand times
You lov'd me best of all things?
Elder Loveless.   I doe confesse it: make your best of that.
Lady.   Why doe you say, you doe not then?   230
Elder Loveless.   Nay Ile sweare it,
And give sufficient reason, your owne usage.
Lady.   Doe you not love me now then?
Elder Loveless.   No faith.
Lady.   Did you ever thinke I lov'd you dearely?
Elder Loveless.   Yes, but I see but rotten fruits on't.
Lady.   Doe not denie your hand, for I must kisse it,
And take my last farewell: now let me die
So you be happy.
Elder Loveless.   I am too foolish: Lady, speake deere Ladie.   240
Lady.   No let me die.   *Shee swounes.*
Martha.   O my sister.
Abigail.   O my Ladie, helpe, helpe.
Martha.   Run for some *Rosasolis*.
Elder Loveless.   I have plaid the fine asse: bend her bodie, Lady,
Best, dearest, worthiest Ladie, heare your servant:
I am not as I shew'd: O wretched foole
To fling away the Jewel of thy life thus.
Give her more aire, see she begins to stir,
Sweete Mistres heare me.
Lady.   Is my servant well?   250
Elder Loveless.   In being yours I am so.
Lady.   Then I care not.
Elder Loveless.   How doe ye,——reach a chaire there:——
          I confesse
My fault not pardonable, in pursuing thus

Upon such tendernesse my wilful errour:
But had I knowne it would have rought thus with yee,
Thus strangely; not the world had wonne me to it,
And let not (my best Lady) any word
Spoke to my end disturbe your quiet peace:
For sooner shall you know a generall ruine,
Then my faith broken. Doe not doubt this Mistres: 260
For by my life I cannot live without you.
Come come, you shall not greeve, rather be angry,
And heape infliction on me: I wil suffer.
O I could curse my selfe, praye smile upon me.
Upon my faith it was but a tricke to trie you,
Knowing you lov'd me dearly, and yet strangely
That you would never shew it, though my meanes
Was all humilitie.

All. Ha, ha.

Elder Loveless. How now? 270

Lady. I thanke you fine foole for your most fine plot:
This was a subtile one, a stiffe device
To have caught Dottrels with. Good sencelesse Sir,
Could you imagine I should swoune for you,
And know your selfe to be an arrant asse?
I, a discoverd one? Tis quit I thanke you Sir. Ha, ha, ha.

Martha. Take heede sir, she may chance to swoune againe!

All. Ha, ha, ha.

Abigail. Step to her sir, see how she changes colour.

Elder Loveless. Ile goe to hel first, and be better welcome. 280
I am fool'd, I doe confesse it, finely fool'd,
Ladie fool'd Madam, and I thanke you for it.

Lady. Faith 'tis not so much worth Sir:
But if I know when you come next a burding,
Ile have a stronger noose to hold the woodcock.

All. Ha, ha, ha.

Elder Loveless. I am glad to see you merry, pray laugh on.

Martha. H'ad a hard heart that could not laugh at you Sir. Ha, ha.

Lady. Praye Sister doe not laugh, youle anger him,
And then hee'l raile like a rude Costermonger, 290

That Schooleboies had cozned of his apples,
As loud and sencelesse.

Elder Loveless.   I will not raile.

Martha.   Faith then lets heare him sister.

Elder Loveless.   Yes you shall heare me.

Lady.   Shall we be the better
For it then?

Elder Loveless.   No. He that makes a woman
Better by his words, Ile have him Sainted:
Blowes wil not doe it.

Lady.   By this light hee'l beate us.

Elder Loveless.   You doe deserve it richly, and may live
To have a Beadle doe it.

Lady.   Now he railes.

Elder Loveless.   Come scornefull Folly,   300
If this be railing, you shall heare me raile.

Lady.   Pray put it in good words then.

Elder Loveless.   The worst are good enough for such a trifle,
Such a proud peece of Cobweb lawne.

Lady.   You bite Sir.

Elder Loveless.   I would til the bones crackt, and I had my will.

Martha.   We had best mussell him, he grows mad.

Elder Loveless.   I would twere lawfull in the next great sicknesse
To have the dogs spared; those harmelesse creatures,
And knocke ith head these hot continuall plagues,
Weomen, that are more infectious.   310
I hope the state will thinke on't.

Lady.   Are you wel sir?

Martha.   He lookes as though he had a greevous fit ath Collick.

Elder Loveless.   Greeneginger wil you cure me?

Abigail.   Ile heate a trencher for him.

Elder Loveless.   Durty *December* doe.
Thou with a face as olde as *Erra Pater*,
Such a prognosticating nose: thou thing
That ten yeares since has left to be a woman,
Outworne the expectation of a Bawde;
And thy dry bones can reach at nothing now,   320

But gords or ninepinnes; pray goe fetch a trencher,
Goe.

Lady.   Let him alone, 'is crackt.

Abigail.   Ile see him hang'd first, 'is a beastly fellow, to use a
woman of my breeding thus; I marry is a: would I were a man,
Ide make him eate his knaves words.

Elder Loveless.   Tye your she Otter up, good Lady Folly,
She stinkes worse then a beare-bayting.

Lady.   Why will you be angry now?

Elder Loveless.   Goe paint and purge,
Call in your kennel with you: you a Lady?   330

Abigail.   Sirra, looke too't against the quarter Sessions, if there
be good behaviour in the world, Ile have thee bound to it.

Elder Loveless.   You must not seeke it in your Ladyes house then:
Pray send this Ferret home, and spinne good *Abigall.*
And Maddame, that your Ladyshippe may know,
In what base manner you have us'd my service,
I doe from this hower hate thee heartily:
And though your folly should whip you to repentance,
And waken you at length to see my wronges,
Tis not the indeavour of your life shall win me: 340
Not all the friends you have in intercession,
Nor your submissive letters, though they spoke
As many teares as words; not your knees growne
Toth' ground in penitence, not all your state,
To kisse you: nor my pardon nor will
To give you Christian buriall, if you dye thus:
So farewell.
When I am married and made sure, Ile come
And visit you againe, and vexe you Lady.
By all my hopes Ile be a torment to you,   350
Worse then a tedious winter.
I know you will recant and sue to me,
But save that labour: Ile rather love a Fever
And continuall thirst, rather contract my youth
To drinke, and safer dote upon quarrells,

324 use] Q3; loose Q1-2

Or take a drawne whore from an Hospitall,
That time, diseases, and *Mercury* had eaten,
Then to be drawne to love you.
Lady.   Ha, ha, ha, pray doe, but take heed though――
Elder Loveless.   From thee, false dice, Jades, Cowards, and plaguy
    Summers,   360
Good Lord deliver mee.   *Exit* Elder Loveless.
Lady.   But harke you servant, harke ye: is he gone? call him
againe.
Abigail.   Hang him Padocke.
Lady.   Art thou here still? fly, fly, and call my servant, fly or
nere see me more.
Abigail.   I had rather knit againe then see that rascall, but I must
doe it.   *Exit* Abigail.
Lady.   I would be loth to anger him too much:
What fine foolery is this in a woman,   370
To use those men most frowardly they love most?
If I should loose him thus, I were rightly served.
I hope 'is not so much himselfe to take it
To'th heart: *Enter* Abigail.

How now? will he come backe?
Abigail.   Never he sweares whilst he can heare men say ther's any
woman living: he swore hee wood ha me first.
Lady.   Didst thou intreat him wench?
Abigail.   As well as I could Madam. But this is still your way, to
love being absent, and when hee's with you, laugh at him and 380
abuse him. There is another way if you could hit on't.
Lady.   Thou saist true, get me paper, pen, and inke, Ile write
to him, Ide be loth he should sleepe in's anger.
Women are most fooles, when they thinke th'are wisest.
                                            Exeunt Omnes.

374.1] Q1 prints after backe (l. 375)

Musicke. Enter Young Lovelesse *and* Widdow, *going*   [IV.ii]
to be married: with them his Comrades [Captain, Poet,
Traveller, Tobacco-Man].

Widow.   Pray Sir cast off these fellowes, as unfitting
For your bare knowledge, and farre more your company:
Ist fit such Ragamuffins as these are
Should beare the name of friends? and furnish out
A civill house? y'are to be marryed now,
And men that love you must expect a course
Farre from your old carrire: If you will keepe um,
Turne um toth' stable, and there make um groomes:
And yet now I consider it, such beggars
Once set a horse back, you have heard will ride,   10
How farre you had best to looke to.
Captain.   Heare you, you
That must be Lady, pray content your selfe
And thinke upon your carriage soone at night,
What dressing will best take your knight, what wastcote,
What cordiall will doe well i'th morning for him,
What tryers have you?
Widow.   What doe you meane Sir?
Captain.   Those that must switch him up: if he start well,
Feare not but cry *Saint George*, and beare him hard:
When you perceive his wind growes hot, and wanting,
Let him a little downe, 'is fleet nere doubt him,   20
And stands sound.
Widow.   Sir, you heare these fellowes?
Young Loveless.   Merry companions, wench, merry companions.
Widow.   To one another let um be companions,
But good Sir not to you: you shall be civill
And slip off these base trappings.
Captain.   He shall not need, my most sweet Lady grocer,
If hee be civill, not your powdered Suger,
Nor your Reasens shall perswade the *Captaine*
To live a Coxcome with him: Let him be civill
And eate i'th *Arches*, and see what will come ont.   30

Poet.   Let him bee civill, doe: undoe him: I,
  Thats the next way.
  I will not take (if hee be civill once)
  Two hundred pounds a yeare to live with him:
  Bee civill? theres a trimme perswasion.
Captain.   If thou beest civill Knight, as *Jove* defend it,
  Get thee another nose, that wil be puld
  Off by the angry boyes, for thy conversion:
  The Children thou shalt get on this Civilian
  Cannot inherit by the law, th'are *Ethnickes*,   40
  And all thy sport meere Morrall lechery:
  When they are growne having but little in um,
  They may proove Haberdashers, or grosse Grosers,
  Like their deare damme there: prethe be civill Knight,
  In time thou maist read to thy houshold
  And be drunke once a yeare: this would shew finely.
Young Loveless.   I wonder sweet heart you will offer this,
  You doe not understand these Gentlemen:
  I will be short and pithy: I had rather
  Cast you off by the way of charge: these are Creatures,   50
  That nothing goes to the maintenance of
  But Corne and Water. I will keepe these fellowes
  Just in the Competency of two Hennes.
Widow.   If you can cast it so Sir, you have my liking;
  If they eat lesse, I should not be offended:
  But how these, Sir, can live uppon so little
  As Corne and Water, I am unbeleeving.
Young Loveless.   Why prethee sweet heart what's your Ale?
  Is not that Corne and Water my sweet Widdow?
Widow.   I but my sweet Knight, wheres the meat to this,   60
  And cloathes that they must looke for?
Young Loveless.   In this short sentence Ale, is all included:
  Meate, Drinke, and Cloth: these are no ravening foot-men,
  No fellowes that at Ordinaries dare eat
  Their eighteene pence thrice out before they rise,
  And yet goe hungry to a play, and crack

66 to a play] Q4; to play Q1–3

523

More nuts then would suffice a dozen Squirrels;
Besides the din, which is damnable:
I had rather raile, and be confin'd to a *Boatemaker*,
Then live among such rascalls; these are people 70
Of such a cleane discretion in their dyet,
Of such a moderate sustenance, that they sweat
If they but smell hot meate. *Porredge* is poyson,
They hate a kitchen as they hate a counter,
And show em but a Fetherbed they swound.
Ale is their eating, and their drinking surely,
Which keeps their bodies cleere, and soluble.
Bread is a binder, and for that abolisht
Even in their ale, whose lost roome fills an apple,
Which is more ayrie, and of subtiller *Nature*. 80
The rest they take, is little, and that little,
As little easie: For like strict men of order,
They doe correct their bodies with a bench,
Or a poore stubborne table; if a chimney
Offer it selfe with some few broken rushes,
They are in downe: when they are sick, that's drunke,
They may have fresh straw, else they doe despise
These worldly pamperings. For their poore apparrell,
Tis worne out to the dyet; new they seeke none,
And if a man should offer, they are angry: 90
Scarse to be reconcyl'd againe with him:
You shall not heare em aske one a cast doublet,
Once in a yeare, which is a modesty
Befitting my poore friends: you see their *Wardrope*,
Though slender, competent: For shirts I take it,
They are things worne out of their remembrance.
Lowsie they will be, when they list, and *Mangie*,
Which showes a fine variety: and then to cure em,
A Tanners lymepit, which is little charge,
Two dogs, and these two may be cur'd for three pence. 100
Widow. You have halfe perswaded me, pray use your pleasure:

80 ayrie] F; ayre Q1–10
100 these two] Dyce; these; these two Q1+

And my good friends since I doe know your dyet,
Ile take an order, meate shall not offend you,
You shall have ale.
Captain. Wee aske no more, let it be mighty, Lady:
And if wee perish, then our owne sinnes on us.
Young Loveless. Come forward gentlemen, to Church my boyes,
When we have done, Ile give you cheere in boules.

              Exeunt.

       Enter Elder Lovelesse.   V. i

Elder Loveless. This senselesse woman vexes me toth' heart,
She will not from my memory: would she were
A man for one two houres, that I might beate her.
If I had bin unhansome, old, or jealous,
T'had bin an even lay she might have scorn'd me:
But to be yong, and by this light I thinke
As proper as the proudest; made as cleane,
As straight, and strong backt; meanes and manners equall
With the best cloth of silver Sir i'th kingdome:
But these are things at some time of the Moone,   10
Below the cut of Canvas: Sure shee has
Some Meeching raskall in her house, some hinde,
That she hath seene beare (like another *Milo*)
Quarters of Malte upon his backe, and sing with't,
Thrash all day, and ith evening in his stockings,
Strike up a hornepipe, and there stink two houres,
And nere a whit the worse man; these are they,
These steelechind rascalls that undoe us all.
Would I had bin a carter, or a Coachman,
I had done the deed ere this time.   20

       Enter Servant.

Servant. Sir ther's a Gentleman without would speak with you.
Elder Loveless. Bid him come in.

    V.i] *Finis Actus Quarti.* | *Actus 5. Scæna Prima.* Q1

Enter Welford.

Welford.   By your leave Sir.

Elder Loveless.   You are welcome, whats your will Sir?

Welford.   Have you forgotten me?

Elder Loveless.   I doe not much remember you.

Welford.   You must Sir.
I am that gentleman you pleas'd to wrong,
In your disguise, I have inquired you out.

Elder Loveless.   I was disguised indeed Sir if I wrongd you.
Pray where and when?

Welford.   In such a Ladies house Sir: 30
I need not name her.

Elder Loveless.   I doe remember you:
You seem'd to be a suter to that Lady.

Welford.   If you remember this, doe not forget
How scurvyly you usd me: that was
No place to quarrell in, pray you thinke of it:
If you be honest you dare fight with me,
Without more urging, else I must provoke yee.

Elder Loveless.   Sir I dare fight, but never for a woman,
I will not have her in my cause, she's Mortall
And so is not my anger: If you have brought   40
A Nobler subject for our swords, I am for you:
In this I would be loth to prick my finger.
And where you say I wrongd you, 'tis so far
From my profession, that amongst my feares,
To doe wrong is the greatest: credit me
We have bin both abusd, not by our selves,
(For that I hold a spleene no sinne of Mallice,
And may with man enough be left forgotten,)
But by that wilfull, scornefull peece of hatred,
That much forgetfull Lady: For whose sake,   50
If we should leave our reason, and runne on
Upon our sense, like *Rams*: the little world
Of good men would laugh at us, and despise us,
Fixing upon our desperate memories

526

The never-worne out names of Fooles, and Fencers.
Sir tis not feare, but reason makes me tell you:
In this I had rather helpe you Sir, then hurt you,
And you shall finde it, though you throw your selfe
Into as many dangers as she offers,
Though you redeeme her lost name every day,   60
And finde her out new honours with your sworde,
You shall but be her mirth, as I have bin.
Welford.   I aske you mercy Sir, you have tane my edge off:
Yet I would faine be even with this Lady.
Elder Loveless.   In which ile be your helper: we are two,
And they are two: two sisters, rich alike,
Onely the elder has the prouder dowry:
In troth I pitty this disgrace in you,
Yet of mine owne I am senselesse: doe but
Follow my counsell, and ile pawne my spirit,   70
We'le overreach em yet; the meanes is this——

                    Enter Servant.

Servant.   Sir theres a Gentlewoman will needs speake with you:
I cannot keep her out, she's entered Sir.
Elder Loveless.   It is the waitingwoman, pray be not seene:——
Sirra hold her in discourse awhile:——
Harke in your eare, goe, and dispatch it quickly,
When I come in Ile tell you all the project.
Welford.   I care not which I have.
Elder Loveless.   Away, tis done,
She must not see you: *Exit* Welford.

                    Enter Abigall.

Now Lady *Gwiniver*, what newes with you?   80
Abigail.   Pray leave these frumps Sir, and receive this letter.
Elder Loveless.   From whom good vanity?
Abigail.   'Tis from my Lady Sir: alas good soule, shee cries and
takes on.
Elder Loveless.   Do's she so good soule? wod she not have a

                    79.1] Q1 *prints after* you? (*l.* 80)
                    527

Cawdle? do's she send you with your fine Oratory goody *Tully*
to tye me to beleife againe? Bring out the Cat hounds, ile make you
take a tree whore, then with my tyller bring downe your *Gibship*,
and then have you cas'd, and hung up ith warren.

Abigail. I am no beast Sir: would you knew it. 90

Elder Loveless. Wod I did, for I am yet very doubtfull: what will
you say now?

Abigail. Nothing not I.

Elder Loveless. Art thou a woman, and say nothing?

Abigail. Unlesse youle heare mee with more moderation; I can
speake wise enough.

Elder Loveless. And loud enough: will your Lady love me?

Abigail. It seemes so by her letter, and her lamentations: but you
are such another man!

Elder Loveless. Not such another as I was, Mumps; nor will not 100
be: ile reade her fine Epistle: ha, ha, ha: is not thy Mistresse mad?

Abigail. For you she will be, 'tis a shame you should use a poore
gentlewoman so untowardly: she loves the ground you tread on:
and you (hard hart) because she jested with you, meane to kill
her: 'tis a fine conquest as they say.

Elder Loveless. Hast thou so much moysture in thy whitleather
hyde yet, that thou can'st cry? I wod have sworne thou hadst
beene touchwood five yeare since: Nay let it raine, thy Face chops
for a shower like a dry dunghyll.

Abigail. Ile not endure this Ribaldry: Farwell ith' Divels name: 110
if my Lady die, ile be sworne before a Jurye, thou art the cause
on't.

Elder Loveless. Doe Maukin doe: deliver to your Lady from me
this: I meane to see her, if I have no other businesse; which before
ile want to come to her, I meane to goe seeke byrds nests: yet I
may come too: but if I come, from this doore till I see her, will I
thinke how to raile vildly at her; how to vexe her, and make her
cry so much, that the Phisition if she fall sick upon't shall want
uryne to finde the cause by: and she remedilesse die in her heresie:
Farwell old Adage, I hope to see the boyes make Potguns on thee. 120

Abigail. Th'art a vyle man; God blesse my issue from thee.

89 cas'd] Q5; cast Q1–4

Elder Loveless. Thou hast but one, and thats in thy left crupper, that makes thee hobble so; you must be ground ith breech like a top, youle nere spin well else: Farwell Fytchocke.

Exeunt.

Enter Lady *alone.*   [V. ii]

Lady. Is it not strange that every womans will
Should tracke out new waies to disturbe her selfe?
If I should call my reason to accoumpt,
It cannot answere why I stoppe my selfe
From mine owne wish; and stoppe the man I love
From his; and every houre repent againe,
Yet still goe on: I know 'tis like a man,
That wants his naturall sleep, and growing dull,
Would gladly give the remnant of his life
For two howers rest: yet through his frowardnesse,   10
Will rather chuse to watch another man,
Drowsie as he, then take his owne repose.
All this I know: yet a strange pevishnes
And anger, not to have the power to doe
Thinges unexpected, carryes me away
To mine owne ruine: I had rather dye
Sometimes then not disgrace in publike him
Whom people thinke I love, and doo't with oaths,
And am in earnest then: O what are wee!
Men, you must answer this, that dare obey   20
Such thinges as wee command.———

Enter Abigail.

How now? what newes?
Abigail. Faith Madam none worth hearing.
Lady. Is he not come?
Abigail. No truly.
Lady. Nor has he writ?
Abigail. Neither. I pray God you have not undone your selfe.
Lady. Why, but what sayes hee?

Abigail.   Faith he talkes strangely.

Lady.   How strangely?   30

Abigail.   First at your Letter he laught extreamly.

Lady.   What in contempt?

Abigail.   He laught monstrous loud, as he would dye, and when
you wrote it, I thinke you were in no such merry mood, to provoke
him that way: and having done he cryed alas for her, and violently
laught againe.

Lady.   Did he?

Abigail.   Yes till I was angry.

Lady.   Angry, why?

Why wert thou angry? he did doe but well,   40
I did deserve it, hee had beene a foole,
An unfit man for any one to love,
Had he not laught thus at mee: you were angry,
That show'd your folly; I shall love him more
For that, then all that ere he did before:
But said he nothing else?

Abigail.   Many uncertaine things: he said though you had mock't
him, because you were a woman, he could wish to doe you so
much favour as to see you: yet he said, he knew you rash, and was
loth to offend you with the sight of one, whom now he was   50
bound not to leave.

Lady.   What one was that?

Abigail.   I know not, but truely I doe feare there is a making up
there: for I heard the servants, as I past by some, whisper such
a thing: and as I came backe through the hall, there were two or
three Clarkes writing great conveyances in hast, which they said
were for their Mistris joynture.

Lady.   'Tis very like and fit it should be so,
For he does thinke, and reasonably thinke,
That I should keepe him with my idle tricks   60
For ever ere he maried.

Abigail.   At last he said, it should goe hard but he would see you
for your satisfaction.

Lady.   All we that are cal'd Women, know as well
As men, it were a farre more Noble thing

To grace where wee are grac't, and give respect
There where wee are respected: yet we practise
A wilder course, and never bend our eyes
On men with pleasure, till they finde the way
To give us a neglect: then we, too late,　　　　　　　70
Perceive the losse of what we might have had,
And dote to death.

Enter Martha.

Martha.　Sister, yonders your Servant, with a gentlewoman with
him.
Lady.　Where?
Martha.　Close at the dore.
Lady.　Ahlas I am undone, I feare he is betroth'd.
What kind of woman is she?
Martha.　A most ill favoured one, with her Masque on:
And how her face should mend the rest I know not.　　　80
Lady.　But yet her minde is of a milder stuffe
Then mine was.——

Enter Elder Lovelesse, and Welford in womans apparrell.

　　　　[*Aside*] Now I see him, if my heart
Swell not againe (away thou womans pride)
So that I cannot speake a gentle word to him,
Let me not live.
Elder Loveless.　By your leave here.
Lady.　How now, what new tricke invites you hither?
Ha' you a fine device againe?
Elder Loveless.　Faith this is the finest device I have now:——
How dost thou sweet heart?　　　　　　　　　　　　90
Welford.　Why very well, so long as I may please
You my deare Lover: I nor can, nor will
Be ill when you are well, well when you are ill.
Elder Loveless.　O thy sweet temper: what would I have given,
That lady had beene like thee: seest thou her?
That face (my love) joynd with thy humble minde,
Had made a wench indeede.

531

Welford.   Alas my love,
What God hath done, I dare not thinke to mend:
I use no paint, nor any drugs of Arte,
My hands and face will shew it.   100
Lady.   Why what thing have you brought to shew us there?
Doe you take money for it?
Elder Loveless.   A Godlike thing,
Not to be bought for money: tis my Mistres:
In whom there is no passions, nor no scorne:
What I will is for law; pray you salute her.
Lady.   Salute her? by this good light I would not kisse her
For halfe my wealth.
Elder Loveless.   Why, why pray you?
You shall see me do't afore you: looke you.
Lady.   Now fie upon thee, a beast would not have don't;
I would not kisse thee of a month to gaine   110
A Kingdome.
Elder Loveless.   Marry you shall not be troubled.
Lady.   Why was there ever such a *Meg* as this?
Sure thou art madde.
Elder Loveless.   I was mad once, when I lov'd pictures:
For what are shape and colours else, but pictures?
In that tawny hide there lies an endles masse
Of vertues; when all your red and white ones want it.
Lady.   And this is she you are to marry, is't not?
Elder Loveless.   Yes indeed is't.
Lady.   God give you joy.
Elder Loveless.   Amen.
Welford.   I thanke you, as unknowne, for your good wish.
The like to you, when ever you shall wed.   120
Elder Loveless.   O gentle spirit.
Lady.   You thanke me? I pray
Keepe your breath neerer you, I doe not like it.
Welford.   I would not willingly offend at all:
Much lesse a lady of your worthy parts.
Elder Loveless.   Sweet, Sweet.
Lady.   I doe not thinke this woman can by nature

532

Be thus, thus ugly: sure shee's some common Strumpet,
Deform'd with exercise of sinne.
Welford.   O Sir
Beleeve not this: for heaven so comfort me
As I am free from foule pollution   130
With any man: my honour tane away,
I am no woman.
Elder Loveless.   Arise my dearest soule:
I doe not credit it. Alas, I feare
Her tender heart will breake with this reproach:
Fie that you know no more civillitie
To a weake virgin. Tis no matter Sweet,
Let her say what she will, thou art not worse
To me, and therefore not at all: be carelesse.
Welford.   For all things else I would, but for mine honour:
Me thinks——
Elder Loveless.   Alas, thine honour is not stain'd.——   140
Is this the businesse that you sent for me about?
Martha.   Faith Sister you are much to blame, to use a woman,
whatsoe're she be, thus: Ile salute her: You are welcome hither.
Welford.   I humbly thanke you.
Elder Loveless.   Milde still as the Dove, for all these injuries.
Come, shall we goe? I love thee not so ill to keepe thee heere a
jesting stocke.——
Adue to the worlds end.
Lady.   Why whither now?
Elder Loveless.   Nay you shal never know, because you shal not 150
finde me.
Lady.   I pray let me speake with you.
Elder Loveless.   Tis very well: come.
Lady.   I pray you let me speake with you.
Elder Loveless.   Yes for another mocke.
Lady.   By heaven I have no mocks: good Sir a word.
Elder Loveless.   Though you deserve not so much at my hands,
yet if you be in such earnest, I will speake a word with you: but I
beseech you bee briefe; for in good faith there's a Parson, and a

142 blame] Q2; balme Q1

533

licence stay for us i'th Church all this while: and you know tis 160
night.

Lady.   Sir, give mee hearing patiently, and whatsoever I have
heretofore spoke jestingly, forget: for as I hope for mercy any
where, what I shall utter now is from my heart, and as I meane.

Elder Loveless.   Well, well, what doe you meane?

Lady.   Was not I once your Mistres, and you my Servant?

Elder Loveless.   O 'tis about the old matter.

Lady.   Nay good Sir stay me out: I would but heare you excuse
your selfe, why you should take this woman, and leave me.

Elder Loveless.   Prethee why not, deserves she not as much as 170
you?

Lady.   I thinke not, if you will looke
With an indifferencie upon us both.

Elder Loveless.   Upon your faces, tis true: but if judicially we
shall cast our eies upon your mindes, you are a thousand weomen
of her in worth: She cannot sound in jest, nor set her lover tasks,
to shew her peevishnes, and his affection: nor crosse what he
saies, though it bee Canonicoll. Shee's a good plaine wench, that
will doe as I will have her, and bring mee lusty boyes to throw
the Sledge, and lift at Pigs of lead: and for a wife, shee's farre 180
beyond you: what can you doe in a houshold, to provide for your
issue, but lye a bed and get um? your businesse is to dresse you,
and at idle houres to eate; when she can doe a thousand profitable
things: She can doe pretty well in the Pastry, and knows how
pullen should be cram'd: she cuts Cambricke at a thrid: weaves
bone-lace, and quilts balls: And what are you good for?

Lady.   Admit it true, that she were farre beyond me in all respects,
do'es that give you a licence to forsweare your selfe?

Elder Loveless.   Forsweare my selfe, how?

Lady.   Perhaps you have forgot the innumerable oathes you have 190
uttered in disclaiming all for wives but mee: Ile not remember
you: God give you joy.

Elder Loveless.   Nay but conceive mee, the intent of oaths is ever
understood. Admit I should protest to such a friend, to see him
at his lodging to morrow: Divines would never hold me perjur'd,
if I were struck blinde, or he hid him where my diligent search

534

could not finde him: so there were no crosse act of mine owne in't.
Can it bee imagined I meant to force you to marriage, and to have
you whether you will or no?

Lady.   Alas you neede not. I make already tender of my selfe, and   200
then you are forsworne.

Elder Loveless.   Some sinne I see indeede must necessarily fall
upon me, as whosoever deals with women shal never utterly
avoide it: yet I would chuse the least ill; which is to forsake you,
that have done me all the abuses of a malignant woman, contemn'd
my service, and would have held me prating about marriage, till
I had beene past getting of children: then her that hath forsooke
her family, and put her tender bodie in my hand, upon my word.

Lady.   Which of us swore you first to?

Elder Loveless.   Why to you.   210

Lady.   Which oath is to be kept then?

Elder Loveless.   I prethee doe not urge my sinnes unto me,
Without I could amend um.

Lady.   Why you may
By wedding me.

Elder Loveless.   How will that satisfie
My word to her?

Lady.   Tis not to be kept,
And needs no satisfaction, tis an error
Fit for repentance onely.

Elder Loveless.   Shall I live
To wrong that tender hearted virgin so?
It may not be.

Lady.   Why may it not be?

Elder Loveless.   I sweare I had rather marry thee then her: 220
But yet mine honesty?

Lady.   What honesty?
Tis more preserv'd this way: Come, by this light
Servant thou shalt, Ile kisse thee on't.

Elder Loveless.   This kisse
Indeede is sweet, pray God no sin lie under it.

Lady.   There is no sinne at all, trie but another.

Welford.   O my heart.

Martha.   Helpe sister, this ladie swounes.

Elder Loveless.   How doe you?

Welford.   Why very well, if you be so.

Elder Loveless.   Such a quiet minde lives not in any woman: I
shal doe a most ungodly thing. Heare me one word more, which
by all my hopes I will not alter. I did make an oath when you 230
delaid me so; that this very night I would be married. Now if you
will goe without delay, suddenly, as late as it is, with your owne
Minister to your owne Chappel, Ile wed you, and to bed.

Lady.   A match deare servant.

Elder Loveless.   For if you should forsake me now, I care not,
she would not though for all her injuries, such is her spirit. If I
bee not ashamed to kisse her now I part, may I not live.

Welford.   I see you goe, as sliely as you thinke
To steale away: yet I wil pray for you;
All blessings of the world light on you two,   240
That you may live to be an aged paire.
Al curses on me if I doe not speake
What I doe wish indeede.

Elder Loveless.   If I can speake to purpose to her, I am a villaine.

Lady.   Servant away.

Martha.   Sister, wil you marry that inconstant man?
Thinke you he wil not cast you off to morrow?
To wrong a ladie thus, lookt she like durt,
Twas basely done. May you nere prosper with him.

Welford.   Now God forbid.   250
Alas I was unworthy, so I told him.

Martha.   That was your modesty, too good for him.
I would not see your wedding for a world.

Lady.   Chuse, chuse, come *Yonglove.*

                         Exeunt Lady, Elder Loveless, *and* Abigail.

Martha.   Drie up your eies forsooth, you shall not thinke
We are all uncivill, all such beasts as these.
Would I knew how to give you a revenge.

228 Such] Dyce; Suce Q1; Since Q2–3, F; *om.* Q4–10
228 quiet] Q2; puiet Q1
254.1 Abigail] Langbaine; *Yong.* Q1–3, F; *om.* Q4–10

Welford.   So would not I: No let me suffer truly,
  That I desire.
Martha.   Pray walke in with me,
  Tis very late, and you shal stay all night: 260
  Your bed shal be no worse then mine; I wish
  I could but doe you right.
Welford.   My humble thankes:
  God grant I may but live to quit your love.

                                              Exeunt.

                Enter Yong Lovelesse *and* Savill.   [V. iii]

Young Loveless.   Did your Master send for me *Savil?*
Savil.   Yes he did send for your worship sir.
Young Loveless.   Doe you know the businesse?
Savil.   Alas Sir I know nothing, nor am imployed beyond my
  howers of eating. My dancing daies are done sir.
Young Loveless.   What art thou now then?
Savil.   If you consider me in little, I am with your worships
  reverence sir, a rascal: one that upon the next anger of your brother,
  must raise a sconce by the high way, and sel switches. My wife
  is learning now sir to weave inckle.   10
Young Loveless.   What dost thou meane to doe with thy children
  Savill?
Savil.   My eldest boy is halfe a rouge already, he was borne
  bursten, and your worship knowes, that is a pretty steppe to
  mens compassions. My youngest boy I purpose sir to binde for
  ten yeeres to a Joaler, to drawe under him, that he may shew us
  mercy in his function.
Young Loveless.   Your family is quartered with discretion: you
  are resolved to cant then: where *Savil* shall your sceane lie?
Savil.   Beggars must be no choosers: 20
  In every place (I take it) but the stockes.
Young Loveless.   This is your drinking, and your whoring *Savil,*
  I tould you of it, but your heart was hardned.
Savil.   Tis true, you were the first that tolde me of it, I doe

  10 now] Q4; new Q1–3   15 compassions] Q5; capassions Q1–4

remember yet in teares, you told me you would have whores, and in that passion sir, you broke out thus; Thou miserable man, repent, and brew three strikes more in a hogshed. Tis noone ere we be drunke now, and the time can tarry for no man.

Young Loveless. Y'are growne a bitter Gentleman. I see misery can cleere your head better then mustard. Ile be a sutor for your 30 keyes againe sir.

Savil. Wil you but be so gratious to me sir? I shal be bound——

Young Loveless. You shall sir,
To your bunch againe, or I'le misse fouly.

Enter Moorcraft.

Morecraft. Save you gentlemen save you.

Young Loveless. Now Pole-cat, what young Rabets nest have you to drawe?

Morecraft. Come, prethee bee familiar Knight.

Young Loveless. Away Fox, Ile send for Terriers for you.

Morecraft. Thou art wide yet: Ile keepe thee companie.   40

Young Loveless. I am about some businesse; Indentures, if ye follow me Ile beate you: take heede, as I live Ile cancell your Coxcombe.

Morecraft. Thou art cozen'd now, I am no usurer: what poore fellow's this?

Savil. I am poore indeede sir.

Morecraft. Give him money Knight.

Young Loveless. Doe you begin the offring.

Morecraft. There pore fellow, heer's an angel for thee.

Young Loveless. Art thou in earnest *Moorcraft*?   50

Morecraft. Yes faith Knight, Ile follow thy example: thou hadst land and thousands, thou spendst, and flungst away, and yet it flowes in double: I purchasde, wrung, and wierdraw'd for my wealth, lost, and was cozend: for which I make a vowe, to trie all the waies above ground, but Ile finde a constant meanes to riches without curses.

26 out] Q 2; our Q 1
29 Gentleman] Q 2; Gentlememan Q 1
30 can] Q 2; can can Q 1

Young Loveless.   I am glad of your conversion Master *Moorcraft*:
Y'are in a faire course, praye pursue it still.
Morecraft.   Come, we are all gallants now, Ile keepe thee company;
Heere honest fellow, for this gentlemans sake, theres two angels 60
more for thee.
Savil.   God quit you sir, and keepe you longe in this minde.
Young Loveless.   Wilt thou persever?
Morecraft.   Til I have a penny. I have brave clothes a making, and
two horses; canst thou not helpe me to a Match Knight, Ile lay a
thousand pound upon my crop-eare.
Young Loveless.   Foote this is stranger then an *Affrick* monster,
There will be no more talke of the *Cleave* wars
Whilst this lasts, come, Ile put thee into blood.
Savil.   Would all his damb'd tribe were as tender hearted. I 70
beseech you let this gentleman joyne with you in the recovery of
my Keyes; I like his good beginning sir, the whilst Ile pray for
both your worships.
Young Loveless.   He shall sir.
Morecraft.   Shall we goe noble Knight? I would faine be acquainted.
Young Loveless.   Ile be your servant sir.

                                                    Exeunt.

                Enter Elder Lovelesse *and* Ladie.   [V.iv]

Elder Loveless.   Faith my sweet Ladie, I have caught you now,
Mauger your subtilties, and fine devises,
Be coy againe now.
Lady.   Prethee sweeteheart tell true.
Elder Loveless.   By this light,
By all the pleasures I have had this night,
By your lost maidenhead, you are cozend meerely.
I have cast beyond your wit. That gentlewoman
Is your retainer *Welford.*
Lady.   It cannot be so.
Elder Loveless.   Your sister has found it so, or I mistake:
Marke how she blushes when you see her next.   10

    65–66 a thousand] Q2; a a Thousand Q1   67 this] Q2; thit Q1
    *7 gentlewoman] Sympson; gent. Q1; Gentleman Q2+

                            539

Ha, ha, ha, I shall not travell now,
Ha, ha, ha.
Lady.   Prethee sweet heart be quiet,
Thou hast angerd me at heart.
Elder Loveless.   Ile please you soone againe.
Lady. Welford.
Elder Loveless. I *Welford*, hee's a young hansome fellow,
Well bred and landed: your sister can instruct you
In his good parts better then I by this time.
Lady. Udsfoote, am I fetcht over thus?
Elder Loveless.   Yes ifaith.
And over shall be fetcht againe, never feare it.
Lady. I must be patient, though it torture me: 20
You have got the Sunne Sir.
Elder Loveless. And the Moone too, in which Ile be the man.
Lady. But had I knowne this, had I but surmiz'd it,
You should have hunted three traines more, before
You had come to'th course,
You should have hanckt o'th bridle, Sir, ifaith.
Elder Loveless. I knew it, and min'd with you, and so blew you up.
Now you may see the Gentlewoman: stand close. [*They retire.*]

Enter Welford *and* Martha.

Martha. For Gods sake Sir be private in this busines,
You have undone me else. O God, what have I done?   30
Welford. No harme I warrant thee.
Martha. How shall I looke upon my friends againe?
With what face?
Welford. Why e'ne with that:
Tis a good one, thou canst not finde a better:
Looke upon all the faces thou shalt see there,
And you shall finde um smooth still, faire still, sweet still,
And to your thinking honest: those have done
As much as you have yet, or dare doe Mistres,
And yet they keepe no stirre.   40
Martha. Good Sir goe in, and put your womans cloathes on:
If you be seene thus, I am lost for ever.

540

Welford.   Ile watch you for that Mistres: I am no foole,
Heere will I tarry till the house be up
And witnes with me.

Martha.   Good deare friend goe in.

Welford.   To bed againe if you please, else I am fixt heere, till
there be notice taken what I am, and what I have done: If you
could juggle me into my woman-hood againe, and so cog me
out of your company, all this would be forsworne, and I againe
an *asinego*, as your Sister left me. No, Ile have it knowne and 50
publisht; then if you'le be a whore, forsake me, and be sham'd:
and when you can hold out no longer, marry some cast *Cleve
Captaine*, and sell Bottle-ale.

Martha.   I dare not stay sir, use me modestly, I am your wife.

Welford.   Goe in, Ile make up all.

                    [Elder Loveless *and* Lady *come forward.*]

Elder Loveless.   Ile be a witnes to your naked truth Sir:——this is
the gentlewoman, prethee looke upon him, this is he that made me
breake my faith Sweet: but thanke your sister, she hath soderd
it.

Lady.   What a dull asse was I, I could not see this wencher from 60
a wench: twentie to one, if I had beene but tender like my sister,
he had served me such a slippery tricke too.

Welford.   Twenty to one I had.

Elder Loveless.   I would have watcht you Sir, by your good
patience, for ferretting in my ground.

Lady.   You have beene with my Sister.

Welford.   Yes, to bring.

Elder Loveless.   An heire into the world he meanes.

Lady.   There is no chafing now.

Welford.   I have had my part on't: I have beene chaft this three 70
houres, thats the least, I am reasonable coole now.

Lady.   Cannot you fare well, but you must cry rost-meat?

Welford.   He that fares well, and will not blesse the founders, is
either surfetted, or ill taught, Ladie: for mine owne part, I have
found so sweet a diet, I can commend it, though I cannot spare it.

Elder Loveless.   How like you this dish, *Welford*, I made a supper
on't, and fed so heartily, I could not sleepe.

Lady.   By this light, had I but sented out your traine, ye had slept with a bare pillow in your armes, and kist that, or else the bed-post, for any wife yee had got this twelve-month yet: I would 80 have vext you more then a tyr'd post-horse: and bin longer bearing, then ever after-game at *Irish* was. Lord, that I were unmaried againe.

Elder Loveless.   Lady, I would not undertake yee, were you againe a *Haggard*, for the best cast of sore Ladies i'th Kingdome: you were ever tickle footed, and would not trusse round!

Welford.   Is she fast?

Elder Loveless.   She was all night lockt here boy.

Welford.   Then you may lure her without feare of loosing: take off her Creance. You have a delicate Gentlewoman to your sister: 90 Lord what a pretty fury she was in, when she perceived I was a man: but I thanke God I satisfied her scruple, without the Parson o'th towne.

Elder Loveless.   What did ye?

Welford.   Maddame, can you tell what we did?

Elder Loveless.   She has a shrewd guesse at it I see by her.

Lady.   Well you may mocke us: but my large Gentlewoman, my *Mary Ambree*, had I but seene into you, you should have had another bedfellow, fitter a great deale for your itch.

Welford.   I thanke you Lady, me thought it was well,   100
You are so curious.

Enter Young Lovelesse, *his Lady* [Widow], Moorecraft,
Savill *and two* Servingmen.

Elder Loveless.   Get on your dublet, here comes my brother.

Young Loveless.   Good morrow brother, and all good to your Lady.

Morecraft.   God save you, and good morrow to you all.

Elder Loveless.   Good morrow.——Here's a poore brother of yours.

Lady.   Fie how this shames me.

Morecraft.   Prethee good fellow helpe me to a cup of Beere.

First Servingman.   I will Sir.   [*Exit.*]

*90 Creance] Sympson (Creyance); Cranes Q1+
109, 128 S.P. *First Servingman.*] Dyce; *Ser.* Q1+

542

Young Loveless.   Brother what make you here? will this Lady doe? 110
Will she? is she not nettel'd still?
Elder Loveless.   No, I have cur'd her.
Master *Welford*, pray know this Gentleman, 'is my brother.
Welford.   Sir, I shall long to love him.
Young Loveless.   I shall not be your debter Sir.——But how is't
with you?
Elder Loveless.   As well as may bee man; I am married: your
new acquaintance hath her Sister: and all's well.
Young Loveless.   I am glad on't. Now my pretty Lady Sister,
How doe you finde my brother?   120
Lady.   Almost as wilde as you are.
Young Loveless.   A will make the better husband: you have tride
him?
Lady.   Against my will Sir.
Young Loveless.   Hee'le make your will amends soone, doe not
doubt it. But Sir, I must intreat you to be better knowne to this
converted *Jew* here.

[*Re-enter* First Servingman.]

First Servingman.   Here's Beere for you Sir.
Morecraft.   And here's for you an angell:
Pray buy no Land, twill never prosper Sir.   130
Elder Loveless.   How's this?
Young Loveless.   Blesse you, and then Ile tell: He's turn'd Gallant.
Elder Loveless.   Gallant?
Young Loveless.   I Gallant, and is now called, *Cutting Moorecraft*:
The reason Ile informe you, at more leisure.
Welford.   O good Sir let me know him presently.
Young Loveless.   You shall hug one another.
Morecraft.   Sir I must keepe you company.
Elder Loveless.   And reason.
Young Loveless.   Cutting *Moorcraft* faces about. I must present 140
another.
Morecraft.   As many as you will Sir, I am for um.
Welford.   Sir I shall doe you service.
Morecraft.   I shal looke for't in good faith sir.

Elder Loveless. Prethee good sweet-heart kisse him.

Lady. Who, that fellow?

Savil. Sir will it please you to remember me: my keyes good sir.

Young Loveless. I'le doe it presently.

Elder Loveless. Come thou shalt kisse him for our sport sake.

Lady. Let him come on then: and doe you heare, doe not instruct 150
me in these tricks, for you may repent it.

Elder Loveless. That at my perill. Lusty Master *Moorecraft*,
Heere is a Ladie would salute you.

Morecraft. She shall not loose her longing Sir: what is she?

Elder Loveless. My wife Sir.

Morecraft. She must be then my Mistres.

Lady. Must I sir?

Elder Loveless. O yes, you must.

Morecraft. And you must take this ring, a poore pawne,
Of some fifty pound.   160

Elder Loveless. Take it by any meanes, tis lawfull prise.

Lady. Sir I shall call you servant.

Morecraft. I shall be proud on't: what fellow's that?

Young Loveless. My Ladies Coach man.

Morecraft. Ther's something (my friend) for you to buy whips,
And for you sir, and you sir.   [*Gives money to Servants.*]

Elder Loveless. Under a miracle this is the strangest,
I ever heard of.

Morecraft. What shall we play, or drinke? what shall we doe?
Who will hunt with me for a hundred pound?   170

Welford. Stranger and Stranger!
Sir you shall finde sport after a day or two.

Young Loveless. Sir I have a sute unto you, concerning your old
servant *Savill*.

Elder Loveless. O, for his keyes, I know it.

Savil. Now sir, strike in.

Morecraft. Sir I must have you grant me.

Elder Loveless. Tis done Sir, take your keyes againe: but harke
you *Savill*, leave of the motions of the flesh, and be honest, or
else you shall graze againe. Ile trie you once more.   180

Savil. If ever I be taken drunke, or whoring, take off the biggest

key i'th bunch, and open my head with it Sir: I humbly thanke
your worships. *Enter* Roger *and* Abigall.

Elder Loveless. Nay then I see we must keepe holiday,
Heers the last couple in hell.
Roger. Joy be amongst you all.
Lady. Why how now sir, what is the meaning of this Embleme?
Roger. Marriage an't like your worship.
Lady. Are you married?
Roger. As well as the next priest could doe it, Madam. 190
Elder Loveless. I thinke the signes in *Gemini,* heer's such coupling.
Welford. Sir *Roger,* what will you take to lie from your sweete-
heart to night?
Roger. Not the best benifice in your worships gift Sir.
Welford. A whorson, how he swels.
Young Loveless. How many times to night Sir *Roger?*
Roger. Sir you grow scurrilous:
What I shall doe, I shall doe: I shall not neede your helpe.
Young Loveless. For horse flesh *Roger.*
Elder Loveless. Come prethee be not angry, tis a day 200
Given wholly to our mirth.
Lady. It shall be so sir:
Sir *Roger* and his Bride, we shall intreate
To be at our charge.
Elder Loveless. *Welford* get you to Church: by this light,
You shall not lie with her againe, till y'are married.
Welford. I am gone.
Morecraft. To every Bride I dedicate this day:
Six healths a peece, and it shall goe hard,
But every one a Jewell: Come be mad Boyes.
Elder Loveless. Th'art in a good beginning: come who leads? 210
Sir *Roger,* you shall have the *Van:* leade the way:
Would every dogged wench had such a day.

Exeunt.

FINIS.

TEXTUAL NOTES

II.ii

44 stiver] The emendation (of *striuer* in Q1–10, F, and L) was proposed by Theobald and introduced into the edition of 1750 (S) with the following note: '*Stive* was the old and obsolete Term for the *Stews*; and consequently, a *Stiver*, as it should be restored in the Text, was a Girl, a Strumpet, who ply'd there. Hence, perhaps, might come the Word *Stiver* too, to signify that inconsiderable Coin (the fifth Part of an *English* Penny) the Pay of these mean Prostitutes, these *Meretrices diobolares*, as Plautus styles them.' Weber notes that 'the word *stives*, for stews, occurs in Chaucer's Frerer's Tale, l. 6914'; and the Variorum cites *Piers the Plowman*, A Text, vii.65: 'Jonete of the stuyues.'

101 Drinke to my friend Captaine.] The line was omitted in Q3 and has never appeared in any text of the play since then. It is certainly authentic, being very much in Young Loveless' manner. Regularly he ends a speech with an abrupt shift of attention—and address—to another in his company, to propose a toast or to see if the glasses are filled. Cf. below, l. 118, and III.ii.45–47, 103–105.

IV.i

22 laye] Q1–10, F, and L read *lape ground*, of which Sympson, whose emendation this is, writes in the edition of 1750: 'I believe, there is no such Term in the *English* Tongue, as *lape* Ground. The Word must have been *Lay*, or *Ley*: i.e. *Terra inculta, Novale*: unplow'd, uncultivated, Land.'

84–85 never your reverend person more] 'I suspect some such word as *mock* or *revile* has been dropped before *your reverend person*; though, possibly, the word *reproach* [l. 83]... may be held as repeated' (Weber). In the redaction of this scene in *The Wits*, the word *abuse* is inserted after *never*.

V.iv

7 gentlewoman] Q1 prints simply *gent.*; Q2–10, F, and L *Gentleman*. Theobald proposes the present emendation, received into the text of 1750 and all subsequent editions, thus: 'I think, the Poets certainly wrote *Gentlewoman*, i.e. that seeming Gentlewoman; for *Welford* was now in Woman's Habit.' He cites in confirmation l. 28, below: 'Now you may see the Gentlewoman: stand close.'

90 Creance] Theobald's emendation, received into the text of 1750, of Q1–10, F, L *Cranes*. He explains: 'The *Creyance* is a fine small long Line of strong, and even twin'd Packthread, which is fasten'd to the Hawk's Leash before she is *reclaim'd*, or fully tamed.'

PRESS-VARIANTS IN Q (1616)

[Copies collated: BM (British Museum), Bodl¹ (Mal. 242[7]), Bodl² (4° T.38. Art [4]), Dyce (Victoria and Albert Museum), CLUC (W. A. Clark Memorial Library), CSmH (Henry E. Huntington Library), MB (Boston Public Library), MH (Harvard University Library), NLS (National Library of Scotland). These comprise the known extant copies.]

Sheet B (*outer forme*)

Corrected: Bodl², Dyce, MB, MH, NLS, CLUC
Uncorrected: BM, Bodl¹, CSmH

Sig. B3.
  I.i.134 signe] singne
Sig. B4ᵛ.
  I.i.238 seruant] sernant

Sheet G (*outer forme*)

1st stage corrected: Bodl¹.
Uncorrected: BM, Bodl², MH (wants leaves G2–3), NLS, CLUC

Sig. G1.
  III.ii.206 vnfold]   vnfold [*The 'uncorrected' reading* (unsold) *has been received into the present edition, the 'corrected' reading* (unfold) *being in fact in error.*]

2nd stage corrected: Dyce, CSmH, MB (wants leaves G2–3)

Sig. G1.
  IV.i.2 thee? to] thee to? to
  IV.i.6 but for an apprition]   hut for an apperition
Sig. G3.
  IV.i.147 it] yet
  IV.i.156 God] gods

Sheet G (*inner forme*)

Corrected: BM, Bodl¹, Dyce, CSmH, NLS, CLUC
Uncorrected: Bodl²

Sig. G2 (wanting in MB and MH).
  IV.i.69 long] logng

SHEET H (*outer forme*)

1st stage corrected: BM, Bodl¹, Dyce, MH, NLS, CLUC
Uncorrected:　　Bodl²

Sig. H4ᵛ.
　V.ii.53 not, but]　~ ₐ ~
　　　2nd stage corrected: CSmH, MB

Sig. H1.
　IV.i.363 againe]　aine

SHEET H (*inner forme*)

1st stage corrected: CSmH, MB
Uncorrected:　　Bodl².

Sig. H2.
　IV.ii.58 Ale?] ~ ₐ
　　　2nd stage corrected: BM, Bodl¹, Dyce, MH, NLS, CLUC

Sig. H2.
　IV.ii.68 din] dyn

Sig. H3ᵛ.
　V.i.82 *Eld. lo.*] *Eed. lo.*

Sig. H4.
　V.i.114 businesse] busiuesse

EMENDATIONS OF ACCIDENTALS

I.i

62 you;] ~ , Q1–10, F
70 see——] ~ . Q1–10, F
72 Mistres——] ~ . Q1–10, F
76 obedience——] ~ . Q1–10, F
80 speake——] ~ . Q1–10, F
90 next?] ~ . Q1–10, F
96 third?] Q5; ~ . Q1–4
109 waterhouse‸] ~ ; Q1–8, F; ~ , Q9–10

110 victuals——] ~ . Q1–10, F
113–114 post- | horse]post-horse Q1
114 tongue——] ~ . Q1–10, F
121–122 chamber- | maids] chamber-maids Q1
231 this:] Q5; ~ , Q1–4
289 wit.] ~ , Q1–4; ~ ; Q5–8, 10, F; ~ : Q9

I.ii

12 you——] Q9; ~ . Q1–2, 4–8; ~ ? Q3, F
17 I——] Q5; ~ ‸ Q1–3; ~ . Q4
26 it——] ~ . Q1–10, F
63.1 *Comrades:*] ~ . Q1; ~ , Q2–6, Q8–10, F; ~ ‸ Q7

68 love——] ~ . Q1–10, F
75 out.——] ~ . ‸ Q1–6, Q8–10, F; ~ ‸‸ Q7
80 Colours——] ~ . Q1–10, F
138–139] Q1–8, F *line*: What... smoking? | Well...home.

II.i

9 rest?] Q4; ~ . Q1–3
20 it?] Q3; ~ . Q1–2
22 Reume!] ~ ? Q1–3, F; ~ . Q4–10
30 whom?] ~ ; Q1–8, F; ~ , Q9–10
50 fast.] ~ ? Q1–2; safe? Q3–5, F; safe. Q6–10

70 Sir!] ~ ? Q1–3, F; ~ . Q4, 6–10; ~ : Q5
85 indeed.——] ~ . ‸ Q1–5, F
113 alone——] ~ . Q1–10, F
142 house!] F; ~ ? Q1–5; ~ . Q6–10
150 Sir——] ~ . Q1–10, F
155 Palsie——] ~ . Q1–10, F

II.ii

2 boyes:] Q4; ~ ‸ Q1–3
10–11] *One line in* Q1–10, F
29–31] *Prose in* Q1–10, F
29 ifaith.] ~ , Q1–8, F; ~ : Q9–10
33–36 Peasant...thee.] *Prose in* Q1–10, F

63 too't——] ~ , Q1–8, F; ~ : Q9–10
67 more——] ~ , Q1–3; ~ . Q4–10, F
85–101] *Prose in* Q1–10, F

108 Sir——] ~ . Q 1–2, 4–10, F;
   ~ ? Q 3
110–128] *Prose in* Q 1–10, F
117 Gentleman.——] ~ . ∧ Q 1–10,
   F

122 you.——] ~ . ∧ Q 1–10, F
130 againe.——] ~ . ∧ Q 1–5, 9–10,
   F; ~ : ∧ Q 6–8
159 Gentleman——] ~ . Q 1–10, F

II.iii

20 hundreds;] ~ ∧ Q 1–10, F

32 little——] ~ ; Q 1–2, 10; ~ :
   Q 3–9, F

III.i

10–11 Dialogue.——] ~ . ∧ Q 1–
   10, F
16 Bell.——] ~ . ∧ Q 1–10, F
53 busines.——] ~ . ∧ Q 1–10, F
56 quicke,] Q 3; ~ ∧ Q 1–2
56 him.——] ~ . ∧ Q 1–10, F
72 wearing: Shall] Q 4; ~ ∧ ~ Q 1;
   ~ , ~ Q 2–3
145 'is] is Q 1–2
201 things.——] ~ . ∧ Q 1–5, F;
   ~ ∧ ∧ Q 6; ~ , ∧ Q 7–8; ~ : ∧
   Q 9; ~ ; ∧ Q 10
205–215] *Prose in* Q 1–10, F

209 it:——] ~ : ∧ Q 1–8; ~ . ∧ Q 9–
   10, F
217–218 Ile…there?] *One line in*
   Q 1–10, F
220 will——] ~ . Q 1–10, F
221–231 And…too.] *Prose in* Q 1–
   10, F
237–239] Prose in Q 1–10, F
257 about:——] ~ : ∧ Q 1–8, F;
   ~ . ∧ Q 9–10
268–271] *Prose in* Q 1–10, F
285–290] *Prose in* Q 1–10, F
343 conditions!] ~ ? Q 1–3, F; ~ :
   Q 4, 6–9; ~ ; Q 5, 10

III.ii

1–8] *Prose in* Q 1–10, F
12–19] *Prose in* Q 1–10, F
22–25 Or…Criticks.] *Prose in*
   Q 1–10, F
48–53] *Prose in* Q 1–10, F
48 Knight.——] ~ . ∧ Q 1–10, F
57 bare-one] bare- | one Q 1
61 Sir!] ~ ? Q 1–5, F; ~ : Q 6–10
65 neats-tongue] neats- | tongue
   Q 1
67 head.——] ~ . ∧ Q 1; ~ : ∧
   Q 2–9, F; ~ ; ∧ Q 10
70–75] *Prose in* Q 1–10, F
83–122] *Prose in* Q 1–10, F

103 time.——] ~ . ∧ Q 1–10, F
105 boy!] ~ ? Q 1–3, F; ~ ∧ Q 4;
   ~ . Q 5–10
114 lungs,] Q 2; ~ ∧ Q 1
135 about!] Q 9; ~ ? Q 1–8, F
138 measures!] ~ ? Q 1–3; ~ : Q 4–
   10; ~ ; Q 3
149 you.] Q 3; ~ ∧ Q 1–2
151 money!] ~ ∧ Q 1; ~ , Q 2–6, F;
   ~ . Q 7–8; ~ : Q 9; ~ ; Q 10
203 house?] ~ ∧ Q 1–5, Q 9–10, F;
   ~ , Q 6–8
205 walles!] ~ ? Q 1–10, F

IV.i

10 (plague...for't)] Q9; ˄~ ... ~
 ˄ Q1–8, F
43 time——] ~ , Q1–10, F
53 sake——] ~ . Q1–10, F
77 Mistres˄] Q2; ~ , Q1
93 sweet ˄ *Abigail.*] Q2; ~ , *Abi.*
 Q1
104–107] *Prose in* Q1–10, F
113–118] *Prose in* Q1–10, F
139–147] *Prose in* Q1–10, F
147 hang——] ~ . Q1–10, F
149–151] *Prose in* Q1–10, F
151 so——] ~ . Q1–10, F
154 unhansome——] ~ . Q1–4,
 6–10, F; ~ , Q5
156–158] *Prose in* Q1–10, F
165–180] *Prose in* Q1–10, F
185 see——] ~ . Q1–10, F
187–195] *Prose in* Q1–10, F
201–221 Neither...this.] *Prose in*
 Q1–10, F
219 me.——] ~ . ˄ Q1–10, F
224 man——] ~ . Q1–4, 6–10, F;
 ~ , Q5
227–228] *Prose in* Q1–10, F
237–239] *Prose in* Q1–10, F

243 Ladie,] Q2; ~ . Q1
245–250 I...me.] *Prose in* Q1–10, F
252–268] *Prose in* Q1–10, F
252 ye,——...there:——] ~ , ˄
 ...~ : ˄ Q1–2; ~ , ˄ ...~ ; ˄
 Q3–5,F; ~ ? ˄ ...~ ; ˄ Q6–8;
 ~ ? ˄ ...~ : ˄ Q9–10
271–276] *Prose in* Q1–10, F
276 one?] ~ . Q1–10, F
277 againe!] ~ ? Q1–5, F; ~ .
 Q6–10
288 H'ad] F; Had Q1–9
294–295 Shall...then?] *One line in*
 Q1–10, F
295–297] Q1–10, F *line*: No...
 words, | Ile...it.
298–299] Q1–10, F *line*: You...
 richly, | And...it.
307–311 I would...on't.] *Prose in*
 Q1–10, F
315–322] *Prose in* Q1–10, F
327–330] *Prose in* Q1–10, F
333–358] *Prose in* Q1–10, F
359 though——] ~ . Q1–10, F
360–361] *Prose in* Q1–10, F
369–375] *Prose in* Q1–10, F

IV.ii

1–108] *Prose in* Q1–10, F

V.i

1–79 *Prose in* Q1–10, F
46–47 ˄ not... | (For] (not... ˄ for
 Q1–10, F
71 this——] F; ~ . Q1–9
74 seene:——] ~ : ˄ Q1–10, F

75 awhile:——] ~ : ˄ Q1–9, F; ~ ;
 Q10
99 man!] ~ : Q1–3; ~ . Q4–6,
 Q9–10, F; ~ ˄ Q7–8

551

V.ii

1–22] *Prose in* Q 1–10, F
21 command.——] ~ . ‸ Q 1–10, F
39–46] *Prose in* Q 1–10, F
58–61] *Prose in* Q 1–10, F
64–72] *Prose in* Q 1–10, F
81–85 But...live.] *Prose in* Q 1–10, F
82 was.——] ~ . ‸ Q 1–10, F
89 now:——] ~ : ‸ Q 1–10, F
94–107 O thy...wealth.] *Prose in* Q 1–10, F
109–111 Now...Kingdome.] *Prose in* Q 1–10, F
113–116 I was...it.] *Prose in* Q 1–10, F
126–127] Q 1–10, F *line*: I...thus, | Thus...Strumpet,
128–138 O Sir...carelesse.] *Prose in* Q 1–10, F
140 thinks——] ~ . Q 1–10, F
140 stain'd.——] ~ . ‸ Q 1–2; ~ , ‸ Q 3, F; ~ ; ‸ Q 4–10
146 goe?] Q 9; ~ , Q 1–8, F
147 stocke.——] ~ . ‸ Q 1–4, 6–10, F; ~ ‸‸ Q 5
211 then?] Q 4; ~ . Q 1–3
213–214 Why...me.] *One line in* Q 1–10, F

214–215 How...her?] *One line in* Q 1–10, F
215–217 Tis...onely.] Q 1–10, F *line*: Tis...satisfaction, | Tis... onely.
217–219 Shall...be.] *Prose in* Q 1–10, F
220–221 I sweare...mine honesty?] *Prose in* Q 1–10, F
221 honesty?] Q 3; ~ . Q 1–2
221–223 What...on't.] Q 1–10, F *line*: What...way: | Come... on't.
223–224 This...it.] *One line in* Q 1–10, F
238–243] *Prose in* Q 1–10, F
246–249] *Prose in* Q 1–10, F
247 morrow?] Q 9; ~ , Q 1–3, F; ~ ; Q 4–8
250–251] *One line in* Q 1–10, F
255–257] *Prose in* Q 1–10, F
258–259 So...desire.] *One line in* Q 1–10, F
259–262 Pray...right.] *Prose in* Q 1–10, F

V.iii

6 then?] Q 5; ~ . Q 1–4
19 lie?] Q 5; ~ . Q 1–4
32 bound——] ~ . Q 1–10, F
41–45] Q 1–10, F *line*: I...Inden-

tures, | If...heede, | As...Coxcombe. | *Mo.* Thou...vsurer: | What...this?
55 ground,] Q 2; ~ . Q 1

V.iv

1–17] *Prose in* Q 1–10, F
23–26] *Prose in* Q 1–10, F
34–40] *Prose in* Q 1–10, F

43–99] *Prose in* Q 1–10, F
56 Sir:——] ~ : ‸ Q 1–10, F
79–80 bed-post] bed-|post Q 1

86 round!] ~ ? Q1–3; ~ . Q4–10,
  F
105 morrow.——] ~ . ₍ Q1–10, F
113 'is] is Q1–4
115 Sir.——] ~ . ₍ Q1–10, F
125–127] Q1–8, F *line*: Hee'le…it.
  | But…knowne | To…here.
157 sir?] Q2; ~ : Q1
163 that?] Q2; ~ : Q1
173–174] Q1–10, F *line*: Sir…you,
  | Concerning…*Sauill*.

178–183] Q1–10, F *line*: Tis…
  againe: | But…motions | Of
  …againe. | Ile…more. | *Sa.* If
  …whoring, | Take…open |
  My…worships.
184 holiday,] Q2; ~ ₍ Q1
192–193 sweete-heart] sweete-|heart
  Q1
201–203 It…charge.] Q1–10, F
  line: It…Bride, | We…charge.

I.i

8 a] an Q 2+
12 *Savill* make] *Sauil.* Make Q 2 (*where the name is regarded as a speech-prefix*); *Yo.Lo.* Make Q 3–9 (*thereby assigning lines* 12–14 *to Young Loveless*); Make F, Q 10, L, S, D (*thus keeping lines* 12–14 *as part of Elder Loveless' speech at lines* 10–11); *Yo.Lo.* Make the boat stay. C (*but assigning remainder of lines* 12–14 *to Elder Loveless*)
16 home, and marry] home marry Q 5–10
17 your Countrey] your own Country Q 7; our Country F, L
17–18 for diseases,...nightcap,] *om.* Q 3+ (–D, V)
28 for] from Q 3+ (–D, V)
34 about] above C, W
36 for] *om.* V
37 doe't] do it Q 9–10
39 S.D. *Exit.*] *om.* Q 5–10
43 heard] D, V *query* 'had'?
48 murtherers] murthers Q 3–4, F, L
51 Clark that shall] Clarke shall Q 3+ (–W, D, V)
57 first part of] first of part Q 7
61 I shall...to me] *assigned to close of Elder Loveless' preceding speech in* D, V
67 occasions] Occasion S
73 heer] there Q 7
86 or] of Q 7; and V
97 Yes] *om.* Q 5–10
100 one can] one that can Q 5–10
117 and to put] and put Q 9–10

119 you for] your Q 3+ (–W, D, V)
121 at at your] at your Q 6, Q 8–9; at, on your V
130 satisfied] told Q 3+ (–W, D, V)
135 your pure] you pure Q 10
143 chose] choose Q 3
147 drunke off] drank of C, W
150 said,] said she: Q 9
153 this] his Q 1–2
159 servant, your] Servant, and your S
166 doth your imagination] doth imagination V
166 you with] with you Q 4–6, Q 8
174 that that man] that man Q 6–10
174 but] *om.* Q 10
176 Why live] Why ile live Q 6–10
188 em] them Q 3+
194 stockins] Stockings Q 5–10, S, C, W, D, V
194 three] the Q 3+ (–D, V)
195 nere] never Q 7
200 further] farther Q 10
205 hastily] happily Q 5–10, S
212 call] cast Q 6–10, F, L, S
216 on them] of them C
216 as on] than on F, L, S, C, W, D, V
216 for they] for that they F, Q 10, L, S
220 beginnings] beginning Q 3+ (–D, V)
221 at] *om.* L
221 maids] Maid Q 9
222 beds] bed Q 5–10
223 not you] you not Q 4–10, C
227 a] *om.* L, S, C

229 hard] *om.* Q3–10, F, L, S
231 servant] Servants Q7
250 will] well Q7
251 other weomen the] other women of the Q2–10, F, L, C, W; There are other Women of the S
251 house holds] housholds Q1–4; house-hold's Q5–10; household F, L, S, W; households' C
251–252 of good] of as good Q9–10, L, S
253 and] tho Q6, Q7, Q9; though Q8, Q10
259 will] well Q7
268 Call] Calld Q6–10
276 have] *om.* Q8
277 names] name Q2+

291 the] *om.* Q2+ (−D, V)
292 an] a Q3–4, F, L, S, D, V; *om.* Q5–10, C, W
292 heres the] here comes the Q6, Q8–10, S; her comes the Q7
295 must] *om.* Q8
299–300 of all] all Q5–10
303 I inculcate] I doe inculcate Q6–10
303 service] Homilies Q6–10, S
309 man to neglect] Man neglect Q7–10
311 ye] you Q3+
311 and] the F, L, S
311 your] you Q5
315 ingenious] ingenuous Q3–8

I.ii

2 beate] beare Q2–10, F, L
4 one] then Q6–10, C, W; *om.* F, L, S; me D, V
13 goe] grow Q3–10, F, L, S, C
14 our] *om.* V
19 one] on Q2
25 keep] maintain F, L, S
32 whilst] while L, S, C, W
33 selfe gentleman-like] selfe like a Gentleman Q6–10
34 mee] *om.* Q7
41 Next] Yet Q4–10, C
43 this *Apocripha*] this is *Apocrypha* Q6–10, C; of this *Apocrypha* F, L, S, W, D, V
48 comes] come Q7, F, L, S, C, W, D, V
50 remnant] remnants W
63 *Ephimerides*] *Ephemeris* S, C
64 helpe all] help us all F, L
65 well] will L
74 not] *om.* C, W; but D, V
79 that cries] and cryes Q3+
84 have] has Q9–10

85 horses, and their] Horses, | Their S
89 even] *om.* Q4–10
89 and] end Q5
91 you] *om.* W
95 let um] ~ them Q3+
101 pounds] pound Q5–10
106 We will have nobody talke] We will not talk Q3–6, Q8–10, F, L, S, C; Will you not talk Q7
114 th'are] they are F, L, S, C, W; they're D, V
114 men] mee Q4–5
120 that] *om.* Q6–10
122 Sir.] sir, to expound it. Q6, Q8–10; to expound it Q7
132 drinke,] drinke Sir Q3+ (−D, V)
134 that live] that I live L, S
135 keep] *om.* Q7
136 part, Ile] part, *Savil,* Ile Q6–10
After line 141, Q6–10, S, C, W *add the following speech:* Omnes. O brave *Lovelace.*

II.i

1 now you see] now see Q7
3 Lady] *om.* Q6–10
4 complement] complaint Q6–10
18 loves] loveth Q6–10
20 you] ye Q6–7, Q9–10
24 premised] promised Q2–10, F, L
27 so] *om.* Q6–10
31 visible] risible S
36 tould] reprov'd Q4–10, C, W
42 Gentleweomen] Gentlewoman Q10
43 Not] No Q4–8
47 has] hath Q5–10, C, W
48 with the] with a Q6–10, C, W
50 fast] safe Q3+ (–D, V)
56 and a Gentleman] and Gentleman Q4
57 into] into into Q1
62 Sir] *om.* Q5–10
66 Gentlewoman] Gentlewomen Q3–8, F, L, S, D
77 you] *om.* S
83 will] would Q8
85 indeed] *om.* Q6–10

89 has] hath Q5–10
94 mornings] morning Q3+
96 quarters] Carcass S
96 meditation] meditations Q4–10, D
96 *Heroycall*] Heroic S
98 expence] experience Q6–10
98 recollection] collection Q5–10
100 *Nicholas Breton*] *Ni. Br.* Q1–5, F, L; *N. B.* Q6–10; *Nich. Broughton* S, C; Nich. Breton D, V
107 to you what you] to what yon Q8
110 keepe] kept Q8
119 make] made Q2
122 you] your Q2
127 verdugo] vertigo S, C, W
145 and their fornication] and fornication Q9–10
146 an other] another Tribe S
148 knowledge;] Knowledge, Sir; S
153 or this cooling] or cooling S
154 kils] kill C, W, D

II.ii

1 thy] my Q7
2 set] sit F, L, S, V
2 turne] tune S
12 this thigh] this puissant Thigh S
22 appeares] appear F, L, S, C, W, D, V
23 drownd] drown Q1
24 *Amias*] *Æneas* Q9–10
44 stiver] striuer Q1–10, F, L
45 till] still Q8
46 Gentlewomen] Gentlewoman Q1–2
63 sworne] sworm Q7

65 a Gods] i' Gods F, L, S, C, W, D, V
68 heere's] her's Q2–3; Here is S, C, W, D, V
71 unto] to S
92 pudder] pother C, W
96 dry] a-dry S
101 Drinke...Captaine.] *om.* Q3+
104 Sir] *om.* Q3–5, F, L, S, C, W
105 little] tittle Q7
106 would be glad] will strive Q6–10
107 You] And you V

115 chance to feede] Chance too to feed S
115 more fishes] Haddockes Q2+ (−W, D, V)
120 scape] escape Q2, Q8
123 'Pray let] pray you let Q5–10
127 rouse] carouse Q2+
130 they] I Q4–10, L, S
143 little as to] little to L
145 finde] feele Q3+

148 will, which] Will behind him, which S
148 behinde a] Behind the L, S, C
153 you] your Q7
154 nor] or Q4–5
165 *Savil.* Let's give] *Cap.* Let's giue Q1–5, F, L, S, C; *Sav.* Let's in and drink, and give Q6–10
165 for't] for it Q2+

II.iii

1 be your] be you your Q6–10
13 And] *om.* S
13 for my] or my Q2
13 for I] I S
17 dreg'd] drudg'd S; dredged C, W, D, V
18 reasons] Raisins Q9+
20 my widdow] *om.* S
22 takes a] takes him a S
22 lone] loue Q3–5
22 dare] dares Q9–10
22 not] nor Q1
29 will not stoope] will stoope Q1–3
30 fede] feede Q1; fed Q2+
31 for I] for that I F, L, S, C, W, V
31 I gave] and gaue Q1–10
33 penitence] patience Q7
36 whom] whence Q5–10
40 perisht] perish Q7
42 drown'd] crown'd Q7
43 saidst] sayst Q7
54 have money] have the money Q5–10
56 any] my Q6–10, L, S
58 Hee's] Here's Q7
62 Angell gold] Angel o' Gold S
63 yours] thine Q6–10
64 well] *om.* Q7

66 brothers] brother Q7
72 the] my Q3, F, L, S
72 my] *om.* S
83 Sir] fit Q4–10
85 afore] before F, L, S, C
86 all] *om.* Q6–10
90 tun] turne Q4–10, L, S, C, W, D
92 ships] ship Q9–10
94 men] man Q9–10, L, S, C, W, D, V
98 againe] against Q4–10, L, S, C, W, D, V
100 thy staffe] my staffe F
101 sed] fed Q3+ (−D, V)
102 seat] eat F
106 eternall] immortall Q6–10, L, S
109 shall] will Q3+ (−D, V)
110 or] and Q3+ (−D, V)
112 meane] men were Q2+
120 pound] pounds Q6–10, C, W
121 the Sunne] this hand Q6–10
125 There's a Gods penny for thee.] There is six Angels in earnest. Q6–10
126 Farme] frame Q8
129 in] *om.* Q2+ (−D, V)
136 so be it] *om.* Q6–10
145 Shee's] She's is Q2
146 at charge] at the charge Q3+ (−D, V)

III.i

0.1 and...Glove] om. Q1, D

1 tels] tell Q4+

2.1 *Enter* Welford.] *om.* Q5–10

3–4 towards] toward Q7–8

8 to do] do you Q8

8 beside] besides F, Q10, L, S

10 enter] enter enter Q8

12 Not] No Q5–10

14 'Twill] It wil Q6–10

23 halfe a] a halfe Q5–9

42 come to speake here] come here to speake Q4–10, L, S, C, W

44 I am] am I Q8

49–50 house, say] hous, I say Q4–10

51 am not I] am I not S

58 calkt] ralkt Q1

58 her] the Q6–10, C, W

61 Guesse] Troth guesse Q6–10, C

65 Gentlewoman] Gentlewomen Q7

66 S.P. *Abigail.*] *Wel.* C

68 one, I] one, one, I Q3+

68 nor] or Q3

73 not you] you not Q2+

80 i'th] i'th the Q1–2

86 have] hath Q4

88 such] *om.* F, L

91 you, tender Sir, whose gentle bloud] you, Sirtender whose gentle blood Q3; you, Sir, whose tender gentle blood F, L, S

97 Ornaments] Ornament Q10

98 Sir] *om.* Q8

99 be] *om.* Q1

104] *After 'still'* Q2+ *add S.D.:* 'They drawe.'

106 Jesus] *om.* Q6–10

110 What] Why what Q3+ (−D, V)

114 I] *om.* Q10

117 not] none Q6–10

131 these] those Q9–10

131 wilde] vild Q2–9, D, V; vile F, L, S, C, W

136 swords] sword Q6, Q9–10

136 come] comes Q6–8

138 With hazard] With a hazard Q5–10

145 'is] is Q1–2; are Q3–10; he's F, L, S, C, W, D, V

149 anger] anger's Q2+

152 curse] share Q6–10

165 you are] are you Q5–10

170 So he] So that he Q8

172 selfe from such temptations] selfe out from temptations Q3–6, F, L, S, C; selfe out from temptation Q7–8; self from temptations Q9–10

173 Pray] *om.* F, L

173 this] the Q4–10

173 whither] whether Q3

176 should] shall F, L; I shall S

184 a] *om.* Q6–10

189 see] saw Q4+

190 If] of Q5

197 this] his Q4–10, S, C, W

200 to great] too great Q2+

204 him] *om.* Q3

204 those] these Q5–10

210 Were] Where L

214 I pull] pull I Q3; I put Q5–10

216 to love] them to Q5–7, Q9–10; me to Q8

218 amaine] amine Q2–3

225 youth] mouth Q8

232 certaine] certainly Q3+ (−D, V)

236 spoke] spoken Q5–10, C, W

237 your] you Q5–8

238 froward] forward Q5–10

247 an't] and't F+ (−Q10)

249 hard creature] hard hearted creature Q4–10, C
251 me doe] me to doe Q5–7, 9–10
253 and] om. S
255 Love] Lover S
260 would redeeme] could redeeme Q4–10, C
265 That] This Q6–10, C, W
270 tricks] trick Q10
277 have] om. Q2+ (–W, D, V)
280 By this, and] By this light, and Q5–10
286 your] you Q8
297 warpt] wrapt Q8
299 my troth] your troth Q7–8
300 could] would Q2+ (–D, V)
305 take your] Take to your C, W

311 I] om. Q6; we Q7–10
314 you are] thou art Q6–10
316 you] thee Q6–10
320 offending] offence Q3+ (–W, D, V)
321 Y'are] Thou art Q6–10; You're L+
321 Gods love] loves sake Q6–10
326 way] ways C, W
329 I hope] om. Q9–10
332 and] an Q8
334 Conster] Construe S, C, W
339 your face] thy face Q6–10
340 staies you] stayes for you F, L, S
344 horses] horse Q8
347 companions] companion Q6–10
351 amble] amable Q1

III.ii

2 thy] my C
2 back-sword] black-sword Q8
11 too.] too, I hope. Q6–10
18 Ile] I will Q9–10
22 yee] you D, V
25 saies] say Q6+
28 shall] may Q5–10
29 whilst] while L, S, C, W
33 All] Mr. *Morecraft*, all Q6–10, C, W
36 your keys] you Keys L
36 ease] easy L, S
39 ther's] there is Q4–10
43 and they] and yet they Q6–10; yet they C, W
45 praie] om. Q7–8
52 of war] o war Q4–10
56 not you] you not Q3+
59 is much] is much is much Q1–2
61 him] me Q1–10, F, L, S, C
62 and a witty] and witty Q9–10
64 but] om. Q3+ (–D, V)
66 to a fat] to fat a Q8
69 and *Savil*] and servant, Savil C

70 ornaments] tenements Q6–10, C
76 I dare not shew] I shall not dare to shew Q6–7, Q9–10, C; I shall dare to shew Q8; as I shall not dare to shew L, S
77 Be] By Q1–2
81 bought] brought Q2
82 ye] you Q5–10, C, W, D, V
89 of] om. Q3–10, F, L
90 forfeits] surfets Q1+ (–W, D, V)
95 of] om. Q8
95 a] and Q4–9
96 a] om. Q8
96 necessary] necessarily F+ (–Q10)
106 you can] can you C, W
116 it] yet Q1–10, F, L, S
123 these Morrals] the Morals Q6, Q9–10; the Morall Q7–8
125 Gentlemen] Gentleman Q8
128 Gentlewoman] Gentleman L, S
129 on's] on't F, L
133 your] you Q2–10, F, L

136 paid againe] paid back again
    Q6–10, C, W
139 S.P. *Widow.*] *Wel.* Q2
139 has] hath Q8
141 where] were L
143 such dismall] such a dismal Q8
144 al] *om.* Q6–10, C, W
145 Heaven] the houre Q6–10
150 goe] to Q8
153 S. P. *Widow.*] *Wil.* Q2; *Well.*
    Q7–8
154 S. P. *Elder Loveless.*] *Yo.Lo.* Q1
155 The] A Q6–10, L, S
157 Sir] *om.* Q6–10, C, W
159 Am I] I am Q10
160 raile] raue Q2+ (–D, V)
164 o'th] to'th Q4–8; to the Q9–10
169 get] yet Q5–8
170 will] shall Q3
173 and] to Q8
179 Sir] *om.* Q8
179 hee's] he is Q6–10
180 your] you Q2+

181 hee's] he is Q3+ (–D, V)
184 observances] observance C
184 fall] fail F, L, S, W, D, V
186 I doe] do I S, C, W
195 you] your Q7–8
195 your] you Q5
199 who] whom, F, L, S, C, W, D, V
200 for] *om.* Q6–10
203 leaping] leading Q1–5, F, L, W
204 night] nights Q5, Q6, Q9
205 all my] all Q7–8
206 unsold] unfold Q1 (corrected),
    Q2–4, Q8
207 three hundred] thirtie Q5
214 get a] Get you a S, C, W
217 Yee] Yea Q2–3; You Q4+
217–218 sir to] fit to F, L, S
220 fornications] fornication Q4+
    (–S, D, V)
222 must I] I must Q10
224 not] no Q5–10
225.1 *Exit* Savill.] *om.* Q10

IV.i

2 brought] now brought S
2 what scurvy] what a scuruy
    Q2+
2 a] *om.* S, C, W
3 for Noble men] of Noblemen Q5
3 those] *om.* S
8 profit] profits Q3–4, F, L+
10 our] out Q6–10
14 all one] all as one S
15–16 his dolefull] this doleful F
17 learning] Learning now S
17 leap't] leap Q8
18 hee's] he is Q6–10
19 is] in Q4–5
19 state] estate Q9–10
21 hadst] hast L
22 laye] lape Q1–10, F, L
25 See how] See, see, how S

25 neglectingly] negligently Q3+
    (–D, V)
26 broke] broken Q3+ (–D, V)
39 too] like me Q6–10
39 *Dalida*] *Dalila* Q6–10; *Dalilah*
    F, L, S, C, W
41 Well, well,] Well well, well, Q8
41 man] men Q8
41 dilate] you may dilate Q6–10, C
48 me] *om.* Q8
53 Worships] worship Q7–8
55 qualm'd] quaum'd Q1; quam'd
    Q2–10
56 could expound] could not ex-
    pound Q6–10, C
57 at prayers once] *om.* Q2–10, F,
    L, S, C
58 mine] my Q2+

58 royall] *om.* Q2–5, F, L

61 Poet] Poets Q4, Q8

63 thee] you Q4–5

64 this] thus Q2

65 as a Father saith] *om.* Q2–5, F, L, S

67 you not] not you Q8

68 in't] in 'em S, C, W

69 chapter with a] *om.* Q2–5, F, L; Chapter with Q7–8

72 lovely] louingly Q2+

73 true] due Q6–10, C, W

76 and] but Q6–10, L, S, C

77 a great] *om.* S

86 Priests in a hanging] Priests a hanging Q1; Priests in the hanging Q6–10; priests i' th' hanging C

87–88 with the great Booke of Martyrs] *om.* Q2–5, F, L

91 if I should bee] should I be S

92 beloved, and] beloved *Abigall*, and Q6–10, C

92 doe even] even do Q8

98 clap] chop Q5–10, C

102 Ha, ha, ha.] Ha, ha, ha, ha. Q8

108 Sir] *om.* Q3+ (−D, V)

112 make] makes F, L, S, C, W

114 verie merrie] very mery merry Q10

120 I] Is Q3

120 God] heaven Q6–10

120 one] on Q2

120 lesse] the less S

125 Lord] *om.* Q5–10

128 some] a Q3–10, F, L, S, C

129 brought such] brought forth such Q5–10

132 shall] will Q5–10, C, W

134 you are] y'are Q5–10

135 cleane] cleere Q5

137 you would] yould Q10

142 the] a L, S, C

143 play withall] playal, with Q10

144 talke] take Q5–9

150 errant] errand Q9+

152 be gone] by gon F

156 the God knowes] the gods knowes Q1(u); God the knowes Q3; God he knowes Q4–5, F, L, S; heaven knowes Q6–10, C; the gods know W, D, V

157 kept] keep C, W

161 our] *om.* Q10

162 There is] There's Q4–10

165 not much] not so much Q2+ (−W, D, V)

167 stay you] stay for you Q4+ (−W, D, V)

178 None] no one C, W, D, V

187 hath] has Q5–10

191 turn him into] turne in to Q2; turne him to Q3+ (−W, D, V)

193 many] any Q7–8

194–195 old, | Keepe] old, pray keepe Q3+ (−S, D, V)

199 my] *om.* Q8

201 amend] mend S

205 you have] have you Q4–10, C, W

206 and] as Q5–10

208 To be] to to be Q9

208 ones] owns Q8

210 heare] Then hear S

214 Wastcoats] Ribbons Q10

215 hand] hands Q8

215 sheepskins] Q6–7, Q9

217 my] *om.* Q7–10

218 eighteene pence] Half a Crown Q10

218 my Lady.] my Lady, I can. Q6–9, L, S, C; Madam, I can Q10

225 is] *om.* Q5–8

229 best] use Q6–10

233 now] *om.* F, L, S

235 ever] never Q7–8

244 *Rosasolis*] *Rosalis* F

253 pursuing] presuming Q5–6, Q8–
   10; persuming Q7
258 my] any Q4–10
259 generall] generally Q2
263 infliction] affliction Q4–10, S
263 on] *om.* Q8; upon F, L
264 curse] course Q7–8
268 humilitie] Humanity S
269 Ha, ha.] Ha, ha, ha. Q6–10, C,
   W
276 I, a] I, ha' Q4; ~ ∧ ~ Q5–10
279 sir] *om.* Q5–10
280 be] *om.* Q8
281 finely] finely finely Q10
282 Ladie ∧ fool'd] ~ , ~ Q4–10,
   F, L; ~ ; ~ C, W; Lady-fool'd
   S, D, V
283 not] no Q9–10
284 know] knew Q2+ (−D, V)
287 see] *om.* Q8
288 that] *om.* Q7–8
288–289 laugh at you Sir. Ha, ha. |
   Lady. Praye Sister doe not
   laugh, youle] laugh, youle Q4–5
   (*thereby assigning remainder of
   Lady's speech at lines 289–292 to
   Martha*); laugh at you. | *Lady.*
   You'l Q6–10
288 Ha, ha.] ha, ha, ha. F, L, S, C,
   W, D, V
295 For it] by it Q3+ (−W, D, V)
298 and may] And you may Q5–10

305 crackt] crack Q8–10
309 knocke] knockt Q6
309 these] those L, S, C, W
313 you] *om.* Q3+ (−D, V)
323 'is] he's Q4+
324 'is] he's Q4+ (−F, L)
324 use] loose Q1–2
325 is a] is he F+ (−Q10)
327–328 Folly, | She] folly, foh, she
   Q6–10
336 you] ye Q5–10
337 thee] yee Q6–10; you L, S, C,
   W
340 shall] can Q8
341 in] *om.* Q3, F, L; make Q4–10;
   nor S, C
344 not] nor Q3+
345 nor will] and will Q5–10; nor
   my Will S, C
355 safer dote] sacerdote Q3–7, Q9–
   10, F, L; sacredote Q8; swagger,
   Doat S; rather Dote C
357 diseases] disease Q7–8
358 Then to be] than be Q8
370 What fine] What a fine S
373 'is] he's Q4+
374.1 *Enter* Abigail.] *om.* Q6–10
376 whilst] while Q8, L, S, C, W, V
379 I] *om.* Q8
381 There is] There's Q3–10, F, L
383 be] *om.* Q10

IV.ii

0.2 *his*] *om.* Q10
7 carrire] carrier Q2–3, F; carriage
   Q4–10
9 I] *om.* F, L
11 best to looke] best looke Q8
11 looke to.] look. F, L, S
20 'is] h'is Q4–5; he's Q6+
28 Nor your Reasens] not your
   rotten Reasons Q6–10

28 Reasens] Raisins F+
30 eate] feed Q6–10
34 pounds] pound F, L
36 defend] defends Q2–5, F
41 Morrall] mortal Q7–8, C, W
42 but little] but a little Q8
45 read to] read [prayers] to D
51 the] *om.* Q8
57 As] *om.* Q8

64 dare] do Q 6–10
66 a] *om.* Q 1–3, F, L
68 is damnable] is most damnable
    S, C, W
69 *Boatemaker*] *Boot-maker* Q 5;
    bear-baiting Q 6–10
70 among] amongst Q 3–4, F, L
73 *Porredge*] *Porrenge* Q 4–9
76 surely] solely C, W
77 bodies] body Q 5
80 ayrie] ayre Q 1–10
82 As] is Q 3+ (− W, D, V)

86–87 drunke, | They] drunke, if
    they Q 4–5
92 one] mee Q 6–10, D
93 is a modesty] is modesty   Q 3–
    10, F, L
94 *Wardrope*] *Wardrobe* Q 6+
99 is little] is a little Q 8
100 Two dogs] to dogs Q 4–10
100 these two] these; these two Q 1–
    10, F, L; these too S, C, W
101 me, pray] me, and pray Q 8
108 cheere] cheate Q 5

V.i

8 and strong] as strong Q 5–10
9 silver ˄ Sir˄] ~ , ~ , Q 4–10
9 i'th] 'th Q 2
14 with't] with it Q 4–10
15 ith] 'th Q 8
15 stockings] stockins Q 6–7, 9–10
24 You] Your Q 2
27 that] the Q 4–10
30 Sir] *om.* Q 3+ (− D, V)
39 she's] she is Q 4–10
41 Nobler] noble Q 7–8
41 our] your Q 2
48 left] best F, L, S
67 has] hath Q 6–10
86 goody] goodly Q 9–10
87 beleife] believe F, L, S

89 cas'd] cast Q 1–4, F, L
98 so] *om.* Q 8
106 Hast] Has Q 8
106 thy] the F
107 I] *om.* Q 9
108 yeare] yeares Q 4–10, C, W
108 chops] chaps C
115 goe] *om.* Q 8
117 vildly] vilely Q 6+ (− F, D)
118–119 want uryne to finde the
    cause by] want vryne finde the
    cause be Q 2–3; find the cause
    to be want of Urine F, L
120 on] of S, C, W
122 and] *om.* Q 7–8

V.ii

1 Is it] It is Q 3
3 accoumpt] account Q 4+
4 stoppe] keepe Q 3+
10 through] though Q 8
10 frowardnesse] forwardness Q 8
12 as he] as as he Q 2
18 oaths] oates Q 3
40 he did doe] he doe Q 5; he does
    Q 6–10
57 joynture] ioynter Q 2–6

61 he maried] he be married Q 3+
    (− D, V)
72 to] till Q 4–10
72.1 *Enter*] *Exit* Q 7–8
77 Ahlas] Ah las Q 3; Ah! las Q 4;
    Ah! Alas Q 5–10
81 is] was Q 3+ (− D, V)
82.1 *womans*] Womens Q 7–10
87 tricke] tricks Q 8
102 Godlike] *om.* Q 6–10

104 passions] passion Q3+
105 for] her Q6–10, S, C
107 Why, why∧] ~ ? ~ ∧ Q3+
      (– C, W)
114 colours] colour Q4–10
115 an] and Q5, Q8
119 as] though Q6–10
128 Deform'd] Defrom'd Q7
129 so] to Q5–10
137 will] well Q7–8
142 blame] balme Q1
145 still] yet Q3+ (– W, D, V)
146 ill to] ill as to Q5–10
149 whither] whether Q8
150 not] never Q5–10
154 pray you let] pray let Q8, S
154 with] om. Q10
156 mocks] mock Q7–8
158 I will] Ile Q3+
163 spoke] spoken Q6–10
172 will looke] will but look S
174 judicially] judiciously F, L, S
176 lover] lovers Q7–8; Love Q9–
      10
178 bee Canonicoll] be not Canonical
      S
185 thrid] third Q2, Q4
186 balls:] balls admirably Q6–10,
      L, S, C
190 forgot] forgotten F, L, S
191–192 Ile…joy.] om. Q6–10

195 lodging] lodgings C, W
196 him] om. L, S, C
197 were] was Q9–10
198 meant] meane Q3–5, F, L, S, C,
      W
198 you] om. Q9–10
200 already] a ready S
207 then] rather then Q9–10, L, S,
      C, W
207 forsooke] forsaken Q6–10, F,
      L, S
219 may not be] may be not Q8
224 God] Heav'n Q10
225 There is] There's Q6–10
228 Such a quiet] Suce a piuet Q1;
      Since a quiet Q2–3, F, L, S, C,
      W; om. Q4–10
228–229 minde…doe] om. Q4–10
229 a most ungodly thing.] printed
      after 'so' as part of Welford's
      speech, line 227, in Q4–10, which
      then begin Elder Loveless' follow-
      ing speech with 'Heare me'.
254.1 and Abigail.] om. Q4–10
256 all uncivill, all such beasts as
      these] vnciuill, all such beasts as
      these Q3; vncivill, as such
      beasts as these Q4–5; all uncivil
      Q6–10; all such uncivil beasts
      as these F, L, S

V.iii

6 art thou] are you Q9–10
8 your] you Q4
10 learning now] learning new Q1–
      3; now a learning Q8
10 sir] om. Q5–10
11 dost] does Q8
14 that is] that's Q6–10
15 compassions] capassions Q1–4
20 choosers] chooses Q2
24 it, I] it indeed, I Q6–10, C

26 out] our Q1
29 bitter] better Q8
30 can cleere] can can cleere Q1
34 I'le] I Q8
35 gentlemen] gent. Q1; Gentle-
      man Q2–7, Q9–10, F, L, S, C,
      W
40 wide] wild Q8
40 thee] the Q8, Q10
41 ye] you Q5–10, L+

52 thousands, thou] thousands,
 which thou C
55 all the waies] all ways S, C, W
60 gentlemans] Gentlewomans Q2
62 God] Heaven Q6–10
65 not] *om.* Q6–10

65 Match Knight] Match, good
 Knight S
68 the *Cleave*] *om.* Q6–10
69 Whilst] While L, S, C, W
70 his] this Q7–8

V.iv

7 gentlewoman] gent. Q1;
 Gentleman Q2–10, F, L
18 ifaith] faith Q8
26 hanckt o'th] hankt it o'th Q7–8
30 God] heaven Q6–10
32 friends] friend Q7–8
34 that] this Q6–10
47 what I am] who I am Q5–10
47 and] *om.* Q9–10
51 sham'd] asham'd Q2+ (−W,
 D, V)
52 out] *om.* Q3–5, F, L, S
56 to] of Q2+
60 wencher] *Welford* Q6–10
61 but] *om.* Q8
74 mine] my Q8
80 yee] you Q6–10, C, W, D, V
81 vext] vex Q8
81 tyr'd] try'd Q3, F
85 sore] *om.* Q4–10, L, S, C, W;
 four F
90 Creance] Cranes Q1–10, F, L
90 your] you Q7–8
92 thanke God] think Q6–10
95 we] you Q8
96 shrewd] shred Q5
96 see by] see it by Q2+ (−D, V)
110 make] makes Q9–10, F, L, S
113 'is] he is Q5–10, L, S, V; he's C,
 W, D

122 A will] I will Q3; Hee'l Q4–10,
 C, W, D, V; He will F, L, S
125 your will] you well Q5–10
127 converted] unconverted Q9–10
132 tell] tell you Q6–10
145 good] *om.* Q8
146 Who] Who's Q6–10
149 sport] sports Q9–10
151 these] *om.* Q8
153 Heere is] here's Q10
159 take] weare Q6–10
160 Of] *om.* Q9–10
161 tis lawfull] 'tis a lawful Q8–10
170 a] an Q5–10
170 pound] pounds Q3+
173 a] *om.* Q5–7, S
180 more] againe Q5–10
183 worships] worship Q6–10
186 amongst] among Q2+ (−W,
 D, V)
187 how] *om.* Q9–10
190 well] fast Q6–10, S
201–202 so sir: | Sir] so; Sir S
204 to Church] to the Church Q3+
205 y'are] y'e are Q3–4; you're L,
 D; *om.* S; you are W
211 leade] and lead Q5–10, C, W
212.1 *Exeunt*] *om.* Q5–10

LOVE'S PILGRIMAGE

edited by

L. A. BEAURLINE

TEXTUAL INTRODUCTION

Since no records mention *Love's Pilgrimage* until long after Fletcher's death, we can only guess about its date and textual history, from mostly ambiguous internal evidence. The source, Cervantes' tale *Las dos Doncellas* in *Novelas Exemplares*, was published in Spain about August 1613 and in France not until early 1615. Fletcher was once thought to have used the French edition as a source of *The Island Princess*; hence he may have used it for this play as well. But an earlier work could have been the source of that play (see Edward M. Wilson, 'Did John Fletcher Read Spanish?', *PQ*, [1948], XXVII, 187–90), leaving us back where we started. An allusion to the French controversy over their king's marriage to a Spanish princess limits the date to about 1615 or early 1616. Incubo asks Philippo

> Sir, the French,
> They say are divided 'bout their match with us,
> What think you of it? (I.i.247–9)

In England there was talk of this by February 1615: 'France is divided into so great factions as trouble is expected.' The nobles began a virtual civil war, but the opposition was reconciled by September 1616. The allusion, therefore, would have had little point after the latter date. Baldwin Maxwell ('The Date of *Love's Pilgrimage* and its Relation to *The New Inn*', *SP*, [1931], XXVIII, 702–9) prefers 1616, but I do not see the need to push it that late, especially if Beaumont is the collaborator. Beaumont was married to a Kentish heiress by 1615 and died by 6 March 1616 (E. K. Chambers, *Elizabethan Stage*, III, 215). A mention of the incipient arrival of 'our *Indian* Fleet', I.i.255, cannot be restricted to any single year. Maxwell suggests November 1616, when a particularly large gold shipment was expected in Spain. However, such anticipation was a normal, annual event, of much interest in England.

The first solid external evidence appears in the Master of the Revels' account book, 'renewing' the licence to act *Love's*

Pilgrimage, 16 September, 1635. Only one pound was paid Herbert's assistant, the usual price charged for a revised play (J. Q. Adams, *The Dramatic Records of Sir Henry Herbert* [1917], pp. 34–9). The King's Men acted the play before the King and Queen at Hampton Court, 16 December 1636, presumably in its revised form. We next hear of it in a list of sixty unpublished plays belonging to the King's Men. At their request the Lord Chamberlain wrote the Stationers' Company 7 August 1641, asking the company to prevent the unauthorized printing of certain plays in the repertory. Third from the last is 'The Louers Pilgrimage' followed by 'The Louers Progress', which probably explains the error in title (*M.S.C.* ii, 398–9). In precisely the same position on another list, the play was entered at Stationers' Hall, 'The Louers Pilgrimage', 6 September 1646, in preparation for its first publication in the folio of 1647.

In the folio, it stands at the beginning of section eight, rather a haven for fugitive pieces that were handled at the last minute. Sigs. 8 A–C are the work of an unidentified printer, but *8 D 1 recto and verso was printed by Edward Griffin. Johan Gerritsen hypothe sizes that originally there were six groups of plays in the folio, divided into clusters of threes and sixes among various printers, and that six plays, including *Love's Pilgrimage*, *The Honest Man's Fortune* and *Valentinian*, were assigned to Ruth Raworth's shop. She finished only three, as the deadline approached, and *Love's Pilgrimage* was taken out of her hands and transferred to another printer. That shop still did not finish, and Griffin, who had just finished *The Honest Man's Fortune* as an extra job, completed the last two pages of this play. ('The Printing of the Beaumont and Fletcher Folio of 1647', *Library*, 5th ser., [1949], III, 233–64. Other interpretations may be found in R. C. Bald, *Bibliographical Studies in the Beaumont & Fletcher Folio of 1647* [1938], and in Greg's *Bibliography*, [1957], III, 1017.)

Although one skeleton-forme persists through 8 A–C, there can be no doubt that two compositors shared the task. Some singularly clear spelling habits separate the two. Compositor *X* prefers *will*, *shall*, and terminal *-ll*, in polysyllables, *O*, *little*, *els*, termina l-*esse*, and sometimes he will use *onely*. Compositor *Y* prefers *wil*, *shal*,

-l, only, wel, else, and sometimes he will use *Oh, litle,* and terminal
-ess. On the basis of these spellings, I assign the following pages
to *X*: A1, A2, A3, A3^v, B3–4^v, C3–C4^v; and the following to
Y: A1^v, A2^v, A4, A4^v, B1–2^v, and C1–2^v. In the present edition
that gives *X*: I.i.1–87, 189–279$\frac{1}{2}$, 391–I.ii.183$\frac{1}{2}$, III.i.1–III.iv.43,
and IV.iii.59–V.iv.184; and it gives *Y*: I.i.88–188, 280–390,
I.ii.184–II.iv.89, and III.iv.44–IV.iii.58$\frac{1}{2}$. Edward Griffin's compositor did V.iv.185 to the end and the prologue. Compositor *X*
punctuates lightly or not at all. *Y* is somewhat more generous with
commas, periods, and colons. *Y* is the more inaccurate: he makes
more literal errors, more misreadings, mislining, and erroneous
speech prefixes. In nearly twice as many such instances I have found
reason to emend in his portions. If we knew some other work by
this printer, perhaps more could be said about their habits.

It is as definite as we can be in these matters that the manuscript
copy came from the King's Men, probably a prompt copy. The
names of three minor actors appear in stage-directions. Many
entrances come a few lines early, and there is a particular concern
with props, off-stage noises, and the other details of a performance,
such as 'Enter Hostesse and Servants with Table', 'Enter Diego
with wine', 'carried by two Servants in a chair', 'two chairs set
out', and 'Ioh: Bacon ready to shoot off a Pistol'. The known actors
mentioned in the text, John Bacon and Rowland Dowle, were hired
men for the King's company in the 1630s; therefore we can be
confident that the prompt copy was for the revival of 1635–6. (The
textual notes to II.i.9.1 and IV.i.24 give further details.)

That we are dealing with the revised form of *Love's Pilgrimage*
complicates any interpretation of authorship. Setting aside the
possible revisions for the moment, we have evidence from linguistic
eccentricities, investigated by Professor Cyrus Hoy (*SB*, [1958],
XI, 85–106) suggesting that Beaumont was originally responsible
for I.i, IV, and V, because of his use of *ha'* and *hath.* Fletcher
apparently wrote I.ii, II, and III, on the strength of the Fletcherean
ye, 'em, and other elisions. Lacking other facts, in contrast with the
fancies of F. G. Fleay and E. H. C. Oliphant, we must for the
time being agree with Hoy. Controversy about revisions in 1635
focuses on the first scene. Parts of two long passages in I.i.25–63

and 330–411 correspond to speeches in Ben Jonson's *The New Inn*, II.v.48–73 and III.i.57–93, 130–68. It is manifestly clear that the conversation between Lazaro and Diego, 330–411, is awkward and artistically inferior to Jonson's version. In *The New Inn*, acted in 1629, the dialogue is more extensive and it is divided among several characters, who speak similarly in other scenes. Furthermore the talk fits the action of Jonson's play. In *Love's Pilgrimage* the episode, as well as the unceremoniousness of the Host Diego, does not function in any way. It is superfluous, plainly. Percy Simpson thought that the passages were borrowed and adapted from Jonson, at the time when our play was 'renewed' for the stage. G. E. Bentley and Hoy agree. Simpson observes that in Incubo's description of a certain 'master of ceremonies' he casts the material in the third person:

> I wil tell thee of him:
> He would not speak with an Ambassadors Cook,
> See a cold bake-meat from a forreign part
> In cuerpo [.]

Jonson's Tipto, 'flaunting his Spanish ceremony upon the homely Host of Barnet', speaks this in the first person. Apparently such a characterization was too extreme for the 'reviser' (*Ben Jonson*, [1925], I, 198–200). Subtleties in *The New Inn* III.i.149–50 are glossed over in *Love's Pilgrimage* 387–90. (For ease of comparison, the relevant parts of *The New Inn* are printed in an appendix of the present edition.)

However, artistic superiority is no test for a source, and Jonsonian scholars should not have to be reminded of that. Jonson's acknowledged habit was to adapt inferior writing—sometimes long passages from contemporary as well as ancient authors, usually with more changes than we find in this case, but he was an inveterate adapter. And we must openly admit that many comic scenes by Beaumont and Fletcher have absolutely no dramatic function, the beginning of II.ii of *King and No King*, for instance. Therefore it is possible that *Love's Pilgrimage* originally contained the speeches that were later used by Jonson in a more skilful way. (I pass over Maxwell's awkward suggestion that Jonson is the reviser of

Love's Pilgrimage, sometime in the mid-1620s.) Another troubling detail is the presence of the jokes about *in cuerpo* in both plays. Fletcher uses the expression elsewhere, in *Love's Cure* II.i, and although the joke first appears in the 'Jonsonian' passages, it is found in other dialogue in Act I of *Love's Pilgrimage*. No earlier use has been recorded in the *OED*. This circumstance makes the priority of the passages from *The New Inn* harder to explain.

One other possible revision. Perhaps II.iv was inserted later, because the first entrance to the scene mistakenly reproduces the entry to III.i. The dialogue in that scene iv, like the supposed inter-polated speeches in Act I, is strictly irrelevant to the action. What goes on in the kitchen of an inn is lively and revolting, but it comes from nowhere and leads to nothing. The linguistic evidence, 14 *ye*'s and 6 *'em*'s, presents a barrier to this interpretation, but some of Fletcher's revisers in other plays—Ford for instance—have similar preferences. I urge this suggestion no more strongly than I do the revisions in Act I; there is not enough evidence in either case.

The present edition is based on the University of Virginia copy 1 of the first folio, collated against Virginia copy 2, The Cambridge University Library copy 1 (Aston a.Sel.19) and copy 2 (SSS.10.8), the Bodleian Library copy (B.1.8.Art.), The Duke University Library copy, The University of North Carolina Library copy and the Folger copy. The play has never been printed outside of the standard collections of the canon, the most important of which have been compared and variants duly recorded in the Historical Collation.

The Persons Represented in the Play

[*Alonso*,] GOVERNOR of *Barcellona*
LEONARDO, a noble *Genoese*, Father to *Mark-antonio*
Don SANCHIO, an old lame angry Soldier, Father to *Leocadia*
ALPHONSO, a cholerick Don, Father to *Theodosia*
PHILIPPO, Son to *Alphonso*, Lover of *Leocadia*
MARK-ANTONIO, Son to *Leonardo*
PEDRO, a Gentleman and friend to *Leonardo*
RODORIGO, General of the *Spanish* Gallies
INCUBO, Bayliff of *Castel Blanco*
DIEGO, Host of *Ossuna*   10
LAZARO, Hostler to *Diego*
[2.] HOST, of *Barcellona*

THEODOSIA, Daughter to *Alphonso* ⎱ Love-sick Ladies in
LEOCADIA, Daughter to Don *Sanchio* ⎰ pursuit of *Mark-antonio*
EUGENIA, Wife to the Governor of *Barcellona*
HOSTESS, Wife to *Diego*
[2.] HOSTESS, Wife to the Host of *Barcellona*

Chirugeons, Soldiers, Attendants, Townsmen, [Gentlemen, Boy,
  Friar, Passengers, Ship-master, Servants.]

The Persons...Townsmen] F2; *om.* F1; The Scene Barcellona and the Road. F2

574

PROLOGUE

To this place Gentlemen, full many a day
We have bid ye welcome; and to many a Play:
And those whose angry soules were not diseasd
With law, or lending money, we have pleasd;
And make no doubt to do again. This night
No mighty matter, nor no light,
We must intreat you looke for: A good tale
Told in two houres, we will not faile
If we be perfect to rehearse ye: New
I am sure it is, and hansome; but how true   10
Let them dispute that writ it. Ten to one
We please the women; and I would know that man
Follows not their example. If ye mean
To know the Play well, travell with the Scene.
For it lies upon the road; if we chance tire,
As ye are good men leave us not i'th mire,
Another bayt may mend us: If you grow
A little gald or weary; cry but hoa,
And we'l stay for ye. When our journey ends
Every mans Pot, I hope, and all part friends.   20

20 Every mans Pot] *i.e.* every man has his pot

LOVES PILGRIMAGE

Enter Incubo *the Bayliff*, Diego *the Host*.

Incubo.   Signior Don *Diego*, and mine Host, save thee.

Diego.   I thank you Master Bayly.

Incubo.   O the block.

Diego.   Why, how should I have answered?

Incubo.   Not with that
   Negligent rudeness: But I kiss your hands
   Signior Don *Incubo de Hambre*, and then
   My titles; Master Bayly of *Castil-blanco*:
   Thou nere wilt have the elegancy of an Host;
   I sorrow for thee, as my friend and gossip:
   No smoak, nor steam out-breathing from the kitchen?
   There's litle life i'th harth then.

Diego [aside].   I, there, there,   10
   That is his friendship, hearkning for the spit,
   And sorrow that he cannot smel the pot boil.

Incubo.   Strange
   An Inne should be so curst, and not the sign
   Blasted, nor withered; very strange, three days now,
   And not an egg eat in it, or an onyon.

Diego.   I think they ha' strew'd the high-wayes with caltraps, I,
   No horse dares pass 'em; I did never know
   A week of so sad doings, since I first
   Stood to my sign-post.

Incubo.   Gossip, I have found   20
   The root of all; kneel, pray; it is thy self
   Art cause thereof: each person is the founder
   Of his own fortune, good or bad; but mend it,
   Call for thy cloak, and rapier.

Diego.   How?

Incubo.   Do, call,
   And put 'em on in haste: Alter thy fortune,

I.i] *Actus Primus. Scæna Prima.*

By appearing worthy of her: Dost thou think
Her good face ere wil know a man in cuerpo?
In single body, thus? in hose, and doblet?
The horse boyes garb? base blank, and half blank cuerpo?
Did I, or Master Dean of *Civil* our neighbor　　　　　30
Ere reach our dignities in cuerpo, thinkst thou,
In squirting hose, and doublet? Signior, no,
There went more to't: there were cloaks, gowns, cassocks
And other paramentos; Call, I say,
His cloak, and rapier here.

Enter Hostesse.

Hostesse.　　　　　What means your worship?
Incubo.　Bring forth thy husbands Sword: so, hang it on;
　And now his cloak, here, cast it up; I mean
　Gossip, to change your luck, and bring you guests.
Hostesse.　Why? is there charm in this?
Incubo.　　　　　Expect; now walk,　　　　　40
　But not the pace of one that runs on errands;
　For want of gravity in an Host, is odious:
　You may remember Gossip, if you please,
　(Your wife being then th'Infanta of the Gipsies,
　And your self governing a great mans Mules then)
　Me a poor Squire at *Madrid* attending
　A Master of Ceremonies; But a man, beleeve it,
　That knew his place to the gold weight, and such
　Have I heard him oft say, ought every Host
　Within the Catholique kings dominions
　Be in his own house——
Diego.　　　　　How?
Incubo.　　　　　A Master of Ceremonies:　　　　　50
　At least vice-master, and to do nought in cuerpo,
　That was his maxime; I wil tell thee of him:
　He would not speak with an Ambassadors Cook,
　See a cold bake-meat from a forreign part

　　　27 cuerpo] *i.e.* undress, without cloak or upper garment
　　　30 *Civil*] *i.e.* Seville

In cuerpo: had a dog but staid without,
Or beast of quality, as an *English* cow,
But to present it self, he would put on
His *Savoy* chain about his neck, the ruff
And cuffs of *Holland*, then the *Naples* hat
With the *Rome* hat-band, and the *Florentine* agat, 60
The *Millain* Sword, the Cloak of *Genua*, set
With *Flemish* buttons, all his given peeces
To entertain 'em in, and complement   *Knock within.*
With a tame Coney, as with the Prince that sent it.
Diego.   List, who is there?
Incubo.   A guest and't be thy wil.
Diego.   Look Spowse, cry luck, and we be encounter'd: ha?
Hostesse.   Luck then, and good, for 'tis a fine brave guest,
With a brave horse.
Incubo.   Why now, beleeve of cuerpo
As you shal see occasion: go, and meet him.

        Enter Theodosia [*disguised as a man*].

Theodosia.   Look to my horse, I pray you, wel.
Diego.   He shal Sir. 70
Incubo.   Oh how beneath his rank and call was that now?
Your horse shal be entreated as becomes
A horse of fashion, and his inches.
Theodosia.   O.   [*Faints.*]
Incubo.   Look to the Cavalier: what ailes he? stay,
If it concern his horse, let it not trouble him,
He shal have all respect the place can yeeld him
Either of barley, or fresh straw.
Diego.   Good Sir
Look up.
Incubo.   He sincks: somewhat to cast upon him,
Hee'l go away in cuerpo else.
Diego.   What, wife!
O your hot waters quickly, and some cold 80
To cast in his sweet face.
Hostesse.   Alas, fair flowre!   [*Exit.*]

Incubo.   Do's any body entertain his horse?
Diego.   Yes, *Lazaro* has him.

Enter Hostesse *with a glasse of water.*

Incubo.   Go you, see him in person.   [*Exit* Diego.]
Hostesse.   Sir, taste a litle of this, of mine own water,
  I did distil't my self; sweet Lilly look upon me,
  You are but newly blown, my pretty Tulip.
  Faint not upon your stalk, 'tis firme and fresh;
  Stand up, so, bolt upright, you are yet in growing.
Theodosia.   Pray you let me have a chamber.   90
Hostesse.   That you shall Sir.
Theodosia.   And where I may be private, I intreat you.
Hostesse.   For that introth Sir, we ha' no choice: our house
  Is but a vent of need, that now and then
  Receives a guest, between the greater towns
  As they come late; only one room——
Incubo.   She means Sir, it is none
  Of those wild, scatter'd heaps, call'd Innes, where scarce
  The Host is heard, though he wind his horn t'his people,
  Here is a competent pile, wherein the man,   100
  Wife, Servants, all doe live within the whistle.
Hostesse.   Onely one room——
Incubo.   A pretty modest quadrangle
  She will describe to you.
Hostesse.   Wherein stands two Beds Sir,
  We have, and where, if any guest do come,
  He must of force be lodg'd, that is the truth Sir.

Enter Diego.

Theodosia.   But if I pay you for both your beds, methinks
  That should alike content you.
Hostesse.   That it shall Sir.
  If I be paid, I am praid.
Theodosia.   Why, ther's a Ducket;

*82 *Incubo.*] Sympson; *Die.* F 1–2
*83 *Diego.*] Sympson; *Host.* F 1–2   *108 praid] *stet* F 1; paid F 2

Will that make your content?

Hostesse.   O the sweet face on you: 110
A Ducket? yes, and there were three beds Sir,
And twice so many rooms, which is one more,
You should be private in 'em all, in all Sir;
No one should have a peece of a bed with you,
Not Master Deane of *Civill* himself, I swear,
Though he came naked hither, as once he did
When h'had like t'have been tane a bed with the *Moore*
And guelt by her Master: you shall be as private,
As if you lay in's owne great house, that's haunted,
Where no body comes, they say.

Theodosia.   I thank you Hostesse.   120
Pray you will you shew me in.

Hostesse.   Yes marry will I Sir,
And pray that not a flea, or a chink vex you.

                        Exeunt Hostesse *and* Theodosia.

Incubo.   You forget supper: Gossip: move for supper.

Diego.   'Tis strange what love to a beast may do, his Horse
Threw him into this fit.

Incubo.   You shall excuse me;
It was his being in Cuerpo, meerly caus'd it.

Diego.   Do you think so Sir?

Incubo.   Most unlucky Cuerpo,
Naught els; he looks as he would eat partridge,
This guest; ha' you em ready in the house?
And a fine peece of kid now? and fresh garlick,   130

                        Enter Hostesse.

With a Sardina, and Zant oile? how now?
Has he bespoke? what, will he have a brace,
Or but one partridge, or a short leg'd hen,
Daintyly carbonado'd?

Hostesse.   'Lasse the dead
May be as ready for a Supper as he.

Incubo.   Ha?

Hostesse.   He has no mind to eat, more then his shadow.

Incubo.   Say you.
Diego.   How do's your worship?
Incubo.   I put on
My left shoo first to day, now I perceive it,
And skipt a bead in saying 'em ore; els   140
I could not be thus cross'd: He cannot be
Above seventeen; one of his years, and have
No better a stomach?
Hostesse.   And in such good clothes too.
Diego.   Nay, those do often make the stomach worse, wife,
That is no reason.
Incubo.   I could at his years Gossips
(As temperate as you see me now) have eaten
My brace of ducks, with my half goose, my cony,
And drink my whole twelve Marvedis in wine
As easie as I now get down three olyffs.
Diego.   And with your temperance-favour, yet I think   150
Your worship would put to't at six and thirty
For a good wager; and the meal in too.
Incubo.   I do not know what mine old mouth can do,
I ha not prov'd it lately.
Diego.   That's the grief Sir.
Incubo.   But is he without hope then gone to bed?
Hostesse.   I fear so Sir, has lock'd the door close to him.
Sure he is very ill.
Incubo.   That is with fasting,
You should ha told him Gossip, what you had had,
Given him the inventury of your kitchen,
It is the picklock in an Inne, and often   160
Opens a close barr'd stomach: what may he be, troh?
Has he so good a Horse?
Diego.   Oh a brave Jennet,
As ere your worship saw.
Incubo.   And he eats?
Diego.   Strongly.
Incubo.   A mighty solascisme, heaven give me patience,

149 olyffs] *i.e.* olives

581

What creatures has he?

Hostesse.   None.

Incubo.   And so well cloath'd,
And so well mounted?

Diego.   That's all my wonder Sir,
Who he should be; he is attir'd and hors'd
For the Constables son of *Spaine*.

Incubo.   My wonders more
He should want appetite: well a good night
To both my Gossips: I will for this time   170
Put off the thought of supping: In the morning
Remember him of breakfast pray you.

Hostesse.   'T shall Sir.

Diego.   A hungry time Sir.

Incubo.   We that live like myce
On others meat, must watch when we can get it.   *Exit* Incubo.

Hostesse.   Yes, but I would not tell him: Our fair guest
Says, though he eat no supper, he will pay
For one.

Diego.   Good news: we'l eat it spouse, t' his health;
'Twas politickly done t'admit no sharers.

Enter Philippo.

Philippo.   Look to the Mules there, wher's mine Host?

Diego.   Here Sir.
Another Fayerie.

Hostesse.   Blesse me.

Philippo.   From what sweet Hostesse?   180
Are you affraid o' your guests?

Hostesse.   From Angels Sir,
I think ther's none but such come here to night,
My house had never so good luck afore
For brave fine guests; and yet the ill luck on't is
I cannot bid you welcome.

Philippo.   No?

Hostesse.   Not lodge you Sir.

*172 'T shall] *stet* F 1; I shall F 2

Philippo.   Not, Hostesse?

Hostesse.   No in troth Sir, I do tell you
Because you may provide in time: my beds
Are both tane up by a yong Cavalier   190
That wil, and must be private.

Diego.   He has paid Sir
For all our Chambers.

Hostesse.   Which is one: and Beds
Which I already ha' told you are two: But Sir,
So sweet a creature, I am very sorry
I cannot lodge you by him; you look so like him,
Yo'are both the loveliest peeces.

Philippo.   What train has he?

Diego.   None but himself.

Philippo.   And wil no less then both beds
Serve him?

Hostesse.   H'as given me a ducket for 'em.

Philippo.   O.
You give me reason Hostesse: Is he handsome,   200
And yong do you say?

Hostesse.   O Sir, the delicat'st flesh
And finest clothes withall, and such a horse,
With such a Sadle.

Philippo.   Shee's in love with all.
The horse, and him, and Sadle, and clothes: good woman,
Thou justifiest thy Sex; lov'st all that's brave:

Enter Incubo.

Sure though I lye o'th ground, ile stay here now
And have a sight of him: you'l give me house-room,
Fire, and fresh meat for money, gentle Hostesse:
And make me a pallat?

Incubo.   Sir shee shal do reason:——
I understood you had another guest: Gossips,   210
Pray you let his Mule be lookt too: have good straw,
And store of bran: And Gossip do you hear,
Let him not stay for supper: what good fowle ha' you?

This gentleman would eat a pheasant.

Hostesse.   'Lass Sir;
We ha' no such.

Incubo.   I kiss your hands fair Sir.——
What ha' you then? speak what you have? I'me one, Sir,
Here for the Catholique King, an Officer
T'enquire what guests come to these places; you Sir
Appear a person of quality, and 'tis fit
You be accommodated.——Why speak you not,   220
What ha' you woman? are you afraid to vent
That which you have?

Philippo [*aside*].   This is a most strange man;
T'appoint my meat.

Hostesse.   The half of a cold hen Sir,
And a boil'd quarter of kid, is all i'th house.

Incubo.   Why all's but cold; let him see it fourth,
Cover, and give the eye some satisfaction,
A Travellers stomach must see bread and salt,
His belly is neerer to him, then his kindred:
Cold hen's a pretty meat Sir.

Philippo.   What you please;
I am resolv'd t'obey.

Incubo.   So is your kid,   230
With pepper, garlick, and the juice of an Orenge,
She shal with sallads help it, and cleane lynnen.——
Dispatch.   [*Exeunt* Diego *and* Hostesse.]
            What news at Court Sir?

Philippo.   Faith, new tires
Most of the Ladies have: the men old Suits,
Only the Kings fool has a new coat
To serve you.

Incubo.   I did ghess you came from thence Sir.

Philippo.   But I do know I did not.

Incubo.   I mistook Sir.
What hear you of the Archdukes?

Philippo.   Troth, your question.

Incubo. Of the French business, What?

Philippo.   As much.
Incubo.   No more?
They say the French——

       Enter Hostesse *and Servants with Table.*

             O that's wel: come I'le help you: 240
Have you no jibblets now? or a broild rasher
Or some such present dish t'assist?
Hostesse.   Not any Sir.
Incubo.   The more your fault: you nev'r should be without
Such aydes: what cottage would ha' lackt a pheasant
At such a time as this? wel, bring your hen
And kid forth quickly.   [*Exeunt* Hostesse *and Servants.*]
Philippo [*aside*].   That should be my prayer
To scape his inquisition.
Incubo.   Sir, the French,
They say are divided 'bout their match with us,
What think you of it?
Philippo.   As of naught to me Sir.
Incubo.   Nay it's as litle to me too: but I love   250
To ask after these things, to know the affections
Of States, and Princes, now and then for bettring.
Philippo.   Of your own ignorance.
Incubo.   Yes Sir.
Philippo.   Many do so.
Incubo.   I cannot live without it: what do you hear
Of our *Indian* Fleet; they say they are well return'd.
Philippo.   I had no venture with 'em Sir; had you?
Incubo.   Why do you ask Sir?
Philippo.   'Cause it might concern you,
It do's not me.

       Enter Hostesse *and Servants with meat.*

Incubo.   O here's your meat come.
Philippo.   Thanks,
I welcome it at any price.
Incubo.   Some stools here,

And bid mine Host bring Wine.——   [*Exeunt Servants.*]
                                    Ile try your kid,   260
If he be sweet: he looks wel: yes, he is good;
Ile carve you sir.
Philippo.   You use me too too princely:
  Tast, and carve too.
Incubo.   I love to do these offices.
Philippo. I think you do: for whose sake?
Incubo.   For themselves sir,
  The very doing of them is reward.
Philippo. 'Had little faith would not beleeve you Sir.

                Enter Diego *with Wine.*

Incubo. Gossip some wine.
Diego.   Here 'tis: and right Saint *Martyn.*
Incubo. Measure me out a glass.
Philippo. I love the humanity us'd in this place.
Incubo. Sir, I salute you here.
Philippo.   I kiss your hands Sir.   270
Incubo. Good wine; it wil beget an appetite:
  Fil him; and sit down, Gossip, entertain
  Your noble guest here, as becomes your title.
Diego. Please you to like this wine Sir?
Philippo.   I dislike
  Nothing mine Host, but that I may not see
  Your conceal'd guest: here's to you.
Diego.   In good faith Sir,
  I wish you as wel as him: would you might see him.
Incubo. And wherefore may he not?
Diego.   'Has lock'd himself Sir
  Up, and has hir'd both the beds o' my wife
  At extraordinarie rate.
Philippo.   Ile give as much   280
  If that will do't, for one, as he for both;
  What say you mine Host, the door once open
  Ile fling my self upon the next bed to him
  And there's an end of me till morning; noise

                        586

will make none.

Diego.   I wish your worship well——but——

Incubo.   His honour is engag'd: And my she Gossip
Hath past her promise, hath she not?

Diego.   Yes truely.

Incubo.   That toucheth to the credit of the house:
Well, I will eate a little, and think: how say you sir
Unto this brawn o'th hen?

Philippo.   I ha' more minde   290
To get this bed sir.

Incubo.   Say you so: Why then
Giv't me agen, and drink to me: mine Host,
Fill him his wine: thou'rt dull, and do'st not praise it,
I eate but to teach you the way Sir.

Philippo.   Sir:
Find but the way to lodge me in this chamber
Ile give mine Host two duckets for his bed,
And you sir two realls: here's to you.

Incubo.   Excuse me,
I am not mercenary: Gossip pledge him for me,
Ile think a little more; but ev'n one bit
And then talke on: you cannot interrupt me.   300

Diego.   This peece of wine sir cost me——

Incubo.   Stay: I have found:
This little morcell: and then: here's excellent garlick:
Have you not a bunch of grapes now: or some Bacon
To give the mouth a rellish?

Diego.   Wife, do you hear?

Incubo.   It is no matter: Sir, give mine Host your duckets.

Diego.   How Sir?

Incubo.   Do you receive 'em: I will save
The honesty of your house: and yours too Gossip,
And I will lodge the Gentleman: shew the Chamber.

Diego.   Good Sir do you hear.

Incubo.   Shew me the Chamber.

Diego.   Pray you Sir,   310
Do not disturb my guests.

Incubo.   Disturb? I hope
The Catholique King sir, may command a lodging
Without disturbing in his vassails house,
For any Minister of his, emploid
In business of the State. Where is the door?
Open the door, who are you there? within?
In the Kings name.
Theodosia within.   What would you have?
Incubo.   Your key sir,
And your door open: I have here command
To lodge a Gentleman, from the Justice, sent
Upon the Kings affairs.
Theodosia.   Kings and necessities   320
Must be obey'd: the key is under the door.
Incubo.   How now sir, are you fitted? you secur'd?
Philippo.   Your two reals are grown a peece of eight.
Incubo.   Excuse me Sir.
Philippo.   'Twill buy a hen and wine
Sir, for to morrow.   *Exit* Philippo.
Incubo.   I do kisse your hands Sir.
Well this will bear my charge yet to the Gallies
Where I am owing a ducket: whither this night
By the Moons leave Ile march: for in the morning
Early they put from *Port Saint Maries.*   *Exeunt al but* Diego.
Diego.   Laʒaro.   330

Enter Lazaro.

How do the horses?
Laʒaro.   Would you would go and see Sir;
A——of all Jades, what a clap h'as given me:
As sure as you live master he knew perfectly
I couzend him on's Oats: he lookt upon me
And then he sneerd, as who should say take heed sirrah:
And when he saw our half peck, which you know
Was but an old Court dish: lord how he stampt:
I thought 't had been for joy, when suddenly

*332 A——] F 1–2; A plague Colman
588

He cuts me a back caper with his heels
And takes me just o'th' crupper: down came I   340
And all my ounce of Oates: Then he neigh'd out
As though he had had a Mare by'th taile.
Diego.   Faith *Lazaro*,
We are to blame to use the poor dumb serviters
So cruelly.
Lazaro.   Yonder's this other gentlemans horse
Keeping our Lady eve: the devill a bit
Has got since he came in yet: there he stands
And looks, and looks, but 'tis your pleasure sir
He shall look lean enough: has hay before him,
But 'tis as big as hemp, and will as soon choak him,   350
Unless he eate it butter'd: he had four shoos
And good ones when he came: 'tis a strange wonder
With standing still he should cast three.
Diego.   O *Lazaro*,
The devils in this trade: truth never knew it,
And to the devill we shall travell *Lazaro*,
Unless we mend our manners: once every week
I meet with such a knock to molefie me,
Sometimes a dozen to awake my conscience;
Yet still I sleep securely.
Lazaro.   Certain Master,
We must use better dealing.
Diego.   'Faith for mine own part   360
Not to give ill example to our issues,
I could be well content to steal but two girths,
And now and then a saddle cloth: change a bridle
Onely for exercise.
Lazaro.   If we could stay there,
There were some hope on's Master: but the devill is
We are drunk so early we mistake whole Saddles,
Sometimes a horse; and then it seems to us too
Every poore Jade has his whole peck, and tumbles
Up to his ears in clean straw, and every bottle
Shews at the least a dozen; when the truth is Sir,   370

Ther's no such matter, not a smell of provinder,
Not so much straw, as would tye up a horse tail,
Nor any thing ith' rack, but two old cobwebs
And so much rotten hay as had been a hens nest.
Diego.   Well, these mistakings must be mended *Lazaro*,
These apparitions, that abuse our sences,
And make us ever apt to sweep the manger
But put in nothing; these fancies must be forgot
And we must pray it may be reveal'd to us
Whose horse we ought in conscience to couzen,   380
And how, and when: A Parsons horse may suffer
A little greazing in his teeth, 'tis wholsome;
And keeps him in a sober shuffle: and his Saddle
May want a stirrop, and it may be sworn
His learning lay on one side, and so brok it:
Has ever Oates in's cloak-bag to prevent us
And therefore 'tis a meritorious office
To tythe him soundly.
     Lazaro.   And a Grazier may
(For those are pinching puckfoysts, and suspitious)
Suffer a myst before his eyes sometimes too,   390
And think hee sees his horse eat half a bushel:
When the truth is, rubbing his gums with salt,
Till all the skin come off, he shal but mumble
Like an old woman, that were chewing brawn,
And drop 'em out again.
     Diego.   That may do wel too,
And no doubt 'tis but venial: But good *Lazaro*,
Have you a care of understanding horses,
Horses with angry heels, gentlemens horses,
Horses that know the world: let them have meat
Till their teeth ake; and rubbing till their ribbs   400
Shine like a wenches forehead; they are devils.
     Lazaro.   And look into our dealings: as sure as we live
These Courtiers horses are a kind of Welsh prophets,
Nothing can be hid from 'em: For mine own part
The next I cozen of that kind, shal be founderd,

And of all four too: Ile no more such complements
Upon my crupper.
Diego.　　　　　Steal but a litle longer
Till I am lam'd too, and wee'l repent together,
It wil not be above two daies.
Laȝaro.　　　　　　　By that time
I shal be wel again, and all forgot Sir.　　　　　410
Diego.　Why then ile stay for thee.

　　　　　　　　　　　　　　　　Exeunt.

　　　　Enter Theodosia, *and* Phillipo *on several Beds.*　　　I. ii

Theodosia.　Oh,——ho! oh——ho!
Philippo.　Ha?
Theodosia.　Oh——oh! heart——heart——heart——heart!
Philippo.　What's that?
Theodosia.　When wilt thou break?——break, break, break!
Philippo.　Ha?
　I would the voice were strong, or I neerer.
Theodosia.　Shame, shame, eternal shame! what have I done?
Philippo.　Done?
Theodosia.　　　　And to no end: what a wild Jorney
　Have I more wildly undertaken?
Philippo.　　　　　　　Jorney?　　　　　　　　　10
Theodosia.　How without counsel? care? reason? or fear?
Philippo.　Whither wil this fit carry?
Theodosia.　　　　　　O my folly!
Philippo.　This is no common sickness.
Theodosia.　　　　　　　How have I left
　All I should love, or keep? ô heaven.
Philippo.　　　　　　　Sir.
Theodosia.　　　　　　　Ha?
Philippo.　How do you gentle Sir?
Theodosia.　　　　　　Alas my fortune.
Philippo.　It seems your sorrow oppresses: please your goodness

　　　406 of all four] *i.e.* off all four feet
　　　I.ii] *Scæna secunda.*

Let me bear half Sir: a divided burthen
Is so made lighter.
Theodosia.　　　　　Oh!
Philippo.　　　　　　　That sigh betrayes
The fulness of your grief.
Theodosia.　　　　　I, if that grief
Had not bereft me of my understanding,　　　　　20
I should have wel remembred where I was,
And in what company; and clapt a lock
Upon this tongue for talking.
Philippo.　　　　　　　Worthy Sir,
Let it not add to your grief, that I have heard
A sigh, or groan come from you: That is all Sir.
Theodosia.　　Good Sir no more: you have heard too much I fear,
Would I had taken poppy when I spake it.
Philippo.　　It seems you have an ill belief of me
And would have feard much more, had you spoke ought
I could interpret. But beleeve it Sir,　　　　　30
Had I had means to look into your breast,
And tane you sleeping here, that so securely
I might have read, all that your woe would hide
I would not have betrayd you.
Theodosia.　　　　　　Sir that speech
Is very noble, and almost would tempt
My need to trust you.
Philippo.　　　　　At your own election,
I dare not make my faith so much suspected
As to protest again: nor am I curious
To know more then is fit.
Theodosia.　　　　　Sir I wil trust you,
But you shal promise Sir to keep your bed,　　　　　40
And whatsoe'er you hear, not to importune
More, I beseech you from me――――
Philippo.　　　　　　Sir I wil not.
Theodosia.　　Then I am proan to utter.
Philippo.　　　　　　My faith for it.
Theodosia.　　If I were wise, I yet should hold my peace.

You wil be noble?

Philippo.　　　　　You shal make me so

If you'l but think me such.

Theodosia.　　　　　　I do: then know

You are deceiv'd with whom you have talkt so long.

I am a most unfortunate lost woman.

Philippo.　Ha?

Theodosia.　　　Do not stir Sir: I have here a Sword.

Philippo.　Not I sweet Lady: of what blood, or name?　　　50

Theodosia.　You'l keep your faith.

Philippo.　　　　　　　Ile perish else.

Theodosia.　　　　　　　　Beleeve then

Of birth too noble for me; so descended——

I am ashamd, no less then I am affrighted.

Philippo.　Fear not: by all good things, I will not wrong you.

Theodosia.　I am the daughter of a noble Gentleman

Born in this part of *Spain*: my fathers name Sir——

But why should I abuse that reverence

When a childs duty has forsaken me.

Philippo.　All may be mended: in fit time too: speak it.

Theodosia.　*Alphonso*, sir.

Philippo.　　　　　*Alphonso?* what's your own name?　　　60

Theodosia.　Any base thing you can invent.

Philippo.　　　　　　　　Deal truely.

Theodosia.　They call me *Theodosia.*

Philippo.　　　　　　Ha? and love,

Is that that hath chang'd you thus?

Theodosia.　　　　　　　Ye have observ'd me

Too neerly Sir, 'tis that indeed: 'tis love Sir:

And love of him (oh heavens) why should men deal thus?

Why should they use their arts to cozen us

That have no cunning, but our fears about us?

And ever that too late to; no dissembling

Or double way but doating: too much loving!

Why should they find new oaths, to make more wretches?　　　70

Philippo.　What may his name be?

*47 talkt] F 2 (talk'd); talk F 1

Theodosia.   Sir a name that promises
Me thinks no such ill usage: *Mark-antonio*,
A noble neighbours Son: Now I must desire ye
To stay a while: else my weak eyes must answer.
Philippo.   I will:——Are ye yet ready? what is his quality?
Theodosia.   His best a theef Sir: that he would be known by
Is, heir to *Leonardo*, a rich Gentleman:
Next, of a handsome body, had heaven made him
A minde fit to it. To this man, my fortune,
(My more then purblind fortune) gave my faith,   80
Drawn to it by as many shews of service
And signs of truth, as ever false tongue utter'd:
Heaven pardon all.
Philippo.   'Tis wel said: forward Lady.
Theodosia.   Contracted Sir, and by exchange of rings
Our souls deliver'd: nothing left unfinish'd
But the last work, enjoying me, and Ceremony.
For that I must confess was the first wise doubt
I ever made: yet after all this love sir,
All this profession of his faith; when dayly
And hourly I expected the blest priest   90
Hee left me like a dream, as all this story
Had never been, nor thought of, why I know not;
Yet I have called my conscience to confession,
And every sillable that might offend
I have had in shrift: yet neither loves law, Signiour,
Nor ty of maidens duty, but desiring
Have I transgrest in: left his father too,
Nor whither he is gone, or why departed
Can any tongue resolve mee: All my hope
(Which keeps mee yet alive, and would perswade mee   100
I may be once more happy, and thus shapes mee
A shame to all my modest sex) is this Sir,
I have a Brother and his old Companion,
Student in *Sallimanca*, there my last hope
If hee bee yet alive, and can be loving

80 gave] F2; grave F1

594

Is left mee to recover him: For which travel
In this Sute left at home of that dear Brothers
Thus as you find mee, without fear, or wisdom,
I have wander'd from my father, fled my friends,
And now am only child of hope and danger:　　　　　　110
You are now silent Sir: this tedious story
(That ever keeps mee waking) makes you heavy:
'Tis fit it should do so: for that, and I
Can be but troubles.

Philippo.　　　　　　No, I sleep not Lady:
I would I could: oh heaven is this my comfort?

Theodosia.　　What aile you gentle Sir?

Philippo.　　　　　　Oh.

Theodosia.　　　　　　Why do you groan so?

Philippo.　　I must, I must; oh misery.

Theodosia.　　　　　　But now Sir
You were my comfort: if any thing afflict yee
Am not I fit to bear a part on't? and by your own rule.

Philippo.　　No; if you could heal, as you have wounded me,　　120
But 'tis not in your power.

Theodosia.　　　　　　I fear intemperance.

Philippo.　　Nay do not seek to shun mee: I must see you:
By heaven I must:——hoa, there mine Host: a Candle.
Strive not, I wil not stir ye.

Theodosia.　　　　　　Noble Sir,
This is a breach of promise.

Philippo.　　　　　　Tender Lady,
It shal be none but necessary:——hoa, there,
Some light, some light for heavens sake.

Theodosia.　　Wil ye betray mee?
Are ye a gentleman?

Philippo.　　　　Good woman!

Theodosia.　　　　　　Sir.

Philippo.　　If I be prejudicial to you, curse mee.　　　　130

*129 Good woman!] Mason; ~ : F 1–2

Enter Diego *with a light.*

Diego.   Ye are early stirring sir.
Philippo.   Give mee your Candle
  And so good morrow for a while.
Diego.   Good morrow Sir.   *Exit.*
Theodosia.   My Brother Don *Philippo*: nay Sir, kil mee.
  I ask no mercy Sir, for none dare know me,
  I can deserve none: As ye look upon me,
  Behold in infinite these foul dishonors,
  My noble father, then your self, last all
  That bear the name of kindred, suffer in mee:
  I have forgot whose child I am, whose Sister:
  Do you forget the pity tyed to that: 140
  Let not compassion sway you: you wil be then
  As foul as I, and bear the same brond with me,
  A favourer of my fault: ye have a sword sir,
  And such a cause to kil me in.
Philippo.   Rise Sister:
  I wear no sword for women: nor no anger
  While your fair chastity is yet untouch'd.
Theodosia.   By those bright starrs, it is Sir.
Philippo.   For my Sister,
  I do beleeve ye: and so neer blood has made us
  With the dear love I ever bore your vertues
  That I wil be a Brother to your griefs too: 150
  Be comforted, 'tis no dishonor Sister
  To love, nor to love him you do: he is a gentleman
  Of as sweet hopes, as years, as many promises,
  As there be growing truths, and great ones.
Theodosia.   O sir!
Philippo.   Do not despair.
Theodosia.   Can ye forgive?
Philippo.   Yes Sister,
  Though this be no smal error, a far greater.
Theodosia.   And think me stil your Sister?
Philippo.   My dear Sister.

596

Theodosia.   And wil you counsel mee?

Philippo.   To your own peace too:
Ye shal love stil.

Theodosia.   How good ye are!

Philippo.   My business,
And duty to my father, which now drew mee   160
From *Salimanca*, I wil lay aside
And only be your Agent to perswade ye
To leave both love, and him, and wel retyre ye.

Theodosia.   Oh gentle Brother.

Philippo.   I perceive 'tis folly:
Delayes in love, more dangerous.

Theodosia.   Noble Brother.

Philippo.   Fear not, ile run your own way: and to help you,
Love having rackt your passions beyond counsel,
Ile hazard mine own fame: whither shal we venture?

Theodosia.   Alas, I know not Sir.

Philippo.   Come, 'tis bright morning.
Let's walk out, and consider: you'l keep this habit.   170

Theodosia.   I would sir.

Philippo.   Then it shal be: what must I cal ye?
Come, do not blush: pray speak, I may spoil all else.

Theodosia.   Pray cal me *Theodoro.*

Enter Diego.

Diego.   Are ye ready?
The day draws on a pace: once more good morrow.

Theodosia.   Good morrow gentle Host: now I must thank ye.

Philippo.   Who do'st thou think this is?

Diego.   Were you a wench Sir
I think you would know before me.

Philippo.   Mine own Brother.

Diego.   By'th Masse your noses are a kin: should I then
Have been so barbarous to have parted Brothers?

Philippo.   You knew it then.

Diego.   I knew 'twas necessary   180

*165 more dangerous] *stet* F 1–2

You should be both together: Instinct Signior
Is a great matter in an Host.
Theodosia.   I am satisfied.
Pedro [*within*].   Is not mine Host up yet?
Philippo.   Who's that?
Diego.   Ile see.   [*Exit.*]
Philippo.   Sister, withdraw your self.   [*She retires.*]

Enter Pedro.

Pedro.   Signiour *Philippo.*
Philippo.   Noble Don *Pedro*, where have you been this way?
Pedro.   I came from Port Saint *Maries*, whence the Gallyes
  Put this last tide, and bound for *Barcellona*,
  I brought *Mark-antonie* upon his way——
Philippo.   *Marc-antonie?*
Pedro.   Who is turn'd Soldier
  And entertain'd in the new Regiment,   190
  For *Naples.*
Philippo.   Is it possible?
Pedro.   I assure you.
Philippo.   And put they in at *Barcellona?*
Pedro.   So
  One of the Masters told me.
Philippo.   Which way go you Sir?
Pedro.   Home.
Philippo.   And I for *Civill*: pray you Sir, say not
  That you saw me, if you shall meet the question;
  I have some little businesse.
Pedro.   Were it lesse Sir,
  It shall not become me, to loose the caution:
  Shall we break-fast together?
Philippo.   Ile come to you Sir.——

                              [*Exit* Pedro.]

  Sister you hear this: I beleeve your fortune   200
  Begins to be propitious to you: we will hire
  Mules of mine host here: if we can, himself
  To be our guid, and streight to *Barcellona*;

This was as happy news, as unexpected.
Stay you, till I rid him away.
Theodosia.   I will.

                                                   Exeunt.

                    Enter Alphonso *and a* Servant.   II. i

Alphonso.   Knock at the door.
1. Servant.   'Tis open Sir.
Alphonso.   That's all one.
   Knock when I bid you.
1. Servant.   Will not your worship enter.
Alphonso.   Will not you learn more manners Sir, and do that
   Your Master bids ye; knock ye knave, or ile knock
   Such a round peal about your pate: I enter
   Under his roofe, or come to say god save ye
   To him, the Son of whose base dealings has undone me?
   Knock lowder, lowder yet: ile starve, and rot first;
   This open ayr is every mans.
2. Servant within.   Come in Sir.

                    Enter 2. Servant.

Alphonso.   No, no Sir, I am none of these come in Sirs,   10
   None of those visitants: bid your wise Master
   Come out, I have to talk unto him: go Sir.
2. Servant.   Your worship may be welcome.
Alphonso.   Sir, I will not,
   I come not to be welcome: good my three duckets,
   My pickell'd sprat a day, and no oyl to't,
   And once a year a cotten coat, leave prating
   And tell your Master, I am here.
2. Servant.   I will Sir.
   This is a strange old man.   *Exit.*
Alphonso.   I welcome to him!

          II.i] ACT. II. SCÆNA I.   1 *1. Servant.*] Dyce; *Ser.* F 1–2
          2 *1. Servant.*] Dyce; *Ser.* F 1–2
          *9.1 2. Servant.] *two Servants, Rowl: Ashton.* F 1; *two Servants.* F 2

                              599

Ile be first welcome to a Pesthouse: Sirhah,
Lets have your valour now casde up, and quiet   20
When an occasion calls, 'tis wisdom in ye,
A Servingmans discretion: if you do draw,
Draw but according to your entertainment;
Five nobles worth of fury.

Enter Leonardo, *and* Don Sanchio (*carried by
two Servants in a chair.*)

Leonardo.   Signiour *Alphonso.*
I hope no discontent from my will given,
Has made ye shun my house: I ever lov'd ye.
And credit me amongst my fears 'tis greatest
To minister offences.
Alphonso.   O good Signiour,
I know ye for *Italian* breed, fair tongu'd,
Spare your Appologies, I care not for 'em,   30
As little for your love Sir; I can live
Without your knowledge, eat mine own, and sleep
Without dependances, or hopes upon ye.
I come to aske my daughter.
Leonardo.   Gentle Sir.
Alphonso.   I am not gentle Sir, nor gentle will be
Till I have justice, my poor child restor'd
Your caper-cutting boy has run away with:
Yong Signior-smooth-face, he that takes up wenches
With smiles, and sweet behaviours, songs, and sonnets,
Your high fed Jennet, that no hedge can hold;   40
They say you bred him for a Stallion.
Sanchio.   Fie Signiour, there be times, and terms of honour
To argue these things in, descidements able
To speak ye noble gentlemen, ways punctuall
And to the life of credit; ye are too rugged.
Alphonso.   I am too tame Sir.
Leonardo.   Will ye hear but reason?

20 casde] *i.e.* cas'd
27 And] An F 1–2; *in* F 1 *an extra space after 'n' suggests that 'd' has dropped out.*

600

Alphonso.   No, I will hear no reason: I come not hither
  To be popt off with reason; reason then.
Sanchio.   Why Signior, in all things there must be method.
  Ye choak the child of honour els, discretion.   50
  Do you conceive an injury?
Alphonso.   What then Sir?
Sanchio.   Then follow it in fair terms; let your sword bite
  When time calls, not your tongue.
Alphonso.   I know, Sir,
  Both when and what to do without directions,
  And where, and how, I come not to be tutur'd,
  My cause is no mans but mine own: you Signior,
  Will ye restore my daughter?
Leonardo.   Who detains her?
Alphonso.   No more of these sleight shifts.
Leonardo.   Ye urge me Signior
  With strange unjustice: because my Son has err'd——
Sanchio.   Mark him.
Leonardo.   Out of the heat of youth: do'st follow   60
  I must be father of his crimes?
Alphonso.   I say still,
  Leave off your rhetorick, and restore my daughter.
  And sodainly: bring in your rebell too,
  Mountdragon, he that mounts without commission,
  That I may see him punished, and severely,
  Or by that holy heaven, ile fire your house,
  And ther's my way of honour.
Sanchio.   Pray give me leave.
  Was not man made the noblest creature?
Alphonso.   Well Sir.
Sanchio.   Should not his mind then answer to his making,
  And to his mind his actions? If this ought to be,   70
  Why do we run a blind way from our worths,
  And cancell our discretions, doing those things
  To cure offences, are the most offences?
  We have rules of justice in us; to those rules

*64 Mountdragon] stet F1

Let us apply our angers: you can consider
The want in others of these terminations,
And how unfurnish'd they appear.
Alphonso.   Hang others,
And where the wrongs are open, hang respects;
I come not to consider.
Leonardo.   Noble Sir,
Let us argue cooly, and consider like men.   80
Alphonso.   Like men!
Leonardo.   Ye are too sodain still.
Alphonso.   Like men Sir?
Sanchio.   It is fair language, and ally'd to honour.
Alphonso.   Why, what strange beast would your grave reverence
Make me appear? like men!
Sanchio.   Taste but that point Sir,
And ye recover all.
Alphonso.   I tell thy wisdome
I am as much a man, and as good a man——
Leonardo.   All this is granted Sir.
Alphonso.   As wise a man——
Sanchio.   Ye are not tainted that way.
Alphonso.   And a man
Dares make thee no man; or at best, a base man.
Sanchio.   Fy, Fy, here wants much carriage.
Alphonso.   Hang much carriage. 90
Leonardo.   Give me good language.
Alphonso.   Sirrah Signiour, give me my daughter.
Leonardo.   I am as gentle as your self, as free born——
Sanchio.   Observe his way.
Leonardo.   As much respect ow'd to me——
Sanchio.   This hangs together nobly.
Leonardo.   And for Civill,
A great deal more it seems: go look your daughter.
Sanchio.   There ye went well off, Signiour.
Leonardo.   That rough tongue

---

*91–92 Leonardo...language. | Alphonso. Sirrah Signiour, give] F2; Leo....
language sirrah Signiour. | Alph. Give F1

602

You understand at first: you never think Sir,
Out of your mightinesse, of my losse: here I stand,
A patient anvill to your burning angers,   100
Made subject to your dangers; yet my losse equall:
Who shall bring home my son?
Alphonso.   A whipping Beadle.
Leonardo.   Why, is your daughter whorish?
Alphonso.   Ha, thou dar'st not,
By heaven I know thou dar'st not.
Leonardo.   I dare more Sir,
If you dare be uncivill.
Alphonso.   Laugh too, Pidgeon.
Sanchio.   A fitter time for fames sake: two weak Nurses
Would laugh at this; are there no more days coming,
No ground but this to argue on? no swords left
Nor friends to carry this, but your own furies?
Alas! it shows too weakly.
Alphonso.   Let it show;   110
I come not here for shews: laugh at me sirrah?
Ile give ye cause to laugh.
Leonardo.   Ye are as like Sir,
As any man in *Spaine*.
Alphonso.   By heaven I will,
I will brave *Leonardo*.
Leonardo.   Brave *Alphonso*,
I will expect it then.
Sanchio.   Hold ye there both,
These terms are noble.
Alphonso.   Ye shall hear shortly from me.
Sanchio.   Now discreetly.
Alphonso.   Assure your self ye shall: do ye see this sword Sir?
He has not cast his teeth yet.
Sanchio.   Rarely carried.
Alphonso.   He bites deep: most times mortall: Signiour,   120
Ile hound him at the fair and home.
Sanchio.   Still nobly.

*117 *Sanchio.* Now] F 2; *Leo.* Now F 1   121 the] *i.e.* thee

Alphonso.   And at all those that dare maintain ye.
Sanchio.   Excellent.
Leonardo.   How you shall please Sir, so it be fair, though certain,
  I had rather give you reason.
Sanchio.   Fairly urg'd too.
Alphonso.   This is no age for reason, prick your reason
  Upon your swords point.
Sanchio.   Admirably follow'd.
Alphonso. And there ile hear it: so till I please, live Sir.   *Exit.*
Leonardo.   And so farewell, you'r welcome.
Sanchio.   The end crowns all things.
  Signiour, some little businesse past, this cause ile argue
  And be a peace between ye, ift so please ye,   130
  And by the square of honour to the utmost:
  I feel the old man's master'd by much passion,
  And too high rackt, which makes him overshoot all
  His valour should direct at, and hurt those
  That stand but by as blenchers: this he must know too,
  As necessary to his judgement, doting women
  Are neither safe nor wise adventures, conceive me,
  If once their wills have wander'd; nor is't then
  A time to use our rages: for why should I
  Bite at the stone, when he that throws it wrongs me?   140
  Do not we know that women are most wooers,
  Though closest in their carriage? Do not all men know,
  Scarce all the compasse of the globe can hold 'em
  If their affections be afoot? Shall I then covet
  The follys of a she-fool, that by nature
  Must seek her like, by reason be a woman,
  Sink a tal ship because the sales defie me?
  No, I disdain that folly; he that ventures
  Whilst they are fit to put him on, has found out
  The everlasting motion in his scabbard.   150
  I doubt not to make peace: and so for this time
  My best love, and remembrance.
Leonardo.   Your poor Servant.

133 all~] F2; ~ . F1   *Exeunt.*

604

Enter Diego [*the*] *Host,* Philippo, *and* Theodosia.

Philippo.   Where will our Horses meet us?
Diego.   Fear not you Sir,
  Some half mile hence, my worships man will stay us.
  How is it with my young bloods? come, be joviall,
  Let's travell like a merry flock of wild geese,
  Every tongue talking.
Philippo.   We are very merry;
  But do you know this way Sir?
Theodosia.   Is't not dangerous?
  Methinks these woody thickets should harbour knaves.
Diego.   I fear none but fair wenches: those are theeves
  May quickly rob me of my good conditions
  If they cry stand once: but the best is, Signiours,   10
  They cannot bind my hands; for any else,
  They meet an equall knave, and there's my pasport:
  I have seen fine sport in this place, had these trees tongues,
  They would tell ye pretty matters: do not you fear though,
  They are not every days delights.
Philippo.   What sport Sir?
Diego.   Why to say true, the sport of all sports.
Philippo.   What was't?
Diego.   Such turning up of taffataes; and you know
  To what rare whistling tunes they go, far beyond
  A soft wind in the shrowds: such stand there,
  And down ith thother place; such supplications   20
  And subdivisions for those toys their honours;
  One, as ye are a gentleman in this bush,
  And oh sweet Sir, what mean ye? ther's a bracelet,
  And use me I beseech ye like a woman,
  And her petition's heard: another scratches,
  And crys she will die first, and then swones: but certain
  She is brought to life again, and does well after.
  Another, save mine honour, oh mine honour,
  My husband serves the Duke, Sir, in his kitchen;

II.ii] *Scæna secunda.*

605

I have a cold pie for ye; fy, fy, fy gentlemen,   30
Will nothing satisfie ye, where's my husband?
Another crys, do ye see Sir how they use me,
Is there no law for these things?
Theodosia.   And good mine Host,
Do you call these fine sports?
Diego.   What should I call 'em,
They have been so call'd these thousand years and upwards.
Philippo.   But what becomes o'th' men?
Diego.   They are stript and bound,
Like so many *Adams*, with fig leafs afore 'em,
And there's their innocence.
Theodosia.   Would we had known this
Before we reacht this place?
Philippo.   Come, there's no danger,
These are but sometimes chances.

Enter [Incubo *the*] *Bayliffe.*

Diego.   Now we must through.   40
Theodosia.   Who's that?
Diego.   Stand to it Signiors.
Philippo.   No it needs not,
I know the face; 'tis honest.
Incubo.   What mine Host,
Mine everlasting honest Host.
Diego.   Masse Bayly,
Now in the name of an ill reckoning,
What make you walking this round?
Incubo.   A——of this round,
And of all businesse too, through woods, and rascalls,
They have rounded me away a dozen duckets,
Besides a fair round cloke: Some of 'em knew me,
Els they had cased me like a cony too,   50
As they have done the rest, and I think rosted me,
For they began to baste me soundly: my young Signiors,
You may thank heaven, and heartily, and hourly,

*46 A——] F 1–2; A pox Colman; *See the textual note on* I.i.332.

606

You set not out so early; ye had been smoak'd els,
By this true hand ye had Sirs, finely smoakt,
Had ye been women, smockt too.

Theodosia.　　　　　　Heaven defend us.

Incubo.　Nay, that had been no prayer; there were those
　That run that prayer out of breath, yet fail'd too:
　There was a Fryer, now ye talk of prayer,
　With a huge bunch of beads, like a rope of onyons,　　　60
　I am sure as big, that out of fear and prayer,
　In half an houre wore 'em as small as bugles,
　Yet he was flea'd too.

Philippo.　　　　　At what houre was this?

Incubo.　Some two houres since.

Theodosia.　　　　　Do you think the passage sure now?

Incubo.　Yes, a rope take 'em, as it will, and blesse 'em,
　They have done for this day sure.

Philippo.　　　　　Are many riffled?

Incubo.　At the least a dozen,
　And there left bound.

Theodosia.　　　　　How came you free?

Incubo.　　　　　　　　　A curtesie
　They use out of their rogueships, to bequeath
　To one, that when they give a signe from far　　　70
　Which is from out of danger, he may presently
　Release the rest; as I met you, I was going,
　Having the signe from yonder hill to do it.

Theodosia.　Alas poor men.

Philippo.　　　　　Mine Host, pray go untie 'em.

Diego.　Let me alone for cancelling: where are they?

Incubo.　In every bush like black birds, you cannot misse 'em.

Diego.　I need not stalk unto 'em.

Incubo.　　　　　　　No, they'l stand ye,
　My busy life for yours Sir.——　　　　*Exit* [Diego.]
　　　　　　　　　You would wonder
To see the severall tricks, and strange behaviors
Of the poor rascals in their miseries.　　　80
One weeps, another laughs at him for weeping,

A third is monstrous angry he can laugh,
And crys, go too, this is no time; he laughs still.
A fourth exhorts to patience, him a fift man
Curses for tamenesse, him a Fryer schools,
All hoot the Fryer: here one sings a Ballad,
And there a little Curat confutes him, and in
This linsey woolsey way, that would make a dog
Forget his dinner, or an old man fire,
They rub out for their ransoms: Amongst the rest,   90
There is a little Boy rob'd, a fine child,
It seems a Page: I must confesse my pitty
(As 'tis a hard thing in a man of my place
To shew compassion) stir'd at him; so finely
And without noyse he carrys his afflictions,
And looks as if he had but dreamt of loosing.
This boy's the glory of this robbery,
The rest but shame the action: now ye may hear 'em.

    Enter Host *and* Leocadia [*disguised as a boy, a* Fryer],
           and other [*Passengers*] *as rob'd.*

Diego.   Come lads, 'tis holy-day: hang clothes, 'tis hot,
And sweating agues are abroad.
1. Passenger.   It seems so;   100
For we have met with rare Phisitians
To cure us of that mallady.
Diego.   Fine footing,
Light and deliver: now my boys: Master Fryer,
How do's your holinesse, bear up man; what,
A cup of neat sack now and a toast: ha, Fryer,
A warm plaister to your belly Father,
There were a blessing now.
Fryer.   Ye say your mind Sir.
Diego.   Where my fine Boy: my poynter.
Incubo.   Ther's the wonder.
Diego.   A rank whore scratch their sides till the pox follow

98.2 *other*] others F 1–2
100 *1. Passenger.*] Colman; *1.* F 1–2
108 Where] *i.e.* Where is

For robbing thee, thou hast a thousand ways
To rob thy self boy, dyce, and a chamber devill——
Leocadia.   Ye are deceiv'd Sir.
Diego.   And thy Master too Boy.
Philippo.   A sweet fac'd Boy indeed: what rogues were these?
What barbarous brutish slaves to strip this beauty?
Theodosia.   Come hither my boy: alas! he's cold, mine Host,
We must intreat your Cloak.
Diego.   Can ye intreat it?
Philippo.   We do presume so much, you have other garments.
Diego.   Will you intreat those too?
Theodosia.   Your Mule must too,
To the next town, you say 'tis neer; in pity
You cannot see this poor Boy perish. I know   120
Ye have a better soul; we'l satisfie ye.
Diego.   'Tis a strange foolish trick I have, but I cannot help it;
I am ever cozen'd with mine own commendations;
It is determin'd then I shall be robb'd too,
To make up vantage to this dozen: here Sir,
Heaven has provided ye a simple garment
To set ye off: pray keep it hansomer
Then you kept your own, and let me have it render'd,
Brush'd, and discreetly folded.
Leocadia.   I thank ye Sir.
Diego.   Who wants a doblet?
2. Passenger.   I.
Diego.   Where will you have it?   130
2. Passenger.   From you Sir, if you please.
Diego.   Oh, there's the poynt Sir.
Philippo.   My honest friends, I am sorry for your fortunes,
But that's but poor relief: here are ten Duckets,
And to your distribution holy Sir,
I render 'em: and let it be your care
To see 'em, as your wants are, well divided.
Diego.   Plain dealing now my friends: and Father Fryer,
Set me the sadle right; no wringing Fryer,

130 *and* 131 2. *Passenger.*] Colman; 2. F 1–2

Nor tithing to the Church, these are no duties;
Scowre me your conscience, if the Devill tempt ye   140
Off with your cord, and swing him.
Fryer.   Ye say well Sir.
All.   Heaven keep your goodnesse.
Theodosia.   Peace keep you, farewell friends.
Diego.   Farewell light-horse-men.   *Exit the rob'd* [*Passengers*].
Philippo.   Which way travell you Sir?
Incubo.   To the next town.
Theodosia.   Do you want any thing?
Incubo.   Only discretion to travell at good houres,
   And some warm meat to moderate this matter,
   For I am most outragious cruell hungry.
Diego.   I have a stomach too such as it is
   Would pose a right good pasty, I thank heaven for't.
Incubo.   Chees that would break the teeth of a new handsaw,   150
   I could endue now like an Eastrich, or salt beeffe
   That *Cesar* left in pickell.
Philippo.   Take no care,
   Wee'l have meat for you and enough: Ith' mean time
   Keep you the horse way lest the fellow misse us,
   We'l meet ye at the end o'th wood.
Diego.   Make hast then.
                              Exit Diego *and* Incubo.
Theodosia.   My pretty Sir, till your necessities
   Be full supplied, so please you trust our friendships,
   We must not part.
Leocadia.   Ye have pull'd a charge upon ye,
   Yet such a one, as ever shall be thankfull.
Philippo.   Ye have said enough: may I be bold to ask ye,   160
   What Province you were bred in? and of what parents?
Leocadia.   Ye may Sir: I was born in *Andoluʒia*,
   My name *Francisco*, son to Don *Henriques*
De Cardinas.
Theodosia.   Our noble neighbour.
Philippo.   Son to Don *Henriques*:

*151 endue] Sympson; endure F 1–2

610

I know the gentleman: and by your leave Sir,
I know he has no son.
Leocadia.   None of his own Sir,
  Which makes him put that right upon his brother
  Don *Sanchio's* children: one of which I am,
  And therefore do not much err.
Philippo.   Still ye do Sir,   170
  For neither has Don *Sanchio* any son;
  A daughter, and a rare one is his heire,
  Which though I never was so blest to see,
  Yet I have heard great good of.
Theodosia.   Urge no further;
  He is ashamed, and blushes.
Philippo.   Sir,
  If it might import you to conceal your self,
  I ask your mercy, I have been so curious.
Leocadia.   Alas! I must ask yours Sir: for these lies,
  Yet they were usefull ones; for by the claiming
  Such noble parents, I beleev'd your bounties   180
  Would shew more gracious: The plain truth is gentlemen,
  I am Don *Sanchios* stewards son, a wild boy,
  That for the fruits of his unhappinesse,
  Is faigne to seek the wars.
Theodosia.   This is a lie too,
  If I have any ears.
Philippo.   Why?
Theodosia.   Mark his language,
  And ye shall find it of too sweet a relish
  For one of such a breed: ile pawn my hand,
  This is no boy.
Philippo.   No boy? what would you have him?
Theodosia.   I know, no boy: I watcht how fearfully,
  And yet how sodainly he cur'd his lies,   190
  The right wit of a woman: Now I am sure.
Philippo.   What are ye sure?
Theodosia.   That 'tis no boy: ile burn in't.

172 his heire] F2; heire F1

Philippo.   Now I consider better, and take councell,
    Methinks he shows more sweetnesse in that face,
    Then his fears dare deliver.
Theodosia.   No more talk on't,
    There hangs some great waight by it: soon at night
    Ile tell ye more.——
Philippo.   Come Sir, what ere you are,
    With us; embrace your liberty, and our helps
    In any need you have.
Leocadia.   All my poor service
    Shall be at your command Sir, and my prayers.   200
Philippo.   Let's walke a pace; hunger will cut their throats els.

                                        Exeunt.

                    Enter Rodorigo, Markantonio.   II.iii]
                        Two Chairs set out.

Rodorigo.   Call up the Master.
Master within.   Here Sir.
Rodorigo.   Honest Master,
    Give order all the Gallys with this tyde
    Fall round, and neer upon us; that the next wind
    We may waigh off together, and recover
    The Port of *Barcelona*, without parting.
Master within.   Your pleasures done Sir.
Rodorigo.   Signior *Markantonio,*
    Till meat be ready, let's sit here and prepare
    Our stomachs with discourses.
Mark-antonio.   What you please Sir.
Rodorigo.   Pray ye answer me to this doubt.
Mark-antonio.   If I can Sir.
Rodorigo.   Why should such plants as you are, pleasures children   10
    That ow their blushing years to gentle objects,
    Tenderly bred, and brought up in all fulnesse,
    Desire the stubborn wars?

        II.iii] SCÆNA TERTIA.
        *0.1 Markantonio.] Sympson; *Markantonio, and a Ship-master.* F 1–2

Mark-antonio.   In those 'tis wonder,
  That make their ease their god, and not their honour:
  But noble Generall, my end is other,
  Desire of knowledge Sir, and hope of tying
  Discretion to my time, which only shews me,
  And not my years, a man, and makes that more,
  Which we call handsome, the rest is but boys beauty,
  And with the boy consum'd.
Rodorigo.   Ye argue well Sir.   20
Mark-antonio.   Nor do I wear my youth, as they wear breches,
  For object, but for use: my strength for danger,
  Which is the liberall part of man, not dalliance;
  The wars must be my Mistresse Sir.
Rodorigo.   O Signiour,
  You'l find her a rough wench.
Mark-antonio.   When she is won once,
  She'l show the sweeter Sir.
Rodorigo.   You can be pleas'd, though,
  Sometimes to take a tamer?
Mark-antonio.   'Tis a truth Sir,
  So she be hansom, and not ill condition'd.
Rodorigo.   A Soldier should not be so curious.
Mark-antonio.   I can make shift with any for a heat Sir.   30
Rodorigo.   Nay, there you wrong your youth too: and however
  You are pleas'd to appear to me, which shews wel Signior,
  A tougher soul then your few yeers can testifie;
  Yet my yong Sir, out of mine own experience
  When my spring was, I am able to confute ye,
  And say, y' had rather come to th' shock of eys,
  And boldly march up to your Mistresse mouth,
  Then to the Cannons.
Mark-antonio.   That's as their lading is Sir.
Rodorigo.   There be Trenches
  Fitter, and warmer for your years, and safer   40
  Then where the bullet plaies.
Mark-antonio.   Ther's it I doubt Sir.
Rodorigo.   You'l easily find that faith: But come, be liberall,

What kind of woman could you make best wars with?
Mark-antonio.   They are all but heavy marches.
Rodorigo.   Fy *Marckantonio,*
  Beauty in no more reverence?
Mark-antonio.   In the Sex Sir,
  I honour it, and next to honour, love it,
  For there is onely beauty, and that sweetnesse
  That was first meant for modesty: sever it
  And put it in one woman, it appears not;
  'Tis of too rare a nature, she too grosse   50
  To mingle with it.
Rodorigo.   This is a meer heresie.
Mark-antonio.   Which makes 'em ever mending; for that glosse
  That cosens us for beauty, is but bravery,
  An outward shew of things well set, no more;
  For heavenly beauty is as heaven it self Sir,
  Too excellent for object, and what is seen
  Is but the vail then, airy clowds; grant this,
  It may be seen, 'tis but like stars in twinklings.
Rodorigo.   'Twas no small study in their Libraries
  Brought you to this experience: But what think ye   60
  Of that fair red and white, which we call beauty?
Mark-antonio.   Why? 'tis our creature Sir, we give it 'em,
  Because we like those colours, els 'tis certain
  A blew face with a motley nose would do it,
  And be as great a beauty, so we lov'd it;
  That we cannot give, which is only beauty,
  Is a fair Mind.
Rodorigo.   By this rule, all our choices
  Are to no ends.
Mark-antonio.   Except the dull end, Doing.
Rodorigo.   Then all to you seem equall?
Mark-antonio.   Very true Sir,
  And that makes equall dealing: I love any   70
  That's worth love.
Rodorigo.   How long love ye Signiour?

57 then] *stet* F 1–2

Mark-antonio.   Till I have other businesse.
Rodorigo.   Do you never
  Love stedfastly one woman?
Mark-antonio.   'Tis a toyle Sir
  Like riding in one rode perpetually;
  It offers no variety.
Rodorigo.   Right youth,
  He must needs make a Soldier; nor do you think
  One woman, can love one man?
Mark-antonio.   Yes that may be,
  Though it appear not often; they are things ignorant,
  And therefore apted to that superstition
  Of doting fondnesse; yet of late years Signior,   80
  The worlds well mended with 'em, fewer are found now
  That love at length, and to the right mark; all
  Stir now as the time stirs; fame and fashion
  Are ends they aym at now, and to make that love
  That wiser ages held ambition;
  They that cannot reach this, may love by Index;
  By every days surveying who best promises,
  Who has done best, who may do, and who mended
  May come to do again; who appears neatest
  Either in new stampt cloths, or curtesies,   90
  Done but from hand to mouth neither; nor love they these things
  Longer then new are making, nor that succession
  Beyond the next fair feather. Take the City,
  There they go to't by gold waight, no gain from 'em,
  All they can work by fire and water to 'em,
  Profit is all they point at: if there be love
  'Tis shew'd ye by so dark a light, to bear out
  The bracks, and old stayns in it, that ye may purchase
  French velvet better cheap: all loves are endlesse.
Rodorigo.   Faith, if ye have a Mistresse, would she heard you.   100
Mark-antonio.   'Twere but the ventring of my place, or swearing
  I meant it but for argument, as Schoolmen
  Dispute high questions.

Rodorigo.   What a world is this
When yong men dare determine what those are,
Age and the best experience ne'r could aym at?
Mark-antonio.   They were thick eyd then Sir; now the print is bigger,
And they may read their fortunes without spectacles.
Rodorigo.   Did you ne'r love?
Mark-antonio.   Faith yes, once after supper,
And the fit held till midnight.
Rodorigo.   Hot, or shaking?
Mark-antonio.   To say true, both.
Rodorigo.   How did ye rid it?
Mark-antonio.   Thus Sir,   110
I laid my hand upon my heart, and blest me,
And then said over certain charms I had learn'd
Against mad dogs, for love, and they are all one;
Last thought upon a windmill, and so slept,
And was well ever after.
Rodorigo.   A rare Phisitian,
What would your practise gain ye?
Mark-antonio.   The wars ended,
I mean to use my art, and have these fools
Cut in the head like Cats, to save the kingdome
Another Inquisition.
Rodorigo.   So old a Soldier
Out of the wars I never knew yet practised.   120
Mark-antonio.   I shall mend every day; But noble Generall,
Beleeve this, but as this you nam'd, discourses.
Rodorigo.   O ye are a cunning Gamster.
Mark-antonio.   Mirths and toys
To cosen time withall, for O my troth Sir,
I can love (I think, well too) well enough:
And think as well of women as they are,
Pretty fantastick things, some more regardfull,
And some few worth a service: I am so honest,
I wish 'em all in heaven, and you know how hard Sir
'Twill be to get in there with their great farthingalls.   130

129 wish] F2; with F1

616

Rodorigo. Well *Marckantonio*, I would not loose thy company
 For the best Galley I command.
Mark-antonio. Faith Generall,
 If these discourses please ye, I shall fit ye
 Once every day. *Knock within.*
Rodorigo. Thou canst not please me better: hark, they call
 Below to Dinner: ye are my Cabbin guest,
 My bosome's, so you please Sir.
Mark-antonio. Your poor Servant.
  Exeunt.

  Enter 2. Host [*of Barcellona*] *and 2.* Hostesse. II.iv

2. Host. Let 'em have meat enough woman, half a hen;
 There be old rotten pilchers, put 'em of too,
 'Tis but a little new anoynting of 'em,
 And a strong onyon, that confounds the stink.
2. Hostesse. They call for more Sir.
2. Host. Knock a dozen eggs down,
 But then beware your wenches.
2. Hostesse. More then this too?
2. Host. Worts, worts, and make 'em porridge: pop 'em up wench,
 But they shall pay for Cullyses.
2. Hostesse. All this is nothing;
 They call for kid and partridge.
2. Host. Well remembred,
 Where's the half Falconers dog he left?
2. Hostesse. It stinks Sir, 10
 Past all hope that way.
2. Host. Run it ore with garlick,
 And make a *Roman* dish on't.
2. Hostesse. Pray ye be patient,
 And get provision in; these are fine gentlemen,

II.iv] *Scæna quarta.*
 0.1 Enter . . . 2. Hostesse.] *Enter second Host and his wife.* F 2; *Enter Philippo, and second Host.* F 1
 *10 half Falconers dog] stet F 1; Falconers half dog F 2

And liberall gentlemen; they have unde quare
No mangey Muleters, nor pinching Posts
That feed upon the parings of musk-millions
And radishes, as big and tough as rafters:
Will ye be stirring in this businesse? Here's your brother,
Mine old Host of *Ossuna*, as wise as you are,
That is, as knavish; if ye put a trick,   20
Take heed he do not find it.
2. Host.   Ile be wagging.
2. Hostesse.   'Tis for your own commodity.   [*Exit* 2. Host.]
                                        Why, wenches.
[*Wench*] *within.*   Anon forsooth.
2. Hostesse.   Who makes a fire there? and who gets in water?
Let *Oliver* go to the Justice, and beseech his worship
We may have two spits going; and do you hear *Druce*,
Let him invite his worship, and his wives worship,
To the left meat to morrow.

Enter [Incubo] *Bayliff.*

Incubo.   Where's this Kitchen?
2. Hostesse.   Even at the next dore Signior: what, old Don?
We meet but seldome.
Incubo.   Prethee be patient Hostesse,   30
And tell me where the meat is.
2. Hostesse.   Faith Master Baylie,
How have ye done? and how man?
Incubo.   Good sweet Hostesse,
What shall we have to dinner?
2. Hostesse.   How do's your woman,
And a fine woman she is, and a good woman.
Lord, how you bear your years?
Incubo.   Is't veale, or mutton,
Beefe, bacon, pork, kid, pheasant, or all these,
And are they ready all?
2. Hostesse.   The howers that have been
Between us two, the merry howers: Lord!
Incubo.   Hostesse, dear Hostesse do but hear; I am hungry.

2. Hostesse.   Ye are merrily dispos'd Sir.

Incubo.   Monstrous hungry,   40
And hungry after much meat. I have brought hither
Right worshipfull to pay the reckoning,
Mony enough too with 'em, desire enough
To have the best meat, and of that enough too:
Come to the point sweet wench, and so I kisse thee.

2. Hostesse.   Ye shall have any thing, and instantly,
Ere you can lick your ears, Sir.

Incubo.   Portly meat,
Bearing substantiall stuffe, and fit for hunger:
I do beseech ye Hostesse first, then some light garnish,
Two pheasants in a dish, if ye have leverits,   50
Rather for way of ornament, then appetite,
They may be look'd upon, or larks: for fish,
As there is no great need, so I would not wish ye
To serve above fowre dishes, but those full ones;
Ye have no cheese of *Parma?*

2. Hostesse.   Very old Sir.

Incubo.   The lesse will serve us, some ten pound.

2. Hostesse.   Alas Sir,
We have not half these dainties.

Incubo.   Peace good Hostesse,
And make us hope ye have.

2. Hostesse.   Ye shall have all Sir.

Incubo.   That may be got for mony.

Enter Diego *the Host, and a Boy.*

Diego.   Wher's your Master?
Bring me your Master boy: I must have liquor   60
Fit for the Mermedons; no dashing now child
No conjurings by candle light, I know all;
Strike me the oldest Sack, a peece that carrys
Point blank to this place boy, and batters; Hostesse,
I kisse thy hands through which many a round reckoning
And things of moment have had motion.

2. Hostesse.   Still mine old Brother.

619

Diego.   Set thy Seller open,
  For I must enter, and advance my colours,
  I have brought thee Dons indeed wench, Dons with duckets;
  And those Dons must have dainty wine, pure *Bacchus*   70
  That bleeds the life bloud: what, is your cure ended?
Incubo.   We shall have meat man.
Diego.   Then we will have wine man,
  And wine upon wine, cut and drawn with wine.
2. Hostesse.   Ye shall have all, and more then all.
Incubo.   All, well then.
Diego.   Away, about your businesse, you with her
  For old acquaintance sake, to stay your stomach.
                               Exit Hostesse *and* [Incubo] Bayliffe.
  And Boy, be you my guid ad inferos,
  For I will make a full descent in equipage.
Boy.   Ile shew you rare wine.
Diego.   Stinging geer?
Boy.   Divine Sir.
Diego.   O divine boy, march, march my child, rare wine boy?   80
Boy.   As any is in *Spaine* Sir.
Diego.   Old, and strong too,
  O my fine Boy, clear too?
Boy.   As christall Sir, and strong as truth.
Diego.   Away boy,
  I am enamour'd, and I long for Dalliance.
  Stay no where child, not for thy fathers blessing,
  I charge thee not to save thy sisters honour,
  Nor to close thy dams eys were she a dying,
  Till we arrive; and for thy recompence
  I will remember thee in my Will.
Boy.   Ye have said Sir.
                                                 Exeunt.

Enter Philippo *and* 2. Host.   III.i

Philippo.   Mine Host, is that apparrel got ye spoke of?
  Ye shal have ready money.
2. Host.   'Tis come in Sir, he has it on sir,
  And I think 'twil be fit, and o' my credit
  'Twas never worn but once Sir, and for necessity
  Pawnd to the man I told ye of.
Philippo.   Pray bargain for it,
  And I wil be the pay-master.
2. Host.   I wil Sir.
Philippo.   And let our meat be ready when you please,
  I mean as soon.
2. Host.   It shal be presently.
Philippo.   How far stands *Barcellona?*
2. Host.   But two leagues off Sir,   10
  You may be there by three a clock.
Philippo.   I am glad on't.

                              Exeunt.

Enter Theodosia, *and* Leocadia.   III.ii

Theodosia.   Signior *Francisco* why I draw you hither
  To this remote place, marvel not, for trust me
  My innocence yet never knew ill dealing,
  And as ye have a noble temper, start not
  Into offence, at any thing my knowledge,
  And for your special good, would be inform'd of,
  Nor think me vainly curious.
Leocadia.   Worthy Sir,
  The courtesies you and your noble Brother,
  Even then when few men find the way to do 'em,
  I mean in want, so freely showrd upon me,   10
  So truly and so timely minister'd,
  Must if I should suspect those minds that made 'em,
  Either proclaim me an unworthy taker,

  III.i] Act. III. Scæna I.   III.ii] *Scæna secunda.*

                    621

Or worse, a base beleever; Speak your mind Sir
Freely, and what you please; I am your Servant.
Theodosia.   Then my yong Sir, know since our first acquaintance
Induc'd by circumstances that deceive not,
To clear some doubts I have (nay blush not Signior)
I have beheld ye narrowly (more blushes!)
Sir, ye give me so much light, I find ye   20
A thing confest already (yet more blushes?)
You would ill cover an offence might sink ye
That cannot hide your self; why do ye shake so?
I mean no trouble to ye; this fair hand
Was never made for hardness, nor those eys
(Come do not hide 'em) for rough objects; heark ye,
Ye have betrayd your self, that sigh confirms me;
An other? and a third too? then I see
These Boyes clothes do but pinch ye. Come be liberal;
Ye have found a friend that has found you; disguise not   30
That loaden soul that labors to be open:
Now you must weep, I know it, for I see
Your eys down laden to the lidds, another
Manifest token that my doubts are perfect;
Yet I have found a greater; tel me this,
Why were these holes left open; there was an error,
A foul one my *Francisco*, have I caught ye?
O pretty Sir, the custome of our Country
Allows men none in this place: Now the showre comes.
Leocadia.   O Signior *Theodoro*.
Theodosia.   This sorrow showes so sweetly   40
I cannot chuse but keep it company:
Take truce and speak sir: and I charge your goodness,
By all those perfect hopes that point at vertue,
By that remembrance these fair tears are shed for,
If any sad mis-fortune have thus form'd ye,
That either care or counsel may redeem,
Pain, purse, or any thing within the power
And honor of free gentlemen, reveal it,

36 holes] *i.e.* holes in her ears

622

And have our labors.
Leocadia.   I have found ye noble
And ye shal find me true; your doubts are certain,   50
Nor dare I more dissemble; I am a woman,
The great example of a wretched woman;
Here you must give me leave to shew my sex;
And now to make ye know how much your credit
Has won upon my soul, so it please your patience,
Ile tell you my unfortunate sad story.
Theodosia.   Sit down and say on Lady.
Leocadia.   I am born Sir
Of good and honest parents, rich, and noble,
And not to ly, the daughter of Don *Sanchio*,
If my unhappy fortune have not lost me: 60
My name call'd *Leocadia*, even the same
Your worthy brother did the special honor
To name for beautiful; and without pride
I have been often made beleeve so Signior;
But that's impertinent: Now to my sorrows;
Not far from us a gentleman of worth,
A neighbor and a noble visitor,
Had his aboad; who often met my Father
In gentle sports of chase, and river hawking,
In course and riding, and with him often brought   70
A Son of his, a yong and hopeful gentleman,
Nobly train'd up, in years fit for affection,
A sprighty man, of understanding excellent,
Of speech, and civil 'havior, no less powerful;
And of all parts, else my eys lyed, abundant:
We grew acquainted, and from that acquaintance
Neerer into affection; from affection
Into belief.
Theodosia.   Well.
Leocadia.   Then we durst kisse.
Theodosia.   Go foreward.
Leocadia.   But ô man, man, unconstant, careless man,

73 sprighty] *i.e.* sprightly

623

Oh subtle man, how many are thy mischiefs?   80
O *Marck-antonio*, I may curse those kisses.
Theodosia.   What did you call him Lady?
Leocadia.   *Marck-antonio*,
The name to me of misery.
Theodosia.   Pray foreward.
Leocadia.   From these we bred desires sir; but lose me heaven
If mine were lustful.
Theodosia.   I beleeve.
Leocadia.   This neerness
Made him importunate; When to save mine honor,
Love having ful possession of my powers,
I got a Contract from him.
Theodosia.   Sealed?
Leocadia.   And sworn too;
Which since for some offence heaven laid upon me
I lost among my moneys in the robbery,   90
The losse that makes me poorest: this won from him,
Fool that I was, and too too credulous,
I pointed him a by-way to my chamber
The next night at an hour.
Theodosia.   Pray stay there Lady;
And when the night came, came he, kept he touch with ye?
Be not so shamefast; had ye both your wishes?
Tell me, and tell me true, did he injoy ye,
Were ye in one anothers arms, abed? the Contract
Confirm'd in ful joys there? did he lie with ye?
Answer to that; ha? did your father know this,   100
The good old man, or kindred privy to't?
And had ye their consents? did that nights promise
Make ye a Mother?
Leocadia.   Why do you ask so neerly?
Good Sir, do's it concern you any thing?
Theodosia.   No Lady,
Only the pity why you should be used so
A litle stirs me, but did he keep his promise?
Leocadia.   No, no Signior,

624

Alas he never came nor never meant it;
My love was fool'd, time numbred to no end,   110
My expectation flouted, and ghesse you Sir,
What dor unto a doating Maid this was,
What a base breaking off.
Theodosia.   All's wel then Lady;
Go forward in your Story.
Leocadia.   Not only fail'd Sir,
Which is a curse in love, and may he find it
When his affections are full wing'd, and ready
To stoop upon the quarry, then when all
His full hopes are in's arms: not only thus Sir,
But more injurious, faithless, treacherous,
Within two dayes fame gave him far remov'd   120
With a new love, which much against my conscience
But more against my cause, which is my hell,
I must confess a fair one, a right fair one,
Indeed of admirable sweetness, Daughter
Unto another of our noble neighbors,
The theef cal'd *Theodosia*; whose perfections
I am bound to ban for ever, curse to wrinckles,
As heaven I hope wil make 'em soon; and aches,
For they have rob'd me poor unhappy wench
Of all, of all Sir, all that was my glory,   130
And left me nothing but these tears, and travel:
Upon this certain news, I quit my Father,
And if you be not milder in construction,
I fear mine honor too; and like a Page
Stole to *Ossuna*: from that place to *Civill*,
From thence to *Barcellona* I was travelling
When you o'er-took my misery, in hope to hear of
Gallies bound up for *Italy*; for never
Wil I leave off the search of this bad man,
This filcher of affections, this love Pedler,   140
Nor shal my curses cease to blast her beauties
And make her name as wandring as her nature

*129 wench] *stet* F 1–2   131 travel] *i.e.* travaile

Till standing face to face before their lusts
I cal heavens justice down.
Theodosia.   This showes too angry,
Nor can it be her fault she is belov'd,
If I give meat, must they that eat it surfeit?
Leocadia.   She loves again sir, there's the mischief of it,
And in despight of me, to drown my blessings,
Which she shal dearly know.
Theodosia.   Ye are too violent.
Leocadia.   She has Devils in her eys, to whose devotion   150
He offers all his service.
Theodosia.   Who can say
But she may be forsaken too? he that once wanders
From such a perfect sweetness, as you promise,
Has he not still the same rule to deceive?
Leocadia.   No, no they are together, love together,
Past all deceit of that side; sleep together,
Live, and delight together, and such deceit
Give me in a wild desert.
Theodosia.   By your leave Lady,
I see no honor in this cunning.
Leocadia.   Honor?
True, none of her part, honor, shee deserves none,   160
'Tis ceas'd with wandring Ladies such as she is,
So bold and impudent.
Theodosia.   I could be angry,
Extreamly angry now beyond my nature,
And 'twere not for my pity: what a man
Is this to do these wrongs: beleeve me Lady,
I know the maid, and know she is not with him.
Leocadia.   I would you knew she were in heaven.
Theodosia.   And so well know her that I think you are cozend.
Leocadia.   So I say Sir.
Theodosia.   I mean in her behaviour,
For trust my faith, so much I dare adventure for her credit,   170
She never yet delighted to do wrong.

149 she] F 2; ye F 1

Leocadia.   How can she then delight in him; dare she think,
Be what she will, as excellent as Angels,
My love so fond, my wishes so indulgent,
That I must take her prewnings; stoop at that
She has tyr'd upon: No Sir, I hold my beauty,
Wash but these sorrows from it, of a sparkle
As right and rich as hers, my means as equall,
My youth as much unblown; and for our worths
And waight of vertue——

Theodosia.   Do not task her so far.   180

Leocadia.   By heaven she is cork, and clouds, light, light sir, vapor;
But I shal find her out, with all her witchcrafts,
Her paintings, and her powncings: for 'tis art
And only art preserves her, and meer spels
That work upon his powers; let her but shew me
A ruin'd cheek like mine, that holds his colour
And writes but sixteen years in spight of sorrows,
An unbathed body, smiles, that give but shadows
And wrinckle not the face; besides she is little,
A demy dame that, that makes no object.

Theodosia.   Nay,   190
Then I must say you err; for credit me
I think she is taller then your self.

Leocadia.   Why let her.
It is not that shal mate me; I but ask
My hands may reach unto her.

Theodosia.   Gentle Lady,
'Tis now ill time of further argument,
For I perceive your anger voyd of councel,
Which I could wish more temperate.

Leocadia.   Pray forgive me
If I have spoke uncivilly: they that look on
See more then we that play: and I beseech ye,
Impute it loves offence, not mine; whose torments,   200
If you have ever lov'd, and found my crosses,
You must confesse are seldom ty'd to patience;
Yet I could wish I had said lesse.

Theodosia.   No harm then;
Ye have made a ful amends; our Company
You may command, so please you in your travels,
With all our faith and furtherance; let it be so.
Leocadia.   Ye make too great an offer.
Theodosia.   Then it shal be.
Go in and rest your self, our wholsom dyet
Will be made ready straight: But heark ye Lady,
One thing I must entreat, your leave, and sufferance   210
That these things may be open to my Brother
For more respect and honor.
Leocadia.   Do your pleasure.
Theodosia.   And do not change this habit by no means
Unless ye change your self.
Leocadia.   Which must not yet be.
Theodosia.   It carries ye concealed and safe.
Leocadia.   I am counsel'd. *Exit.*

Enter Philippo.

Philippo.   What's done?
Theodosia.   Why all we doubted; 'tis a woman,
And of a noble strain too, ghesse.
Philippo.   I cannot.
Theodosia.   You have heard often of her.
Philippo.   Stay, I think not.
Theodosia.   Indeed ye have; 'tis the fair *Leocadia*,
Daughter unto Don *Sanchio*, our noble neighbor.   220
Philippo.   Nay?
Theodosia.   'Tis she Sir, o' my credit.
Philippo.   *Leocadia*,
Pish *Leocadia*, it must not be.
Theodosia.   It must be, or be nothing.
Philippo.   Pray give me leave to wonder, *Leocadia?*
Theodosia.   The very same.
Philippo.   The damsel *Leocadia.*
I ghest it was a woman, and a fair one.
I see it through her shape, transparant plain,

But that it should be she; tell me directly.

Theodosia.　　By heavens 'tis shee.

Philippo.　　　　　　　　By heaven then 'tis a sweet one.

Theodosia.　　That's granted too.

Philippo.　　　　　　　　But heark ye, heark ye Sister,　　230
How came she thus disguis'd?

Theodosia.　　　　　　　　Ile tell you that too;
As I came on the self-same ground, so us'd too.

Philippo.　　By the same man?

Theodosia.　　　　　　　　The same too.

Philippo.　　　　　　　　　　As I live
You lovers have fine fancies, wonderous fine ones.

Theodosia.　　Pray heaven you never make one.

Philippo.　　　　　　　　　　Faith I know not,
But in that mind I am, I had rather cobble,
'Tis a more Christian trade; pray tell me one thing:
Are not you two now monstrous jealous
Of one another?

Theodosia.　　　　She is much of me,
And has rayl'd at me most unmercifully　　　　　　240
And to my face, and o' my conscience,
Had she but known me, either she or I
Or both had parted with strange faces,
She was in such a fury.

Philippo.　　　　　*Leocadia?*
Do's she speak hansomly?

Theodosia.　　　　　　Wondrous wel Sir,
And all she do's becomes her, even her anger.

Philippo.　　How seem'd she when you found her?

Theodosia.　　　　　　　　　　Had you seen
How sweetly fearfull her pretty self
Betray'd her self, how neat her sorrow show'd,
And in what hansom phrase shee put her story,　　250
And as occasion stir'd her how she started,
Though roughly, yet most aptly into anger
You would have wonder'd.

Philippo.　　　　　　Do's she know ye?

629

Theodosia.   No,
Nor must not by no means.
Philippo.   How stands your difference?
Theodosia.   Ile tell ye that some fitter time, but trust me,
My *Marck-antonio* has too much to answer.
Philippo.   May I take knowledge of her?
Theodosia.   Yes she is willing.
Philippo.   Pray use her as she is, with all respects then,
For she is a woman of a noble breeding.
Theodosia.   Ye shal not find me wanting.
Philippo.   Which way bears she?   260
Theodosia.   Our way, and to our end.
Philippo.   I am glad on't; heark ye,
She keeps her shape?
Theodosia.   Yes, and I think by this time
Has mew'd her old.

                    Enter Leocadia.

Philippo.   She is here: by heaven a rare one,
An admirable sweet one, what an eye
Of what a full command she bears, how gracious
All her aspect shows; bless me from a feavor,
I am not well o'th sodain.
Leocadia.   Noble friends,
Your meat and all my service waits upon ye.
Philippo.   Ye teach us manners Lady; all which service
Must now be mine to you, and all too poor too;   270
Blush not, we know ye; for by all our faiths,
With us your honor is in sanctuary
And ever shal be.
Leocadia.   I do well beleeve it,
Will ye walk neerer Sir.   *Exeunt* Philippo *and* Leocadia.
Theodosia.   She shows still fairer,
Yonger in every change, and clearer, neater;
I know not, I may fool my self, and finely
Nourish a wolfe to eat my heart out; Certain
As she appears now, she appears a wonder,

A thing amazes me; what would she do then
In womans helps, in ornaments apt for her   280
And deckings to her delicacy? without all doubt
She would be held a miracle; nor can I think
He has forsaken her: Say what shee please,
I know his curious eye; or say he had,
Put case he could be so boy-blind and foolish,
Yet stil I fear she keeps the Contract with her,
Not stolne as she affirms, nor lost by negligence;
She would loose her self first, 'tis her life, and there
All my hopes are dispatch'd; O noble love,
That thou couldst be without this jealousie,   290
Without this passion of the heart, how heavenly
Would thou appear upon us? Come what may come
Ile see the end on't: and since chance has cast her
Naked into my refuge, all I can
She freely shal command, except the man.

                                                   Exit.

                Enter Leonardo, *and* Don Pedro.   III. iii

Leonardo.   Don *Pedro*, do you think assuredly
   The Gallyes will come round to *Barcellona*
   Within these two dayes?
Pedro.   Without doubt.
Leonardo.   And think ye
   He will be with 'em certainly?
Pedro.   '   He is sir;
   I saw him at their setting off.
Leonardo.   Must they needs
   Touch there for water as you say?
Pedro.   They must sir,
   And for fresh meat too: few or none go by it;
   Beside so great a Fleet must needs want trimming
   If they have met with fowle seas, and no harbour
   On this side *Spain* is able without danger   10

                III.iii] Scæna Tertia.

To moore 'em, but that haven.
Leonardo.   Are the warrs
His only end?
Pedro.   So he professes.
Leonardo.   Bears he
Any command amongst 'em?
Pedro.   Good regard
With all, which quickly will prefer him.
Leonardo.   Pray Sir tell me,
And as you are a gentleman be liberal.
Pedro.   I will Sir, and most true.
Leonardo.   Who saw ye with him?
Pedro.   None but things like himself; yong soldiers
And gentlemen desirous to seek honor.
Leonardo.   Was there no woman there, nor none disguis'd   20
That might be thought a woman? in his language
Did he not let slip something of suspition
Touching that wanton way?
Pedro.   Beleeve me Sir,
I neither saw, nor could suspect that face
That might be doubted womans, yet I am sure
Aboard him I see all that past, and 'tis impossible
Among so many high set bloods there should be
A woman, let her close her self within a cockle,
But they would open her; he must not love
Within that place alone, and therefore surely   30
He would not be so foolish, had he any,
To trust her there; for his discourse, 'twas ever
About his business, war, or mirth to make us
Relish a Can of wine wel; when he spoke private
'Twas only the remembrance of his service,
And hope of your good prayers for his health Sir,
And so I gave him to the seas.
Leonardo.   I thank ye,
And now am satisfied, and to prevent
Suspitions that may nourish dangers Signior,

21 woman? in his language$_\wedge$] Sympson; woman $_\wedge$ in his language? F 1–2

(For I have told you how the mad *Alphonso*   40
Chafes like a Stag i'th toyl, and bends his fury
'Gainst all, but his own ignorance;) I am determin'd
For peace sake and the preservation
Of my yet untouch'd honor, and his cure,
My self to seek him there, and bring him back
As testimony of an unsought injurie
By either of our actions; That the world,
And he if he have reason, may see plainly
Opinion is no perfect guide; nor all fames
Founders of truths: In the mean time this courtesie   50
I must entreat of you Sir, Be my self here
And as my self command my family.
Pedro.   Ye lay too much trust on me.
Leonardo.   'Tis my love Sir,
I wil not be long from ye; if this question
Chance to be call'd upon ere my return,
I leave your care to answer; So farewell Sir.
Pedro.   Ye take a wise way; All my best endeavors
Shal labor in your absence; peace go with ye.   *Exit* Leonardo.
A noble honest gentleman, free hearted
And of an open faith, much loving, and much loved,   60
And father of that goodnesse only malice
Can truly stir against; what dare befall
Till his return Ile answer.

                                Exit Pedro.

Enter Alphonso, *and* Servant.   [III. iv]

Alphonso.   Walk off Sirha,
But keep your self within my call.
Servant.   I will Sir.
Alphonso.   And stir my horse for taking cold: within there,
Hoa people; you that dwel there, my brave Signior,
What are ye all a sleep? is't that time with ye?
Ile ring a little lowder.

                III.iv] *no scene division* F 1–2

Enter Pedro.

Pedro.   Sir who seek ye?
Alphonso.   Not you Sir; Where's your Master?
Pedro.   I serve no man
In way of pay sir.
Alphonso.   Where's the man o'th house then?
Pedro.   What would you have with him Sir?
Alphonso.   Do you stand here Sir,
To ask men questions when they come?
Pedro.   I would sir,   10
Being his friend, and hearing such allarums,
Know how men come to visit him.
Alphonso.   Ye shall sir,
Pray tell his mightiness here is a gentleman
By name *Alphonso*, would entreat his conference
About affairs of state sir, are ye answer'd?

Enter Sanchio *carried [by servants].*

Pedro.   I must be sir.
Sanchio.   Stay, set me down, stay Signior,
You must stay, and ye shall stay.
Alphonso.   Meaning me sir?
Sanchio.   Yes you Sir, you I mean, I mean you.
Alphonso.   Well Sir,
Why should I stay?
Sanchio.   There's reason.
Alphonso.   Reason Sir?
Sanchio.   I, reason sir,   20
My wrong is greatest, and I will be serv'd first.
Call out the man of fame!
Alphonso.   How serv'd sir?
Sanchio.   Thus sir.
Alphonso.   But not before me.
Sanchio.   Before all the world sir,

20 I,] Colman (Ay,); ~ ₐ F 1–2

As my case stands.

Alphonso.   I have lost a daughter sir.

Sanchio.   I have lost another worth five score of her sir.

Alphonso.   Ye must not tel me so.

Sanchio.   I have, and heark ye?

Make it up five score more: Call out the fellow,

And stand you by sir.

Pedro.   This is the mad morrisse.

Alphonso.   And I stand by?

Sanchio.   I say stand by, and do it.

Alphonso.   Stand by among thy lungs.

Sanchio.   Turn presently   30

And say thy prayers, thou art dead.

Alphonso.   I scorn thee

And scorn to say my prayers more then thou do'st,

Mine is the most wrong, and my daughter deerest,

And mine shal first be righted.

Sanchio.   Shal be righted?

Pedro.   A third may live I see, pray hear me gentlemen.

Sanchio.   Shalbe?

Alphonso.   I, shal be righted.

Sanchio.   Now?

Alphonso.   Now.

Sanchio.   Instantly?

Alphonso.   Before I stir.

Sanchio.   Before me?

Alphonso.   Before any.

Sanchio.   Dost thou

Consider what thou sayst? hast thou friends here

Able to quench my anger, or perswade me   40

After I have beaten thee into one main bruise

And made thee spend thy state in rotten apples,

Thou canst at length be quiet? shal I kil thee,

Divide thee like a rotten Pumpion,

And leave thee stincking to posterity?

Ther's not the least blow I shall give, but do's this.

*41 bruise] Colman; bruist F 1–2

635

Urge me no further: I am first.

Alphonso.   Ile hang first.
No goodman glory, 'tis not your bravado's,
Your punctuall honor, nor soldadoship——
Sanchio.   Set me a little neerer.
Pedro.   Let him sally.   50
Alphonso.   Lin'd with your quircks of carriage and discretion,
Can blow me off my purpose. Wher's your credit
With all your school points now? your decent arguing
And apt time for performing: where are these toys,
These wise ways, and most honourable courses,
To take revenge? how dar'st thou talk of killing,
Or think of drawing any thing but squirts
When letchery has dry founderd thee?
Sanchio.   Neerer yet,
That I may spit him down: thou look'st like a man.
Pedro.   I would be thought so Sir.
Sanchio.   Prethee do but take me,   60
And fling me upon that Puppy.
Alphonso.   Do for heavens sake,
And see but how ile hug him.
Sanchio.   Yet take warning.
Pedro.   Faith gentlemen, this is a needlesse quarrell.
Sanchio.   And do you desire to make one?
Pedro.   As a friend Sir,
To tell you all this anger is but lost Sir,
For *Leonardo* is from home.
Alphonso.   No, no Sir.
Pedro.   Indeed he is.
Sanchio.   Where dare he be, but here Sir,
When men are wrong'd, and come for satisfactions.
Pedro.   It seems he has done none Sir; for his businesse
Cleer of those cares, hath carried him for sometime   70
To *Barcelona*; if he had been guilty,
I know he would have staid, and cleer'd all difference
Either by free confession, or his sword.

*50–51 Pedro. Let him sally. | Alphonso. Lin'd] Alph. Let him sally. | S. Lin'd F 1–2

Sanchio.   This must not be.

Pedro.   Sure, as I live, it is Sir.

Alphonso.   Sure, as we all live,
He's run away for ever: *Barcelona*,
Why? 'tis the key for *Italy*, from whence
He stole first hither.

Sanchio.   And having found his knaveries
Too grosse to be forgiven, and too open,
He has found the same way back again: I beleeve too   80
The good grasse gentleman, for his own ease,
Has taken one oth' Fillyes: Is not his stuffe sold.

Alphonso.   I fear his worships shoos too, to escape us;
I do not think he has a dish within dores,
A louse left of his linnage——

Pedro.   Ye are too wide Sir.

Alphonso.   Or one poor wooden spoon.

Pedro.   Come in and see Sir.

Alphonso.   Ile see his house on fire first.

Pedro.   Then be pleas'd Sir
To give better censure.

Sanchio.   I will after him,
And search him like conceal'd land; but ile have him,
And though I find him in his shrift, ile kill him.   90

Alphonso.   Ile bear ye company.

Sanchio.   Pray have a care then,
A most especiall care, indeed a fear,
Ye do not anger me.

Alphonso.   I will observe ye,
And if I light upon him hansomly.

Sanchio.   Kill but a peece of him, leave some, *Alphonso*,
For your poor friends.

Pedro.   I fear him not for all this.

Alphonso.   Shall we first go home,
For it may prove a voyage, and dispose
Of things there; heaven knows what may follow.

Sanchio.   No,

*90 shrift] *stet* F 1–2

637

Ile kill him in this shirt I have on: let things   100
Govern themselves, I am master of my honor
At this time, and no more; let wife, and land,
Lie lay till I return.
Alphonso.   I say amen to't:
But what care for our monies?
Sanchio.   I will not spend
Above three shillings, till his head be here;
Foure is too great a sum for all his fortunes.
Come take me up instantly.
Alphonso.   Farewell to you Sir,
And if your friend be in a featherbed,
Sow'd up to shroud his fears, tell him 'tis folly,
For no course but his voluntary hanging   110
Can get our pardons.   *Exeunt* [Alphonso *and* Sanchio].
Pedro.   These I think would be
Offence enough, if their own indiscretions
Would suffer 'em: two of the old seditious,
When they want enemies, they are their own foes:
Were they a little wiser, I should doubt 'em:
Till when ile ne'r break sleep, nor suffer hunger
For any harm he shall receive: For 'tis as easie
If he be guilty, to turn these two old men
Upon their own throats, and look on, and live still,
As 'tis to tell five pound: a great deal sooner,   120
And so ile to my meat, and then to hawking.

Exit.

Enter Markantonio, *and a* Gentleman.   IV. i

Mark-antonio. Sir, this is complement; I pray you leave me.
Gentleman. Sir, it is not.
Mark-antonio.   Why? I would only see
The Town.
Gentleman. And only that I come to shew you.

*113 seditious] F 2; seditions F 1
IV.i] Act. IV. Scæna I.   2 it is] F 2; is it F 1

638

Mark-antonio.　Which I can see without you.

Gentleman.　　　　　　　　　　　　　So you may

Plainly, not safely: For such difference
As you have seen betwixt the sea and earth
When waves rise high, and land would beat 'em back
As fearfull of Invasion, such we find
When we land here at *Barcelona.*

Mark-antonio.　　　　　　　Sir——

Gentleman.　Besides our Generall of the Gallyes, fearing　　　10
Your hasty nature, charg'd me not return
Without you safe.

Mark-antonio.　　　O Sir, that *Rodorigo*
Is noble, and he do's mistake my temper.
There is not in the world, a mind lesse apt
To conceive wrongs, or do 'em; ha's he seen me
In all this voyage, in the which he pleases
To call me friend, let slip a hasty word?

Enter Eugenia, *with divers Attendents.*

'S'light Sir: yonder is a Lady vaild,
For propernesse, beyond comparison,
And sure her face is like the rest: we'l see't.　　　　　20

Gentleman.　Why? you are hasty Sir already: know you
What 'tis you go about?

Mark-antonio.　　　　Yes, I would see
The womans face.

Gentleman.　　　By heaven you shall not do't:
You do not know the custome of the place:
To draw that curtain here, though she were mean,
Is mortall.

Mark-antonio.　Is it? earth must come to earth
At last, and by my troth, ile try it Sir.

Gentleman.　Then I must hold you fast. By all the faith
That can be plac'd in man, 'tis an attempt
More dangerous then death: 'tis death and shame:　　　30

*24 place:] F 2; place: *Ioh. Bacon ready to shoot off a Pistol.* F 1

I know the Lady well.

Mark-antonio.   Is she a Lady?
I shall the more desire to see her Sir.

Gentleman.   She is *Alanso's* wife, the Governor,
A noble gentleman.

Mark-antonio.   Then let me go;
If I can win her, you and I will govern
This Town Sir, fear it not, and we will alter
These barbarous customes then; for every Lady
Shall be seen daily, and seen over too.

Gentleman.   Come, do not jest, nor let your passions bear you
To such wild enterprises: hold you still,   40
For as I have a soul, you shall not do't.
She is a Lady of unblemish'd fame,
And here to offer that affront, were base:
Hold on your way, and we will see the Town,
And overlook the Ladyes.

Mark-antonio.   I am school'd,
And promise you I will: But good Sir, see,
She will passe by us now; I hope I may
Salute her thus far off.

Gentleman.   'Sfoot, are you mad?
'Twill be as ill as th'other.

1. Attendant.   What's the matter?
What would that fellow have?

Gentleman.   Good Sir forbear.   50

1. Attendant.   It seems you are new landed: would you beg
Any thing here?

Mark-antonio.   Yes Sir, all happinesse
To that fair Lady, as I hope.

Gentleman.   *Marckantonio.*

Mark-antonio.   Her face, which needs no hiding, I would beg
A sight of.

Gentleman.   Now go on, for 'tis too late
To keep this from a tumult.

1. Attendant.   Sirrah, you

*42 She...fame,] F2; *Rod.* She...fame, *above.* F1

Shall see a fitter object for your eyes,
Then a fair Ladies face.
Eugenia.   For heavens sake, raise not
A quarrell in the streets for me.
1. Attendant.   Slip in then;   60
This is your door.
Eugenia.   Will you needs quarrell then?
1. Attendant.   We must, or suffer
This outrage: is't not all your minds sirs, speak?
All.   Yes.
Eugenia.   Then I do beseech ye, let my Lord
Not think the quarrell about mee; for 'tis not.   *Exit.*

Enter three or four Soldiers.

Gentleman.   See, happily some of our Galley Soldiers
Are come ashore.
1. Attendant.   Come on Sir, you shall see
Faces enough.

Enter certain Townsmen.

Gentleman.   Some one of you call to
Our Generall; the whole rore of the Town
Comes in upon us.
Mark-antonio.   I have seen, Sir, better   70
Perhaps, then that was cover'd; and will yet
See that, or spoil yours.   *Fight.*

Enter Philippo, Theodosia, *and* Leocadia.

Philippo.   On: why start you back?
Theodosia.   Alas Sir, they are fighting.
Leocadia.   Let's begon,
See, see, a hansome man strook down.
Gentleman.   Ho Generall,
Look out, *Antonio* is in distresse.

Enter Rodorigo *above.*

Theodosia. *Antonio?*
Leocadia.   *Antonio*! 'tis he.
Rodorigo [*to*] *within.* Ho, Gunner make a shot into the Town,
Ile part you: bring away *Antonio*   *A shot.*
Into my Cabben.   *Exit Attendents and Townsmen.*
Gentleman.   I will do that office.
I fear it is the last, that I shall do him.   80
                    Exit Soldiers and Gentleman *with* Marckantonio.
Theodosia. The last, why will he die?   [*Faints.*]
Leocadia. Since I have found him: happinesse leave me,
When I leave him.   *Exit.*
Philippo.   Why *Theodosia?*
My Sister; wake: alas, I griev'd but now
To see the streets so full; and now I grieve
To see 'em left so empty: I could wish,
Tumult himself were here, that yet at least
Amongst the band, I might espie some face
So pale and fearfull, that would willingly
Embrace an arrand for a Cordiall,   90
Or Aquavitæ, or a cup of sack,
Or a Phisitian: But to talk of these——
She breaths: stand up, O *Theodosia,*
Speak but as thou wert wont, give but a sigh,
Which is but the most unhappy peece of life,
And I will ever after worship Sadnes,
Apply my self to grief; prepare and build
Altars to sorrow.
Theodosia.   O *Philippo,* help me.
Philippo. I do; these are my arms; *Philippo's* arms,
Thy Brothers arms that hold thee up.
Theodosia.   You help me   100
To life: but I would see *Antonio*
That's dead.
Philippo.   Thou shalt see any thing; how dost thou?

77 Gunner] F2; Governor F1

642

Theodosia.   Better, I thank you.
Philippo.   Why that's well: call up
  Thy sences, and uncloud thy cover'd spirits.
  How now?
Theodosia.   Recover'd: but *Antonio*,
  Where is he?
Philippo.   We will find him: art thou well?
Theodosia.   Perfectly well, saving the misse of him;
  And I do charge you here, by our allyance,
  And by the love which would have been betwixt us,
  Knew we no kindred; by that killing fear,   110
  Mingled with twenty thousand hopes and doubts,
  Which you may think, plac'd in a Lovers heart,
  And in a Virgins too, when she wants help,
  To grant me your assistance, to find out
  This man alive, or dead, and I will pay you
  In service, tears, or prayers, a world of wealth:
  But other treasure, I have none: alas!
  You men have strong hearts; but we feeble maids
  Have tender eyes, which only given be
  To blind themselves, crying for what they see.   120
Philippo.   Why do'st thou charge me thus? have I been found
  Slow to perform, what I could but imagine
  Thy wishes were? have I at any time
  Tender'd a businesse of mine own, beyond
  A vanity of thine? have I not been
  As if I were a senslesse creature, made
  To serve thee without pow'r of questioning?
  If so, why fear'st thou?
Theodosia.   I am satisfied.
Philippo.   Come, then let's go: wher's *Leocadia?*
Theodosia.   I know not Sir.
Philippo.   Wher's *Leocadia?*   130
Theodosia.   I do not know.
Philippo.   *Leocadia*,
  This Tumult made the streets as dead as night,
  A man may talk as freely: what's become

Of *Leocadia?*

Theodosia.   She's run away.

Philippo.   Begone, and let us never more behold
Each others face, till we may both together
Fasten our eyes on her: accursed be
Those tender cozening names of charity,
And naturall affection; they have lost
Me only by observing them, what cost,   140
Travell, and fruitlesse wishes may in vain
Search through the world, but never find again.

Theodosia.   Good Sir be patient, I have done no fault
Worthy this banishment.

Philippo.   Yes, *Leocadia*,
The Lady so distress'd, who was content
To lay her story, and to lay her heart
As open as her story to your self,
Who was content, that I should know her Sex,
Before dissembl'd, and to put her self
Into my conduct, whom I undertook   150
Safely to guard, is in this Tumult lost.

Theodosia.   And can I help it Sir?

Philippo.   No, would thou couldst;
You might have done, but for that seal'd religion
You women bear to swownings; you do pick
Your times to faint, when some body is by
Bound or by nature, or by love, or service
To raise you from that well dissembled death:
Inform me but of one that has been found
Dead in her private chamber by her self,
Where sicknesse would no more forbear, then here,   160
And I will quit the rest for her.

Theodosia.   I know not
What they may do, and how they may dissemble;
But by my troth, I did not.

Philippo.   By my troth,

150 whom] F2; when F1
*153 seal'd] zeald F2; scale F1   154 women] F2; woman F1

Would I had try'd; would I had let thee layen,
And followed her.
Theodosia.　　　　　I would you had done so,
Rather then been so angry: wher's *Antonio?*
Philippo.　Why do'st thou vex me with these questions?
Ile tell thee where, he's carried to the Gallyes,
There to be chain'd, and row, and beat, and row,
With knotted ropes, and pizzels; if he swound,　　　170
He has a dosis of bisket.
Theodosia.　　　　　I am glad
He is alive.
Philippo.　Was ever man thus troubled?
Tell me where *Leocadia* is.
Theodosia.　　　　　Good brother
Be not so hasty, and I think I can:
You found no error in me, when I first
Told you she was a woman, and beleeve me,
Something I have found out, which makes me think,
Nay, almost know so well, that I durst swear
She follow'd hurt *Antonio.*
Philippo.　　　　　What do we
Then lingring here; we will aboard the Gallyes　　　180
And find her.

　　　Enter the Governor, *two Attendents, and the Townsmen.*

Governor.　Made he a shot into the Town?
1. Attendant.　　　　　He did Sir.
Governor.　Call back those Gentlemen.
1. Attendant.　The Governour, commands you back.
Philippo.　We will obey him Sir.
Governor.　You gave him cause to shoot, I know; he is
So far from rash offence, and holds with me
Such curious friendship: could not one of you
Have call'd me while 'twas doing, such an uproar,
Before my dore too?　　　190
1. Townsman.　By my troth Sir, we were so busy in the publick

cause, of our own private falling out, that we forgot it; at home
we see now you were not, but as soon as the shot made us fly,
we ran away as fast as we could to seek your honour.

Governor.   'Twas gravely done; but no man tels the cause
Or chance, or what it was that made you differ.

1. Townsman.   For my part Sir, if there were any that I knew of,
the shot drove it out of my head: do you know any neighbours?

All.   Not we, not we.

Governor.   Not we! nor can you tell?

1. Attendant.   No other cause,   200
But the old quarrell betwixt the Town and the Gallyes.

Governor.   Come neerer Gentlemen: what are your names?

Philippo.   My name *Philippo.*

Theodosia.   And mine *Theodoro.*

Governor.   Strangers you are it seems.

Philippo.   Newly ariv'd.

Governor.   Then you are they begun this Tumult.

Philippo.   No Sir.

Governor.   Speak one of you.

1. Attendant.   They are not, I can quit 'em.

Theodosia.   Yet we saw part, and an unhappy part
Of this debate, a long sought friend of ours
Strook down for dead, and borne unto the Gallyes,
His name is *Markantonio.*

Philippo.   And another   210
Of our own company, a Gentleman
Of noble birth, besides accompanied
With all the gifts of nature, ravish'd hence,
We know not how, in this dissention.

Governor.   Get you home all, and work; and when I hear
You meddle with a weapon any more
But those belonging to your Trades, ile lay you
Where your best Customers shall hardly find you.

                                   Exeunt Townsmen.

I am sorry gentlemen, I troubled you,
Being both strangers; by your tongues, and looks,   220

206 quit] F2; quiet F1

Of worth: To make ye some part of amends
If there be any thing in this poor Town
Of *Barcelona* that you would command,
Command me.
Theodosia.   Sir, this wounded Gentleman,
If it might please you, if your pow'r and love
Extend so far, I would be glad to wish
Might be remov'd into the Town for cure:
The Gallyes stay not, and his wound I know
Cannot endure a voyage.
Governor.   Sir, he shall,
I warrant you: Go call me hither Sirrah,   230
One of my other Servants.   *Exit* 1. Attendant.
Philippo.   And besides
The gentleman we lost, Signior *Francisco*,
Shall he be render'd too?

                    Enter a Servant.

Governor.   And he Sir too: Go sirrah, bear this ring
To *Rodorigo*, my most noble friend,
The Generall of the Gallys: Tell him this.
                    Whispers to his servant. *Exit servant.*
Theodosia.   Now we shall have 'em both.
Philippo.   Blest be thy thoughts
For apprehending this: blest be thy breath
For utring it.
Governor.   Come gentlemen, you shall
Enter my roof: and I will send for Surgeons,   240
And you shall see your friends here presently.
Theodosia.   His name was *Markantonio*.
Governor.   I know it,
And have sent word so.
Philippo.   Did you not forget
Francisco's name?
Governor.   Nor his: you'ar truly welcome:

                *233.1 *Servant.*] F 2; *Servant, Rowl: Ashton.* F 1
                236.1 *Whispers*...servant.] F 2; *om.* F 1

To talk about it more, were but to say
The same word often over: you are welcome.

Exeunt.

Enter Markantonio, *carried.* Leocadia *following,*   IV. ii
and the Servant. *Two* Soldiers *carrying him.*

Servant.   This is the house Sir.
Mark-antonio.   Enter it, I pray you,
For I am faint, although I think my wound
Be nothing. Soldiers, leave us now: I thank you.
1. Soldier.   Heaven send you health Sir.
Servant.   Let me lead you in.
Mark-antonio.   My wounds not in my feet; I shall entreat 'em,
I hope, to bear me so far.   *Exeunt.*
2. Soldier.   How seriously these land men fled, when our Generall
made a Shot, as if it had been a warning to cal 'em to their Hall.
1. Soldier.   I cannot blame 'em: What a man have they now in the
Town, able to maintain a Tumult, or uphold a matter out of 10
square if need be: O the quiet hurley burleys that I have seen in
this Town, when we have fought four howrs together, and not a
man amongst us so impertinent or modest to ask why? But now
the pillars that bare up this blessed Town in that regular debate,
and scambling, are dead, the more's the pity.
2. Soldier.   Old *Ignatio* lives still.
1. Soldier.   Yes, I know him: he will do pretily well at a mans
liver: but where is there a man now living in the Town that hath
a steady hand, and understands Anotomy well? if it come to a
particular matter of the lungs, or the spleen, why? alas *Ignatio* is 20
to seek; are there any such men left as I have known, that would
say they would hit you in this place? is there ever a good heartist,
or a member percer, or a small-gut man left in the Town, answer
me that.
2. Soldier.   Masse, I think there be not.
1. Soldier.   No, I warrant thee. Come, come, 'tis time we were at
the Gallys.

Exeunt.

IV.ii] Sꜱᴄᴀ̃ɴᴀ Sᴇᴄᴜɴᴅᴀ.   *8 it] he F 1–2

648

Enter Governour, Eugenia, Markantonio, Philippo,   [IV.iii]
           Theodosia, Leocadia, *Attendants.*

Governor.   Sir, you may know by what I said already,
You may command my house; but I must beg
Pardon to leave you; if the publique businesse
Forc'd me not from you, I my self should call it
Unmannerly: but good Sir, do you give it
A milder name: it shall not be an houre
Ere I return.
Mark-antonio.   Sir, I was nere so poor
In my own thoughts, as that I want a means
To requite this with——
Governor.   Sir, within this houre.   *Exit.*
Mark-antonio [*aside*].   This the Lady that I quarrell'd for: 10
O lust, if wounds cannot restrain thy power,
Let shame: nor do I feel my hurt at all,
Nor is it ought, only I was well beaten:
If I pursue it, all the civill world
That ever did imagine the content
Found in the band of man and wife unbroke,
The reverence due to housholds, or the blemish
That may be stuck upon posterity,
Will catch me, bind me, burn upon my forehead,
This is the wounded stranger, that receiv'd   20
For charity into a house, attempted——
I will not do it.
Eugenia.   Sir, how do you now?
That you walk off.
Mark-antonio.   Worse Madam, then I was;
But it will over.
Eugenia.   Sit, and rest a while.
Mark-antonio.   Where are the Surgeons?
Eugenia.   Sir, it is their manner,
When they have seen the wound, especially
The patient being of worth, to go consult,

Which they are now at in another room,
About the dressing.
Mark-antonio.   Madam, I do feel
My self not well.
Theodosia.   Alas!
Leocadia.   How do you Sir?   30
Eugenia.   Will you drink waters?
Mark-antonio.   No good Madam, 'tis not
So violent upon me; nor I think
Any thing dangerous: But yet there are
Some things that sit so heavy on my conscience
That will perplex my mind, and stop my cure,
So that unlesse I utter 'em a scratch
Here on my thumb will kill me.——Gentlemen,
I pray you leave the room, and come not in
Your selves, or any other till I have
Open'd my self to this most honour'd Lady.   40
Philippo.   We will not.
Theodosia [*aside*].   O blest! he will discover now
His love to me.
Leocadia [*aside*].   Now he will tell the Lady
Our Contract.   [*Exeunt.* Eugenia *and* Mark-Antonio *stay.*]
Eugenia [*aside*].   I do beleeve he will confesse to me
The wrong he did a Lady in the streets;
But I forgive him.
Mark-antonio.   Madam, I perceive
My self grow worse and worse.
Eugenia.   Shall I call back
Your friends?
Mark-antonio.   O no; but ere I do impart
What burthens me so sore, let me entreat you,
(For there is no trust in these Surgeons)
To look upon my wound; it is perhaps   50
My last request: But tell me truly too,
That must be in: how far you do imagine
It will have pow'r upon me.
Eugenia.   Sir, I will.

Mark-antonio.   For heavens sake, softly: oh, I must needs lay
  My head down easily, whilst you do it.
Eugenia.   Do Sir,
  'Tis but an ordinary blow; a child
  Of mine has had a greater, and been well;
  Are you faint hearted?
Mark-antonio.   Oh.
Eugenia.   Why do you sigh?
  There is no danger in the world in this;   60
  I wonder it should make a man sit down;
  What do you mean, why do you kisse my breasts?
  Lift up your head, your wound may well endure it.
Mark-antonio.   O Madam, may I not expresse affection,
  Dying-affection too I fear, to those
  That do me favors, such as this of yours.
Eugenia.   If you mean so, 'tis well; but what's the busines
  Lies on your conscience?
Mark-antonio.   I will tell you Madam.
Eugenia.   Tel me, and laugh?
Mark-antonio.   But I wil tel you true
  Though I do laugh, I know as well as you   70
  My wound is nothing, nor the power of earth
  Could lay a wound upon me, in your presence,
  That I could feel; But I do laugh to think
  How covertly, how far beyond the reach
  Of men, and wisemen too, we shal deceive 'em,
  Whilst they imagine I am talking here
  With that short breath I have, ready to swound
  At every full point; you my ghostly Mother
  To hear my sad confession, you and I
  Will on that bed within, prepar'd for me,   80
  Debate the matter privately.
Eugenia.   Forbear,
  Thou wert but now as welcome to this house
  As certain cures to sick men, and just now
  This sodain alteration makes thee look
  Like plagues come to infect it; if thou knewst

How loathsom thou wilt be, thou wouldst intreat
These walls, or postes to help thee to a hurt,
Past thy dissimulation.
Mark-antonio.   Gentle Madam
Cal 'em not in?
Eugenia.   I will not yet; this place
I know to be within the reach of tongue,   90
And ears; thou canst not force me; therefore hear me
What I will tell thee quickly: thou art born
To end some way more disesteem'd then this,
Or which is worse, to dye of this hurt yet.
Come gentlemen.

Enter Leocadia.

Mark-antonio.   Good Madam.
Eugenia.   Gentlemen.
Leocadia.   Madam how is't? is *Mark-antonio* well?
Methinks your looks are alter'd, and I see
A strange distemper in you.
Eugenia.   I am wrought
By that dissembling man, that fellow worth
Nothing but kicking.

Enter Philippo, *and* Theodosia.

Leocadia.   Gentle Madam speak   100
To me alone, let not them understand
His fault; he wil repent it I dare swear.
Eugenia.   Ile tell it you in private.   [*They whisper apart.*]
Philippo.   *Mark-antonio,*
How do you?
Mark-antonio.   Stand further off I pray you;
Give me some ayre.
Theodosia.   Good Brother, wil he scape?
The Surgeons say there is no danger.
Philippo.   Scape?
No doubt he wil.

89 yet] F 2; yee F 1

652

Leocadia [*aside*].   Alas wil he not leave
  This trying all?——Madam, I do beseech you,
  Let me but speak to him, you and these by,
  And I dare almost promise you to make him   110
  Shew himself truly sorrowful to you,
  Besides a story I shal open to you,
  Not put in so good words but in it self
  So full of chance, that you wil easily
  Forgive my tediousnesse, and be wel pleas'd
  With that so much afflicts me.
Eugenia.   Good Sir do.
Leocadia.   And I desire no interruption
  Of speech may trouble me, till I have said
  What I wil quickly do.
Theodosia.   What wil she say?
Eugenia.   Come gentlemen, I pray you lend your ears,   120
  And keep your voyces.
Leocadia.   Signior *Mark-antonio*,
  How do you?
Mark-antonio.   Oh the Surgeons——
Leocadia.   Let me tel you
  Who know as wel as you, you do dissemble;
  It is no time to do so; leave the thoughts
  Of this vain world, forget your flesh and blood,
  And make your spirit an untroubled way
  To passe to what it ought.
Mark-antonio.   You'r not in earnest?
  Why I can walk Sir, and am wel.
Leocadia.   'Tis true
  That you can walk, and do beleeve you'r wel:
  It is the nature, as your Surgeons say   130
  Of these wounds, for a man to go, and talk,
  Nay merrily, till his last hour, his minute:
  For heaven sake sir, sit down again.
Mark-antonio.   Alas,
  Where are the Surgeons?
Leocadia.   Sir, they will not come,

If they should dresse you, you would dye they say
Ere one told twenty; trouble not your mind,
Keep your head warm, and do not stir your body,
And you may live an hour.
Mark-antonio.   Oh heavens, an hour?
Alas, it is to little to remember
But half the wrongs that I have done; how short   140
Then for contrition, and how least of all
For satisfaction?
Leocadia.   But you desire
To satisfie?
Mark-antonio.   Heaven knows I do.
Leocadia.   Then know
That I am he, or she, or what you will
Most wrong'd by you, your *Leocadia*;
I know you must remember me——
Mark-antonio.   Oh heaven!
Leocadia.   That lost her friends, that lost her fathers house,
That lost her fame, in loosing of her Sex,
With these strange garments. There is no excuse
To hinder me; it is within your power   150
To give me satisfaction; you have time
Left in this little peece of life to do it:
Therefore I charge you for your conscience sake,
And for our fame, which I would fain have live
When both of us are dead, to celebrate
That Contract, which you have both seal'd and sworn,
Yet ere you dye, which must be hastily
Heaven knows.
Mark-antonio.   Alas, the sting of conscience
To death-ward for our faults; draw neerer all
And hear what I unhappy man shal say;   160
First Madam I desire your pardon; next
(I feel my spirits fail me) Gentlemen
Let me shake hands with you, and let's be friends,
For I have done wrong upon wrong so thick,

137 your body] F 2; you body F 1

654

I know not where, that every man methinks
Should be mine enemy; Forgive me both.
Lastly 'tis true (oh I do feel the power
Of death seize on me) that I was contracted
By seal and oath to *Leocadia*;
(I must speak fast, because I fear my life   170
Will else be shorter then my speech would be)
But 'tis impossible to satisfie
You *Leocadia*, but by repentance,
Though I can dyingly, and boldly say
I know not your dishonor, yet that was
Your vertue, and not mine, you know it wel;
But herein lies th' impossibility,
O *Theodosia*, *Theodosia*,
I was betroth'd to *Theodosia*
Before I ever saw thee; heaven forgive me,   180
She is my wife this half hour whilst I live.
Theodosia.   That's I, that's I, I'me *Theodosia*.
Hear me a litle now, who have not suffer'd
Disgrace at all methinks, since you confess
What I so long have sought for; here is with me
Philippo too, my Brother.
Mark-antonio.   I am glad;
All happiness to him; Come let me kiss thee,
Beg pardon of that Maid for my offence,
And let me further, with a dying breath
Tell in thine ear, the rest of my desires.   190
Eugenia.   I am afraid they wil all four turn women
If we hold longer talk.
Leocadia.   Alas there is
No hope for me; that's *Theodosia*
And that her Brother; I am only sorry
I was beholding to 'em; I will search
Over the world, as carelesse of my fortunes,
As they of me, till I can meet a curse
To make these almost-killing sorrows worse.   *Exit.*
Theodosia.   Sir, as I live she ly'd, only to draw

A just confession from you, which she hath,   200
A happy one for me; ask of this Lady,
Ask of my Brother.
Eugenia.   Sir, she did dissemble,
Your wound is nothing.
Philippo.   *Leocadia*'s gone.   *Exit.*
Theodosia.   Rise up, and stir your self, 'tis but amazement
And your imagination that afflicts you;
Look you Sir now.
Mark-antonio.   I think 'tis so indeed.
Theodosia.   The Surgeons do not come, because they swear
It needs no dressing.
Eugenia.   You shal talk with 'em
Within, for your own fancy.
Mark-antonio.   Where's your Brother
And *Leocadia?*
Eugenia.   Within Belike.   210
Mark-antonio.   I feel my self methinks as well as ever.
Eugenia.   Keep then your mind so too; I do forgive
The fault you did to me; But here is one
Must not be wrong'd hereafter.
Mark-antonio.   Neither shall shee.
When I make jests of oathes again, or make
My lust play with religion, when I leave
To keep true joyes for her, and yet within
My self true sorrow for my passed deeds,
May I want grace, when I would fain repent,
And find a great and sodain punishment.   220

                                        Exeunt.

                    Enter Philippo, Diego, *and* Incubo.   V. i

Philippo.   Where is mine Host, did not he see him neither?
Diego.   Not I, y'faith Sir.
Philippo.   Nor the muleter?
Incubo.   Nay he is past seeing, unlesse it be in's sleep,

By this time; all his visions were the pots,
Three hours since Sir.
Philippo.   Which way should she take?
Nay, look you now; do you all stand stil? good god,
You might have lighted on him, now, this instant?
For loves sake seek him out; who ever find him
I will reward his fortune as his diligence;
Get all the Town to help, that will be hir'd;   10
Their pains ile turn to an annall holiday,
If it shal chance, but one bring word of her.
Pray you about it.
Incubo.   Her sir? who do you mean?
Philippo.   (I had forgot my self) the Page I meant
That came along with us.
Diego.   He you give the clothes too?
Philippo.   I ga' the clothes to, Rascal.
Diego.   Nay good Sir.
Philippo.   Why do'st thou mention, or upbraid my courtesies,
Slave?
Diego.   For your honor Sir.
Philippo.   Wretch; I was honor'd,
That she would wear 'em (he, I would say) 'sdeath!   20
Go, get, and find him out, or never see me.——
[*Aside*] I shal betray my love ere I possess it,
Some star direct me, or ill planet strike me.   *Exit* Philippo.
Incubo.   Best to divide.
Diego.   Ile this way.
Incubo.   And I this.
Diego.   I, as you, find him for a real.
Incubo.   'Tis done.
Diego.   My course is now directly to some piehouse;
I know the Pages compasse.
Incubo.   I think rather
The smock side o' the Town, the surer harbor
At his years to put in.
Diego.   If I do find
The hungry haunt, I take him by the teeth now.   30

Incubo.   I by the tail, yet I as you.
Diego.   No more.

Exeunt.

Enter Philippo.   V. ii

Philippo.   Dear *Leocadia,* where canst thou be fled
Thus like a spirit hence? and in a moment?
What cloud can hide thee from my following search
If yet thou art a body? sure she hath not
Tane any house? she did too late leave one
Where all humanity of a place receiv'd her,
And would (if she had stayd) have help'd to right
The wrong her fortune did her; yet she must
Be inter'd somewhere, or be found; no street,
Lane, passage, corner, turn, hath scap'd enquiry: 10
If her dispair had ravish'd her to ayre,
Shee could not yet be rarefied so
But some of us should meet her! though their eyes
Perhaps be leaden, and might turn; mine would
Strike out a lightning for her, and divide
A mist as thick as ever darknesse was,
Nay see her through a quarry; they do lye,
Lye grosly that say love is blind; by him,
And heaven they lye; he has a sight can pierce
Through Ivory as clear as it were horn,   20
And reach his object.

Enter Incubo.

Incubo.   Sir hee's found, hee's found.
Philippo.   Ha? where? But reach that happy note again
And let it relish truth; thou art an Angel.   [*Gives money.*]
Incubo.   Hee's here; fast by sir, calling for a Boat
To go aboard the Gallies.
Philippo.   Where, where; hold thee.   *Exit.*
Incubo.   He might ha' kept this now, I had nought to shew for't

V.ii] SCÆNA SECUNDA.   9 inter'd] *i.e.* enter'd

658

If he had had the wit t'have gone from's word.
These direct men, they are no men of fashion,
Talk what you will, this is a very smelt.

Exit.

Enter Leonardo *with a* Surgeon.

Leonardo.   Upon your art Sir, and your faith to assist it,
Shal I beleeve you then his wounds not mortal?
Surgeon.   Sir 'tis not worth your question; lesse your fear.
Leonardo.   You do restore me Sir; I pray you accept
This smal remembrance of a fathers thanks
For so assur'd a benefit.
Surgeon.   Excuse me.
Leonardo.   Sir I can spare it, and must not beleeve
But that your fortune may receive't, except
You'ld ha' me think you live not by your practise.
Surgeon.   I crave your pardon Sir; you teach me manners.   10
Leonardo.   I crave your love and friendship, and require
As I have made now, both my self and businesse
A portion of your care, you wil but bring me,
Under the person of a call'd assistant,
To his next opening, where I may but see him,
And utter a few words to him in private,
And you will merit me; For I am loth,
Since here I have not to appear my self,
Or to be known unto the Governor,
Or make a tumult of my purpose.
Surgeon.   Neither   20
I hope wil be your need Sir; I shal bring you
Both there and off again without the hazard.

Exeunt.

V.iii] Scæna Tertia.

Enter Philippo, *and* Leocadia.   V. iv

Philippo.   Wil you not hear me!

Leocadia.   I have heard so much
Wil keep me deaf for ever; No, *Mark-antonie*,
After thy sentence, I may hear no more:
Thou hast pronounc'd me dead.

Philippo.   Appeal to reason,
She will reprieve you from the power of grief,
Which rules but in her absence; Hear me say
A soveraign message from her, which in duty,
And love to your own safety, you ought hear:
Why do you strive so? whither would you fly?
You cannot wrest your self away from care,   10
You may from councel; you may shift your place
But not your person; and another Clyme
Makes you no other.

Leocadia.   Oh.

Philippo.   For passions sake,
(Which I do serve, honor, and love in you)
If you will sigh, sigh here; If you would vary
A sigh to tears, or out-cry, do it here.
No shade, no desart, darknesse, nor the grave
Shal be no more equal to your thoughts then I;
Only but hear me speak.

Leocadia.   What would you say?

Philippo.   That which shall raise your heart, or pul down mine,   20
Quiet your passion, or provoke mine own;
We must have both one balsame, or one wound,
For know (lov'd fair) since the first providence
Made me your rescew, I have read you through,
And with a wondring pity, look'd on you;
I have observ'd the method of your blood,
And waited on it even with sympathy
Of a like red, and palenesse in mine own;
I knew which blush was angers, which was loves,

V.iv] Scæna Quarta.

660

Which was the eye of sorrow, which of truth;   30
And could distinguish honor from disdain
In every change; And you are worth my study:
I saw your voluntary misery
Sustain'd in travel: A disguised Maid
Wearied with seeking, and with finding lost;
Neglected, where you hop'd most, or put by;
I saw it, and have laid it to my heart,
And though it were my Sister, which was righted,
Yet being by your wrong, I put off nature,
Could not be glad, where I was bound to triumph,   40
My care for you, so drown'd respect of her,
Nor did I only apprehend your bonds,
But studyed your release: and for that day
Have I made up a ransom, brought you health,
Preservative 'gainst chance, or injury,
Please you apply it to the grief, my self.
Leocadia.   Humh.
Philippo.   Nay do not think me lesse then such a cure;
Antonio was not; And 'tis possible
Philippo may succeed: My blood and house   50
Are as deep rooted, and as fairly spread,
As *Mark-antonio's*, and in that all seek,
Fortune hath given him no precedency:
As for our thanks to Nature I may burn
Incense as much as he; I ever durst
Walk with *Antonio* by the self-same light
At any feast, or triumph, and nev'r car'd
Which side my Lady or her woman took
In their survey; I durst have told my tale too,
Though his discourse new ended.
Leocadia.   My repulse——   60
Philippo.   Let not that torture you, which makes me happy,
Nor think that conscience (fair) which is no shame.
'Twas no repulse, it was your dowry rather:
For then methought a thousand graces met

63 it] Colman; I F 1–2

To make you lovely, and ten thousand stories
Of constant vertue, which you then out-reach'd,
In one example, did proclaim you rich,
Nor do I think you wretched, or disgrac'd
After this suffring, and do therefore take
Advantage of your need; but rather know   70
You are the charge and businesse of those powers,
Who, like best Tutors, do inflict hard tasks
Upon great Natures, and of noblest hopes;
Read trivial lessons, and half lines to sluggs;
They that live long and never feel mischance,
Spend more then half their age in ignorance.
Leocadia.   'Tis wel you think so.
Philippo.   You shal think so too,
You shal sweet *Leocadia*, and do so.
Leocadia.   Good Sir no more; you have too fair a shape
To play so foul a part in, as the Tempter: 80
Say that I could make peace with fortune, who,
Who should absolve me of my vow yet; ha?
My Contract made?
Philippo.   Your Contract?
Leocadia.   Yes, my Contract;
Am I not his? his wife?
Philippo.   Sweet, nothing lesse.
Leocadia.   I have no name then?
Philippo.   Truly then you have not;
How can you be his wife, who was before
Anothers husband?
Leocadia.   Oh, though he dispence
With his faith given, I cannot with mine.
Philippo.   You do mistake (cleer soul); his precontract
Doth annul yours, and you have giv'n no faith   90
That ties you in religion, or humanity;
You rather sin against that greater precept,
To covet what's anothers; Sweet, you do
Beleeve me, who dare not urge dishonest things:
Remove that scruple therefore, and but take

Your dangers now, into your judgements skale
And weigh them with your safeties: Think but whither
Now you can go: what you can do to live?
How neer you ha' barr'd all Ports to your own succor,
Except this one that I here open: Love,   100
Should you be left alone, you were a prey
To the wild lust of any, who would look
Upon this shape like a temptation
And think you want the man you personate,
Would not regard this shift, which love put on,
As vertue forc'd but coveted like vice;
So should you live the slander of each Sex,
And be the child of error, and of shame,
And which is worse, even *Mark-antonie*
Would be cal'd just, to turn a wanderer off,   110
And Fame report you worthy his contempt;
Where if you make new choyce, and setle here,
There is no further tumult in this flood;
Each currant keeps his course, and all suspitions
Shal return honors: Came you forth a Maid?
Go home a Wife? alone? and in disguise?
Go home a waited *Leocadia*:
Go home, and by the vertue of that Charm
Transform all mischiefs, as you are transform'd;
Turn your offended Fathers wrath to wonder,   120
And all his loud grief to a silent welcome:
Unfold the Riddles you have made; what say you?
Now is the time; delay is but despair,
If you be chang'd, let a kisse tell me so.
Leocadia.   I am: but how, I rather feel then know.

   Enter Sanchio *carried,* Alphonso, *and Servants.*

Sanchio.   Come Sir; you are welcome now to *Barcellona*;
 Take off my hood.
Philippo.   Who be these? stay, let's view 'em?
Alphonso.   'Twas a long journey: are you not weary Sir?

Sanchio.   Weary? I could have rid it in mine Armour.
Leocadia.   Alas!
Philippo.   What ayl you deer?
Leocadia.   It is my Father.   130
Philippo.   Your Father: which?
Leocadia.   He that is carried: oh,
Let us make hence——
Philippo.   For loves sake: good my heart.
Leocadia.   Into some house before he see me.
Philippo.   Deer,
Be not thus frighted.
Leocadia.   O, his wrath is tempest.
Philippo.   Sweet, take your spirit to you, and stay: bee't he,
He cannot know you in this habit, and me
I'me sure he lesse knows, for he never saw me.
Alphonso.   Ha? who is that? my Son *Philippo*?
Philippo.   Sir.
Alphonso.   Why, what make you here? Is this *Salamanca*?
And that your study? ha? nay stay him too,   140
Wee'l see him by his leave.
Servant.   You must not strive Sir.   [*Holding*
Alphonso.   No, no, come neer.   Leocadia.]
Sanchio.   My daughter: *Leocadia*?
Alphonso.   How Sir: your daughter?
Sanchio.   Yes Sir, and as sure
As that's your Son: Come hither: what now? run
Out o' your sex? breech'd? was't not enough
At once to leave thy Father, and thine honor,
Unlesse th'hadst quit thy self too.
Philippo.   Sir what fault
She can be urg'd off, I must take on me
The guilt, and punishment.
Sanchio.   You must Sir: how
If you shal not, though you must? I deal not   150
With boys Sir, I; you have a Father here
Shal do me right.

148 off] *i.e.* of   151 Sir, I;] ~ ; ~ , F1–2

Alphonso.   Thou art not mad, *Philippo?*
Art thou *Mark-antonie?* Son to *Leonardo?*
Our businesse is to them.   [*Exit* Leocadia.]
Sanchio.   No, no, no, no,
Ile ha' the businesse now: with you, none else,
Pray you let's speak, in private: (carry me to him)
Your Son's the ravisher Sir, and here I find him:
I hope you'l give me cause to think you noble,
And do me right, with your sword sir, as becomes
One gentleman of honor to another;   160
All this is fair Sir: here's the sea fast by,
Upon the sands, we will determine.
'Tis that I call you too; let's make no days on't,
Ile lead your way.——To the seaside Rascals.
Philippo.   Sir,
I would beseech your stay; he may not follow you.
Sanchio.   No? turn, ile kill him here then: Slaves, Rogues,
    Blocks,
Why do you not bear me to him? ha' you been
Acquainted with my motions, loggs, so long
And yet not know to time 'em?
Philippo.   Were you Sir,
Not impotent——
Alphonso.   Hold you your peace Boy.
Sanchio.   Impotent!   170
'Death ile cut his throat first, and then his Fathers.
Alphonso.   You must provide you then a sharper razor
Then is your tongue, for I not fear your sword.
Sanchio.   'Heart bear mee to either of 'em.
Philippo.   Pray Sir, your patience.

Enter Governor *and Attendants.*

Alphonso.   My curse light on thee if thou stay him.
Philippo.   Hold.
Governor.   Why, what's the matter, Gentlemen, what tumult
Is this you raise i'th street? before my door?
Know you what 'tis to draw a weapon here?

Sanchio.   Yes, and to use it (bear me up to him, Rogues)   180
Thus, at a Traytors heart.
Alphonso.   Truer then thine.
Governor.   Strike, strike; Some of the people disarm 'em;
Kil 'em if they resist.
Philippo.   Nay generous sir,
Let not your courtesie turn fury now.
Governor.   Lay hold upon 'em, take away their weapons;
I wil be worth an answer, ere we part.
Philippo.   Tis the Governour sir.
Alphonso.   I yield my selfe.
Sanchio.   My Sword? what thinkst thou of me? pray thee tell me.
1. Attendant.   As of a Gentleman.
Sanchio.   No more?
1. Attendant.   Of worth
And quality.
Sanchio.   And I should quit my Sword   190
There were small worth or quality in that friend;
Pray thee learn thou more worth and quality
Then to demand it.
Governor.   Force it I say.
1. Attendant.   The Governour
You heare, commands.
Sanchio.   The Governour shall pardon me.
Philippo.   How, *Leocadia* gone again?   *Exit* Philippo.
Sanchio.   He shall friend,
I'th point of honour; by his leave, so tell him;
His person and authority I acknowledge,
And do submit me to it; but my Sword,
He shal excuse me, were he fifteen Governours;
That and I dwell together, and must yet   200
Till my hands part, assure him.
Governor.   I say force it.
Sanchio.   Stay, heare me. Hast thou ever read *Caranʒa?*
Understandst thou honour, Noble Governour?
Governor.   For that we'l have more fit dispute.
Sanchio.   Your name sir.

666

Governor.   You shall know that too: But on colder termes,
Your blood and brain are now too hot to take it.
Sanchio.   Force my Sword from me? this is an affront.
Governor.   Bring 'em away.
Sanchio.   You'l do me reparation.

                                             Exeunt.

                Enter Philippo.   [V. v]

Philippo.   I have for ever lost her, and am lost,
And worthily: my tamenesse hath undone me;
She's gone hence, asham'd of me: yet I seek her.
Will she be ever found to me again,
Whom she saw stand so poorly, and dare nothing
In her defence, here, when I should have drawn
This Sword out like a meteor, and have shot it
In both our parents eyes, and left 'em blind
Unto their impotent angers? O I am worthy
On whom this losse and scorn should light to death   10
Without the pity that should wish me better,
Either alive or in my Epitaph.

                                          [*Exit.*]

            Enter Leonardo, Marc-Antonio.   [V. vi]

Leonardo.   Well son, your father is too neere himselfe
And hath too much of nature to put off
Any affection that belongs to you.
I could have onely wishd you had acquainted
Her father, whom it equally concerns,
Though y'had presum'd on me: it might have open'd
An easier gate, and path to both our joyes:
For though I am none of those flinty Fathers
That when their children do but naturall things,
Turn rock and offence streight: yet *Marc-antonio,*   10
All are not of my quarry.

V.v] *no scene division* F 1–2   V.vi] *no scene division* F 1–2

Mark-antonio.   Tis my feare sir;
And if hereafter I should ere abuse
So great a piety, it were my malice.

Enter Attendants.

1. Attendant.   We must intreat you Gentlemen to take
Another room; the Governour is comming
Here, on some businesse.

Enter Governour, Sanchio, Alphonso, *Attendants.*

Mark-antonio.   We will give him way.
Sanchio.   I will have right sir on you; that believe,
If there be any Marshals Court in *Spaine.*
Governor.   For that sir we shall talke.
Sanchio.   ——Doe not slight me,
Though I am without a Sword.
Governor.   Keep to your chaire sir.   20
Sanchio.——Let me fall, and hurle my chaire! (slaves) at him.
Governor.   You are the more temperd man sir: let me intreat
Of you the manner how this brawle fell out.
Alphonso.   Fell out? I know not how: nor do I care much:
But here we came sir to this Town together,
Both in one businesse and one wrong, engag'd
To seeke one *Leonardo* an old *Genoese*;
I ha' said enough there; would you more? false father
Of a false sonne, cal'd *Marc-antonio*,
Who had stole both our daughters; and which father   30
Conspiring with his sonne in treachery,
It seemd, to fly our satisfaction,
Was, as we heard, come private to this Town
Here to take ship for *Italy.*
Leonardo.   You heard
More then was true then, by the feare, or falshood:
And though I thought not to reveale my selfe
(Pardon my manners in't to you) for some
Important reasons; yet being thus character'd

19 *and* 21 ——] F 1–2; Pox! Colman; *see the textual note on* I.i.332.

And challeng'd, know I dare appeare, and doe
To who dares threaten.
Mark-antonio.   I say he is not worthy   40
The name of man, or any honest preface,
That dares report or credit such a slander.
Doe you sir say it?
Alphonso.   Sir, I doe say it.
Governor.   Hold,
Is this your father Signior *Marc-antonio?*
You have ill requited me thus to conceale him
From him would honour him, and do him service.

Enter Eugenia.

Leonardo.   Twas not his fault sir.
Eugenia.   Where's my Lord?
Governor.   Sweet heart.
Eugenia.   Know you these Gentlemen? they are all the fathers
Unto our friends.
Governor.   So it appeares my Dove.
Sanchio.   Sir I say nothing: I doe want a Sword,   50
And till I have a Sword I will say nothing.
Eugenia.   Good sir command these Gentlemen their Armes;
Entreat 'em as your friends, not as your prisoners.
Where be their Swords?
Governor.   Restore each man his weapon.
Sanchio.   It seems thou hast not read *Caranza*, fellow;
I must have reparation of honour,
As well as this: I finde that wounded.
Governor.   Sir,
I did not know your quality, if I had,
Tis like I should have done you more respects.
Sanchio.   It is sufficient, by *Caranza's* rule.   60
Eugenia.   I know it is sir.
Sanchio.   Have you read *Caranza* Lady?
Eugenia.   If you mean him that writ upon the duell,
He was my kinsman.
Sanchio.   Lady, then you know,

669

By the right noble writings of your kinsman,
My honour is as deere to me, as the Kings.
Eugenia.   Tis very true sir.
Sanchio.   Therefore I must crave
Leave to goe on now with my first dependance.
Eugenia.   What ha you more?
Governor.   None here good Signior.
Sanchio.   I will refer me to *Caranʒa* still.
Eugenia.   Nay love, I prethee let me mannage this.   70
With whom is't sir?
Sanchio.   With that false man *Alphonso*.
Eugenia.   Why he has th'advantage sir in legs.
Sanchio.   But I
In truth, and hand and heart, and a good Sword.
Eugenia.   But how if he will not stand you Sir?
Alphonso.   For that,
Make it no question Lady; I will sticke
My feet in earth down by him, where he dare.
Sanchio.   O would thou wouldst.
Alphonso.   Ile do't.
Sanchio.   Let me kisse him.
I feare thou wilt not yet.
Eugenia.   Why Gentlemen,
If you'l proceed according to *Caranʒa*,
Me thinks an easier way, were too good chaires;   80
So you would be content sir to be bound,
'Cause he is lame, ile fit you with like weapons,
Pistols and Ponyards, and ev'n end it. If
The difference between you be so mortall,
It cannot be tane up.
Sanchio.   Tane up? take off
This head first.
Alphonso.   Come bind me in a chaire.
Eugenia.   Yes, do.
Governor.   What mean you, Dove?
Eugenia.   Let me alone,
And set 'em at their distance: when you ha' done,

Lend me two Ponyards; ile have Pistols ready
Quickly.   *Exit.*
                          Enter Philippo.

Philippo.   She is not here. *Marc-antonio,*   90
Saw you not *Leocadia?*
Mark-antonio.   Not I brother.
Philippo.   Brother let's speak with you; you were false unto her.
Mark-antonio.   I was, but have ask'd pardon: why do you urge it?
Philippo.   You were not worthy of her.
Mark-antonio.   May be I was not;
But tis not well, you tell me so.
Philippo.   My sister
Is not so faire.
Mark-antonio.   It skils not.
Philippo.   Nor so vertuous.
Mark-antonio.   Yes, she must be as vertuous.
Philippo.   I would faine——
Mark-antonio.   What brother?
Philippo.   Strike you.
Mark-antonio.   I shall not beare strokes,
Though I do these strange words.
Philippo.   Will you not kill me?
Mark-antonio.   For what good brother?
Philippo.   Why, for speaking well 100
Of *Leocadia.*
Mark-antonio.   No indeed.
Philippo.   Nor ill
Of *Theodosia?*

               Enter Eugenia, Leocadia, Theodosia,
                    and one with two Pistols.

Mark-antonio.   Neither.
Philippo.   Fare you well then.
Eugenia.   Nay you shall have as Noble seconds too,
As ever duellists had; give 'em their weapons:
Now Saint *Iago*——
                    [Leocadia *and* Theodosia *stand between them.*]

Sanchio.   Are they charg'd?
Eugenia.   Charg'd sir,
I warrant you.
Alphonso.   Would they were well discharg'd.
Sanchio.   I like a Sword much better I confesse.
Eugenia.   Nay wherefore stay you? shal I mend your mark?
Strike one another, thorough these!
Philippo.   My love.
Alphonso.   My *Theodosia.*
Sanchio.   I ha' not the heart.   110
Alphonso.   Nor I.
Eugenia.   Why here is a dependance ended.
Unbind that Gentleman; come take here to you
Your sonnes and daughters, and be friends. A feast
Waites you within, is better then your fray:
Lovers, take you your own, and all forbeare
Under my roofe, either to blush or feare.——
My love, what say you; could *Caranʒa* himselfe
Carry a businesse better?
Governor.   It is well:
All are content I hope, and we well eas'd,
If they for whom we have done all this be pleas'd.   120

                                                Exeunt.

TEXTUAL NOTES

I.i

82–83 *Incubo...Diego.*] Since the Hostess needs time to go off-stage to bring water, she cannot answer 'Yes, *Laʒaro* has him' as in F 1. Diego later in the scene is the character who consorts with Lazaro. Incubo, furthermore, habitually used the affected language 'Do's any body entertain his horse?' and he is normally the one who asks questions and gives orders. Therefore Sympson's reassignment is probably correct.

108 praid] F 2 *If I be paid, I am paid,* followed by all editors, misses the homely witticism of the Hostess. She plays on the proverb, 'He that cannot pay, let him pray' (*Oxford Dictionary of English Proverbs,* 1948 edition).

172 'T shall] All editors follow F 2 *I shall,* but F 1 seems correct if the meaning is 'He shall be reminded of breakfast'. See the *OED s.v. remember, v* 3 c for this sense of 'remember of'. The substitution of 'it' for 'he' is common in Elizabethan English, as in 'It is a peerelesse Kinsman' referring to Banquo, *Macbeth* I.iv.58 (1623 edition).

332 A——] In Jonson's *The New Inn,* III.i.57 which these lines parallel, the expression is 'A plague', a rather mild oath to censor. Other plays in the 1647 folio, however, show sporadic excision of oaths of a similar sort. Sometimes, as in *Bonduca,* censorship occurs in different ways in both the manuscript and the folio (see Bald, pp. 72–73). In *Love's Pilgrimage* 'god' is permitted to stay at V.i.6 whereas other oaths were cut from II.ii.46, and V.vi.19 and 21. 'A pox' or 'A plague' will fit equally well here and at II.ii.46. 'God' seems more appropriate than 'pox' at V.vi.19 and 21.

I.ii

47 talkt] F 1 *with whom you have talk so long* needs the correction given in F 2 *talk'd,* but the spelling 'talkt' provides the easier basis for a misreading. Of course 'have talk' is possible, if we take 'talk' as a noun, but Fletcher prefers the participial form.

129 Good woman!] As Mason observed in his *Comments on the Plays of Beaumont and Fletcher* (1797), Philippo addresses the Hostess here, in the same way he did at I.i.204. He calls Theodosia 'Lady'. Therefore the speech is not broken off, 'Good woman—', as we might first suppose.

165 Delayes in love, more dangerous.] The simplest interpretation assumes an elipsis [are] after 'love', and there is little need to emend or indicate an interruption after 'dangerous', as most editors have done.

II.i

9.1 2. Servant.] F1's *Rowl: Ashton* is a prompter's warning for the two
players to prepare to enter at line 24, carrying Sanchio in a chair. Rowland
Dowle was a hired player for the King's Men, other references to him
being made in 1631–1638. Ashton is not otherwise known, unless he be
'Edward Ashborne' cited in a list of attendants of the King's Men in 1624
(see Bentley, *Jacobean and Caroline Stage*, II, 350–351, 425–426). The same
two bit players are alerted in this play at IV.i.233.1, a dozen lines before
two soldiers enter carrying Mark-antonio. Also see the note on IV.i.24.

64 Mountdragon] Although 'Mountdragon' is not in the *OED*, it is
surely not an error for 'Mount dragoon'. The dragon was the female
whom St George, the amorous male, mounted. 'How our St Georges will
bestride the dragon, The red and ramping dragons!' (*The Mad Lover*,
I.i.271–272 (ed. R. W. Bond, 1908)). See Farmer and Henley's *Slang and
its Analogues* (1890–1904), *s.v.* St. George.

92 *Alphonso*. Sirrah Signiour] Although F1 assigns this to Leonardo, F2,
as all editors agree, rightly gave it to the rude and blustering Alphonso.

117 *Sanchio*. Now discreetly.] Sanchio is a commentator from the sidelines,
encouraging the other two to argue by the book, making this remark
appropriate for him, not for Leonardo, as in F1.

II.ii

151 endue] Sympson noticed that 'endue' rather than 'endure' is the right
reading, because it means 'digest'. Mason saw that the special point in the
speech depends on the vulgar error that an ostrich can digest iron.

II.iii

0.1 Markantonio.] 'and a Ship-master' probably crept into F1 because
the manuscript had a notation by the prompter for the actor to supply the
off-stage voice. See other signs of a prompter's notes at II.i.9.1, IV.i.24,
and IV.i.42, as well as the concern for props, such as, 'Two Chairs set out'.

81 The] 'That' entered F1, perhaps, by attraction to 'That' in the line below.

II.iv

0.1 *Enter...2. Hostesse.*] It is hard to explain the presence of the
erroneous entrance of '*Philippo and second Host*' in F1, but the fact that
III.i correctly begins with the same entry means something. Possibly, the
fourth scene is an interpolation for the revival of 1635–36, as has been
said of the discussion between Diego and Lazaro in I.i.330 ff. Certainly,

this scene, like the similar matter from *The New Inn*, does not further the action in any way. If my surmise is correct, the entry to III.i was possibly written at the bottom of a page of the manuscript in the original version, ending II.ii, as a warning for the forthcoming entry on the top of the following page. Playhouse manuscripts have this feature often. Then in the process of 'renewing' the play, an additional scene was inserted between II.iii and III.i, making the warning irrelevant. The compositor of F1, in this case, set the first entry he saw and ignored the proper entrance to II.iv, if there was an entrance there. See the present textual introduction for further comment.

10 half Falconers dog]   F2 *Falconers half dog* is a commoner word order, but the earlier form is still found in recent writers. Otto Jesperson (*A Modern English Grammar*, section 7.43 [1909–1949]) cites 'the barren wasp's nest' from Carlyle and 'the celebrated Lady's doctor' from Thackeray.

III.ii

129 wench]   The temptation to emend to 'wretch' should be resisted, although the *OED* does not list 'wench' in the sense of one in deep distress. Jonson, *Every Man in His Humour*, folio version, V.i.36–37, 'alas, poore wench, wert thou beaten for this?' (ed. Herford and Simpson, vol. III [1927]) and Shakespeare, *Henry VIII*, III.i.188, 'Alas (poore Wenches) where are now your Fortunes' (1623 edition) are appropriate parallels.

III.iv

41 bruise]   Theobald first suggested this emendation, in place of F1 *bruist*, and Colman introduced it to the text, because of the mention of rotten apples in the following line. 'Bruist' is not recorded as a spelling variant of 'bruise'.

50–51 *Pedro.* Let him sally. *Alphonso.* Lin'd]   Pedro the peacemaker is the most likely to say 'Let him sally'. The folios give this line to Alphonso, and all editors have agreed—even though Alphonso is the one 'sallying' at this moment. Sanchio, who is nearing the boiling point, seems least appropriate. The second line and the following long speech, given to Sanchio in F1, clearly belongs to Alphonso, since he continues the sentence broken off at line 49.

90 shrift]   F1's reading must stand, although 'shirt' is tempting. 'In his shrift' means in a state of penance, hence not affording Sanchio perfect vengeance.

113 seditious]   'The seditious' is the common expression cited in the *OED*, and I have found no example of F1 *seditions* in this use. Possibly 'seditions' results from a turned letter.

IV.i

24 place]   'Joh: Bacon ready to shoot off a Pistol' comes safely fifty lines before the gunner's shot. John Bacon is listed as an attendant of the King's company, January 1636–1637 (*M.S.C.* II, 380).

42 She...fame,]   F1 *Rod.* She...fame, *above.* may be a compositor's misreading of a prompter's note, in advance of Rodorigo's later entry.

153 seal'd]   F1 *scale religion* makes little sense, but F2 *ʒeald* seems somewhat better, meaning, 'consumed with zeal'. This passage is the only one cited in the *OED* for this form of the word however, always a suspicious sign. All editors have followed F2. The most satisfactory reading is 'seal'd', *i.e.* sworn or secret, the sworn religion of women with respect to swooning. For that matter, 'zeal'd' is a variant spelling of 'seal'd', and possibly the corrector of F2 meant that.

171 dosis]   F2 *dose* is essentially right, I think, but the earlier spelling 'dosis' helps explain the misreading of F1 *dotes.* Cf. 'a sugerd Dosis Of Wormwood, and a Deaths-head crown'd with Roses' (Henry Vaughan, *Silex Scintillans*, 1655, 'Joy', lines 5–6 (ed. Martin, second edition [1957])).

233.1 Servant.]   For comment on 'Rowl: Ashton' see the note on II.i.9.1.

IV.ii

8 it]   Since 'yt' and 'he' are often difficult to distinguish in the secretary hand and since the gun shot, not the general, was the call to their hall, I emend.

IV.iii

10 This]   All editors since Sympson have felt the need to emend here. The sense remains 'Is this the lady I quarrelled for?' whether we supply a verb or not. I find the line more emphatic without a verb: 'Ye Gods, this, the lady I quarrelled for!'

V.iv

100 open: Love,]   All editors since Langbaine have, with slight variation, associated 'Love' with the foregoing sentence. That is a possible reading, although it is somewhat loose. It seems to me that he offers marriage not love as a port of succour; she already has love. In my reading, closer to F1, he addresses her in the fashion of romance, as 'Love', *i.e.* my beloved.

106 coveted]   The syntax is tangled here, but the sense requires that 'covet' should parallel 'forc'd'; hence I emend. F1 *covet it* suggests that the lustful young men would covet her masculine shape, an implication that is far from the point.

PRESS-VARIANTS IN F1

[Copies collated: ViU¹ (University of Virginia, copy 1), ViU² (copy 2), Bodl (Bodleian B.1.8.Art.), Camb¹ (University Library Cambridge, Aston a.Sel.19), Camb² (SSS.10.8), NcD (Duke University), NcU (University of North Carolina), DFo (Folger Library).]

SHEET 8 C. II (*inner forme*)

Corrected: ViU¹,², Camb¹,², NcD, DFo
Uncorrected: Bodl, NcU

Sig. 8C2ᵛ.
   IV.iii.54 It] Ir

Sig. 8C3.
   IV.iii.95 Madam] Modam

EMENDATIONS OF ACCIDENTALS

Prologue

18 little] F 2; litte F 1

20 Pot,] ~ ∧ F 1–2

I.i

17 caltraps] cal-|traps F 1–2
21 pray;] pray, F 1; *om.* F 2
23 good∧] F 2; ~ , F 1
36 so,] ~ ∧ F 1–2
36 on;] ~ , F 1–2
38 luck,] F 2 *and probably a broken comma in* F 1
50 house——] ~ . F 1–2
67 *Hostesse.*] *In* F 1 *all her prefixes are* Host. *in this scene*
69.1 *Enter* Theodosia.] *one line earlier* F 1–2
74 stay,] ~ ∧ F 1–2
78 sincks:] ~ , F 1–2
81 flowre!] ~ ? F 1–2
84 you,] ~ ∧ F 1–2
88 fresh;] ~ ∧ F 1–2
96 room——] ~ , F 1–2
102 room——] ~ . F 1–2
103 Sir,] ~ ∧ F 1; ~ . F 2
105.1 *Enter* Diego.] *two lines earlier* F 1–2
108 Ducket;] ~ ∧ F 1–2
113 Sir;] ~ , F 1–2
114 you,] ~ ∧ F 1–2
115 swear,] ~ ∧ F 1; ~ . F 2
122.1 *Exeunt*] *Exit* F 1–2
125 me;] ~ ∧ F 1–2
128 els;] ~ , F 1–2
132 what,] ~ ∧ F 1–2
138 worship?] ~ ∧ F 1–2
156 him.] ~ ∧ F 1–2
161 be,] ~ ∧ F 1–2
163 eats?] F 2; ~ ∧ F 1

176–177 Says...one.] *One line in* Ff
177 t'] F 2; 't F 1
177 health;] ~ , F 1–2
195 him,] ~ ∧ F 1–2
197 beds] F 2; deds F 1
208 money,] F 2; ~ : F 1
208 Hostesse:] ~ ∧ F 1; ~ ; F 2
209 reason:——] ~ : ∧ F 1; ~ ∧... F 2
210 Gossips,] F 2; ~ ∧ F 1
215 Sir.——] ~ . ∧ F 1–2
216 one, Sir,] ~ ∧ ~ ∧ F 1–2
220 accommodated.——Why] ~ : ∧ why F 1–2
223 T'appoint] F 2; 'T appoint F 1
232 lynnen.——] ~ ; ∧ F 1–2
233 Dispatch. What] ~ : what F 1; ~ ; what F 2
233 Faith,] F 2; ~ ∧ F 1
238 Troth,] ~ ∧ F 1–2
240 French——] ~ : F 1–2
240 *Enter...Table.*] *One and a half lines earlier in* Ff
245 hen∧] ~ , F 1–2
249 it?] ~ . F 1–2
258 *Enter...meat.*] *One and a half lines earlier in* Ff
260 Wine.——Ile] ~ , ∧ ile F 1; ~ , ∧ Ile F 2
269 I...place.] Ff *line:* I...humanity | Us'd...place.
278 not?] ~ : F 1–2
285 but——] ~ ∧ F 1–2

292 Host,] ~ ∧ F 1–2
301 me——] ~ ∧ F 1–2
324 hen∧] ~ ; F 1–2
325 Sir.] ~ ∧ F 1–1
330 *Laȝaro.*] F 2; ~ ∧ F 1
331 Sir;] ~ , F 1–2
343 *Laȝaro,*] ~ ∧ F 1–2
349 him,] ~ ∧ F 1–2
353 *Laȝaro,*] ~ ∧ F 1; ~ . F 2
354 it,] ~ ∧ F 1–2
355 *Laȝaro,*] ~ ∧ F 1–2
357 me,] ~ ∧ F 1–2

358 conscience;] ~ ∧ F 1–2
359 Master,] ~ ∧ F 1–2
364 there,] ~ ∧ F 1–2
366 Saddles,] ~ ∧ F 1–2
370 Sir,] F 2; ~ ∧ F 1
389 (For...suspitious)] F 2; ∧ ~ ...
        ~ : F 1
389 puckfoysts,] F 2 *and probably a*
        damaged comma in F 1
393 off,] ~ : F 1–2
396 *Laȝaro,*] ~ ∧ F 1–2
411.1 *Exeunt.*] *Exit.* F 1–2

I.ii

1 ho!...ho!] ~ - ?...~ ? F 1;
     ~ ∧ ?...~ ? F 2
3 oh!] ~ ? F 1–2
3 heart!] ~ ? F 1–2
5 break!] ~ ? F 1–2
8 shame!] ~ ? F 1–2
12 folly!] ~ : F 1; ~ , F 2
18 Oh!] ~ , F 1–2
23 Sir,] ~ ∧ F 1–2
30 Sir,] ~ ∧ F 1–2
39 you,] ~ ∧ F 1–2
42 More,] ~ ∧ F 1–2
42 me——] ~ . F 1; ~ ∧ F 2
44 peace.] ~ ∧ F 1–2
45 noble?] F 2; ~ . F 1
50 name?] ~ . F 1–2
52 me;] ~ , F 1–2
56 Sir——] ~ : F 1–2
62 love,] ~ ∧ F 1–2
66 us∧] ~ ? F 1–2
69 loving!] ~ ? F 1–2
72 *Mark-antonio,*] ~ ∧ F 1–2
76 by∧] F 2; ~ ; F 1
95 law,] ~ ∧ F 1–2
115 comfort?] F 2; ~ . F 1

123 must:——] ~ : ∧ F 1–2
123 Candle.] ~ : F 1–2
124 Sir,] ~ ∧ F 1–2
125 Lady,] ~ ∧ F 1–2
126 necessary:——] ~ : ∧ F 1–2
130.1 *Enter...light.*] *One line earlier*
        in Ff
133 mee.] ~ ∧ F 1–2
135 me,] ~ ∧ F 1–2
136 dishonors,] F 2; ~ ∧ F 1
137 self,] F 2; ~ : F 1
147 Sister,] ~ ∧ F 1–2
159 are!] ~ ? F 1–2
167 counsel,] ~ : F 1–2
169 morning.] ~ ∧ F 1–2
184 *Enter* Pedro.] *Two lines earlier in*
        Ff
188 way——] ~ . F 1; ~ ∧ F 2
196 question;] ~ , F 1–2
197 Sir,] ~ . F 1–2
199 Sir.——] ~ : ∧ F 1–2
202 can,] F 2; ~ ∧ F 1
203 *Barcellona*;] ~ , F 1–2
204 unexpected.] ~ ∧ F 1–2

II.i

1 one.] ~ ∧ F 1; ~ , F 2
7 me?] F 2; ~ . F 1

8 first;] ~ , F 1–2
10 Sirs,] F 2; ~ ∧ F 1

14 duckets,] F2; ~ ∧ F1
19 Sirhah,] ~ ∧ F1–2
22 draw,] ~ ∧ F1–2
24 Enter . . . chair.)] Two lines earlier
  in Ff
24 Sanchio] Zanchio F1–2
28 Signiour,] ~ ∧ F1–2
37 with:] ~ ∧ F1; ~ ? F2
40 hold;] ~ ∧ F1–2
42 Sanchio.] All his prefixes are
  Zanch. in this scene of F1
45 credit;] ~ , F1–2
49 method.] ~ ∧ F1; ~ , F2
50 discretion.] ~ , F1–2
52 terms;] ~ , F1–2
53 know, Sir,] ~ ∧ ~ ∧ F1–2
56 Signior,] F2; ~ ∧ F1
59 err'd——] ~ ∧ F1–2
61 crimes?] ~ . F1; ~ , F2
61 still,] ~ ∧ F1; ~ . F2
64 commission,] ~ ∧ F1–2
67 leave.] ~ ∧ F1–2
68 creature?] F2; ~ ∧ F1
70 actions?] ~ , F1–2

70 If] if F1–2
78 respects;] ~ , F1–2
83 reverence] re-|verence F1; reve-
  |rence F2
86 man——] ~ . F1–2
87 man——] ~ . F1–2
92 give] Give F1–2
93 born——] ~ . F1–2
94 me——] ~ . F1–2
95 Civill,] F2; ~ ∧ F1
97 off,] ~ ∧ F1–2
98 Sir,] ~ ∧ F1–2
99 stand,] ~ ∧ F1–2
100 anvill∧] ~ , F1–2
100 angers,] ~ ∧ F1–2
104 Sir,] ~ ∧ F1–2
110 show;] ~ , F1–2
112 Sir,] ~ ∧ F1–2
120 Signiour,] ~ ∧ F1–2
123 certain] F2; cer-|tain F1
128 things.] ~ ∧ F1–2
137 adventures,] ~ : F1–2
141 wooers,] ~ ∧ F1–2
144 Shall] shall F1–2

II.ii

1 Diego.] His first two prefixes in
  this scene are Host Dieg. and
  Host Die. F1; in the rest of the
  scene they are Host.
2 us.] ~ , F1–2
10 is, Signiours,] ~ ∧ ~ ∧ F1–2
14 though,] thongh ∧ F1; though ∧
  F2
21 honours;] ~ , F1–2
23 ther's] ther·s F1; there's F2
28 Another,] F2; ~ ∧ F1
34 'em] F2; ·em F1
35 call'd] F2; call·d F1
38 there's] F2; there·s F1
38 this∧] ~ ? F1–2
39 place?] ~ . F1–2
41 Who's] F2; Who·s F1

43 Incubo.] In F1 his prefixes are
  Bayl. throughout this scene.
43 Host,] ~ : F1–2
44 Bayly,] ~ : F1–2
45 reckoning,] ~ ∧ F1–2
54 els,] ~ ∧ F1–2
57 prayer;] ~ , F1–2
60 onyons,] ~ ; F1; ~ : F2
64 now?] ~ . F1–2
71 danger,] ~ ; F1–2
72 rest;] ~ , F1–2
78 Sir.——You] ~ : ∧ you F1–2
78 Exit Diego.] Exit. one line earlier
  F1–2
80 miseries.] ~ , F1–2
82 laugh,] ~ ∧ F1–2
83 still.] ~ , F1–2

84 patience,] ∼ : F 1–2
85 tamenesse,] ∼ ; F 1–2
87–88 And...dog] Ff *line*: And...
   him, | And...dog
89 fire,] F 2; ∼ ∧ F 1
93–94 place ∧...compassion)] ∼)
   ...∼ , F 1–2
98.1–2 *Enter*...*rob'd*.] *Two lines*
   earlier in F 1–2
99 *Diego*.] *In* F 1 *all his prefixes are*
   Host. in this scene.
104 what,] ∼ ∧ F 1–2
111 devill——] ∼ . F 1–2
116 it?] ∼ . F 1–2
117 garments] F 2; gar-|ments F 1
120–121 You...ye.] Ff *line*: You...
   perish. | I...ye.

121 soul;] ∼ , F 1–2
122 it;] ∼ , F 1–2
124 too,] ∼ . F 1–2
136 see] F 2; se F 1
143 Sir?] ∼ . F 1–2
144 thing?] ∼ . F 1–2
150 handsaw] F 2; hand-|saw F 1
153 Ith'] F 2; I th' F 1
155.1 Diego *and* Incubo.] Host &
   Bayl. F 1–2
169 *Sanchio's*] *Zanchio's* F 1–2
171 *Sanchio*] *Zanchio* F 1–2
174 further;] ∼ , F 1–2
184 too,] ∼ . F 1–2
197 more.——] ∼ . ∧ F 1–2
197 are,] ∼ ∧ F 1–2
198 us;] ∼ , F 1–2

II.iii

8 *Mark-antonio*.] *In* F 1 *his prefixes*
   in this scene are Marc. and Mar.
10 children] F 2; chil-|dren F 1
13 'tis] F 2;˙tis F 1
18 more,] ∼ . F 1–2
21 breches,] F 2; ∼ ∧ F 1
23 dalliance;] ∼ , F 1–2
26 though,] ∼ ∧ F 1–2
47 beauty,] ∼ ; F 1–2
49 not;] ∼ , F 1–2
54 more;] ∼ , F 1; ∼ : F 2
55 beauty∧] ∼ , F 1–2
57 this,] ∼ ∧ F 1–2
74 perpetually;] ∼ , F 1–2

77 man?] F 2; ∼ . F 1
82 mark;] ∼ , F 1–2
88 and who] F 2; and wo F 1
93 feather.] ∼ : F 1–2
94 'em,] ∼ ∧ F 1–2
104 are,] ∼ ? F 1; ∼ ∧ F 2
105 at?] ∼ . F 1–2
109 shaking?] ∼ . F 1–2
118 kingdome∧] ∼ , F 1–2
120 wars ∧] ∼ , ∧ F 1–2
122 nam'd,] ∼ ∧ F 1; ∼ . F 2
125 love (I...too)] ∼ ;...∼ ; F 1–2
125 enough:] ∼ ∧ F 1–2

II.iv

1 2. *Host*.] *In this scene in* F 1 *he*
   and his wife have speech prefixes
   Host. and Hostess.
18 Here's] here's F 1–2
18 brother,] F 2; ∼ ∧ F 1
19 *Ossuna*] F 2; *Ossuva* F 1
21 Take] F 2; Takc F 1

22 commodity. Why,] ∼ : why ∧
   F 1–2
28 *Incubo*.] *In* F 1 *in this scene all his*
   prefixes are Bayl.
29 what,] ∼ ∧ F 1–2
39 Hostesse...hungry.] Ff *line*
   Hostesse, | Dear...hungry.

41 meat.] ~ , F 1–2
46 instantly,] ~ ₐ F 1–2
51 appetite,] ~ ₐ F 1–2
59 *Diego.*] *1. Host. Diego.* F 1; *the rest of his prefixes in this scene are 1. Host Die.*

69 duckets;] duck-|ets, F 1; duckets ₐ F 2
71 what,] ~ ₐ F 1–2
76 stomach.] F 2; ~ ₐ F 1
79 geer?] ~ . F 1–2
80 boy?] ~ . F 1–2
84 Dalliance.] ~ , F 1–2

III.i

4 'twil] 't wil F 1

III.ii

8 Brother,] F 2; ~ ₐ F 1
15 please;] ~ , F 1–2
17 not,] ~ ₐ F 1–2
18 have (nay...Signior)] ~ ;...
    ~ , F 1–2
19 narrowly (more blushes!)] ~ ;
    ...~ ? ₐ F 1–2
21 already (yet...blushes?)] ~ :
    ...~ ? ₐ F 1–2
25 eys ₐ] F 2; ~ . F 1
26 (Come...'em)] F 2; ₐ~ ...~ ,
    F 1
26 objects;] ~ , F 1–2
29 ye. Come] ~ , come F 1–2
29 liberal;] ~ , F 1–2
30 you;] ~ , F 1–2
35 this,] ~ ₐ F 1–2
36 open;] ~ , F 1–2
42 goodness,] ~ ₐ F 1–2
43 vertue,] ~ ₐ F 1–2
59 *Sanchio*] *Zanchio* F 1–2
84 heaven] F 2; hea-|ven F 1
86 honor,] ~ ₐ F 1–2
91 him,] ~ ₐ F 1–2
105 Lady,] ~ ₐ F 1–2
109 it;] ~ , F 1–2
114 Sir,] ~ ₐ F 1–2
118 Sir,] ~ ₐ F 1–2
122 hell,] ~ ₐ F 1–2
125 neighbors,] ~ ₐ F 1–2

130 glory,] ~ ₐ F 1–2
132 Father,] ~ ₐ F 1–2
133 construction,] ~ ₐ F 1–2
139 man,] ~ ₐ F 1–2
144 angry,] ~ ₐ F 1–2
147 it,] ~ ₐ F 1–2
148 me,] ~ ₐ F 1–2
148 blessings,] ~ ₐ F 1–2
153 promise,] ~ ₐ F 1–2
155 love together,] ~ ₐ F 1–2
158 Lady,] ~ ₐ F 1–2
162 angry,] ~ ₐ F 1–2
163 nature,] ~ ₐ F 1–2
165 Lady,] ~ ₐ F 1–2
168 And...cozend.] Ff *line* And...
    her | That...cozend.
169 behaviour,] ~ ₐ F 1–2
170 faith,] ~ ₐ F 1–2
170 credit,] ~ ₐ F 1–2
172 think,] ~ ₐ F 1; ~ ? F 2
173 Angels,] ~ ₐ F 1–2
174 indulgent,] ~ ₐ F 1–2
176 beauty,] ~ ₐ F 1–2
177 it,] ~ ; F 1–2
180 vertue———] ~ . F 1; ~ ₐ F 2
181 vapor] F 2; va-|por F 1
187 sorrows,] ~ ₐ F 1–2
189 little,] F 2; ~ ₐ F 1
194 her.] ~ ₐ F 1–2
194 Lady,] ~ ₐ F 1–2

199 ye,] ~ ∧ F 1–2
201 crosses,] ~ ∧ F 1–2
202 patience;] ~ , F 1–2
205 travels,] ~ ∧ F 1–2
207 be.] ~ ∧ F 1–2
209 Lady,] ~ ∧ F 1–2
218 Stay,] ~ ∧ F 1–2
219 *Leocadia,*] ~ ∧ F 1–2
220 *Sanchio*] *Zanchio* F 1–2
221 Sir,] F 2; ~ ∧ F 1
225 *Leocadia.*] ~ ∧ F 1–2
226 one.] ~ ∧ F 1–2
227 plain,] ~ ∧ F 1–2
231 too;] ~ ∧ F 1–2
234 You...ones.] Ff *line* You...
    fancies, | Wondrous...ones.
237 thing:] ~ ∧ F 1–2
239 me,] ~ ∧ F 1–2

241 conscience,] ~ ∧ F 1–2
243 both∧] ~ , F 1–2
243 faces,] ~ ∧ F 1–2
245 Sir,] ~ ∧ F 1–2
251 started,] ~ ∧ F 1–2
255 me,] ~ ∧ F 1–2
263 *Enter* Leocadia.] *One and a half*
    lines earlier in Ff
266 feavor,] ~ ∧ F 1–2
267 friends,] ~ ∧ F 1–2
271 faiths,] ~ ∧ F 1–2
274 *Exeunt...*Leocadia.] *Exit.* F 1–
    2
284 eye;] ~ , F 1–2
286 her,] ~ ∧ F 1–2
287 negligence;] ~ , F 1–2
289 love,] ~ ∧ F 1–2

III.iii

4 sir;] ~ ∧ F 1–2
6 sir,] ~ ∧ F 1–2
7 it;] ~ ∧ F 1–2
10 *Spain*∧] ~ , F 1–2
14 all,] ~ ; F 1–2
23 way?] ~ . F 1–2
23 Sir,] ~ ∧ F 1–2

29 her;] ~ , F 1–2
40–42 (For...ignorance;)]∧ ~ ...
    ~ ; ∧ F 1–2
40 *Alphonso*] F 2; *Alphenso* F 1
44 cure,] ~ ∧ F 1
47 world,] F 2; ~ ∧ F 1
55 return,] ~ ∧ F 1–2

III.iv

1 Sirha,] F 2; ~ ∧ F 1
2 call.] ~ ? F 1–2
4 Signior,] ~ ∧ F 1–2
9 Sir,] ~ ∧ F 1–2
10 sir,] ~ ∧ F 1–2
11 allarums,] ~ ∧ F 1–2
20 sir,] ~ ∧ F 1–2
21 first.] ~ , F 1–2
22 fame!] ~ ? F 1–2
23 sir,] ~ ∧ F 1–2
33 deerest,] ~ ∧ F 1–2
34 righted?] ~ . F 1–2
36 Shalbe?] ~ . F 1–2
37 Instantly?] ~ . F 1–2

38 me?] ~ . F 1–2
38–39 Dost...here] *One line in Ff*
43 quiet?] ~ , F 1–2
43 thee,] ~ ∧ F 1–2
45 posterity?] ~ , F 1–2
46 give,] ~ ; F 1–2
46 this.] ~ ∧ F 1–2
49 soldadoship——] ~ . F 1–2
51 discretion,] ~ ∧ F 1–2
83 too,] ~ ; F 1–2
83 us;] ~ , F 1–2
85 linnage——] ~ . F 1–2
95 some, *Alphonso,*] ~ ∧ ~ ∧ F 1–2
105 here;] ~ , F 1–2

IV.i

1 *Mark-antonio.] In* F 1 *his prefixes
are Marc. throughout this scene.*
2 not.] F 2; ~? F 1
2–3 Why. . . Town.] *One line in* Ff
8 Invasion,] ~ ; F 1–2
9 Sir——] ~ . F 1
17.1 *Enter. . .* Attendents.] *One line
earlier in* Ff
22 about?] ~ . F 1–2
34 go;] ~ , F 1–2
42 unblemish'd] F 2; unblemishd'd
F 1
55 hiding,] ~ : F 1–2
65 *Enter. . . Soldiers.] One line
earlier in* Ff
68 *Enter. . . Townsmen.] One half
line earlier in* Ff
69 Generall;] ~ , F 1–2
70 seen, Sir,] ~ ∧ ~ ∧ F 1–2
72 *Enter. . . Leocadia.] One line
earlier in* Ff
80 it] F 2; It F 1
80.1 Gentleman] Gentlemen F 1–2
92 Phisition:] F 2; *and probably a
broken colon in* F 1
92 these——] ~ ∧ F 1–2
115 dead,] ~ ; F 1–2
120 To] F 1 *cw,* F 2; Yo F 1 *text*
123 were?] ~ ; F 1–2
127 questioning?] ~ , F 1–2

139 affection;] ~ , F 1–2
140 cost,] ~ ∧ F 1–2
152 couldst;] ~ , F 1–2
154 swownings;] ~ , F 1–2
156 by∧] ~ : F 1–2
165 so,] ~ ∧ F 1–2
166 Rather∧] ~ , F 1–2
169 beat, and row,] ~ , ~ ∧ F 1–2
172 troubled?] ~ , F 1–2
173 is.] ~ ? F 1–2
173–174 Good. . . can:] *One line in*
Ff
175 me,] ~ ∧ F 1–2
181.1 *Enter. . .* Townsmen.] *Two
lines earlier in* Ff
191–194 By. . . honour.] Ff *line as
verse* By. . . own | Private. . .
now | You. . . ran | Away. . .
honour.
197–198 For. . . neighbours?] Ff *line
as verse* For. . . knew | Of. . .
neighbours.
200 tell?] ~ . F 1–2
213 hence,] ~ ∧ F 2; *punctuation in*
F 1 *doubtful*
218.1 *Exeunt] Exit* F 1–2
231 besides∧] ~ . F 1–2
233 too?] ~ . F 1–2
244 welcome:] ~ , F 1–2

IV.ii

1 *Mark-antonio.] In* F 1 *his prefixes in this scene are Mar. and
Mark.*
5 'em,] ~ ∧ F 1–2
6 hope,] ~ ∧ F 1–2
6 *Exeunt.] Exit.* F 1–2
7–15 How. . . pity.] Ff *line as verse*
How. . . a | Shot. . . Hall. | I. . .
the | Town. . . out | Of. . . I |

Have. . . howrs | Together. . .
or | Modest. . . bare | Up. . .
and | Scambling. . . pity.
7 Generall] Ge-|nerall F 1–2
13 But] but F 1–2
17–24 Yes. . . that.] Ff *line as verse*
Yes. . . liver: | But. . . Town |
That. . . Anotomy | Well. . .
lungs, | Or. . . are | There. . .

that | Would...there | Ever
...a | Small-gut...answer |
Me that.

26–27 No...Gallys.] Ff *line as
verse* No...time | We...
Gallys.

IV.iii

3 you;] ~ , F 1–2
7 *Mark-antonio.*] *In* F 1 *his first
nine prefixes in this scene are
Marc.; thereafter his prefixes are
Mar.*
9 with——] ~ . F 1–2
18 posterity,] ~ ∧ F 1–2
21 attempted——] F 2; ~ : F 1
26 wound, especially∧] ~ ∧ ~ ,
F 1–2
30 Sir?] ~ . F 1–2
36 'em a] 'em. A F 1–2
37 me.——] ~ : ∧ F 1–2
43 *Exeunt...stay.*] *Exit.* F 1–2
47–48 Shall...friends?] *One line in*
Ff
63 wound∧] ~ , F 1–2
72 me,] *Probably a damaged comma
in* F 1; ~ ∧ F 2
89 yet;] F 2; ~ , F 1
91 ears;] ~ , F 1–2
92 quickly:] ~ , F 1–2
94 yet.] ~ , F 1–2
102 fault;] ~ , F 1–2
104 you;] ~ , F 1–2
105 scape?] ~ , F 1–2
108 all?——] ~ ; ∧ F 1–2
108 you,] ~ ∧ F 1–2
111 Shew...you,] *One line in* Ff
121 *Mark-antonio,*] ~ ∧ F 1–2

122 Surgeons——] ~ . F 1–2
123 dissemble;] ~ , F 1–2
133 Alas,] ~ ∧ F 1–2
143 satisfie?] F 2; ~ . F 1
145 you,] ~ ; F 1–2
145 *Leocadia;*] ~ , F 1–2
146 me——] ~ . F 1–2
149 garments. There] ~ , there F 1–
2
150 me;] ~ , F 1; ~ ∧ F 2
155 dead,] F 2; ~ ; F 1
156 Contract,] ~ ; F 1–2
156 sworn,] ~ ∧ F 1–2
164 thick,] ~ ∧ F 1–2
178 *Theodosia, Theodosia,*] ~ , ~ ∧
F 1–2
180 me,] ~ ∧ F 1–2
182 *Theodosia.*] ~ , F 1–2
185 for;] ~ , F 1–2
187 thee,] ~ ∧ F 1–2
194 Brother;] ~ , F 1–2
200 hath,] ~ ∧ F 1–2
201 me;] ~ , F 1–2
205 you;] ~ , F 1–2
209–210 Where's...*Leocadia?*] *One
line in* Ff, *although* And *is begun
with a capital letter*
214 shee.] ~ ∧ F 1–2
218 deeds,] ~ ∧ F 1–2

V.i

6 god,] ~ ∧ F 1–2
8 out;] ~ , F 1–2
10 be hir'd] F 2; behir'd F 1
10 hir'd;] ~ , F 1–2
12 her.] ~ , F 1–2

17 to,] ~ ; F 1–2
18 courtesies,] ~ ∧ F 1–2
20 'sdeath!] ~ ? F 1–2
21 me.——] ~ , ∧ F 1–2
26 piehouse;] ~ ∧ F 1–2

V.ii

9 found;] ~ , F 1–2
11 ayre,] ~ ⋀ F 1–2
13 her!] ~ ? F 1–2

21 *Enter* Incubo.] F 2; *ten lines earlier in* F 1
23 truth;] ~ , F 1–2
27 word.] ~ , F 1–2

V.iii

1 it,] ~ ⋀ F 1–2
4 Sir;] ~ , F 1–2
13 me,] ~ ⋀ F 1–2

14 assistant,] ~ ⋀ F 1–2
17 loth,] ~ ⋀ F 1–2
22 there⋀] ~ , F 1–2

V.iv

2 *Mark-antonie,*] ~ ⋀ F 1–2
3 more:] ~ , F 1–2
10 care,] ~ ⋀ F 1–2
18 I;] ~ , F 1–2
25 you;] ~ , F 1–2
35 seeking,] ~ : F 1–2
35 lost;] ~ , F 1–2
36 most,] F 2; ~ ; F 1
44 health,] ~ ⋀ F 1–2
45 injury,] ~ ⋀ F 1–2
46 grief,] ~ ; F 1–2
48 cure;] ~ , F 1–2
51 rooted,] ~ : F 1–2
52 that⋀] ~ , F 1–2
59 too,] ~ ⋀ F 1–2
60 repulse——] ~ . F 1–2
61 happy,] ~ ⋀ F 1–2
62 shame.] ~ ⋀ F 1–2
67 rich,] ~ ⋀ F 1; ~ : F 2
83 Contract;] ~ , F 1–2
89 soul);] ~) ⋀ F 1–2
91 humanity;] ~ , F 1–2
94 things:] ~ , F 1–2
104 personate,] ~ ⋀ F 1–2
105 on,] ~ ⋀ F 1–2
112 here,] ~ ⋀ F 1–2
113 flood;] ~ . F 1; ~ , F 2

122 made;] ~ , F 1–2
125.1 *Enter...Servants.] Three lines earlier in* Ff
126 Sanchio.] *In* F 1 *his prefixes in this scene are* Sanc. San. *and* Sanch.
126 *Barcellona;*] ~ , F 1–2
131 oh,] ~ ⋀ F 1–2
132 hence——] ~ . F 1–2
134 O,] ~ ⋀ F 1–2
135 stay:] ~ ⋀ F 1–2
152 mad,] ~ ⋀ F 1–2
162 determine.] ~ ⋀ F 1–2
164 way.——To] ~ ; ⋀ to F 1–2
164 Sir,] ~ ⋀ F 1–2
166 No?] ~ , F 1–2
166 turn,] F 2; ~ ⋀ F 1
166 Blocks,] ~ ⋀ F 1; ~ . F 2
169 'em?] ~ . F 1–2
169 Sir,] ~ ⋀ F 1–2
170 impotent——] ~ . F 1–2
170 Impotent!] ~ ⋀ F 1; ~ , F 2
175 Sir,] ~ ⋀ F 1–2
179 here?] F 2; ~ . F 1
182 'em;] ~ , F 1–2
183 sir,] ~ ⋀ F 1–2
185 weapons;] ~ , F 1–2

189 more?] F 2; ~ . F 1
189 worth ₐ] ~ , F 1–2
195 friend,] ~ ₐ F 1–2

196 him;] ~ , F 1–2
202 *Caranza*] F 2; *Curanza* F 1

V.v

12 alive ₐ] ~ , F 1–2

V.vi

14 *1. Attendant.*] *Atten.* F 1–2
15 room;] ~ , F 1–2
17 *Sanchio.*] *In* F 1 *in this scene all his prefixes are Sanch.*
19 ——Doe] ——doe F 1–2
27 *Genoese*;] ~ , F 1–2
35 then,...falshood:] ~ : ~ , F 1–2
47 Lord?] F 2; ~ . F 1
48 fathers] F 2; fa-|thers F 1
55 *Caranza*] F 2; *Curanza* F 1
55 fellow;] ~ ₐ F 1–2
58 had,] ~ ₐ F 1–2
63 know,] ~ ₐ F 1–2
69 will ₐ] ~ , F 1–2
69 *Caranza*] F 2; *Claranza* F 1

74 Sir?] F 2; ~ . F 1
75 Lady;] ~ , F 1–2
79 *Caranza*] F 2; *Curanza* F 1
80 chaires;] ~ , F 1–2
84 mortall,] ~ . F 1–2
87 Dove?] ~ . F 1–2
88 done,] ~ ₐ F 1–2
90 here.   *Marc-antonio,*] ~ ₐ ~ .
    F 1–2
98 Strike] F 2; Srike F 1
103 too,] ~ ₐ F 1–2
105 *Iago*——] ~ . F 1–2
109 these!] ~ ? F 1–2
116 feare.——] ~ ₐ ₐ F 1–2
117 *Caranza*] F 2; *Cuzanza* F 1

HISTORICAL COLLATION

[The following editions are collated: F1 (1647), F2 (1679), L (*Works*, 1711, ed. Gerard Langbaine the Younger), S (*Works*, 1750, ed. Theobald, Seward, and Sympson), C (*Works*, 1778, ed. George Colman the Younger), W (*Works*, 1812, ed. Henry Weber), D (*Works*, 1843–1846, ed. Alexander Dyce).]

The Persons Represented in the Play

The Persons...Townsmen] *om.* F1
  9 *Blanco*] *Bianco* F2
 12 *Barcellona*] *Barcellona.* | Bailiff of *Barcellona.* F2
 18 Attendants, Townsmen,] Atten-
dants, Townsmen. Attendants. F2
19.1] The Scene Barcellona and the Road. F2

I.i

 12 sorrow] sorry S, C, W, D
 16 or] nor F2, L, S, C
 17 caltraps, I,] caltraps, S
 21 pray;] *om.* F2, L
 33 cassocks] and Cassocks S
 38 bring] brink F2
 45 Squire] Esquire S
 48 oft] ought F2
 82 *Incubo.*] *Die.* F1–2, L
 83 *Diego.*] *Host.* F1–2, L
103 stands] stand S, C, W, D
108 praid] paid F2+
128 partridge] a Partridge S
144 those] these F2, L, S
148 drink] drank L, S, C, W; drunk D
156 has] h'as F2, L, S, D; h'has C; he has W
164 give] grant W
172 'T] I F2+
176 eat] eats F2, L, S

183 afore] before C, W
188 Not] No S
245–246 W *transposes the two lines to read:* And kid forth quickly, | *Exeunt Hostess and Servants.* | At such a time as this? Well, bring your hen.
299 think a] think. A C, W, D
300 then talke] then—Talk C, W, D
311 guests] guest C, W, D
332 A——] A plague C, W, D
346 Lady eve] Lady's eve S; Lady-eve W, D
347 Has] H'as F2, L, S, D; H'has C; He has W
349 has] h'as F2, L, S, D; H'has C; He has W
386 Has] H'as F2, L, S, D; H'has C; He has W
398 Horses...horses,] *om.* F2, L, S

I.ii

7 strong] stronger S, C, W, D
38 curious] curio W
47 talkt] talk F 1; talk'd F 2+
63 that that] that C
80 gave] grave F 1
113 it] you L, S
127–128 light   for   heavens   sake.

Theodosia. Wil] light! *Theod.*
For Heav'n's sake! Will C
129 woman!] ∼ : F 1–2, L, S
154 O sir!] O sir, I—— F 2, L, S
165 Delayes] Delay's W
165 more] are S
165 dangerous.] ∼ —— C, W, D

II.i

1 *1. Servant.*] *Serv.* F 1–2, L, S, C, W
2 *1. Servant.*] *Serv.* F 1–2, L, S, C, W
9.1 2. Servant.] *two Servants.* F 2, L, S; *two Servants, Rowl: Ashton.* F 1
14 good my] my good S
26 I ever lov'd ye] *om.* F 2, L, S
27 And] An F 1–2
59 unjustice] injustice F 2+

61 father] the Father S
91–92 language. | *Alphonso.* Sirrah Signiour, give] language sirrah Signiour. | *Alph.* Give F 1
97 went] were L, S
117 *Sanchio.* Now] *Leo.* Now F 1
128 crowns] crown C
133 all∧] all. F 1
137 adventures] Adventurers F 2, L, S, C, W
138 wills] will F 2, L, S

II.ii

13 trees] three F 2
31 satisfie ye] satisfy F 2, L
46 A——] A pox C, W, D
50 cony] Cunny L, S
55 ye] he F 2
60 a huge] an huge S, C, W
98.2 *other*] *others* F 1–2, L, S, C

100 *1. Passenger.*] *1.* F 1–2, L, S
108 Where] Where's S, C, W, D
125 this] his L, S
130 *and* 131 *2. Passenger.*] *2.* F 1–2, L, S
151 endue] endure F 1–2, L
172 his] *om.* F 1

II.iii

0.1 Markantonio.] *Markantonio, and a Shipmaster.* F 1–2, L
1 *within*] *om.* F 2, L, S
6 Sir.] Sir. *Ex.* F 2, L, S
10 pleasures] pleasure F 2
44 marches] marchers W
54 An] And D
57 vail∧ then] Vail, thin S, D

81 The] That F 1–2, L, S, C
81 fewer] few S
83 as] as as F 2
89 appears neatest] appear nearest F 2
105 and] *om.* L
129 wish] with F 1
133 please ye,] please, S

689

II.iv

0.1 Enter . . . 2. Hostesse.] *Enter
    Philippo and second Host.* F 1
2 pilchers] Pilchards F 2+
10 half Falconers] Falconers half
    F 2+
42 worshipfull] worshipfuls S

74 All,] All's S; All ^ C, D
79 geer] Beer L
81–82 Sir. | *Diego.* Old, and strong
    too, O] Sir, old and strong too. |
    Diego. O S (*conjecture*)
83 strong] *om.* L

III.ii

79 man, man,] man, F 2, L
90 among] amongst L, S, C, W
147 the] thy L
149 she] ye F 1
175 stoop] stop F 2, L
188 An] And S

190 that, that] that F 2+
198 spoke] spoken F 2, L
229 heaven] Heavens W, D
248 fearfull] fearfully C
292 Would] Wouldst F 2+
292 upon] unto F 2, L, S

III.iii

21 woman? in his language ^] wo-
    man ^ in his language? F 1–2;
    Woman? in his language? L

26 see] saw S, D

III.iv

20 I,] Ay ^ L, S; I ^ F 1–2
30 Turn] Tuin F 2; Tune L
36 I,] I ^ F 2
41 beaten] beat S
41 bruise] bruist F 1–2, L, S
50–51 *Pedro.* Let him sally. |

Alphonso. Lin'd] *Alph.* Let him
    sally. | *S.* Lin'd F 1–2, L; *Alph.*
    Let him sally!—— | Lin'd S+
92 especiall] special F 2, L
113 seditious] seditions F 1, C, W, D

IV.i

2 it is] is it F 1
13 he] *om.* F 2, L, S
24 place:] place: *Ioh. Bacon ready
    to shoot off a Pistol.* F 1
42 She . . . fame,] *Rod.* She . . . fame,
    above. F 1
77 Gunner] Governor F 1, C, W
150 whom] when F 1

153 seal'd] zeald F 2+ ; scale F 1
154 women] woman F 1
154 to] no C
171 dosis] dotes F 1; dose F 2+
206 quit] quiet F 1
207 *Theodosia*] *Philippo* C
233 he] *om.* F 2, L
236.1 *Whispers* . . . servant.] *om.* F 1

IV.ii

8 it] he F 1+
9 a] *om.* F 2, L, S, D
15 scambling] scrambling C, W

17 at a mans] at Man's L, S
18 a man] any man F 2, L, S
22 heartist] Artist L, S, C, W

IV.iii

10 This] Is this S, C, W; This is D
22 do you] do you do F 2, L, S
53 you do] do you F 2, L, S, C
61 man sit] man——Sit C, W, D
87 These] Those S
89 yet] yee F 1

102 it] *om.* F 2, L
122 do you?] do you do? F 2, L
133 heaven] Heav'ns L, S, C
136 told] would tell F 2, L
137 your body] you body F 1

V.i

1 not he] he not L, S
6 god] Heaven F 2+
8 seek] see F 2, L
8 find] finds S+
11 an] *om.* F 2, L, S, C

16 give] gave F 2+
20 she would] she should C, W
21 him] 'em F 2, L, S
22 betray my] my betray my L

V.iv

25 wondring] wandring L
40 was] must F 2
44 health] a health F 2, L
47 Humh] Humph F 2, L, S, C
52 *Mark-antonio's*] *Mark-antonio*
F 2
63 it] I F 1–2, L, S

81 could] could not F 2
100 open: Love,] ~ : ~ ∧ F 1; ~ ∧
~ ∧ F 2; ~ , ~ : L+
106 coveted] covet it F 1+
121 And] Add F 2
151 Sir, I;] ~ ; ~ : C, W, D; ~ ;
~ , F 1–2; ~ ; Ay, L, S

V.vi

19 ——] Pox! C, W, D
21 ——] Pox! C, W, D
37 in't to you)] in't) to you, C, W,
D

43 Sir] *om.* F 2, L, S
73 and hand] in hand F 2, L, S
86 Come] Come, come S
100 brother] Bother L

APPENDIX

PASSAGES FROM *THE NEW INN*

The following extracts are the parallels that have a bearing on possible revisions in *Love's Pilgrimage* I.i.25–63, and 330–411. The first passage is from II.v.48–73; the second from III.i.57–93 and 130–168, in the text of the 1631 octavo. Speech-prefixes and abbreviations are expanded, the long s, u, v, i, and j modernized, and commas replaced by dashes in lines 132, 150, and 153.

Tipto.   But why in *Cuerpo*?
  I hate to see an host, and old, in *Cuerpo*.
Host.   *Cuerpo*? what's that?
Tipto.   Light, skipping hose and doublet.   50
  The horse boyes garbe! poore blank, and halfe blank *Cuerpo*,
  They relish not the gravity of an host,
  Who should be King at Armes, and ceremonies,
  In his owne house! know all, to the goldweights.
Beaufort.   Why that his *Fly* doth for him here, your Bird.
Tipto.   But I would doe it my selfe, were I my Host,
  I would not speake unto a Cooke of quality,
  Your Lordships footman, or my Ladies *Trundle*,
  In *Cuerpo*! If a Dog but stay'd below
  That were a dog of fashion, and well nos'd,   60
  And could present himselfe; I would put on
  The *Savoy* chaine about my neck; the ruffe;
  And cuffes of *Flanders*; then the *Naples* hat;
  With the *Rome* hatband; and the *Florentine* Agate;
  The *Millan* sword; the cloake of *Genoa*; set
  With *Brabant* buttons; all my given pieces:
  Except my gloves, the natives of *Madrid*,
  To entertaine him in! and complement
  With a tame cony, as with a Prince that sent it.
Host.   The same deeds, though, become not every man.   70

What fits a *Colonel*, will not fit an Host.

Tipto.   Your *Spanish* Host is never seen in *Cuerpo*,
Without his *Paramento's*, cloake, and sword

. . . .

Peck.   A plague of all Jades, what a clap he has gi'n me!

Fly.   Why how now Cossen?

Tipto.   Who's that?

Ferret.   The Hostler.

Fly.   What ayl'st thou Cossen *Peck?*

Peck.   O me, my hanches!
As sure as you live, Sir, he knew perfectly   60
I meant to Cossin him. He did leere so on me,
And then he sneerd. As who would say take heed Sirrah.
And when he saw our halfe-pecke, which you know
Was but an old court-dish, Lord how he stamp't!
I thought, 't had beene for joy. When suddainly
He cuts me a backe caper with his heeles,
And takes me just o' the crouper. Downe come I
And my whole ounce of oates! Then he neighed out,
As if he had a Mare by the tayle.

Fly.   Troth Cossin,
You are to blame to use the poore dumbe Christians,   70
So cruelly, defraud 'hem o' their *dimensum*,
Yonder's the Colonels horse (there I look'd in)
Keeping our Ladies Eve! The divell a bit
He ha's got, sin'e he came in yet! There he stands,
And lookes and lookes, but t'is your pleasure, Cosse,
He should looke leane enough.

Peck.   He ha's hay before him.

Fly.   Yes, but as grosse as hempe, and assoone will choake him,
Unlesse he eat it butter'd. H'had foure shoes,
And good ones, when he came in: It is a wonder,
With standing still he should cast three.

Peck.   Troth Quarter-Master,   80
This trade is a kind of mystery, that currupts
Our standing manners quickely: Once a weeke,
I meet with such a brush to mollifie me.

Sometimes a brace, to awake my Conscience,
Yet still, I sleepe securely.
Fly.   Cossin *Peck,*
You must use better dealing, fayth you must.
Peck.   Troth, to give good example, to my successors,
I could be well content to steale but two girths,
And now and then a saddle-cloth, change a bridle,
For exercise: and stay there.
Fly.   If you could   90
There were some hope, on you, Cosse. But the fate is
You' are drunke so early, you mistake whole Saddles:
Sometimes a horse...

Peck. Truly it seemes to me   130
That every horse has his whole peck, and tumbles
Up to the eares in littour——
Fly.   When, indeed
There's no such matter; not a smell of provander.
Ferret.   Not so much straw as would tie up a horse-taile!
Fly.   Nor any thing i' the rack, but two old cobwebs!
And so much rotten hay, as had beene a hens nest!
Trundle.   And yet he's ever apt to sweepe the mangers!
Ferret.   But puts in nothing.
Peirce.   These are fits, and fancies,
Which you must leave, good *Peck.*
Fly.   And you must pray   140
It may be reveal'd to you, at some-times,
Whose horse you ought to cosen; with what conscience;
The how; and when; a Parsons horse may suffer——
Peirce.   Who's master's double benefic'd; put in that.
Fly.   A little greasing i' the teeth; 'tis wholesome:
And keepes him in a sober shuffle.
Peirce.   His saddle too
May want a stirrop.
Fly.   And, it may be sworne,
His learning lay o' one side, and so broke it.
Peck.   They have ever oates i' their cloake-bags, to affront us.

Fly. And therefore 'tis an office meritorious,
To tith such soundly.
Peirce. And a graziers may——   150
Ferret. O they are pinching puckfists!
Trundle. And suspicious.
Peirce. Suffer before the masters face, sometimes.
Fly. He shall thinke he sees his horse eate halfe a bushell—
Peirce. When the slight is, rubbing his gummes with salt,
Till all the skin come off, he shall but mumble,
Like an old woman that were chewing brawne,
And drop 'hem out againe.
Tipto. Well argued Cavalier.
Fly. It may doe well: and goe for an example:
But Cosse, have care of understanding horses,
Horses with angry heeles, Nobility horses,   160
Horses that know the world; let them have meat
Till their teeth ake; and rubbing till their ribbes
Shine like a wenches forehead. They are Divels else
Will looke into your dealings.
Peck. For mine own part,
The next I cossen o' the pampred breed,
I wish he may be found'red.
Fly. Foun-de-red.
Prolate it right.
Peck. And of all foure, I wish it,
I love no crouper complements.